"Is Hollywood shifting its accent on sex?" asked *Silver Screen* after the release of *Sabrina:* "She's changing Hollywood's taste in girls. From the full-bosomed, sweater-filling type with more curves than the New York Central Railroad, to the lean, umbrella-shaped variety." They were speaking, of course, of Audrey . . . Newspapers in 1954 were reporting on a "new cult" around Audrey Hepburn. "Today," said one, "It is no secret in the magazine world that a picture of the lady on a cover is like a Benzedrine pill to sales." *Vogue* was calling her "today's wonder-girl . . . she has so captured the public imagination and the mood of the time that she has established a new standard of beauty, and every other face now approximates to the 'Hepburn look' . . . This slim little person, with the winged eyebrows and Nefertiti head and throat, is the world's darling."

Barry Paris is an award-winning journalist, film and music critic, Slavic linguist and translator of Chekhov. His writing appears in the *New Yorker, Opera News, Vanity Fair* and *Art and Antiques.* He lives in Pittsburgh, USA.

By the same author

Louise Brooks
Garbo
Tony Curtis: The Autobiography (co-author)

AUDREY HEPBURN

Barry Paris

ORION

An Orion paperback
First published in Great Britain by Weidenfeld & Nicolson in 1997
This paperback edition published in 1998 by
Orion Books Ltd,
Orion House, 5 Upper St Martin's Lane, London WC2H 9EA

Ninth impression 2003

First published in the USA in 1996 by G. P. Putnam's Sons

A CIP catalogue record for this book is available
from the British Library.

ISBN: 0 75281 540 7

Printed and bound in Great Britain by
Clays Ltd, St Ives plc

CONTENTS

For George Coleman

FOREWORD

AUDREY HEPBURN IS THE BIOGRAPHER'S dream and nightmare simultaneously. No other film actress was so revered—inspired and inspiring—both for her on-screen appearances and for her passionate, off-screen crusade. She remains so beloved that virtually no one has a bad word to say about her. The worst thing she ever did, it seems, was forget to mention Patricia Neal at the 1964 Oscars. She left no lurid secrets or closet cruelties to be exposed. Beneath her kind, warm surface lay more kindness and warmth to the core.

The challenge is to capture but not canonize her, to find the real woman beneath the icon. If this effort succeeds at that, it is due to all those who shared their knowledge of her with me. A full list of them is found in the Acknowledgments.

But certain contributors warrant special recognition.

I am indebted most of all to the family and Estate of Audrey Hepburn: Robert Wolders, Mel Ferrer, Sean Ferrer, Ian Quarles van Ufford, Hako and Christine Sixma van Heemstra, Yvonne Quarles van Ufford, Leopold Quarles van Ufford (former Dutch Consul General to the U.S.), Michael Quarles van Ufford, Mrs. Cemelia Wolders, Rick and Claudia Wolders de Abreu, Hans and Margaret Wolders Schouten, Dr. Ronald and Grada Wolders Glegg, Kirk Hallem and Rose Ganguzza. But I must stress that this is not an "authorized" biography; that it was not subject to the approval of the Hepburn family; that the family members who participated in this book did so in a limited way as individuals, not members of her Estate, and do not necessarily agree with any conclusions or characterizations herein. The Hepburn Estate reserves all rights to publish a book of its own in the future.

I am very grateful for unprecedented access to the close friends of Audrey Hepburn who have rarely or never spoken about her before. Chief among them were Lord James Hanson, Connie Wald, Doris and Victoria Brynner, Hubert de Givenchy, Michael Tilson Thomas, Ralph Lauren, Anna Cataldi, Arabella Ungaro, Countess Lorean Gaetani-Lovatelli, Camilla Pecci-Blunt McGrath and Alfred Heineken III.

Hepburn worked with many of the most distinguished directors in Anglo-American cinema, and I was honored to interview five of them: Fred Zinnemann, Richard Lester, Terence Young, Peter Bogdanovich and Billy Wilder. In a class by herself is Audrey Wilder, Billy's wife, whose salty remarks pepper this narrative.

Among Hepburn's colleagues, the most valuable insights were provided by André Previn, musician and observer extraordinaire, and Roddy McDowall, a human archive whose generosity knows no bounds. Other marvelous reflections came from Leslie Caron, R. J. Wagner, James Coburn, Tony Curtis, Deborah Kerr and Peter Viertel, Eli Wallach, Patricia Neal, Valentina Cortesa, Sophia Loren, Ginny Mancini, Theodore Bikel, Katharine Dunham, Marni Nixon, Leonard Gershe, Efrem Zimbalist, Jr., and the late Jeremy Brett and Eva Gabor. Photographer Bob Willoughby was essential, as were Janis Blackschleger and Julie Leifermann of "Gardens of the World"—Audrey's last, beautiful film project.

My accounts of the Battle of Arnhem and Audrey's experiences during the Nazi occupation of Holland are based on previously untapped material, located and translated by the foremost Dutch military historian and author, Paul Vroemen. I am deeply grateful to him and to Wyoming B. Paris II—an excellent military historian in his own right—for leading me to Mr. Vroemen. Another generous Dutchman, Leendert de Jong, programming director of the Hague Film Foundation, provided me with rare film footage from Hepburn's early years.

For film-historical information and advice, I relied as always on Steven Bach, Kevin Brownlow, James Card, Hugo Vickers, Lawrence Quirk, Leonard and Alice Maltin, Richard Lamparski and David Stenn. I also benefitted from the spadework of previous Hepburn biographers Charles Higham, Ian Woodward, Caroline Latham, Warren Harris, Alexander Walker, Sheridan Morley and James Robert Parish.

The final sections on Audrey Hepburn's dynamic labors for UNICEF could not have been written without the insights of Robert Wolders, Christa Roth, John Isaac, Prince Sadruddin Aga Khan, Jack Glattbach, Ian MacLeod and many other UNICEF personnel, as well as Senator Nancy Kassebaum, Anne Cox Chambers and William Banks. And I am grateful to G. P. Putnam's Sons for agreeing to donate a portion of this book's revenues to UNICEF and the Hepburn Estate's "Hollywood for Children" foundation.

It was a great loss to be deprived of George Coleman, the Putnam editor who conceived this book. But it was a privilege to have the ongoing support of Phyllis Grann and editors Laura Yorke, David Groff and especially David Highfill. Ion Trewin and Allegra Huston at Weidenfeld & Nicolson (UK) and Martin Appelmann at Bosch & Kuening (Netherlands) gave valuable assistance in Europe.

No such sweeping, intercontinental project as this is possible without enormous domestic and moral support. In my case, it came from Robert ("le Diable") Gottlieb, ace agent Dan Strone, the Deco duo of Charles Busch and Eric Myers, Jack Larsen, Wallace Potts, Rick and Deborah Geary, Ron Wisniski, Albert French, Stephen Baum, Rose Hayden, James and Queen Christina O'Toole, Pamela and David Loyle, Wyoming B. Paris I, Merica Paris and Wyoming B. Paris III.

The most crucial come last: Writer-researcher Maria Ciaccia is simply the best in the business, and the most devoted. John Barba (with the long-suffering Margie's support) is my brilliant friend, closest advisor and, in many ways, the coauthor of this book. And finally, Myrna—Diva and pillar of strength—whom I thank and love, as ever.

BARRY PARIS
Pittsburgh
March 7, 1996

CHAPTER 1

Holland and
the Bridge Too Far
(1929–1947)

> "I had an enormous complex about my
> looks. I thought I was ugly and I was
> afraid nobody would ever marry me."
> AUDREY HEPBURN

ON THE DAY OF THE greatest airborne invasion in history, Audrey Hepburn was a skinny girl of fifteen—stunned and exhilarated by the prospect of imminent liberation from the Nazis and incredulous that it was taking place in her own provincial Dutch town of Arnhem. Now, on September 17, 1944, Arnhem found itself the scene of the single most daring Allied gambit of World War II. That day—combined with 1,800 other days under the Nazi occupation—would have repercussions on her life forever.

Strange circumstances had brought her there, and even stranger circumstances would turn the teen who stood watching that invasion into the most beautiful icon of her era. "Audrey Hepburn looks like every girl and like no girl," said a friend. "She doesn't even look like Audrey Hepburn."[1] She was a ballet dancer, who never performed a full ballet. She was the world's highest paid film actress, who never studied acting.

The pessimists said no new feminine ideal could emerge from the war, wrote Cecil Beaton, but the rubble of Holland, an English accent, and an American success would produce a wistful child who embodied the spirit of a new day. "Nobody ever looked like her before," said Beaton, except maybe "those wild children of the French Revolution." She had enormous eyes and thick eyebrows, an incredibly long and slender neck, and was "too tall" by the standard of the day. And yet, like a Modigliani portrait, "the distortions are not only interesting in themselves but make a completely satisfying composite."[2]

She would come to represent not just a new look but a new femininity—the diametric European opposite of the American sex goddess. Diva Maria Callas, and a few million others, would use her as a model.[3] "She comes at an historical moment," wrote critic Molly Haskell, "just before feminism, easy divorce and the sexual revolution." She was the vulnerable waif, discreet and ambiguous to the end. That persona in *Love in the Afternoon*, said Stanley Kauffmann, was typical: "The sign of her preparing to take the plunge was when she removes a glove."

Child-women have fascinated film audiences since Lillian Gish, but Hepburn's version came with a paradoxical glamour and sophistication. Most glamour queens began as waitresses or shop girls and had to be groomed for the throne by their studios. Not Audrey Hepburn. She arrived more or less in complete form, like Botticelli's Venus on the half-shell. Beauty and glamour may coincide but are by no means the same thing. Beauty is visual—necessary but not sufficient for glamour, which is more abstract. And if glamour is a form of mass hypnosis, Hepburn was the finest film hypnotist of her time.[4]

Of the great movie goddesses, only Marilyn Monroe and Elizabeth Taylor decorated more covers of *Life* than Audrey Hepburn, and only Garbo held more aloof from Hollywood. Over forty years, she starred in just twenty films but imbued them all with a remarkable, original presence. When she sings "Moon River," softly confiding her melancholy to her guitar, "she is not an actress we judge but a person we know and love," wrote one admirer. "That face would have excused a lot of awkward performances and bad movies. Happily, it didn't have to."[5]

What shined through, too, was her regal aura. "She is one of us," Queen Mother Elizabeth reportedly told her daughter after they met Hepburn. It seemed to Haskell "as if she dropped out of the sky into the fifties, half wood-nymph, half princess, and then disappeared... leaving no footprints... a changeling of mysterious parentage, unidentifiable as to nationality or class."

Perhaps, then, it is no surprise to learn that she was the daughter of a real-life baroness.

AUDREY HEPBURN'S MOTHER BELONGED TO an ancient family of the Dutch nobility. Her grandfather, Baron Aernoud van Heemstra (1871–1957), was a lawyer and familiar figure at the court of Queen Wilhelmina. His ancestors had held high positions in the Netherlands as statesmen and soldiers from the twelfth century. Audrey's life had its share of problems, but she would never suffer from an identity crisis: Portraits of her ancestors hung in museums and aristocratic homes throughout Holland.

The van Heemstras' original wealth derived from colonial trading, but Baron Aernoud preferred government service to commerce. In 1896, he married Elbrig van Asbeck, who bore him five daughters and a son. Ella, the third child and future mother of Audrey, was born in 1900 in the province of Gelderland.

Ella wanted to study for the opera, but the stage was out of bounds. "Whatever you do, don't associate with actors and actresses," the Baron decreed. "You'd bring disgrace on the family." Ella's friend Alfred ("Freddie") Heineken III, of the Dutch brewery family, calls her "a born actress, very dramatic, highly emotional, with a great sense of fun. But in those times, a daughter of the nobility was forbidden to have a career. She was expected to marry well and have lots of children."

Ella would lament that she "grew up wanting more than anything else to be English, slim, and an actress." The dutiful daughter forsook those yearnings but vowed that if she ever had a talented daughter, she would encourage her. Her own comfortable childhood was spent at several family estates—notably Doorn Castle near Utrecht (now the Huis-Doorn Museum), a gorgeous manse surrounded by beautifully landscaped grounds and a swan-filled moat. But Ella's generation of van Heemstras did not occupy it for long.

Dwarfed by the powerful memory of World War II is World War I: Few recall that Holland was neutral in that conflict, at the end of which Kaiser Wilhelm II fled Germany for the Netherlands. The victorious Allies declared him a war criminal, but the ever-clement Dutch declined to hand him over. The van Heemstras were obliged not only to accommodate him at Doorn but, in 1920, to sell it to him. There he fantasized about his restoration and, in noxious Prussian fashion, cut down a tree a day "for exercise." Joseph J. O'Donohue IV—a future in-law of the future actress Audrey Hepburn—recalls visiting Doorn in the early 1930s at the invitation of the Kaiser's grandson, Prince Louis Ferdinand:

> One was received by Baron von Grancy, the Hofmarshall, and escorted across the moat to the castle. There, one was introduced to the other guests in a large room notable for [its German] furnishings. [After sherry] a lackey opened a large door [and] a plump Dachshund waddled regally into the room, followed by the Kaiser whose gait was considerably livelier. [After presentations], we proceeded into the handsome dining room where I was seated on the Emperor's right. [Following lunch], we retired to the Smoking Room, largely dedicated to paintings and memorabilia of Frederick the Great, for whom the Kaiser had a hero-worship almost as great as his love for his grandmother, Queen Victoria.[6]

The last of the kaisers lived at Huis-Doorn until his death in 1941 (when Hitler granted him a military funeral). The van Heemstras, long before that, had taken up residence at another of their estates just outside the western Dutch town of Arnhem: Zijpendaal, a pristine mini-castle, dating to 1743, was nestled in a picturesque rustic setting with stables and a water mill and outbuildings for the keepers of its well-manicured

park and horses.* The Baron and his brood lived there in aristocratic
fashion from 1910 through 1920, during which he served as the burgomaster—or mayor—of Arnhem.

He would soon be called to a more exotic locale but first attended to
the matrimonial disposition of his nineteen-year-old Ella. She was married
in Arnhem on March 11, 1920, to Hendrik Gustaaf Adolf Quarles van
Ufford, Knight of the Order of Orange-Nassau. A former lieutenant in the
Queen's equerry, he was now an oil executive of Bataafsche Petroleum
(later Dutch Shell), newly assigned to the Netherlands East Indies. He took
his bride to Batavia (now Jakarta, Indonesia's capital) where, precisely
nine months after the wedding, their son Alexander was born.

The Dutch empire was far-flung, and Ella's father now headed for its
most remote outpost: In 1921, he was appointed Governor of Surinam
(Dutch Guiana) on the northeast coast of South America. It was a territory
roughly the size of Georgia, running from the Caribbean seaboard to Brazil,
received in a 1667 trade with Britain in exchange for New Amsterdam—
the present state and city of New York. It seemed like a good deal at the
time.

Nearly half the colony's population of 300,000 lived in Paramaribo,
the capital. In the colorful Asian market area near the waterfront were
several Hindu temples and the Caribbean's largest mosque, peacefully
located next to a synagogue. All in all, Paramaribo was an ecumenical
city, unmistakably Dutch in character despite its bizarre population mix.‡
The relative lack of racial tensions was due largely to the tradition of
Dutch tolerance: Surinamese knew how to get along with one another.

Paramaribo boasted many beautiful eighteenth-and nineteenth-century
colonial buildings in the Dutch neo-Norman style. Not least of them was
the Governor's Mansion, situated on a plaza with the impossible Dutch
name of Onafhankelijkheidsplein. As Baroness Elbrig was often ill, her
seventeen-year-old daughter Jacqueline took her place as hostess, serving
in that role for the length of her father's administration. In the future, she
would become lady-in-waiting to Princess (later Queen) Juliana; for now,
Surinam would provide her with a perfect—and perfectly beautiful—
training ground. The official residence, surrounded by orchids that grew
twelve feet tall, greatly impressed the van Heemstras from the moment
they laid eyes on it.

The Surinamese, in turn, were impressed with Baron van Heemstra.

---

* Zijpendaal now houses the Foundation of Friends of the Geldersche Castles, dedicated to preserving
the province's twenty-one castles and their contents and gardens.

‡ Native Indians and "Bush Negroes" (descendants of runaway slaves) inhabited the interior tropical
rain forest, much of which has still not been explored. They were outnumbered by Creoles and Asians
who came as plantation laborers from Java, India and Pakistan. The official language is Dutch, but
the main Creole dialect—a pidgin English called Taki-Taki—is the lingua franca.

He was the first governor to travel deep into the interior, where white Europeans seldom penetrated. His purpose was business, not pleasure: He was scouting new ways to exploit the country's extraordinary natural resources, including its huge deposits of bauxite. Soon, Surinam's bauxite/aluminum industry would account for 72 percent of its exports.

The atmosphere of Paramaribo was charmed. Among its customs were birdsong competitions in the public parks. People routinely carried their pet songbirds in cages when out for a stroll, and even to work. Life was good, and so was the cuisine—as exotic as Surinam's ethnic makeup—featuring *pom*, a puree of cassava, and peanut soup with plantain dumplings. The climate was moist but not terribly hot, thanks to the northeast trade winds year round. It was truly, in many ways, a tropical paradise.

But there was trouble in another paradise, halfway around the globe in Batavia, where Ella's marriage was not going well. The constant quarrels between her and Quarles van Ufford ended in 1925, a year after their second son Ian was born, when they were divorced in the Netherlands East Indies. Divorce was quite rare for an aristocratic Dutchwoman of that time, said a friend, "but she preferred that to taking a lover, like most."[7] Ella was a strong-willed, energetic woman who loved the good life and had a fatal weakness for good-looking men. She took herself and the boys to join her family in the colonial splendor of Paramaribo—but not for long. For Ella, unlike sister Jacqueline, the novelty of Surinam wore off in less than a year, and after returning briefly to Arnhem, she went back to Indonesia.

Her real agenda was to renew and pursue her relationship with an Anglo-Irish businessman, Joseph Hepburn-Ruston, whom she had met there earlier. He, too, had recently been divorced—in San Francisco, of all places. In Ella's set, marriages and divorces were more easily conducted in exotic locales: On September 7, 1926, she and Joe were wed in Batavia.

Ruston was born in 1889 in Slovakia, where his British father had business. His claims to have studied at Cambridge and served in the British Army during World War I are unverified, but after the war he did join the diplomatic service and was assigned to the Dutch East Indies as vice-consul at Semarang, a town between Batavia and Surabaja. He later gave that up for a job with the Batavia arbitrage house of Maclaine Watson & Company, which handled trading in East Indian tin.

The allure of Java did not include its oppressive heat or its limited social excitement, and the couple soon opted for Europe again. But Ruston's transfer to Maclaine Watson's London headquarters lasted only for a year. Always restless, he next joined an Anglo-French credit society dealing in home loans and the like. That company armed him with the title of vice president and deputy administrator and sent him to open a new branch office in Belgium, where he, Ella and the two boys settled down in the Ixelles district of Brussels.

Half a century later, most chroniclers would characterize Audrey Hepburn's father as a "banker" who was employed in the Bank of England's Brussels branch and who, after marrying Ella, handled the van Heemstra family's properties and finances. Late in life, Audrey bluntly denied it: "They speak of my father having been a banker, which he wasn't at all. He never really held down a job."[8]

The Bank of England was an exchequer or treasury, not a conventional bank, and in fact had no foreign branch in Brussels or anywhere else. Ruston's initial interest in Ella was enhanced by his incorrect assumption that her family had vast wealth, but he was sadly if not bitterly disabused of that notion early on.

The term "international banker" described him less well than "international adventurer." The term "pregnant" now described his wife.

AUDREY KATHLEEN VAN HEEMSTRA RUSTON was born in Brussels on May 4, 1929. "Audrey" was a feminine form of "Andrew," which was to have been her name if she'd been a boy. Her birth certificate omits the hyphenated "Hepburn" before Ruston; Ella allegedly added it later to spiff up her own and her daughter's future calling card. According to biographer Warren Harris, it was the only aristocratic name Ella could find in Ruston's family tree—the surname of his grandmother, who was descended from James Hepburn, Earl of Bothwell, the third husband of Mary, Queen of Scots. Since the baby's father and Dutch mother were both British citizens in the eyes of the law, the new baby was likewise certified by the British consulate in Brussels.

"If I were to write a book about myself," Audrey once told her son Sean, "it would start like this: I was born on May 4, 1929, and I died three weeks later." At twenty-one days of age, she contracted such a terrible case of whooping cough that her heart stopped. Ella, who was a rather strict Christian Scientist and had not called a doctor, revived her by spanking. "There was no giving up on this baby," said Sean. "I think that had an effect on her whole life, [as if she'd been given] a second chance."[9]

Her early years were chaotic, with constant traveling back and forth between London and Brussels, Arnhem and The Hague. Alexander and Ian stayed often in those days with Ella's parents and saw little of stepfather Hepburn-Ruston. Ella was as restless as her husband and, when Audrey was a toddler of two, insisted on moving the family from Brussels to a small estate called Castel Sainte-Cecile in the nearby village of Linkebeek.

Baron van Heemstra had by then resigned as Governor of Surinam and returned to live with his daughter Mies and her husband, Count Otto van Limburg Stirum, at Zijpendaal Castle, where Audrey often visited and roamed the gorgeous grounds. But, by and large, she did not recall her early childhood fondly. She was a puny, introverted little girl who had trouble making friends and preferred the tomboyish companionship of her much older half-brothers. She cared much less for dolls, which "never seemed real to me," she said, than for animals.

Her happiest moments by far were in the country. "I had a passion for the outdoors, for trees, for birds and flowers," she said—and for Rudyard Kipling, inspired by brother Alexander, "the original bookworm.... When we were children he was devoted to Kipling [and] I read all Kipling's books because I wanted to be like him. I followed everything else he read, too. Before I was thirteen I had read nearly every book by Edgar Wallace and Edward Phillips Oppenheim, who wrote a long series of romantic mysteries about secret international documents, shifty diplomats and seductive adventuresses.... To me as a girl they had far more appeal than books like *Topsy Goes to School*."[10]

Reading became a lifeline for her. She spoke of *The Secret Garden* as one of her favorite books and of the fact that, at the age of nine, her mother gave her a copy of *Heidi* just before they embarked on a train trip from Holland to Italy. She started it instantly and, by the time she finished, they were in Italy without her having seen a glimpse of Switzerland.[11]

Ian was also a voracious reader, and also close to his little sister. "We were very naughty," he said. "We did a lot of tree climbing." Ella would reprimand sharply and "threaten to disown me," Audrey recalled:

> My mother was not a very affectionate person. She was a fabulous mother, but she had a Victorian upbringing of great discipline, of great ethics. She was very strict, very demanding of her children. She had a lot of love *within* her, but she was not always able to show it. I went searching all over the place to find somebody who would cuddle me, and I found it, in my aunts and nannies.[12]

Several of her aunts encouraged Audrey to begin piano lessons, which she did. But there would be no escaping her mother's overbearing presence. Robert Wolders, the soft-spoken Dutchman with whom Audrey spent the last dozen years of her life, knew Ella well as "a superior woman, very humorous, extremely well read and well educated—but critical of everyone, including Audrey. Biased, intolerant."[13]

Audrey's childhood was fairly cloistered and indeed full of nannies and private tutors. Though never wanting for a thing, she was keenly aware of the tension between her parents, who fought incessantly over money and other matters. She became increasingly withdrawn and hypersensitive, often seeking refuge in the fields of her family's estates. Hiding and eating became preoccupations: "It was either chocolates, bread or my nails."

Her father's work took him abroad a great deal, and only when he was away did the child seem to find moments of peace. But when he returned, the bickering resumed, and so did Audrey's introversion. To draw her out, her mother decided to try the "shock" treatment: She sent Audrey, at age five, to a boarding school in England.

At first, "I was terrified about being away from home," said Hepburn in adulthood. She was teased for being shy and plump, unlike her hockey-playing peers, and for her imperfect English. She missed her mother terribly. Her father, nearby in London, made little effort to see her. Even so, she concluded stoically, "it turned out to be a good lesson in independence."[14]

The school was run by the six unmarried Rigden sisters in Elham, Kent. To immerse the girl further in English customs and language, Ella arranged for her to spend holidays with a coal miner's family in the country, where she learned the names of all the flowers—and never forgot them.[15]

"Those people had a remarkable effect on her," says Wolders. "She always kept a picture of their terrier on her dressing-room table." Many years later, she went back to look them up and helped their son adopt a child through the UN.

AUDREY WAS ADJUSTING WELL TO England, but English politics and the gathering storm over Europe were now compounding the maladjustment of her parents. In mid-1930s Britain, the growth and appeal of fascism were by no means universally condemned. Sir Oswald Mosley, once a top minister in Ramsay MacDonald's Labour government, had formed the British Union of Fascists (BUF). His companion and future wife was Diana Mitford, whose sister Unity was also sympathetic to the movement. Ella was friendly with the Mitfords and evidently encouraged her rabidly anti-Communist husband to join up.

As the BUF grew in strength, the Hepburn-Rustons were openly involved in its fund-raising and recruitment. Ella was so devoted to Mosley that she publicly endorsed him in the April 26, 1935, edition of BUF's weekly paper, *The Blackshirt*, a glamorous photo of herself accompanying her article:

> We who have heard the call of Fascism, and have followed the light on the upward road to victory, have been taught to understand what dimly we knew, and now fully realize. . . . At last we are breaking the bondage and are on the road to salvation. . . . We who follow Sir Oswald Mosley know that in

him we have found a leader whose eyes are not riveted on earthly things, whose inspiration is of a higher plane, and whose idealism will carry Britain along to the bright light of the new dawn of spiritual rebirth.

A few weeks later, in May, Ella and her husband joined Mosley's BUF delegation to Germany to observe conditions under the Nazis. They toured autobahns, factories, schools and housing developments, and had the heady honor of meeting Hitler himself at the Nazis' Brown House headquarters in Munich. A group photo taken there—showing the Hepburn-Rustons with Unity Mitford, her sisters Pamela and Mary, and others— was long enshrined in a silver frame on Ella's mantelpiece.

The extent to which Ella's fascist involvement was sincere or merely in misguided support of her husband's ambitions is still unknown. Her article and the Brown House photo are the only clear pieces of evidence, and she never elaborated to her daughter in later years. In any case, the thrill of meeting the Führer had no magical effect on their domestic situation. Almost immediately after their return from Germany, in that same month of May 1935, Ruston walked out on his wife and six-year-old girl.

Dutch sources claim Joseph Hepburn-Ruston was a heavy drinker and that he and Ella argued about it.[16] But more compelling reasons for departure were contained in his increasing radicalism: He soon quit the BUF to join an even more violently anti-Semitic splinter group. Ella's father was said to be incensed not only by his son-in-law's politics but by the belief that Ruston was mismanaging the van Heemstras' money and— worse—channeling some of it to fascist causes. By one account, Queen Wilhelmina herself urged the old Baron to silence Ella and pay off Ruston, if necessary to get him out of the family.[17]

Audrey called her father's disappearance "the most traumatic event in my life" and "a tragedy from which I don't think I've ever recovered. I worshiped him and missed him terribly from the day he disappeared.... If I could have just seen him regularly, I would have felt he loved me, and I would have felt I had a father. But as it was, I always envied other people's fathers, came home with tears, because they had a daddy."[18] Equally painful was her mother's reaction and the haunting memory of it:

You look into your mother's face, and it's covered with tears, and you're terrified. You say to yourself, "What's going to happen to me?" The ground has gone out from under you....[19] He really left. He just went out and never came back. Watching her agony was one of the worst experiences of my life. She cried for days until I thought she'd never stop, even when we went shopping. I was left with a sense of helplessness, of... not ever really understanding why Daddy had gone away.[20]

There was a frightening physical manifestation of the disaster, too. When her father left, she said, "my mother's hair turned white overnight. [But she] never ever put him down." Instead, "of necessity, my mother became a father too."[21] Ella began to spend more time in England with Audrey, who, despite her parents' breakup, made the school's honor roll and was making friends more easily. Most important, one of the many Miss Rigdens—a disciple of Isadora Duncan—was now helping her discover the art form that would captivate her for life.

"I fell in love with dancing," she recalled. "In this village in Kent where I stayed, there was a young dancer who would come up from London once a week and give ballet classes. I loved it, just loved it."[22]

Her life now settled down into a rather pleasant routine, largely undisturbed until the formal divorce of her parents in 1938. Ella got primary custody of nine-year-old Audrey. Hepburn-Ruston insisted that she remain in England and that he be given visitation rights. Ella resisted the second demand but gave in when Audrey pleaded for it. It turned out to be a moot point, in view of his subsequent failure to exercise those rights.

A year later came another upheaval for Audrey in the monumental upheaval of the world. Her mother came to collect her one day from school and was chatting with the dance instructor, who wanted to develop the girl's talent. Audrey overheard their conversation: "The teacher said, 'Would you let me take her to London?' 'No,' she said. 'I'm taking her back to Holland.'"[23]

Ella and her sons had been visiting relatives in Arnhem when England declared war on Germany, following the Nazi invasion of Poland, in September 1939. Travel could be curtailed at any moment; she might be separated from her daughter for years. Ella returned in panic to Britain and hastily obtained court approval (over Hepburn-Ruston's objections) to remove Audrey to Holland.

"She thought London was about to be bombed and that she and Audrey would be safer in Arnhem," recalls Freddie Heineken.[24] The notion seems foolish in hindsight but was not at the time: Holland was neutral and certain to remain so. Ella and most of her countrymen clung to the naive belief that Hitler would respect the neutrality of his "Dutch cousins." Very few commercial planes were still permitted to fly, but Ella pulled strings to get Audrey on one of them.

"Somehow she had contacted my father and asked him to meet me at the train in London where I was coming in [from Kent]," she told writer Dominick Dunne half a century later. "They put me on this bright-orange plane [the Dutch national color], and it flew very low. It really was one of the last planes out. That was the last time I saw my father."[25]

Her widowed grandfather, the old Baron, was now living with his eldest daughter Mies back at Zijpendaal Castle. Ella, Audrey and the boys stayed there briefly before finding their own apartment in Arnhem's Sonsbeek area. With no support from Hepburn-Ruston, Ella turned her attention to money and discovered that most of her inheritance was gone—frittered away by herself or her ex-husband? No one ever quite knew.[26] But that was a relatively minor disaster. She was terribly relieved at having brought her family to Arnhem, certain that it was the safest place to be.

"Famous last words," mused Audrey.[27]

ARNHEM IS A TYPICAL GELDERLAND town whose surrounding landscape is a mix of quaint villages, castles, lovely woods and meadows. Nature and geography were good to it in all respects but one: It is situated just twelve miles from the German border.

Civilization in and around Arnhem is ancient, dating to a Roman fortress there in the second century A.D. Urban Arnhem began in 893 and, from 1312 on, its citizens and Guild Masters played an active role in governing the city. In the fifteenth century it became the capital of the province of Gelderland. The English poet and war hero Philip Sidney fought for Dutch independence from Spain, was killed and is buried in Arnhem. The great Eusebius Church was a late-Gothic wonder; its striking eight-sided tower was Arnhem's chief landmark from 1560 to 1944, when it was destroyed in the last and worst foreign occupation.

By the mid-nineteenth century many Dutch people who had grown rich in the East Indies colonies moved to the Arnhem area, and living there became fashionable for such upper-class families as the van Heemstras. Baron Aernoud was elected burgomaster, but during his tenure, in 1911, the *Arnhemse Courant* saw fit to attack him for saying Arnhem's future was as "a luxury town," failing to mention its development as a shipping and trade center. Under leadership like his, said the paper, Arnhem would end up a ghost town.

That teapot tempest was long forgotten by 1939. Others had taken up the old Baron's slack, and he was now just an elder in retirement. The "new" Arnhem had an industrial purpose, indeed, in which the transportation of people and goods by river was most essential. Arnhem's first bridge over the Rhine had been constructed in 1603. Its newest, most spectacular span had just been completed in 1935—a sleek commercial convenience to which no one, at the moment, attached much larger significance.

Certainly not Ella, who had concerns of her own. In December 1939, she packed up her possessions and her children and moved from Sonsbeek to a modest terrace house at 7 Sickeslaan. She was also busy commuting to a part-time job with Panders, an exclusive interior-design company in the Hague. She enrolled Audrey in the fifth form of the Tamboersbosje (Drummer's Wood) public school. But the girl's Dutch at that point was primitive, and her fluent English a potentially dangerous liability in a town so close to the German border:

"My mother was worried about [my] speaking English in the streets with Germans all around." To make her appear more Dutch, Ella had enrolled her under van Heemstra instead of Hepburn. For Audrey, the surname made no difference. She hated being "in a huge classroom not knowing a word that was being said and every time I opened my mouth, everyone roaring with laughter.[28] The first morning in school, I sat at my little bench, completely baffled. For several days I went home weeping. But... I was forced to learn the language quickly. And I did."[29]

Years later, when asked if she felt more Dutch or English, she said she leaned toward English "because I was more English than Dutch when I went to Holland" in 1939. But little by little, as she learned the language and discovered her family in the Netherlands, "my Dutch roots were reborn."[30]

Her social life was limited, but it did exist, thanks to her mother's involvement in the Christian Science church, located in the local Masonic Temple. David Heringa was living just outside Arnhem in late 1939, when he and several other teens were asked to come to Sunday school because a new girl "needed kids who could speak English." Arnhem's Christian Science community was small—perhaps thirty families. Heringa remembers a "very quiet" ten-year-old "whose mother came to our house in Velp to practice reading the Scripture and *Science and Health*."[31]*

Ella was also involved with the local arts council, but there is no truth to the claim that she was president of something called the British-Netherlands Society in Arnhem or even that such a society existed. Her cultural activity centered on the stage—and not just the audience side of the footlights. She gave one public reading of a poem entitled "Daughter," to which Audrey listened proudly in the balcony of the Arnhem Theater. And at an amateur theatrical there in late 1939, Ella and her children appeared together in an elaborate Mozart tableau with eighteenth-century costumes, stage decor and music.

As a very small girl, Audrey had been taken to several ballet per-

---

* Ella and Heringa's parents alternated as regular readers. Arnhem's Christian Science Church was shut down early in the German occupation because of its "internationalism" and the suspected Jewish sympathies of its members.

formances in Brussels and had declared her intention to become a ballerina. But the older she got, the more she disliked what she saw in the mirror: Ballerinas were slender with perfect features. She was chubby. She thought her eyes were too big. She hated her irregular teeth. "I had an enormous complex about my looks," she said. "I thought I was ugly and I was afraid nobody would ever marry me."[32] But the desire to dance stayed with her, rekindled by her lessons in Kent. There are reports that she briefly attended a high school in Arnhem, but no proof. Others say she was privately tutored. Either way, upon entering puberty, she was far more interested in ballet than school.

Audrey's serious ballet training began at age twelve, in 1941, under Winja Marova at the Arnhem School of Music. Billed as "the former Russian ballerina," Marova was in fact a good Dutch lady named Winnie Koopman, who was married to the school's director, Douwe Draaisma, and had romanticized her professional name. Audrey would slim down and study with her through the summer of 1944, becoming her star pupil in the process, as Marova recalled:

> She was long, slender, very sweet, very eager to learn, and obsessed with dancing. She was willing to give everything for it. She was very musical. I always enjoyed teaching her. She just took everything you told her. At her first performance, I could see how good she was. When she was on stage, even though she just knew a little bit, you immediately saw that a flame lit the audience.

"Pavlova was my ideal," she said years later, but "Winja was the first [dancer] I really got to know and could call a friend. She was a beautiful world-class dancer [and she] helped this very young girl in Arnhem to believe that she could become one, too.[33] I was going to be a ballerina. I was very fanatic about it."[34]

Ella supported her—powerfully. "She was always at the rehearsals and stood behind the curtains during a performance," says Carel Johan Wensink, who often played the piano for Audrey's lessons with Marova. "Her mother had hair on her teeth!"—a fine Dutch vulgarism for something like "too much chutzpah."

She was a stage mother, all right, but not a stereotypical one. After one modest poetry reading and a Mozart tableau, Ella never again sought the limelight herself. Age and aristocratic reticence finally vanquished the private longing. From now on, full energy and attention were diverted to the little dancing daughter who was almost—but not quite—a prodigy.

*

THE SADLER'S WELLS BALLET WAS the most stellar company in England. Before, during and after the war, its choreography—by Frederick Ashton—was on the cutting edge. Director Ninette de Valois presided over a close-knit company of brilliant dancers, headed by Margot Fonteyn (who joined at age fourteen) and Robert Helpmann, the greatest mime of his era.

On May 4, 1940, nine months after the outbreak of World War II, the Sadler's Wells embarked on a courageous goodwill tour of Holland, Belgium and France. Under the auspices of the British Council, the trip was intended to boost morale in those jittery countries. Its patron, Lord Esher, had one unsettling caveat: "I hope that they may get there before Hitler does."[35]

Annabel Farjeon, a twenty-one-year-old corps member, kept a diary of that journey, starting with Bobby Helpmann's anxiety about his newly waved hair. "If the ship gets hit," he declared, "I shall swim breaststroke, with my head well back. I could never look the Dutch in the face if my perm got wet and went into a frizz, like one of those cheap ten-shilling do's."

Their Dutch home base was The Hague, from which the young troupe would sally forth in busses to the smaller towns and return each night. The company's first performance took place May 6 at The Hague's Theatre Royal. The next day they traveled to the industrial town of Hengelo, about seven miles from the German border. "It was swarming with spies and Nazi supporters," wrote Farjeon. People in the streets spat and jeered, "Ingleesh! Leepstick-leepstick!" Ninette de Valois wanted to send the younger girls back to The Hague, but the road was temporarily blocked. "The knowledge that our retreat was cut off intensified the excitement," Farjeon recorded. "The brothel scene of 'Rake's Progress' was at its most vulgar, with Helpmann mouthing lewd remarks to conductor Constant Lambert."

The following night's venue was the huge Philips Electronics factory in Eindhoven. The next day, Thursday, May 9, it was Arnhem—where Farjeon wandered about, unimpressed: "Along the river stood opulent houses with gardens down to the water, where wealthy Dutchmen retired for their well-fed old age, streets strewn with rubbish, dirty children playing in the gutter, and the smell of drains."[36]

A mile away, in a better part of the town, eleven-year-old Audrey Hepburn was excitedly anticipating the performance:

"For the occasion, my mother had our little dressmaker make me a long taffeta dress. I remember it so well. I'd never had a long dress in my life. There was a little round collar, a little bow here, and a little button in front. All the way to the ground, and it rustled. The reason she got me this, at great expense—we couldn't afford this kind of thing—was that I was to present a bouquet of flowers at the end of the performance to Ninette de Valois, the director of the company."[37]

The Sadler's Wells program that night at Arnhem's City Theater featured "Horoscope," a tale of young lovers ruled by the zodiac; and "Façade," Ashton's great comic ballet, with music by William Walton and an all-star cast of Fonteyn, Helpmann, Pamela May and Michael Somes. The audience was enthralled—none more so than Baroness van Heemstra and her daughter. Ella, who had helped arrange the company's visit, took the opportunity to deliver an extended thank-you speech first in Dutch, then in English, after which Audrey was summoned to present her bouquet to de Valois. If the presentation was especially touching, no one but the girl and her mother felt it at the time.

"A little kid brought some flowers," says company member Jane Edgeworth. "Just a nice little girl, like hundreds of other little girls, who wanted to study the ballet."[38]

The performance was followed by a supper and more of "those dull speeches that officials love to make," Annabel Farjeon noted. "The town was black and empty when we came out for the journey back to The Hague. Trucks which had lined the road the previous night [were] now rumbling toward the German frontier filled with soldiers and guns."

Earlier that day on the way into Arnhem, company member Elizabeth Kennedy saw felled trees all along the roadside: "They had the trees cut, and so they closed the roads by pushing the trees across as we passed. They were expecting an invasion."[39] Shortly after the company left Arnhem—around midnight—all roads into and out of the town were closed. "It was lucky that we had not dawdled longer and been trapped," says Farjeon.*

Hepburn folklore holds that the Sadler's Wells company fled Arnhem in panic that night, to the sound of bombs, "ten minutes" before the Germans crossed the Rhine and turned the town into a battlefield. In fact, there was no streetfighting in Arnhem that night—or for the next four years. But just three hours later, at three a.m. on May 10, the Germans indeed crossed into Holland, Belgium and Luxembourg—and Arnhem was one of their first stops.

"There was no noise," says Paul Vroemen, an Arnhem boy of eight at the time. "My dad switched on the radio at about five a.m. and they said planes were bombing Rotterdam, Amsterdam and The Hague with no declaration of war. The first Germans who arrived in Arnhem passed our

* The Sadler's Wells tale is tangential to our own, but balletomanes must not be denied its conclusion: The next morning, with Rotterdam in flames in the distance, the Germans dropped pamphlets proclaiming, "The Hague is surrounded, it is useless to resist." The dancers were taken to a temporary refuge near Velsen; forty-eight hours later, they boarded a cattle ship at Ijmuiden, arriving at Harwich the next day. Left behind in their flight were all sets, costumes and music for the ballets "Rake's Progress," "Checkmate," "Dante Sonata," "Façade," "Les Patineurs" and "Horoscope"—lost forever in a van somewhere between Arnhem and Haarlem, where they were scheduled to perform the night after Audrey saw them.

house about nine-thirty in the morning—three soldiers, well-equipped, in camouflage jackets. Just three. An hour later came lots of troops, artillery and infantry."*

Audrey recalled the disbelief and confusion on which the Germans capitalized:

> All civilians were ordered to remain indoors and to close their shutters, and we were warned not to look out of the windows. Naturally, we all peeped.... It was uncannily strange. In an invasion, one expects fighting; but there was no fighting. We saw the grey uniforms of the German soldiers on foot. They all held machine-guns and marched in looking spick-and-span and disciplined; then came the rumble of trucks—and the next thing we knew was that they had taken complete charge of the town.[40]

May 10, not coincidentally, was momentous in England as well. During the "Phony War" of late 1939 and early 1940, British Secretary of State for Air Kingsley Wood had refused to authorize air raids against German munitions factories on the grounds that they were "private property"! For such idiocy, and the Holland invasion's proof of it, the government now fell. On the evening of May 10, Neville Chamberlain resigned and the king sent for Churchill.

Thousands of men, women and children were burned or buried alive and 11,000 buildings destroyed in the barbaric Nazi firebombing of Rotterdam.‡ General H. G. Winkelman, the Dutch commander-in-chief, had planned to give up northern and eastern Holland and hold out for reinforcements from England and France. But the wild, wishful rumors of British war vessels and troops rushing to the defense of Holland were false.[41] The small Dutch army fought bravely, inflicting heavy casualties on the Germans especially around The Hague, where Nazi paratroopers were rushing to capture the queen. Feisty Wilhelmina reportedly told her secretary to shoot her if necessary to prevent her from falling into Hitler's hands.

But the situation was quite hopeless. Had Winkelman's forces continued to resist, Rotterdam's destruction would have been followed by similar attacks on Amsterdam and other cities. Three days after the invasion, the queen and her ministers left for London—as bitterly disappointing to the Germans as it then was to the Dutch. Two days later, to spare more carnage, Winkelman capitulated. Holland had been crushed in five days.

---

* The wartime account of this chapter owes much to Paul Vroemen, foremost Dutch military historian and author of seven books about Arnhem; and to *The Lion Rampant: The Story of Holland's Resistance to the Nazis*, by L. de Jong and Joseph W. F. Stoppelman.

‡ Among the Rotterdam survivors were four-year-old Robert Wolders and family (see Chapter 9).

In the despair of the moment, many castigated the queen for her flight, but others thought her wise and pointed out that the king of Belgium—who stayed—was just a hapless prisoner of war. Soon enough, she would begin her new job as the symbol of Dutch Resistance. When Radio Orange made its broadcast debut from London in July, Wilhelmina delivered the inaugural speech. Hers was a captive audience in every way, and she exhorted them forward to liberation. From then on, whenever Radio Orange announced a speech of the queen, all Holland knew and listened—the extended van Heemstra family included.

From childhood, Ella had known the queen slightly and always found her more stiff than inspirational. But nowadays, Ella and her children cheered with the rest of Holland "when the old girl used the rude word *moffen* for Germans [or] called Dutch Nazis *lummels* (nitwits)."[42] Listening to Radio Orange was strictly forbidden, and at the end of each broadcast, it was Audrey's job to turn the dial elsewhere in case of any surprise inspection.

After the capitulation, Dutch officials were forced to release all imprisoned members of the Dutch Nazi Movement (Nationaal-Socialistische Beweging, or NSB), who now became the country's hated ruling class. But by and large, the first weeks went by with no rampant murder or pillaging, and by June, rail connections, mail service, and telephones were restored.

"The Germans tried to be civil and to win our hearts," Audrey remembered. "The first few months we didn't know quite what had happened.... A child is a child is a child, [and] I just went to school."[43]

Vroemen, too, recalls life during the occupation as "quite normal" at first: "Life went on, though the rations were getting lower and lower. We had football and swimming matches, we went to the movies—not American or British, only German, of course, lots of propaganda and films of the victorious German army."

Holland had been a part of the historic Holy Roman Reich, or Empire, and the Dutch were given a chance to prove "willing" to rejoin it. They would not be crushed like the Poles and others. Germans did not take over civil authority; stamps were not, as elsewhere, imprinted with the words "Occupied Territory."

Soon enough, however, the brutal truth was that half a million German soldiers were being fed, clothed and paid from Dutch resources. Civilians were required to "board" soldiers for ten Dutch cents per night, and the country's riches were fully exploited for the German war machine. A partial list of the immense wealth stolen from the Netherlands and sent to Germany included virtually all Dutch tea, coffee, butter, vegetable oils, fruit and woolen goods. In 1940, the entire apple harvest was requisitioned by Germany, along with fourteen million of twenty-two million chickens and most of the cattle.

By spring of 1941, it was hard to get the single weekly egg to which rationing entitled everyone, let alone meat. By summer there was no tea or coffee left at all. Most dire was the fuel shortage: In the freezing winter, only one room per home was allowed to be heated. Entire woods disappeared. The death rate for children from cold and malnutrition soared 40 percent over that in 1939.[44]

Like everyone else, the van Heemstras had little food or heat, and—like everyone else—no choice but to endure. The Germans even confiscated bicycles. Insult to many injuries was the "personal identification card" which people now had to carry. Pre-invasion Holland had been the least-regimented state in Europe. In occupied Holland, Audrey was learning a harsh discipline very different from that of ballet.

But she was still learning ballet, too—with the help or hindrance of Ella's intense hovering. "Her mother was very dominant—a real ballet mother," says Winja Marova, "and the other girls didn't like it. They were also jealous, because Audrey was always the one that was mentioned."

Wartime reviews of her dance-school performances were, in fact, invariably enthusiastic about Audrey—the embryonic positive publicity of a lifetime. Wrote one critic, in July 1941, of a Marova school performance in the Musis Sacrum theater: "As all of them are just at the start of their dance development, we do not want to mention any names except for Audrey Hepburn who, in spite of the age of only twelve, was noticed because of her very individual personality and performance. She danced the 'Serenade' of Moszkowski with her own choreography."[45]

A year later, she was singled out again by the *Courant:* Audrey Hepburn "is only thirteen years old and has a natural talent that is in good hands with Winja Marova." And again, in 1943: "She has a beautiful figure, posture [and] gave the most beautiful performance of the evening."

Such public praise helped brighten her days and her life inside the house on Sickeslaan. It was modest for a baroness, but then the Dutch have always had a wide range of poor nobility. "My mother didn't have a dime," Audrey often protested later. "I don't know why people always think that just because my mother had a title, she was also wealthy."[46]

From Sickeslaan, they moved up to a brand-new rental house at 8A Jansbinnensingel, in a sector whose fountains and sculptures are still the jewels of Arnhem. The house was tastefully decorated by Ella to serve both as a domicile and as a showcase for her freelance design business. Audrey and Ella would remain there through the rest of the war, having no contact with neighbors and keeping entirely to themselves. They were so short of funds that Ella also gave bridge lessons to bring in a little extra cash, and felt no shame in doing so.[47]

Virtually all of the van Heemstra family's property had by then been confiscated: property, homes, bank accounts, securities and even jewelry. Old Baron Aernoud was barely able to secure permission to stay in his own home, Zijpendaal. Ella's sister and brother-in-law, Miesje and Otto, who were living with him, had to leave to make room for some Nazi officers. Eventually, the Baron himself was evicted, with permission to join Miesje and Otto in another of his houses in Oosterbeek.[48]

Due to her British citizenship, Audrey was in some danger of internment, if and when it suited German needs, and Ella warned her ever more fiercely never to speak English in public. The reverse of that dilemma was taking place in England, where Joseph Ruston was among hundreds of pro-Nazi activists—including Oswald Mosley—imprisoned without trial by the government under the infamous Regulation 18b (much as the Americans were interning Japanese), despite a row in Parliament over its legality. Most of them, including Audrey's father, spent two to three years in London jails before being moved to a detention camp on the Isle of Man. His treatment was severe in both places.

The wife and daughter he had abandoned knew nothing of it.

THE SUFFERING OF ENGLISH FASCISTS, at its worst, was nothing compared to the Nazi crimes against the Jews. Nowhere were the atrocities worse than in Holland where, during the previous forty years of Queen Wilhelmina's long liberal reign, all barriers between Christians and Jews had been erased. In 1933, when Hitler began his persecutions in earnest, thousands of German Jews fled—and were welcomed—to the Netherlands.

The first major blow to Dutch Jewry came in October 1940, when Jewish enterprises were forced to register, for eventual confiscation. A month later, all Jewish teachers, doctors and civil servants were dismissed. In December, Jews were barred from theaters and, soon, from parks and hotels. When the first physical attacks on Jews began the following February, Gentiles declared a strike in Amsterdam, paralyzing public services. As a result of that act of rebellion, municipal councils were dissolved and their powers transferred to Nazi commissioners.

In June 1941, more than seven hundred young Jewish men were rounded up at random and sent to Buchenwald. Their parents were later informed that the ashes of their sons could be obtained in exchange for "adequate payment." Arthur Seyss-Inquart, the Nazi Reichskommissar of the Netherlands, declared: "We do not consider the Jews a part of the Dutch people. They are the enemy with whom we neither wish to come to a truce, nor to a peace."

By 1942, Jewish-owned industries and real estate had been "Aryanized." Most Jews were transported to the larger cities and herded into ghettos. Their household goods were sent to Germany as "gifts to the victims of RAF bombings." Dutch Jews were now obliged to wear a yellow Star of David with the inscription "Jood" in mock-Hebrew letters. The number of Jewish suicides grew; some also took the lives of their children. About 30,000 went into hiding, assisted by Gentiles with forged ration books.

Both the Catholic and Protestant clergy opposed the madness from the start. Priests were forbidden to say Mass for dead Nazi soldiers. The Dutch Reformed Church urged disobedience to all anti-Semitic Nazi decrees, declaring: "The Jews have lived among us for centuries and are bound up with us in a common history." Infuriated by such opposition, the Nazis stepped up the arrests and deportations to a rate of six hundred per day. The adolescent Audrey Hepburn was a terrified witness:

> I'd go to the station with my mother to take a train and I'd see cattle trucks filled with Jews ... families with little children, with babies, herded into meat wagons—trains of big wooden vans with just a little slat open at the top and all those faces peering out. On the platform, soldiers herding more Jewish families with their poor little bundles and small children. They would separate them, saying "The men go there and the women go there." Then they would take the babies and put them in another van. We did not yet know that they were going to their death. We'd been told they were going to be taken to special camps. It was very hard to understand because I was eleven or so. I tell you, all the nightmares I've ever had are mingled with that.[49]

The people she saw were mostly being taken to Transit Camp Westerbork, some seventy-five miles northeast of Arnhem, a "holding" center before deportation to Auschwitz and other death camps. Among them were some of her neighbors from Jansbinnensingel.[50]

Non-Jews were victims as well. In May of 1942, seventy-two Dutchmen were executed in a single day for alleged crimes against their oppressors. Scores of others paid with their lives for helping British pilots who were downed over Dutch territory. When Dutch sabotage increased, the Germans announced a new policy of taking and executing hostages if the saboteurs were not turned in.

"The Germans were very good at reprisals," says Vroemen. "Once they knew they were losing, they were much more brutal to the people in the occupied countries."

For two years, the van Heemstras had escaped fatalities, but their luck now ran out. After a Dutch underground attempt to blow up a German train, the Nazis took five hostages from different sections of Holland, none of whom had any connection to the sabotage but all of whom had prominent Dutch family names. One of them was Count Otto van Limburg

Stirum, an Arnhem magistrate and the husband of Ella's elder sister, Miesje.

"The Germans thought people with titles were very popular with the population and that they were all connected with the court, which was not true," says Hako Sixma van Heemstra, a distant relative of Audrey's and family historian. "The Germans never really knew much about our way of living."

Uncle Otto was one of Audrey's favorites. For several weeks, he and the others were held at a monastery in the province of North Brabant. When no one came forth to confess to the train plot, they were taken into the woods and shot on August 15, 1942.[51] Her uncle had the grim distinction of being in the first group of civilians executed purely for publicity and retribution.

More reprisals followed, some of which Audrey witnessed in Arnhem, until the horror became almost a routine: "We saw young men put against the wall and shot, and they'd close the street and then open it and you could pass by again.... Don't discount anything awful you hear or read about the Nazis. It's worse than you could ever imagine."[52]

For self-preservation as well as effective insurgency, more and more Dutchmen were going underground, and her brother Alexander now became one of them. He had no wish to be caught in the round-up of young men—tens of thousands of them—now being "enlisted" to work in the German war industry as forced laborers.

Her younger brother Ian did not escape that fate. He was caught and sent to work fourteen hours a day in a munitions factory in Berlin or—for all his family knew—to his death. Audrey and her mother were beside themselves. After Otto van Limburg Stirum's arrest and execution, his widow and old Baron van Heemstra left Oosterbeek and moved to a home of the Baron's called Villa Beukenhof on Rozendaalselaan in the town of Velp. With no other male protection or sanctuary left to them, Ella and Audrey now turned to him in desperation, and he took them in.

Late in life, when an interviewer dwelled on her absent father and "lack of a man," Audrey bristled: "I had my grandfather and we lived with him; he became the father figure in my life. I adored him. He and I would do very old crossword puzzles, sitting around a little lamp with no heat."[53] She remembered those days in Velp as an endless waiting game. "Had we known we were going to be occupied for five years, we might have all shot ourselves. We thought it would be over next week... six months... next year.... That's how we got through."[54]

That, and by resisting the enemy—in whatever large or small ways they could. Resistance leaders and the queen demanded that Dutchmen "must undo all Nazi measures in the struggle for liberation." But Dutch Resistance was, in fact, quite late in organizing. The prewar leaders had failed to lay the groundwork for any underground espionage or communications network. Yet the Dutch were masters of obstruction when they wanted to be. Once the movement got going, Dutch youth presented an especially united front: Of 4,500 students at Utrecht University, for example, a total of twenty joined the Dutch Nazi party.

In Arnhem, as elsewhere, the Resistance had many levels and was not highly unified, and the roles played by many of its citizens were ambiguous—including the van Heemstras. It is possible, as later claimed, that Ella engaged in some fund-raising for the cause and may have passed along information from certain of her pro-Nazi friends to the underground. But she is nowhere mentioned in the city's 2,000 archival files on the subject. Local Resistance leaders must have known of her fascist past and would not have considered her very trustworthy.

The far-fetched report that Ella was overtly pro-fascist in order to hide her covert work in the Resistance is debunked by her own daughter-in-law, Alexander's wife, Miep, who says Ella's German sympathies were no cover but a kind of fashion that was "in" for a long time before the invasion of Holland: "Ella was very English, but she was also pro-German. A lot of people in the aristocratic class were pro-German. She even went out with a German general, although it's said she did this to protect her children, as many did. Later on, she became anti-German."[55] David Heringa and his mother, Ella's Christian Science friends, once dropped by Ella's and were surprised to find a German officer "who was introduced to us as one of her relations."[56]

Many Hollanders still cannot accept the fact that, while some actively resisted the Germans, many—perhaps most—did not. The retroactive outrage against "collaborators" contains much hypocrisy and sheds little light. In Ella's case, it can only be said that she did what she had to do to survive and take care of her children. As a good Dutchwoman, she could not have held on to her erstwhile Nazi views much after her husband's desertion and her firsthand experience of the occupation. She certainly never benefitted in any way from her former fascist leanings. The bottom line is that no one really knows what Ella was up to politically—if anything—during the war.

More is known about the activities of her daughter; there was never any doubt where Audrey's sympathies lay. Resistance work was a sensitive subject long after the war ended. From the heroic to the humble, most Netherlanders wanted to forget and not relive the experience. "Interviewers try to bring it up so often, but it's painful," she would say. "I dislike talking about it because I feel it's not something that should be linked to publicity."[57] In her case, the publicity put forth after she became a star contained some truth and much melodrama.

"Audrey did have contacts with the underground forces," confirms historian Vroemen after extensive research of her Arnhem activities, "but there was no espionage. She was only twelve or so, after all. And yet it's true that youngsters had an advantage because they had less fear and more freedom. I was about eleven, by the middle of the war, and could go where I liked. I was mostly interested in stealing things from the Germans if I got a chance. I'm sure Audrey had similar experiences."[58]

Chief among the Hepburn legends—and quite true—are her exploits as a courier and occasional secret messenger. Her son Sean remembers that "she told us stories about carrying messages as an eleven-year-old for the Resistance in her shoes."[59] Children often did such things, as Vroemen noted, because they could move about with relative freedom, especially going to and from school.

"Once I had to step in and deliver our tiny underground newspaper," she said. "I stuffed them in my woolen socks in my wooden shoes, got on my bike and delivered them."[60] The illegal leaflets came from Dr. Visser 't Hoofd, a general practitioner and Resistance worker in Velp. Regular shoes were tightly rationed and extremely expensive. Her mother once got her a pair of brown lace-up boots that were two sizes two big, in the hope they'd last longer. "I never grew into them," Audrey recalled, but she made good use of the extra space inside.[61]

Her performing talents were also put to use for the cause and, equally, for herself. In 1943, the Germans confiscated all radios. Thenceforth, in more ways than one, a girl had to make her own music. "I was left to my own devices," she said, and those devices drew her more deeply into music and dance, "where one didn't have to talk, only listen.[62] There was a war, but your dreams for yourself go on [and] I wanted to be a dancer."

Her personal ambition linked up with the Resistance in a series of "blackout performances" that served both as an outlet for the dancers and a fund-raising activity for the underground: "We would literally do it in somebody's house with locked windows, drawn blinds. I had a friend who played the piano and my mother would run up costumes out of old curtains and things. I'd do my own choreography—not to be believed!"[63]

They were her own condensed versions of classic ballets, performed behind locked doors with lookouts posted to watch for German soldiers, several times at the home of Dr. Wouders, a local homeopath, and at least once at her own house. "The best audience I ever had," she said years later, "made not a single sound at the end of my performance."[64] After a silent curtain call, the hat was passed and "the money we made helped saboteurs in their work against the Nazis."[65]

They were never caught, and Audrey's involvement in those recitals continued until late in the war when the lack of food weakened her so much she could hardly walk, let alone dance. "Every loyal Dutch schoolgirl and boy did their little bit to help," she said. "Many were much more courageous than I was. I'll never forget a secret society of university students called *Les Gueux* [The Beggars], which killed Nazi soldiers one by one and dumped their bodies in the canals. That took real bravery, and many of them were caught and executed by the Germans. They're the type who deserve the memorials and medals."[66]

Neither her days nor her life felt heroic. In later years, and with great emotion, she would identify with Anne Frank, whose life was "very much a parallel to mine":

[Anne Frank and I] were born the same year, lived in the same country, experienced the same war, except she was locked up and I was on the outside. [Reading her diary] was like reading my own experiences from her point of view. I was quite destroyed by it. An adolescent girl locked up in two rooms, with no way of expressing herself other than to her diary. The only way she could tell the change in season was by a glimpse of a tree through an attic window.[67]

It was in a different corner of Holland, [but] all the events I experienced were so incredibly accurately described by her—not just what was going on on the outside, but what was going on on the inside of a young girl starting to be a woman... all in a cage. She expresses the claustrophobia, but transcends it through her love of nature, her awareness of humanity and her love—real love—of life.[68]

Audrey's favorite passage in the diary, which she could quote from memory, was written in 1944, just six months before Anne Frank was taken to a death camp:

I go to the attic and from my favorite spot on the floor, I look up at the blue sky at the bare chestnut trees on whose branches little raindrops shine, like silver. And I can see gulls and other birds as they glide on the wind. As long as this exists and I may live to see it, this sunshine and the cloudless sky, while it lasts, I cannot be unhappy.... As long as this exists, and it certainly always will, I know there will be comfort for every sparrow.

Audrey's comfort came from dance, despite all difficulties and debility. By now it was impossible to buy ballet clothes or shoes, but "as long as there were any old sweaters to pull out, my mother would re-knit my tights," she said. "Sometimes we were able to buy felt to make slippers, but they never lasted more than two classes."[69] She danced endless hours in shoes that were worn to shreds, finally resorting to the only painful alternative—wooden ones.

By 1944 she was Winja Marova's star pupil, sufficiently advanced to help instruct the youngest students, one of whom was kindergartner Rose-Marie Willems:

"Ballet was something that belonged to your education, like swimming and gymnastics. [Audrey at fourteen] was tall and skinny, with big hands and feet. Her teeth were a little bit crooked, but her big eyes were really remarkable. She was very serious for her age, and she really tried to make something out of the lessons. They had an old gramophone, and she would clap her hands. I wasn't always the best-behaved child and once in a while [she] would say, 'You there in the brown suit. Don't be so bad! You have to behave better.'"[70]

Audrey also gave some under-the-table private lessons in those days, which Winja Marova pretended not to know about. Marova felt her protégée might pass along the wrong technique, but others were doing it too and she couldn't blame them for trying to earn an extra guilder or two for their families.

One of Audrey's "private" students was Hesje van Hall, who lived in Velp. The lessons took place in the family dining room, and Hesje's brother Willem remembers them well: "I was starting puberty then. Audrey was very slender and walked so gracefully. When she came in, the whole house would look different."[71]

The biggest dance moment of Audrey's young life came on January 8, 1944, in a student showcase choreographed by Winja Marova at Arnhem's City Theatre. "Audrey Hepburn-Ruston," as the program billed her, featured in many numbers, from Burgmüller's *March Militaire* to Debussy's *Danseuse de Delphus*, returning late in the show for her tour de force—the "Morgenstimmung" (Morning Mood) and "Death of Aase" sections of Grieg's *Peer Gynt*.

She was quite "magnificent" that night, says music teacher Carel Wensink, "no doubt the best of Marova's pupils." Audrey the dancer was getting better, but things in Arnhem were getting worse. A local fan found her looking "slightly dazed" one day and asked when she had last eaten. "I had some bread yesterday morning," she said, "but I'm not hungry." "You're a very good dancer, but a very poor liar," he replied.[72]

Under such circumstances, "I could not go on dancing," she said. "It was the war diet and the anxiety and the terror."[73] Audrey was growing fast—"really tall, skinny and pale," Marova says. "She didn't get the right nutrition, and she fell apart. I agreed with her mother that she should stop dancing temporarily."

As the war dragged on, food and money became even scarcer. She and her family were now subsisting on watery soup and a kind of "green bread" made from peas. "We ate nettles, and everyone tried to cook grass, only I couldn't stand it," she said.[74] At one point, there was nothing to eat for days but endive, and they thanked God for that. But like Scarlett

O'Hara in *Gone With the Wind,* "I swore I'd never eat it again as long as I lived."[75]

AS AUDREY OFTEN SAID, NO one believed the war could last five years. Even less believable was that Arnhem could be the site of the greatest airdrop operation in twentieth-century warfare.

Eight weeks after the June 6, 1944, invasion of Normandy, the Allies reached Paris. Now, with much of Belgium and France liberated, British Field Marshall Montgomery conceived "Operation Market Garden." It was a bold plan to end the war by Christmas and make military history: A vast number of airborne troops would be dropped behind enemy lines to capture the Dutch towns of Eindhoven, Grave, Nijmegen and Arnhem— and most important, their bridges over the Maas, Waal and Rhine rivers. Land forces would join them for a quick advance into the German heartland and on to Berlin, thus ending the war in a lightning stroke.

The Germans were raggedly retreating east on foot, poorly armed and demoralized. But the Allies failed to finish the job, allowing 80,000 enemy troops to escape into Holland. The Allied command did not imagine how quickly they might reorganize. Nor did they believe Dutch underground reports that two powerful Panzer divisions were regrouping just outside Arnhem.

Five crucial bridges had to be taken, according to Montgomery's plan. If any one of them failed to fall, so did the entire operation. The 101st U.S. Airborne Division was to capture the bridges by Eindhoven and Veghel, which it did. The 82nd U.S. Airborne was ordered to grab the bridges at Grave and Nijmegen—likewise taken, with great difficulty.

Last and most important was the Rhine bridge in Arnhem, which had been blown up by the Dutch early in the war but since rebuilt. The unenviable task of retaking it was assigned to the First British Airborne Division and the Polish Independent Parachute Brigade Group. The parachutists were ordered to take and defend the Arnhem bridge for forty-eight hours while the ground troops pushed up from the south to join them.

The Battle of Arnhem—the largest air-land operation of the Second World War—began Sunday, September 17, 1944, with the first drop of British paratroopers under the command of Major-General Roy Urquhart, an infantry officer who had never been in command of an airborne division. The Germans were stunned, but the drop had been made some ten kilometers from the center of Arnhem. Every minute is precious in an airborne landing, but this one was afflicted with terrible delays and a failure to capitalize on the Germans' surprise. Most of the 3,000 men dropped that first day were left on the landing zones. Only one battalion of seven hundred, under Lieutenant-Colonel John Frost, made it to the bridge. Worse, a breakdown of communications equipment left them without information as well as reinforcements.

When the great drop began, many German soldiers ran away in terror, recalls Paul Vroemen, whose best friend was killed that day by a British—not a Nazi—bomb as he was leaving church after Mass. Vroemen remembers the Germans running past his house, shouting, "The tommies are coming!" and throwing down their weapons: "About forty-five minutes later, we saw one lone jeep with some English paratroopers—that was all." Immediately, the townsfolk began to celebrate, filling the streets, showering the advance guard with flowers and otherwise getting in their way.

But in the next seventy-two hours, Arnhem became a slaughterhouse. Reinforcements in C-47 transports and gliders landed the second day under heavy fire—an incredible feat in which many men lost their lives while floating to earth under their parachutes, easy marks for the German artillery below. The following morning, a desperate attempt was made to break through to Frost's men at the bridge. But General Urquhart's troops were simply too far away, forced to defend themselves on three sides at suburban Oosterbeek—including the grounds of the van Heemstra family.

"There was fighting in our garden in Oosterbeek," says Audrey's cousin Michael Quarles van Ufford. "My grandfather was an amateur moviemaker, and we have footage of those gliders coming in and people scattered all over the front lawn."[76]

The Baron was shuttling back and forth between his bomb-damaged properties in both Oosterbeek and Velp. Ella and Audrey were living at the latter place, three miles outside Arnhem, when Audrey was summoned—in view of her good English—to deliver a message to one of many British airmen stranded in the nearby woods. According to a widely published story later, by Audrey's friend Anita Loos, it happened like this:

Audrey entered the woods, found the paratrooper, explained he was surrounded, and led him to a nearby house for some food. When he could hide no longer, "he gave himself up, refreshed and prepared for his forthcoming ordeal as a prisoner of war," wrote Loos. "Before they parted, the young man gave Audrey his only possession of value, a silver locket with the Lord's Prayer engraved on it. After the war, she heard from the young paratrooper and at Christmas, 1947, went to England to visit his family and to receive his mother's thanks."[77]

It is a poignant story—and mostly nonsense. Loos was a notorious embellisher. The accurate version is contained in a 1956 *Dance* magazine article for which Audrey was actually interviewed: She went into the woods to a designated rock, found the man, traded information quickly, and then skipped off, picking flowers. Encountering a German soldier on the way back, she smiled and sweetly handed him her bouquet and proceded on into town to signal a street cleaner that the soldier would be coming in that night to hide out with him.[78]

Similar civilian efforts to aid the British, singly and en masse, were taking place all over the area, which was infested with German units. On Thursday, September 21, the brave and bloody—almost suicidal—landing of General Sosabowski's Polish parachutists did not improve the situation, which degenerated to streetfighting in Arnhem itself. Heavy fighting raged around St. Elizabeth's Hospital, where the wounded on both sides were taken and treated, indiscriminately, by Dutch and German doctors alike.

The tide was fast turning against the liberators, many of them now dependent on the townspeople. One of the most desperate was Major Anthony Deane-Drummond, an officer of the First Airborne Division Signals. He had gone into Arnhem to investigate the communications breakdown between Frost and Urquhart but was caught in the fighting and ended up leading the remnants of a company in search of homes in which to hide. Deane-Drummond and three others sought cover in a corner house near the foot of the bridge, at 69 Eusebius Buitensingel. It belonged to Countess Miesje van Limburg Stirum—Otto's widow and Audrey's aunt—who had strong reasons to offer help, and did so.

But their asylum was in the eye of the hurricane. The Germans were rushing to reinforce that exact spot, and within hours the Englishmen were trapped. After three days in hiding, with Miesje's direction, they dashed east to Velp but were caught and detained there in a large manor house with hundreds of other British prisoners. In the confusion, they located a hidden wall space where they managed to elude notice for thirteen days, existing on water and bits of bread. Helpful Dutch servants inside made their plight known to a woman in the adjacent home—Ella van Heemstra—who dug into her father's secret reserves to provide the men with food on the night they escaped.*

"On opening up the basket," wrote Deane-Drummond in his memoirs, "I found a bottle of vintage Krug champagne, a jar full of beef tea and some coffee. . . . I would have been even more incredulous if someone had told me that the daughter would one day grow up into the beautiful stage and film actress Audrey Hepburn. The delicacies that they had sent round were literally more valuable than gold in wartime Holland, and were freely given to a complete stranger. I later heard that the Heemstra family were themselves suffering shortages of food and that little Audrey was even too weak to dance. Such was true generosity which I will always remember."[79]

---

* The Deane-Drummond events, unlike most Hepburn-related war stories, are recounted in *A Bridge Too Far*, Cornelius Ryan's meticulously researched book on the Battle of Arnhem, and confirmed by Deane-Drummond in his own reliable book, *Return Ticket*.

The Deane-Drummond story had a happy ending; the Battle of Arnhem did not. The British defended their ground at Oosterbeek until September 26, when 2,400 men were evacuated back across the Rhine. Frost and his men held the bridge twice as long as they were ordered to, but at a terrible cost. In the end, Allied casualties at Arnhem were far greater than in the D-Day invasion of Normandy—17,000 vs. 12,000. Hundreds of civilians died, as well. Virtually all of Arnhem's historic buildings were destroyed and 75 percent of its homes left uninhabitable.

The Arnhem invasion has been refought a thousand times on paper: Had the Allies moved in a week earlier, the town might have been taken without a fight. The German officers were incredulous: "If they wanted the bridge," said one, "why would they land ten kilometers away?" The same question was asked in the Allied high command, where British-American rivalry led both to ignore reliable information from the Dutch underground. As usual in war, the problem was at the top.

Today, the landing zones outside Arnhem look just as they did fifty years ago, green and deceptively inviting. Vroemen points out shell holes and monuments containing the emblems of the various parachute units—the famous Pegasus, for instance, with its inscription: "They shall mount up with wings as eagles," from Isaiah 40:31. Some veterans still like to jump, he says. During a recent reunion, one of them—at age seventy-three—did a double.

THE BATTLE WAS OVER, BUT worse was in store for the shell-shocked locals. Expecting a British counterattack over the Rhine at any moment, the Germans now ordered all citizens to leave the town "for their own protection." If that was humanitarian in part, it was mostly retaliatory: The Germans were enraged by the cooperation and support given the British by the populace.

The evacuation of Arnhem was brutal in the extreme. The day after the British capitulation, every man, woman and child was forced to leave within twenty-four hours or risk being shot on sight. An exodus of 90,000, with what little they could carry on foot, began at dawn. Most headed north toward Apeldoorn, others south or west. Some 3,000 would die on the way to their destinations.

With its people gone, Arnhem was now ransacked. "Special troops came from Germany to do the looting," says Vroemen. In good German fashion, "they kept a careful, itemized list of what they stole—clothes, raincoats, underwear, shoes. They sent it all to Germany and said it was 'a gift from the Dutch people.'"

The Germans had taken over the attic and installed a radio transmitter at Baron van Heemstra's villa in Velp, but Ella and her daughter continued to live there in relative safety, watching the evacuation in horror and doing what they could.

"I still feel sick when I remember the scenes," Audrey would recall. "It was human misery at its starkest—masses of refugees on the move, some carrying their dead, babies born on the roadside, hundreds collapsing of hunger.... [80] 90,000 people looking for a place to live. We took in forty, but... there was literally nothing to eat."[81] She was told to drink as much water as she could so her stomach might at least *feel* full.[82]

Previous hardships in the Netherlands had been monumental, but that last winter of the war—known in Holland as "the hunger winter"—was the worst by far. Starvation deaths were augmented by a tuberculosis epidemic in early 1945, and the demand for caskets could not be met. Life in Holland was at its lowest ebb, but fifteen-year-old Hepburn felt more hope than despair.

"I wanted to start dancing again," she said, and so Velp's village carpenter was asked to put up a barre in one of her grandfather's rooms with a marble floor. "I gave classes for all ages, and I accepted what was about a dime a lesson. We worked to a gramophone wound by hand." Some of her pupils lived in the house, and the lessons helped keep their minds off the horror outside. But soon enough, the Germans ordered everybody out: "It was unspeakably hard to turn [them] into the cold night. Even my brother, who was hiding there, had to leave."[83]

Her own close brush with disaster came soon after, in March 1945, two months before the liberation, when she was stopped on the street by soldiers with machine guns, rounding up young women to staff their military kitchens. Herded into the group, Audrey and the other sobbing girls were marched toward German headquarters—but poorly guarded.

"I was picked right off the streets with a dozen others," she said. "As they turned to get more women, I nipped off and ran, and stayed indoors for the next month."[84] Her hiding place was not the cellar of the County Council building, as often reported later, but her own home. By the end of the war, she was in broken health but good spirits:

> I had jaundice during that last six months. My mother and aunt and I ate very little. We ate a few turnips, we made flour from tulip bulbs, which is actually very fine flour. In the winter there was nothing; in the spring we picked anything we could in the countryside.... [85]
>
> I was very sick but didn't realize it. It wasn't until after the war that I started to realize how my mom must have suffered. She wanted to give me an orange or something. She often looked at me and said, 'You look so pale.' I thought she was just fussing, but now I understand how she must have felt.[86]
>
> I was given an outlook on life by my mother.... It was frowned upon

not to think of others first. It was frowned upon not to be disciplined. . . .
During the last winter of the war, we had no food whatsoever, and my aunt
said to me, "Tomorrow we'll have nothing to eat, so the best thing to do is
stay in bed and conserve our energy." That very night, a member of the
underground brought us food—flour, jam, oatmeal, cans of butter. . . . When
I hit rock-bottom, there [was] always something there for me.[87]

Adolf Hitler committed suicide on April 30, 1945. The liberation of
Holland was completed four days later on Audrey's sixteenth birthday,
May 4, which also became Holland's official day of mourning for the
victims of the war. Arnhem, largely a ghost town, had been liberated a
fortnight earlier. "That was the day I learned that freedom has a bouquet,
a perfume all its own —the smell of English tobacco and petrol," Audrey
recalled:[88]

We were in our cellar, where we'd been for weeks. Our area was being
liberated practically house to house, and there was lots of shooting and
shelling from over the river and constant bombing: explosions going on all
night. . . . Once in a while you'd go up and see how much of your house was
left, and then you'd go back under again. Then early in the morning all of
a sudden there was total silence. Everybody said, my God, now what's
happening? We listened for a while, and strangely enough, I thought I could
hear voices and some singing—and I smelt English cigarettes.[89]

We crept upstairs to the front door, opened it very carefully and to our
amazement, our house was completely surrounded by English soldiers, all
aiming their guns at us. I screamed with happiness, seeing all these cocky
figures with dirty bright faces and shouted something in English. The corporal
or sergeant walked up to me, and in a very gentle English voice—so different
from all the German shouting we'd been used to—said, "We hear you have
a German radio station in your house and we've come to take it away.
We're sorry to disturb you." I laughed and said, "Go right on disturbing
us." Then a cheer went up that they'd liberated an English girl. I was the
only one for miles.[90]

Equally vivid in her memory of liberation day were the seven chocolate
bars given to her by an English soldier. She ate them all at once—and
was violently ill. Far better nutritionally was the food she and thousands of
others received soon after from the United Nations Relief and Rehabilitation
Administration, the forerunner of UNICEF. Her commitment to that
organization began then and there. She would never forget the first two
incongruous things they gave her: condensed milk and cigarettes.[91]

"They filled the schools [with] UNRRA crates—boxes of food that we
were allowed to take home, and blankets, medication and clothes," she

said. "I remember going to a huge classroom where we could pick out clothes, sweaters and skirts, and they were so pretty and had come from America. We thought, how could people be so rich to give away things that looked so new?[92]

"I remember lots of flour and butter and oatmeal and all the things that we hadn't seen in ages!... One of the first meals I had was oatmeal made with canned milk, and I put so much sugar on it and I ate a whole plateful and was deadly ill afterwards because I couldn't absorb it. I wasn't used to rich food anymore. I was hardly used to *food* anymore, let alone that kind of thing. But it was everything we dreamed of."[93]

She was sixteen years old, five-foot-six and weighed ninety pounds. After five years, she was suffering from asthma, jaundice and other diseases stemming from malnutrition, including anemia and severe edema, a swelling of the joints and limbs in which the blood literally turns to water. "It begins with your feet," Audrey recounted clinically, "and when it reaches your heart, you die. With me it was above the ankles when we were liberated."[94]

She was also having problems with colitis and irregular periods—possibly endometriosis, common among women dancers and athletes with little body fat—and her metabolism would be permanently affected. In some ways, she would never fully recover from the war: To the end of her life, she never weighed more than 110 pounds. It would be claimed that she also suffered from some form of anorexia or bulimia, of which the war was the source; and that she later deprived herself of, or felt she could do without, food. (See Chapter 9, pp. 303–304.)

But past and future pain were set aside for the moment, in celebration of the present. A few nights after the liberation, Canadian troops plugged a projector into an outdoor electric generator in the town square and—to the joy of Audrey and her teenage friends—gave them an alfresco screening of the first Hollywood film they had seen since before the war.

Audrey and Ella's joy was more profound a few weeks later when Alexander suddenly emerged from years as an *onderduiker*—in underground hiding—with a pregnant wife. On July 17, 1945, Audrey became an aunt with the birth of their son Michael. More miraculously, soon after, Ian showed up at their door—having walked most of the 325 miles from Berlin to Arnhem. Five thousand Dutch boys sent for forced labor in Germany had died there. Ian's family now thanked God that he was not one of them.

"We had almost given up," said Audrey, "when the doorbell rang and it was Ian....[95] We lost everything, of course—our houses, our possessions, our money. But we didn't give a hoot. We got through with our lives, which was all that mattered."[96]

AS SOON AS IT WAS possible to do so, they returned to Arnhem and their little house at 8A Jansbinnensingel. "Unfortunately," Audrey concluded, "people basically learn little from war. We needed each other so badly that we were kind, we hid each other, we gave each other something to eat. But when it was over, people were just the same—gossipy and mean."[97]

But Audrey was neither of those, and she was exhilarated by the existential liberation that came with the military one: "Life started again and all the things you'd never had, never seen, never eaten, never worn, started to come back again. That was such a stimulus."[98] So was the freedom to choose and do what she wished.

Her first choice, in the summer of 1945, was to volunteer for work in the Royal Military Invalids Home, a facility for injured and retired veterans in the Arnhem suburb of Bronbeek. It was, and remains, a sprawling, beautiful white structure, built in 1862 by King Willem III, Queen Wilhelmina's father. There, Audrey helped minister to soldiers of many nationalities, one of whom would happily link up with her twenty-two years later.

"While she was being shelled in Arnhem, I was in a tank a few miles away," said Terence Young, the future director of a fine thriller called *Wait Until Dark*. "We were stuck on that single road into the town and never able to come to the relief of the unfortunate parachutists stuck there."[99]

Wounded in the last weeks of the war, Young was now lying in the Arnhem hospital. "In the next room to mine," he recalled, "was a legendary figure in the parachute regiments, 'Mad Mike' Calvert, a brigadier general. When he found out I was a filmmaker, he asked me about doing a film on Arnhem. That same afternoon, director Brian Desmond Hurst arrived with the head of Gaumont-British news to ask if I would write a script about Arnhem, using the real-life characters."

The resulting *Men of Arnhem*, codirected by Hurst and Young, is one of the most powerful of all World War II documentaries, and though Audrey had nothing to do with it, she had her own encounter with those filmmakers at the time. In September 1945, recalls David Heringa, Audrey's friend from the Christian Science classes, "her mother brought her to our house to see if we could introduce her to some big shots of Gaumont-British who were staying with us and making [*Men of Arnhem*]. But they could only suggest [that she] continue ballet lessons and then, when things were more normal, come to England. We all thought Mother van Heemstra a bit pushy about Audrey."[100]

Characterizations of Ella were always remarkably consistent. With typical resilience, she now reapplied herself to Audrey's career, which could no longer be served in the ruins of Arnhem. At twenty-five and twenty-one, her brothers were on their own. Alexander worked first in government reconstruction projects and then in Indonesia for British Petroleum Matape. Ian joined the multinational firm Unilever (a merger of Britain's Lever Brothers and the Dutch Margarine Company), whose postwar product line featured such previously unavailable delicacies as peanut butter. Only Audrey remained in the nest—and Ella decided it was time to move the nest to Amsterdam.

No great immediate prospects awaited most of the thousands of displaced Hollanders who jammed that city in October of 1945. But Ella had a large network of friends and was not too proud to take the first honest work she could find, which turned out to be cook-housekeeper for a wealthy family who also provided her a small basement flat. She soon left for a slightly better post as a florist's shop manager, and a slightly better apartment nearby.

The overriding reason for relocating to Amsterdam was Audrey: Winja Marova had given her a glowing recommendation to study with Sonia Gaskell, then the leading name in Dutch ballet. Holland had been on the cutting edge of dance since 1658 when "The Ballet of Maidens" featured female dancers, decades before women were allowed on stage in more sophisticated Paris.

In that tradition, Gaskell nowadays ran a school and soon founded a company that would evolve into the Netherlands (Dutch National) Ballet.* "The classic dance is dead," she declared. Gaskell's school was known in Europe and America for avant-garde choreography and the hard-edged modern music to which it was often set—jazz and atonal included. She was also adept at discovering, encouraging and harboring young talent.

Audrey was one of her discoveries and now joined Gaskell's "Balletstudio '45," where she danced classroom roles to such dissimilar composers as Bach, Debussy, Villa-Lobos, Stravinsky and Shostakovich, sometimes choreographing the exercises herself. Audrey, said Gaskell, "had no money to pay for the lessons. Yet I thought she deserved a chance. In the two floors of studio space below my apartment, I found her a tiny room in which she barely could move, but she loved it and became a very serious pupil."[101] What Audrey learned from Gaskell was "the work ethic—don't complain, don't give in even if you're tired, don't go out the night before you have to dance. Sonia taught me that if you really worked hard, you'd succeed, and that everything had to come from the inside."[102]

In May 1946, Audrey was chosen to dance with Gaskell's top student

---

* Sonia Gaskell (1904–1974), a Lithuanian Jew, danced with the Russian ballet of Serge Diaghilev from 1927–1929 and later had her own studio in Paris. In 1933, she followed her husband, Dutch interior architect Philip Aukens, to Amsterdam and taught ballet there until the German occupation, when she went into hiding. After the war, she immediately picked up where she left off.

star, Beatrix Leoni, in a matinee performance at Amsterdam's Hortus Theater. "She didn't have a lot of great technique," wrote the *Algemeen Handelsblad* newspaper critic of her three solos, "but she definitely had talent."

For her seventeenth birthday that month, Ella gave her a season ticket for the upcoming season of Amsterdam's great Concertgebouw Orchestra, and for Christmas she got tickets to a series of Beethoven string quartets. Her living arrangement with Gaskell ended. She was back with her mother and so broke that she couldn't even afford to ride the tram, but even in the most inclement weather, she walked the considerable distance from their flat to the Concertgebouw and never missed a concert.*

She often took along Anneke van Wijk, her friend and fellow dance student. Van Wijk remembers her as a hard worker who practiced incessantly—spontaneous, funny, cultivated and never arrogant or competitive to the point of rivalry:

"Audrey's expression was fabulous. The way she used her hands and eyes showed that she also had talent for acting. Her enormous eyes were not to be believed. I asked her once, 'What are you doing to make them seem so wide?' She said, 'Nothing. They've always been this way.'"[103] When van Wijk knew her, she was just "a normal Dutch girl with chubby cheeks," by no means heavy but not thin, either. "I remember that because I used to take showers with her after the lessons. It wasn't until later, when she started to act, that she became so skinny."

Van Wijk thought they were both a bit old to be starting with Gaskell and that they had lost too much time because of the war. Partly with that in mind, she and her husband introduced Audrey to photographer Helena Voute, at whose studio Audrey began to do some posing. With her innate stage presence and good posture, she quickly developed her natural feel for it.

Ella was still moving around considerably in those days. Her network of friends included the Heineken brewery family, whose son Freddie recalls seeing Audrey and passing along the esoteric skill he was then cultivating:

"I gave her her first tap-dance lesson. Her nickname was Rimple, for some reason, because when she laughed, she had a little dimple or 'rimple.' She and Ella lived for a while in Noordwijk [just southwest of Amsterdam], where I lived, too. They spent a lot of time at my mother's house. Ella was taking care of our little poodle. She was a funny, down-to-earth

---

* Painful political baggage was attached to the Concertgebouw. In 1941, its famous conductor Willem Mengelberg had accepted a post on the Nazi "Culture Council" shunned by loyal Dutchmen. Throughout the war, many Dutch musicians displayed their anti-Nazi sentiment. The Nazi weekly *De Misthoorn* (The Foghorn) complained in 1942 that the Arnhem orchestra, for example, "took particular pleasure" in honoring Jewish musicians. After the war, Mengelberg was fired and exiled, and a cleansed Concertgebouw was under new management.

woman with enormous problems. I don't think Audrey would have gotten anywhere without her."[104]

Ella was now subsidizing her daughter's lessons by doing facials and makeup at the fashionable beauty salon of P. C. Hoofstraat. By one account, she was also selling cosmetics door-to-door. For a time, Audrey developed a little avocation as a hatmaker, selling her creations to her mother's clients.

"Audrey had exquisite taste," said her friend Loekie van Oven, a Gaskell dancer who was several years older and took her under her wing. "She and her mother had no money, but they had class and style. Audrey used to go to department stores in Amsterdam and buy plain-looking hats and, with her artistic talent, easily change them into something really nice."[105]

Audrey and Loekie spent a lot of time together, talking and dreaming. As there was never enough money for proper dance gear, "We used to wear ballet shoes made by a Belgian shoemaker that were like wooden shoes—very heavy. Audrey was quite ingenious. She used to make tights from Ace bandages and dye them by soaking them in water with red crepe paper."[106]

Audrey in Amsterdam was "very shy and withdrawn," says van Oven, partly because of her monastic living conditions and lack of money, but mostly because of the strict nature of ballet life itself: "Love or *érotique* do not play an important part in it. . . . It had nothing to do with sexuality. We flirted sometimes, but that was it. The dancing was physically very fatiguing, so we had to put all our energy into that. Dancing was everything for Audrey. . . . She could put a spell on an audience and subdue them. There was poetry and motion in anything she touched."

Though Audrey was ambitious, Loekie felt she chafed at the even greater ambition of her mother. Ella longed for a return to prominence in the class in which she (and Audrey, for that matter) had been raised. She wanted Audrey to meet more of "the right kind of people" and preferably to marry one of them. Her pressure contributed to Audrey's withdrawal, says van Oven· "A lot of people thought it was interesting and exciting to know the daughter of a baroness. But Audrey didn't want to have anything to do with that. She really kept her distance from it."

Audrey was one of Gaskell's best and favorite pupils, but not everyone was happy with the mistress. Gaskell believed a dancer's expression "was prettier when the person felt bad," says van Oven, and often helped to induce such feelings. Dancer Ida de Jong, who had attended Gaskell's school before the war, gone to England and then returned to Gaskell in 1948, calls her "not very kind." When Ida later left to join the Dutch Opera ballet, "Sonia never spoke to me again."[107]

More than once before leaving, Ida told Audrey, "You must not stay in Holland—you must go to England. You'll have a lot more opportunities there, and you don't have to ask to come in because you are half English."[108] As an afterthought, she added that Audrey could also get movie parts in London, which was "an easy way to make some money."

Immigration into Britain was then quite difficult indeed, requiring much documentation and a work permit. But Ida was right: With a British father and British passport, Audrey could go there if she chose, and after almost three years with Gaskell, she finally decided to do so. During a short preliminary visit to London with her mother, she auditioned for the celebrated Marie Rambert ballet school and was accepted, with scholarship.

The bad news was that she would have to pay her own living expenses. That, combined with Ella's current financial crunch, meant her enrollment would have to be postponed, and Audrey was hugely disappointed. But the goal was in sight.

CHAPTER 2

England and
the Chorus Line
(1948–1951)

"I can't stand it! I know I've got the best
tits on stage, and yet they're all staring at
a girl who hasn't got *any.*"

AUD JOHANSSEN, *chorine*

LONG AFTERWARD, AUDREY WAS ASKED if she felt her career had been carried along by some predestined momentum. The romantic question got an unromantic reply. No, she said—simply "by the need to work." She had a desire "to wear a tutu and dance at Covent Garden. That was my dream, but not a plan. I never thought I'd make it."[1]

She later said she realized, even in Holland, that she was "a little too old" for the rigors of becoming a ballerina, and that any human or divine momentum nudging her toward London was "because I wanted very much to become a choreographer and Rambert was known for developing young choreographers. So I wanted to be Margot Fonteyn and a choreographer as well."[2] But London was on hold due to the cash shortage. She would stay put in the present for an interlude that heralded her art form of the future.

Elsewhere in Amsterdam in 1948, a pair of Dutch freelance filmmakers had a clever idea—on paper, at least. Director Charles Huguenot Van der Linden (1909–1987) and his associate Henry M. Josephson were making a low-budget travelogue about Holland for Britain's Rank film company. With KLM "celebrity pilot" A. Viruly at the controls, they had flown over the country and, from the cockpit, shot scenes of the meadows, farmlands, Golden Age houses and modern Amsterdam below. They now concocted a thin story—for export—about a British cameraman who has seven days in which to learn Dutch. Some loose farce and as many pretty girls as they could find would be intercut with the landscape footage they already had in the can.

There are multiple versions of every legendary "discovery," and Audrey's case was no different. By one account, the two filmmakers came to

Gaskell's studio on their talent search and instantly agreed on "the tall, thin girl with the *eyes*."[3] Over the years, Van der Linden and Josephson squabbled about who saw her first. Most likely, she just showed up at their office under the watchful eye of her mother, who stated the obvious: Audrey needed work. Could they find some little role for her?

"I saw a dream coming into the room," Van der Linden recalled. She was fetchingly dressed in a little print frock, gloves and hat, and he decided to do a screentest then and there. She was taken outside and directed to cross a street and walk toward the camera. She did so, stopping in close-up. A voice behind the camera asked if she wanted to be in a movie. She smiled a bit quizzically and nodded. That was it. Smitten by her fresh look, Van der Linden and Josephson offered her a job on the spot. They were amused—though Ella was not—by her response: "I am not an actress. You will regret it."[4]

There would be no reason to regret Audrey, if many to lament the film. She played the KLM stewardess who welcomes cameraman "George" to Holland. That starring role went to Wam Heskes, a radio comedian better known as "Koes Koen"—a sort of Dutch Will Rogers—on his down-home broadcasts. This would be his screen debut as well as the stewardess's.[5]

Van der Linden had been so pleased with Audrey's little test that he recycled it, in thrifty Dutch fashion, to help establish the premise of his self-conscious film-within-a-film: *Nederlands in Zeven Lessen (Dutch in Seven Lessons, or Dutch at the Double)*, "A G-B Instructional Production," opens with George arriving in Amsterdam from England. He has only a week to make a film about Holland, and he keeps getting distracted by all the pretty Dutch girls—starting with Audrey, whom he spots on the street. In their exchange of pleasantries, we hear Hepburn's first words on screen, spoken softly (and incongruously, to American ears) in that odd "foreign" language called Dutch.

That's the test footage. It cuts sharply from Audrey the pedestrian to Audrey the flight attendant. Her character's name? "Audrey." She shows George around the Amsterdam airport, then glances at him coquettishly and says "Goodbye"—in English, for some reason—with a wry look in her almond eyes. "The drinks he had later with Audrey were his own personal business," says the narrator, hinting at naughty doings.

A tedious train tour is followed by more aerial footage shot from KLM's new state-of-the-art "PH-TAF" commercial craft, while the narrator relentlessly dispenses facts: "The Dutch live four hundred people to the square mile...." The conclusion is a cheesecake sailing sequence in swimsuits.

It was Dutch-British corn of the stalest kind. The premiere took place May 7, 1948, three days after Audrey turned nineteen. *Dutch in Seven*

Lessons survives in both the seventy-nine-minute Dutch original and a mercifully truncated thirty-eight-minute English version. Audrey's dialogue was of course cut out of the latter, and she was not mentioned by the reviewers of either. Most charitable was the *Handelsblad's* critic, who called it "no masterpiece."

Van der Linden had hoped to get in on the ground floor of the postwar Dutch movie industry and European coproductions. He also hoped to develop the talents of young Audrey, signing her up to a half-year contract with the intention of starting a new picture in six months. But when *Dutch* flopped on both sides of the channel, Van der Linden wasn't able to raise the money.

By her own admission, having been isolated in Nazi-occupied Arnhem for so many years, she was still ignorant of (and largely disinterested in) the "real" film world of America, Britain and France. But however modestly, her screen career had begun—even though she herself was hardly aware of it.

SHE WAS MORE AWARE OF modeling and more interested in the one or two beneficial results of her stint with Van der Linden: a part-time modeling job at Tonny Waagemans fashion salon in Amsterdam, and a chance to sit for artist Max Nauta, portraitist to the queen.[6] Both engagements were prestigious, but neither produced any work in her field, which was dance. It was time to get serious and get to England, to partake of that Rambert scholarship. The pooled resources of Audrey and her mother were about one hundred pounds, sufficient to get them there and not much more.

They finally made the crossing in late 1948, but the London that greeted them was grim compared to Amsterdam, and so was the British economy, compared with the faster Dutch recovery. Ella was shocked to find that one and four-pence-worth of meat was the weekly ration per person. It was almost as bad as wartime. The déjà vu specter of hunger was worrisome again, as was Audrey's health. She had arrived in one piece, "but I had no stamina."[7]

Ella had hoped to unlock some funds left behind in 1939, but all attempts to get at her money failed.[8] She and Audrey found no help from Ruston—nor did they find *Ruston*. In view of Ella's pride and the fact that he was in great disrepute, she probably did not look hard for him. But Audrey did, in spite of her strong and lingering feelings of rejection:

"I never heard from him or knew anything about him during the war. But after the war, curiosity took over. I wanted to know where he was, whether he was still alive, and through the Red Cross I found out that he lived in Ireland. But it took me many years before I could write to him, before I could say, 'I want to see you.' "[9]*

Ruston's release from internment on the Isle of Man had been a long time coming and, by the time it was accomplished, he was ill, broke and unemployable. It was years before Audrey learned that he obtained sanctuary at a monastery in County Waterford, Ireland, where the Trappist abbot eventually helped him find a job with an insurance brokerage in Dublin.

Needing sanctuary of their own, Audrey and her mother spent their first few weeks with old friends in Kent before Ella got down to finding the series of humble jobs that would sustain them in London—a virtual repetition of her experience in Amsterdam: first, in a florist's; next as a cook and beautician; then some interior decorating and door-to-door cosmetics peddling. But she soon found the "situation" they really needed— a job combined with a flat—managing a block of apartments at 65 South Audley Street, Mayfair. The neighborhood was elegant; their unpretentious walk-up was not. But Ella had extraordinary faith in her daughter's future and a commitment to it that dwarfed all sacrifice. There was joy as well, Audrey recalled:

"My mother was delighted [to be] in London because we had a room together and could be together.... To be able to buy a pair of shoes when you wanted to, or to take a taxi when you wanted.... We always took undergrounds and buses [so] that if it rained we could afford a taxi or go to the movies."[10] With the memories of Arnhem still fresh, one counted one's blessings and was thankful for such luxuries.

One was even more thankful for Marie Rambert (1888–1982), whose assistance and inspiration to Audrey were typical in the three generations of dancers she cultivated. To describe Rambert is to describe the history of British ballet. Agnes de Mille called her "Queen hornet, vixen mother." By age sixty, when Audrey met her, she was legendary, her credentials dating to the days when she coached Nijinsky in *The Rite of Spring*. With Ninette de Valois and Frederick Ashton, Rambert had founded the companies that would evolve into the Sadler's Wells and the Royal Ballet. Diaghilev himself came to watch her dynamic rehearsals.

In 1931, Rambert and her playwright husband, Ashley Dukes, opened The Ballet Club in a former church hall (vintage 1840) near Notting Hill Gate, part of which they would later rent to the famous Mercury Theatre. It was the first permanent ballet center in England—a theater, company and school—where the tiny production budgets went hand in hand with tiny salaries.

---

* And it took another dozen years for the actual father-daughter reunion to take place. (See Chapter 5, p. 166.)

Rambert was ever short of money but ever generous. She not only gave Audrey a scholarship to study but also took her into her home, housing and feeding her there for six months. That arrangement was a lifesaver for Ella and Audrey both.

"They'd had a rotten time during the war," recalls Rambert's daughter Angela Dukes Ellis, "and mother took pity on them. My sister and I had already left home, and the enormous house in Campden Hill Gardens had plenty of spare rooms.

"When the war came, the ballet theater closed down, and after the war, it became difficult to run because the unions were much stronger and you had to pay West End fees. The theater only seated 120 people and was impossible commercially, so it was turned once again into a studio and run as the Rambert School of Ballet until 1979."[11]

There, Audrey took her lessons in a drafty practice hall with a Dickensian coal fire and a battered upright piano, around the corner from Rambert's house to which she returned in the early evening. Angela called around often to visit:

"My mother had no idea whatsoever about running a house, cooking, or anything like that. This wonderful woman Helen Welton was with her for forty years did all that for her. When I would pop in to see Helen, Audrey and her own mother would be sitting in the kitchen talking to her.... My mother had always complained about the size of my feet, but Audrey had the same as mine—size 7. I bought a marvelous pair of warm, fur-lined shoes from her, which we'd never seen in England. She had had them for the Dutch winters, and I had them for many years."

Angela was struck by Audrey's "lovely, elfin quality." But Audrey was struggling with a variety of inferiority complexes beyond just her shoe size.

"My technique didn't compare with that of the girls who had had five years of Sadler's Wells teaching, paid for by their families, and who had always had good food and bomb shelters," she later said, in a rare expression of resentment.[12] "I also sensed that I was very tall...."[13]

Her sense, put more bluntly on another occasion, was that "I was an Amazon, towering over the boys," and she was tremendously self-conscious about it.[14] "I tried everything to make it an asset. Instead of working on allegro—little small tight movements—I took extra courses in adagio, so I could use my long lines to advantage."[15]

Ida de Jong, her petite colleague at Gaskell's in Amsterdam, had been particularly aware of it: "Audrey's big handicap for the ballet was her height. If I was sitting next to her, my head only reached up to her shoulders. Tall people have a hard time in ballet, because it's very difficult to find a proper partner."[16]

One who disagreed from firsthand experience was her fellow dancer

Ronald Hynde, who had come to the Rambert studio the previous year at age fifteen: "She was this very pretty, strange Dutch girl who suddenly arrived at the Rambert school—slight accent, beautiful face, everyone's idea of Cinderella or Sleeping Beauty, but with something different about her. I used to partner her in exercises, and she had a tiny waist. She was tallish, but one was never aware he was behind a giant when supporting her."[17]

But Audrey thought otherwise. And to her real or imagined problem of height was added one of weight. In London, she said, "I went on an eating binge. I would eat anything in sight and in any quantity. I'd empty out a jam jar with a spoon. I was crazy about everything I could lay my hands on when the food started appearing. I became quite tubby and put on twenty pounds."[18]

Some remembered her then as a "balloonlike teenager" who, with the determination that became her trademark, acquired a gazelle-like frame in two months. Soon enough—too soon and more than enough—she lost thirty pounds by ruthlessly eliminating all starches and sweets from her diet. "You have to look at yourself objectively," she would say, "as if you were some kind of tool, and then decide exactly what you must do."[19]

Her assessment of her own tools was severe. She made few new friends and concentrated totally on dance until the need for money led her to moonlight, on weekends and holidays, as a model for several commercial photographers who were beguiled by her unique, pixieish face. One of them snapped that face and put it in a thousand British drugstores, advertising the benefits of Lacto-Calamine complexion lotion.

These initial forays into English modeling reinforced her awareness of fashion and lifelong resolve—if not compulsion—to find the designs and colors that showed her to best advantage. Black and white and muted colors such as beige and pink "tend to make my eyes and hair seem darker," she felt, "whereas bright colors overpower me and wash me out." Low-heeled shoes, to deemphasize her height, were always a must.

Many other aspiring performers, men as well as women, were dabbling in fashion photography then. One of them was the future James Bond, Roger Moore, whom Audrey enlisted in her UNICEF work four decades later: "We modeled together about 455 years ago in London," Moore would say, "when Audrey was very young and I was middle-aged in the late forties."[20]

A job was a job. Anything to pick up a few extra pounds.

AUDREY AT TWENTY HAD THE increasingly sinking feeling that she was not destined to become a solo ballerina. Aside from the other issues, she still needed five more years of training even to qualify for a corps de ballet position. "I couldn't afford to put in all those years to end up earning five pounds a week, which was the going rate then," she said.

Rambert now told her, gently but firmly, that she had neither the physique nor the talent to make it as a classical dancer. Yet soon after, when a recruiter from a government-sponsored company visited Rambert's studio in search of dancers for a South American tour, Audrey was offered a position. She might have viewed that as evidence that Rambert's verdict was wrong. She was badly in need of money. But Audrey declined the tour, with her customary realism, and pondered the alternatives.

A dancers' casting call had just been announced for the London version of *High Button Shoes*, the American hit musical with Jule Styne music and Jerome Robbins choreography to be recreated intact by British producer Archie Thomson. Highlight of the show was Robbins's comic "Mack Sennett Ballet," a Keystone Kops chase in black-and-white makeup, simulating a silent movie, that called for unusual virtuosity on the part of the dancers.

Audrey was one of a *thousand* who tried out for the chorus line and—to her own amazement—one of ten who got the job, at eight pounds ten shillings ($35) a week. Her fellow bathing beauties included sixteen-year-old Alma Cogan, the future "Miss Show Business" of England, and Kay Kendall, the future wife of Rex Harrison—both of whom she would befriend, and both of whom would die of cancer in their early thirties. "I was stiff as a poker as a jazz dancer," she said, "always off beat on the simplest syncopation.... Going into a musical was the best thing that could have happened to me."[21]

The show opened at London's Hippodrome on December 22, 1948, for a 291-performance run. Audrey never forgot her one and only line—the first she ever spoke on a professional stage:

"Lou Parker, the star, stood in the middle and I went tearing across holding another girl by her hand and said, 'Have they all gone?' Believe me, I was nervous every single night. I used to repeat it to myself over and over before going on."[22]

The show's featured male dancer was Nickolas Dana, who today recalls the beautiful seventeen-minute pas de deux, choreographed by Robbins for Dana and a girl who often missed rehearsal and required a stand-in:

"Once the boy picked up the girl, she didn't touch the floor until the end of it. Just gorgeous. Audrey was the prettiest girl in the show, and one day I asked her to try it and she went up like a feather. I recommended she be the understudy and from then on, she was. I thought she was a beautiful dancer."[23]

Dana also has a vivid recollection of Audrey's offstage wardrobe at the time: "She had one skirt, one blouse, one pair of shoes, and a beret, but she had fourteen scarves. What she did with them week by week, you wouldn't believe. She'd wear the little beret on the back of her head, on one side, on the other side—or fold it in two and make it look very strange. She had the gift, the flair of how to dress."

Dana's agents, Dorothy McAusland and Olive Bridges, were always on the lookout for new talent, and when Dana told them about Audrey, "They came to see the show and called me a couple days later and said, 'There's not very much talent. She's a nice little dancer, but nothing spectacular.'"

Talent was in the eye of the beholder, of course, and perhaps also in the beholder's gender. In early 1949, London impresario Cecil Landeau came to see *High Button Shoes* and left thinking that nice little dancer worth capturing. Nobody liked the overbearing Landeau, but he was powerful in the West End and currently preparing a lavish new revue of Ziegfeld proportions.

Sauce Tartare was a song-and-dance extravaganza with twenty-seven comic sketches and musical episodes satirizing different nationalities in a mock travelogue. Landeau claimed to have travelled 14,000 miles to find the perfect international cast. His coup was singer Muriel Smith, the black American star of Broadway's *Carmen Jones*. The British members of cast were top-notch, too: Renee Houston, Jack Melford, Audrey's friend Alma Cogan—and Audrey herself among the five chorus hoofers.

Produced and directed by Landeau, *Sauce Tartare* opened to raves on May 18, 1949, and enjoyed a healthy run of 433 performances at the Cambridge Theatre. Even before that sauce grew cold, Landeau was stirring up a fresh one, *Sauce Piquante*, which likewise opened at the Cambridge, on April 27, 1950, and likewise starred Muriel Smith. This time the cast was mostly British and included some of the country's hottest entertainers. Chief among them was female impersonator Douglas Byng, whose rendition of "I'm One of the Queens of England" always brought down the house. Moira Lister did a riotously funny burlesque of Vivien Leigh's Blanche DuBois in *A Streetcar Named Desire*.

Audrey was back, too—with bigger bits and bigger paycheck, raised by Landeau to a downright affluent fifteen pounds a week. One of her jobs was to walk across the stage in a skimpy French-maid outfit, holding up the title card for each new skit. Though she was cast primarily as a dancer, Landeau upgraded her role and she figured in several comedy sketches, much to the annoyance of her peers.

"I can't stand it!" complained the big-busted dancer Aud Johanssen. "I've got the best tits on stage, and yet they're all staring at a girl who hasn't got *any*."[24]

One of the show's most popular performers was Bob Monkhouse, soon to become the BBC's first contract comedian and later a writer for Bob Hope and Jack Benny. Monkhouse and Hepburn became friends, though he disagreed with Nick Dana's assessment of her dance skill, as he told biographer Ian Woodward:

> The standard of dancing in *Sauce Piquante* was ... superior, but Audrey's was the poorest.... If she'd been a good dancer, the other girls would not have minded so much.... They all loved her offstage, but hated her on, because they knew that even if she jumped up and down, the audience would still be attracted to her. What Audrey had in *Sauce Piquante*, and what has sustained her through [her] career, was an enormous, exaggerated feeling of "I'm helpless—I need you." When people sense this, they respond to it immediately, perhaps not realising why they're doing so. Audrey had it in abundance.... Everybody in the audience thought, "I want to look after little Audrey." She seemed to be too pretty, too unaware of the dangers.
>
> It was quite extraordinary. [That] impish grin seemed to go from one earhole to the other. She looked incredibly radiant because, at that time, it was uncontrolled. The lips actually turned inside-out and the eyes went sort of potty, like a Walt Disney character. It was so lovely, one stepped back a pace. She later learned to tone it down a bit.[25]

Monkhouse remembered that during their first conversation, in rehearsals, she had said: "I'm half-Irish, half-Dutch, and I was born in Belgium. If I was a dog, I'd be in a hell of a mess!" Animals were a running theme. One night during the run, when Muriel Smith showed up with a bedraggled cat she had just rescued off the street, Audrey immediately adopted the thing.

"We called the cat Tomorrow, at Audrey's suggestion," says Monkhouse. "It was rather a rude joke, stemming from the fact that [it was] a male cat that had been castrated, and you know what they say about tomorrow never coming."[26]

But for the most part, she tended to keep her distance from the other performers, and the insecurity they perceived in her was real. "In musicals," she said, "I was the tense, rigid girl trained for ballet who had to watch everyone else to find out what to do."[27] Nobody was quite sure if she was a dancer, an actress or a model—including Audrey herself.

Fashion photographer Anthony Beauchamp had seen and admired her in the first of the *Sauces* at a time when the magazines he worked for were looking for "a new face." He went backstage after the show and asked to photograph her. She said she was flattered but couldn't afford his fee. Beauchamp assured her there would be no charge. "I kept looking again and again at the startling eyes which were never still," he said. When his pictures appeared in British *Vogue*, her unusual wide-eyed "look" produced a nice stir—and another modeling job with British press agents Frederic Mullally and Suzanne Warner.

"The sweater was doing nothing for Audrey," said Warner, "and Audrey was doing near as nothing for the sweater." Invoking the eleventh commandment of fashion ("What God's forgotten, we stuff with cotton"), they coaxed her into shooting in falsies. Others might speak of her "splendid emaciation," but she didn't find it so splendid. "I'd like to be not so flat-chested," she said. "I was too thin and I had no bosom to speak of. Add [it] up, and a girl can feel terribly self-conscious."[28]

There was no reason to feel that way in the opinion of Marcel le Bon, a handsome young French crooner who had several featured spots in *Sauce Piquante* and dreamed of becoming the next Maurice Chevalier. Early in the production, he and Audrey began dating and fell madly, if briefly, in love. By the final weeks of the show's run, le Bon was leaving roses in her dressing room nightly and had become the first serious boyfriend of her life. Backstage gossip was much livened by rumors of a marriage.

When Landeau heard of it, he was furious, claiming to have inserted a "no-marriage" clause in Audrey's contract. Reports that he was threatening to sue her if she married le Bon appeared in the tabloids. She also had to endure the wrath of her mother, who believed Marcel was plotting to cash in on Audrey's greater talent.

In fact, le Bon was more her pal than her paramour, but it didn't seem so at the time. Landeau's testy mood was related to the fact that his show was sinking, despite good notices, and would soon close—in June 1950—after just sixty-seven performances. He lost 20,000 pounds and found himself in bankruptcy court. For the moment, he was staving off that disaster by cannibalizing some sketches from *Sauce Piquante* into a shorter revue called *Summer Nights* for Ciro's, one of the most chic nightclubs in London. Moonlighting there was financially welcome but exhausting, Audrey later told Dominick Dunne:

"I did two shows at the same time, a musical revue at the Cambridge Theatre, twelve performances a week, and then we were all shipped to Ciro's nightclub right after the show, and there we did a floor show."[29] She would finish up at Ciro's around two a.m., walk home with some of the other girls through Piccadilly ("so lovely and safe then"), and sleep until noon. In the afternoons, she and Marcel and others from *Sauce Piquante* worked on a new cabaret act they were trying to concoct. As if that weren't enough, she was also doing "a bit of TV" at the time though, unfortunately, none of her television work from that pre-videotape era has survived.[30]

The trade publications were now starting to take notice. In early 1950, *Picturegoer* called her "a heart-shattering young woman with a style of her own, no mean acting ability, and a photogenic capacity for making the newspaper pages."[31]

Nudged as always by her mother, Audrey took steps to improve the raw skills that such press notices insisted she possessed. Earlier, when informed that people had trouble hearing her one and only line in *High Button Shoes*, she had taken a few singing lessons—not to learn how to sing, but how to speak. Shades of Eliza Doolittle. Soon after, in between the two *Sauces*, she enrolled in the Saturday morning movement classes of Betty and Philip Buchell, prominent London teacher-choreographers.

With Landeau's financial help, she now graduated to elocution lessons with Felix Aylmer (1889–1979), a delightful old character actor who subsidized his modest income as a supporting actor in films and plays by taking a few pupils on the side—Vivien Leigh and Charles Laughton among them, and now Audrey.

She had seen precious few "serious" pictures in her life, but Laurence Olivier's two great Shakespearean films, *Henry V* (1944, Aylmer as the Archbishop of Canterbury) and *Hamlet* (1948, Aylmer as Polonius) were among them. Having admired him in both, Audrey now drank in Aylmer's instruction in diction and his techniques for "responsive stillness" to lure an audience into watching her even when she was doing nothing in a scene.

"He taught me to concentrate intelligently on what I was doing," she said, "and made me aware that all actors need a 'method' of sorts to be even vaguely professional."[32]

She was all the while performing two and sometimes three shows daily, one of which was attended by the actor and future director Richard Attenborough: "Everybody knew there was something totally remarkable about her [and] that sooner or later, she was going to become a major, major movie star."[33]

The wisdom of hindsight may have been at work there, but Attenborough was not alone. Countless others claimed to have "discovered" Audrey during her brief cabaret stint. Stanley Holloway, who later played Alfred Doolittle to Audrey's Eliza in *My Fair Lady*, mocked the many people "who have genuinely kidded themselves into believing that they were the first to recognise Audrey Hepburn's potential radiant talent."[34] Britain's *Picturegoer* magazine had the inside track in 1950:

"The fact that some people went night after night to see her in cabaret at Ciro's was a good enough reason for Associated British to talk of signing her for the screen."[35]

ROBERT LENNARD CAUGHT AND LIKED her act at Ciro's, if not night after night, at least once. Having entered the British film industry in 1930, Lennard was now casting director of Associated British Pictures Corporation (ABC). He had a sixth sense and a distinguished reputation for finding and signing up future stars. But the reputation of his studio was not so lustrous.

"ABC pictures were generally second features," says Britain's greatest film historian, Kevin Brownlow. "I can't think of a major ABC film. In England, you went to the movies to see American pictures in those days. When you saw the credits and heard companies like Columbia or RKO, you got a buzz out of just the name. When you heard ABC, your heart sank."[36]

Located in London, ABC was protected from its overwhelming Hollywood competition by a government requirement that exhibitors show at least one British film for every two American ones. The result was a plethora of generally dismal "quota quickies"—125 of them a year—most ending up as the lesser half of double features headed by Hollywood films.

Artistic virtues aside, those pictures were the bread-and-butter of Britain's postwar film industry, of which Lennard was both an employee and a champion. Smitten by Audrey in the Ciro's show, he arranged a meeting between her and Italian director Mario Zampi, who was in London preparing a new comedy for ABC called *Laughter in Paradise*. At the start of the war, Zampi had been arrested under Regulation 18b (like Joseph Hepburn-Ruston) for his alleged pro-fascist beliefs, but was soon released. He claimed to have seen Audrey in *Sauce Piquante* fourteen times and now offered her a major role in *Laughter in Paradise*. But she turned it down "for personal reasons," apologizing that "I've just signed to do a short tour in a show. I can't break the contract."

The real reason was Marcel le Bon. He and Audrey and their *Sauce* pals had worked out a new cabaret act and were all set to take it on the road when, suddenly, the bookings fell through. Le Bon blamed himself and, in impulsive Gallic fashion, now abandoned Audrey and England both and boarded a ship for America.

Though upset by his departure, she was not really devastated and—now that her "personal reasons" had evaporated—rushed back to tell Zampi, "If the part's still available, and you're not too mad with me, I'd be thrilled to do it." He wasn't mad, but he had already given her role to Beatrice Campbell. "The only role not yet cast is a bit-part of a girl who sells cigarettes," he said. "Do you want to do it?"

Yes, she did.

Laughter in Paradise was a major cut above ABC's average "quota quickie." Its witty story, by Michael Pertwee and Jack Davies, has a dying eccentric (Hugh Griffith) leaving his heirs a fortune—on condition that they carry out the most embarrassing tasks: His sister (Fay Compton), who terrorizes her domestic help, must work as a servant for a month. His pompous nephew (Alastair Sim) must spend a month in jail and postpone his wedding to a female soldier. ("What am I to say to Commandant Bulthwaite and the girls?" she exclaims. "They've bought us a toast rack!") His nephew (Guy Middleton), a shameless womanizer, must marry the first unattached woman he speaks to.

Audrey's big scene—as a cigarette girl in short black dress and white apron—comes thirty minutes into the film. She wanders up to Middleton in a bar, flashes a dazzling smile and says, "Hello! Who wants a ciggy?" She has two more brief appearances in the film, which is a morality tale: The greedy heirs all perform their assignments, but it turns out Griffith was really flat broke, and none of them will get a penny.

Laughter in Paradise was one of the top-grossing British films of its year and—on the strength of "Who wants a ciggy?"—Audrey's film career was launched. ABC offered her a seven-year contract but, for the time being, she preferred to keep her options open. Girls who signed long-term British contracts in those days rarely made it to stardom. A few, such as Natasha Parry and Honor Blackman, survived, but most—Carol Marsh, Susan Shaw, Joan Dowling, Patricia Plunkett, Jane Hylton, Patricia Dainton, Hazel Court—were never heard from again.[37]

So as a freelance rather than contract actress, Audrey went straight from *Laughter in Paradise* into production of *One Wild Oat*, an ABC comedy directed by Charles Saunders, based on a bedroom farce of the 1948 West End season. She had three days' work playing a hotel receptionist, but most of her bits ended up on the cutting-room floor: It seems that Audrey was the "wild oat" and that the British censors objected to both the visual and verbal insinuations of her character.

Forty-five years later, director Saunders recalls *One Wild Oat* as "one of the nicest films I worked on, shot entirely in the studio in about three weeks." He, too, had seen Audrey in *Sauce Piquante* and cast her on the basis of that alone. "Her only line was, 'Good afternoon, this is the Regency Hotel.' That's all."

Was he surprised by the speed of her subsequent fame?

"Surprised and bloody annoyed, quite frankly," says Saunders. "We tried hard but we just didn't have the means at that time to get her under contract."[38]

In the gentle hands of Saunders and Zampi, Audrey's film work thus far had been pleasant. She would be exposed to a very different kind of director in her next film, *Young Wives' Tale*, a static romantic comedy about England's postwar housing shortage. Its stars were Joan Greenwood, Helen Cherry and Nigel Patrick. Its director was the tyrannical Henry Cass, and Audrey, in the minor role of a typist, somehow ran afoul of him.

"I was his whipping boy, that was for sure," she said. "Half the time I was in tears, but adorable Joan Greenwood and Nigel Patrick—the stars—were very sweet and protective.[39] [It was] the only unhappy picture

I ever made because Cass had it in for me, and I was miserable. I didn't like Henry Cass."[40]

She had her revenge of sorts when *Young Wives' Tale* opened in New York in November of 1951. *New York Times* critic Bosley Crowther berated it for being as "dismal [a comedy] as ever leaked from an uninspired brain" but, even so, made it a point to mention "that pretty Audrey Hepburn."[41]

By now she had signed a contract and, after *Young Wives' Tale*, ABC loaned her out to Michael Balcon's Ealing Studios, which specialized in sophisticated, irreverent comedies. *Kind Hearts and Coronets* was its most recent success. The Ealing film at hand was *Lavender Hill Mob*, directed by Charles Crichton and starring Alec Guinness as a timid bank clerk who conceives and executes a most daring robbery. It would be one of Ealing's— and England's—finest comedies, and Guinness, who had met Audrey through Felix Aylmer, helped her obtain a small part in it. She is "Chiquita" in an airport lounge, where Guinness calls her over and hands her a wad of bills. "Oh, but how *sweet* of you!" she coos, and deposits a thank-you kiss on his forehead.

Lavender Hill Mob was named the best film of 1951 by the British Film Academy, but Audrey's contribution was unnoticed. "I paid no particular attention to her," said Balcon.

But Alec Guinness did.

"She only had half a line to say, and I don't think she said it in any particular or interesting way," Guinness recalls. "But her faunlike beauty and presence were remarkable."[42]

Audrey had just tested for the lead in ABC's *Lady Godiva Rides Again*. Guinness now recommended her to director Mervyn LeRoy, who was then in London to cast the MGM epic *Quo Vadis?*. She duly made that test, too, in full Roman costume. But there were no callbacks. Audrey was judged too thin for the first part, which went to Pauline Stroud, and too inexperienced for the second, which went to Deborah Kerr.

"Quo vadis?" indeed. Where to go from here?

HEPBURN WAS AMBITIOUS AND FOCUSED on her career, but she was also, privately, a very traditional and romantic woman determined to avoid the disastrous experience of her parents. After Marcel le Bon's departure, she continued to seek a serious relationship and, in summer 1950, she found it in the person of James Hanson.

They met shortly after she finished *Lavender Hill Mob* and immediately hit it off. She was twenty-two. He was twenty-eight, six-foot-four and the multimillionaire scion of a Yorkshire trucking industry family. He served dynamically in World War II from 1939 (at age seventeen) to its end, with the Duke of Wellington's regiment, among others, in North Africa, Italy and Greece. Nowadays he was a horseman, yachtsman and master of foxhounds, and a trustee of the D'Oyly Carte opera company.

Hanson was an elegant socialite and a dashing lover of the good life. He dressed impeccably, commanded a fleet of expensive cars, owned his own plane, and frequented the best nightspots of London and New York. He adored beautiful women—beautiful actresses in particular—and they invariably returned the favor. In recent months, he had been Jean Simmons's escort in London, but she was quickly forgotten when Audrey entered his life.

"When I met her, she had just finished with [Marcel le Bon]," he recalls today. "I got lucky and found her when she was on her own." Hanson—now Lord Hanson—is one of the wealthiest men in England. Still trim and engaging, he sits back in the London headquarters of Hanson PLC, his $17-billion global conglomerate, locks his hands behind his head, and smiles at the recollection of Audrey:

> We met at a cocktail party in Mayfair at Les Ambassadeurs, a very popular place, and we were attracted to each other right away. I invited her for lunch next day, we soon fell in love, became engaged a few months later. She was a one-man woman, and it was a relationship of that kind. We became extremely good friends. Everybody saw in her this wonderful life and brightness and terrific strength of character. She was a very strong young woman who clearly had the determination she was going to need in order to achieve what she did. She had done a couple of small parts in movies, and her career was just about to blossom. There was no doubt about that by anybody who saw her.[43]

The Hanson family's transport business, in Huddersfield, Yorkshire, had thrived for a hundred years. But in 1948, the Labour government nationalized all railways, airlines, trucking and shipping companies, and Hanson found himself out of a job. At that point, he bought a trucking firm in Canada, shuttling back and forth across the Atlantic thereafter.*

During that time, he did not neglect romance, as one of the all-time authorities on that subject—Zsa Zsa Gabor—confirms:

"Audrey and I started together in London. She was a beautiful Dutch girl, engaged to James Hanson. I was making my first movie, *Moulin Rouge*. His partner Gordon White was chasing me, and Jimmy was chasing

---

* In the later fifties and sixties, Hanson, his brother, and their associate Gordon White gradually rebuilt the family businesses after the transport industry was *de*-nationalized by the second Churchill government. Today, more than half of Hanson PLC's interests are in North America and Lord Hanson spends five months a year in Palm Springs.

her. They were *dahling*—such a handsome couple. Jimmy was not only rich, but charming."[44]

Audrey thought so, too. "Jimmy," for his part, observed his girl closely and remembers her as "not particularly strong" but largely recovered from her postwar debility. He debunks the claims that she suffered from any kind of anorexia at the time.

"She had dancer's legs and a dancer's upper body, which is often wasted because of the perspiration from all that practicing," says Hanson. "I would have thought that she might have difficulty with her health in the future. But she was an extremely healthy young girl then, apart from the fact that like many dancers, she looked as if she should be built up a bit. Yet she ate well and enjoyed her food. She could eat like a horse! Any problem that developed certainly wasn't evident then."

One evident problem, however, was her mother. Though impressed with Hanson's social and financial status, Ella was reportedly horrified at the thought of Audrey's marriage and exile to the Yorkshire boondocks, just when her career was at the takeoff point. Such, at least, was the story repeated in most later books and articles about Audrey—but quite untrue.

"I liked Ella very much," Hanson insists. "It was certainly not true that my relationship with her was poor. She was always very encouraging about me with Audrey. She felt the age difference—about six years—was right and that somebody in a solid business was right for somebody on the artistic side. She would be marrying somebody with his feet on the ground, not in show business, with all its uncertainties. We talked about it many times. We'd already worked that out: Audrey was going to make one movie a year with the option to do a play whenever she wanted to—pretty much the pattern Audrey followed anyway. That was partially because she wanted to have a life also as my wife.

"We were a very happy 'family' in the two years we were together. I spent a good deal of time with Ella. She thought we were well suited. She had no reservations about my being in business and Audrey being an actress. Ella was not fond of show business people. I did a lot for her, as I would a future mother-in-law. I tried to develop a relationship, and it worked."[45]

Audrey often described her mother as "a lady of very strict Victorian standards." But Dutch Victorian was different from British Victorian, and on the subject of sex, at least, her liberal attitude astonished Hanson a year or so later in Rome.

"I must have been twenty-nine or thirty at the time," he recalls. "It was the first time in my life I had ever slept in the same bed as my fiancée—with her mother bringing the breakfast in. That was something I had never experienced. There was always a rather furtive dashing back to your room. But Ella was completely different. I remember her bringing the breakfast into that room. She was a very earthy woman."

AUDREY'S FILM ROLES TO DATE were small, and so were the films. Now, for the first time, she was about to play a major supporting role in a major movie by a major British filmmaker.

Director Thorold Dickinson had seen "the girl with the eyes" in *Sauce Piquante* and tucked her away in his mind. A former supervising editor at Ealing Studios, he was a significant figure in British cinema. His brilliant *Gaslight* (1940) was made four years before the Ingrid Bergman version and was far better. His most recent picture, *Queen of Spades* (1949), was a tour de force for Edith Evans and both a critical and commercial success.

Dickinson and producer Sidney Cole were now readying *Secret People*, a downbeat melodrama of prewar political intrigue. It was the furthest thing in the world from ABC's fluffy comedies. The screenplay, written by Dickinson and novelist Joyce Cary (*The Horse's Mouth*), was the tale of Maria Brent, living in London in 1937 with her little sister Nora—a very young and very beautiful ballet student. They are exiles from an unnamed foreign country, where their pacifist father is murdered. Maria abandons his ideals and turns violent revolutionary—but with deep guilt and a desperate desire to protect the innocent Nora.

Secret People's broad, political scope was the talk of British film circles—so much so that a young film intern decided to chronicle it from start to finish. The result was a full-length book, *Making a Film: The Story of "Secret People,"* by Lindsay Anderson, who would become an important director himself in the sixties. Anderson's behind-the-scenes account makes it clear that casting went down to the wire. Both Maria and her radical boyfriend Louis had to have believable accents, but the budget ruled out the major English-speaking Europeans in Hollywood.

The eventual choices were two talented but little-known Italians, Valentina Cortesa and Serge Reggiani—a Paul Muni lookalike. But the perfect Nora still eluded them. "An actress would have to be found who could dance, or a dancer who could act," said Anderson, whose journal for October 30, 1950, reads:

> Interview with Audrey Hepburn, possible Nora. With [Cortesa and Reggiani as] the leads, the height of potential cast members begins to assume importance. Neither of them is tall, so to a certain extent the rest of the cast must be scaled to them. This applies particularly to Nora—a slight discouragement to Audrey Hepburn. From now on all actors interviewed are sternly measured against the office wall.

On November 10, the cameras turned for the first time on *Secret*

People—still without a Nora, even as composer Roberto Gerhard finished the elaborate ballet music to which Nora would dance in the most violent, climactic scene. In all his films, said Dickinson, he liked to have at least one sequence "of pure and unmistakable cinema," and Nora's ballet was going to be it.

Various candidates for Nora had been rejected. Valentina Cortesa was now responsible for the breakthrough.

"There were four girls that did the test," says Cortesa today, "and I saw at the barre this beautiful little thing, like a little deer, with this long neck and those big eyes. She looks at me and says, 'Do you think I have a chance?' I was so touched that I went to the director and said, 'Listen, if you really love me, I would like to have as the sister that little girl.' They said, 'We were going to look at some others.' I said, 'No, I beg you— I want her.'"[46] In the follow-up test, Cortesa further assisted by suggesting Audrey remove her shoes and by playing the scene herself on tiptoe, to minimize their height difference.

Hepburn got the role of Nora on February 26, 1951, and art imitated life in almost all of her scenes. She's the ingenue of ingenues, a gay wisp of a girl always rushing to or from an audition. Her barre exercises are those of her Rambert days, her dance form is marvelous, and her dialogue with Charles Goldner (as Anselmo, the landlord) might have been taken from her life:

ANSELMO:	Now you are British. You feel different, Nora?
NORA	I'll say! No more labour permits!... I might get some cabaret work in the autumn.
ANSELMO	Cabaret work? What for?
NORA:	(calling back as she jumps on a bus) Money! For more classes! For more cabaret work!

The big challenge, aside from nine grueling days filming the ballet sequence, was her greatest dramatic moment in the film—in fact, the first tragic scene she had ever played: an emotional encounter with her sister after a terrorist bomb produces mayhem and death at the party where Nora has just finished dancing. The scene and its graphic dialogue unnerved her, bringing back nightmares from Arnhem. "I just can't seem to say it," she told Dickinson. "Don't bother about how you're going to say it," he advised. "Just think of the experience that lies behind the words. During the war, perhaps you saw something like that.... Get the feeling right, and the words will look after themselves."

While the stand-ins were being lit, Audrey went off by herself to a corner. "By the time we come to the take," wrote Anderson, "the words have become spontaneous and heartfelt and tears come naturally to her eyes."

With Valentina Cortesa, Audrey developed a warm, big-and-little sister relationship off the set as well as on. "We used to go out in London at night, all dressed up," Cortesa recalls. "Once we went to a very chic restaurant and both of us smoked a cigar. Like little idiots, we smoked a cigar and laughed. Well, why not? I adored her."[47]

But by mid-March, Cortesa was greatly agitated. For one thing, she was secretly pregnant by actor Richard Basehart, whose current visit to the set was creating much tension. (A few weeks later, they would marry.) Besides that, she was annoyed and besieged constantly by publicity requests. One day in the presence of Anderson and Hepburn, Cortesa unloaded:

"We must be allowed to have our own lives. In Hollywood it is terrible; they expect you to be their slave; you have to be ready to do anything for them, at any time, not just when you're making a picture." She shuddered and turned to Audrey: "Think hard before you sign a long-term contract. Liberty is the most wonderful thing of all."

At this embryonic stage, Audrey was thus alerted to the danger of overexposure and the contempt bred of familiarity. That very week she was booked for a photo session at South Downs, feeding ducks and paddling in the village pond, followed by some "breast skyline" pictures for a cover story in *Illustrated*—too much publicity before her "serious" work had even been seen by the public. "They'll get sick of it," she fretted. "I'd much rather wait until I have [more] to show."

By its final reel, *Secret People* becomes a metaphor for the Cold War. Maria, threatened by both sides ("You wouldn't want anything to happen to Nora, would you?"), breaks down and turns state's evidence. It is then Scotland Yard's turn to manipulate her until her final confrontation with Louis, in which she is stabbed to death and the sobbing Nora is led away.

The rough cut of *Secret People* ran almost two hours, twenty minutes of which were chopped before its premiere in November of 1951. Cortesa's underplayed performance was acclaimed, and photographer Gordon Dines praised for his moody, high-contrast lighting in the postwar neo-realist style. The film's gritty feel and restraint were remarked. But all in all, the critical response to *Secret People* did not fulfill Dickinson's hopes.

Variety called the script "hackneyed" but said Hepburn "combines beauty with skill" in the fine ballet scenes.[48]* Indeed, forty-five years later,

* Aside from those sequences, there was no incidental music in the film. But a nightclub scene between the unhappy lovers Cortesa and Reggiani called for a tango with French lyrics. The song was written by none other than Marcel le Bon, Audrey's former boyfriend who had almost—but not quite—disappeared forever from her life. He seems to have resurfaced once or twice in London, and she was evidently still kindly enough disposed to get him the job.

Secret People provides our last glimpse of her as a young, working dancer.[49]

Though her part was small, Hepburn received above-the-title credit, just below Cortesa and Reggiani—"which reflected how pleased we were with her performance," said producer Cole. Dickinson, convinced of her star potential, tried hard to persuade Ealing to sign her up, but in vain. She would soon go the way of Cary Grant, James Mason, Charles Laughton, Vivien Leigh, Boris Karloff, Deborah Kerr, David Niven and a host of others lost by England to Hollywood.[50]

But first, she would be temporarily lost to France.

IN THE MIDDLE OF *SECRET People* production, while she was still very much "an unknown," Audrey's new agent Kenneth Harper went to director Terence Young in London and told him she was someone special and to be reckoned with.

"From the moment she came into my office, I realized he was right," recalled Young, shortly before his death in 1994. "But she was the last person in the world I needed for the role of a tough Lapland woman in the wilds of Norway, who had to move around all day on skis. I told her she was completely wrong for the picture [*Valley of the Eagles*] and said, 'I bet you can't even ski.' Her reply was, 'But I can learn.' She was utterly enchanting and she stayed on in my office talking for half an hour. I told her I'd certainly remember her for something else. I even added that I thought she was going to make it, and I hoped one day *she* would remember *me*, and get me to direct."[51]*

Around the same time, writer-editor Alfred Shaughnessy—later a cocreator of the *Upstairs, Downstairs* PBS-TV series—suggested her for a comedy film called *Brandy for the Parson*. Shaughnessy gave her a copy of the screenplay, which she soon returned with a mischievous smile. "Lovely," she said, "but I couldn't play Scene 42. The censor wouldn't allow it." He grabbed his "thoroughly wholesome" script, turned to Scene 42 and read: "Petronilla is awake, dressed in Bill's pyjamas. *She is peeing out of the porthole.*"[52] A crucial "r" had been omitted.

In April, while still filming *Secret People*, Audrey had received a call from Harper saying he had an offer for her to play in a film with bandleader Ray Ventura, who was also its producer. The part was small but the money was good, she would get to wear a Dior dress, and—best of all—the picture would be shot in Monte Carlo, which meant a month in the sun.

Audrey went immediately to Valentina Cortesa, asking whether she should take it. Cortesa's response was unhesitant, as always: "I said,

* Which she did. Sixteen years later. Young directed one of her finest films, *Wait Until Dark*.

'Listen, if the cast is number one, if the director is number one, even if the part is not number one—do it. Maybe something else comes out of it.'"[53]

Nous irons à Monte Carlo [We Go to Monte Carlo] was a sequel to Ventura's mildly successful *Nous irons à Paris* (1949). Audrey was cast as much for her bilingual fluency as for her charms: The film would be made both in French and English (with the snappier title *Monte Carlo Baby*). It was a series of skits loosely—*very* loosely—connected by the musical appearances of Ventura and his band. Audrey played a movie star chasing after her missing baby.

Compared with her serious role in *Secret People*, it was absurd. Her misgivings were compounded by a report that the jazz musician who would be her leading man was a notorious womanizer. She mentioned that to Nick Dana, her *High Button Shoes* pal, who replied, "It's true, but Frenchmen are usually not as good as their words." At that point, says Dana, "She looked at me and smiled and said, 'What do *you* think I should do?' I said, 'What did they offer you?' She told me. I said, 'Ask for fifty pounds more.' She went back and said, 'If I have to work with this man, I need more money.' And she got it."

Three days before departure, she showed up at Dana's apartment in the St. John's Wood area of London with an announcement: "I feel like I should look different if I'm going to do a French movie."

Dana, who had a few salon skills of his own, reflects on that moment with delight at his home in Rochester, New York, and is not too modest to deny credit for what happened next:

"I said, 'You have the kind of face that needs a gamine haircut. I would almost take the ends of your eyebrows off so that you have a quizzical look. You have the kind of face for it —a pixie face. Let's make it a pixie.' So we did the eyebrows and I gave her a gamine cut. It was that simple."[54]

Thorold Dickinson was accommodating, too, moving up her dialogue post-synching session for *Secret People* to May 28, since she had to leave for France that very evening.

"Everything significant in my life has happened gloriously and unexpectedly—like the trip to Monte Carlo tomorrow," she told writer Radie Harris the previous night. "I've always longed to go to the French Riviera, but I could never afford it."

A day later, she was installed at the Hotel de Paris, the most splendid Belle Epoque structure on the Riviera, and ready to start shooting *Monte Carlo Baby* under the direction of Jean Boyer. Boyer, one of France's most prolific directors, was a master of mass-audience fluff. His next assignment would be to direct Brigitte Bardot in her first film, *Crazy for Love* (1952). His current stars were less titillating. The biggest name in *Monte Carlo Baby* was sad-faced comic Jules Munshin. He was supported—not hugely—

by Cara Williams, Michelle Farmer (Gloria Swanson's daughter) and John van Dreelen. Audrey would appear in the film for a total of twelve minutes.

Monte Carlo was released in France and England in 1952, and poorly received. There was no interest in American distribution until May 1954, after Hepburn had become famous, when producer Collyer Young and his wife Ida Lupino bought the U.S. rights and exhibited *Monte Carlo Baby* in a few art houses, where confused American audiences could not understand why such a big new star was appearing in such a small part.[55] *The New York Times* called it "as witless a film exercise as ever was spewed from an ingenuous camera." Audrey's role of the film star? "She made this film before she became one in reality. It is rather astonishing how she stands out in that seared desert of mediocrity."[56]

THE HOLLYWOOD "STAR SEARCH" WAS typically full of sound and fury, most often signifying nothing other than publicity. The more dignified theater world usually disdained it—with the exception of *Gigi*. It was the last fiction work of Sidonie-Gabrielle Colette (1873–1954), written during the Nazi occupation of Paris. When published in 1945, it was just the sort of escapist fare Europeans wanted to read, and a huge hit. In 1948, it was made into a pleasant French film starring Danièle Delorme, which in turn led to the idea of a stage version.

But Colette's New York agent was having trouble trying to sell *Gigi* as a Broadway play: The first dramatization by a French playwright called for nineteen sets and a cast of thirty-eight—much too much. The agent now asked Anita Loos (of *Gentlemen Prefer Blondes* fame) to streamline it, and she duly produced a version with just eight actors and four sets. But there were other obstacles.

"First of all," said Loos, "the stage rights were acquired by Gilbert Miller, who hadn't the least intention of producing *Gigi*. Gilbert's main interest in life was to be an international playboy. At the same time, he didn't want some other producer to acquire a likely property, so he followed his usual custom: paid me an advance of a thousand dollars, tossed my script into the lower drawer of his desk, and went merrily off to Europe."[57]

Miller was a powerful theatrical czar on both sides of the Atlantic. *Victoria Regina, What Price Glory?* and *The Cocktail Party* were among his hits, and he was a millionaire long before marrying the additional fortune of heiress Kitty Bache. He had his own airline, bank, estates in four countries, and was hugely fat. In London, he and Kitty lived royally in their Savoy suite overlooking the Thames.[58] He was there now, laying plans to produce both Cleopatra plays—the Shakespeare and the Shaw—with Laurence Olivier and Vivien Leigh.

Before leaving New York, Miller had asked an ambitious young assistant named Morton Gottlieb to look after his affairs. Gottlieb found Loos's manuscript and took it upon himself to put it into production. Miller returned, furious to learn that *Gigi* had been announced in the trade papers.

"Gilbert then thought of one more chance to ditch the production," said Loos. "Colette herself might possibly come to his aid by turning down my adaptation." Miller sent Loos to the ancient Palais Royale apartment in Paris where Colette had long been bed-ridden with arthritis. "I presently realized that Colette's mind was wandering," said Loos, "and her gaze was directed toward my feet.... 'Where did you buy those adorable shoes?' she asked. From that moment on we hit it off."[59]

Loos came away with Colette's approval of her *Gigi* script. That delighted Gottlieb as much as it annoyed Miller, who was now obligated to move forward—but there was still no Gigi:

> With Miss Loos I combed the roster of Equity for a young American actress who could meet the requirements— without result. We must have seen at least two hundred girls in New York. For a time we considered the Italian actress Pier Angeli, but her accent seemed too high a hurdle to surmount. Briefly we pondered the potential of Leslie Caron, but Miss Caron was *too* French.[60]

They were about to compromise "on a none-too-pristine Hollywood starlet," said Loos, when a telegram arrived from Colette via her husband Maurice Goudeket in Monte Carlo, where they regularly spent their summers as guests of Prince Rainier at the Hotel de Paris: "Don't cast your Gigi until you receive my letter." The letter that followed told a remarkable tale:

Colette, seventy-eight, was being propelled through the hotel lobby— sipping a liqueur and resplendent in her red corkscrew curls—when her wheelchair was blocked by a group of actors, technicians and their film equipment. The chair got tangled in some wires, and director Jean Boyer was cross about the interruption. But he fell respectfully silent when he recognized Colette, and shooting was halted while he went over to pay his respects. During that interaction and the time it took to get her chair sorted out, Colette studied the activity with her usual curiosity. Several cast members came up to meet her, but her attention was drawn to one who did not: A girl in the background, oblivious to Colette, was taking advantage of the unplanned break to frolic with two of the musicians off to the side. She was dancing around them in playful fashion; she seemed graceful and awkward at the same time; she was extremely pretty. The old author's eyes narrowed. Suddenly she announced, "Voilà! There is my Gigi!"

"What author ever expects to see one of his brain-children appear suddenly in the flesh?" she would later add. "Not I, and yet, here it was. This unknown young woman was my own thoroughly French Gigi come alive!"[61]

Colette thought the girl might be fifteen or sixteen—far younger than her twenty-two years—and summoned a crew member to enquire about her. "She's here with her mother, the Baroness van Heemstra," the man reported. Ella, it turned out, knew Colette's novel well and was thrilled by the idea of Audrey in its title role.

Anita Loos was in New York with Paulette Goddard, getting ready to leave for a vacation in Paris, but after Colette's letter arrived, they arranged for a stopover first in London. There, at the Savoy, Colette's discovery paid them a visit:

"The girl came in, dressed in a simple white shirtwaist and skirt, but Paulette and I were bowled over by her unusual type of beauty. After talking for a moment, we arranged an audition for her to read for Gilbert the following day. But after she left, Paulette said to me, 'There's got to be something wrong with that girl!' I asked, 'What?' 'Anyone who looks like that would have been discovered before she was ten years old.'

"There was nothing wrong, except the strange fact that perfection is almost impossible for the ordinary eye to see.... She had been in full view of the London public for two years, [but] it had taken Colette to see Audrey Hepburn."

When Miller heard her read for the part, he was unimpressed. But such was Colette's insistence that he engaged her anyway and called on his old friend Cathleen Nesbitt for help. Nesbitt, a veteran character actress (formerly a leading lady and lover of Rupert Brooke), agreed to critique Audrey's delivery. Audrey did a reading. Nesbitt couldn't hear her. Serious coaching was in order, and Nesbitt told Miller she'd provide it if the girl would come regularly to her country home outside New York City.

No one was more aware of her deficiencies than Audrey. "I'm sorry, Madame, but it is impossible," she told Colette the day they met. "I wouldn't be able to, because I can't act."

Valentina Cortesa had told her something might come out of *Monte Carlo Baby*, and it did. "Fortuna!" Cortesa called it.[62] And now, while Audrey waited for Miller and ABC pictures to sort out the business arrangements, more *fortuna* was on the way.

RURITANIAN PRINCESS VISITS FOREIGN COUNTRY, eludes her guardians, goes madcap for twenty-four hours, falls in love with American journalist, returns to her senses in bittersweet ending.

Dalton Trumbo and Ian McLellan Hunter had come up with that screenplay idea in the mid-forties and sold it to Frank Capra, who wanted but failed to make it at Paramount with Elizabeth Taylor and Cary Grant. William Wyler read it in 1951 and told Paramount he'd do it, but only if he could shoot on location in Rome. The studio agreed, Capra released the property to Wyler, and casting for *Roman Holiday* began. Everything hinged on the princess.

Wyler's first idea was Jean Simmons, but Howard Hughes—who owned her contract—refused to make her available. The search continued on two continents through July 1951, when Paramount's London production chief Richard Mealand wrote the home office: "I have another candidate for *Roman Holiday*—Audrey Hepburn. I was struck by her playing of a bit-part in *Laughter in Paradise*."

At the time, said Audrey, "I had no idea of who William Wyler was [and] no sense of what Mr. Wyler could do for my career. I had no sense, period. I was awfully new, and awfully young, and thrilled just to be going out on auditions and meeting people who seemed to like me."[63]

She was busy enough trying to prepare for *Gigi*, and it boggled her mind to think of making a movie—before, during or even after. But if Paramount of Hollywood wanted her to do a screen test, she could hardly refuse. Upon returning to London from Monte Carlo, just prior to leaving for America, she acquiesced to Mealand's hasty arrangements.

"I wanted a girl without an American accent to play the princess, someone you could believe was brought up a princess," Wyler recalled.[64] He was in London and "sort of picked out a few girls but didn't want to stay and do the tests," said Audrey. "So he put Thorold Dickinson in charge of testing me because I'd worked with him in *Secret People*, and he understood me."[65]

Her *Roman Holiday* test took place at Pinewood Studios in London, September 18, 1951, under Dickinson's direction. "We did some scenes out of the script," he said, but "Paramount also wanted to see what Audrey was actually like not acting a part, so I did an interview with her. We loaded a thousand feet of film into a camera and every foot of it went on this conversation. She talked about her experiences in the war, the Allied raid on Arnhem, and hiding out in a cellar. A deeply moving thing."[66]

All of which was a prelude to the *real* test: In order to assess the *spontaneous* Audrey, Wyler had instructed Dickinson to keep the film rolling when she thought she was finished. After a scene in which the princess flings herself onto her bed, Audrey was told she could relax and leave. But she stayed put.

"I didn't hear anybody say 'Cut!'" she said. "Only one man here has the right to say 'Cut' [and] I won't move until I hear him."

"Cut!" said Dickinson. But the camera kept rolling as Audrey sat up in her royal bed, stretched sexily, clasped her hands around her knees, smiled and asked how she'd done.

Lionel Murton, who played the Gregory Peck part for the purposes of the audition, was also smiling. "This little doe-eyed charmer is a very smart cookie," he thought to himself. "She knows perfectly well that the camera is still running—and is giving it the works."

The test results were flown to Rome, where Wyler found them irresistible: "First, she played the scene from the script, then you heard someone yell 'Cut!' but the take continued. She jumped up in bed and asked, 'How was it? Was I any good?' She saw that everybody was so quiet and the lights were still on. Suddenly, she realized the camera was still running and we got *that* reaction, too.... She had everything I was looking for—charm, innocence and talent. She also was very funny. She was absolutely enchanting, and we said, 'That's the girl!'"[67]

The studio fired off a cable to Mealand: "Exercise the option on this lady. The test is certainly one of the best ever made in Hollywood, New York or London." Even Don Hartman, Paramount's tough-as-nails production chief, was impressed: "We were fascinated," he said. "It's no credit to anyone that we signed her immediately."[68] Mealand now received a routine follow-up telegram: "Ask Hepburn if okay [to] change her last name to avoid conflict [with] Katharine Hepburn." The answer was not routine: Audrey politely but emphatically refused; if Paramount wanted her, they'd have to take her name, too.*

"I tried to explain to all of them that I wasn't ready to do a lead," said Audrey, "but they didn't agree, and I certainly wasn't going to argue with them."[69]

For *Gigi*, she would be getting $500 a week, from which she would have to pay her own living expenses in New York. The *Roman Holiday* offer was $12,500 with an option for a second picture at $25,000. Paramount wanted a seven-year contract, but she balked at such length and—with a little help from her fiancé—negotiated a shrewder deal. James Hanson is modest about it. "The only contribution I made," he says, was to help her get around her long-term obligations to ABC. As an old friend of Jack Dunfee and Lew Wasserman of MCA, "I was able to put in my two cents' worth to improve on her contract with Paramount."

The final result was a two-year movie deal with a clause allowing her

---

* The two Hepburns may have been distantly related: Both had a great-grandfather called James Hepburn, but that was a common name in Scotland, and no one has proven the genealogical connection.

to act in stage plays as well. With Hanson's help, she also fought and won the battle with Paramount for permission to do television work, too, if and when she chose.

"Heaven help me live up to all this," she wrote Richard Mealand in London.[70]

So she was in—signed up to do *Roman Holiday* after the run of *Gigi*, regardless of how long that might be. It was a big risk for Paramount. The play could have run for years, and Gregory Peck had been signed only for a very narrow window of shooting time the following summer of 1952. Cautiously, in view of those uncertainties, the studio decided to hold off a bit on announcing her contract. Everything now depended on *Gigi*: if it worked, Paramount would have a star; if it flopped, they'd have an unknown London failure on their hands.[71]

The pressure was on, personally and professionally. *Gigi* rehearsals began in October 1951. In late September, Gilbert Miller sent her a first-class ticket on the *Queen Mary*. For the first time on any momentous occasion in her life, her mother would not be with her: Ella couldn't leave her apartment manager's job in London. James Hanson, kind as always, promised to fly both Ella and himself to New York for *Gigi*'s opening.

The press had the Hanson-Hepburn relationship thoroughly confused at this point: One magazine, for example, in a big feature called "Audrey, the New Hepburn," ran their photos with the caption: "They were married last month." For that matter, Hanson himself was a bit confused. Throughout all her amazing career breaks of the last eighteen months, their mutual affection remained strong—if anything, it had grown stronger. He'd been supportive in every way, and Audrey had been grateful and reliant on his support. But she seemed less willing than ever to fix a firm wedding date, and though they never argued about it, Hanson was privately upset at the ongoing delay.

Audrey was upset, too, but not about that. During the leisurely eighteen-day crossing to America—her first and last such leisure for many years—it crossed her mind that, at twenty-two, she was the first girl signed simultaneously to star in a Broadway play and a Hollywood film without ever having set foot in either place—and with virtually no experience in either medium.

CHAPTER 3

Stardom Beyond Belief
(1951–1954)

"I think sex is overrated."
AUDREY HEPBURN

IN THE WEE HOURS OF October 3, 1951, Broadway publicist Arthur Cantor dispatched an "Urgent" release to the New York newspapers and wire services: "New British actress named Hepburn arriving this morning at Pier 90 to appear in Broadway play. She is a great find. Suggest you send reporters and photographers."

The response was much like that which greeted Greta Garbo at the same location in 1925. "Without benefit of telepathy," wrote Martin Abramson for *Cosmopolitan*, "every editor who received the communiqué impaled it on a spike reserved to useless trivia, and Miss Hepburn arrived in New York harbor to be greeted by a crashing yawn. The anxious Mr. Cantor scurried around the dock, found one ship-news reporter with time on his hands, and begged him to ask the new arrival a few questions. 'Nah,' the reporter told him. 'I'd rather go have a cup of coffee.' "[1]

Morton Gottlieb, general manager of the *Gigi* company, was the only other person there, and even *he* went grudgingly:

"I had to get up at six in the morning to make the boat and I'd been working most of the night. I was bleary-eyed. I had a splitting headache, the weather was nasty.... Even Lady Godiva on her horse would have made a negative impression on me. Yet when I saw this girl standing on the dock, tired out from her trip, wearing only a plain two-piece suit, I said to myself, 'Ye gods, this is Garbo, this is Bergman!' "[2]

Audrey recalled that "the first thing I saw when I came to America was the Statue of Liberty. The second—Richard Avedon." She was stretching the facts, but only by a little. Gottlieb took her straight from the dock to a photo studio where, "before I knew it, I was in front of Avedon's cameras, lights flashing, music going, Richard snapping away a mile a minute, darting from one angle to the other like a hummingbird, everywhere at once, weaving his spell."[3] Avedon was then working for *Bazaar*, which wanted first crack at any new and noteworthy face.

From Avedon, she was taken to modest accommodations ($125 a week) at the Blackstone Hotel on East Fifty-eighth Street and given just enough time to check in and change clothes before being whisked off to a World Series game at Yankee Stadium, where she cheered happily in complete ignorance of what was going on.[4]

She got a restrained reception the next day in Gilbert Miller's lavish Rockefeller Center suite, where the producer was not pleased to find her appearance changed from London.

She had gained fifteen pounds on the ship and when Miller saw her, "He was appalled," said Anita Loos. "He had engaged a sprite who had suddenly turned into a dumpling. Gilbert, as a gourmand, couldn't believe that his Gigi could ever get down to weight. Rehearsals began, with Gilbert regarding his ingenue's weight with a skeptical eye. But Mortie [Gottlieb] put her on a diet of steak tartare at Dinty Moore's, next door to our Forty-sixth Street theater. Her pounds slowly began to melt."[5]

Not so slowly, in fact. She shed all fifteen pounds in two weeks, and was soon looking emaciated. Miller now wanted the pendulum to swing back, and called in his wife Kitty for help: "I want you to come over and watch a rehearsal with little Audrey," he told her. "She seems to conk out in the afternoon." Kitty went, watched and then took her by the hand, saying, "You're going to have a good square meal and don't let me hear any of this dieting nonsense! How about a fat, juicy steak?"[6]

Audrey never tried—or needed—to lose weight again.

Miller had his thin Gigi back, but still no director. He wanted Raymond Rouleau, a forty-seven-year-old Belgian who had recently staged the successful French version of *A Streetcar Named Desire*—but who spoke no English. Loos volunteered a solution: If Miller could persuade Rouleau to come to America, she would facilitate by translating her adaptation into French. Loos, Hepburn, Cathleen Nesbitt and most of the rest of the *Gigi* cast were fluent in French. Rouleau agreed and was soon in New York.

As dramatized by Anita Loos—in both languages—*Gigi* is a two-act play set in the Paris of 1900. Gilberte—Gigi for short—is the gawky adolescent daughter of a mediocre soprano at the Opéra Comique. They come from a long line of *grandes cocottes*, in whose footsteps Gigi is expected to follow. Luck has provided them with a new and fabulously wealthy young man-about-town to whom Gigi's grandmother Madame Alvarez (Josephine Brown), and Aunt Alicia (Cathleen Nesbitt) are the "consultant bawds."[7] But high-spirited Gigi is more interested in her schoolwork, despite the relentless efforts of her grandma and aunt to interest her in the lucrative tricks of the *cocotte* trade:

MME. ALVAREZ: You see, my Gigi, lessons can give a girl ideas of a career. And a career is the ruination of any woman. . . .

	How often must I tell you to keep your knees together when you're sitting on a stool?...
GIGI:	But I've got my drawers on, Grandma.
MME. ALVAREZ	Drawers are one thing, and decency is another. It's all in the point of view....
GIGI	... With my skirts so short I always have to remember to bend my knees in the shape of a Z, on account of my you-know-what.
MME. ALVAREZ	(shocked to the heart) Gigi! Where did you ever hear such language?...
GIGI	But what do you call it, then?
MME. ALVAREZ	(a pause) Nothing! It has no name.... Can't you keep your legs together? When you stand like that, the river Seine could flow between them....
GIGI	(studies a gem) Mmmmmm—a—topaz!
ALICIA	A topaz! A topaz, among my jewels!
GIGI	I'm sorry, Aunty...
ALICIA:	It's a jonquil diamond, you little barbarian. (holds ring closer to Gigi) Study it closely for color, or you'll wind up your career with topazes.... You must learn never to accept a second-rate jewel, even from a king. [Men] are not as intelligent as we are. So it's only good manners to play the fool for them.[8]

All the "arrangements" are explained to her, but at the moment of truth, Gigi balks. The moral: It pays to say no.

The role wasn't simple. A subtle sophistication was required to portray innocence, and Hepburn lacked it. She tended to scamper about frantically, either shout or whisper her lines, and exhaust rather than pace herself. "She didn't have much idea of phrasing," said Nesbitt. "She had no idea how to project, and she would come bounding onto the stage like a gazelle."[9]

After five days of rehearsals, said Gottlieb, "Miller fired her. By the next morning, he realized it was too late to replace her, so he gave her another chance, and then he fired her again a few days later. This went on up to opening night. Poor Audrey was on the verge of a nervous collapse. They were working her eighteen hours a day, sneaking into the theater at night because Gilbert didn't want to pay the union technicians overtime."[10]*

* There was a lot of nighttime activity at the Fulton during *Gigi*. The set designer was Lila de Nobilli, whose Paris Opéra designs would become legends. But the backstage unions opposed the hiring of foreigners. Gottlieb used a well-known ploy: "He engaged an American stooge, whose name was on

Years later, in a letter to biographer Charles Higham, Raymond Rouleau's widow attributed the problem to extracurricular activities, and the solution to her husband:

> She was acting extremely badly, totally failing to understand the meaning of the text, going out late at night and arriving very tired at the theater in the mornings. [Raymond] on the eighth day took Audrey aside and told her quite firmly that she must improve, or else. She must work with more dedication, obtain enough sleep, eat properly, devote herself to the text and, in a word, become properly professional, or he would decline all responsibility for her future.... He was very severe with her....
>
> From that moment, she progressed steadily and became better and better every day, using every bit of advice Raymond had given her, as though he had been in charge of a childbirth.... When Raymond was inspired by an artist, he became a magician.[11]

Perhaps so—but Rouleau had some crucial assistance from Cathleen Nesbitt, who was once again enlisted by Miller. The veteran Nesbitt, who first played New York in works by Shaw and Yeats in 1911, would celebrate her sixty-third birthday on *Gigi*'s opening night. She agreed to take Audrey to her country place on weekends for additional coaching on vocal projection, among other things. Progress was rocky. Even with rehearsal audiences, Audrey kept pushing too hard. "I didn't get my laugh," she would lament after a scene. "What did I do wrong?" But Nesbitt had confidence because "she had that rare thing—audience authority, the thing that makes everybody look at you when you are on stage."[12]

Anticipation was heightened by an extraordinary amount of pre-opening publicity and the "vibration" that something theatrically important was in the works. *New York World Telegram and Sun* interviewer Norton Mockridge went so far as to predict that "within a few weeks, or months at most, Miss Hepburn's elfin features and gamine hair-do will be known and acclaimed throughout the country. Her hair, snipped short and scraggly, is virtually a mess. But most people, who see it for the first time, sigh and say something like: 'How breathlessly enchanting.'"

Mockridge further observed, during his luncheon meeting with her, that she "is always hungry. And after being starved for years for a taste of fresh meat, she eats almost nothing else over here. 'Look,' she'll say to a waitress. 'The tenderloin steak, please, but very rare. You know what I mean? Raw rare. With the blood in it. Dripping. Very rare. Almost raw.'... Some of the meat Audrey eats is rare enough to have walked into the

the program as set designer," said Loos, "and Lila herself painted the scenery, sneaking into the theater after dark, mounting a stepladder and painting all night."

restaurant five minutes before." In between bites, she expressed her own high state of anticipation:

"Right now, I am living only for the opening night of *Gigi*. It's my whole life. There is nothing else. I live or die. [The cards] are on the table, and we don't know if there is an ace among them."[13]

Previews started November 8, 1951, at the Walnut Street Theater in Philadelphia, where Rouleau kept her prisoner for the forty-eight hours before the opening, still trying to cajole the right moves from her.[14] Miller wanted to fire her again, restrained only by the lack of a replacement. He hated her first-night performance, telling Loos after the show that he would either fold it or find another Gigi, but he was persuaded to hold off at least until he saw the morning reviews.

They were raves.

"The acting find of the year," declared one critic. "She gives a wonderfully buoyant performance which establishes her as an actress of the first rank," wrote Henry P. Murdoch in the *Inquirer*. There were more raves in New Haven, where the show had its three final trial runs.

On to New York, where Audrey discovered another young imported actor with the jitters back at the Blackstone. In that amazing Broadway season of 1951–52, no fewer than forty-four new plays and nine new musicals were premiering. One of them was called *Nina*, starring Gloria Swanson and David Niven and set to open within a week of *Gigi*, with which it was often confused.

"Audrey and I shook with fear as our opening nights on Broadway grew inexorably nearer," Niven recalled. "We met when a body crashed down from the eighteenth floor and bounced off Audrey's windowsill on its way to the ground. Anyway, she rushed into our room and we later discovered that some poor man had committed suicide."[15]

It seemed a fairly bad omen.

"I'm frightened," she told a reporter, with excessive candor, a few days before the opening. "I have no stage training whatever. Why, others spend their lives at it before they get anywhere.... I'll have to act by intuition until I learn."[16]

The out-of-town success had not much calmed either the star or the producer. "Everybody still worked on poor Audrey," Loos remembered. "Cathleen Nesbitt helped... Gilbert stepped in and hindered. By opening night we were all on tenterhooks." To make matters worse that November 24 evening, Audrey had acquired a bad cold. Backstage, someone in the cast got a hold of the Fulton's *Gigi* Playbill and read aloud: "In the event of an air-raid alarm, remain in your seats and obey the instructions of the management. Signed, Arthur H. Wallander, Director of Civil Defense." After a glum silence, he deadpanned, "They've got to have *some* way of making people stay for the second act."

The second act was the problem, all right, and it went none too smoothly. "On the final scene rested the whole reason for the play being a play," Audrey recalled, "and right at the climax I forgot my lines and everything stopped. A whole speech was missed out. But I managed to pull round and last out until the final curtain."[17]

As she left the stage after her last bow, stage manager Dick Bender told her, "I don't know how you're going to get inside your dressing room. It's full of flowers."[18] It was also full of celebrities, including Marlene Dietrich and Helen Hayes (for whom the Fulton Theatre would later be renamed), many comparing her with Maude Adams and suggesting she was the new *Peter Pan*. But as always, everything hinged on "The Seven Butchers of Broadway"—Anita Loos's term of endearment for the all-powerful newspaper critics. In a split decision, the majority of them gave low marks to the play but kudos to Audrey.

"The delightful Miss Hepburn obviously is not an experienced actress," said Richard Watts, Jr., in the *Post*. "But her quality is so winning and so right that she is the success of the evening. [She] is as fresh and frisky as a puppy out of a tub. She brings a candid innocence and a tomboy intelligence to a part that might have gone sticky."

Walter Kerr, writing for both the *Herald-Tribune* and *Commonweal*, doled out the brickbats first. Anita Loos, in his opinion, "has no style at all. She follows the Colette outline patiently and perfunctorily." Director Rouleau "is a belligerent stylist" who "comes close to dashing the play's brains out." But Audrey Hepburn was "a young actress of great charm . . . who pulls the whole thing into focus. . . . Instead of shifting styles with her colleagues, she manages to wrap them all into a simple, coherent, and delectable pattern of her own, and this is a major achievement for a fledgling performer."[19]

In *The New Yorker*, Wolcott Gibbs confessed that "I, for one, was quite disappointed when . . . a purer kind of love intruded itself into the proceedings and the young couple decided to get married. [But] Audrey Hepburn, who has never acted in New York before, is nearly perfect as Gigi."[20]

Newsweek's dry conclusion was that "Nothing, really, happens on the stage of the Fulton Theatre except a gradual rapprochement between Michael Evans and Audrey Hepburn (no relation to Katharine)."[21]

The *Theatre Arts* critic, however, was especially rough on Audrey: "[Rouleau] has propelled her into such a jumping over furniture and such a breathless sprinting about the premises as would better suit a trained dog act. The girl's personal acting qualifications leave me much in doubt. . . . She acts innocence in accordance with the script's demands, but she never for a moment is successful in suggesting it."[22]

A private pan came from Noel Coward to his diary: "Went to *Gigi*—

an orgy of overacting.... Audrey Hepburn inexperienced and rather too noisy, and the whole thing badly directed."[23] He was more diplomatic to her face. "Noel Coward came backstage to tell me something he found wrong with my performance," she said, "and I was terribly flattered."[24]

By and large, however, the collective assessment concurred with the December 10 *Life* headline, "Audrey Is a Hit": "The only trouble was that the authors and producer had set their sights too low. They had once thought of making *Gigi* a musical but were convinced that they would never find anyone who could sing and dance and also act the difficult role. It happens that Audrey can dance and sing as well as act. Broadway hopes to see her sooner or later in a triple-threat role in the style of Gertrude Lawrence."[25]

Funny they should mention that. When *Gigi* was still in its embryonic stage, composer-lyricist Frank Loesser (*Where's Charley?*, *Guys and Dolls*) had asked Gilbert Miller to consider coproducing it as a musical. Miller rejected the idea instantly, and Lerner and Loewe would later prove him wrong. Now, several performances into the run, Lawrence herself came backstage after the show to tell Audrey that if her own life were ever filmed, she would want Hepburn in the role.[26]*

Hepburn was surprised and truly modest about her success and generous as always in dispensing the credit for it.

"I find out more about the part all the time," she told a reporter for the *Brooklyn Eagle*. "Dick Bender is the person I rely on completely. He's our stage manager, a wonderful person. I have to have a master I can go to and ask if my sums are correct. He keeps close watch on the show, since the director isn't around anymore and he'll say, 'This was good,' or 'You're starting to miss out there.' He'll say, 'It's strange, but for two nights you didn't do this, and it was so attractive before, but you're not doing it now.'"[27]

But she was not too humble to savor the day they moved her name from below to above the title—in lights—on the Fulton's marquee. Photographers snapped away as Miller held the ladder while Audrey climbed and lifted up the "A." (The other twelve letters were already in place.) Yet she gave the newsmen only the most self-deprecating little quote when she climbed down: "Oh dear, and I've still got to learn how to act."[28]

Little known, in the wake of her "triumph," is that she not only continued coaching with Nesbitt but now renewed her dance instruction— at the Tarassova School of Ballet on West Fifty-fourth Street. It was run by Mme. Olga Tarassova and her eccentric husband, Vladimir Bell, whom

---

* Among intersecting ironies is the fact that, when 20th Century-Fox finally decided to film the Gertrude Lawrence story, *Star!* (1968), the Lawrence role was played by Julie Andrews.

Audrey knew three years earlier when Tarassova was located in Amsterdam.[29] In *Saturday Review*, Audrey sang the virtues and importance of dance to an actor:

> [Dancers] do a lot of technical things out of good habit. When we relax we never get sloppy. In my case that's because when my ballet teacher, Madame Rambert, would catch us folding our arms or slouching our shoulders she'd give us a good rap across the knuckles with a stick.... Dancers learn to feel when their posture is not graceful....
>
> Our director, Raymond Rouleau, used to be very amused at the way I stood with my toes pointing out and my legs stiff whenever I'd lean down to pick something up. [She jumps up and demonstrates the bending action.] I wasn't conscious of doing it. It just came automatically.
>
> I'm halfway between a dancer and an actress. I've got to learn. Ballet is the most completely exhausting thing I have ever done. But if I hadn't been used to pushing myself that hard, I could never have managed the tremendous amount of work necessary to learn in three weeks how to play a leading role in my first real acting job.[30]

She was smart enough to know it and honest enough to say it. Though she was frequently mentioned as a contender for the Best Actress Tony Award, it was won by Julie Harris for *I Am a Camera*. Audrey was not disappointed.

Neither was Colette. Across the ocean, she congratulated herself and sent her discovery an autographed photo inscribed, *For Audrey Hepburn, a treasure which I found on the sands.*[31] Ah, how Colette adored her. But there is no confirmation of the report that, when Colette died three years later, she left her personal jewels to Audrey. She didn't adore her quite *that* much.

ACROSS THE SAME OCEAN, JAMES Hanson also adored Audrey and was also congratulating himself. During his three-day surprise visit to New York for the *Gigi* premiere, she had accepted his diamond ring and they had formalized their engagement.

"I didn't know he was coming over," said Audrey to a nosy reporter. "I left the theater a few hours before the opening performance to get into a car and there he was. Actually, we have been informally engaged for some time. There is nothing definite about a wedding date as yet."[32]

Both restrained and strained, the reply suggests she might not have appreciated the unexpected distraction of her fiancé just before the most important and frightening night of her professional life. But she confirmed the marriage, if not the date, and an announcement appeared almost immediately in *The London Times'* "Forthcoming Marriages" on December 4, 1951:

Mr. J. E. Hanson and Miss A. Hepburn: The engagement is announced between James, son of Mr. and Mrs. Robert Hanson, of Norwood Grange, Huddersfield, Yorkshire, and Audrey Hepburn, daughter of Baroness Ella van Heemstra, of 65, South Audley Street, London, W.1.

Subsequent updates said the wedding was scheduled for spring 1952, between the end of the *Gigi* run and the start of *Roman Holiday* shooting in Italy. Bridesmaids names were given out, and it was suggested that, after *Roman Holiday*, Mr. and Mrs. Hanson would take up residence in Huddersfield. That came as a shock to Ella—but was never really the couple's intention. They were too cosmopolitan by then, and Hanson was more often in his New York or Toronto office than in Britain.

"Our engagement and affair had mainly to do with New York," Hanson recalls. "I worked there and had a flat in New York and was able to spend a lot of time with her when she was in *Gigi*.

"The great thing about Audrey was her international ability. She spoke many different languages. Once I went with her to see my parents, who had an apartment in the Ritz Tower at Fifty-seventh and Park when they were in America. We were going up in the lift with two women. You know how older women sometimes look down their nose at a young beauty? Well, they were talking in Dutch about her, assuming that nobody else in the world, let alone in the elevator, would speak Dutch. Audrey looked at me and gave me a wink. We didn't say a word to each other, but just before we got out, she rattled a stream of Dutch at me as if I was just as much a native speaker as she. They had been talking about her in a rather bitchy way, and they were in shock as we got out. She was very amusing and very good at that sort of thing."[33]

Hanson's own internationalism was useful to Audrey. He introduced her to his lawyer Abraham Bienstock in New York, who helped improve upon her contract arrangements. He suggested that she avoid making films in England or the United States, if possible, in favor of other countries where the tax rates weren't nearly so high. When Audrey called him in Canada, much perplexed about the need to convert and merge her ABC option with the option Paramount had on her, Hanson rang up his friend Lew Wasserman in Beverly Hills and arranged to organize it along beneficial lines. From then on—long before she became one of his major clients—Wasserman took a personal interest in her.

"The only advice I was able to give her was financial," says Hanson. "It was just a natural thing that, with my knowledge, I could do. By knowing the people that I did here and in the U.S., I was able to make personal contact for her with them. That possibly helped to advance her career in a very small way."

Was there a plan for him to become her business manager?

"That was never the thought. Obviously, if you marry a successful businessman, it might come up. But I was careful not to interfere. I only planned to run my own career."[34]

All was well, in Hanson's view, but a certain "if and when" hesitation was detectable in Audrey. "When I marry James, I want to give up at least a year to just being a wife to him," she told her journalist friend Radie Harris. "James is being wonderfully understanding about it. He knows it would be impossible for me to give up my career completely. I just can't. I've worked too long to achieve something. And so many people have helped me along the way, I don't want to let them down."[35]

An ominous report said she had removed the framed picture of Hanson from her dressing-table at the Fulton. Asked why, she replied, "So many people whom I hardly know asked me what was his name and when were we going to be married, that I simply had to put the picture into a drawer. My private life is my own."[36]

Her professional life was not. Paramount was champing at the bit to get started on *Roman Holiday* and had given Miller a $50,000 incentive to release her from *Gigi* at the end of May, though she was still committed to do the road-show tour that fall. Thus on May 31—after a short but wildly successful run of 217 performances—*Gigi* closed in New York.

Shortly before, while *Gigi* was still on the boards, Hollywood costume czarina Edith Head met with Audrey for a preliminary discussion of her *Roman Holiday* wardrobe, and a warm friendship between them began. Head later told Charles Higham:

"She would laugh and curl up on the floor (which she always preferred to a chair) and tuck her legs under her like an adorable, naive, utterly innocent schoolgirl, and then she would say, with a sweetness that cut like a knife to the heart of the problem, 'I don't think the princess [in *Roman Holiday*] would be quite so shrewd, Edith, darling, as to use that *particular* décolletage!' and I would think, 'Oh, my God, if she doesn't get to the top I'll eat Hedda Hopper's hats.'"

Her personality dazzled or melted everyone. She could just as easily conduct a conversation with Dean Martin and Jerry Lewis as with visiting Queen Juliana of the Netherlands. A friend summed it up: "It broke my heart. Just the look of that girl. It's one of those magic things."[37]

SOMETHING WAS HAPPENING ON A grander scale, and "the look of that girl" was making it happen. It had to do with the changing standards of beauty and with film and fashion overall, but perhaps most with the era itself.

"I remember the fifties as a time of renewal and of regained security," Audrey would later write. "There was a rebirth of opportunity, vitality and enthusiasm... a return to laughter and gaiety—the world was functioning again. Above all there was a wonderful quality of hope, born from relief and gratitude for those greatest of all luxuries—freedom and peace."[38]

It was this brave new world that Audrey was somehow coming to epitomize, and in which she would set the pace. Nobody looked like her before the war, Cecil Beaton had written in *Vogue*, but now there were "thousands of imitations [and] the woods are full of emaciated young ladies with rat-nibbled hair and moon-pale faces."[39] When she was young, Audrey said later, "I wanted to be a cross between Elizabeth Taylor and Ingrid Bergman. I didn't do either."[40]

Instead of some "cross," Hepburn and her look were original. To embryonic feminist Molly Haskell, she was "alert, full of the ardor of an explorer, with nothing of the lassitude or languor of such voluptuous and earthbound sex goddesses as Elizabeth Taylor, Sophia Loren or... the overeager Monroe. The qualities that made her more desirable to us were precisely those that made her less desirable to masses of red-blooded American men."[41]

More about those physical qualities and the fashion phenomenon they inspired later. For now, suffice to say that she was unique among her contemporaries in refusing to pose for cheesecake photos, and that her private view was both unusual and refreshingly simple. "I think sex is overrated," she said.[42]

ROMAN HOLIDAY WOULD BE SHOT entirely "around" Audrey. Filming was to begin in Italy in June 1952, after *Gigi* closed in New York. She and Hanson were to be married in the interlude, but as it turned out, there *was* no interlude, and the wedding had to be postponed. Paramount's schedule was so tight that she was required to go straight from the closing night of *Gigi* to Rome.

The film she was about to make was Cinderella in reverse. Some say it derived from an old Ferenc Molnar story. Others insist it was inspired by a telephoto-lens shot of Princess Margaret in a swimsuit on Capri. The screenplay was written by Dalton Trumbo, one of the blacklisted Hollywood Ten, working under the pseudonym of "John Dighton," with Ian McLellan Hunter.

Roman Holiday was a bit reminiscent of Capra's *It Happened One Night*, with a big difference in tone: It was no screwball comedy of the thirties, but a sentimental escape of the fifties, unlike such other "realistic" new films as *A Place in the Sun*.[43] Director William Wyler's brilliant credits included *Wuthering Heights, The Little Foxes, Mrs. Miniver* and *The Best Years of Our Lives*. Paramount had approved his request to make it on location for self-serving reasons: It could be financed with "frozen" lira earned in (but not removable from) Italy. For economy's sake, Wyler agreed to shoot *Roman Holiday* in black and white, "and by the time I'd realized my error it was too late to get enough color stock over to Italy," he said.[44]

"He was the classiest filmmaker that ever lived," says his friend Billy Wilder, who was determined not to cry during *Best Years of Our Lives* but did so throughout. "And I'm not a pushover. I laugh at *Hamlet*. There was a finesse in that guy that you would never expect, sitting across from him at a card table."*

With *Roman Holiday*, Wyler first had to finesse Gregory Peck, a major star at thirty-six, thanks to his performances in *The Keys of the Kingdom* (1945), *The Yearling* (1946) and *Gentleman's Agreement* (1947)—all of which had earned him Oscar nominations.

"When he told me that an unknown girl, a little dancer from London, was going to play the princess, I said, 'Well, Willy, no one has better judgment than you, but have you seen her on film?' " Peck recalls. "He said, 'Let me show you something.' "[45]

Wyler showed Audrey's screen test to Peck, who had read the *Roman Holiday* script and realized now, more than ever, that "it was not going to be about me, it was about the princess." On that basis, he rejected it. But Wyler knew just what button to push. "You surprise me, Greg," he said. "If you didn't like the story, okay, but because somebody's part is a little better than yours, that's no reason to turn down a film. I didn't think you were the kind of actor who measures the size of the roles."[46]

Peck capitulated. Moreover, he phoned his agent George Chasin to say, "The real star of this picture is Audrey Hepburn. [Tell] the studio I want Audrey Hepburn to be billed on the same line."[47] It was an unusually generous gesture, and the Paramount executives were initially much opposed. But soon enough, says Peck, "We all knew that this was going to be an important star and we began to talk off-camera about the chance that she might win an Academy Award in her first film."[48]

Audrey knew no such thing. "Willie was a great, famous director when I met him," she said, "but I didn't really know much about directors [and I was] not really aware of his importance."[49]

---

* Throughout the careers of Audrey Hepburn's two most beloved directors, there was endless confusion between "Billy Wilder" and "Willie Wyler." Wilder, who was slightly younger and more annoyed by the mistake, says Wyler "would put his arm around me and say, 'Come on, now—Monet/Manet? What's the difference?' "

Neither Hepburn nor Wyler was aware of the hazards of filming in Rome: The noise was incessant, the summer heat was intense, and the logistics of clearing the crowded streets for shooting were a nightmare. Bribes were paid all around but provided no insurance against political violence: Fascists and Communists battled in the streets, as if the Christian Democrats' election victory in May had never happened. At one point, five bundles of explosives were discovered under a bridge over the Tiber River, where filming was about to take place.

Wyler, undaunted, adhered to his perfectionist ways and made countless takes of each scene—modified only by the hordes of Roman gawkers who were always on hand, as Gregory Peck recalled:

> One of the first scenes we shot was at the Piazza di Spagna.... There were at least 10,000 people assembled at the foot of the Spanish Steps and in the street. The police couldn't stop them from whistling and heckling. For Audrey and me, it was like acting in a huge amphitheater before a packed house of rowdies. I asked her if she didn't find it very intimidating. "No, not at all..." She took it as calmly and serenely as a real princess would have....
>
> Italians are all born film actors [and] were quite hands-on about the whole thing.... Wyler would say, "Good, that's it, print it." They might say, "No, no, no, let's have another one." Or Wyler would say, "Let's do it again," and they'd say, "No, no, *molto bene!*"—they wanted to print that one. And Wyler usually followed their advice.[50]

The single most famous scene in *Roman Holiday* is the one in which Peck and Hepburn dare each other to stick a hand inside the mouth of an ancient Roman cave dragon: To get a spontaneous reaction, Peck resorted to an old vaudeville trick—drawing his hand up into his cuff so that it looked severed. Unforewarned, Audrey reacted perfectly, with a shriek. "It was the only scene Wyler ever did in one take," she said.[51]

Peck recalls "a girl who was good at everything except shedding tears—wacky and funny, a very lovable girl who was always making faces and doing backflips and clowning around. But when it came to a poignant scene, she couldn't find that within herself; she just couldn't find the right kind of emotion."[52]

He was referring to one of the most touching final scenes in which the princess must leave the journalist and return to royal imprisonment.

"I don't know how to say goodbye," she says. "I can't think of any words."

"Don't try," he replies, as the music swells.

It seemed straightforward, but "I had no idea how to come by those tears," Audrey recalled. "The night was getting longer and longer, and Willy was waiting. Out of the blue, he came over and gave me hell. 'We can't stay here all night. Can't you cry, for God's sake?' He'd never spoken to me like that, ever, during the picture. He'd been so nice and gentle. I broke into such sobs and he shot the scene and that was it. Afterwards he said, 'I'm sorry, but I had to get you to do it somehow.' "[53]

Years later, when a BBC interviewer asked how much she had learned from Wyler, Audrey replied, "I'd say almost everything. His attitude was that only simplicity and the truth count. It has to come from the inside. You can't fake it. That is something I long remembered."

Then and thereafter, Audrey did not watch the rushes, but Wyler did: "She was every eager young girl who has ever come to Rome for the first time and I, crusty veteran that I was, felt tears in my eyes watching her. Audrey was the spirit of youth—and I knew that very soon the entire world would fall in love with her, as all of us on the picture did."[54]

Gregory Peck was first among them. "It was my good luck," he said, "during that wonderful summer in Rome, to be the first of her screen fellows, to hold out my hand, and help her keep her balance as she did her spins and pirouettes. Those months [were] probably the happiest experience I ever had making movies."[55]

Peck, her screen lover, was friendly with James Hanson, her offscreen lover, who was present and accounted for on the *Roman Holiday* set. "I was able to spend time with her in the flat that the company found for her and her mother on the Via Boncompagni," says Hanson. "They would do shots of Audrey, and Greg would be in a trailer waiting to do his stuff. He and I would go into the Caffè Greco on the Via Condotti and play gin rummy for hours. I enjoyed being there, encouraging her and watching her. We were going to be married as soon as *Roman Holiday* was finished. All the plans were made."[56]

But once again the best-laid plans went awry. When *Roman Holiday* filming ended in September 1952, there was not even a hiatus let alone a wedding for Audrey, who had to go directly into the American road tour of *Gigi*. She returned to the United States, opened at the Nixon Theater in Pittsburgh on October 13, 1952, and continued for eight months, through Boston, Cleveland, Chicago, Detroit, Washington and Los Angeles. She was exhausted long before the tour was over and, according to Cathleen Nesbitt, under heavy pressure from her mother to break off the engagement. Midway during the tour, she announced it was over.

"When I couldn't find time to attend to the furnishing of our London flat, I suddenly knew I'd make a pretty bad wife," she told Anita Loos. "I would forever have to be studying parts, fitting costumes and giving interviews. And what a humiliating spot to put a husband in ... making him stand by, holding my coat, while I signed autographs for the bobbie soxers!"[57]

Pestered endlessly by the media, she gave variations on that theme—some more diplomatic than others:

"I felt it would be unfair to James to marry him when I was also in love with my work."

"It was a mutual decision and a very personal matter about which I have nothing more to say."[58]

"The time will come when I can afford the luxury of a husband. Just now, I haven't got the time."

"When I get married, I want to be *really* married."[59]

Zsa Zsa Gabor says Ella wasn't the only one pressuring Audrey to get unengaged: "When she got the part in *Roman Holiday*, the studio advised her not to get married."[60] Indeed, Paramount and most film companies encouraged "romances" but generally opposed star marriages (especially to non-stars) in the belief that millions of lovestruck fans would be disappointed thereby.

Forty years later, Lord Hanson reflects on the breakup in his candid, magnanimous way:

[After *Roman Holiday*], she came to me and said, "I really don't think I want to get married at this time. I hate to do this to you. I love your family...." She made her decision as much based on what she felt would be best for me as what would be best for her. I said, "Fine, okay." If somebody makes a decision they think is best for them, I say one of two things: "Think it over," or else, "I agree with you—do what's best for you." There was disappointment, yes. But there was no rift or rupture, just a natural decision made by both sides.

So I went my way and started to build up businesses, while she went her way and continued to build up her career. Had she married me, Audrey would have continued with her career. No doubt about it. I believed in that. There was never any "either/or" [marriage/career] problem. She was somebody whose star and whose destiny had been set by her talent. It would have been pointless to try to persuade her to do anything else.... I loved Audrey very much. I've not loved very many women in my life in that way. Yet I have no regrets whatsoever about her decision.[61]

If anyone, Audrey was the one with regrets. The amicable nature of their split was proven by the fact that they continued to see each other. In December, Hanson went to visit and spend Christmas with her in Chicago:

"I got the impression Audrey had reflected upon it and wanted to take it up again that Christmas. But I believed she had made the right decision and that it wouldn't be right to backtrack on it—not for any reasons of spite. You couldn't be spiteful about Audrey. She was just too delightful.

She tried to make a reconciliation but by that time, I felt I could not go back. We spent a happy Christmas together in Chicago, after which we parted as good friends."[62]*

The subject of her romantic life remained a hot topic for many months, even after the *Gigi* road show came to a close, on May 16, 1953, in San Francisco. When no-nonsense columnist Dorothy Kilgallen asked her if she had always had "beaus buzzing around her," Audrey replied, "Well, I'll say this. I've never wanted for one—not since I was seventeen, anyway."[63]

They came in all shapes, sizes and ages. The day after she accepted a dinner invitation from sixty-two-year-old Groucho Marx, the newspapers wasted no time in speculating on their betrothal.

"Nonsense," replied Groucho. "I don't want to be ungallant, but Audrey's too old and wrinkled for me."

UNTIL NOW, NOBODY BUT THE studio had seen *Roman Holiday*. When it finally opened, in August 1953, audiences and critics alike loved it. Mostly it was the doe-eyed little star they loved. In the opening sight gag, the princess's shoes are killing her during a royal reception; she kicks one of them off beneath her floor-length gown and then can't find it.

Audrey's performance captivated throughout. Irate about being a royal prisoner, the princess throws a tantrum and is given a tranquilizer—but sneaks out of the palace before it takes effect. Journalist Gregory Peck finds her snoozing in a public square and promises his editor a scoop. Peck and the film are aided by the beautiful cinematography of Franz Planer and the romantic background music of Georges Auric.‡

But most of all, they were aided by the face and mesmerizing voice of Audrey Hepburn—a soft mezzo that turned soprano in excitement. And everyone was caught off-guard by the film's conclusion—perhaps the first romantic comedy with an unhappy ending. Molly Haskell called it a "heartbreaking moment of renunciation."[64]

Roman Holiday turned out to be strangely relevant to the moment. Nineteen fifty-three was a busy year for English royalty: The coronation of Queen Elizabeth II and the "commoner" romance of her sister, Princess Margaret, had both received saturation news coverage. Paramount denied

---

* In later years, Hepburn always spoke affectionately of Hanson. In 1959, he married Geraldine Kaelin, with whom he has remained happily for thirty-seven years. They have two sons and a daughter.

‡ Auric—with Francis Poulence, Darius Milhaud, Arthur Honegger, Germaine Tailleferre and Louis Durey—was one of France's legendary "Les Six" composers. The brilliant Czech-born cameraman Franz Planer had recently filmed Max Ophuls's *Letter from an Unknown Woman* (1948) and *Death of a Salesman* (1951). He became Audrey's cinematographer of choice for many future films.

any connection but slyly exploited the similarities between Princess Anne's love for a reporter in the film and Princess Margaret's involvement with Captain Peter Townsend in real life. In publicity terms, there could have been no more fortuitous a coincidence.

The picture earned back a third of its production costs in Japan alone (where it is the no. 1 favorite foreign film of all time, ahead of *Gone With the Wind*). *There and in Europe and America, Audrey and her "look" became the rage.*

The trade papers were talking of a great new star, but the tabloids were talking scandal. The New York Mirror said Peck's wife Greta was "giving him the bounce because of his affection for the sylph-like nymph, a willowy boyish miss" named Hepburn.[65] Audrey bristled: "I saw her coming out of Romanoff's the other day and she asked me to spend next Sunday swimming in the pool at her home. Does that sound like I'm a home-breaker?"[66]

There was, in fact, never any romance between Hepburn and Peck, whose marriage was dissolving before he and Audrey ever met. He would soon be divorced and, a year later, marry French journalist Veronique Passani, with whom he has remained.

But in truth, few cared about Gregory Peck these days. They cared about *Audrey Hepburn.* Young Senator John F. Kennedy was among many declaring *Roman Holiday* to be his favorite film and Hepburn his favorite actress. September 7, 1953, found her on the cover of *Time* magazine— never before occupied by an unknown star of a newly released film. Peck was temporarily left in the dust, but never resented it. Three decades later, returning from a trip to China, he gave her a grand cross-cultural tribute:

"When we climbed out of the airplane [in Beijing], to my amazement I saw about two hundred little Chinese Audrey Hepburns waiting at the airport. *Roman Holiday* was playing in China for the first time—thirty years after we made it—and attracting enormous crowds. Everywhere we went we saw little Audrey Hepburns with the bangs and the long skirts."[67]

"SHE WAS A ONE-MAN woman, very loving," says Lord James Hanson. "Once she gave up one man, it was then the next man. She didn't play the field."[68] To the disappointment of the tabloids, the "next man" was not Gregory Peck—but he was a close friend of Peck's. It was party time in London, where Audrey returned in July 1953 for the British opening of *Roman Holiday.* One of those fêtes was hosted by her mother, at Ella's South Audley Street flat, where Cecil Beaton met Audrey for the first time and that night recorded in his diary:

"[She has] a huge mouth, flat Mongolian features, heavily painted eyes, a coconut coiffure, long nails without varnish, a wonderfully lithe figure, and a long neck.... She appears to take her wholesale adulation with a pinch of salt, and gratitude rather than puffed-up pride.... Without any preliminaries, she cuts through to a basic understanding that makes people friends." Beaton added that the other guests included American actor Mel Ferrer—"a charming, gangling man, [who] described A.H. to me as 'the biggest thing to come down the turnpike.' "[69]

Ferrer's invitation had come through Gregory Peck, who was in London making *Night People* and had hosted his own party for Audrey in his Grosvenor Square flat. Ferrer was likewise in London at the moment, shooting MGM's *Knights of the Round Table* at Pinewood Studios.* Mel was the twice-divorced father of four by then. But Peck wanted him to meet Audrey and gave him her phone number at Ella's.

"She answered herself and said, 'This is Audrey,' " Ferrer remembers. "When I told her Greg had suggested I call, she answered very cheerily, 'Oh, I loved you in *Lili!*' "[70] That lovely musical, released just a few months before *Roman Holiday*, starred Ferrer as a lame carnival puppeteer and Leslie Caron as the orphan girl with whom he falls in love.

"My first impression of Audrey when we finally saw each other was how simple and direct she was," says Ferrer today. "She was gentle, delicate and sensitive. But full of life and sparkle."[71] The chemistry between them was instant.

Nearly six-foot-three in height, Mel was "gangly" indeed, as well as handsome, and his prospects for serious leading-man status and film stardom were on the rise. But he was not "just" an actor. He was also a stage and film director, producer and cofounder of the pioneering La Jolla Playhouse. Some thought of him—and he perhaps thought of himself—as the next Orson Welles.

Actor James Coburn first knew Ferrer at La Jolla, where Coburn and many other prominent young actors got their Actors Equity cards. A decade later, during a break on the set of *Charade*, Coburn and Audrey had an intimate discussion that was rare for both of them.

"She told me about first meeting and falling in love with Mel," Coburn recalls, "and I asked, 'What was the attraction?' She said, 'The way he looked me in the eyes—the way he just penetrated me with his eyes.' That was the thing that really got her, she said."[72]

MELCHOR GASTON FERRER WAS BORN a dozen years before Audrey Hepburn, in Elberon, New Jersey, on August 25, 1917, and spent most of his early life in New York City. His father, Dr. José Ferrer, a prominent

* Ferrer played King Arthur opposite Ava Gardner's Guinevere. Merlin was old Felix Aylmer—Audrey's former acting coach.

Cuban-Spanish surgeon at St. Vincent's Hospital in New York, died when Mel was four. His mother was Irene O'Donohue, whose family was socially important in Manhattan and Newport.

"She was a Gibson-girl type, spoilt, arrogant, opinionated and tactless," says Joseph J. O'Donohue IV, who was her grandnephew and godson. The cousins were great friends, and when Mel once ran away from home, it was to Joe's big summer home near Newport that he fled. "He stayed about a week before returning to the fold," O'Donohue recalls. "In those days Mel wrote very agreeable poetry, surreptitiously, which he let me read."[73]

Upon graduation from Canterbury Preparatory School in 1935, Mel entered Princeton, where he immersed himself in theater and, in his sophomore year, won an award for best original play. In the summers, he stage-managed at the Cape Playhouse in Dennis, Massachusetts, and played the lead in *Our Town* there. When a Princeton friend tried to convince Mrs. Ferrer of her son's talent, she replied haughtily that writing and theater were out of the question "for one of Mel's breeding."[74]

After two years, Mel left Princeton and spent a year in Taxco, Mexico, struggling to write a novel but ending up instead with a successful children's book, *Tito's Hats*, published by Doubleday Doran, which sold out its edition of 20,000. Thus encouraged, he took a job at Stephen Daye Press in Brattleboro, Vermont, in the hope of making it as a professional writer.

"I drove a bookwagon all over New England for the first few months and then got promoted to editing," Ferrer recalls. While there, he was fascinated by a collection of New England graveyard epitaphs that had been assembled by Robert E. Pike. He took all the photos and chalked all the inscriptions and epitaphs himself, compiling them—uncredited—for the whimsical Stephen Daye book, *Granite Laughter and Marble Tears*, in 1938.

The previous year, he had married Frances Pilchard, an artist-sculptress he met at Princeton. But it was soon clear that he couldn't support a family as an editor. At that late date in the Depression, the theater was hardly a more secure occupation—but it was the one he'd always wanted and would now pursue in earnest. As a result, "his money was cut off and he had a hard time of it," says Joseph O'Donohue, who had provided crucial assistance by introducing him to actor Clifton Webb.

"When Fran and I lost our first child," Mel recalls, "I took a long weekend off, went to New York and landed in a Shubert musical *You'll Never Know* with music by Cole Porter," starring Webb and Libby Holman. It was his first Broadway job—and first ever as a hoofer. Webb advised him to acquire "the rudiments of the dance before opening night," says

Ferrer, and taught him "a few basic steps as a tap dancer so I could keep the job."[75]

One critic called Mel "the only Social Registerite chorus boy," which did not amuse his mother. "Mrs. Ferrer removed Mel's listing in the S.R.," says O'Donohue, who always respected him for not giving a hoot. "I was fond of Mel and still am."[76]

The Porter show brought more dance work in the Marc Connelly musical, *Everywhere I Roam* (1938). Next came Mel's acting debut in *Cue for Passion* (1940) with Otto Preminger, recently returned to New York as an actor—in some disgrace—from his rocky first stint as a director in Hollywood. And then came disaster.

"Toward the end of the *Cue for Passion* run, I contracted polio," Ferrer recalls. "No doctor—of the many I consulted— diagnosed it correctly, and I lost the use of my right arm and shoulder. Not until two years later, after I had gone into radio (which required only one hand), did I meet the remarkable Sister Kenny. She finally explained that I had been crippled by polio. And she helped me restore the use of my arm and right side."[77]

His recuperation was slow and painful, but Ferrer was never a man to give up. He had divorced Pilchard, by whom he had a son and a daughter, and married Barbara Tripp, by whom he had another son and daughter. Soon, he would divorce Tripp and *remarry* Pilchard! During that period of marital confusion, radio work took him to Longview, Texas, and Little Rock, Arkansas, before he got back to where he wanted to be—New York—in 1943.

There, he was hired by NBC as a producer-director for some of its best radio programs: *The Hit Parade*, *The Durante-Moore Comedy Hour*, *Mr. District Attorney* and *Dr. I.Q.* He helped create NBC's first jazz program and won a Peabody Award for *The Eternal Light* series he directed and produced for the Jewish Theological Seminary. And then came the call of the movies:

"Columbia Pictures approached me with an offer to come to Hollywood, do an apprenticeship as a dialogue director and then graduate to directing. It meant a big salary boost and preparation for what I thought would be my future—television." He wanted to direct teleplays and felt films would provide good training. Instead, he became hooked forever on film.

One day early on, in Los Angeles, Columbia publicist Herb Sterne asked Mel if he wanted to be introduced to the director he most admired. "That," says Ferrer, "is how I met D. W. Griffith. We had Orange Blossoms with him at the Hollywood Roosevelt Hotel, his habitat. D. W. befriended me and I was lucky enough to sit next to him every Saturday night for the next few months while he screened his oldest and rarest prints for us."[78]

Asked if it's true that Orson Welles was his role model in those days, Ferrer replies that he considered *Citizen Kane* one of the ten best pictures ever made, and still does: "I admired Orson and I laughed at his jokes, which meant we became friends."

Ferrer's first shot at directing was a low-budget remake of Gene Stratton Porter's *Girl of the Limberlost* (1945) in the Columbia "B" unit. On the last day of *Limberlost* shooting, he got a call from actor José Ferrer in New York.* José was directing a stage version of Lillian Smith's *Strange Fruit*, a controversial novel about miscegenation and racial prejudice in the South, and was calling to offer Mel the lead in it. "I informed Joe—loftily—that I was directing my first film and that I intended to keep on that course," says Ferrer, but he agreed to read the script—and loved it. "Naturally, I flew to New York a few days later and went straight into rehearsal."

So much for Columbia. *Strange Fruit* turned out to be a wise career move, as a result of which Mel was offered several new Hollywood contracts. He chose the one from David O. Selznick, obtaining a delay in its starting date long enough for the two Ferrers to switch positions again. "I decided that Joe should become our American Olivier," says Mel, "and I proposed he do *Cyrano de Bergerac*.... He said he would but he wanted me to direct, and I'm happy to say that José Ferrer's *Cyrano* was the biggest step forward in his career. He became our flag-bearer."

Back on the West Coast, Selznick gave Mel wide-ranging assignments as an actor, director and producer of screen tests. (No lesser legend than Joseph von Sternberg had shot Mel's own first screen test for Selznick, and now Mel shot Patricia Neal's initial test.) Selznick soon loaned him to John Ford as an assistant director on *The Fugitive*. "Ford was another of my idols," says Ferrer, and "taught me a great deal.... A gruff, hidden, tortured and inspired director."

These were Hollywood's "glory days," he recalls. By 1947, he, Joseph Cotten, Dorothy McGuire, Jennifer Jones and Gregory Peck were all working successfully under Selznick. "But there was one definite void which each of us felt acutely," Mel felt. "We had all come from the legitimate theatre and [hankered] for an audience. We wanted to start a summer theatre where we could get back... with audiences, people who would laugh out loud, whom you could hear applaud, whose presence you could feel."[79]

Gregory Peck, born and raised in La Jolla, made a brief reconnaisance trip there and came back with the report that the high school theater was available, and the local Kiwanis Club would help them build a list of subscribers. A budget was worked out: It would take $15,000 to open the

---

* José and Mel Ferrer are not related, though they have spent most of their professional lives being confused with one another. Further complicating the matter is that, in addition to his father, Mel's brother was also named José Ferrer and was also a leading surgeon in New York (and later Dean of the College of Physicians and Surgeons at Columbia University).

doors for a nine-week season. Ferrer and Peck went to Selznick and left his office with a check for $15,000. Selznick had a few shrewd reasons of his own for bankrolling the effort. His best performers were pining for live stage work in between films. This outlet would keep them happy and might also become a recruiting ground for future film talent.

The La Jolla Playhouse now began an ambitious season of ten shows a summer. Ferrer staged many himself and, in 1948, Norman Lloyd was also hired to direct. The group's prestige increased steadily with such productions as *The Cocktail Party* with Patricia Neal, Vincent Price and Estelle Winwood; *The Lady's Not for Burning* with Marsha Hunt; *I Am a Camera* and *The Postman Always Rings Twice*. Ferrer recalls *Summer and Smoke* (1950) with special fondness: "Dorothy McGuire gave a moving performance and Tennessee came all the way from Florida to see it. He hugged me with tears in his eyes when the curtain came down and told me it was 'the best production of mah play I ever had.'"

Personally, says Mel, "the biggest romp I had there was our version of Oscar Wilde's *The Importance of Being Earnest*, in which Hurd Hatfield and I played opposite Jane Wyatt and Dorothy McGuire. Constance Collier played Lady Bracknell. Hysterical."[80] Eventually, he turned over the administrative reins to John Swope, McGuire's photographer-husband, and a fund was established that led to a new facility for the La Jolla Playhouse, which continues to this day.

"Greg and I ran it for nine years," Ferrer reflects, "and we never took a cent."[81]

His management of the operation had been brilliant: By 1953, all of David O. Selznick's initial loan had been repaid—a rare occurrence in Selznick's professional life.

In those days, says Mel, "David was busy going broke, so all of us under contract were happy to do loan-outs so that he could make a little money." Howard Hughes now called Selznick looking for a director to do three days of shooting for a new ending of a Preston Sturges film, *Vendetta*, and Mel got the nod. "It took me two years to execute Howard's directives," says Ferrer. "A long three days! During that time, we remade the entire film and Howard negotiated for and bought RKO. I was the first person he signed to a contract. [By that time,] David was bankrupt. He graciously gave me a release, and I went to work for Howard Hughes as a director, producer and midnight chum."

Ferrer worked daily with his billionaire boss in the reorganization of RKO. When Hughes asked for suggestions for top executive posts, Mel proposed his friends, producer Jerry Wald and screenwriter Norman Krasna: "Once the studio had two such capable people at the helm, Howard promptly sold RKO to General Tire Company and betook himself to the desert and other remote outposts" to concentrate on his aircraft and oil interests.[82] Mel, too, now departed RKO temporarily for something new and daring—something akin to *Strange Fruit* a few years before: The offer to make his film-acting debut—as a black man.

Lost Boundaries (1949), based on a *Reader's Digest* article by William L. White, was the true story of a light-skinned Negro doctor who passed for white for twenty years in the little town of Keene, New Hampshire. Louis de Rochemont, creator of *The March of Time* newsreels, had bought the story and would turn it into one of the first important American racial films, starring a number of fine Negro stage performers, including Canada Lee. Ferrer was cast for his indeterminate ethnic swarthiness.

Under Alfred L. Werker's clear-eyed direction, *Boundaries* treated its theme bluntly. The blacks in med school trade bleak jokes about their job chances. "If we can't be doctors, we can always be Pullman car redcaps," says one. Another recites the ruling verse of the day:

"If you're white you're all right,
If you're brown you hang around,
If you're black you stand back."

Ferrer's character, Dr. Scott, is proud of his race and objects to "passing." But he and his wife have a baby on the way and, desperate for a job, he gives in: "For one year of my life I'm gonna be white." It stretches into half a lifetime.

Ferrer's understated portrayal of the hero got glowing reviews, as did the film. "De Rochemont almost lost his home and his career—he had to mortgage his house to do it," says Mel, "but he was vindicated. It was produced for $250,000, and in two years it grossed over $5 million."[83]

Mel had done it out of conviction—and a total salary of $7,500. The film was screened at the White House for President Truman, who was influenced by it to initiate legislation permitting blacks to become officers in the U.S. Navy. Ferrer calls it "a ground-breaker and a 'moving' picture in every sense of the word, light-years ahead" of the other racial-theme movies that year, *Intruder in the Dust, Home of the Brave* and *Pinky*.

"I still consider it the best movie I was ever lucky enough to be in," he says today. "I had never appeared on the screen before, only directed, so I could not be identified as being white or black. Career-wise, it was a huge risk. But the end result was spectacular and I cherish it."[84]

It also fueled his personal interest and activity in the civil-rights movement—convictions soon shared and combined with the humanitarian concerns of Audrey Hepburn.

BACK AT RKO AFTER THAT loan-out, Ferrer next directed Claudette Colbert and Robert Ryan in a melodrama called *The Secret Fury* (1950). But with such positive reinforcement for his *Lost Boundaries* performance, he now wanted to concentrate on acting. His next role would be another stunning one—back at Columbia, on loan-out again—as a Mexican matador in *The Brave Bulls* (1951), directed with gritty realism by Robert Rossen.

"Rossen had just done *All the King's Men* and had made an exciting prizefighting picture before that, and I wanted very much to play the bullfighter," says Ferrer. "Rossen's response was that I was the first candidate he'd met who could fit his behind into the *taleguilla* [breeches]. I got the part."[85]

The praise for Ferrer and the movie alike were lavish. *Newsweek* put *The Brave Bulls* "squarely alongside such milestones as *Citizen Kane*" and observed, "for his professional good, it is perhaps a pity that so superb a young actor should find his first great part in so superb a film; he is not *in* the film, he *belongs* to it, along with the dust and bells of Mexico."[86] Many thought Ferrer's performance worthy of an Oscar, but he and the film fell victim to a radical past: Rossen once belonged to the Communist Party, and during *Bulls* filming in Mexico, the House Un-American Activities Committee witch hunt had heated up in Hollywood.

"I felt Bob had a good chance of winning the Academy Award for [the previous year's] *All the King's Men*," says Mel, who persuaded Rossen to fly to Hollywood for the Oscars. "He felt sure that Harry Cohn would prevail against him but he went, reluctantly, [and] it won Best Picture. It was a triumph for Rossen. But Cohn got his revenge when *Brave Bulls* was released. In spite of outstanding notices, Cohn issued the edict that *no* funds would be available for promotion, ads or publicity. [So it was] a critical success, but a financial failure."

Ferrer finished his much-loaned-out RKO contract by costarring with Marlene Dietrich in *Rancho Notorious* (1952). At that point, MGM signed him up as an actor, using him first in the hit swashbuckler *Scaramouche* and then in one of the most successful "sleepers" in that studio's history.

Lili (1953) was the unpretentious little musical in which Audrey had seen and loved the thirty-five-year-old Ferrer at his sexiest. It was directed and choreographed by Charles Walters, based on a Paul Gallico story. In its title role was Audrey's only real screen "rival," Leslie Caron.* At its outset, orphan Caron arrives, forlorn, in a little French village. A carnival has just arrived, and she encounters the lame, unfriendly puppeteer Paul (Ferrer). "He's always angry," Jean-Pierre Aumont tells her, "—a disagreeable man." Aumont, in real life, was a Free French war hero

---

* Eight years later, *Lili* became the first film musical to be converted into a stage musical, instead of the other way around: *Carnival*, directed and choreographed by Gower Champion, had Anna Maria Alberghetti in Caron's role and Jerry Orbach in Ferrer's.

(whose wife Maria Montez had recently died under mysterious circumstances in her bathtub). Here he is "Marcus le Magnifique," a magician with a sexy sidekick, Zsa Zsa Gabor.

Paul's puppets (their voices all truly Ferrer's) are his alter egos: Carrot Top, the nice guy; Reynardo, the Fox; Golo, a villain; Marguerite, the diva-forerunner of Miss Piggy. Through them, unhappy Paul talks unhappy Lili out of suicide. Together, they sing the lovely "Hi Lili, Hi Lo" theme song—without dubbing—that became popular throughout the world.*

Caron is thoroughly enchanting in her fantasy dance sequences, trading places (and slinky red-sequinned dresses) with Gabor.‡ In the final number, the puppets come to life for a cross between "Yellow Brick Road" in *The Wizard of Oz* and the great Caron-Kelly dream ballet of *An American in Paris*.§ The result is a naive, charming romance, with Ferrer at his most appealing—Audrey told him she saw it three times.

"Mel is a very complex person," says Leslie Caron, guardedly. "On the one hand, he was very generous and very paternal to Audrey and to me when we worked on *Lili*. On the other hand...."[87]

She trails off and declines to finish the sentence.

Charles Higham calls Ferrer a man of too many parts—"adept in so many fields that no single achievement placed him quite in the first class"—fragmented by the range of his own abilities, and thus volatile and high-strung. "He lacked the warmth, sheer animalism, and brute force" to cross the great divide between leading man and star. "He did not provoke sexual longings in millions of women; he did not evoke fantasies."

Except in Audrey Hepburn. She had fallen in love with the sensitive, soulful character in *Lili* and projected it onto him in real life. She also loved his voice, and the way he jokingly signed his name—"Mellifluous." Clearly, her notion of Mel Ferrer was romanticized from the start.

AUDREY WAS EVOKING SIMILAR FANTASIES in her own adoring fans, who clamored for scraps of information about her. Her publicist, scrambling for a few new factoids, sent her a questionnaire and hastily released her answers when he got them:

---

* "I still get royalties from 'Hi Lili,'" says Ferrer, "and I hope Leslie does, too."

‡ Zsa Zsa was the Miss Hungary of 1936. *Lili* is, far and away, the highlight of her filmography.

§ Charles Walters (1911–1982) choreographed such MGM musicals as *Meet Me in St. Louis* and was Judy Garland's favorite director. He made *Easter Parade* (1948), *The Barkleys of Broadway* (1949) and Joan Crawford's camp classic, *Torch Song*. "After a few days of shooting we all realized that Leslie was giving an extraordinary performance," recalls Ferrer. Walters wanted to expand the numbers, increase the budget and make a typical MGM big musical, [but] Dore Schary ruled that the picture would stay in its small, modest, intimate form. How right he was."

"Still finds it exciting to buy food. . . .

"Has a large collection of long-playing records—from classics, Broadway musicals, to hot jazz. Believes one of the greatest things about the U.S. is the long-playing record. . . .[88]

"Speaks seven languages in faultless diction, lives in a New York apartment-hotel with her mother. . . .

"Likes rain. . . ."[89]

Favorite films? She listed her own *Lavender Hill Mob, Les Enfants du Paradis*—and *Lili*. Asked for her opinion of TV and radio, she responded, "I miss the audiences."[90]

"TV" was not a pleasant set of initials for Paramount, which like all big studios, was beset with antitrust suits and the devastating competition of the new medium. Paramount had again tried unsuccessfully to buy out Audrey's Associated British Pictures contract and was now paying even more for her services. But since its other "major" female players were Arlene Dahl, Rhonda Fleming, Polly Bergen, Rosemary Clooney and Dorothy Malone, there was no choice but to be grateful to have Audrey, whatever her cost, for top projects.[91]

The top project at hand, in September 1953, was a Samuel Taylor stage hit known in Britain as *Sabrina Fair*, shortened to *Sabrina* in America to avoid confusion with *Vanity Fair*. Audrey had recently seen it on Broadway, starring Margaret Sullavan and Joseph Cotten, and asked Paramount to buy it as a vehicle for her. The studio did so, agreeing to pay her all of $15,000.

"It's the second big film," said Audrey, "which will prove if I was really worthy of the first."

Sabrina was Cinderella redux: a chauffeur's daughter becomes a sophisticate. She loves both sons of her father's employer, despite Dad's warning that "Nobody poor has ever been called democratic for marrying somebody rich." Director Billy Wilder—after *Double Indemnity, Lost Weekend, Sunset Boulevard* and *Stalag 17*—would complete his Paramount contract with this film.

Sabrina was filmed on location at the Glen Cove, Long Island, estate of Paramount chairman Barney Balaban in just nine weeks, between September and November 1953, plus a few trips to Hollywood for retakes. William Holden played the younger brother. The role of the debonair older brother had been rejected by Cary Grant. It was accepted by Humphrey Bogart, who had spent most of his career at Warner Brothers but was now finishing up his own three-picture contract with Paramount.

Bogart's hectic schedule that year included *Beat the Devil, The Caine Mutiny* and *The Barefoot Contessa*. When shooting began on frothy *Sabrina*, he had just finished playing Captain Queeg in *Caine Mutiny* and seemed to carry over Queeg's paranoia. Bogart "was in totally unfamiliar territory," said Wilder, "and very uncomfortable." He had "the occupational insecurity of most actors," said Lauren Bacall, the last of his four wives. "He was never sure when he would work again."[92]

Bogart's insecurities were aggravated by Wilder's jocular comment to a reporter that the reason Bogart, not Holden, wound up with Audrey in the end was "because Bogart gets $300,000 a picture and Holden gets $125,000." Despite (or because of) that, Bogart fussed and worried. "I'm gonna get fucked," he told a friend. "Billy's going to throw it to his buddy Holden."[93]

Holden (real name: William Franklin Beedle, Jr.) was thirty-five and at the peak of his career, having just starred in two of Wilder's greatest pictures—*Sunset Boulevard* and *Stalag 17*. He and Bogart had fallen out years earlier while making *Invisible Stripes* (1939). Nowadays, Bogart referred to him as "Smiling Jim," mocked his bleached-blond look in *Sabrina*, and called him a "dumb prick" to the press. Bogey had a special loathing for Holden's macho display of rolling Gaulois cigarettes with one hand. Audrey smoked English Gold Flakes—in a long, filtered holder—and Bogart smoked heavily, as well. The air quality on the set was as woeful as the interpersonal relationships.

If Holden and Bogart did not get along, Holden and Hepburn certainly did—so much so that it may have constituted an affair. Holden was married to actress Brenda Marshall (real name: Ardis Gaines) but was notoriously promiscuous and had an odd habit of bringing women home to meet his wife.[94]

Audrey was infinitely more prim and proper. Back in California after the Long Island shooting, she lived alone in a modest two-room apartment ($120 a month) on Wilshire Boulevard. There, she said, her biggest joy was "to unlock my door and find the new record that the store down the street delivered during the afternoon. I get into old, soft, comfy clothes and then I play the new music while I cook." She boasted of having over a hundred records—from Brahms and Beethoven to "a mess of good jazz like Benny Goodman, Mel Powell and Gerry Mulligan."[95]

In those days, Holden and Audrey were often seen at fancy restaurants, after which they would repair to her apartment. But Audrey's most intimate friends doubt she ever went to bed with Holden, and her journalist acquaintance Henry Gris claims she had "very little sexual drive" in general.[96] All such opinions, of course, were speculative: Did she really love Holden? Was she expecting him to get a divorce?* And what about Mel Ferrer? But there was no doubt that Holden passionately adored *her*: "She was the love of my life," he later declared.

---

* However shaky, the marriage of William and Aridis Holden lasted another twenty years, into the 1970s.

Audrey, for her part, was at least infatuated with the warm, demonstrative side of Holden's personality—when it was not submerged in alcohol. Holden's biographer Bob Thomas quoted her as saying she and Bill could "make beautiful babies together."

Baby-making was, in the end, the issue. Compounding Holden's obsession with sex was a secret he eventually had to tell Audrey: A few years before, at his wife's insistence after the birth of their second son, he had undergone an irreversible vasectomy. When Audrey learned of it, she dropped all thought of marriage. Her deepest desire—even above career—was to be a mother.

Another Audrey—Billy Wilder's wife—knew the score long before. The Wilders and Holdens were friends, and Audrey Wilder recalls a down-to-earth talk she had with Holden's wife: "Brenda said, 'The doctor told me I can't have any more children, so I had Bill have a vasectomy.' I said, 'Why didn't you have your tubes tied? The minute you do that to a guy, he's going to try to screw everybody.'"[97]

Holden was already trying—though he claimed to exempt his leading ladies: "I just don't want anything in a relationship with an actress to be misunderstood at the time," he told Donald Zec, the biographer of Sophia Loren, with whom Holden starred in The Key (1958). "You have to work with them terribly intimately, particularly in the love scenes, and unless you play it neutral you may have a situation on your hands. I've had that difficulty with Jennifer Jones, Grace Kelly, Audrey Hepburn and Kim Novak."

Zec observed that such a problem was better than being held prisoner by the Viet Cong. But Holden continued:

"In all the relationships I've had with leading ladies, I found that the less involved I was with them, the better. [Two or three of them] I absolutely adored... and if they had ever been willing to change their way of life and say 'I'll go with you,' it would have been fine. But we never stepped over the boundaries. So after all these years we have the same kind of respect for each other that we had in the beginning. I'll tell you, it's worth a lot more to me than a piece of ass."[98]

Holden's satyriasis was matched by his compulsion to talk about it. Even in reference to the greatest screen beauties, he could never discuss women in less than batches of half a dozen. At the moment, in the wake of his vasectomy confession, he was distraught about Audrey's reaction and rejection of him. "I was really in love with Audrey but she wouldn't marry me," he said. When Sabrina shooting ended, he set out on a 'round-the-world publicity tour with a private plan of action that was typical:

"I was determined to wipe Audrey out of my mind by screwing a woman in every country I visited. My plan succeeded, though sometimes with difficulty. When I was in Bangkok, I was with a Thai girl in a boat in one of the klongs [canals]. I guess we got too animated, because the boat tipped over and I fell into the filthy water. Back at the hotel I poured alcohol in my ears because I was afraid I'd become infected with the plague." He poured alcohol into more than just his ears, and, "When I got back to Hollywood, I went to Audrey's dressing-room and told her what I had done. You know what she said? 'Oh, Bill!' That's all. 'Oh, Bill!' Just as though I were some naughty boy."[99]

SABRINA WAS SUPPOSED TO BE a romantic comedy, but there were more dramatic than comic moments on the set, and no romance between Humphrey Bogart and anyone. Everyone said Bogart hated Holden. Some said Bogart also hated Audrey—for her inability to do a scene in less than ten takes, and for "conspiring with Holden against him because she was giving Holden a tumble."[100]

Audrey never spoke negatively about any of her leading men. The closest she came was, "I was rather terrified of Humphrey Bogart—and he knew it. [But] if he didn't like me, he certainly never showed it."[101] She later told Rob Wolders "how reasonable Bogart was with her, a little rougher with other people around—but a jovial roughness." Bogart himself once paid her a rare if backhanded compliment: "You take the Monroes and the Terry Moores, and you know just what you're going to get every time. With Audrey it's kind of unpredictable. She's like a good tennis player—she varies her shots."[102]

The final authorities on the subject are the redoubtable Billy and Audrey Wilder, jointly interviewed at their Wilshire Boulevard home in 1995.

"He did not hate Hepburn," says Wilder. "Nobody could hate Hepburn. He did not hate Holden. He hated *me!* Why? Because he knew that I wanted to have Cary Grant but I couldn't get him. Bogart did me a favor [by taking the role]. Holden I had made pictures with before, and Holden fell in love with Hepburn, so that was kind of a nice cozy arrangement. But Bogart we got at the last minute, and so I did not know what to do with him."

One of many sources of tension was the script:

"It was written for Cary Grant and we had to rewrite a lot. One time, I handed him a new page and he looked at it and said, 'You must be kidding. Who wrote that, your five-year-old daughter?' He said it loud, for the gallery of electricians and everybody. But they were all my pals. He didn't get a laugh."[103]

But the worst problem between Bogart and Wilder stemmed from a social faux pas. One day after shooting, Wilder invited Holden, Hepburn and several others over for drinks—either consciously or unconsciously excluding Bogart. "At the time," says Audrey Wilder, "I said to Billy, 'You can't do that. He's a big star. You can't have Audrey and Bill and not ask Bogart. He's going to be furious.' And he was." She turns to her husband and adds, "You just didn't get it. I did right away."

Billy shrugs and pleads nolo contendere: "I got it, but it was too late."

In fact, Bogart was often left out of the after-hours fraternizing, simply because he wasn't much fun to have around. Feeling ostracized and offended, he became even more irritable—and downright offensive to Wilder. "Kraut bastard" and "that Nazi" and various anti-Semitic epithets were said to be his pet terms for Wilder. But the Wilders say they don't remember it.

"Billy *is* a kraut," says Audrey Wilder with a laugh. "Anyway, a kraut isn't a Jew. Neither is a Nazi."

Says Billy: "He hated me so much—everything, my German accent—but ultimately, when he got sick and was lying there in his house, dying of cancer [in 1957], I went up to him and he was wonderful. We didn't say, 'Let's make up' or anything like that, but he was absolutely wonderful. He completely changed."

Mrs. Wilder elaborates on the last Mrs. Bogart's theme: "Bogart was insecure. They're all insecure about something. He was insecure about Billy's love for Audrey and Bill Holden."[104]

There was no doubt about the Wilder-Hepburn love affair—as real and as sweetly platonic as that of any director for any actress in Hollywood history. Says Billy Wilder today:

> The very first day, she came on the set prepared. She knew her lines. I did not have to squeeze it out of her. She was so gracious and graceful that everybody fell in love with her after five minutes. Everybody was in love with this girl, I included. My problem was that I am a guy who speaks in his sleep. I toss around and talk and talk.... But fortunately, my wife's first name is Audrey as well.[105]

The most famous of all Billy Wilder statements about Hepburn was made midway in *Sabrina* shooting: "This girl, singlehanded, may make bosoms a thing of the past."[106] Henceforth, he later added, "The director will not have to invent shots where the girl leans way forward for a glass of Scotch and soda."

Life magazine called her "the director's joy" and quoted Wilder's comment that, "She gives the distinct impression that she can spell schizophrenia."[107] She was so diligent that—with Wilder's approval—she insisted on doing her own singing. The *Sabrina* script called for her to croon a few verses of "Yes, We Have No Bananas" in English and the pretty "La Vie en Rose" in French. She often spent two hours a day with a vocal coach. "I had to," she said. "I had no voice at all. It was terribly monotonous, shrill and inflexible."[108] But Sabrina's breathy little singing voice would be perfect, and very much her own.

In Hollywood, Wilder gave her a fancy green chrome-and-aluminum bicycle, on which she careened back and forth across the Paramount lot thereafter. In New York, he hovered around her—uncharacteristically—even off the set, as on the October day in 1953 when *New York Herald* reporter Otis Guernsey interviewed her in the lobby of the St. Regis Hotel.

"May I present the female Mickey Mantle?" said Wilder to the writer, with a light pat on Audrey's head, adding that, like the Yankee switch-hitter, "She can do anything." But when the talk turned to stardom, he said, "Shhh! Don't wake my Sleeping Beauty. She doesn't know how big a star she really is."[109]

Her rapport with Wilder was lasting, and so was her relationship with the two great designers who worked with her on *Sabrina*. Edith Head's costumes for *Roman Holiday* would soon win an Oscar. She and Audrey had enjoyed each other throughout that production, often shopping and dining together. (Head marveled at Hepburn's ability to consume five chocolate éclairs at a time, or a jumbo banana nut sundae.) Naturally enough, Head had been rehired for *Sabrina*. But early on, Wilder made a daring move: Audrey's high-fashion costumes would be designed by the young Parisian couturier Hubert de Givenchy. Edith Head's work would be limited to the "Cinderella clothes" before the transformation. With abject apologies to Edith, Audrey now flew to Paris.[110]

At twenty-six, Givenchy—a devotee of Cristobal Balenciaga—was already challenging Christian Dior and Yves St. Laurent to inherit the fashion throne of Chanel and Lanvin. Givenchy's designs reflected his love of classic Greek lines. His wealthy family, owners of the Gobelin and Beauvais tapestry factories, had recently financed the opening of his salon on Avenue Georges Cinq, where he and Audrey met in the summer of 1953 and a legendary association began.

"One day," Givenchy recalled, "someone told me that 'Miss Hepburn' was coming to Paris to select some clothes [for her new film]. At that time, I had never heard of Audrey Hepburn. I only knew of Katharine Hepburn. Of course, I was very happy to receive Katharine Hepburn." When the confusion was cleared up upon her arrival, he tried to hide his disappointment. "My first impression of her was that she was like a very fragile animal. She had such beautiful eyes and she was so skinny, so thin.... an adorable young girl with large hazel eyes. She was wearing a sweater, straight slacks and flats; she was charming."[111] But however charmed, he was a busy man, as he recounted to Warren Harris:

I told her the truth: I was in the midst of putting together my next collection and didn't have the time to spend with her. She insisted. For the sake of peace and quietude, I said she could choose anything she liked from my current collection. That satisfied her and she selected several.... She knew exactly what she wanted. She knew perfectly her visage and her body, their fine points and their faults. [Later] I tried to adapt my designs to her desires. She wanted a bare-shouldered evening dress modified to hide the hollows behind her collar bone. What I invented for her eventually became a style, so popular that I named it "décolleté Sabrina."[112]

Audrey's angular figure was perfectly suited to the austere, geometric simplicity of Givenchy's lines and to his preference for black, off-whites and subdued pastels. She loved what she saw and flew back to Hollywood with a portfolio of Givenchy sketches that Edith Head was now asked to execute. According to folklore, Head was furious. The Wilders deny it.

"She was one of the great dames of all time," Audrey Wilder says. "There's no real truth to that. Maybe she was hurt a little but—" Billy interrupts:

"Did you know that Edith Head won the most Oscars, with the exception of Walt Disney? Even when he had nothing to do with the picture, it was always 'Walt Disney, the producer,' and he got the Oscar. The same with Cedric Gibbons, who was listed on every MGM picture as the set designer, whether he did it or not. It was in his contract. The same with Edith Head."

Audrey Wilder recalls her excitement the day Hepburn brought Givenchy's sketches and left them at the house for Billy. "I saw one and took it over to my mother, who was a fantastic seamstress and worked in the studios," says Aud Wilder. "She ripped it off right away, and I wore it one night a few days later. Billy said, 'That's not fair! The picture isn't even out!' "[113]

Everyone went gaga over Givenchy's designs, and Hepburn went gaga over Givenchy. She found him the epitome of cultivation and *politesse.* "He's my great love," she would say. "He made the first dresses I ever wore from a good fashion house. I consider him one of my best and most important friends."[114]

Toward the end of shooting on Long Island, a humorous moment helped relieve the tension of the dueling designers and leading men. The visiting king and queen of Greece wished to see the set. Wilder borrowed two thrones from the Bob Hope film *Monsieur Beaucaire* and set them up at the top of some stairs, with a red carpet leading up to them. As the embarrassed royal couple was being led to their thrones, an electrician shouted, "Hey, Queen, where were you last night when I needed you to fill a straight?"

Audrey would call Sabrina "a dreamer who lived a fairy tale, and she was a *romantic*, an incorrigible romantic, which I am." Otis Guernsey in the *New York Herald* pegged the young star's forte: "Fairy tales are her natural element."[115]

Enter Prince Charming.

MEL FERRER, ONCE CALLED THAT "nerve in perpetual motion," had not only fallen in love with Audrey but had been pondering how to advance her career—and his own. The answer came to him in the form of a prewar French play he now discovered.

Jean Giraudoux's *Ondine* had been a great success when first performed in Paris in 1939 and his status as France's preeminent dramatist secured by *The Madwoman of Chaillot*, which not only dazzled Europe but won the New York Drama Critics' Award as best foreign play of the 1949–50 Broadway season.

Ondine, based on an early nineteenth-century German fairy tale, was later turned into two operas, symphonic works by Debussy and Ravel, and—in 1958—Frederick Ashton's definitive ballet for Margot Fonteyn. It was a fable of man's inability to comprehend and need to destroy innocence. The mythological "undine" is a water sprite who can only acquire a soul by marrying a mortal. In Giraudoux's play, the knight she chooses is unfaithful and—by virtue of a sacred pact—he must die and she must return to the water, never to remember him. The knight charges that she "adored him beyond endurance." Ondine's view is whimsical. "So it takes twenty minutes to catch a man," she muses when he proposes. "It takes longer than that to catch a bass."

When Ferrer sent Hepburn the script, she loved both the play and the obvious casting. She told him she'd do it and instructed her MCA agent Kay Brown to approach the Playwrights Company, which jumped at the chance to land her: She was offered a minimum guarantee of $2,500 per week against a percentage of the box office, a big improvement on her $500 a week salary for *Gigi*. She secured Mel as her costar and—in appreciation of his suggesting the idea—insisted not only on sharing cobilling but also on splitting her percentage with him.

"If this isn't love," said her friend Radie Harris of the arrangement, "what is?"[116]

When the word got out, she was deluged with questions about the nature of the role.

"It's a wonderful part," she told an interviewer, "the kind I feel would be good for me. As opposed to *Gigi*, which was a comedy, and *Roman Holiday*, which is a light comedy, too, this is a very serious dramatic part, and an unusual one."[117] It was the closest she would ever get to Peter

Pan—the role everyone wanted her to play—a combination of Ariel and Miranda.

In her two-week "vacation" between the end of *Sabrina* and the start of *Ondine* rehearsals, she packed up and moved to New York, where her mother would arrive three days later. "I want everything to be perfect," she said. "I've ordered tickets for all the new plays, and I'm going to lay it on real thick—New York, that is. I want mother to love it as much as I do. I plan to spoil her as she's never been before!"[118]

She accomplished that in and around her reunion with Ferrer and their rapidly intensifying relationship. Soon after *Ondine* rehearsals began, she and Mel began living together in Greenwich Village, and Frances Ferrer once again consulted her lawyers. Mel was said to believe he and Audrey could become the next Olivier and Leigh, or Lunt and Fontanne.

There was coincidence and irony in that: Alfred Lunt and Lynn Fontanne had scored a great triumph in Giraudoux's *Amphitryon 38* in 1937. Before he died in 1944, the playwright reportedly "entrusted" the English debut of *Ondine* to them, and they had since tried (and failed) to persuade Olivier and Leigh to do it.[119] Beyond that, in London the previous year, Radie Harris had taken Audrey to see Fontanne and Lunt in Noel Coward's *Quadrille*, "and when I took her to the dressing room to meet them," said Harris, "she was like a wide-eyed child meeting Santa Claus for the first time."[120] Now, to Audrey's joy, Lunt accepted the Playwrights Company's offer to direct *Ondine*.

In addition to Hepburn and Ferrer, *Ondine*'s cast included Marian Seldes, whose initial problem was similar to Givenchy's. When she auditioned for Princess Bertha, Ondine's haughty rival for the knight, all Seldes knew was her agent's description of the part: "It's the heavy in a play with Hepburn."

"I thought he meant *Katharine* Hepburn," says Seldes. "But when I worked with Audrey in *Ondine*, she behaved in such a way that my admiration for her was on a par with what I felt for my early idols. I expected so little, I got so much.... I loved watching her rehearse and act. How beautiful [she made] other people feel! That was her magic on and off the screen. [And] how obediently she followed Mr. Lunt's suggestions."

That was more than could be said for Ferrer.

"The gossip in the company was that since she had fallen in love with Mel Ferrer, he was giving her different directions after the rehearsals," says Seldes. "I did not believe it.... He did not respond to direction as Audrey did, was ungracious to the older man in front of the company at times, but the production of *Ondine* had been largely Mel's idea and it would have been ridiculous for him to sabotage it by redirecting Audrey.

"Lynn Fontanne came to many rehearsals to watch her husband

direct.... Occasionally [Lunt] would show Mel how to play part of a scene and step into his place. He would become Hans, the knight who loved the water nymph Ondine, and for a few moments I would be acting with this marvel. Afterward he would mutter to Mel, 'I am doing this badly, of course.' By that time Mel's attention would have wandered....[121]

"Mel was in a difficult position. Lunt made a much greater connection with Audrey and the others. Because Mel was somewhat cool, distracted, he didn't really work on the part from his inner self. At the time I thought he was rude, but looking back, perhaps he felt a little out of his depth in *Ondine* waters."[122]

The Playwrights Company had engaged him with an ulterior motive. "We bought Hepburn and the price was Ferrer," said a staff member. "It turned out to be much too expensive."[123] There was tension from the first day of rehearsal: Ferrer thought Lunt's direction dull and resented Fontanne's presence. He reportedly asked for revisions in the play to expand his own role, but Robert Sherwood refused to alter a word, even when it was suggested that Ferrer might quit and take Audrey with him.

Inevitably, Hepburn was drawn into the fray. One night after rehearsals, she showed up unexpectedly at Sherwood's apartment, upset and fearful of the show's failure. She and Mel were to be married, she told him, and she could hardly remain neutral in the conflict. She offered to withdraw from the production, but Sherwood reassured her, and she agreed to stay on.[124]

Less serious but vexing up to the last minute was the matter of Audrey's hair: Lunt felt it should be blond, since Ondine was a creature of the washed-out, watery deep. Just before previews opened in Boston, she gave in, allowed her hair to be bleached—and quickly regretted it. She then had its real color restored and switched to a blond wig. But the wig felt "stiff and hot and horrible," she said. The eventual solution was to tint her hair with gold dust each night and wash it out after every show.

Her costumes were built by the great Valentina Schlee, designer for Fontanne in *Idiot's Delight*, Norma Shearer and the Duchess of Windsor. Audrey spent days in Valentina's East Sixty-seventh Street studio, standing six hours at a time to supervise the sewing of her costume, which consisted of fishnet and a few strategically placed leaves—censorable on anyone but Audrey, whose innate decorum gave even the scantiest outfit an almost Quakerish propriety.

All trials and tribulations were vindicated when *Ondine* premiered—with incidental music by Virgil Thomson—on February 18, 1954, at the Forty-sixth Street Theater in New York.

"Hepburn moves with the fleet freedom that testifies to her ballet training, and she speaks with a voice of strange and vibrant beauty," said

Variety. "Largely because of her personal incandescence..., *Ondine* is a resounding hit."

"*Ondine* was worth writing, translating and producing just to place Miss Hepburn on stage," wrote Eric Bentley in *The New Republic*. "It is not time to speak of a great actress, yet no one would doubt the possibility of greatness."[125]

Most critics cited her amazing leap—from a standing position into Ferrer's lap—as one of the show's most memorable moments.* Her smash success in *Roman Holiday*, released just a fortnight earlier, made *Ondine*'s opening night even more the gala event of the season. "The box-office lines are a block long," said *Newsweek*. "The reason is Audrey Hepburn."[126]

James Hanson was sitting next to Baroness Ella van Heemstra on opening night. As with the *Gigi* premiere, he had flown over from London to surprise Audrey, even though he was no longer her fiancé. Neither Hanson nor the Baroness failed to notice the subtext at the end of that night's performance: The audience cheered on and on, demanding a solo curtain call by Audrey. But with every bow, Mel appeared at her side. Finally, the house lights were turned on, and Mel held up his hand to hush the crowd for a speech—surely to acknowledge Audrey. "Instead," said Radie Harris, "we heard a flowery expression of thanks to Alfred Lunt," which most everyone knew to be insincere.[127]

After the premiere, Hanson disappeared and Mel accompanied Audrey and her mother to a supper party sponsored by the cultural attaché of the French Embassy. There, someone made the mistake of asking Lunt, "Did you learn anything from working with a movie star like Mel Ferrer?" Yes, he replied, "I learned that you cannot make a knight-errant out of a horse's ass!"[128] In New York theatrical circles, it was a mini-scandal that Ferrer would not let Audrey take her last curtain call alone. One critic called him "churlish" for not doing so. The late Eva Gabor was in that opening-night audience and remembered it vividly:

I can still see this beautiful wisp of a girl come on stage and the whole audience gave a big sigh—'Ahhh!' She was incredibly beautiful, captivating. In the curtain call, she came out first but turned to the wings and waited till he came out, because it would have been a terrible letdown for him to come out alone, after her. I never forgot that look on her face: The audience went wild, applauded, screamed—but she would not turn until he came out. I don't know of another actress who would have done that. She was in love with him.[129]

Most of the bouquets for Audrey came with thorns for Mel.

---

* Exactly a decade later, she amazed filmgoers with the same trick in *My Fair Lady*, jumping from a stand-up posture to a perfect sitting position on the bed during "I Could Have Danced All Night."

"Occasionally, during the times when Audrey Hepburn was absent from the stage of the Forty-sixth Street Theater, it occurred to me that Ondine had the makings of a quite majestic bore," wrote Wolcott Gibbs in *The New Yorker*. "On each of her entrances, however, [Hepburn] set about creating a queer, personal miracle.... Her performance [is] a beautiful and astonishingly intelligent piece of work, and I don't believe there is an actress in our theatre physically or mentally equipped to duplicate it."

And Mel Ferrer?

"Reasonably attractive," said Gibbs, "but I don't believe he has quite the style, of either conduct or diction, that this difficult part demands. It is a heavy task to oppose the kind of acting Miss Hepburn is offering, and I can think, offhand, of nobody except perhaps Olivier and Gielgud who could manage it, and Mr. Ferrer is certainly neither of these men."[130]

The harshest verdict was Lunt's, in a private letter to Sherwood: "All the medals and praise in the world will never convince me that beautiful play comes off.... She jumps on his lap & he holds her like a potted palm—he sits beside her at the table & treats her like a tired waitress at Child's.... If he played his scenes on top of her, you'd have the feeling he was laying a corner stone. Personally, I'd call the whole show a fucking failure."[131]

Audrey was much praised—"too much indeed," *Commonweal* dissented. "She is not yet a very accomplished actress [and] must learn to manipulate her voice with some of the grace and variety she brings to her body movements."[132]

In "Nymph Mania," the *Ondine* review in *Saturday Review*, the perceptive Henry Hewes said Audrey was giving "a performance and not a piece of acting. This is not to discredit Miss Hepburn [but] rather to clarify what it is that this clever youngster does.... Perhaps if she could join a repertory company, as Claire Bloom has, she would gradually acquire the acting skill to go with her performing talents. As it is, she is faced with being a star rather than becoming one."[133]

A variation on that theme was Harold Clurman's "Open Letter to Audrey Hepburn" in *The Nation*, which began by observing that the response to her *Ondine* performance was "as if everybody were asking for your telephone number":

[You are] a wonderful instrument with a soul of your own. But, said old Grandpa Ibsen, talent is not just a possession, it is a responsibility. You are at the beginning of your career; because this beginning is so dazzling you must not allow the beginning to become the end. You do not yet know how to transform the outward aspects of a characterization into an inner characterization....

You can learn to be a real actress if you do not let the racket, the publicity, the adulation rattle you away from yourself. Keep on acting, studying, working.... Play parts that are risky, parts that are difficult, and do not be afraid to fail! Above all, play on the stage.... Do not trust those who tell you that screen and stage acting are the same species or of equal artistic value.[134]

For Audrey, that was both a concrete and a cosmic issue of major importance. Just the day before *Ondine* opened, she had filled out a new questionnaire from her publicist:

Any special role you most wish to play?

"One day I would like to try the classics, yardsticks by which an actress's technique and variety are measured."

What is your greatest ambition as an actress?

"To some day be considered as good an actress and as faithful to her public as was Maude Adams or is Helen Hayes.... A stage and screen career each benefits from the other."

Now, as if to confirm that, came the news that she had been nominated for an Academy Award for *Roman Holiday*.

"*ONDINE* AND *GIGI* WERE ENTIRELY different," says actress Celeste Holm, who saw Audrey in both. "*Gigi* was an American version of a French farce. *Ondine* was almost a ballet. In both cases, she had something that couldn't be manufactured. People who are very *definite* are more interesting than the paste-ups. The effects of the war, her dancer's sense of communicating physically—all that carried through to her work. So many people in theater have no specific idea of what they're communicating, just a vague idea of showing off. But not Audrey. The moment you saw her, you realized she was an artist."[135]

Two Broadway hits and an Oscar nomination were proof of her spontaneous romance with the public, but still, "I wouldn't say I've learned to act yet," she said during *Ondine*. "Often I think I'll never learn anything. Some of the things I do on stage depress me beyond measure."[136] Compounding that angst, she was emotionally drained—by Mel Ferrer as much as *Ondine*.

"It often happens that actors and actresses fall in love during a play that moves them deeply," says Celeste Holm. "They think it's the other person, but it's really the play."

Audrey and Mel really fell in love because of *Ondine*?

"I think so," says Holm. "Look at Gary Merrill and Bette Davis—the same thing."

While Ella was issuing statements that her daughter and Ferrer were not romantically involved, they were, in fact, seriously discussing marriage. And as those marital pressures mounted—pro and con, from Mel and her mother—so did the extravagant attention of the media, in anticipation of the Academy Awards. "Not since Garbo has a new actress been welcomed with such fervor and adulation," declared *Cosmopolitan*.[137]

The Oscar ceremony of March 25, 1954, was a bicoastal affair, dually hosted by Donald O'Connor at the Pantages Theater in Los Angeles and Fredric March at the NBC Century Theater in New York. When Audrey arrived breathless and very late at the latter place, a great shout of "Hepburn's coming!" rose from the media area, and all the photographers rushed to the door.

"Hepburn, still wearing makeup of water nymph in *Ondine*, did the fastest dash I've ever seen," wrote one reporter, "straight through the animal pack to a small room off the inner lobby." As she was rushing to change clothes, she ran into fellow nominee Deborah Kerr, just arrived—equally breathless—from her own Broadway hit, *Tea and Sympathy*. They wished each other luck and agreed Leslie Caron was going to win for *Lili*.[138]

"Ladies predominantly blond this year," continued the reporter, "hair drooping and matted, like seaweed.... Hepburn emerged. Vision of love-liness in white lace dress. Animal pack, momentarily bowled over by beauty, soon regained composure and screamed for pictures."[139] Audrey briefly obliged, then ducked into the theater just in time to join her agent, Jack Dunfee, and her imperturbable mother before the moment of truth.

From Here to Eternity dominated the awards, winning Best Film, Director (Fred Zinnemann), Supporting Actor (Frank Sinatra), Supporting Actress (Donna Reed) and four other awards, tying the all-time *Gone With the Wind* record. The odds were in Deborah Kerr's favor. But the Oscar went to Audrey.*

"I was so surprised when they called my name that I didn't know what to do," she said the next day. "Mother and I wanted to celebrate, so we bought a bottle of champagne on the way home. It was warm—but it was the best champagne I ever tasted!"[140]

From then on, she regularly gave Ella credit for her achievement—seriously and humorously—at every chance: "My mother taught me to stand straight, sit erect, use discipline with wine and sweets, and to smoke only six cigarettes a day."

Ella just as regularly demurred: "I can really take no credit for any

---

* In addition to Hepburn, Kerr and Caron, the other nominees were Ava Gardner for *Mogambo* and Maggie McNamara for *The Moon Is Blue*. William Holden was named best actor for *Stalag 17*. Ian McLellan Hunter—Dalton Trumbo's front—won the story-writing award for *Roman Holiday*. Forty years later, a posthumous Oscar was presented to Trumbo's widow and children.

talent that Audrey may have. If it's real talent, it's God-given. I might as well be proud of a blue sky, or the paintings in the Flemish exhibition at the Royal Academy."

Neither of them knew how important the Oscar really was. "Having lived in England for some time," Audrey said years afterward, "I wasn't extremely familiar with the Academy Awards. I knew it was a coveted prize, but I didn't realize until later what an honor it was to win it for the first time out."[141]

Paramount production chief Don Hartman was cautious. "There is no evidence that Audrey is a full star yet," he said a few days after the ceremony. "The question which has to be answered is: 'Can she hold up a picture on her own?' Audrey has been called a star after *Roman Holiday*, and she has certainly had a lot of publicity. But we haven't tested yet whether the Hepburn name *by itself*, above a film title, will fill cinemas."[142]

It was a candid, pragmatic statement. But Audrey was even more candid. Mel once read her a list of adjectives that had been applied to her *Ondine* performance—words like "coltish," "gazelle-like" and "otherworldly."

"What they mean is tall and skinny," she replied.

Her eyes had been described as "lake-haunted," he told her.

"Maybe I need some sleep," she said.

Beauty experts hailed her innovative "bat-wing" eyebrows.

"I wish I had the courage to tell them that I just don't pluck them," she remarked.[143]

Exactly three days after the Oscars, before the shock had worn off, came yet another stunning prize: the Antoinette Perry ("Tony") award for best stage actress in *Ondine*. There were no announced "nominees" for the Tonys until 1956, but Hepburn had been chosen over Deborah Kerr in *Tea and Sympathy*, Geraldine Page in *The Immoralist*, and Margaret Sullavan in *Sabrina Fair*. Only one other actress had ever managed to win an Oscar and a Tony in the same year—Shirley Booth for *Come Back, Little Sheba* and *The Time of the Cuckoo*.*

"How will I ever live up to them?" she told a throng of reporters. "It's like being given something when you're a child—something too big for you that you must grow into."

Now and in the future, she would keep her distance from the social whirl of both the British and the American film-theater worlds—to concentrate on her work, she said: "Acting doesn't come easy to me. I put a tremendous amount of effort into every morsel that comes out."[144] One of

---

* Ellen Burstyn would do so again in 1974 for *Alice Doesn't Live Here Anymore* and *Same Time Next Year*.

her non-fans complained: "This training thing is a pose. She's made it—why doesn't she relax and have fun?"[145]

A year after her arrival in America—just six years from her start in the chorus of a London musical—she was at the top. At twenty-four, she had vaulted into the public heart and was generating more excitement than Marilyn Monroe. It was unbelievable. It was nerve-wracking. It might suddenly disappear at any time.

"I believe in fixing a goal for myself and not being diverted in any way from pursuing that goal," she said the night she won her *Roman Holiday* Oscar. "I can't allow this award or all this public acclaim to turn my head or induce me to ease up."

A veteran Hollywood producer summed her up a bit ominously: "She charts each day's schedule like a timetable so there will be no wasted minutes or wasted energies. She operates more like an engineer with a slide rule than a young, single girl turned loose in this emotional world of show business."[146]

CHAPTER 4

Ruling the World
(1954–1957)

"A woman looks good either in clothes or
out of clothes, never both."

MARLENE DIETRICH

UDREY HEPBURN WAS AN UNLIKELY fashion revolutionary. "I
never thought I was pretty," she told Ralph Lauren years later.
She felt too skinny, too flat, too tall. Her insecurities kept her from
seeing her beauty, but she instinctively knew the value of her looks. She
said she used to be so self-conscious about the unevenness of her front
teeth that she tried not to smile. Yet during *Roman Holiday*, she declined
the studio's offer to cap her teeth. Nor would she let them pluck her heavy
eyebrows.[1]

William Wyler, early in *Roman Holiday* shooting, looked at her and
said, "I think you should wear some falsies, if you don't mind my saying
so." Audrey looked back and said, "I am!"[2]

The last word belonged, as always, to Billy Wilder: "If that girl had
tits, she could rule the world."

She would rule it anyway, in their absence. *Photoplay* called her "flat-
chested, slim-hipped and altogether un-Marilyn Monroeish"—a stringbean,
in Hollywood. But she would march straight into the bosom boom and
pioneer a look of her own. "You have to look at yourself objectively," she
advised her fans. "Analyze yourself like an instrument. You have to be
absolutely frank with yourself. Face your handicaps, don't try to hide
them. Instead, develop something else."[3]

Hepburn's vital statistics were the same from age twenty-three to the
end of her life: 32–20–35.* Givenchy says she never altered more than a
centimeter in forty years. Anita Loos observed that her hat size (21) was
bigger than her waist—"the slimmest since the Civil War," said Edith

---

* For the record, here are the slight variances. From William Fields, her Playwrights Company
publicist (1953): height: 5'6¾"; weight: 110; dress size: 8; hat size: 21; shoe size: 8; waist: 20";
glove size: 6½. The *New York Post* (1956) said 32½-20–35. *Photoplay* (1954) said 32–20½-34.

Head. "You could get a dog collar around it." (A prankster friend once actually used Audrey's belt as a collar for her St. Bernard—and it fit perfectly!)[4]

Head told Charles Higham that Hepburn understood fashion better than any actress except Marlene Dietrich. "Like Dietrich, Audrey's fittings became the ten-hour not the ten-minute variety. She knew exactly how she wanted to look or what worked best for her, yet she was never arrogant or demanding. She had an adorable sweetness that made you feel like a mother getting her only daughter ready for her prom."

She compensated for her height by making flats and ballet slippers an integral part of apparel; her daily uniform consisted of slacks or skirts with a blouse. But gradually, this "wistful child of the war era" turned into something else. Her 1952 publicity photos showed a girl largely removed from fashion, in toreador pants and men's shirts tied at the waist— charming but not particularly chic.[5] *Sabrina* and Givenchy brought the look that became legendary: From now on, her clothes are not only glamorous but deliberately *emphasize* the slender silhouette.

Her beauty secrets—such as they were—were revealed in William Fields's press release of December 29, 1953:

Shade of powder?

"None."

Lipstick?

"Pale shades at all times."[6]

"She looks so pure," said Audrey Wilder at the time. "She doesn't wear jewels or hats or furs like the rest of us, and half the time her only makeup is around those huge eyes of hers. The result is that, through no fault of hers, she makes me feel fat and tacky. Also, I suddenly realize that I probably drink and smoke too much."[7]

Hepburn's reasons for not indulging in luxuries had nothing to do with their expense. "Jewelry just doesn't suit me," she said, "and if I wear too much makeup, my face looks like a mask instead of me.... Put me in furs and jewels, and I look like something off a barrel organ."[8]

"Is Hollywood shifting its accent on sex?" asked *Silver Screen* after the release of *Sabrina:* "She's changing Hollywood's taste in girls. From the full-bosomed, sweater-filling type with more curves than the New York Central Railroad, to the lean, umbrella-shaped variety." They were speaking, of course, of Audrey, and quoting her: "I know I'm not very well built. I'm not very shapely and not very voluptuous.... It may be that the accent has gone off sex slightly and gone on to femininity."[9]

Newspapers in 1954 were reporting on "a new cult" around Audrey Hepburn. "Today," said one, "it is no secret in the magazine world that a picture of the lady on a cover is like a Benzedrine pill to sales."[10] *Vogue* was calling her "today's wonder-girl.... She has so captured the public imagination and the mood of the time that she has established a new standard of beauty, and every other face now approximates to the 'Hepburn look.'... This slim little person, with the winged eyebrows and Nefertiti head and throat, is the world's darling."[11]

From now on, *Vogue* would record her every minute change of appearance. So would everyone, and every other publication in Europe and America, with any interest in fashion.

PRIVATELY, THE LITTLE FASHION PLATE'S situation was less grand. "I have had no time to shop for 'Audrey' clothes," she lamented. "I have two dinner dresses and slacks, and horrible gaps in between."[12] It illustrated the discrepancy between an international phenomenon and a real-life young woman. The roller coaster was exhilarating, but it was moving much too fast.

Three months into the run of *Ondine*, she was suffering from exhaustion. She was smoking a pack of cigarettes a day and was fifteen pounds underweight. Her doctors said she had to quit and get some rest, and she reluctantly followed their advice: *Ondine* closed on July 3, 1954, after 157 performances.

"Audrey was worn out," says Mel Ferrer. "She had been working nonstop since before *Roman Holiday*, supporting her mother and herself. Dancing in musicals and cabaret. Playing an occasional bit-part in films. From *Roman Holiday* she had jumped into *Sabrina* and then decided she wanted to do *Ondine*, in spite of her agents' and Paramount's objections....

"I urged her to take a complete rest in Switzerland—most importantly [to] cure herself of a debilitating case of asthma. When we first saw each other in London she often had to stop and rest in the street as I walked her home. She had very raspy breathing and a deep-seated asthmatic condition."[13]

Mel felt the good Swiss air would help her overcome it. At the end of July, she flew to an Alpine resort in Gstaad, only to be greeted by a crowd of photographers and reporters. After a week of media imprisonment there, she fled to Bürgenstock—a lavish mountaintop retreat overlooking Lake of Lucerne. The drive up was almost perpendicular, rising 3,000 feet in twenty minutes. The windows of her villa looked out onto the Alps, and she found both the views and the climate a tonic—unmolested at last.

"I love to wake up in the early morning, throw open the shutters and drink in the sight of the tall mountain peaks and the lake down below," she enthused.

Going to Bürgenstock was one of the most significant decisions of her life. There, wrote Charles Higham, she luxuriated in a private kingdom created by the great Frey hotelier family, whose current scion Fritz became her close friend. He ruled over a mountain peninsula of five hundred acres—a former wilderness transformed into three hotels with golf course, beach, funicular railway, forested park, and staff of hundreds. In that regal resort, Audrey found her first real respite since leaving England for America nearly three years before.

Forgotten, for the moment, were the complex business arrangements of her career. Paramount had once again tried to buy out her British contract—this time, for a cool million dollars, but Associated British refused. It was the highest-ever rejected Hollywood bid for a British star. Though still bound to ABC, Audrey subsequently agreed to a multiple-picture Paramount contract, with an optional year off between films for the theater.

"My bosses at Paramount realize I am very sincere about the stage," she said. "I feel I wouldn't last long if I were to do pictures only. I have learned the little I know about acting from my stage work."[14]

There were discussions of her playing Juliet at Stratford-upon-Avon, but she was in no condition to do so. In August 1954, the *New York Herald Tribune* reported that she might be enticed to New York in the winter to play the title role in Maxwell Anderson's *Mary of Scotland*, with Helen Hayes as Queen Elizabeth. Hayes, who had created the part of Mary in 1933, wanted to do the show again: "Suddenly, I thought of Audrey. She'd be the ideal Mary Stuart." Perhaps recalling that Audrey had been ordered to rest, Hayes added, "It's only for two weeks. I should think she could do it. That's a wonderful part for a girl."[15]

And a wonderful idea: Hayes and Hepburn in a great stage vehicle to showcase them both. But Audrey Hepburn would never return to the theater again.

AT THAT POINT, IT WAS all she could do to rally from the edge of a nervous breakdown. And it was Mel Ferrer for whom she rallied. In August, for his thirty-seventh birthday, Audrey sent him a platinum Rolex watch engraved, "Mad About the Boy." (They were both avid Noel Coward fans.) He flew to Switzerland and formally proposed, and she formally accepted—over Ella's objection.

During *Ondine*, she was asked where she wanted to "settle down" permanently. "That's hard to answer," she replied, "because one changes all the time. What strikes me most about America is the gaiety and the speed and the vitality. If I had my choice, and if I had the money, I'd have an apartment in London, an apartment in New York, and someplace in the country—providing, of course, I could travel a lot and go to Paris and Rome a great deal! But of course, the day I marry a man I'm very much in love with, and he lives in Timbuktu, that's where I'll live."[16]

It would be Switzerland, not Timbuktu.

On September 24, 1954, Audrey and Mel Ferrer were married in a civil ceremony at Buochs, on the shores of Lake of Lucerne, in the parlor of the local mayor's house. The next day they repeated their vows at a religious ceremony in a thirteenth-century Protestant chapel below the mountain at Bürgenstock, presided over by Pastor Maurice Eindiguer. She wore a Pierre Balmain white organdie robe, a small crown of white roses, and white gloves. Among the twenty-five guests were Mel's children Pepa and Mark and his sister Terry; London Paramount chief Richard Mealand; and Sir Neville Bland, a friend of Ella's and former British ambassador to Holland. Best man Gregory Peck had to cancel due to his film schedule and was replaced by Fritz Frey. Freddie Heineken was an usher. James Hanson was invited but sent regrets.

For the rest of her life, Audrey would call Switzerland home. Bürgenstock was a town where doctors still made house calls and people took care of sick neighbors. "There is no place in the world where I feel so much at peace," she would say. "It's my very private stomping ground. I've become one of these people. We're loyal to each other."

After a four-day honeymoon near Bürgenstock, she and Mel enjoyed a week together in the Italian vineyard country near Cinecittà, where he was filming *La Madre*. "We were pursued by five carloads of photographers when we arrived in Rome," Mel recalled. "I had rented us a delightful farmhouse outside of Rome.... We had to establish a cordon of security around the farm, so that she could continue to rest while I went off each day to the studio. It was a beautiful and peaceful spot."[17]

There, while Mel completed his picture, they billed and cooed and awaited the release of *Sabrina*.

SABRINA'S AMOROUS EXPOSITION UNFOLDS BENEATH a fake Long Island moon with the Rodgers and Hart theme, "Isn't It Romantic" endlessly driven home in the background.

"That song is repeated in every Paramount picture because it was totally owned by Paramount," Billy Wilder explains. "It was first composed for *Love Me Tonight* (1932), the Mamoulian picture with Chevalier and Jeanette MacDonald. There was no ASCAP, so they bought it from Rodgers and Hart and used it forever."[18]

It even plays as Sabrina (Hepburn) is contemplating suicide over David (Holden) and writing a farewell note to her father: "Don't have David at the funeral. He probably wouldn't even cry."

Sabrina is shipped off to France, where she tries to forget David while attending a Parisian academy of cuisine. The cooking school provides the film's funniest, most "Wilderesque" sequences, thanks to Marcel Hillaire as the chief chef. His lecture-demonstrations are a comic tour de force:

> Today, we will learn the correct way how to crack an egg. Voilà! Egg! Now, an egg is not a stone. It is not made of wood. It is a living thing. It has a heart. So when we crack it, we must not torment it. We must be merciful and execute it quickly—it is done with one hand. Kindly watch the wrist. Voilà! One, two, three, crack! You see? It is all in the wrist. Now, everybody— one, two, three crack your egg! One, two, three, crack your egg!

They all do so in unison—Sabrina most clumsily.

Back on Long Island, Humphrey Bogart as David's diligent elder brother, Linus, dictates a letter to his playboy sibling over a state-of-the-art 1954 car phone:

> Interoffice memo, Linus Larabee to David Larabee. Dear David, this is to remind you that you are a junior partner of Larabee Industries. Our building is located at Thirty Broad Street, New York City. Your office is on the twenty-second floor. Our normal week is Monday through Friday. Our working day is nine to five. Should you find this inconvenient, you are free to retire under the Larabee Pension Plan.

Their crotchety, frothing-at-the-mouth father (Walter Hampden) sneaks cigars and martinis behind their mother's back and fulminates about David's prior marriages, including "that Twyman girl—her family fifty years on the social register, and she has the audacity to wear on her wedding dress, not a corsage but a Stevenson button!" It was one of the script's many good political jokes nowadays lost on most viewers.

Sabrina returns from Paris transformed into a sophisticate —the birth of Hepburn's partnership with Givenchy. David fails to recognize her in her chic new suit. But he invites her to a party that evening, where she wears another fabulous Givenchy creation—a white organdy strapless sheath with a sweeping, floor-length overskirt, open in front, giving the impression that she has wings from the waist down!

In the hasty twist ending, Audrey gets her man—not flashy Holden, but stuffy Bogart, who undergoes a transformation. "Look at me," he says, "—Joe College with a touch of arthritis." Their age difference is huge, but Hepburn's magic eyes lure us into suspending disbelief, as they would often be called upon to do in her future films.

Opinion differed sharply over Bogart's long-in-the-tooth character. Bosley Crowther in *The New York Times* thought his performance "one of the most surprising and affecting he has ever done."[19] A later critic, on the other hand, declared, "Every time Bogie pitches the woo, you feel like calling the cops."[20]

Britons were offended by "the Wilder vulgarity," as when Holden sits on a pair of wineglasses. "The subsequent scenes, where the affected region is constantly being prodded and kicked by hearty fellow characters, firmly overstep the narrow dividing line between slapstick and viciousness," wrote reviewer (later director) Karel Reisz.[21] But American audiences loved the running gag of Holden's injured rear-end, especially the absurd plastic hammock with "trap door" in the middle, helpfully devised by the older brother for the younger's recuperation.

In general, the critics were less effusive about Audrey's second outing. *Films in Review* said she was "fey and gaminish" and "costumed to emphasize her lack of what are technically known as secondary sexual characteristics." *Time*'s love affair with her in *Roman Holiday* seemed to be over: "Actress Hepburn's appeal, it becomes clearer with every appearance, is largely to the imagination; the less acting she does, the more people can imagine her doing, and wisely she does very little in *Sabrina*."

The meanest pan came from Clayton Cole in the British magazine *Films and Filming*: "Sabrina is the prick that bursts the fair bubble that was Audrey Hepburn in *Roman Holiday*. Surely the vogue for asexuality can go no further than this weird hybrid with butchered hair. Of course none of this would really matter if the charm and grace were sincere, but I am afraid that she is letting her calculation show."

Cole dismissed Bogart brutally as "a frail, lisping old man."[22] But the only ballot box that counted was at the box-office, where the fans' mandate was clear: *Sabrina* was the No. 3 top money-making film of 1954.*

AFTER HONEYMOONING IN ITALY, AUDREY and Mel returned to Bürgenstock, where her happiness about *Sabrina*'s success was soon dwarfed by a greater ecstasy: She was pregnant.

She so longed for a child and was now "infanticipating" with great excitement. Discussions of the baby occupied them in November on their way to Holland for Audrey's first visit "home" since achieving movie fame. She had been invited by the League of Dutch Military War Invalids for a five-day fund-raising tour and to receive an award for her efforts during the war. But the sensation she created was rather too great. At a department store in Amsterdam, where Mel accompanied her to sign photographs for the benefit of war victims, thousands of teenagers stormed the place, breaking showcases and wreaking havoc in an effort to get close to her. Police had to be called in to control the mob.

The following month, just before the 1955 New Year, they rented a

---

* Audiences are still casting their votes for *Sabrina*, remade in 1995 by Sidney Pollack, with Julia Ormond in Hepburn's role and Harrison Ford in Bogart's. Billy Wilder served as a consultant.

furnished flat in London near Marble Arch, while Mel filmed *Oh Rosalinda!* there. Ella had found the place, which was just a few minutes from her own flat in Mayfair. Audrey enjoyed the proximity to and reunion with her mother. Mel, less so. In any case, it marked the start of their firm policy to schedule their professional lives to be never, or rarely, apart.

Oh Rosalinda!, under Michael Powell's direction at Elstree, was a non-musical version of Johann Strauss's *Fledermaus*, and there was some tension during its making. By one account, when Audrey dropped by the set to watch Mel at work, he refused to let her appear in any publicity photos, not wanting to share the limelight. Asked about that, Ferrer says, "I never refused to allow Audrey to do anything. She always had very precise ideas about what she did and did not want to do."[23]

Other allegations soon made the rounds concerning Ferrer's dominance of her and Audrey's insistence on only accepting films in which he would costar with her. She supposedly turned down the "perfect" role of Joan of Arc in Otto Preminger's *Saint Joan*—the part that would make Jean Seberg famous—when Preminger refused to cast Ferrer as the Dauphin. But Ferrer denies it:

"*Saint Joan* was not a project which appealed to Audrey. Her agent, Kurt Frings, was a chum of Otto Preminger and he wanted Audrey to do it, [but she] decided otherwise. There was never any question of my playing the Dauphin—it would have been totally wrong casting."[24]

Their own pet film project was *Ondine*, which they championed at every opportunity in England. Mel wanted Associated British to do the project as part of Audrey's commitment to them, but ABC declined on the theory that water-sprites were death at the box office. He then pushed for MGM to make *Ondine* in the States, with Charlton Heston in the role of the knight, but the Giraudoux estate would not approve.

"We spoke often of trying to film *Ondine*," says Ferrer, "but it was such a tenuous, gossamer work that we were advised against it as a motion picture." Perhaps it wouldn't have worked, he admits, "although I would have loved to have seen Audrey's mesmerizing performance preserved on film."[25]

Her affairs were in some turmoil then. She was inundated with offers, but Associated British was contesting her Paramount contract. Mel helped crucially by proposing that Audrey hire the aggressive Kurt Frings as her new agent and by arranging for veteran Henry Rogers to take charge of her publicity. "We all had a difficult and complicated time steering a way through the exigencies of two long term contracts [ABC and Paramount] signed by Audrey before I met her," says Ferrer. "Kurt became a devoted and fanatical defender of her interests."[26]

Frings bore assorted grudges against the studios and was said to enjoy gouging them by turning his star clients into freelancers and getting them bigger fees plus a percentage. A former boxer, he was colorful and smart—and Audrey liked him a lot. Frings and his screenwriter-wife, Ketti, who won a Pulitzer Prize for the play of *Look Homeward, Angel*, were now among the Ferrers' few close friends in Hollywood, along with Gregory Peck.[27]

Speaking of whom... Peck and Hepburn had just been voted the world's most popular film stars of 1954 in the Foreign Press Association's poll of fifty countries. Soon after, in February 1955, Audrey received her second Oscar nomination, for *Sabrina*. She lost to Grace Kelly for *The Country Girl* (who should have lost to Judy Garland for *A Star Is Born*).

Sabrina's sole Oscar winner was—Edith Head for costumes. The real credit belonged to Givenchy, who was much too polite to register a protest. Audrey phoned him in Paris to apologize, but he told her "not to worry because *Sabrina* had brought me more new clients than I could handle. But Audrey was still upset, and she made a promise to me that in the future she would make sure that it never happened again. And she kept her promise."[28]

Life for Audrey seemed glorious, until a miscarriage intruded into it that March. She and Mel grieved privately. Publicly, she was perched at the top—which was a kind of trap. In the accepted career-tracking of the day, she could never again take a supporting role and now faced the need to "top" herself with every new film. Her next role had to be something big, sweeping and serious.

WHEN DINO DE LAURENTIIS DESERTED the Fascists and was hiding out on the isle of Capri during World War II, he had a total of two books to while away the time: *The Odyssey* and *War and Peace*. The former inspired his later movie *Ulysses*—which was but a "finger exercise," he said, for the latter.[29]

Tolstoy's two-thousand-page manuscript, written between 1863 and 1869, conjured three hundred characters with a panoramic backdrop of Russia and the Napoleonic wars. It was arguably the greatest of all novels. One critic called it "a combination of everything ever written by anyone." No film version of *War and Peace* had ever been made, though some of the greatest names in film history had plotted to do so over the years—D. W. Griffith, Ernst Lubitsch, Erich von Stroheim and Irving Thalberg among them.

Now, all of a sudden, everybody wanted to do *War and Peace* at once. It was a time of epics and new widescreen techniques to make motion pictures more competitive with television. Aside from De Laurentiis, Mike Todd said he had a Robert Anderson screenplay of the Tolstoy novel to be filmed in his new Todd-AO 65 mm process in May 1955. David O. Selznick boasted a Ben Hecht script that would start shooting in June 1955. MGM was said to have a *War and Peace* set for August 1955.[30]

The book's central figure is Natasha Rostov—"a dark-eyed girl full of life, with a wide mouth, slender bare arms... , her shoulders thin, her bosom undefined," wrote Tolstoy. "Such was Natasha with her wonder, her delight, her shyness."[31] He might have had Audrey Hepburn in mind. All the film producers now did, and so did the actress herself. She could powerfully identify with an adolescent whose life is turned upside down by war and who ages quickly through three terrible years of conflict.

Todd seemed to lead the pack by getting Fred Zinnemann's agreement to direct. "Mike's suggestion that Audrey Hepburn should play the part of Natasha made things even more exciting," said Zinnemann. "Unfortunately, Dino De Laurentiis thought so too. [Todd] was shattered; his heart was set on that picture. He had been courting Marshal Tito, and already two Yugoslav cavalry divisions had been earmarked to work with us."[32]

De Laurentiis, for reasons of practicality and national pride, thought the Italian army more photogenic—and easier to hire. Two smart moves made him the *War and Peace* sweepstakes winner: his teaming with producer Carlo Ponti (future husband of Sophia Loren) and his hiring of Mel Ferrer to play Prince Andrei. That cinched the signing of Audrey Hepburn for $350,000 (three and a half times Mel's $100,000 salary) and $500 a week expenses. The prospect of being and working together in such a monumental, prestigious project thrilled them both, and the remaining details were quickly sorted out: De Laurentiis struck loan-out deals with Paramount (in exchange for U.S. distribution rights) and Associated British (for U.K. distribution).

The director of an epic such as this had to be someone of vast experience. De Laurentiis chose King Vidor, craftsman of such silent classics as *The Big Parade* (1925) and *The Crowd* (1928) and, in the sound era, of *Duel in the Sun* (1947)—but little since. Vidor was near the end of a distinguished career and would make only one more film. His tendency to oversimplify complex stories and to indulge in sentimentality had increased with age, yet he seemed a safe enough choice.

Vidor was hired not only to direct but to write, and he now performed the astounding feat of condensing Tolstoy's million and a half words into a shooting script in one month. Needless to say, it took many liberties. "Tolstoy took two hundred fifty pages to tell readers that there was a feeling between [Natasha and Pierre]," said De Laurentiis. "We got it over in one scene in the horse corral at the beginning of the picture."[33] Such solutions had their drawbacks, and the screenplay repairs would end up engaging eight writers for most of a year. Among them was novelist Irwin

Shaw, who later denied that he asked to be removed from the credits—but seemed relieved not to be listed.

The casting of Pierre was one of the biggest problems. Prince Andrei—whom Natasha loves wildly—is not the most important male figure in *War and Peace*. Its masculine soul and true hero is Pierre Bezukhov, her bastard half-brother. Audrey and Mel originally wanted Gregory Peck for the role, but he was engaged. Their next (and best) choice was Peter Ustinov, who was turned down by De Laurentiis for lacking a big enough "name." Marlon Brando was among others under consideration, but they finally settled on Henry Fonda.

In spring of 1955, the Ferrers went to Italy and reoccupied the charming house in Albano, twenty miles outside Rome, where they had spent their honeymoon. One of their visitors was Jeremy Brett, who was playing Natasha's younger brother.

"When I arrived at their house," recalled Brett, shortly before his death in 1995, "Mel met me and under his right arm popped a little girl with no makeup who looked about sixteen years old—an exquisitely delicate, porcelain doll. I was spellbound. I remember swimming with them and banging my head on the side of the pool because I was so busy looking at her."[34]

The Ferrers loved that pool, whose water gushed forth from an antique carved stone head in the center. But there was precious little time to swim in it, once *War and Peace* began shooting on July 4. Ten-hour days were the norm, and they were lucky to get home by eight p.m. for dinner. Due to the miscarriage and her frailty in general, Audrey was at pains to keep up her weight and Ferrer was the imperious liaison for all her needs.

"Mel is like a manager with her as well as a husband," said cinematographer Jack (*The African Queen*) Cardiff, who was annoyed by Ferrer's incessant solicitude: "Is the car ready for Miss Hepburn?" ... "The costume is wrong for Miss Hepburn." ... "It is too hot (or too cold) for Miss Hepburn."[35]

Audrey called Natasha the toughest role she ever did, yet she executed it with her unique toughness. "I did *War and Peace* in velvets and furs in August," she recalled. "In the hunting scene where I'm in the velvet and a high hat, the family was plodding across a big field in the blazing Roman sunshine and, all of the sudden, my horse fainted out from under me. They quickly got me out of the saddle so I didn't end up being rolled over. So when they say I'm strong as a horse, I am. I'm stronger! *I* didn't faint. The *horse* did."[36]

Her toughness included an insistence on the behind-the-scenes artists she trusted. She demanded the husband-and-wife team of Alberto and Grazia de Rossi for her makeup and hair, and kept them through her career. "She had such beautiful bone structure that her features did not need a lot of work," said Alberto, who also served Ava Gardner and Elizabeth Taylor. "She had a strong jawline, which in a sense I reversed by emphasizing her temples. She had thick eyebrows that always needed to be thinned out. Every picture we made together, I tried to reduce them a bit more than the time before, but without going to extremes. She had the kind of face that needed eyebrows."[37] When someone once said she had the most beautiful eyes in the world, Audrey replied: "Oh, no—the most beautiful eye *makeup* perhaps—but all the credit belongs to Alberto." Indeed, some credit de Rossi as most responsible for the "Hepburn look."

Audrey also paid tireless attention to costume details—having studied books on early nineteenth-century fashion—and she annoyed De Laurentiis's costumers by flying in Givenchy from Paris to give his *ex officio* approval of everything. She could stand three hours at a time until a pleat or petticoat was adjusted to her satisfaction. In the end, she wrestled through twenty-four costume changes and ten different hairdos, supervising most of them herself down to the final hairpin.

De Laurentiis had his own staggering problems. It took fabulous bribes and cajolery finally to muster the 15,000 Italian soldiers to play French and Russian troops in the battles of Borodino and Austerlitz. Ten thousand of them—believed to be an all-time record—appeared in one scene. (The buttons alone, for their uniforms, kept ninety tailors busy for months in a Swiss factory.) Some 8,000 horses and 3,000 cannons peppered the battlefields, and the many accidents required De Laurentiis to hire sixty-four doctors, dress them up as soldiers, and sprinkle them among the combatants to provide first aid.

Moscow of 1812, complete with its onion-domed churches and towers, was painstakingly reconstructed on the Tiber River, and, in the intense July heat, snow scenes were created by wind machines blowing cornflakes dipped in gypsum. Audrey spoke of standing on a hill, watching the production assistants go about with torches, setting fire to "Moscow" in De Laurentiis's attempt to outdo Selznick's burning of Atlanta in *Gone With the Wind*.

The gargantuan production required all forty-eight acres and nine soundstages of Rome's massive Cinecittà studios—a fully equipped city in itself. The Ferrers drove there daily from their rented farmhouse and found it, compared to the Hollywood counterparts, a happy and stimulating place. Audrey enjoyed joining the crew for lunch and watching their consumption of large quantities of wine and pasta during breaks.

But the strain was enormous. Scenes of war and carnage by day gave her nightmares by night. Moreover, she hated having to film her scenes out of sequence. *Roman Holiday* and *Sabrina* had been shot chronologically. In *War and Peace*, she was a naive teenager one day and a grief-stricken adult the next. She was also distracted by the many visitors De Laurentiis allowed on the set and later complained about it in a *Photoplay* interview:

> Can you imagine doing a play, and someone during one of the acts says, "Just a moment, please," and you stop? A stranger wanders on the stage, you shake hands, and then you all sit down and you chat. Then after a while he leaves, and you are expected to go on with the play exactly as if nothing had happened.... I forced a smile on my face and muttered a few polite words, because I knew it was expected of me. But the scene was finished as far as I was concerned. The mood had disappeared....
>
>   There are actors, much better actors than I, who can cope with such a situation and not let it disturb them. But I just can't.... There was a time when I even had a complex working in front of my fellow actors. But I'm getting better; I'm learning. I hadn't much choice. I had about half the Italian Army watching me.[38]

She could hardly say so on the record, but the main object of her pique was all-powerful gossip columnist Louella Parsons, who turned up in Rome during *War and Peace* shooting, installed herself in a luxury suite at the Excelsior Hotel, demanded access to Audrey—and got it. Not surprisingly, Audrey was much relieved when the filming of *War and Peace* finally came to an end. Now it was in the hands of King Vidor and his editors. All that remained, for her and Mel, was the verdict.

THE VERDICT, IN A NUTSHELL, was that *War and Peace* was "the least Russian movie ever made."[39] And for once it couldn't be blamed on Hollywood. The picture was quintessentially Italian, despite the odd international cast: Herbert Lom as Napoleon, Oscar Homolka as General Kutuzov, Jeremy Brett as Natasha's brother Nikolai, Vittorio Gassman as Anatole, Anita Ekberg as Helene, May Britt as Sonya and John Mills as Platon.

Worst by far was Henry Fonda—the lanky Yankee whose accent clashed jarringly with Hepburn's soft, pleasant Euro-timbre. Not for a moment is he believable as sensitive Pierre. Mel Ferrer, by contrast, conveys noble dignity throughout, especially in the gorgeous ball scene. But his dramatic deathbed reunion with Natasha lacks much impact, and his dying seems to go on and on.

So does the film. *The Manchester Guardian* said it had "length without depth"—at three hours and twenty-eight minutes, just twelve minutes short of *Gone With the Wind*. It had cost a whopping $6 million, but that was less than half of its $13-million rival, *The Ten Commandments*, which grossed three times as much at the box office. *War and Peace* premiered

August 21, 1956, in a year of "spectacles" that pitted it not only against Moses but also *Around the World in 80 Days* and *Giant*.

Many reviews, as that of *Films in Review*, praised Hepburn's rendering of Natasha: "She dominates an epic picture by refusing to distort her character to the epic mould, letting her... very littleness in the face of history captivate us by its humanity contrasted with the inhumanity of war. She incarnates all that is worth fighting for."

Audrey had acted well—and looked perfect—in a part that was neither well written nor well directed. In the end, she was defeated not by Mel Ferrer but by King Vidor and Henry Fonda.*

THEN AND LATER, PEOPLE SAID Ferrer dictated her career in totalitarian fashion, forcing her to reject good roles if there was no choice role for himself. Then and later, Audrey denied it. There was certainly no truth, for instance, to the claims that Audrey lost roles in *The Diary of Anne Frank* and the musical *Gigi* because Mel insisted on parts for himself. But it was quite true that they didn't like to be apart, which had considerable influence on the film work they did accept.

Toward the end of *War and Peace* shooting, she and Mel experienced their first separation since getting married. His scenes had been finished before hers, and he had flown to France to star with Ingrid Bergman and Jean Marais in Jean Renoir's *Elena and Her Men* [also called *Paris Does Strange Things*].

"We tried our best not to be separated by work," says Mel, but the Renoir film was important. "Audrey and I both adored Ingrid.... We agreed it was something not to be missed, and she subsequently joined me in Paris."[40]

In an April 1956 *Photoplay* story headlined "My Husband Doesn't Run Me," Audrey sang the same tune in an interview with Mary Worthington Jones: "Mel and I both value our careers immensely. We'd be very foolish and irresponsible if we didn't. [But] if we ever said, 'Oh, just this once, what does it matter if we're separated for a few short months,' then the once becomes twice—without realizing it, we might have let material success ruin two lives.... If I were asked to take a step which might jeopardize my marriage, I would delve deep down into my heart to discover *why* I must do this."[41]

In particular, she was incensed by an article calling their relationship

---

* Hepburn was upset in later years by Fonda's disdain for *War and Peace* and refusal to include it in retrospectives of his work. One indirect tribute to Audrey was Sergei Bondarchuk's grand, eight-hour Soviet version of *War and Peace* (1966), in which he cast Ludmila Savelyeva—an Audrey Hepburn lookalike—as Natasha.

"a kind of master-to-slave one, with Mel directing her life, using her career as a stepping stone for his own."[42] In general, she was very touchy about the "Svengali" stories:

> How can people say Mel makes all my decisions, that he decides what I am going to play, and with whom, and where! It so infuriates me. I know how scrupulously correct he is, and how he loathes to give an opinion unless I ask for it. This is *because* we want so badly to keep our careers separate. We don't *want* to interfere with each other....
>
> I've been fending for myself since I was thirteen and thinking very carefully about a lot of important problems, and I don't think I've made many bad decisions. I'm very proud of that, about my ability to think for myself, and no one, not even my husband, whom I adore, can persuade me to do something against my own judgment.[43]

Before that interview was over—and in many others—she again had to debunk the charge that Mel got his *War and Peace* role because of her. She was "indignant," said Jones, and sprang from her chair, pacing up and down as she answered:

"He was asked to play Prince Andrei long before I was even approached—as a matter of fact, before we were even married.... After it was decided, Mel and I were thrilled at the thought of being in the same picture together. But from that moment on, we were put on the defensive. Imagine! Two married people, in the same profession, whose interests and careers are parallel, having to give excuses for playing in the same film together!"[44]

The ever-candid Bernard Schwartz—better known as Tony Curtis—was not an intimate friend of the Ferrers but knew them (and Hollywood) well enough to have his own sharp take on their dynamic. "You couldn't get near her unless he was taken care of somehow," says Curtis. "In the early years of that marriage, she had no confidantes. There was nobody around. The only one she could rely on was Mel, who wasn't a bad guy, but the view that came from him was certainly self-serving."[45]

Variations on the "Mel as villain" theme occupied many fan magazines and newspapers, even in England, where it took cartoon form in the London *Evening Standard*. "Mel had an enormous influence over her in the early days," said director Fred Zinnemann.[46] But that was different from "using" her. Professionally, her stardom outshined his, which privately produced strain. Despite her protestations, she often did try to suppress her own will to conform to his wishes. Mel felt he was trying to do the same. Some thought they were trying too hard.

"She was absolutely charming," recalls actor Theodore Bikel, who met them while filming *The Vintage* (1957) with Mel in France, "—fun and bright and international, just a delight to be with. Mel was decent and workmanlike, but he was a bit of a stick and she was the life of the party. She was very solicitous of him. It seemed that she was taking care of *him* a lot."[47]

Working together as much as possible was the only way they saw to combine marriage with two film careers. Baroness Ella van Heemstra was among those who harbored dark suspicions that Ferrer was subordinating her daughter's budding career to his own. But there is no evidence that he ever did so. In the long run, the "togetherness dilemma" would impair his career more than hers.

PEOPLE IN THE INDUSTRY REMAINED skeptical. In fall of 1955, Audrey received producer Hal Wallis and writer Tennessee Williams in Switzerland to discuss the film version of *Summer and Smoke*. There, said Wallis, servants brought in a platter containing a single enormous fish—no soup, side dishes or dessert. "Audrey, dainty as a Dresden figure in a Givenchy original, consumed a large portion of the sea beast with great relish," said Wallis, who was not pleased with the meal or the subsequent negotiations. They broke down, he claimed, because she wanted Givenchy to design the spinster teacher's wardrobe and because she—not Ferrer—insisted Mel be her leading man. (The roles eventually went to Geraldine Page and Laurence Harvey.)[48]

So what *would* her next film project be?

She was deluged with script offers, including two dozen from Associated British—all of which she declined. From Paramount she now received an intriguing offer to star in the William Wyler film of Edmond Rostand's *L'Aiglon*. It was an extraordinary part, created on stage by Sarah Bernhardt, as the tubercular *son* of Napoleon and Empress Marie Louise. Hepburn would have made a fascinating boy and wanted to play it. Premature reports that she would make *L'Aiglon* praised her "courage" for taking on a male role.[49] But like Garbo's longed-for transsexual roles in *Hamlet* and *The Picture of Dorian Gray*, Audrey's did not materialize. It was too unorthodox for 1956; Paramount never made the film.

She also failed to materialize opposite James Mason in the title role of *Jane Eyre*, which 20th Century-Fox offered her around the same time. Mason objected to her casting from the start: "Audrey Hepburn just happened to be the most beautiful woman in movies. A head-turner. The whole point about Jane was that no one noticed her when she came into a room or left it."

When Audrey's participation fell through, so did the film.

Among other films she rejected were Joseph Mankiewicz's proposed *Twelfth Night* and Mark Robson's *The Inn of the Sixth Happiness*, whose lead was then snapped up by Ingrid Bergman. There was also talk of Billy Wilder's *Ariane*.

But the winner was *Funny Face*.

IT WAS A FANTASY COME true: Audrey's first film musical, dancing and singing with Fred Astaire in the rain, far from Spain—namely, on the Seine. That dream deal involved a lot of horse-trading and was finally achieved by two elemental things: Audrey wanted Fred, and Fred wanted Audrey.

Astaire had just made *Daddy Long Legs* with Leslie Caron. Once again, to retain his appeal to young moviegoers, he would have to be cast opposite a younger woman. Who better than Audrey Hepburn—youth personified?

Astaire was exactly thirty years older than Audrey—fifty-seven to her twenty-seven—almost old enough to be her *granddaddy* long legs. The Hepburn role was originally earmarked for Carol Haney, a recent stage hit in *Pajama Game*, but MGM concluded she wasn't "big" enough for a major film and was about to shelve the picture, when screenwriter Leonard Gershe suggested Hepburn. "Kurt Frings, who had not read the script, sent it over to her in Paris because we had to have an answer right away," Gershe recalls. "When he read it, he was furious. 'How could you send this trivial musical to Audrey Hepburn? Are you crazy?'"

But she was in dire need of something light after *War and Peace*. "Audrey usually takes about three days to read and consider a script," said Mel. "This one she finished in two hours. She burst into the room where I was working and cried, 'This is it! I don't sing well enough, but, oh, if I can only do this with Fred Astaire!'"[50]

She told Frings, "I'm crazy about it," and she was cast. "Without Audrey," says Gershe. "Fred would not have been strong enough alone to have gotten the studio to do it then. But Audrey could have anything she wanted. She was the hottest thing."[51]

She was hot enough to drive a hard bargain, too: $150,000, plus generous expenses for a posh Parisian hotel suite and the right to retain most of her Givenchy wardrobe.

More important than the dancing, at this stage, was the music, on which Gershe and producer-arranger Roger Edens were collaborating. Edens had begun as a pit piano player for George Gershwin and later become a Hollywood producer by way of *Easter Parade* (with Astaire) and other MGM musicals. In his opinion Gershwin's original 1928 score for *Funny Face* was too theatrical. New songs would be written by Gershe and himself, though the bulk of it would still consist of the great Gershwin standards.*

In order to get the Gershwin songs and title, MGM bought the rights to *Funny Face* from Warner Brothers, promptly discarding its dubious libretto about a jewel heist in Atlantic City. MGM now owned the songs, but Paramount owned Audrey and Fred Astaire.

What followed was a classic case of Hollywood wheeling and dealing: Edens, Gershe and director Stanley Donen were now sold by MGM—along with the Gershwin songs—to Paramount. "By the time we'd bought the rights of *Funny Face* and made all the deals," said Donen, "it had cost a million dollars—and that was before a single foot of the film was even shot."[52]

Gershe's original story, *Wedding Bells*, replaced the old script, and he was amazed by how well Ira Gershwin's lyrics suited the new characters and the casting of Audrey. Ella van Heemstra—with whom he was forming a close friendship—thought so, too. "I read the script when it was sent to Audrey in Paris," she told Gershe, "and I could hardly believe it had been written by someone who didn't know her. Every facet of her is there. I mean to say it *is* Audrey."[53]

It was Cinderella again—but in the high-fashion milieux: The top photographer and editor of a trend-setting magazine are desperate to find a sensational new "discovery." Audrey, of course, is the beatnik clerk-cum-fashion-plate they discover. The tale was loosely based on the life of photographer Richard Avedon and his search for a model embodying elegance and intelligence. Once he finds her, he trains and falls in love with her—not unlike Henry Higgins in *My Fair Lady*.

In real life, Avedon had found, trained, and married model Evelyn Franklin in 1951. He and Gershe had become close friends when they were serving in the Merchant Marine and, even then, had spoken of applying slick magazine photo techniques to a big film musical. Soon enough, Donen and Avedon would be spending half the night working out details of the next day's shooting.

Astaire's role was inspired by Avedon; the other inspiration was Diana Vreeland, colorful editor of *Harper's Bazaar* and *Vogue*. She served as the model for Maggie Prescott, manic editor of *Quality* magazine in the movie. That part was tailored to the larger-than-life talents of cabaret star Kay

---

* The final rundown of *Funny Face* tunes and their authors:

By George and Ira Gershwin: "Funny Face," "He Loves and She Loves," "Let's Kiss and Make Up" and " 'S Wonderful" from the original *Funny Face* (1927); "How Long Has This Been Going On?," written for *Funny Face* but not used until *Rosalie* (1928); and "Clap Yo' Hands" from *Oh, Kay!* (1926).

By Roger Edens and Leonard Gershe: "Think Pink," "On How To Be Lovely," and "Basal Metabolism." With Ira Gershwin's permission, Edens and Gershe updated some of the Gershwin songs' lyrics.

Thompson, who would be making her film debut in *Funny Face*.*

Interior shooting commenced at Paramount in Hollywood in April 1956 and continued there for three months, followed by a month on location in Paris, and Audrey and Mel managed to stay together the whole time. In California, they rented director Anatole Litvak's Malibu beach house; in Paris, where Mel was finishing up the Renoir film, they stayed at the Hotel Raphael.

"Home is wherever Mel and I create it, wherever our work takes us—Paris, California, before that Italy, and next Mexico," she said.[54] "We move our home with us, like snails."

The press made much of the extravagance of their traveling and baggage arrangements—upwards of fifty pieces of luggage sometimes being necessary to create the Ferrers' homes-away-from-home in various rented villas and luxury hotels.

"Like an exiled member of royalty," said one report, "she takes with her, wherever she goes, trunks packed with her own candelabra, flat silver, books, records, pictures. She also takes many objects in her favorite color of white: table and bed linen, two hand-knit blankets, sets of china, vases, and her tiny Limoges ashtrays and cigarette boxes."[55] It was claimed that she hand-labeled every piece herself and kept a loose-leaf inventory with her at all times, so that she could find (and repack) everything in the same order. The source of that habit was allegedly her mother, who—like other Euro-aristocrats with multiple residences—had traveled that way in her heyday.

Ella, nowadays, was still based in London but often visited her daughter and made several trips to Paris during the shooting of *Funny Face*. (Friends felt Audrey was still emotionally dependent on her, but financially, "Her mother was completely dependent on Audrey," says Ferrer.[56] The Paris sequences involved virtually all of the city's major landmarks—the Louvre, Eiffel Tower, Paris Opera, Notre Dame, Arc de Triomphe. Audrey and Mel threw a memorable dinner-dance party one night for the cast and crew. Ingrid Bergman was one of their guests, and so was Audrey's favorite *Photoplay* reporter, Mary Jones, at a restaurant with a fabulously romantic view of Montmarte.

Romance was Jones's relentless theme with Hepburn that night. Could Audrey remember the moment her friendship with Mel turned into love? Audrey could not. "After a while," she said, "we both just took it for granted that we would marry.... I was never engaged—just married."

---

* Kay Thompson was also the creator of "Eloise," that irrepressible little heroine of a whimsical book series on which millions of girls were raised in the fifties and sixties. In addition, Thompson was a vocal arranger for Judy Garland and the godmother of Liza Minelli (one of the inspirations for Eloise), with whom the eighty-four-year-old Thompson now lives reclusively in New York.

That didn't sound so romantic, but she was being honest. One aspect of her attraction to Mel was of special importance now, she said: She had been ignorant of jazz and had learned its fine points from him. Their portable phonograph and records were always part of those fifty pieces of baggage.

"I like jazz best now," she said. "It makes me want to move. But I was stiff as a poker as a jazz dancer, always off beat on the simplest syncopation. That was all gradually broken down. I'm so lucky to be married to Mel Ferrer, who is such a good dancer and adores jazz."[57]

It was more than private enjoyment. She was now paired up with Fred Astaire in a major musical—one in which she was called upon to perform a lengthy jazz number and other dances, with and without him. She was determined not to be unprepared. For two months in Europe, before shooting, she put on her size 8AA (high metatarsal) slippers and went back to the barre, taking up practice with Paris Opéra ballet dance master Lucien Legrand. "When I don't dance," she said at the time, "I always get fat in the wrong places. Most of all, I get hippy."[58]

On *Sabrina*, she had worked with stage and film choreographer Eugene Loring and was delighted that he was choreographing *Funny Face* as well. "He's familiar with all my limitations," she said, though the only limitations Loring ever cited for her were "modesty and legs a bit too long."[59] Forty years later, Leonard Gershe remembers watching Audrey rehearse:

"I never saw anyone work so hard. She was tireless in learning both the songs and the dances. It wasn't like Cyd Charisse or Ginger Rogers, who did it all the time. Roger Edens would say, 'Audrey, take tomorrow off. You've been working sixteen hours a day.' She'd say, 'No, I'll be here at nine.' And then she'd be there at eight." It was partly her desire to meet Astaire's standards, "but it had mostly to do with wanting to be good."[60]

Funny Face's choreography was credited to Loring and Astaire, with "song staging" by Donen.* Loring devised her most important numbers, deftly incorporating her mannerisms and elfin sense of comedy. But Hepburn's main inspiration was Astaire—once she survived their introduction. The morning they met at the studio in Hollywood, Audrey was "so shaken that I threw up my breakfast," she wrote in her introduction to Stephen Silverman's biography of Stanley Donen.[61] "I was absolutely terrified, but Fred said, 'Honey, just follow me, I'll take care of everything.'

---

* Donen, then just thirty-one, made his Broadway dance debut at sixteen in *Pal Joey*, which began his long collaboration with Gene Kelly. They codirected *On the Town* (1949) and *Singin' in the Rain* (1952). As solo director, Donen made such stunning film musicals as *Give a Girl a Break* (1953, with Marge and Gower Champion), *Seven Brides for Seven Brothers* (1954), and later *Pajama Game* and *Damn Yankees*.

And he did."[62] Before rehearsing their first number he suggested, "Come on, let's have a little go together," and they took a few delirious, anxiety-reducing spins.[63]

Astaire had had his own bouts with anxiety years earlier, related to this very vehicle. In 1928, he and sister, Adele, won raves for the stage show of *Funny Face*, and Paramount gave them a tryout for a proposed film version. That screen test produced an immortal, famous-last-words studio verdict on Fred: "Can't act, can't sing, balding, can dance a little."

The original unmade *Funny Face* film was to have been shot in May 1929—the month Audrey Hepburn was born. Astaire gallantly told a reporter it was worth the twenty-seven-year wait: "This could be the last and only opportunity I'd have to work with the great and lovely Audrey, and I was not missing it."[64]

The opening dance sequence in *Funny Face* was the famous "Think Pink" fashion number ("Banish the black, burn the blue, bury the beige! Think pink! And that includes the kitchen sink!"). Despite the bevy of top dancers and models in it, including Suzy Parker and Sunny Harnett, this razzle-dazzle routine belonged entirely to Kay Thompson, who utilizes it to start stealing the show early. (Movie audiences at the time often burst into applause at the end of it.)

Audrey's first dance is a downbeat contrast. Astaire, Thompson and crew find Embryo Concepts, the perfect "sinister bookstore" in Greenwich Village, where Audrey as "Jo" works. Donen gives her a brilliant entrance: a ladder is shoved aside and hurtles along a row of bookshelves with the terrified Jo on top. Her passion is the esoteric philosophy of "empathic-alism," not frivolous fashions. She tries to throw them out, but they ignore her protests, tear up the place for their shoot, and then leave her alone in alphabetical disorder. In the wreckage, she sings Gershwin's "How Long Has This Been Going On?," filmed exquisitely from high angles in semi-darkness, and performs a dance built around a single prop: a yellow-and-orange straw hat, the sole dab of color amid all the brown and black. At its end, forlorn little Jo tosses the hat aside and climbs back up the ladder—where she started—to begin replacing a thousand books.

It is the loveliest and most intimate musical moment in any film she ever made. But it is not her most taxing. That comes after she's transported to Paris, in a smoke-filled existential dive on the Left Bank—a send-up of Sartre's Café de Flore.

"I feel like expressing myself," says Jo, in defiance of Astaire. What she expresses, in a routine called "Basal Metabolism," is a satire of avant-garde interpretive dance—a sort of jitterbug-jazz ballet with cardiovascular contortions. Audrey slithers wildly about, clad entirely in black and but for Donen's brilliant touch of white socks. She is supported by two men who manage to keep smoking their cigarettes even standing on their heads. "I'd never done anything so jazzy before," she said. "I'd never even *listened* to that kind of beat."

Astaire had his own shining solo moment in "Let's Kiss and Make Up," a courtship dance performed in a lamplighted courtyard for the benefit of Audrey on her balcony. Midway, he turns it into a Spanish bullfighter's display—a dazzling tour de force for a fifty-seven-year-old who has lost none of his stuff.

But the grand finale—"He Loves and She Loves," an overly gauzy wedding number filmed outdoors near Chantilly—was more final than grand.

"It had been raining for weeks and weeks," Donen told Warren Harris, "but finally we went out to shoot on this little island, which was not much more than a strip of grass between two streams. The grass was ankle deep in bog. Audrey had on white satin dancing shoes made in Paris, very expensive. She had about nine pairs standing by because they kept getting black in the mud. Fred got very crotchety and said to me, 'I can't dance in that. Fix it.'... How?... He said, 'I don't care! Put down a wood floor and paint it green.' Everyone was tense until Audrey suddenly quipped, 'Here I've been waiting twenty years to dance with Fred Astaire, and what do I get? Mud in my eye!'"[65]

Though always humble about her own dancing ("I had a very slender kind of technique"), she had held her own, however worried she may have been about comparisons with Astaire's great partners of the past. Leslie Caron, when asked for her opinion of Hepburn as a dancer, replies with the graceful sidestep equivalent of a *jeté:* "You're asking me a tough one there. I thought uppermost she was a delightful romantic comedienne. I will be a little more silent on her dancing. But it doesn't matter. Whatever she did was so delightful that one was happy to watch her."[66]

The appeal of Hepburn's dancing varies greatly, according to taste. "Where Gene Kelly and Leslie Caron have energy," wrote Sheridan Morley, "Astaire and Hepburn have class and subtlety.... If only she had managed to make *Gigi* for the screen a couple of years later, but by then she was otherwise engaged, and her role went by default to Caron."[67]* The most sharp-eyed assessment comes from dance writer Caroline Latham:

"Hepburn's long legs and slim body make her a good match for

---

* Leslie Caron was then playing *Gigi* at the New Theatre in London "in order to warm myself up for the film." One night she was visited in her dressing room by Baroness Ella van Heemstra. "She was very friendly," Caron recalls, "and felt there was a tie between Audrey and me." Aside from *Gigi*, Caron and Hepburn often vied for the same parts. After Audrey played *Ondine* on Broadway, Caron played it with the Royal Shakespeare Company in London. "When I did *Fanny* (1961) with Josh Logan," says Caron, "it was a toss-up between the two of us." They met frequently "and always we had this sibling recognition. But I was in awe of her, and there was a great deal of shyness on both our parts."

Astaire's own elongation. Watching them, one is struck by their shared quality of benign remoteness. Each seems enclosed by some personal bubble of space and air, a visible separateness. Rather than lovers, they seem when they dance to be brother and sister, twin halves of a whole from some classic myth."[68]

Much like Fred and Adele.

ALMOST LOST IN THE DANCE shuffle of *Funny Face* was the fact that Audrey was under equal pressure to sing—and to sing well enough for a recording. Donen would refer to her "thin little voice," which she went to great pains to improve. An intense round of vocal coaching was in store for her at the Paramount soundstages in Hollywood before her taping sessions: daily rehearsals for nearly four weeks. "I was quite nervous about it, never having recorded before," she said.

Even Kay Thompson was called in to help. She had coached Judy Garland, among other MGM singer-actress stars, and now coached Audrey, urging her to employ a parlando style of speech-song and to concentrate on the lyrics. Astaire helped, too, during the vocal-track recording of their "'S'Wonderful" duet. The third time through, Donen recalled, "she made a mistake and Fred jumped in and did something wrong on purpose. He said, 'Oh, I'm sorry. I've ruined it. Can we do it again?'" Audrey gratefully believed it was his fault instead of hers.[69]

In the end, her "childlike yet trained voice contributes a great deal to the film's sentiment," said Donen. "Here is someone who is actually paying attention to the words." Critics agreed on the "intimate, lyrical and genuinely affecting" qualities of her singing.[70]

Hepburn, Donen and Avedon—jointly and separately—were praised for the picture's great photographic success, from the stylish dazzle of its opening credits through the magnificent Technicolor vistas of Paris, captured with high-contrast clarity by Paramount's new Vista-Vision process. *Funny Face* was a glorification (and spoof) of fashion photography, and its most striking visuals were the freeze-frame montages, frozen first in a negative or color-separated image, then in a positive one.

The process was the talk of both dance and photography circles: When a shot is "frozen" on the screen, the same frame is printed over and over for the desired length, but with a drastic loss in clarity. To get around that, Donen put a two-way mirror over the lens. The movie camera shot *through* the mirror while Avedon focused on the mirror, and the lab later matched the still photo with the film frame.[71] Avedon's fashion photos were a kind of "frozen dance," and Donen wanted the fashion sequences of *Funny Face* to have the same choreographic quality.[72]

Singled out above all was the scene in which Hepburn—in Givenchy gown, with "Winged Victory" behind her—runs briskly down an enormous staircase in the Louvre, snapped all the way by Astaire in a series of freeze frames. How she managed it was semi-miraculous, she recalled:

"I think that was just good luck. I did it once and didn't break my leg. Lynn Fontanne once said to me, 'My dear, whenever you walk downstairs, never look down and don't hold your skirt.' So everything you try to do to save your life, you're not allowed to do. You just hope to God you don't trip."[73]

In *Funny Face*, said Janet Maslin, Audrey became what she would forever be best: "a perfectly balanced mixture of intelligence and froth."[74]

Less complimentary things were said about Fred Astaire. The *Harvard Lampoon* named *Funny Face* one of the Ten Worst Films of 1957 and gave Astaire the award for "Most Appalling Example of the Inadequacy of Our Present Social Security Program." Among others who disliked the film, albeit more tactfully, is composer-conductor André Previn:

"It rubbed me the wrong way. I loved Audrey, but I thought the Kay Thompson business was hard to take, and the beatnik thing is so dated. Audrey and Fred by the edge of the river—you can't get any better than that. But it was just too chic. I didn't think it had any muscle in it. It made me a little edgy. It was all so precious."[75]

Funny Face, at $3 million, wasn't horribly expensive to make. But it was the first of Hepburn's American films not to be among the top ten moneymakers of its year. Its retro-raves, however, are legion. *American Film* put it "among the most lushly gorgeous Technicolor films ever produced."[76] Douglas McVay in *The Musical Film* called it "arguably the most pictorially ravishing of all American pictures." Rex Reed hailed it as "the best fashion show ever recorded on film," and Stanley Donen drew a final, further conclusion: "Audrey was always more about fashion than movies or acting."[77]

IN THE FASHION REALM, GIVENCHY was her indisputable guide. As Avedon was to give *Funny Face* the photographic look of *Vogue*, it was preordained that Givenchy would provide the actual high-fashion wardrobe, and that he and Audrey would spend countless hours together in the fittings.

From now on, her contracts contained a standard clause stipulating that Givenchy would design her film clothes, while his designs for her private use propelled her onto every best-dressed list in the world. "His are the only clothes in which I am myself," she said in 1956, full devoted by then to his spare, simple lines and dominant blacks and whites. Like his mentor Balenciaga, Givenchy heralded the minimalist designs of the sixties. Women who admired "The Hepburn Look" now flocked to his salon, and his sales soared, while the personal bond between him and Audrey became ever more intense.

"I depend on Givenchy in the same way that American women depend on their psychiatrists," she said. "There are few people I love more. He is the single person I know with the greatest integrity."

Long after, Givenchy recalls, "She told me something so touching that I will always remember it. She said, 'When I wear a white blouse or little suit that you create for me, I have the feeling of being protected by that blouse or suit—and this protection is very important to me.' "[78]

Givenchy was humble. "All the responsibility for the way Audrey looked is hers," he says. "She made the selections. I [just] helped her."[79] Clothes made the woman, but even her most beloved designers said she made herself—and perhaps *them*, too. Ralph Lauren, whose designs she often wore in later years, says, "She did more for the designer than the designer did for her."[80]

Leslie Caron believes Hepburn was the first great fashion example of "less is more":

"Simplicity was her trademark. She had the originality never to wear any jewelry, and this at the time of double rows of pearls, little earrings, lots of 'little' everything.... And then suddenly she would appear at a premiere wearing earrings that reached all the way down to her shoulders. Really daring!"[81]

In the anything-goes era of makeup and beauty today, it is hard to grasp how revolutionary Hepburn's look in the fifties really was. It represented "the feminine edge of androgyny," says designer Isaac Mizrahi—"the wonderful things about women that are not just tits or ass... the other side of Marilyn Monroe. [Her] sexiness enters through your heart not through your groin." Mizrahi says her erotic fashion appeal was epitomized by the hooded parka, black turtleneck and tight black pants she wore in *Funny Face*—"the perfect American look."[82]

Yet she *wasn't* American, and both she and her films had a different impact abroad. "For me," said Elizabeth Wilson in Britain's *Sight and Sound*, "her charm lay not in the androgyny of simple hair and a boyish figure, but in a style that seemed the embodiment of sophisticated, existential Europe as opposed to the overripe artificiality of Hollywood."[83] On both sides of the Atlantic, her look in *Funny Face* was a kind of quantum leap.

"Audrey was the first actress to play a fashion model on screen who really could have been one off screen," says Lenny Gershe. "It was always a joke when someone like Lana Turner in *A Life of Her Own* [1950] or Ava Gardner played a model—women who would never have made the cover of *Vogue* because they were too voluptuous. Today it's different. Now they're all bizarre—not *Harper's Bazaar*, just *bizarre*. For high fashion in the fifties, you had to be skinny. You had to look like Audrey Hepburn or Dovima or Suzy Parker. But Audrey was the first one to do it on screen. The audience bought that she could *be* this creature."[84]

Some thought *Funny Face* had changed her personality as well as her image, making her more confident and solid. Others attributed that not to the movie but to marriage—as if she had finally made the passage from girl to woman. "Two years ago," said a friend, "she was a pixie. "You didn't know but what she'd suddenly climb a tree or hurdle a hedge or just vanish in a spiral of smoke. Now you're reasonably sure she'll eat a ham sandwich and go to a ball game, or whatever."[85]

Her husband could certainly be sure of her devotion. One illustration concerned those fifty pieces of luggage with which they traveled: She almost always supervised the packing herself, but once when someone else did it for them, Mel was unable to locate his cuff links upon their arrival. Audrey ransacked six trunks before finding them and, in servile fashion, laid the blame on herself: "I didn't think this was fair to Mel. I considered it my responsibility not to let it happen again."[86]

Despite all dire predictions, her marriage had confounded the critics. She and Mel appeared to enjoy working together as well as being together. Prior to their wedding, her happiness seemed exclusively centered on her work. "I don't think now that I was a whole woman then," she said. "No woman is, without love. . . . I'm not alone anymore. Don't make that sound pathetic. I never minded being alone. But I'd mind it now."[87]

The Ferrers' union had no greater admirer than Sophia Loren, who rented a neighboring chalet in Bürgenstock and knew them there from 1957 during her own "convulsive marriage situation" with Carlo Ponti. "When the law in Italy was persecuting Carlo and me as criminals guilty of bigamy," recalls Loren today, "the marriage of Audrey Hepburn and Mel Ferrer seemed to me like a dream—far away and unreachable. . . . In those days, she was so happy, she inspired *my* dream [of the same]."[88]

Audrey's view of marriage was traditional to the point of subservience, as paradigmatic of the "good" fifties woman as her look and fashion statements were not.

"He is a protective husband, and I like it," she said. "Most women do. . . . It's so nice being a wife and having your husband take over your worries for you. American women have a tendency to take over too much, and in that way they miss out on a lot of fun that their European sisters have."[89]

That seemed to contradict her professed love of independent decision-making—and perhaps to suggest she was still trying get a firm handle on her lingering anxieties:

I have often thought of myself as quite ugly. In fact, I used to have quite a complex about it. To be frank, I've often been depressed and deeply disappointed in myself. You can even say that I hated myself at certain periods. I was too fat, or maybe too tall, or just plain too ugly. I couldn't seem to handle any of my problems or cope with people I met. If you want to get psychological, you can say my definiteness stems from underlying feelings of insecurity and inferiority. I couldn't conquer these feelings by acting indecisive. I found the only way to get the better of them was ... by adopting a forceful, concentrated drive.[90]

"Getting psychological" about her might begin with two quotations, the first from Audrey:

"My greatest asset is my discontent."

The second from an anonymous friend of hers:

"Discontent is her greatest personal liability."[91]

In career terms, she said, "Sometimes I think the more successful you become the less secure you feel. [Originally,] I didn't have the drive because I had the luxury of not needing it. After *Roman Holiday*, the offers came in. It was not in my nature to be terribly ambitious or driven because I didn't have the confidence. My confidence came and went with each movie; once I'd finished one, I didn't know if I'd ever work again."[92]

Chief among her weapons for combatting that insecurity was her intense power of concentration. "In talking about herself—or any subject from artichokes to zebras—she takes up one point at a time, never skips or flashes back," said a *Cosmopolitan* reporter. "When she reads, she reads; when she fits, she fits; when she talks clothes, she talks clothes; when she sits under a drier, she simply sits and dries. 'She is the only actress I've ever had who doesn't gab, read, knit, wriggle, pick her teeth, or eat a lettuce and tomato sandwich,' says her hairdresser."[93]

Equally remarked upon were her gentility and courtesy. She was both the delight and the despair of her publicists—"our nicest and most difficult client," said one of them. "She has politely turned down more than ninety percent of the publicity ideas we've dreamed up for her."

The normally bland *Good Housekeeping*, for one, was a little suspicious: "*Can* anybody really be so noble, so thoughtful, so perennially 'good' "?[94] She seemed a little *too* cool and aloof.

"Today I'm having lunch in my dressing room alone," she told a reporter around this time. "I usually do. Being alone, I recharge my batteries. Anyway, I thought I was being a good girl, giving my all to the picture this way. But then one of the columnists—one I thought I got along with—wrote, 'What goes with snooty Audrey Hepburn, not eating in the commissary.' So now do I have to begin eating in the commissary just to pacify this columnist? I'm afraid it would be cowardly of me. He's committed me to a course of action."[95]

Her comments to and about the press were getting sharper, and she was letting some of her hostilities out. She was asked, "If Mel wished it, would you forsake your career?"

"If you'll forgive me," she replied coldly, "it's not a fair question."[96]

She had an outburst now and then, but few doubted her tenderness and warmth. One day during *Funny Face*, the cast and crew were having a press luncheon on the second floor of the Eiffel Tower when a little French girl, one of the extras, burst into tears from fear of the popping flashbulbs and klieg lights that were blinding her. The empathetic young woman who got up to dry her tears and comfort her was Audrey.

She had become a grown-up version of that little girl:

"Now and then it staggers you. So many people pointing cameras, especially in Europe. Now and then, you find yourself out of your depth. The questions—all the way from what do I think of love or how does it feel to be a star, to enormous ones, even political, with as many prongs as a pitchfork. Here I am, an innocent little actress trying to do a job, and it seems that my opinion on policy in the Middle East is worth something. I don't say I don't have an opinion, but I doubt its worth."[97]

For now. One day, her opinions on such matters would be worth a lot.

AFTER *FUNNY FACE*, AUDREY RETURNED to Bürgenstock for four weeks' rest before her happy reunion and second film with Billy Wilder, whose much-delayed *Ariane* finally began shooting in August 1956. Based on a popular novel by Claude Anet set in pre-Bolshevik Russia, the story had the ring of *Gigi* and *Sabrina*: sophisticated Don Juan falls for innocent young beauty.

It was reworked by Wilder and I. A. L. Diamond—the first of their legendary script collaborations—to make the playboy even more cynical and the girl even more naive: Ariane became the cellist-daughter of a private detective and would fall in love with the rich libertine being investigated by her father for marital infidelity. The mise-en-scène was shifted from Russia to Paris, and the title spiced up to *Love in the Afternoon*. But when the male lead was announced, wags said a better name might be *Beauty and the Beast*.*

Cary Grant had been Wilder's first choice. He was almost *always* Wilder's first choice, and always unavailable. This time, Grant demurred on the grounds that, at fifty-two, he was too old to romance twenty-seven-

---

* *Ariane* had been filmed three times before—once as a French silent and twice with Elisabeth Bergner, whose gamine qualities were similar to Audrey's.

year-old Audrey Hepburn on screen. So the part went instead to an even older man—Gary Cooper, fifty-five.

The old cowboy's career had been in decline since *High Noon* (1952) but was recently revived by William Wyler's *Friendly Persuasion* (1956), which was still filling movie houses as *Love in the Afternoon* was getting under way. He would have to shed several decades to avoid looking like a child molester.

"I don't know why Coop was cast," says Audrey Wilder. "Billy wanted the all-American kind of guy. But if you read the book, you see that Audrey shouldn't have played *her* part, either. She was supposed to be a virgin whose father ran an army post, and all the men were crazy about her and lied about her, so when she goes off with this guy, he's horrified to find out she's never had any experience. But Audrey by nature and her innocent persona made him seem like a dirty old man. When she says she's been with twenty-five guys—you don't believe her for a minute. Brigitte Bardot could say it and you'd believe it."[98]

Many were disturbed by that, but Hepburn and Cooper were not among them. Shooting took place at the Studios de Boulogne and on location around Paris, and—by comparison with the tension on Wilder's *Sabrina* set—the atmosphere on this one was blissful. Audrey loved Cooper and the week it took to shoot a romantic picnic scene with him in the woods of Landru. She liked mastering the finger movements for the cello part in Haydn's Symphony No. 88, which she had to "perform" in one scene.[99]

She also enjoyed the man who played her father—and who almost stole the picture from her—Maurice Chevalier. That old charmer won her heart with a telegram on the first day of shooting: "How proud I would be, and full of love I would be, if I really had a daughter like you." Later, when he learned that her mother was a fan and an autograph collector, he sent Ella a photo inscribed, "To Audrey's *real* mother from her *reel* father."

Not everyone was so bowled over by Chevalier: Audrey Wilder said his only topic of conversation was himself and that "if the conversation veered away from him, his eyes turned to glass."

The other Audrey and her mobile domestic gear were back at the Hotel Raphael. (The Wilders had been there, too, but checked out after a few days in protest against the bartender's inability to make a proper martini.) Mel was filming *The Vintage* with Pier Angeli in the south of France, and on the weekends Audrey joined him in Nice or St. Tropez. On one of those visits, Ferrer gave her a Yorkshire terrier puppy, soon named "Famous," who turned out to be the most beloved gift of her life.

In Paris, the Ferrers and the Wilders, along with Cooper, Diamond, et al., often met after work for drinks or dinner, where Mel kept a close eye

on his girl—to the point of being a drag. At one such soiree, Audrey
Wilder told Charles Higham, Ferrer reminded Audrey that she had to leave
early the next day for the London premiere of *War and Peace* and that
they had to arrange tickets for some mutual friends. Fortified by a few
more cocktails than usual, she replied loudly, "What a crock of shit about
the tickets!" Everyone was astonished. Mel was furious. "You're leaving
here now," he said, and they did.[100]

Another negative report surfaced from unit publicist Herb Sterne
concerning her insistence on seeing and approving all publicity photos.
The photographers had been forbidden to shoot her at too low an angle
because that would accentuate her nostrils, which she felt were too large.
Sterne was amazed by "her obsession with her own face."[101] Her fussiness
in general seems to have left the *Love in the Afternoon* crew less fond of
her than their *Funny Face* counterparts.

In addition, there were problems with Gary Cooper. It took him a full
day—and many flubs—to complete the five-minute scene in which Ariane
is ready to storm out of his life but can't find her shoe. "Somebody wake
up Coop!" ordered Wilder before the umpteenth take. He had the further
difficulty of teaching Cooper some routine ballroom steps for one scene.
No mean dancer himself, Wilder took personal charge of the lessons—and
ended up shaking his head over "Old Hopalong Nijinsky."[102]

Cooper, unlike Humphrey Bogart, was a good sport about such cracks,
and by and large, *Love in the Afternoon* was a happy picture. Wilder enjoyed
trying to get a rise out of prim Audrey by telling her that the film's theme
song, "Fascination," had been the musical accompaniment to his own
loss of virginity.

Wilder's humor was best employed, of course, in the film itself—which
occasionally crossed the line between romantic comedy and bedroom farce.
Wilder's best black-comedic touches belong to Lise Bourdin as a lady who
keeps beating and chastising her dog for offenses it never commits.

Hepburn was filmed to perfection by William Mellor (*A Place in the
Sun*). The final "farewell" scene, with Cooper scooping her up into a
moving train in fine cowboy fashion, is a classic. But audiences and critics
alike had trouble accepting The Age Gap. Despite the aid of gauzy filters,
Cooper still looked old enough to be her father, which made the plot look
more like a tawdry affair than a romance. It was "among the bleakest,
most melancholy of comedies," said *American Film*. "Cooper's face is often
in silhouette, making it appear that Hepburn has fallen in love with a
shadow. Which, in essence, she has."[103]

To thwart charges of bad taste and bad morals, a voice-over was added
at the end, assuring viewers that they were headed for the altar. Even so,
in Spain several scenes were censored, and in France its name reverted to
Ariane because the American title was considered too suggestive.[104]

Audrey at the time made a spirited defense against the claim that her leading men were too old: "The charge is particularly unfair to Coop," she told a *New York World Telegram* reporter. "In *Love in the Afternoon* he's not trying to fool anyone. He's supposed to be a man of fifty. That's the whole point of the story. As for Fred Astaire, who cares how old he is? He's Fred Astaire! If anyone doesn't like it, he can go jump in the lake."[105]*

Later, however, she gave up the fight and said—not so facetiously—that *Love in the Afternoon* might have been more credible if Cooper and Chevalier had switched roles.

WHEN SHE FINISHED SHOOTING THE Wilder film in late fall 1956, Audrey left Europe to spend the Christmas holiday at La Quinta, a desert resort near Palm Springs, with Mel and his children, Pepa and Mark. There— and subsequently—she reverted again to wifely mode: "If a room isn't gay it can be awfully depressing and a male begins to sulk," she said. "I try to keep our trunks tabulated so I will never have to ask myself again, 'Now where did I pack Mel's patent leather pumps?'"[106]

Meanwhile, she was turning down such film offers as Jean Negulesco's *A Certain Smile* and George Stevens's *The Diary of Anne Frank.* She had read *Het Achterhuis* [*The Secret Annex,* retitled *The Diary of Anne Frank*] in 1947 in its Dutch galley form, and "it destroyed me," she said. "There were floods of tears. I became hysterical." Audrey was one of the first pilgrims to the Amsterdam building on Prinsengracht where the Franks had hidden. But Anne's story was too much Audrey's own, and the memories—having survived the occupation in which Anne perished— made it impossible for her, despite great pressure that was brought to bear on her. At the request of George Stevens, Anne's father, Otto Frank, traveled to Bürgenstock from his home in Zurich to try to persuade Audrey to take the role.

"He came to lunch and stayed to dinner," she recalled. "We had the most wonderful day.... He came with his new wife, who had lost her husband and her children [in the Holocaust]. They both had the numbers on their arms. He was a beautiful-looking man, very fine, a sort of transparent face, very sensitive. Incapable of talking about Anne without extreme feeling. I had to ask him nothing because he had a need to talk about it. He struck me [as] somebody who'd been purged by fire. There was something so spiritual about his face. He had been there and back."[107]

Audrey kept a snapshot of the occasion for good luck in her own little Everyman Library edition of *The Diary.* "I read it again when George sent

* For more on the theory and practice of Hepburn's "old men" in films, see Molly Haskell's discussion in Chapter 5. pp. 165–66.

it to me—and had to go to bed for the day," she said. Later, she added other reasons for declining: "I didn't want to exploit her life and her death to my advantage—to get another salary, to be perhaps praised in a movie."[108] A practical problem was cited by her friend Doris Brynner: "She was too old. She knew she couldn't play a fifteen-year-old."[109]

Young Millie Perkins played it instead, quite well, in what turned out to be an excellent picture. Years later, Larry King asked Hepburn if, upon reflection, she thought she might have been the perfect Anne. "No," she replied, "but then I'm not much of an actress.... I could not have suffered through that again without destroying myself."[110]

Perhaps for similar reasons, she also declined Paramount's offer to star in a non-musical biography of Maria von Trapp, whose life story would soon become The Sound of Music on Broadway. But there would be other nuns in Audrey's future, and for the moment, everything else was swept away in favor of the chance to costar with her husband.

In November 1957, the Ferrers attended the twenty-second annual New York Film Critics Awards at Sardi's, where the agenda was film but the talk was of television—and how to compete with it. The winners that night seemed to confirm the success of the new big-screen devices: Around the World in 80 Days (shot in Todd-AO) was chosen best film. The best actor and actress awards went to Kirk Douglas for Lust for Life and Ingrid Bergman for Anastasia—both lush CinemaScope productions.

During NBC radio's live broadcast of that event, commentator Ben Grauer provided the play-by-play: "... There's a little kiss from Ingrid Bergman to Audrey Hepburn ... and a man who's close by Audrey's side. Come here, Mrs. Ferrer! Mel, hello. Mel Ferrer —formerly of NBC."

"Still with NBC," Mel corrected. "We're working for them right now."

Film stars who made television movies were rare in those days, and viewed as slightly traitorous by Hollywood. Some were even subject to reprisals by the studios, but Audrey Hepburn was "too big" for anything like that to occur. Thus, she and Mel had agreed to do Mayerling for NBC-TV—the most lavish made-for-television spectacular up to that time.

It would be a ninety-minute Producers' Showcase color extravaganza— a kind of counterattack to the recent spate of movie epics—with a $620,000 budget, a cast of 107, fabulous costumes and sets. For Audrey, the financial arrangements were as appealing as the choice of her costar: She would get $150,000 for three weeks' work, one of rehearsal and two of indoor taping at the NBC studios on Sixth Avenue in New York City— where the Ferrers arrived on New Year's Day of 1957.

The author of the project at hand was the same Claude Anet who had written Ariane. But Mayerling was no light comedy. It was the true story of Crown Prince Rudolph of Austria, who in 1889 fell in love with a seventeen-year-old commoner named Maria Vetsera and, rather than give her up, made a mutual suicide pact. Its director was Anatole Litvak, who knew the territory well: He had made the successful 1936 French version starring Charles Boyer and Danielle Darrieux. But this time, he had an unusual problem with his leads:

"When Audrey plays Maria, speaking to the prince, she is also Audrey speaking to her husband," Litvak told *Life* magazine in mid-production. "It is very difficult to get Mel to treat her roughly. I had to work with him to get him to do it."[111]

Ferrer himself confirms the accuracy of that—if not of a second Litvak statement: "I had a lot of trouble getting them to turn on the heat. Audrey seemed to have a better rapport with that Yorkshire terrier of hers."[112]

It always took months between the filming and the release of a movie, but—in good television fashion—*Mayerling* was aired on February 4, 1957, just two weeks after the conclusion of production. Reportedly, it garnered the largest audience of any *Producers' Showcase* program since *Peter Pan* two years earlier. But a big audience was not necessarily a happy audience—and the word "flop" was heard more than a little.

"A more pallid or elementary version of *Mayerling* would be difficult to imagine," opined *The New York Times*.[113] "The lovers seem more fated to bore each other to death than to end their illicit alliance in a murder-suicide pact," said TV critic John Crosby.[114] As usual, Hepburn was praised for her beauty, delicacy and poignant vulnerability. Most of the brickbats were reserved for Ferrer as insufficiently dashing or romantic. Even in Europe, where the production was released theatrically, there was no critical or box-office excitement.

Mayerling was Mel and Audrey's last joint appearance, and on the basis of its failure, Paramount would reject several other proposed Hepburn-Ferrer team productions, including Thomas Wolfe's *Look Homeward, Angel* and Jean Anouilh's *The Lark*.

It was finally dawning on Audrey—and more grudgingly on Mel— "that they were not destined to be the next Laurence Olivier and Vivien Leigh," says Sheridan Morley. The public would accept them separately as a leading lady and a downbeat character actor, but not collectively. "From now on, Ferrer began to think of himself as the producer/director rather than costar of the partnership."[115]

So what could, or would, the leading lady take on next? The month of *Mayerling*'s release, she had been voted "Girl of the Year" by Britain's *Picturegoer Film Annual*. New York's Cholly Knickerbocker named her one of the ten most fascinating women in the world, and the New York Dress Institute put her on its best-dressed list. As the accolades poured in, it was increasingly clear that they had more to do with her "look" than with her acting. However beloved by fashion photographers and designers, Audrey was still unusually difficult to cast in films.

She and Mel pondered that dilemma, after *Mayerling*, on a skiing trip to St. Moritz and then in Spain and Mexico, where she accompanied Mel for the making of *The Sun Also Rises*, costarring Tyrone Power, Ava Gardner and Errol Flynn. The Mexican location shoot was charged with electricity. By one account, Ava Gardner had just ended her affair with screenwriter Peter Viertel, losing him to Joan Fontaine, who in turn soon lost him to Deborah Kerr, on top of which there was great tension between Flynn and Power due to their alleged prior affair—all of which Audrey and Ava ignored by shopping and sightseeing together constantly.

"Total bullshit," says Peter Viertel. "Joan Fontaine was in the future, and my affair with Gardner—which wasn't really an affair—was playing nurse to her when she was pissed DURING the *Sun Also Rises* shooting. Audrey and Mel kept very much to themselves, and so did Ava. I never knew of any 'affair' between Errol and Ty—and I very much doubt it."

The truth is more interesting than the fiction. "My first draft of the [*Sun*] script was a hundred percent better than the final one," says Viertel. "Fred Zinnemann said he'd do it. He wanted Audrey for Lady Brett and he sent her the script, but she said she didn't want to play 'a nympho-maniac.' In fact, even though she sleeps with everybody, the character is not a nymphomaniac, but Audrey felt she had an image to keep up. She wouldn't have been right for Lady Brett—but she would have been interesting."[116]

When shooting of the Hemingway film was completed (under Henry King's, not Fred Zinnemann's, direction), the Ferrers went to California for some studio story conferences and a visit with Mel's children in Santa Barbara before returning to Switzerland. Audrey was hugely relieved to be back home: She was expecting a baby. But it was those story conferences in Hollywood that would soon give birth—to twins.

"I'M TERRIBLY SORRY THAT I won't be able to do *The Diary of Anne Frank*," she told a reporter—disingenuously—around this time. "It will come at the same time as *The Nun's Story*, so it will be impossible."[117]

Robert (*Tea and Sympathy*) Anderson had long been working on a script for *The Nun's Story*, which was the subject of one of those story conferences Mel and Audrey attended in California. The second dealt with another book-to-film project, but of a highly allegorical nature. Both would come to fruition. The question was which to make first. Having played mostly ingenues and Cinderellas to date, Hepburn decided it was time to prove herself as a serious dramatic actress in a part that submerged her own sunny personality beneath a much deeper set of emotions. The role of Sister Luke, which she signed to play in December 1957, would offer the greatest screen challenge of her life.

Toward the end of the fifties, Audrey Hepburn was a "glorious anachronism," a member of a cinematic aristocracy whose appeal was on the wane. Her leading men had mostly been over fifty, and their ages had been considered no detriment to her. "She was courted on screen by nearly every hunky Hollywood relic," said Richard Corliss, "until, in *The Nun's Story*, only God could be her best beau."[118]

CHAPTER 5

Huckleberry Friend
(1958–1962)

"Marilyn [Monroe] was my first choice to
play Holly Golightly. I thought she would
be perfect. Holly had to have something
touching about her... unfinished. [But]
Paramount double-crossed me in every
way and cast Audrey."

TRUMAN CAPOTE

FROM NYMPH TO NUN, SAID the wags.[1] Making *The Nun's Story* was a daring decision both for Audrey Hepburn and for Warner Brothers in the year 1958. The narrative seemed better suited to documentary than to big-feature treatment. Moreover, the complex spiritual problems of its heroine were sure to disturb the Roman Catholic Church and many of the faithful. Some ecclesiastical officials charged that Hulme's novel exaggerated and sensationalized such aspects of convent life as flagellation and that its "negative" ending reflected pejoratively on all nuns.

Two things were essential to pulling the film off: a director of great finesse, and the presence of Hepburn. She was the only major star with sufficiently credible "purity," untainted by any scandalous behavior on-or offscreen.

Director Fred Zinnemann (*High Noon, From Here To Eternity, Oklahoma!*) would provide the finesse. The book had been sent to him by Gary Cooper, "who thought I might find it interesting. He was right. Unhappily, my enthusiasm was not shared by any of the studios.... But when Audrey said she wanted to do it the studios suddenly became intensely interested."[2] The only other candidate, Zinnemann revealed, had been Ingrid Bergman—but she failed the purity test.

Reports that Hepburn had hesitated due to the lack of a part for Mel Ferrer were false. Ferrer, in fact, had read *The Nun's Story* first and recommended it with enthusiasm. "I particularly admired Fred Zinnemann," he recalls, "and urged Audrey to play the nun, which changed the direction of her creative life."[3] Forever criticized, Mel never got credit

for this instance—among others—of his positive career advice. His attitude
was all the more generous considering that her casting in *Nun's Story*
complicated his own ambitious project with her, *Green Mansions*. The
schedule was so tight that Audrey would have no break between two
demanding productions in tropical locales, for which she was now taking
an assortment of twelve shots against a host of diseases.

The previous great "Catholic film"—*The Song of Bernadette*, fifteen years
earlier—had been uplifting and devoid of controversy. Kathryn C. Hulme's
Nun's Story, on the other hand, was a bestselling novel that treated its
religious material with respect but also with severe realism and a sad
ending.

It was the true story of Belgian nun Marie-Louise Habets ("Sister
Luke"), whose devotion is ever at war with her vow of obedience. She is
sent to work as a nurse in the Belgian Congo, where her inner struggle
unfolds through a series of medical crises and an intense relationship with
the surgeon she serves. The backdrop is World War II and her moral
dilemma is compounded by the question of whether to assist the Resistance
after her father is killed by the Nazis.

The film, like the book, had to work simultaneously on multiple levels—
dramatic, spiritual, political—with a disturbing relevance to Hepburn's
own war experience. Author and subject had met in 1945 at a UNRRA
camp for displaced persons in Germany. One day, Hulme remarked on the
long hours Habets spent at her nursing work. "You're a saint, Marie-
Lou," she said, to which Habets reacted with great upset. "I was a nun
once," she later confided to Hulme, "but a nun who failed her vows."

The two women became soul mates as well as housemates. Habets
came to the United States in 1951, moved in with Hulme and worked in
a Santa Fe Railroad hospital in Los Angeles, caring for Navajo track
walkers, brakemen and porters. *Nun's Story* had sold three million copies
and been translated into twelve languages by the time film production
began, when Zinnemann arranged for Audrey to meet the real-life Sister
Luke at Hulme's home near Los Angeles.

"She didn't really want to meet me," Habets later said. "She felt the
story was too much of my private life. She just sat there and looked at me
and didn't ask any questions."[4]

On subsequent visits, Hepburn got less tongue-tied and ended up
working so closely with Hulme and Habets that people referred to them
collectively as "The 3-H Club." Audrey consulted the ex-nun on every
detail of her character—from the proper donning of a habit to the correct
kissing of a crucifix. Habets also familiarized her with an operating room
and helped demystify the world of microscopes and Bunsen burners in a
medical laboratory.

The presence of Hepburn allayed Jack Warner's fears but not necessarily those of the Catholic church. She was not, after all, a Catholic herself, and the church was still sufficiently powerful in 1958 to hold up a multimillion-dollar production over a single line of dialogue, as Zinnemann recalled:

> Two things about the project worried them. One was the fact that a professed nun would leave her order after seventeen years—it was not good for recruiting, as one Monsignor put it. The other problem was that we might be tempted to exploit the implicit attraction between the nun and the worldly, cynical, charming Dr. Fortunati....
>
> All film companies approaching the Catholic Church for assistance are [assigned] someone—often a Dominican priest—to work with them. The Dominican Order ... is strong on dogma and not particularly flexible. In our case they were extremely thorough in scrutinizing our shooting script. They went through it line by line and objected, for instance, to a speech by Edith Evans: "The life of a nun is a life against nature." Our advisers said, "You mustn't say that. You have to say, '... a life *above* nature....'" More than two hours were spent in discussion of that one word. We went back and forth without making progress until a Jesuit friend ... said, "Why can't you say, '*in many ways*, it's a life against nature'?" and so, with the Jesuitical addition of "in many ways," into the screenplay it went.[5]

Zinnemann also needed to secure permission for Audrey to do more "homework"—and for the company to shoot—inside an actual nunnery. The bishop of Bruges had refused permission to film at Habets's own Sisters of Charity convent in Ghent, but Warner agents negotiated the use of a similar French convent belonging to the Sisters of the Oblates d'Assomption, at Froyennes—in exchange for some hard, Hollywood cash. The mother superior also agreed to let Audrey stay there briefly for observation purposes.

Casting, by then, had been completed. Audrey had hinted that Ferrer could play Dr. Fortunati, says Warren Harris, but "Zinnemann pretended not to hear."[6] Several other candidates, including Yves Montand, declined the part on the grounds that it was too small. Zinnemann settled wisely on Australian actor Peter Finch, whose name and fee were smaller. Dame Edith Evans was perfectly cast as Mother Emmanuel, Sister Luke's mother general in Belgium. Dame Peggy Ashcroft, Mildred Dunnock and Beatrice Straight would play the other key roles among the nuns.

Never before or after were the logistics of a film—far-flung locations in France, Italy and the Congo—so difficult for Audrey. From Day One, she fretted that delays in *Nun's Story*'s shooting schedule would run into Mel's start-up date for *Green Mansions*, and she couldn't get a straight answer out of the studio. With the clock ticking, Zinnemann sent a red-flag cable to Warners: "We are courting disaster if Audrey left unaware of finishing date much longer. Will decline all responsibility for picture unless Audrey fully aware of true situation. Find myself increasingly unable to cope with endless uncertainty."

Matters were complicated by various sublime and ridiculous snags. It was reported that Hepburn insisted a bidet be airmailed to her in Rome and thence to Africa. (She denied it: "How and where would you hook it up?") What she wanted much more than a bidet was her dog Famous: The Italians were willing to fudge their quarantine rules, but the Congolese were not. Cables flew back and forth among officials on three continents, until Famous finally got his canine visa. Audrey hugged and kissed and fussed over him, and took him everywhere. Once when a car nearly ran over him, "she went crazy, screaming and crying," recalls costar (and later film-biographer par excellence) Patricia Bosworth. "After her outburst, she locked herself in her dressing room until she had herself under control."[7] Fred Zinnemann thought the dog was an obvious child-substitute.

Actress Rosalie Crutchley, who played Sister Eleanor, remembered a chat she and Hepburn had after Crutchley's young son and daughter visited the studio. "How fortunate you are," Audrey said wistfully. "I do terribly want to have a child—more than anything else in the world. How have you managed to have children *and* maintain a career?" Crutchley's reply was rather brusk: "unlike you, I am not a globe-trotting film star."[8]

The real globe-trotting for *Nun's Story* had not yet begun. The "studio" was not in Hollywood but in Rome, where most of the interior photography would be done. In the Cinecittà Studios' Experimental Center, set wizard Alexander Trauner designed an historically correct convent and chapel and perfect replicas of an early Michelangelo "Pieta" and other statues in Bruges. One advantage to filming in Rome related to obtaining the many other nuns required for *Nun's Story*, as Zinnemann explained:

"As it was understood that real nuns were not to be photographed, we needed to find extras for the large complicated ceremonial scenes of walking in procession, kneeling, bowing and prostrating themselves—all more or less on cue; these women had to have special training. In the end, twenty dancers were borrowed from the ballet corps of the Rome Opera and were drilled by two Dominican nuns, one of them a university professor."

Zinnemann took scrupulous care to see that all convent rituals were accurately rendered—literally "choreographed," with the help of those dancers, in the chapel scenes.

"For the nuns' close-ups," he said, "faces of great character and personality were needed. We found them mostly among the embassies and the Roman 'black' aristocracy: a lot of principessas and contessas would turn up in their Rolls-Royces or Mercedes at five a.m. Dressed as nuns they looked marvelous."

As of two weeks before shooting began, all the on-screen nuns were ordered to stay out of the sun, and makeup supervisor Alberto de Rossi emphasized the paleness of their skin and lips. His wife Grazia, again serving as Audrey's hairdresser, was cleverly engaged to play the nun who cuts off Sister Luke's hair at the beginning of her novitiate. (Contrary to legend, the hair she lops off is not Audrey's own, but a wig.)[9]

Otherwise, Zinnemann chose not to cast many Roman Catholics in the film. "It seemed important to keep an objective approach to the work, without the emotional involvement a faithful believer would bring to it," he said, and none of the leads relied on religion to create their roles. Most fascinating was Edith Evans's approach to her part. She told Zinnemann she took the character of the Reverend Mother from a single sentence in the book: "Her back never touched the back of the chair in which she was sitting." Evans held herself absolutely straight to show the gap between the chair's back and her own, and built her whole character from that one physical trait.[10]

Audrey, by contrast, was building her character from the inside out. She began a regimen of simple, convent-type meals and a policy of not looking at herself in mirrors, which were forbidden to real-life nuns. When a makeup man turned on a phonograph one day during a break in shooting, she asked him to turn it off as "Sister Luke wouldn't be allowed to listen to it." The inward essence concerned her deeply. "There's a man in the Congo I want to see, if I possibly can," she told a reporter just before leaving Rome for Africa. "Albert Schweitzer."[11]

ON JANUARY 23, 1958, HEPBURN, Zinnemann, Finch and company flew to the Belgian Congo in high spirits. In that pre-jet age, it took fourteen hours to get to Stanleyville, their headquarters for the next two months. Once they arrived, said Zinnemann, "Except for the occasional snakes in unexpected places, such as under breakfast tables, we lived quite comfortably in the Sabena Guest House on food flown in from Brussels twice a week."[12]

What would Mel eat in her absence? Audrey—dutiful wife as well as dutiful actress—had not failed to take care of that. Before leaving for Africa, she had written out daily menus for the cook to prepare for him—breakfast, lunch, dinner, and even midnight snacks—during the months she would be away.[13]

Audrey's own needs and demands were few. Other than the dog, "The only thing she requested in the Congo was an air conditioner," says Zinnemann. "It was promptly sent from the studio in Burbank but did not seem to do much good. On closer inspection it turned out to be a humidifier."[14]

Audrey recalled that "in the Congo, a cool day was 100, and the weather was often 130. [But] I didn't swelter in my nun's habit.... Actually, all that covering keeps the heat out."[15] Perhaps being thin also made the heat less oppressive for her than for others; Dame Peggy was out for two days with heat stroke. In any case, Zinnemann said he had "never seen anyone more disciplined, more gracious or more dedicated to her work than Audrey. There was no ego.... There was the greatest consideration for her coworkers." She was taking on the characteristics of an actual nun—albeit Hollywood-style.

"Our 'nuns' carried make-up cases and smoked cigarettes between setups," said Zinnemann. "The blacks who came to watch the shooting could not believe their eyes. Then someone said, 'Of course, these are American nuns.' And the blacks said, 'Ah, yes, now we understand.'"[16]

Highlight of the filming was the four days they spent with the celebrated British missionary Dr. Stanley Browne, shooting a sequence in his leper colony on an island in the middle of the Congo river. "Naturally," said Zinnemann, "we asked [Dr. Browne] about the risks involved. 'You have less risk of getting leprosy here than catching a cold in the New York subway,' he said. After we had finished shooting he added, 'Of course you have to understand that the incubation period for leprosy is seventeen years.'" Dr. Browne was using the new sulfone drugs to stop the spread of, though not cure, leprosy. "Each year they were able to release a small number of people who were declared safe and were returned to their villages after a most moving ceremony which ended with everyone singing an anthem in their own language: English, French, Lingala and Swahili."[17] The tune to which they all sang their own words was the "Ode to Joy" of Beethoven's Ninth Symphony, and when Audrey heard it, she wept.

Equally dramatic was the planned sequence in which three men are caught in quicksand on the banks of a raging river during a rainstorm. People along the water's edge were to watch in horror as the men disappeared under the mud, Zinnemann recalled:

A good river was soon found, but the set—with three built-in lifts to show the men slowly sinking out of sight —would cost $40,000. In 1958 this was a staggering sum; Jack Warner wouldn't hear of giving his okay. Finally, [producer Henry Blanke] had to fly with me all the way from the Congo to Hollywood, in order to persuade Warner of the enormous excitement of this scene....

On the day before shooting, we rehearsed the entire sequence, complete with lifts, wind machines and rainbirds. It all worked to perfection. But during the night the river fell by two feet; all the chicken-wire and cement holding together the "quicksand" was glaringly exposed.[18]

It was the $40,000 scene-that-was-never-shot. But of greater concern was the worsening political situation in the Congo, which was coming to the end of nearly a century of bitter Belgian colonialism. Racial tensions were palpable in Stanleyville, where a postal clerk named Patrice Lumumba would soon become premier—and soon after be murdered.

"There was a curfew for the blacks, who were not allowed in the European area after sunset," Zinnemann recalled. "[One year later,] the Belgians would be driven out [and] very many of these extraordinary people were dead—killed in the revolution."[19]

Exterior filming in the Congo was completed early in March 1958, but equally tricky were the interior sexual subtleties of the story—namely, the relationship between Sister Luke and the atheist doctor for whom she works. "He's a genius—also a bachelor and an unbeliever," she is warned in advance. "Don't ever think for an instant that your habit will protect you."

There could be no hint of a physical affair between the doctor and the nun, but Zinnemann felt Finch had the sex appeal to make audiences feel a powerful attraction anyway. Soon enough, there were rumors of a Hepburn-Finch affair—as there were rumors of an affair between Finch and every actress he ever worked with, including Vivien Leigh in *Elephant Walk*. Confirmed, rather than rumored, were his heavy drinking habits, cultivated from an early age in Australia. Audrey's piety, in and out of her role, had nothing in common with Finch's wild, womanizing ways—but made for a perfect complement to him on screen.

"His public image was no myth," said Yolande Finch, his second wife. "He was a piss-pot and a hell-raiser, but he was also a happy drunk, a gigglebum and very, very good company."[20]

Typical of Finch's attachments was one formed on the Sabena airliner en route to the Congo: He was suddenly afflicted by a fear of flying to rival Erica Jong's, finding relief only in close contact with a beautiful, six-foot Belgian stewardess named Lucienne Van Loop.[21] She was regularly assigned to that flight, and they saw a lot of each other during *Nun's Story* shooting. Finch said the reason for her frequent visits was "dental treatment," although Stanleyville was not known to be a mecca of dentistry. Audrey, in one of her rare and charming off-color remarks, observed that, "If she keeps up at the present rate, she'll be giving her Finchy a very gummy smile."[22]

Finch, however, was always respectful of Hepburn. A certain Magistra monkey, on the other hand, was not. It was supposed to be Sister Luke's beloved pet, but it gave Audrey a nasty bite on the right arm. Otherwise, location injuries were minimal.

Audrey's serious medical trouble happened not in Africa but after the company returned to Italy for the conclusion of the marathon 132-day shoot. One midnight at the Hotel Hassler in Rome, she began to feel excruciating back pains, accompanied by vomiting and a urinary obstruction. Stoic as ever, she refused to call anyone she knew for help, not even Zinnemann and his wife, who were on the floor below. "We learned of her illness only the next morning," said Mrs. Zinnemann. "She had telephoned the hotel doctor rather than disturb our sleep."[23]

Partly due to dehydration in the Congo, she had a severe case of kidney stones. Her mother and husband immediately flew to be with her—Ella from London and Mel from Venezuela, where he'd been scouting *Green Mansions* locations. In an effort to avoid surgery, the doctors prescribed drugs and ordered bed rest. Filming continued around her until the treatment achieved its results—successfully—without requiring an operation.

"Someone said that kidney ailments are even more painful than childbirth," said Audrey at the time. "Now I'm perfectly prepared to have a dozen children."[24]

Zinnemann shielded her from the bombardment he was getting from Warner production chief Steve Trilling, who thought Audrey was dogging her recovery and who kept cracking the whip for work to resume—in the same Roman studio where *Ben-Hur* was being shot on an adjacent sound stage.* At any rate, by April, Hepburn was back on the *Nun's Story* set in good shape.

The film's most shocking scenes take place in a grim, Marat-Sade type of insane asylum in Belgium—groaning women in cells and bathtubs, shot in semi-documentary fashion. There, Sister Luke is nearly killed when she disobeys orders and opens the cell of a patient who yanks her inside and attacks her. It's a fierce struggle, and Audrey was only recently over a debilitating illness. "We'd provided a double for that fight," Zinnemann says, "but she wouldn't hear of it."[25] Hepburn insisted on playing the scene herself and took instruction from the double in how to wrestle without tearing a ligament—in full nun's robes. The credible violence of that sequence is riveting.

Credibility was important to Zinnemann in every way, particularly in his visual aspirations for the film:

"I dearly wanted to shoot the European parts in black and white and then, when Sister Luke arrives in the Belgian Congo, to burst out into all the hot, vivid, stirring colors of Central Africa. Jack Warner vetoed it; he

---

* The persistent rumor that Audrey appeared as an extra in a *Ben-Hur* mob scene as a whimsical favor to director William Wyler is a myth, stemming from a visit that she and Patricia Bosworth made one day to watch the filming of the chariot scene. Hepburn took an interest in Bosworth, "maybe because it was my first big break in the movies [and] I was the youngest member of the cast," she says. "During my big scenes, Audrey firmly advised me not to do anything—'just react, don't act'—and that's what I did."

thought it was too tricky and too far ahead of [the] popular imagination."[26]

The director's consolation was Austrian cinematographer Franz Planer, who had photographed Audrey in *Roman Holiday* and whose style was perfectly suited to the somber formality of *The Nun's Story*. Planer's splendid ethnographic footage of Congo village life much enhanced the production.

Zinnemann had lost the black-and-white visual battle, but he would win a major audio victory. There was great internal studio dispute over composer Franz Waxman's score:

> What I didn't know was that Waxman had a strong dislike of the Catholic Church. When we listened to his music it sounded like the background for the dungeons of *The Count of Monte Cristo*. I decided not to use very much of it. Franz was outraged and complained to Jack Warner. The wrangle centered on my wish to have absolute silence at the end of the film as the nun changes into her civilian clothes and walks out of the convent door....
>
> "Why don't you want music at the end?" Warner asked. I answered, "Why do *you* want music at the end?" "Because every Warner Brothers picture has music at the end," replied Jack. I said, "If you have festive music you are saying to the audience, 'Warner Brothers congratulates the nun on quitting the convent.' If the music is heavy, the audience will be depressed; I don't see how you can win." Audrey was allowed to make her exit in silence.[27]

In that chilling final scene, which contains not a word of dialogue, Luke removes her robes, a buzzer pops open a door, and she leaves the convent without ceremony or farewell of any kind. She is being cast out literally, and through the open door, the camera tracks her slow trek down a brick lane and the moment's hesitation before she makes a right turn. It is a sad, stark, beautiful downer of an ending, devoid of any false hope.

The ending was silent, but Warner music executive Rudy Fehr, who accompanied Audrey to the first sneak preview of *The Nun's Story* in San Francisco, remembers the overall resolution of the sound-of-music controversy a bit differently:

> Franz Waxman had researched Bach and Handel and recorded a beautiful score. At the preview, little did he know that 80 percent of the music was out of the picture. He was furious. We had a meeting at the St. Francis Hotel in San Francisco with Steve Sterling, who represented Jack Warner, and Franz was shaking. He said, "I protest! I've never been treated so badly. I worked so hard on this!" Then all of a sudden, the head of the publicity department walks in with the preview cards, where people write down their reactions. He went right up to Franz and said, "Franzie, where was the

fucking music?" [Later,] Jack Warner said, "Rudy, I leave it in your hands. Put in what you think is right." I put all but 15 percent of it back in. A beautiful score.[28]

Indeed, the stark, melancholy Waxman music merged with all the other elements of *Nun's Story* to perfect effect, and chief among those elements was Audrey Hepburn. During six months of shooting, she seemed to be living out her selfless role whether the cameras were rolling or not. Once, when water finally arrived after the cast was stranded for hours in the broiling sun, she poured out cupfuls for thirty natives, leaving none for herself. But not everyone was favorably impressed.

"It's that princess bit again—be a shining example to the populace," said one observer on the set. "Having chosen her noble role, [she] plays it to the hilt, as any superb actress should. Yet her determination to carry it off—even to the extent of suffering unnecessary personal pain—causes one to wonder why she does it."[29] Audrey's explanation was disarmingly honest: "I'm afraid that my strenuous advance preparation is part of my obsessive worry that I won't be ready."[30]

She was ready enough in the opinion of Marie-Louise Habets and Kathryn Hulme, who saw an uncut version that ran nearly four hours. "It was too overwhelming," said Habets. "I'm never going to see it again because if I do I'm going to run right back to the convent.... I could just sit there and cry my eyes out, not with regret, but because of the beauty of it. It is a beautiful life, the religious life, if you ... can accept it without murmuring all the time."[31]

It was said that no matter how outwardly serene a nun might be, her soul remained a battleground until she died. *The Nun's Story* chronicled such a battle with restraint and compassion. *American Film* called it "among the most transcendent of films."[32] Britain's *Films & Filming* cited the "wisdom" of Audrey's performance as "more profound than that of any other character Hepburn has played."[33] The story of Sister Luke was "not a crisis of faith, but a crisis of worthiness," said Zinnemann, who marveled at "the fine, firm line of development" of Audrey's portrayal. He compared her favorably with that other beautiful, fragile actress he loved, Grace Kelly—the strength of Hepburn's self-possession versus the weakness of Kelly's self-doubt.

"I think Audrey was much more comfortable with Sister Luke than with other parts," says Rob Wolders. "It was the story of a woman who investigated life, who was constantly on a search, as Audrey was." It was not about "a woman who wants to be herself," said critic Stephen Whitty, but about "a woman who wants to be a saint. Whether she's holy, or wholly neurotic, is up to you."[34]

Her husband was her biggest fan. Mel Ferrer is still awed, today, at the way she accomplished it "with very little of her face showing ... by showing so little."[35] She had no big-name leading man or high-fashion designers to help her out, and precious few speeches. With her hands and body hidden for most of the film, she had to rely almost entirely on her eyes. "Large and luminous, they become a window to her doubt," wrote Whitty. "They draw us so completely into her world, and to her character, that her self-torture becomes wrenching."

The increasingly dark circles under those eyes seemed etched by pain, not makeup, so much so that it's a shock at the end when Sister Luke becomes Gabrielle again, removing her habit to reveal her hair for the first time since the story began—but not quite enough of a shock, in the director's opinion:

"In retrospect I can see this is where I slipped up. When Audrey takes off her nun's habit, the passage of seventeen years is not clearly enough suggested. [There is] hardly a strand of gray hair when she shakes it free from the confining wimple."[36]

Zinnemann was being polite: Such an important detail had not, in fact, slipped his mind. He had wanted her hair to be streaked with more gray, but Audrey opposed the idea—and won.

The studio was jittery about the picture's release for a plethora of reasons and not at all certain of its success. "To say that Warners were not entirely happy with the film would be an understatement," said Zinnemann. "They thought it would flop. Well, they said, maybe Audrey [would bring] some people in."[37]

She did, indeed. Nun's Story opened at Radio City Music Hall on July 18, 1959, and made more money for Warners than any of its previous films. It cost $3.5 million and grossed more than $6 million then—and much more since. Hepburn was named Best Actress of 1959 by the New York Film Critics and its British equivalent. "Her performance will forever silence those who have thought her less an actress than a symbol of the sophisticated child/woman," said Films in Review. "Her portrayal of Sister Luke is one of the great performances of the screen."[38]

Nun's Story won none of the eight Oscars for which it was nominated. Audrey was a candidate for Best Actress (her third nomination in six pictures) as was Katharine Hepburn for Suddenly Last Summer—rival nominees for the first time. Both Hepburns lost to Simone Signoret for Room at the Top, and MGM's epic Ben-Hur swept away the competition in virtually every other category.

Zinnemann later proposed a flippant alternate title: "I Kicked My Habit." But Audrey always maintained a respectful tone about the film. At the moment, she was issuing carefully phrased denials to reports that she was converting to Roman Catholicism. "I have been educated in the Protestant faith and shall remain Protestant even though I have great respect for those who profess the Catholic faith," she told the (highly disappointed) Italian news agency Italia.[39]

Sister Luke in *Nun's Story* was the subliminal genesis of a real-life role she would play in Africa three decades later. "After looking inside an insane asylum, visiting a leper colony, talking to missionary workers, and watching operations, I felt very enriched," she said. "I developed a new kind of inner peacefulness. A calmness. Things that once seemed so important weren't important any longer."[40]

SHE WOULD NEED ALL THE inner peace and external energy she could muster for the next project, which came so fast on the heels of *Nun's Story* that it ended up in front of it: *Green Mansions*—either the great disaster or the "lost masterpiece" of the Ferrers' joint efforts in film.

Zinnemann very much wanted to work with Audrey again. He offered her the lead in a proposed movie of James Michener's epic *Hawaii*.*[41] But in June, before the *Nun's Story* set was cold, she and Mel flew from Rome to Hollywood for their "leftover" commitment from *Funny Face*: For loaning out that musical property and certain key artists to Paramount, MGM was owed an Audrey Hepburn picture—with Mel Ferrer as director.

It was one of the shrewdest bargains the Ferrers ever struck. Though his three previous efforts had not been hits, Mel still longed for success as a director. But the vehicle he chose had some inherent rust: a turn-of-the-century utopian novel by W. H. Hudson, *Green Mansions: A Romance of the Tropical Forest*. It was the tragic romance of Rima, mysterious "bird girl" of the South American forest, and the adventurer who invades her world.

When Ferrer first read it at Princeton, it made a profound impression on him. For years he had dreamed of turning it into a film, more so since marrying Audrey, who conformed to his own and Hudson's vision: Rima was the feminine symbol of innocence, a victim of male greed and lust. She was much like Ondine, only from the jungle instead of the sea—a delicate Tarzana. But she faced a long, hard journey from the page to the screen.

RKO had bought the screen rights to *Green Mansions* a quarter century earlier, hoping to ape the success of *King Kong*. Dolores Del Rio was to star, but the plan fell through and the rights were acquired by MGM in 1945 for a proposed musical version starring Yma Sumac. In 1953, Alan Jay Lerner was asked to prepare a *Green Mansions* script as a vehicle for Liz Taylor, to be directed by Vincente Minnelli, but it never materialized.

---

* That film didn't materialize until 1966 and starred Audrey's nemesis-to-be, Julie Andrews, when it did.

The film that did materialize, in 1959, opens with an unusual advance thank-you to the governments of British Guiana and Venezuela, where Mel and a unit of thirty spent several months filming background exteriors while Audrey finished *Nun's Story*. Ferrer and his crew traveled 25,000 miles through pristine fog forests—and shipped back 250 tons of props, plants, tree-bark canoes, blowguns, and live snakes.

Totally enchanted, Ferrer wanted to shoot all the exteriors in those green and misty mansions of South America, but had to settle for Hollywood, where art director Preston Ames recreated an Indian village on twenty-five MGM studio acres. The reason was partly budgetary and partly due to Audrey's health: Just after tough duty on *Nun's Story* in Africa, it was too soon to hustle her straight back into the jungle on an even more remote continent.

Screenwriter Dorothy (*Pal Joey*) Kingsley stuck close to the novel: Abel (Anthony Perkins) escapes into the interior from the Caracas revolution in which his family has just been massacred. Ignoring his Indian guides, he enters a "forbidden" village with revenge and gold-lust in his heart. There, Chief Runi (Sessue Hayakawa) and brave Kua-ko (Henry Silva) test Abel's courage, as he tests theirs by nearly talking them to death in a language they don't understand. (An ongoing linguistic suspension of disbelief is required by this film. No accent is like any other; all, of course, are speaking the lingua franca of Hollywoodese.)

Abel regards the Indians with fine racist contempt: "However friendly they might be towards one of a superior race, there was always in their relations with him a low cunning." But one day in the forest, he hears "a low strain of exquisite bird-melody, wonderfully pure," unlike any sound he has ever heard. He spies a girl—"small, in figure slim, with delicate hands and feet."

She is Rima the Bird Girl, a jungle princess who thwarts the native hunters by roaming the woods to warn the animals. The resentful Indians plot to kill her and enlist Abel's help. But he reconsiders when she saves him from a poisonous snakebite and takes him to the hut where she lives with her grandfather (Lee J. Cobb). There, she nurses his body and libido back to health. Rima is always near, yet elusive. Whenever Abel touches her, she becomes silent and constrained. He is intrigued by the idea that she might be one of an undiscovered race. Theirs is an innocent love, like that of Peleas and Melisande.

But when Abel mentions the precipitous mountains of Riolama, Rima is afire: "That is the place I am seeking!" It was the home of her dead mother, and she begs to be taken there. Her grandfather begs *not* to be taken: "Have mercy on me! It is so far—and I am old and should meet my death!" But Rima needs him as a guide and forces him, in a ferocious speech:

"Would he die—old grandfather? Then we could cover him up with palm leaves in the forest and leave him.... Shall you die? Not until you have shown me the way to Riolama.... Then you may die, and... the children and the grandchildren and cousins and friends of all the animals you have slain and fed on shall know that you are dead and be glad at your death."

Hepburn lacks true ferocity but looks great through all the perils and hardships and shrunken heads on the way to Riolama. Scampering about in her bare feet, she manages to keep her single forest frock clean and pressed the whole time. This is surely the lowest costume budget for a Hepburn film ever.

At Riolama, Abel steals a kiss from her unconscious lips, thus ending her illusions by opening her heart to love. But however much he might love her, he can never fully understand her. She goes off alone and is tracked down by her Indian enemies and chased into a tree—which the natives set aflame. It is an apotheosis and martyrdom like Joan of Arc's: Director Ferrer elevates her, once and for all, from princess to goddess.

Depending on one's mind set, this was either a beautiful morality tale or the most bizarre, idealized malarkey. Mel thought the former. Audrey not only agreed with him but also "lived" the part of the pantheistic nature girl. Animal lover that she was, her favorite costar was the dappled fawn that accompanies Rima everywhere. But fawns are temperamental and nervous. Producer Edmund Grainger conferred with Clarence Brown, director of *The Yearling*, who said the only way to handle one was for the actress to adopt it right after birth and raise it as her own baby. Soon enough it would believe Audrey to be its mother.

MGM duly bought a four-week-old fawn at Jungleland, a children's outdoor zoo in Los Angeles. When it arrived, with its huge eyes and skinny legs, everyone thought it looked remarkably like Audrey. From then on, everywhere that Audrey went, the fawn was sure to go—including the supermarket and beauty parlor. It had to be bottle-fed every two hours, and Audrey often had to interrupt a scene or a conference to rush off and give a bottle of warmed goat's milk to "Ip"—so named by Audrey because of the "*ip ip*" sounds he made when hungry.

Ip and Famous, her Yorkshire terrier, soon formed a working partnership: Ip would take the laces out of shoes and give Famous the leather to chew on. Ip also had a fondness for electrical cords, and to keep him from electrocuting himself, Mel and Audrey had to disconnect all their lamps.[42]

"For two and a half months it lived in our house," said Mel (see photo 27). "It ate its bowl of pabulum with us in the dining room, and at night it slept in our bathroom. It got so it actually thought Audrey was its mother; professional animal trainers were amazed at the way it followed her around."[43]

Professional viewers were amazed at the way the camera followed Audrey around—and how it rendered her face: *Green Mansions* and *Ben-Hur* were the first two movies to be filmed in Panavision, a new wide-screen process devised to one-up CinemaScope, Todd-AO and VistaVision. Hepburn had disliked the way CinemaScope exaggerated her angular features. Panavision fixed that by means of an anamorphic lens, and soon outpaced CinemaScope as the industry's standard. Its inventor, Robert E. Gottschalk, recalled the excitement at the first rushes: "The people in the projection room—Audrey and Mel among them—all broke out in spontaneous applause."[44] Gottschalk, ever after, would credit Audrey's "square face" for Panavision's success.

Many had predicted trouble on the set between Mr. and Mrs. Ferrer, working together as director and star for the first time. But Audrey's sheer professionalism disappointed the naysayers. It was lights-out at ten, said a friend, "and more frequently than not she is in bed by eighty-thirty or nine p.m. reading until her ten o'clock curfew"—*Dr. Zhivago*, at the time. She also made it clear that she "knew her place" from the start.

"Mel won't have any trouble with me," she said. "I like being directed. I don't know what to do myself. Of course, there are certain things on the set that I have an instinct about. What I do worry about is that I might hesitate to suggest something because I wouldn't want him to think that I'm interfering. Any contribution of mine would be minimal, but sometimes one does think of something, you know."[45]

It sounds painfully servile now, but it was how she truly felt then. Throughout the making of the film, she was as conscientious a wife at the studio as she was at home, according to photographer Bob Willoughby, who shot her at both places: "If the prop man forgot to bring Mel his morning orange juice, she brought it herself. In the afternoon she'd bring him tea and cookies. I think she's the wife of every man's dreams."[46]

Some members of the crew were so unhappy with Ferrer's direction that they threatened to walk off the set. Audrey, on the other hand, "often did things she knew were wrong just because he told her to," says Willoughby. "No matter how idiotic the directions that Mel would give her, while all the other people on the set were rolling their eyes, she would carry them out perfectly, beautifully, without a hint of disagreement, in an effort to help him save face."[47]

One friend said her desire to win admiration from her husband was part of her desire to win admiration from *everyone*; she was too good to be true: "Someday she'll prove it by finally revealing herself to be like the rest of the human race, both good and bad. When she does, there may be an explosion, but she'll be a lot happier than she is now."[48]

Maybe, maybe not. In any event, she certainly won admiration from her choreographer. Mel hired brilliant Brazilian composer Heitor Villa-Lobos to create the score for *Green Mansions* and the great Katherine Dunham to stage its dances—and to coach Audrey.

"I taught her a number of things to help her get into the atmosphere," recalls Dunham. "She had such a wonderful sense of her body and movement. Technique is a way of life—it's holistic—and she was a holistic person. That film allowed her to have a lot of exposure in a natural setting, and she fit into it practically without direction. I remember feeling that I'd love to have had her as a dancer to handle."[49]

Dunham's main choreographic task in the film involved a rite-of-passage ceremony with Henry Silva and the other "Indian" men: Silva's chest is covered with honey and he must wear a "vest" of stinging bees to prove his manliness. That sado-masochistic ritual ends with one of Dunham's most orgiastic male dances—a kind of aboriginal, aberrational bachelor party.

"It was a very exotic film for its day," she says today. "I wasn't terribly happy with the director, but it was none of my business. As in other films that I did, the director seemed to feel competitive about the dance sequences because they were out of his control to some extent. It happened also on *The Bible:* I thought John Huston and I were in agreement about things, but somehow, a lot of the dance was left out."

Dunham thought Hepburn had a hard time working under Ferrer: "I felt that he was not terribly sympathetic to her." But Audrey herself declared otherwise: "Before we began, many friends asked me how such an artistically touchy situation would turn out.... I can say it was pleasantly uncomplicated. I found that being directed by Mel was as natural as brushing my teeth."[50]

She also professed delight with Anthony Perkins as her leading man—the first of her film career to be close to her own age (he was three years younger). Perkins was one of Hollywood's rising new male stars in the wake of his fine performances in *Friendly Persuasion* (1956) and *Fear Strikes Out* (1957). Forced to sing "The Song of Green Mansions" (accompanying himself on the guitar), he did well enough. But his sexual ambivalence—on-and offscreen—did not make for passionate celluloid. Perkins was too quirky and high-strung—as if anticipating Norman Bates in *Psycho* the next year—to be a convincing lover opposite such an ethereal sprite as Hepburn.

How did it feel to have her husband tell another man how to make love to her?

"Uninhibited," said Audrey. "For the first time in my career, I've lost my shyness.... Love scenes have always been difficult for me. But with Mel directing and leading Tony and me through the emotional passages, everything's fallen into place."[51] Indeed, regardless of the film's ultimate success or failure, only under Mel's direct view could she feel free enough to let herself go and attempt a "new," sexier Audrey Hepburn.

Green Mansions was completed in November 1958 and premiered at Radio City Music Hall in Easter Week of 1959—before *Nun's Story*, which had wrapped much earlier but was not released until July. Much to the Ferrers' distress, *Mansions* did not pan out with either the critics or the public—and Mel got the blame.

"If Miss Hepburn won't change husbands, or directors," said one critic who particularly hated the color photography of Joseph Ruttenberg, "she at least owes it to her public to change her brand of toothpaste. In Ferrer's fiasco, she looks as if she had been given an overdose of chlorophyll.... The whole thing has an appalling greenish patina that makes it look as if it had been filmed in a decaying parsley patch."[52]

Variety said it was "likely to confuse those who haven't read the book and irritate those who have." *Cue* thought it "a mawkishly absurd burlesque of a jungle *al fresco* romance."

But a significant minority was favorable. "Hepburn's doe-like grace probably comes closer to a real-life Rima than we have any reason to expect," wrote Arthur Knight in *Saturday Review*. British critic Simon Brett was positively rhapsodic, ranking it as something of a lost masterpiece:

"It is remarkable that it came to be made at all in the year Hollywood produced *I Want to Live*, *The Big Country* and *Gigi*. [Ferrer has] a control, of space and of movement in space, and a taut skill in telling the story in terms of action with the minimum of dialogue. Audrey Hepburn *is* Rima in the same way that she was Ondine." Brett felt it marked the end of the first phase of her career: "Rima was her most complete, indeed an almost abstract, symbol of innocence, and in a sense her last."[53]

The "maligned masterpiece" view, however, is disputed by Audrey's later friend and Lincoln Center Film Society director Wendy Keys: "It was obviously a gesture to please Mel Ferrer, and she put all the effort into it that she put into everything. But *Green Mansions* does nothing to make me believe he had a sense of anything as a director. It's a miserable piece of work."[54]

Green Mansions failed to recoup its $3 million investment and put an end to the professional teaming of Audrey Hepburn and Mel Ferrer once and for all. In a way, it was fortunate to have been eclipsed quickly by the much better and more ballyhooed *Nun's Story*, whose delayed release by Warners helped limit the damage. But *Mansions'* failure was a bitter blow to Mel—the last nail in his coffin as a director-producer. He never directed another Hollywood film.

For all that and the lumps he took, Ferrer is gracious about it today: "Directing Audrey was a delight. It was more a matter of trying to present

Audrey at her grave and touching best than directing her. She knew what
she felt. Revealing it was my job. Perhaps I did not do it well. But Rima
remains alive for me, and the film was a creative effort we were all glad
we tried."[55]

MEL WAS ALWAYS KEENLY INTERESTED in his wife's personal as well as
professional welfare. Her extreme slimness was a career asset but also a
concern: Though generally healthy, she was ten or fifteen pounds underweight and tired easily—not for lack of nutrition, she insisted. She ate
what she wished and did not preserve her figure by dieting, said Audrey.

Yet with food, as all else, she practiced strict discipline and in a sense
dieted every day of her life. It would later be claimed that she suffered
from anorexia or bulimia (see Chapter 9, pp. 303–4), but Mel Ferrer
categorically denies it:

"Audrey never had an eating disorder. She was always very careful
about her diet, did not drink alcohol except an occasional glass of wine
with dinner, and avoided desserts. She chose her diet as a dancer would:
plenty of protein and lots of vegetables and salads. She ate sparingly and
rarely splurged. But we did have a yearly feast of caviar in a baked
potato."[56]

When cooking for guests, she could turn out such gourmet treats as
egg in aspic, rolled stuffed veal or a Dutch apple torte. But her private diet
was indeed simple, as the press's obsessive coverage of her at the time
confirms. "She always eats the same breakfast," reported *Good Housekeeping*
in 1959, going on to itemize "two boiled eggs, one piece of seven-grain
whole-wheat toast from a health-food store, and three or four cups of
coffee laced with hot milk. Her lunch consists of cottage cheese and fruit
salad or of yoghurt with raw vegetables. For dinner, she has meat and
several cooked vegetables."[57]

Five years of near-starvation in Holland left her with a passion for
sweets that she still had to fight. "I have seen her resist the most tempting
dessert to guard against one inch more on her extraordinary size eight,"
said her friend Radie Harris.[58] Said Audrey herself: "I'm glad I like sweet
things—I expect I'd be tubercular if I didn't. But if I ate all I wanted, it
just wouldn't do. I'm getting better. Now if I get a box of good chocolates,
it will last awhile, maybe for two hours. I used to eat them all without
stopping until every last one was gone.... I guess it's a basic form of
insecurity."[59]

There was clearly a deep ambivalence in her attitude toward food,
stemming from her childhood. "When you have had the strength to
survive starvation," she would say, "you never again send back a steak
simply because it's under-done."

These days, under Mel's watchful eye, Audrey's life was as prudent and safe as possible, though he could not insulate her from every danger. After years of reluctance, she now decided to learn how to drive. But soon after getting her license, she crashed into a parked car containing actress-dancer Joan Lora, twenty-two, who suffered neck and back injuries and sued her for $45,000. Reports that Audrey had been drinking or driving on the wrong side of the road were false and, in the end, Lora was awarded just a tenth of what she asked—$4,500. But Audrey was bitterly upset and vowed never to get behind the wheel of a car again.

A much worse accident was in the offing.

THE UNFORGIVEN WAS AUDREY HEPBURN'S first and last Western—and one of the darkest and most peculiar of all time. It was a product of Hecht-Hill-Lancaster Productions (an independent company co-owned by actor Burt Lancaster, producer Harold Hecht and writer James Hill), which had a growing reputation for bold, socially relevant pictures. Their *Marty*, a few years before, had swept the Oscars for Best Picture, Director and Screenplay.

The Unforgiven, under John Huston's direction, was expected to be in that league. It concerned the deep, mindless prejudice against Indians in frontier Texas, and Huston wanted to make a major statement. This was, after all, the early heyday of the American civil-rights movement. But United Artists and Burt Lancaster just wanted a box-office hit.

"I thought I saw in [Ben] Maddow's script the potential for a more serious—and better—film than either he or Hecht-Hill-Lancaster had originally contemplated," said Huston. "I wanted to turn it into the story of racial intolerance in a frontier town, a comment on the real nature of community 'morality.' [But] what they wanted was what I had unfortunately signed on to make in the first place—a swashbuckler.... This difference of intention did not become an issue until we were very close to shooting time, and quite mistakenly I agreed to stick it out, thus violating my own conviction that a picture-maker should undertake nothing but what he believes in.... From that moment, the entire picture turned sour. Everything went to hell."[60]

Huston never confirmed or denied the claim that he took on *The Unforgiven* to fill the time while Arthur Miller polished up the script for his next (and more important) film, *The Misfits*. In any case, *The Unforgiven* had a huge budget for a Western—nearly $6 million. Three hundred thousand dollars alone went into the construction of an 1860 pioneer sod home replica that might have cost $150 originally. Audrey's salary was $200,000, and not everyone thought she deserved it. "She is not an actress, she is a model, with her stiff meager body and her blank face full of good bone structure," wrote Dwight MacDonald at the time. "She has the model's narcissism, not the actress' introversion."

Her director disagreed. "She's as good as the other Hepburn," Huston declared. This was drama, not melodrama. Audrey's role in *The Unforgiven*, in fact, represented a big departure from her previous princesses and saints: an adopted Indian girl entangled not only in the violence and racial nightmares of frontier Texas but, simultaneously, in an incestuous relationship with her brother (Lancaster).

Since Texas no longer resembled itself in the 1860s, Huston decided to film in Durango, Mexico, which retained the primitive look of the early Lone Star panhandle. But at Durango's Casablanca Hotel, where the cast was ensconced, there was some tension. Audrey got along with everybody, but Lillian Gish, playing her mother, developed an intense dislike for costar Audie Murphy. He was then under a serious charge of cattle rustling that required studio influence and the full manipulation of Murphy's World War II hero status to overcome. He also nearly drowned one day in a boating accident on a nearby lake.

Murphy had escaped disaster by inches. Audrey did not. On January 28, 1959, she attempted to ride bareback on a white stallion, aptly named Diablo and formerly owned by Cuban dictator Fulgencio Batista. Determined to do all her own riding in the film, she had firmly rejected the idea of a stand-in, despite her lack of equestrian experience. For hours, she practiced riding around a corral and did well enough for Huston to make some preliminary shots. Mel Ferrer takes up the account from there:

"[As she was] cantering toward the cameras, they decided to retake the scene and stopped the cameras. A horseman was sent out to tell her to ride back slowly. Arabian stallions are very fiery animals. This one saw the other horse coming, stopped short and threw his head down. Audrey had nothing to hold on to and was pitched over the stallion's head."[61]

She landed on her back, before the horrified eyes of the company, including Huston and Lancaster, who rushed toward her with three wranglers to get the horses under control. Before fainting, she had the presence of mind to joke to Lancaster, "I had to do something to get out of this hellhole."[62]

She was sure her back was broken but was far more concerned about her unborn baby—as yet a secret from the world—and about Mel's reaction. He was doing promotional appearances in New York for *Green Mansions* and a guest shot on *What's My Line?* When informed, he immediately flew to Durango, where he found her in capable hands at the local hospital but horribly afraid she might be paralyzed. "I'd hate to see her become another Susan Peters," said Burt Lancaster, with some lack of tact—referring to the rising young film actress who was injured in a 1944 hunting accident and never walked again.[63]

Mel sent for Dr. Howard Mendelson, Audrey's Hollywood physician, who confirmed what the X rays showed: four broken vertebrae, torn muscles in her lower back, and a badly sprained foot. Dr. Mendelson arrived with none other than Marie-Louise Habets—the real-life Sister Luke—who took personal nursing charge of Audrey. "Sister Lou" persuaded her to return on an ambulance plane to California on February 2 and nursed her for the next month, tending to her injuries and salving her conscience for holding up production of the film.

"In thirty years of experience, I never before had a patient like her," said Habets. "She refused all narcotics and sedatives, and despite her pain she never once complained."[64]

Audrey bore her recuperation with regal stoicism indeed. She wrote more than one hundred thank-you notes to her well-wishers in the first two weeks alone, prompting journalist Eleanor Harris to elaborate on the theme of her need for admiration: "Throughout each day, she strives... to be a shining example of good character and good manners." One friend provided an illustrative account of visiting her in the hospital:

> She lay propped up in an immaculate bed in her immaculate bedroom.... She wore a snow-white Victorian high-necked nightgown. Her hair was pulled back mirror-smooth into a pony tail and tied with white ribbon to match the white ribbon on her beautifully groomed little Yorkshire terrier. Around the room stood white Limoges vases with white tulips and orchids.
>
> I noticed that whenever she smoked a cigarette, she stubbed it out in a tiny white ashtray, then put the butt into a wastebasket beside her bed, wiped out the ashtray with a Kleenex, and dropped that too into the basket. Then she replaced the clean ashtray on her bedside table near the framed pictures of her husband, her four stepchildren, and, believe it or not, the horse that threw her. *That* picture, in a white leather frame, had the front position![65]

Her attitude toward the stallion was typically benevolent. In her first phone conversation with Mel after the accident, she had said, "'Don't get angry at the horse! It wasn't the horse's fault,'" Ferrer recalled.[66]

The doctors assured them there was no danger of paralysis. Though there was some hemorrhaging, the fractures were clean breaks, no surgery was needed and there was little to do but let the hemorrhages drain and the fractures heal. She would have to complete the final work on the picture in an orthopedic brace.

She returned to Durango as she left it—on a stretcher—and was back on the set by March 10. Huston welcomed her with fireworks and a mariachi band, and together they reorchestrated her remaining scenes. There was no getting around the fact that, to match the shots made before the accident, she had to ride Diablo once more. But this time he was sedated, she was properly secured, and all went well.

Thirty-five years later, shortly before his death, costar Doug McClure (who played Audrey's younger brother in the film) recalled being mesmerized by her on the set:

> Audrey Hepburn as an Indian girl raised by a frontier family? It was odd because she had that slight English accent. But so many wonderful things were going on inside her, and she *looked* like such a little girl in Lancaster's arms. I thought she played it very realistically. There was a lot of rewriting; between Hecht, Lancaster and John, I don't think they ever really agreed on the ending. . . .
>
> I played chess with Audrey once. She asked me to come to her trailer. She didn't have makeup on, and I hadn't seen her without makeup—but those eyes! We played chess, and she didn't really know how. We talked about her war experience, and she opened up a lot. I was twenty-three, with a bunch of very big stars. I never matched it later.[67]

Hepburn's opening line of dialogue in the film requires her to say "ain't" for the first time on screen—or probably in her life. Chekhov's Three Sisters longed for Moscow; Audrey and her Three Brothers long for Wichita—the symbol of civilization. Director Huston seems to be preparing for *The Misfits:* The violent horse-breaking scenes harbinger those of Clark Gable a year later. Here, the "code of the West" supplies an analogy for the sixties, and the film overall is so shocking as to be almost—but not quite—politically correct. "Red niggers, all of 'em!" screams one character. Gish has a stunning "mad scene" in which she beats the horse out from under a lynching victim, for having revealed her adopted daughter's Indian origin. And in the chilling climax, Lancaster orders McClure, his brother, to "Kill one!", meaning an Indian—*any* Indian—deliberately provoking a massacre and the death of his own mother.

In the midst of the final siege, Audrey asks Burt if he would "fancy her" if he weren't her brother. His answer takes the form of a passionate kiss. Her next move is to shoot and kill her *real* Indian brother outside.

When released in April 1960, *The Unforgiven* was compared by some to George Stevens's *Shane*—a sincere "adult Western" delving into miscegenation. But it was mostly panned. Lillian Gish, who rarely uttered a critical word, would say "Audrey's talent was never used properly in the film." Stanley Kauffmann said it more brutally: "That Huston cannot get a good performance out of Burt Lancaster can hardly be held against him, but he has achieved here what no other director has ever managed: to get a really bad performance out of the lovely Audrey Hepburn."

Huston felt that all the performances but Burt Lancaster's were doomed from the outset. "Some of my pictures I don't care for," he said, "but *The Unforgiven* is the only one I actually dislike.... The overall tone is bombastic and overinflated. Everybody in it is bigger than life. I watched it on television one night recently, and after about half a reel I had to turn the damned thing off. I couldn't bear it."[68]

Many years later, Audrey privately confided that she took the picture seriously and was "very disappointed that Huston did not, and that he showed disdain for it."[69]* In any case, film historian Molly Haskell feels its erotic and emotional subtexts exemplified the Freudian implications of Audrey's *oeuvre* overall:

> In Hepburn's films, a romantically overlaid incest theme, injecting a note of melancholy and unease, crops up over and over in the feverishly heightened love of father-and brother-surrogates. [In *The Unforgiven*], she and Burt Lancaster are raised as brother and sister only to discover that she is actually an Indian, brought up as white, so they are now free to love and marry, thus sealing an attraction that has been felt subliminally throughout the film.... Her frequent pairing with older men was a pattern that [many] were baffled by. She was fated, as Richard Corliss put it, "to be courted by most of Hollywood's durable... senior citizens." The matching vulnerability was the point: where these stars might have looked ridiculous with lustier females, Hepburn rescued them romantically, both within the film and as stars on the decline....
>
> This was the romantic heroine's traditional vocation—to melt the man's inhibitions, urge him on to a discovery of the forgotten parts of himself, including an awakening to love. But Hepburn's compulsion to idealize involves an identification with the man bordering on the morbid.[70]

IN REAL LIFE, THERE WAS no such dark subtext with Audrey's own two half-brothers, who adored their glamorous little sister and kept in regular touch. Elder brother Alexander, his wife, Miep, and their children, Michael and Evelyn, traveled extensively for Bataafsche Petroleum (Shell), moving

---

* John Huston, of course, was legendary for not taking things seriously. In his memoirs, he said his "one joyful memory" during *Unforgiven* shooting was when his friend Billy Pearson, a horse jockey and fellow prankster, came down to visit: "A new luxury golf club outside Durango was celebrating its opening with a major tournament, and an international cast of golfing celebrities was on hand for it. Billy and I ... bought 2,000 ping-pong balls and inscribed them with the most terrible things we could think of: 'Go home, Yankee sons-of-bitches!' 'Fuck you, dirty Mexican carbones!' and similar sentiments. Then we rented a small airplane and dumped [them] on the fairway while play was under way. It was a triumph. Nobody could possibly locate a golf ball. ... The tournament was canceled and everybody was furious—especially Burt Lancaster, who was one of the sponsors and took his golf quite seriously."

from Indonesia to Japan, then Holland, later Brunei and back to Japan again, remaining with Shell until his retirement in 1970. Currently, Alexander had a new two-year assignment to Congo-Leopoldville.

Brother Ian, too, was a one-company man for life. He, his wife Yvonne and their daughter, "Audrey II," lived in Holland, where Unilever's fast-growing personal-products division now included Pepsodent, Elizabeth Arden, Calvin Klein and Helene Curtis cosmetics, and various perfumes. Ian and family had recently paid a surprise visit to *The Nun's Story* set in Rome, during which "Audrey I" made a big fuss over "Audrey II."

There was never a problem with her brothers. But there was the complex, ongoing dilemma of her father. Around this time, her mother wrote her to say she had heard that Ruston died. "I was so distraught," Audrey recalled. "I realized how much I cared.... I just couldn't bear the idea that I wouldn't see him again. Mel said, 'Maybe it's not true.'... He went about finding him, and discovered that he was still living in Dublin."[71]

The joy and the pain of that news were about equal. "He had never tried to reach me, nor did he ever want to see me," she said. "It is hard for children who are dumped. It tortures a child beyond measure.... I never saw him from the time he left when I was six. [But] at age thirty, I had this great need [and] I traveled to Dublin with Mel. My father was living in a tiny apartment, just two rooms.... He looked the way I remembered him. Older, yes, but much the same. Slim and tall. He was married to a woman some thirty-odd years his junior, almost my age."[72]

Ruston would turn 75 that November. Audrey attributed their long separation to "his sense of discretion" and fear that his fascist politics and imprisonment might hurt her reputation. He was up to date on her fame and unsympathetic about her riding accident on *The Unforgiven*: "He had been a great horseman in his youth, and he said to me, 'Of course you were a fool to ride a gray stallion.' He was cross with me for riding a horse that I should have known was likely to throw me."

From then on, she sent him a monthly check and took care of his every need for two decades, until he died in his nineties. "It helped me to lay the ghost [to rest]," she said.[73]

Audrey and Mel's own little family now occupied her mind: She was a happily pregnant woman and, after completion of *The Unforgiven*, returned to Bürgenstock for the duration of her term. But soon after, she miscarried again. "I blamed God," Audrey recalled. "I blamed myself. I blamed John Huston. I was a bundle of anger and recrimination. I couldn't understand why I couldn't have children. Mel and I were so much in love."[74]

Ferrer called it "a tragedy" and said, "It has broken her heart and mine." Audrey went into a deep depression. Her weight fell to ninety-eight pounds, and she was smoking three packs a day. In an effort to snap her out of it, Mel made her keep a commitment to do a six-city tour for the European release of *The Nun's Story* in October 1959. After London, Stockholm and Paris, they went to Amsterdam, where her reception was more subdued than the 1954 mob scene that greeted her. Reporters found her looking tired from the heavy schedule, but she rose to the occasion and gave "clean Dutch answers" to various weighty questions, while Mel stood by and smiled uncomprehendingly.

Was it true that she cried in Stockholm because the authorities would not let her dog enter Sweden?

No, she hadn't.

Was she afraid of a maniac in England who was said to be stalking her there?

No, she wasn't.

Was she going to do another movie directed by her husband?

No, again.

The Nun's Story premiere in Amsterdam was a benefit for the Dutch war-veterans alliance she had long supported. The last and most poignant event on her Netherlands agenda was a side trip the next morning to Doorn, site of the van Heemstras' erstwhile "castle," where one of the town's streets was to be renamed "Audrey Hepburnlaan" in her honor. Amid much pomp and mountains of red roses, she "unveiled" the road that would bear her name. Veterans Alliance president W. C. J. M. van Lanschot said it was originally to have been called "Audrey Hepburn Way," but "way" seemed too modest and they upgraded it to "lane."

She talked to the veterans a bit and then left. "Everybody was very emotional and happy," said the local paper.[75]

EVERYBODY WAS HAPPY EXCEPT AUDREY. In the wake of the miscarriage, family and children were on her mind more than ever. "From the earliest time I can remember, the thing I most wanted was babies," she said later. "My miscarriages were more painful to me than anything ever, including my parents' divorce and the disappearance of my father.[76] ... If and when [a baby] comes along, it will be the greatest thing in my life."

In the meantime, she told a friend. that Christmas, "I must work to forget. Only work can help me; holidays give me time to think, and that's bad for me."[77] Almost in desperation, she turned back to her work. *The Unforgiven* had not helped her career, but neither had it inflicted any great damage. Living in the Swiss Alps left her relatively insulated from Hollywood's self-absorbed obsession with the hits and failures of the moment.

For some time, negotiations had been under way for her to costar with

Laurence Harvey in the forthcoming Alfred Hitchcock film, *No Bail for the Judge*. She would play a London barrister whose magistrate-father is wrongly accused of a murder she sets out to solve herself. Contracts had been drawn up and casting announced in the press, based on her approval of the initial script she had read. But late in the day, she learned that a new scene called for her to be dragged into Hyde Park and raped. It was typical of Hitchcock to humiliate the "pure" heroine—he would do it often, with Grace Kelly, Doris Day, Janet Leigh, Eva Marie Saint and Tippi Hedren. But Hepburn was notoriously squeamish about violence: She had been unable to watch Susan Hayward's execution scene in *I Want To Live* and had allegedly fainted at the premiere of *A Farewell to Arms* during the scene in which Jennifer Jones dies in childbirth.[78]

"I think the reason I did not do the Hitchcock picture was there was another picture that was conflicting," Audrey told Larry King years later.[79] But that was a polite lie.

"Audrey didn't even like to *watch* Hitchcock films," says Rob Wolders. "She thought they were too cynical. When I asked her about this once, she said she had no recollection at all of any joint project. It seems to have been something her agent, Kurt Frings, was arranging on his own that got leaked prematurely."

No Bail for the Judge was first postponed and then canceled entirely, Hitchcock losing $200,000 in the process. By some accounts, he held Audrey responsible for backing out of the project and hated her for it. It was further said that his resentment against her was what motivated him to cast no major stars at all in his next film—a low-budget thing called *Psycho* that became the biggest box-office hit of his career.

Audrey declined some other historic film parts in 1959: The title role in *Cleopatra* eventually went to another Kurt Frings client, Elizabeth Taylor—perhaps luckily for Hepburn—while the female leads in Otto Preminger's *The Cardinal* and Robert Wise's *West Side Story* were taken by Carol Lynley and Natalie Wood. It had nothing to do with the roles: Audrey was pregnant again—and this time, no film work would jeopardize the child.

"Audrey is a mental wreck," said a friend, even as she was ecstatically knitting baby clothes. Though refusing all picture deals, she did accompany Mel to Rome for the making of Roger Vadim's campy horror yarn, *Blood and Roses* (1961), which had the look and feel of an Ed Wood film. Elsa Martinelli and Annette Vadim both try to seduce handsome Ferrer, who has precious little to work with in a vampire film without bite. Hepburn also joined Mel in France while he made *The Hands of Orlac* (costarring her old acting coach, Felix Aylmer), but otherwise stayed close to home, awaiting the birth of her baby.

His arrival came on January 17, 1960, at Lucerne's Municipal

Maternity Clinic. According to a delivery-room nurse, the thirty-year-old Audrey cried out, "Let me see my baby, let me see it at once. Is it all right? Is it really all right?" When told yes, she uttered a cry of relief and then promptly passed out. At nine and a half pounds, he was a big boy for such a diminutive mama. His parents named him Sean, an Irish form of Ian, meaning "Gift of God," in honor of Audrey's brother, who—with Mel's sister, Terry—served as godparents. He was his father's fifth child.

Sean was baptized in the same Bürgenstock chapel and by the same Pastor Maurice Eindiguer who had married Audrey and Mel six years earlier. The baby yelled heartily at that event, prompting Grandma Ella van Heemstra to quote the Dutch maxim, "A good cry at the christening lets the devil out!" Mother and son were then beautifully photographed by Richard Avedon in their Givenchy-designed christening clothes, and the U.S. ambassador to Switzerland, Henry Taylor, Jr., presented the baby with an American passport and a brand new fifty-star American flag.

"Like all new mothers, I couldn't believe at first he was really for me, and I could really keep him," Audrey said to a reporter from Look at the time. "I'm still filled with the wonder of his being, to be able to go out and come back and find that he's still there.... I would like to mix Sean with all kinds of people in all countries, so that he will learn what the world is all about. He should take his own small part in making the world a better place."[80]

When he read those sentiments back in Hollywood, Alfred Hitchcock responded with icy irony: "Every word she said was pregnant with meaning."[81]

Audrey's joy was mixed with anxiety. She fretted about kidnapping and even about the effect the baby would have on her dog: "This may sound silly, but I took special pains to soften the blow to Famous's self-esteem." Mel's self-esteem concerned her, too—if somewhat as an afterthought. "With the baby I felt I had everything a wife could wish for," she said. "But it's not enough for a man. It was not enough for Mel. He couldn't live with himself just being Audrey Hepburn's husband."[82]

FOR MANY, THE ROLE AUDREY Hepburn was "born to play" most of all was Holly Golightly in Breakfast at Tiffany's. Years later, in her oddly restrained way, she called it "the one I feel least uncomfortable watching. But the two things I always think of when I see it are (1) how could I have abandoned my cat? and (2) Truman Capote really wanted Marilyn Monroe for the part."[83]

Capote confirmed it:

"Marilyn was my first choice to play the girl, Holly Golightly. I had seen her in a film and thought she would be perfect for the part. Holly had to have something touching about her... unfinished. Marilyn had that."[84]

Capote had sold the film rights for $65,000 to producers Martin Jurow and Richard Shepherd for Paramount, and they hired George Axelrod to tailor the screenplay for Monroe. "She wanted it so badly," said Capote, "that she worked up two whole scenes all by herself to play for me. She was terrifically good." But Monroe's dramatic advisor, Paula Strasberg, declared "that she would not have her play a lady of the evening." After Monroe's elimination, "Paramount double-crossed me in every way and cast Audrey," said Capote. "She was just wrong for that part."[85]

Holly was a latter-day Manhattan version of Sally Bowles—a cross, said *Time*, "between a grown-up Lolita and a teen-age Auntie Mame." Holly's agent calls her "a phony, all right—but a *real* phony!" She was really a hooker, but Axelrod converted her into a whimsical ingenue and Audrey found her "irresistible." In October 1960, she left Sean in Bürgenstock with her mother and a nanny and flew to New York to begin filming. There, on Fifth Avenue, in her beehive hairdo, Givenchy gown and evening gloves, Holly sipped coffee from a plastic cup, munched a Danish, and broke the hearts of audiences around the world.*

Director Blake Edwards's big casting mistake was Mickey Rooney as Holly's Japanese neighbor Mr. Yunioshi, complete with buck teeth—a portrayal worthy of the worst World War II racial stereotypes. But George Peppard was an attractive Paul, the aspiring novelist with whom Holly falls in love, and Patricia Neal was superb as Paul's "patroness" and Holly's rival. Neal has piquant memories of making the film:

I had only one scene with Audrey, but she was quite friendly and even invited me to her house for supper. Mel was very strict with her during production, so it was one drink, a light meal and good night. I don't think the sun had set by the time I got home. I'd never seen anything so fast in my life. But I sure knew how she kept her looks.

I was a little pissed off because I'd worked at the Actors Studio with [Peppard], and we got along fabulously—he had a crush on me. So I thought, good, I'm happy to be doing this with him. But my God, he had gotten so bigheaded. My character was a society matron known only as 2-E, the apartment she keeps for the writer. I dominated him in the original story, and he didn't want to be seen in that way. He and Blake almost had a

---

* Hepburn hated Danish pastries and could hardly bring herself to nibble on one for that legendary scene outside Tiffany's. She asked director Blake Edwards if she could lick an ice-cream cone instead, but he said no. Only one scene was actually filmed inside Tiffany's, on a Sunday when the store was closed to the public. Twenty security guards kept a nervous eye on all the extras and technicians within snatching range of millions of dollars worth of jewelry. No pilferage was reported.

fistfight. Unfortunately, I said, 'Let's talk about this,' and Blake gave in and shot it his way. I could have killed myself for getting involved. I had fantastic lines, but they wrote my part down [for] gorgeous George. I always felt that had Blake stood his ground, the film would have been stronger.[86]

Audrey, too, found it difficult to work with Peppard, who was then considered a potential new James Dean. Peppard's reliance on Lee Strasberg's version of "The Method" was the opposite of Hepburn's technique—which was no method at all. But in the end, Peppard's significance was minimal. Of far greater impact was a song by Johnny Mercer and Henry Mancini that won the Oscar that year and inspired ninety-seven subsequent recordings.

"Without Audrey, there'd've been no 'Moon River,'" Mancini told documentarist Gene Feldman. "It was one of the hardest songs I ever had to write, because I couldn't figure out what this lady would be singing up there on the fire escape. Would she sing a pop tune? Would she sing something with a blues thing in it? It took me almost a month to figure it out.... Without Audrey there would have been no 'huckleberry friend.' She sang that song with an honesty and such a dedication to the words. She knew what she was doing. She knew what the words were."[87]

"Moon River," Mancini said, was written to explain that Holly was really just a yearning country girl: "One night after dinner, it hit me that it should be very, very simple ... a 'sophisticated country song.' You can play it all on the white keys. You can throw the black keys away and still play it, which is a trick that I wasn't aware of—it just happened."

Mancini's wife Ginny recalls that he "agonized over it for a long time and wanted it to be true to the scene and appropriate for the character. So although it took him a month to figure it out, once he knew where he was going, it only took maybe twenty minutes. He had listened any number of times to her version of 'How Long Has This Been Going On' [in *Funny Face*] and knew she could handle anything within that range."[88]

Asked later if the song's astounding popularity surprised him, Mancini said, "It was the kind of a song that had [success] written all over it, but Johnny Mercer didn't think so. When we were in recording and Audrey sang it with the guitar, Johnny said, 'Boy, that's pretty, but let's get on to something that's going to make some money here!'"

Its first recording was by black singer Jerry Butler. "Andy Williams grabbed it only because he was asked to do the Academy Awards that year," said Mancini. "Columbia Records knew the song and picture were successful, got geared up and put 'Moon River' as title of the album. Tuesday [after the Monday Oscars], it was all over the country and became number one in a matter of weeks."

In a fabulous career of film compositions, "Moon River" was Mancini's biggest hit—"the one that will go down in history as a true folk song," says his wife. "It gets to the heart of the matter and touches people all over the world. It's a haunting melody, plus Johnny's lyrics—that phrase, 'huckleberry friend.' I never look at a full moon on the water anywhere that I don't see a moon river." But amazingly enough, "Moon River" nearly ended up on the cutting-room floor.

"We previewed the movie in San Francisco and went to a nearby hotel to discuss [the] very good audience reaction," Mancini recalled. "We all deferred to Paramount's new president, who paced the room puffing a cigar and whose first utterance was, 'Well, I can tell you one thing, we can get rid of that song.' Audrey shot right up out of her chair and said, 'Over my dead body!' Mel had to put his hand on her arm to restrain her. That's the closest I ever saw her come to losing control."[89]

As in *Funny Face*, Hepburn's singing voice in *Tiffany's* was intimate, evocative and affecting. Its delicate, breathy quality was perfect for the ballad at hand, though technically a weakness that would plague her down the line. But for now, "Moon River" was the song, and Holly the role, through which she became and remained a huckleberry friend to millions.

There are dissenters, of course. "While it may be the archetypical Audrey Hepburn film," says Frank Thompson, "it's nowhere near her best. Blake Edwards's notion of life in the early sixties is stunningly unauthentic—his idea of a swinging party animal is Martin Balsam."[90] Critic Herbert Feinstein at the time dared to compare Hepburn's latest film with that of Brigitte Bardot, *La Vérité*:

Two gorgeous girls, Brigitte Bardot and Audrey Hepburn, trot down the runway of life as Beat anti-heroines. Hepburn [is] violently, pathologically miscast as [Holly]. Blake Edwards has learned a lot—too much—from his television series *Peter Gunn* and *Mr. Lucky*. He has allowed her to eke out a ballad, "Moon River," shot in a phony, oblique angle down an East Side fire escape. And he has encouraged her worst tendencies [to be] charming. . . .

Here we have two crashing beauties, two personalities of around 30 who have been great at playing themselves for a decade, who now have been convinced by their agents and other film cognoscenti that they can act. Worse, the two have convinced themselves and presently aim for art. . . .

Why is it deeply sad to see two accomplished screen personalities essay the Beat girl? . . . Dominique and Holly lie undulating on their night and day beds, lunging after man after man, really from fantasy to fantasy, dragging along their never comforting, never to be comforted, bodies. After a time, nobody wants them. Nobody gets them. There is no need: they get themselves.[91]

Audrey's own initial misgivings about the role, actually, were quite similar to Feinstein's. "Holly," she told Kurt Frings, "is so contrary to me. She frightens me. This part called for an extroverted character. I am an introvert."[92] But Frings had convinced her that it was the role she needed precisely *because* it was so out of character. "When Audrey saw the finished print," he said, "she made no bones about being proud of herself. She said to me, 'This is the best thing I've ever done, because it was the hardest.'"[93]

Years later, she made a rare statement of self-approval to Rob Wolders when they watched *Tiffany's* one night on TV: "She liked the bit when they come out of the shop wearing the animal masks. She laughed at it and said, 'That's rather good!'"

Breakfast at Tiffany's in film form was Truman Capote's greatest commercial success, but he couldn't stand it: "The book was really rather bitter.... The film became a mawkish valentine to New York City and Holly and, as a result, was thin and pretty, whereas it should have been rich and ugly. It bore as much resemblance to my work as the Rockettes do to Ulanova."[94]

He always missed Monroe in the role, but most did not. In the novella, Holly says she's "only had eleven lovers—not counting anything that happened before I was thirteen." One could believe that of Monroe, but never of Hepburn. When asked about it, Audrey said, "I don't think Holly really has known as many men as she pretends. It's just a jazzy facade she creates, because basically she's a small-town girl who's out of her depth."

Audrey from backwater Texas? Not likely. But she took a Monroe role and successfully invested it with her own image—"as svelte as Jackie Kennedy," said critic Michael Sragow. Holly and "Moon River" seemed an integral part of that short-lived Camelot, even as Hepburn's sanitized hooker presented a whole new, minxlike concept of the cinematic slut. The obverse was a mind-boggling impossibility: Marilyn Monroe as Sister Luke?[95]

Breakfast at Tiffany's did well, if not spectacularly, at the domestic box office ($4 million) and better abroad ($6 million). In France, it was called *Diamants sur Canapé—Diamonds on Toast*. Hepburn was nominated for best actress but lost to Sophia Loren in *Two Women*. Of *Tiffany's* nominations, only Mancini's score and song came away with Oscars.*

But women around the world would be quoting Holly's famous put-

---

* Efforts to translate *Tiffany's* into other forms never quite worked: A 1966 Broadway musical version with Richard Chamberlain and Mary Tyler Moore was aborted, as was a proposed television show in 1968. James Parish quotes Capote's complaint that the TV folks wanted to "make a big, boring Audrey Hepburn thing out of it."

down line ("Quel beast!"), in an Audrey Hepburn cadence, for years. And there was one other sociological result of the film: Animal-rescue leagues and pet stores everywhere reported an unprecedented demand for orange cats.

FRIENDSHIP IN THE FILM WORLD is different from that in other occupational spheres—intense to the point of symbiosis during a production, only to terminate abruptly with the conclusion of shooting. Everyone in the film industry who worked with Audrey found her friendly, but very few came away from her with a real friendship. Among those few was beautiful Deborah Kerr, whose delicacy and vulnerability (in person and in persona) were much like Audrey's. They lived near each other in Switzerland, and their real-life relationship was strong—if difficult to describe.

"To the world it might not have seemed that constant or deep an association," says Deborah Kerr today, "but we became very close, even though we didn't see each other much. I couldn't say, 'She was my best friend in my whole life.' Yet in a way, perhaps she was." Kerr and screenwriter Peter Viertel were married on July 23, 1960, and Audrey's gift to Deborah is still fresh in her mind:

"It was a complete outfit from Givenchy. It had its panics because it was sent from Paris to Klosters and hadn't yet arrived on the morning of the wedding. I recall it vividly—cyclamen pink—a fantastic present. It was so Audrey, the thoughtfulness of it. That sums up our relationship, really."

AFTER FINISHING THE *TIFFANY'S* LOCATION work in New York, Audrey had gone to California to do the bulk of interior shooting in the studio. She and Mel rented a house in Coldwater Canyon, where—to her great relief—they were joined by Sean and Sean's nanny for Christmas. Living there without her baby would have been unendurable. The older she got, the less she liked Hollywood, where her only close friends were Connie and Jerry Wald and, to some extent, the Pecks and the Wilders.

Kurt Frings had tried to foster a friendship between Audrey and his other great star-client, Elizabeth Taylor, who had returned to Los Angeles to convalesce from a near-fatal bout with pneumonia in England. Taylor was then married to crooner Eddie Fisher, whose career was then on the skids as a result of public outrage for his dumping of the much-loved Debbie Reynolds to marry Liz. Mel helped Eddie pick and prepare material for his "comeback" nightclub act at the Desert Inn in Las Vegas.

The Ferrers and the Fishers saw a lot of each other in those days, perhaps partly because of a common dilemma between the men: fabulously beautiful wives whose success outshone their own. They had been together at the previous year's Oscar ceremony, when Taylor was a sympathy winner for the inferior *Butterfield 8*, and the women remained fond of each other for life.

Just after New Year's, on January 8, 1961, Audrey delivered a lovely original poem titled, "What is a Gary Cooper?", at a Friars Club testimonial dinner in Hollywood for her old costar, whose terminal illness was not widely known. Cooper died of cancer, at sixty, the following May.

Otherwise, Hepburn rarely appeared in public or spoke to the press. But one day toward the end of *Tiffany's* retakes on the Paramount lot, a reporter cornered her and asked what role she most wanted to play next. "That's easy to answer," she said. "I'd do anything to play Eliza Doolittle in *My Fair Lady*."

IT WAS A BIT PREMATURE to be thinking about Eliza but never too soon to ponder the next film, even though she preferred her temporary retirement. For as long as possible, she held off a decision, accompanying Mel now and then to his own shootings in France and Yugoslavia, but turning down all offers for herself, reportedly including *A Taste of Honey* and *In the Cool of the Day*. But soon enough, instead, she accepted one of the most controversial roles of her career.

Lillian Hellman's *The Children's Hour*, that playwright's first major success, enjoyed a 601-performance Broadway run in 1934. It was loosely based on Scotsman William Roughhead's story *Bad Company*, about two Edinburgh teachers accused of lesbianism in 1810 by a student whose grandmother spreads the gossip and ruins the school. In Hellman's drama, Martha discovers her love for Karen only after the slander. In a final monologue, she cries, "I'm guilty! I've ruined your life, and I've ruined my own. I feel so damn sick and dirty I just can't stand it anymore." A scene of the play that never appeared on film makes clear that she commits suicide because she really *is* a lesbian: It is not the lie that destroys her, but the awful truth.[97]

The play's first film rendering was the 1936 *These Three*, directed by William Wyler, starring Merle Oberon as Karen and Miriam Hopkins as Martha. Lesbianism being a taboo subject, the story was turned into a heterosexual triangle in which the one woman was accused of being in love with the other's fiancé. Hellman's basic theme—that a lie had the power to destroy people's lives—survived, but any mention of her "lesbian play" was forbidden by the censors. Said *Variety*: "It is verboten to ballyhoo the original source."

Oberon and Hopkins both turned in fine performances in *These Three*, and so did Joel McCrea. But the film was stolen by fabulous Bonita

Granville as evil little Mary. Just thirteen at the time, she won an Oscar nomination for her trouble—long before Patty McCormack's similar work in *The Bad Seed*.

Exactly twenty-five years later, many were stunned by the news that Audrey Hepburn and Shirley MacLaine would star in a remake. The new version, like the original, would be directed by William Wyler, who wanted Oberon and Hopkins to return in the supporting roles of Mary's grandmother and Martha's aunt. Hopkins said yes. Oberon said no, and Fay Bainter took the grandmother's part. Hellman began work on the new script but soon dropped out due to the terminal illness of her beloved Dashiell Hammett. She was replaced by John Michael Hayes, a Hitchcock favorite (*Rear Window, To Catch a Thief*), who worked hard to restore the lesbian angle and update the picture to the 1960s.

"When we made the picture the last time," said Wyler, "what we put out was a watered version. We couldn't put it on the way we wanted to because the public wasn't ready for that sort of thing yet. Now, they are."[98]

Wyler had initially toyed with the intriguing combination of Doris Day and Katharine Hepburn for his leads. In settling on the younger Hepburn and MacLaine, he cast two women who were *both* perceived more as comediennes than tragic heroines. To say the least, it was casting against type, especially for Audrey: The idea of lesbianism ran counter to her image in every way. "The reason I chose Audrey is that she is so clean and wholesome," said Wyler. "I don't want bosoms in this." He had directed her great debut hit, *Roman Holiday*. "We are in [such] close communication we hardly have to talk," said Audrey. "I know when he feels it's wrong." She trusted him implicitly to guide her in breaking this new and possibly dangerous ground.

Wyler and Otto Preminger were then engaged in a bitter battle within the industry. Censorship of scenes such as the Tony Curtis-Laurence Olivier bath sequence in *Spartacus* prompted protests from producers and directors in Hollywood that they could not compete with foreign films that dealt openly with homosexuality. In the summer of 1961, the Mirisch Company, co-producers of *Children's Hour*, attacked the ban against "sex perversion" on screen. In September, Preminger announced he would shoot the Allen Drury novel *Advise and Consent* with its homosexual episodes intact. On October 3, 1961, the Motion Picture Association caved in and announced a change in its Code: "In keeping with the culture, the mores and the values of our time, homosexuality and other sexual aberrations may now be treated with care, discretion and restraint."

In the early sixties, says Vito Russo in *The Celluloid Closet*, homosexuality was "the dirty secret exposed at the end of the last reel," most often a false accusation against a heterosexual character. *The Children's Hour* was the first film to receive an MPAA Code seal after the sexual rules were changed—but with bland results. Shirley MacLaine laid the blame on Wyler:

> In the play, scenes were developed so that you could see Martha falling in love with Karen [but Wyler] thought they'd be too much for Middle America to take. I thought he was wrong, and I told him so, and Audrey was right behind me. But he was the director, and there was nothing we could do. Even so, I conceived my part as though those scenes were still there. I didn't want it to suddenly just hit her when the child tells the lie that maybe she could really be a lesbian.... Lillian had written a slow examination of one woman's personal growth in the area of falling in love with another woman. But Willie Wyler didn't want that.[99]

Audrey was even more nervous than usual, insisting that both Sean and Famous be with her on the set every day. She and MacLaine had gone into the picture with great enthusiasm and confidence in a director they adored. But both were disappointed by the many nuances of their characters' relationship that ended up on the cutting-room floor. Wyler, almost up to the picture's release, wanted to tack on a semi-happy ending suggesting that, after MacLaine's suicide, Hepburn and Garner get together.

Despite all its compromises, *Children's Hour* was attacked for "condoning lesbianism, albeit surreptitiously," even by such normally enlightened publications as *Films in Review*: "There is an explicit scene which asserts that those who choose to practice lesbianism are not destroyed by it—a claim disproved by the number of lesbians who become insane or commit suicide."[100]

Young Karen Balkin as Mary did not measure up to Granville in *These Three*, though Miriam Hopkins was wonderful and Fay Bainter as the grandmother superb in this, her last role, for which she received an Oscar nomination. But the film suffered from the uninspired performance of James Garner, star of TV's *Maverick* series and distinctly out of place here.

Time even attacked Audrey for giving "her standard, frail, indomitable characterization, which is to say that her eyes watered constantly (frailty) and her chin is forever cantilevered forward (indomitability)." MacLaine's notices were better. A more versatile actress than Hepburn, she turned her climactic confrontation scene with Bainter and her final breakdown into a powerfully emotional tour-de-force.

Children's Hour was nominated for five Oscars, all of which it lost. But they had dared to do it. A consolation for Hepburn lay in the personal experience with her costar—and vice versa:

"I had plenty of qualms about Audrey when we met for the first rehearsal," said MacLaine, "but from then on, working with her was one big kick.... Audrey and I decided we'd throw a party for the cast and the crew when the picture was finished. We went all out, had it catered by Romanoff's—nothing but the best. In the middle of the party, Audrey sidled up to me, jabbed me with her elbow and said, out of the corner of her mouth, 'Hey, Shirl-Girl, whattaya think the bruise is gonna be for this bash?' "[101]

NOT FOR NOTHING WAS FAMOUS on "doggie downers"—tranquilizers to calm him down in general, but especially around automobiles and on canine social visits. "She was ga-ga over that dog," remembers Billy Wilder. "She was ga-ga over all the dogs that she had, and she always had one."

"Yippy, yappy, jumpy ones," adds Audrey Wilder. "One day she brought Famous over to see my little female named 'Fifty.' She was much smaller than Famous—same breed, same year, a Yorkie. We had the same lady breeder in Paris, and she named them with the same letter of the alphabet each year. Audrey said, 'Famous is absolutely perfectly behaved.' So he came into our little apartment, took one look at Fifty, and peed on every single chair. She went crazy—'Oh, my God, what are you doing?' I put him out in our backyard, but Famous was strong. He pushed open that gate. I looked out and he was taking Fifty up and down Wilshire Boulevard, smelling all the bushes."[102]

The Ferrers were then renting a place on Sunset Boulevard, and not long after his visit with Fifty, Famous escaped and ran into the street. Before he could be recaptured, he was hit by a car, to the horror of Audrey, who heard a commotion and ran out to find his mangled body stopping traffic.

Her devastation filled her with an even deeper aversion to Los Angeles, from which she was always looking to escape. She now took herself and Sean to Paris, where Mel presented her with the only thing that might dry her tears—a new Yorkshire terrier named Assam of Assam, who looked a lot like Famous and gradually came to replace him in her affection.

Mel would be in France for many months, working on *The Longest Day* (1962), one of the last great World War II epics—Darryl F. Zanuck's $15 million rendering of the Allied invasion of Normandy. Ferrer, as Major General Robert Haines, shared billing with most of the major male film stars of the day: John Wayne, Rod Steiger, Robert Ryan, Robert Mitchum, Henry Fonda, Richard Burton, Sean Connery, Sal Mineo, Jeffrey Hunter, Roddy McDowall, Eddie Albert, Robert Wagner and Kurt Jurgens.

In view of Audrey's skittishness about violent World War II films, she was not with him steadily and spent most of her time with Sean in

Bürgenstock. Mostly, she wanted to relax after her two tiring, closely-spaced films of the previous year. She was less keen than ever on rushing into a new picture, but, as always, others were keen on her behalf.

"You have all the qualities of Peter Pan," Fred Astaire had sung to her in *Funny Face*. Others thought so, too, including George Cukor, who wanted to make a *Peter Pan* with Audrey in the sixties. "Reliable reports" now claimed Audrey had agreed to appear opposite Peter Sellers as Captain Hook and Hayley Mills as Wendy. But there were legal problems on both sides of the Atlantic—with the Great Ormond Street Hospital for Sick Children in London, which owned the rights to the play, and with the Walt Disney company, whose 1953 cartoon version was still in release. Much as she wanted to assay the role, it was not in the cards.

Another report had it that Hitchcock was ready to forgive her for backing out on him previously and to cast her in his next frightful outing *The Birds*. But Audrey was averse to having her eyes pecked out, and the role went to Tippi Hedren.

From now on, Hepburn *the mother* was less inclined to make films in general, and when she did so, her decision was based as much on convenience and logistics as on the merits of the script. The proposed director and costars were important, of course, but the necessity for a tight shooting schedule and a European location were even more important. And if the location happened to be Paris, it was much easier to get her to say yes.

Those circumstances now dovetailed with the fact that her Paramount contract expired at the end of 1962 and she still owed the studio one more picture. So, by coincidence, did William Holden. Production head Martin Racklin, cognizant of the two stars' mutual fondness, hit on the solution of teaming them in a to-be-announced script by George Axelrod, who recalls:

"I got a call one day from Paramount saying, 'We have a problem here—we have Audrey and Bill Holden under old contracts and they both want to shoot in Paris next summer. Do you have something?'" He pauses for effect, then poses the rhetorical question: "What would you have said?"[103]

Thus was Axelrod, still basking in the success of his *Tiffany's* screenplay, tapped to provide his magic touch again. Borrowing a phrase from Cole Porter's "I Love Paris," he called the script *Paris When It Sizzles*. He borrowed the story, as well, from Julien Duvivier's *La Fête à Henriette (Holiday for Henrietta)*, a 1952 film starring Hildegard Knef. Paramount wanted Blake Edwards to direct, but he had prior commitments and recommended his close friend Richard Quine, who had directed Holden in *The World of Suzie Wong* and knew how to control Holden's heavy drinking—or so he thought.

Holden lived in Switzerland near Lausanne, where he was pursuing a fitful affair with French actress Capucine, a former high-fashion model and one of the great beauties of Europe. Born Germaine Lefebvre, she had fashioned her solo stage name on the French word for "nasturtium" and would play a role in Holden's and Hepburn's lives up to the tragic end of her own.

Holden agreed to *Paris When It Sizzles*. It remained only to convince Audrey. Quine made the pilgrimage to Bürgenstock, where he found her jittery about several things. For one thing, Ferrer was preparing to leave for an extended shoot in Madrid, where he featured in yet another all-star epic, *The Fall of the Roman Empire*, with Sophia Loren, Alec Guinness and James Mason. But Audrey was most jittery about reuniting with Holden, who was said to be still wildly in love with her. In the end, Quine overcame her qualms with the lure of Paris and of the lavish expense-account perquisites she would enjoy.

Filming of *Paris When It Sizzles* began in July 1962 at Studios de Boulogne in Paris, with a bad omen right off the bat. Just after she left for France, Audrey's Bürgenstock chalet was burgled. The main items taken seemed to be her *Roman Holiday* Oscar and her underwear. The former was soon recovered in the nearby woods; the latter was never seen—at least by Audrey—again. The thief was a twenty-two-year-old science student named Jean-Claude Thouroude, who turned himself in and told the judge he was motivated by his passion for Audrey and the hope that he'd get to meet her at his trial. She stayed away in a proper huff. He got a fine and a suspended sentence from the avuncular magistrate, who opined, "Love is not a crime!"[104] All over Europe, people were amused by the outcome—the Ferrers not among them.

(It wasn't the first or the last bizarre crime involving Audrey. The previous year, a thief in Australia broke into the Paramount Pictures vault in Sydney, ignored hundreds of more valuable films, and made off only with *War and Peace*, *Funny Face*, *Sabrina* and *Roman Holiday*. "It looks as though whoever stole the films had a wild crush on Audrey Hepburn," speculated a Paramount spokesman, by way of the obvious.)[105]

Meanwhile on the set, there was some unanticipated sizzling over the choice of cinematographer. Audrey watched the first rushes and loathed what she considered the unflattering results by cameraman Claude Renoir, nephew of the great director Jean. She insisted he be replaced by Charles Lang.

"Audrey could be very, very critical of herself on screen," Richard Quine recalled. "She just hated the way that she and Bill Holden looked, which wasn't necessarily Claude Renoir's fault, but I had no option but to discharge him. Of course, firing a Renoir is tantamount to treason in France, so the unions raised hell and threatened to go out on strike."[106]

The lady got her way on that point. But her well-grounded fears on the subject of Holden were not so easily dismissed or resolved. "The day I arrived at Orly Airport to make *Paris When It Sizzles*," Holden told his friend Ryan O'Neal, "I could hear my footsteps echoing against the walls of the transit corridor, just like a condemned man walking the last mile. I realized I had to face Audrey again, and that I had to deal with my drinking, and I didn't think I could handle either situation."[107]

He was right. Holden's casting opposite Hepburn was doomed from the start. He was tormented by being with her again, and by his own worsening inadequacies. Drinking more heavily than ever, he often arrived drunk on the set, flirting with dismissal. Axelrod remembered the night Holden climbed a tree by a wall leading up to Audrey's room. Like Rapunzel, she came to her window and leaned out, whereupon Holden kissed her—and then slipped and plunged from the tree, landing atop a parked car below. His wife Ardis—"bitter and frustrated," said Audrey Wilder—arrived on the scene and harangued him, to no effect. The coup de grace in Paris was his purchase of a new Ferrari that he promptly drove into a wall, further delaying the picture.

In the dubious *Paris When It Sizzles* script, Holden was a screenwriter who can't get his story right and keeps trying to reinvent it with the secretarial and romantic assistance of Audrey, who helps act out his fantasies. Director Quine was striving for a frothy kind of Cary Grant comedy, but Holden wasn't up to it, and Hepburn seemed embarrassed most of the time.

The delays were costing a fortune and Paramount threatened to shut down the production by the time Quine finally persuaded Holden to enter the Château de Garche, an alcoholic recovery hospital, to dry out. He then imported a new guest star—Tony Curtis—who provides his own candid account:

The joke for years after that, when anybody asked how to account for a budget increase, was, "Charge it off to the profits of *Paris When It Sizzles*." I was in London when I got a call from Dick Quine: Bill Holden's liver was really in bad shape. He'd gone out drinking in Paris, and now he couldn't work. It was going to take him a week to recover. Paramount told Quine, "You don't shoot, we shut down."

So Dick said, "Tony, please come and do three or four days. They'll let us run if you'll do that." I said okay and flew to Paris, and they put me up at the George Cinq and gave me some cash. Axelrod and Quine frantically wrote a couple of new scenes, and I worked with Audrey. I did about five or six days, and then finally Holden came back to work. They just needed to fill that time. They had to come up with something, and what they came up with was me.[108]

In the end, several of the film's few funny moments belonged to Curtis as a hip Hollywood heartthrob who keeps appearing when least expected. He's a spoofed-up version of Curtis himself—a cool cat in tight pants, tossing off sixties jargon: "Like, bon jour, baby! Groovy! But I'm gonna have to split." Thanks to Tony, the picture kept rolling, and so did the meter.

Poor Quine was besieged on all fronts.* He had a male star who couldn't stay sober and a female star who was racked by insecurities. Audrey these days had renewed an old obsession about her crooked front tooth and spoke constantly of having it fixed. Quine loved the singularity of the thing and threatened "to absolutely maim her if she changed that tooth."[109]

In addition to Curtis, Quine was calling in every other "star chit" he had in an effort to salvage a very moribund affair. Marlene Dietrich and Noel Coward agreed to make cameo appearances, against their better judgment. Coward's ego needed the gig more than Dietrich's, as his 1962 diary entries suggest:

September 25: George Axelrod rang me up and asked me to play a small... part in the movie he is doing with Audrey Hepburn and Bill Holden. He hurried the script to me and the scene is effective although tiny, but I am being paid $10,000 and all luxe expenses, and so I said yes. I think it will be rather fun. The part is that of a Hungarian movie producer (Alex Korda?) dressed in a Roman toga at a fancy dress party. I shall enjoy doing the accent. . . .

October 1: George A said that they did not want me to play the part with an accent but to be super Noel Coward. This rather threw me; [but] it worked like a charm and I have never had such a fuss made.... Audrey H, unquestionably the nicest and most talented girl in the business, deluged me with praise and roses. Bill Holden, off the bottle and looking 15 years younger, absolutely charming to work with. We exchanged confidences and bottles of eau de cologne in the interminable waits.... George showed me about half of the rough-cut; it really is funny and Audrey and Bill are enchanting. So is Tony Curtis and so, apparently, am I.[110]

Hepburn didn't share his enchantment. "She really hated it," says her nephew Michael Quarles van Ufford, Ian's son, who visited her then on

---

* Richard Quine (1920–1989) was a child prodigy actor-singer-dancer who appeared in many films with the great juvenile stars of the '30s and '40s before becoming a director in adulthood. Among his hits was *My Sister Eileen* (1955) and *Bell, Book and Candle* (1958). In 1943, he married actress Susan Peters, who was shot and paralyzed in a hunting accident a year later. Quine was guilt-ridden about the accident and took his own life on June 10, 1989.

the *Sizzles* set. "She had to get up at four, the limousine would come and fetch her around six, and she would come back at eight at night, exhausted. She'd say, 'All this was for five minutes of filming today.'"[111]

When finally completed, wildly overbudget, Paramount recognized it as a dud and shelved it for two years. It did not improve with age and got a disastrous reception when finally released in 1964 (two years *after* Hepburn's subsequent film).

"Axelrod's dialogue and Holden's gift for comedy amply deserve each other," wrote Stanley Kauffmann. "Noel Coward is briefly on hand at his most repellent." Hollis Alpert in *Saturday Review* called it "a dreadfully expensive display of bad taste." Judith Crist checked in with, "*Paris When It Sizzles?* Strictly Hollywood when it fizzles."

More ridicule was in store as a result of the on-screen credit, "Miss Hepburn's wardrobe and perfume by Hubert de Givenchy." The fragrance was L'Interdit, created for her by Givenchy in 1957. Hepburn chronicler Warren Harris observed it was "the first time since the 1960 *Scent of Mystery* (produced in the Smell-O-Vision process) that a movie left itself wide open for critical branding as a stinker."

IF NOTHING ELSE, THE EMBARRASSMENT of such reviews was postponed for a couple of years. A more immediate embarrassment for Audrey was her fraying relationship with Mel. Ferrer was still working on *The Fall of the Roman Empire* in Madrid, where he was often seen out and about with such ladies as "the vivacious" Duchess of Quintanilla. The gossip columnists had plenty to work with: Hepburn was carrying on with Holden again, they said, "in retaliation." Audrey was furious about the reports and—quite rare for her—lashed out publicly at the writer "who started all that talk while Mr. Holden and I were making *Paris When It Sizzles*. The only thing that really happened was that Bill cracked up his expensive Ferrari one day and came around on crutches. And all I did was 'mother' him a little. Anyway, I'm glad that Capucine is now getting all the publicity."[112]

Mel took it all in stride, stiffly preserving his dignity and exhibiting no special jealousy—which annoyed Audrey even more. In his view, they had survived a variety of marital strains, and would survive the current ones. But the separation and tensions between them were taking a greater toll on Audrey, who now relayed to him her feeling that they should consider divorce. Shocked into action, Mel flew home to talk things over, and the rift was patched up—for the moment.

Thirtysomething years later, the Wilders supply their own piquant view of Hepburn's dilemma:

"I did not think Mel was the proper husband," says Billy, "but then, who *would* have been the proper husband for her?"

It's rhetorical but draws a reply from his wife.

"Well, Bill was a nice guy," answers Audrey Wilder. "Bill would have been better—if he'd been sober."[113]

THERE WAS A GOOD REASON why Audrey now suddenly extended her lease on the lovely old Bourbon chateau she was renting near Fontainebleu: A brand new Paris-based movie had materialized unexpectedly on the heels of *Paris When It Sizzles*—a picture that, for once, she didn't have to be coaxed into but very much wanted to do. It was the best of two worlds for her—a Hitchcock-style thriller without Hitchcock—and filming began exactly one day after *Sizzles* shooting ended.

The delicious soufflé was called *Charade*—a romantic comedy-thriller caper and landmark of its style. Stanley Donen, one of Hepburn's true favorites, would direct in their first reteaming since *Funny Face*. Best of all for Audrey and posterity, Cary Grant would star. She had never worked with him and longed to do so. The script was a both a send-up and celebration of the genre and the great Hitchcock-Grant collaborations of the past.

"I always wanted to make a movie like one of my favorites, *North by Northwest*," said Donen. "What I admired most was the wonderful story of the mistaken identity of the leading man. They mistook him for somebody who didn't exist; he could never prove he wasn't somebody who wasn't alive. I searched [for something with] the same idiom of adventure, suspense and humor."[114]

What he found—and bought—was a short story, "The Unsuspecting Wife," by Peter Stone and Marc Behn, published in *Redbook*. It was the tale of a beautiful widow who is hounded by a group of unsavory rogues looking for her dead husband's hidden fortune. The structure and tone were full of smart dialogue, red herrings, single and double bluffs, and Parisian style.

"It was a wonderful piece of work," says James Coburn, the superb character actor who gave one of his most wryly villainous performances in *Charade*. "Peter Stone knew Paris very well because he'd lived there as a writer on the Île de France, right by Notre Dame. Did you know that he wrote it specifically for Cary Grant and Audrey Hepburn?"[115]

A lot of people wrote a lot of things specifically for Grant and Hepburn. But getting them to do something—separately, let alone jointly—was another matter.

Audrey said yes quickly, but "Cary thought he was going to do a picture with Howard Hawks called *Man's Favorite Sport?* [and so he] said

1. The face that would launch two dozen features: Audrey Hepburn-Ruston's unique features, remarkably in place at five, show no sign of the social "shock treatment" from being sent to an English boarding school that year.

(COURTESY OF THE AUDREY HEPBURN ESTATE)

Act 1

2. Baroness Ella van Heemstra misses—but the camera catches—her seventeen-year-o
daughter's somber look that reflects their relationship, Amsterdam, 1946.
(ARCHIVE PHOTOS, COURTESY OF THE AUDREY HEPBURN ESTATE)

3. British and American
paratroops dropping—
many of them to their
deaths—on Day One of
the disastrous Battle of
Arnhem, September 17,
1944. (ARCHIVE PHOTOS,
COURTESY OF ERIC RACHLIS
AND JANET SOMMER)

4. Engaging in gauging (top): On the *Lavender Hill Mob* set (1951), Audrey and Alec Guinness briefly share the limelight, while the hand of the photographer Douglas Slocombe measures it. (Bottom) The freshly engaged chorine: In her only known bikini shot, Hepburn shares the sunlight with fiancé James Hanson, heir to the British transport fortune, at the time of their betrothal and of *Lavender Hill Mob*'s release. (EALING STUDIOS, BARRY PARIS COLLECTION; AND COURTESY OF LORD JAMES HANSON)

5. Hopeful hoofers Hepburn and Babs Johnston, waiting and worrying in the Hippodrome's melancholy wings during London auditions for *High Button Shoes*, December 1948. (BARRY PARIS COLLECTION)

6. Sister-heroines-in-exile: Valentina Cortesa, the reluctant radical, adoringly watches Audrey Hepburn, aspiring ballerina, in Thorold Dickinson's dark political drama, *Secret People* (1952)—Hepburn's most important British film. (PHOTOFEST)

7. Hepburn soaks up instruction at the feet and on the shoulder of Colette, creator of Gigi's character on the page and of Audrey's chance to render her on the stage. (ARCHIVE PHOTOS)

8. Mel Ferrer, the carnival puppeteer, and two of his alter egos work to cheer up orphan Leslie Caron in *Lili*, the "sleeper" film musical of 1953. (ARCHIVE PHOTOS)

9. A candid snapshot from Rome, perhaps? Audrey looks deliciously casual: In fact, she's in Hollywood on the set of *Sabrina*, fully costumed and made-up as the chauffeur's daughter a few moments before shooting a scene.

(PHOTO BY MARK SHAW FOR *LIFE*, COURTESY OF PHOTO RESEARCHERS & SUZANNE GOLDSTEIN)

PART III: AMERICA'S ARTS AND SKILLS
THE AGE OF HOMESPUN
RUSSIA'S NEW FRIENDLY PITCH
PHOTOGRAPHED IN MOSCOW BY LEONARD McCOMBE

ITALIAN FARM
REY HEPBURN

WHY MORE AND MORE MINISTERS CRACK UP
NEW PHOTOS EXPOSE A HISTORIC HOAX:
THE CASE OF DR. COOK AND MT. McKINLEY

AUDREY HEPBURN
AS TOLSTOY HEROINE
IN 'WAR AND PEACE'

20 CENTS
AUGUST 20, 1956

WHAT MAKES AUDREY CHARM

MISS HEPBURN AT HOME

20 CENTS
DECEMBER 7, 1953

IN COLOR: TH
A LIFE TOU
JUDGE LEIBOW

AUDREY HEPBURN
'THE NUN'S STORY'

MEMORABLE MOMENTS OF THE
EXCLUSIVE POLISH ELECTION
SOCIETY'S STERN DANCING

HEPBURN AND FERRER,
PREVIEW OF TV 'MAYERLING'

20 CE
FEBRUARY

111 COLOR PAGES FOR EASTER
THE GLORY AND
BEAUTY OF ROME

BEN CASEY
The Doctor
Challenges the
Cowboy on TV

ALSO THIS WEEK
An Important
Report
by SYLVIA
PORTER
Your Stake
in the
Common Market

SPRING...
...and a New Hat
for Audrey
Hepburn

APRIL 20 · 1962 · 20¢

10. Center: In her first cover outing for *Life* (December 7, 1953), the straight-faced gamine reveals an alluring phone manner and much more thigh than her Dutch mother condoned. Surrounding are the five other Audrey Hepburn appearances on *Life's* cover over the decades. (©1953, 1955, 1956, 1957, 1959 AND 1962, *LIFE* MAGAZINE AND TIME INC.)

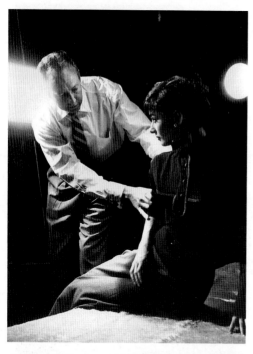

11. Paramount Studios, 1953:
Photographer Bud Fraker guides Audrey
through her first formal portrait session
in Hollywood.

(PHOTO BY BOB WILLOUGHBY)

ABOVE:

12. Even that most unglamorous activity
was subject to Hepburn's stylish
transformation: In 1953, long before a
cigarette holder became Holly
Golightly's symbol, the real-life Audrey
turns a sow's-ear location into a silk-
purse Kodak moment.

(PHOTO BY MARK SHAW FOR *LIFE*,
COURTESY OF PHOTO RESEARCHERS)

13. Audrey and costume designer Edith
Head had what one mutual colleague
termed "a sincere and truly nerdy
friendship." Head marveled most at
Hepburn's waist, "the slimmest since the
Civil War, nineteen-and-a half inches—
you could get a dog collar around it!"
(Someone once actually did so.)

(PHOTO BY BOB WILLOUGHBY)

14. Hepburn and Ferrer on Broadway in *Ondine* (1954): The watersprite's eternal youth and innocence prove unbearable, in the end, to her faithless Knight Errant. (PHOTOFEST)

15. *Ondine* director Alfred Lunt, caught literally and figuratively between his costars' deceptive smiles. (ARCHIVE PHOTOS)

16. Honeymooners Audrey Hepburn and Mel Ferrer, fresh and refreshed from Italy, arrive at the Dorchester Hotel in London, January 1954.

17. Jumping for joy and for photographer Philippe Halsman: One of the finest in Halsman's famous series of celebrity jumps, from the October 1955 *Cosmopolitan*.

18. On the set of *Funny Face* in Paris: Hepburn as the bookworm-turned-fashion-plate—"a perfectly balanced mixture of intelligence and froth"—with her designer-for-life, Hubert de Givenchy. (MGM / TURNER, BARRY PARIS COLLECTION)

. "Winged Victory" is her ckdrop for a shoot at the Louvre *Funny Face:* Hepburn descends a aircase with terrifying speed and ly the Givenchy gown to protect r from Lynn Fontanne's perilous vice: "My dear, never look down d don't hold your skirt." GM / TURNER, BARRY PARIS LLECTION)

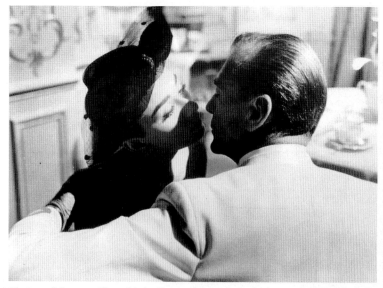

20. One of director Billy Wilder's efforts to finesse the scandalous age difference between his stars in *Love in the Afternoon* (1956): The only excuse for the shadow hiding half of Hepburn's face is that it hides *all* of Gary Cooper's. (ARCHIVE PHOTOS)

21. William Holden rests his injured pride and posterior in the hammock-sling, thoughtfully designed by his brother (and Sabrina rival) Humphrey Bogart, with a hole in the middle. (ARCHIVE PHOTOS)

22. On location in Africa for *The Nun's Story* (1958): A contemplative photo study of the relationship between Hepburn and director Fred Zinnemann, as they talk out a troubling scene. (WARNER BROS.)

23. If a celebrity visited the set of a Richard Quine movie, he often ended up in it—as Tony Curtis (left, with Robert Wagner and Hepburn) found out during the chaotic *Paris When It Sizzles.* (PHOTO BY BOB WILLOUGHBY)

24. The most beloved Hepburn film image of all: Holly Golightly on the outside looking in, munches her Danish and sips Dixie-cup coffee in the wistful opening window shot of *Breakfast at Tiffany's* (1960). (COURTESY OF JOHN BARBA)

25. Hepburn the stenographer and Holden the blocked writer —as the incongruous Guinevere and Lone Ranger— two fantasies too many in the doomed comedy *Paris When It Sizzles* (1963). (COURTESY OF LEONARD MALTIN)

26. Shirley MacLaine and Audrey during a maternity break on the set of *The Children's Hour* (1961): The tormented screen lesbian and her love-object with the latter's real-life son, Sean Ferrer.

(PHOTO BY BOB WILLOUGHBY)

27. At home in Hollywood, Audrey bonds with Ip the fawn, her quadruped costar in the exotic *Green Mansions* (1958). Her biped costar was Anthony Perkins, but the deer got better reviews.

(PHOTO BY BOB WILLOUGHBY)

28. The Odd Couples as a quartet: Mel Ferrer dances with Elizabeth Taylor, Audrey with Eddie Fisher, at the Desert Inn in Las Vegas after the crooner's opening-night performance there on May 18, 1961. (ARCHIVE PHOTOS)

29. Husband guides wife in the studio jungle of *Green Mansions:* Hepburn's first and last role under Mel Ferrer's direction was her least popular with the public. (PHOTO BY BOB WILLOUGHBY)

30. Audrey and Mel Ferrer arrive at Bürgenstock's chapel for the baptism of Sean, pillowed in the arms of Grandma Ella van Heemstra, autumn 1960. When the baby yelled heartily, Ella quoted the Dutch maxim: "A good cry at the christening lets the devil out!"
(PHOTO BY RICHARD AVEDON FOR *LOOK*, COURTESY OF THE AUDREY HEPBURN ESTATE)

no to *Charade*," Donen relates. "Columbia said get Paul Newman. Newman said yes, but Columbia wouldn't pay his going rate. Then they said get Warren Beatty and Natalie Wood. So I got them and Columbia decided they couldn't afford them or the picture. So I sold *Charade* to Universal. In the meantime, Cary had read Hawks's script and didn't like it. So he called me and said he would like to do *Charade*."[116]

The project involved a lot of anniversaries for Grant: *Charade* was his seventieth film, 1962 was his thirtieth year in the film business, Audrey would be precisely his fiftieth leading lady, and he was just one year shy of sixty. He had been spotted in 1933 by Mae West, who was then casting *She Done Him Wrong* and said, "If he can talk, I'll take him." Soon after, on celluloid, she gave him that legendary invitation, "Come up and see me sometime."

Nowadays, he was nervous about his image and afraid that, opposite Audrey, he might look like a dirty old man. He and Donen had Stone change the dynamic to make Audrey the aggressor who finally wears *him* down, instead of the usual reverse. Their age difference was turned into a running joke. But privately, he still worried, as a vignette described by biographers Charles Higham and Roy Moseley illustrates:

"At time of *Charade*, Grant decided to stay not in a hotel but in Barbara Hutton's Paris apartment, whose secretary Mona Eldridge recalled him walking down the long central hall with glass-fronted display cases with priceless antique figurines, jade, etc., not examining contents but glancing from left to right to observe his reflection in the mirrored cabinet doors, fussing over his hair, fretting over wrinkles."[117]

Hepburn and Grant had never met, and Donen couldn't wait to introduce them. He arranged for dinner at "some terribly smart bistro," Audrey recalled, where she and Donen arrived first. When Grant came in, Audrey rose and said, "I'm so nervous," to which Grant replied, "Don't be.... I'm thrilled to know you. Here, sit down.... Put your hands on the table, palms up, put your head down and take a few deep breaths." Donen had ordered a bottle of red wine, and when Audrey put her head down, "she hit the bottle, and the wine went all over Cary's cream-colored suit," the director recalls. "Audrey was humiliated. People at other tables were looking.... It was a horrendous moment."

Grant just "nonchalantly removed his jacket," said Audrey, "and pretended, very convincingly, that the stain would simply go away.... I felt terrible and kept apologizing, but Cary was so dear about it. The next day he sent me a box of caviar with a little note telling me not to feel bad."[118]

James Coburn, just in from Munich after finishing *The Great Escape*, was also meeting Grant for the first time. "Cary was in one of those little dressing-room things on the set," Coburn recalls. "I said, 'Hi.' He said,

'Come on in.' We were talking about the script when Walter [Matthau] came by and said, 'Hey, Jim, how are you? Did you ever see anybody do a better impression of Cary Grant than this guy?' And then walked away. It was the only time I ever saw Cary Grant off balance."[119]

A charade is a guessing game full of tricks, a pantomimed secret to be deciphered in bits and pieces. So is *Charade*, beginning with its spectacular credits—a wild geometric charade in themselves. The names wind in and out of psychedelic mazes, heralding the upcoming game of illusion, set around Paris's most charming landmarks: Les Halles, Notre Dame, the Palais Royale, the Champs Elysées—all lushly photographed by Charles Lang, Jr.

But the opening scenes take place around the swimming pool of Mont d'Arbois in Megeve, Switzerland, playground of the Euro ski-and-jet set of which Audrey was an honorary member.

Charade's trickery begins with the very first shot: Audrey as Reggie (stunningly dressed by Givenchy) is the picture of tranquility as she suns herself on the terrace. Ominously, a gun emerges from a gloved hand and aims straight at her head. The tension mounts, the trigger is squeezed, and—SPLAT!—Hepburn's ear is full of water from a bratty child's water pistol. It's the first of many cunning, unnerving shifts from suspense to humor.

Suddenly, a man named Peter Joshua (Cary Grant) approaches Reggie, initiating a lickety-split repartee that stokes up the scene through the sparring of the stars:

CG:	Do we know each other?
AH	Why, do you think we're going to?
CG	I don't know, how would I know?
AH	Because I already know an awful lot of people and until one of them dies, I couldn't possibly meet anyone else.
CG	Well, if anyone goes on the critical list, let me know.
AH:	Quitter.

In things romantic, our sexy young widow is forceful. In things financial related to her murdered husband, Charles, she hasn't a clue. Only slowly and painfully does she come to the realization that he was either a liar, a thief, a spy, or all three—and that his name wasn't even Charles.

Non sequiturs pepper everyone's discourse. As Hepburn and Grant walk along the Seine, mulling over the recent drowning of a thug named Scobie, she suddenly remarks, "Wouldn't it be nice if we could be like him?" Grant, in surprise, asks, "Scobie?" "No, Gene Kelly," she replies. "Remember when he danced down here by the river without a care in the world in *An American in Paris*?"

Down at the morgue, a drawer—presumably Charles's—is rudely yanked out and then slammed shut from the *corpse's*-eye-view inside. More macabre hilarity follows at Charles's funeral. Aside from the sorrowful widow, his mourners number a total of four very suspicious-looking characters. Grief is low on their agenda. Each has his own Grand Guignol entrance, approaching the coffin to inspect the body—and to become a suspect:

- Leopold Gideon (Ned Glass): chronic sneezer and milquetoast accountant.
- Tex (James Coburn): sticks mirror under the corpse's nose, just to make sure.
- Herman (George Kennedy): has a steel claw instead of a right hand, and keeps a spare; sticks a hatpin deep into the corpse and, convinced by the lack of reaction, stomps out.
- Bartholomew (Walter Matthau): U.S. embassy official, master of lame jokes and slow delivery—"The last time I sent out a tie, only the spot came back."

People get bumped off left and right, but in a rather quiet and civilized manner. *Charade*'s overall violence and villainy are of the stylized kind. "You can't believe these guys could really do anything very bad," says Coburn, "and yet they're trying really hard and they're getting killed for it."

Of our four bad guys, Coburn has the most frightening scene of personal violence against Audrey. As maniacal Tex, he follows her to a garage where she makes the mistake of using a phone booth. He traps her when she tries to come out and subjects her to sadistic intimidation—lighting one match after another and tossing them on her clothes and in her face, all the while threatening worse to come. Cornered and hysterical, she cannot escape until he simply gets tired of monsterizing her.

"I felt really bad about burning Audrey," recalls Coburn, with a gentleman's lament in his voice. "It went against my nature. Of course, we had it down so it wouldn't hurt her. She was wonderful in that. We didn't discuss that scene beforehand at all, except the mechanics of how close we'd be, because you're playing on her face with that flare going off."

Coburn was enthralled with her, but it wasn't until halfway through shooting that they sat down and talked, and she jolted him by asking, "Do you know how you got this role?"

Coburn said he didn't.

"I saw you in *The Magnificent Seven*," said Audrey, "and I told Stanley Donen—he's our Tex!"

A third of a century later, Coburn still wonders, "How do you thank somebody for doing that? 'Thanks, Baby.' It was her suggestion. If it had been up to Stanley, he never would have hired me. He was a song-and-dance man. I don't think Stanley ever gave me a direction. We secondary players were on our own out there. He didn't really give us too much time. I got more help from Charlie Lang, the photographer."[120]

But Donen gave plenty of time to Audrey, whom he cherished as a person and as an actress. They grew closer with each of their movies together. Audrey was fond of teasing him about his hopeless French, which, despite much moviemaking in France, he invariably butchered. On one trans-Atlantic flight to Paris together, she pointed to the NO SMOKING sign above their heads and reminded him, "See Stanley? No fuming!"

On New Year's Eve 1963, the Ferrers held a dinner party at their rented chateau outside Paris for eight: Donen and his wife, Adele, Peter Stone and his wife, Mary, and Cary Grant and his twenty-five-year-old amour (and future wife) Dyan Cannon, who had flown to Paris to lick her wounds after the disastrous three-night stand of her Broadway play, *The Fun Couple*. It was formal and fancy. The servants wore white gloves while serving huge baked potatoes, into which the guests ladled sour cream and Russian caviar from a five-pound tin provided by Grant.

"It was as glamorous an evening as one can imagine," recalled Stone, "but it was truly boring. It wasn't anybody's fault. Nobody there was boring. But it was just one of those terrible evenings where nobody... was in great humor. Cary and Dyan were arguing a bit. Mel and Audrey were arguing a bit, and Stanley and Adele were arguing a bit. The only ones who remained happily married to each other were Mary and me."[121]

But Cary Grant was Cary Grant, even on a bad day. As shooting progressed, James Coburn was ever more fascinated by Grant's idiosyncrasies and firm views on everything from acting and fashion to the battle of the sexes:

"Cary Grant always did things three times. Every shot, every scene he would do big, small, and right in-between. He would find a dynamic that seemed to work, but he explored all the possibilities first. He was always looking for something.

"One night we were sitting around the pool in the Rothschilds' hotel after work. The air was sparkling with little ice crystals. It was Cary's fifty-ninth birthday, and we had just all come up from dinner. We started talking and suddenly he said he was a little nonplussed about Audrey's film clothes: 'She dresses like a kook!' I said, 'It's Givenchy.' He said, 'Yes, but it's too over-the-top. Too *fashionable*.'

"He was always looking for longevity in films. He always dressed right in the middle because he knew very early in his career that for a film to last, it can't be too fashionable. Today, there's no lasting fashion, no style, no nothing. It's out the door, and on to video. So he was critical of Audrey's clothes in that film, but never of Audrey—except that he thought she was much too young for him."[122]

Audrey as the cool, unruffled Reggie in *Charade* thought otherwise. "You know what's wrong with you?" she asks Grant as their romance builds, and answers herself: "Nothing." Both of their performances were facilitated by Stone's fine script, bubbling over with ironic twists and diabolical turns. Everyone in *Charade* lies constantly to everyone else and says "Trust me" all the while, right up to the suspenseful finale—a nighttime chase of Hepburn by Grant and Matthau in the shadowy colonnades of the Palais Royale. Trapped there, she'll win or lose the game—and her life—by deciding which of two armed and dangerous liars might possibly be telling the truth.

HOLLYWOOD PUBLICIST-TO-THE-STARS Herb Sterne has a little light to shed, and a little cold water to throw, on the subject of Grant's and Hepburn's professional bliss during *Charade:*

"Cary wasn't so particular about how he looked in a still, but he didn't want Audrey to look as good as he did. Audrey didn't want Cary to look as good as she did. So I said, 'Let us have two sheets, so each star can kill a still and the other will not know which still they have killed.' This went great until my secretary, who was busy kissing Audrey's ass, sneaked out a print which Cary had killed and made sure it was published."[123]

But aside from that minor bit of sabotage, there was hardly a ripple of discontent between the two stars, evidenced by the fact that Grant wanted to be reteamed with Audrey immediately in *Father Goose*, his next picture for which Peter Stone again wrote the script (and won an Oscar). Audrey demurred, and the part went to Leslie Caron, because her sights were now set on something much bigger. But for the rest of their lives, Grant and Hepburn traded valentines of mutual affection.

"Working with Cary is so easy," said Audrey. "He does all the acting, and I just react."[124] Grant had touched her even more as a person than as a performer. Twenty-five years later, shortly after his death, she exhaled a long, dreamy sigh when asked about him and disclosed the kind of intimate details about their personal dynamic that she rarely shared in public:

"Cary—such a lovely souvenir in my life. Unlike some people might think, he was really a very reserved, very sensitive, very quiet person, very philosophical, rather mystic in some ways. And had enormous empathy for other people. He had me down flat the minute he met me. I

mean, he knew what I was all about and whatever I was uptight
about and was extremely helpful. Terribly helpful because I was quite
inexperienced, really, when I worked with him."[125]

The last part of the statement was quite untrue. She had made
seventeen films before *Charade* and enjoyed major star status for a decade
by then. But that's how it—and Cary Grant—seemed in her mind. Later,
she elaborated on his psychological insight:

> I think he understood me better than I did myself. He was observant and
> had a penetrating knowledge of people. He would talk often about relaxing
> and getting rid of one's fears.... But he never preached. If he helped me, he
> did it without my knowing, and with a gentleness which made me lose my
> sense of being intimidated....
>
> Cary was a vulnerable man, and he recognized my own vulnerability.
> We had that in common.... He said one thing very important to me one
> day when I was probably twitching and being nervous. We were sitting next
> to each other waiting for the next shot. He laid his hand on my two hands
> and said, "You've got to learn to like yourself a little more." I've often
> thought about that.[126]

James Coburn agrees with Hepburn's assessment but adds that Grant
had one advantage over Audrey and all other vulnerable people in the
world: "He had 'Cary Grant' to protect him!"[127]

Though he rarely saw Audrey thereafter, Coburn happily admits being
"wild about her" and coming away from their association with a distinct
perception about her sexuality.

"Audrey was something else," Coburn reflects, "—a real lady, and
there are so few of them. It had to do with her upbringing and those
negative experiences in the war, which I think made her become rather
secretive. On the film just before, *Paris When It Sizzles*, Bill Holden was
having a strong romance with Capucine, who was also close to Audrey.
But Audrey and Bill had a thing, too.... Underneath, Audrey was a very
sexual creature, always secretive and goddesslike. It would take some kind
of a godlike creature to bring her down—but she didn't seem to be too
unwilling. She was the gamine goddess."[128]

ALL *CHARADE* HAD GOING FOR it was an exciting story, witty dialogue,
the ideal cast, a top director, Parisian chic, and yet another Mancini-
Mercer hit. Donen held his breath, hoping for a good reception, but
Charade's ecstatic reviews went beyond all his expectations.

"A Technicolored merry-go-round in which Grant, Hepburn and Paris
never looked better," raved *Look*. "An absolute delight," said *Newsweek*.

Pauline Kael in *The New Yorker* called it "probably the best American film" of the year.

Charade was popular with all segments of the public, but especially with that much-mocked subgroup known as philatelists, since a rare stamp figures as the key to its plot. The glorious and sorrowful mysteries of philately may seem absurd to those who don't share the compulsion. But in 1963, *Charade* exalted and elevated stamp-collecting to the peak of its vogue.

It is arguably Stanley Donen's best non-musical film but, ironically, many remember it most for its smooth, sexy title song. Henry Mancini and Johnny Mercer had just won two best-song Oscars in a row, for "Moon River" and "The Days of Wine and Roses," but the third time wasn't a charm. "Charade" lost to "Call Me Irresponsible" from *Papa's Delicate Condition.*

That minor disappointment was offset by its surprise bonanza at the box-office: *Charade* was Audrey's biggest hit yet—and Donen's biggest hit ever—breaking all records at Radio City in New York. It was the year's fifth most profitable film, grossing $6.15 million and inspiring a flock of comic-thriller imitations with similar titles—*Mirage, Caprice, Masquerade, Kaleidoscope, Blindfold*—all of which lacked the charm of the original.

Among those who tried to imitate Donen's magic formula was Donen himself in *Arabesque* (1966): "Gregory Peck and Sophia Loren asked me to find a movie for them," he said. But that humorless duo turned out to be, in Donen biographer Joseph Caspar's words, about "as exciting as Friday night in a Benedictine abbey."[129]

Back in Hollywood, Grant's delight with *Charade* was expressed in his comment to a reporter, "All I want for Christmas is another movie with Audrey Hepburn."[130] He didn't really need anything else: His share of *Operation Petticoat* (1959) had netted him about $3 million, and he would earn $4 million in percentages from his previous hit, *That Touch of Mink* (1962). With no pressing need to rush immediately into *Father Goose* production, Grant the good liberal took time off for some volunteerism in Washington, lending his name and support to Attorney General Robert Kennedy's campaign to curb high school dropouts.

He was not the only one with New Frontier connections. More than once, President John F. Kennedy had phoned Audrey Hepburn to compliment her on a film and to say she was his favorite actress. On May 29, 1963, she reciprocated at the Waldorf-Astoria Hotel in New York by singing "Happy Birthday, dear Jack" at the President's forty-sixth—and last—birthday party. Audrey's pretty little rendition caused much less stir than that of the previous year's serenader, Marilyn Monroe.

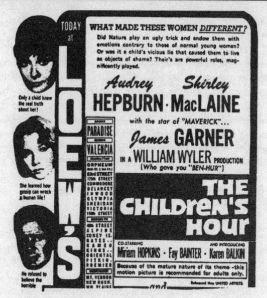

A typical newspaper advertisement for The Children's Hour *(1962): Director William Wyler's original title was* Infamous!.

"WHAT MADE THESE WOMEN DIFFERENT? Did Nature play an ugly trick and endow them with emotions contrary to those of normal young women?"

CHAPTER 6

Fair and Unfair Ladies
(1963–1964)

"Did Rex Harrison want Julie Andrews
instead of Hepburn? No. He didn't want
anybody. He felt whatever fuss was made
about Audrey or Julie was pointless, because nobody was interested in the girl.
They were only interested in *him*."

ANDRÉ PREVIN

IT WAS THE BEST OF roles, it was the worst of roles. . . .
  "You've got *My Fair Lady!*" shouted Kurt Frings triumphantly to
Audrey Hepburn via long-distance telephone in Bürgenstock, where
she had returned for some rest after *Charade*.[1]

It was the call she had been awaiting for months—or years or perhaps
her whole life. "I had to share the magnificent news with somebody close
to me," she said. "Mel was away. But there was Mother upstairs, taking
a shower. I banged on the bathroom door and screamed something
unintelligible about the movie I was to star in and Mother came out
soaking wet, wrapped in a towel, thinking the house was on fire."[2]

Ferrer was in France at the Cannes Film Festival, and Audrey immediately placed a call to him there but had to hang on the line for half an
hour until he could be located. By the time he got to the phone, she was
in tears. When she told him her news, he asked why she was crying.
"Because it's such an important day and we are hundreds of miles apart,"
she replied.[3]

Eliza Doolittle was one of the greatest stage roles of all time. She was
created by George Bernard Shaw, whose favorite subject was women—far
more sane and loving than men, he believed and best asserted in the title,
Man and Superman. Of his many influential plays, *Pygmalion* was the
greatest success. In the Greek myth, that sculptor detests women for their
wicked ways and vows to remain a bachelor but makes the fatal mistake
of carving a statue which is so beautiful that—when Aphrodite brings it
to life—he falls in love. Ovid treated the same subject in his *Metamorphoses*,

as did several Elizabethan writers and eventually, in 1871, Sir William Gilbert. His play *Pygmalion and Galatea* was seen and much admired by the fifteen-year-old Shaw.

It took forty years and the inspiration of Mrs. Patrick Campbell for Shaw to produce his own Pygmalion—a fussy phonetics professor named Henry Higgins. His Galatea was the cockney flower girl Eliza Doolittle— "perhaps eighteen, perhaps twenty, hardly older." "It would be better if I was twenty-five years younger," Mrs. Campbell wrote Shaw, "but thanks for thinking I can be your pretty slut." She was forty-nine when she created the role on the London and New York stages in 1914.

It was a sensation from the start. Audiences gasped at the end of Eliza's first scene with Freddy. "Are you walking across the park, Miss Doolittle?" he asks. "Walk!" she exclaims, "Not bloody likely!" If not the first, it was the most celebrated utterance of that word on the London stage to date.

Subsequent Elizas included Lynn Fontanne in the 1926 Broadway revival, Wendy Hiller (opposite Leslie Howard) in the 1938 British film version, and Gertrude Lawrence in the Broadway production of 1946. Inevitably, it was a candidate for musical treatment—which it repeatedly defied. "Dick Rodgers and I worked on it for over a year, and we gave it up," said Oscar Hammerstein in the early fifties. "It can't be done."[4]

Alan Jay Lerner and Frederick Loewe took their first crack at it around 1952. "It seemed one drawing-room comedy which just resisted expansion," said Lerner, who worked on it for six months but then set it aside. When it finally started to gel a few years later, not everyone was impressed. Mary Martin and her agent were among the first to hear what was then *My Fair Liza*, after which the agent told Lerner, "You boys have lost your talent." The boys kept working but, as late as the show's opening in New Haven, still hadn't settled on a title.... *Lady Liza, My Lady Liza, Come to the Ball, Fanfaroon?*

The nod finally went to *My Fair Lady*, a pun on the cockney pronunciation of "Mayfair lady." On March 15, 1956, with Julie Andrews as Eliza and Rex Harrison as Higgins, it opened at the Mark Hellinger Theatre and stayed there for an astounding 2,717 performances, the longest run of any musical to that time. It won every award and became the biggest hit in musical theater history, ultimately produced in eleven languages and twenty-one countries.

A fierce bidding war for screen rights was eventually won by Warner Brothers: at $5.5 million plus 50 percent of gross revenues above $20 million, it was the most expensive stage-to-film deal ever made in Hollywood.* With a budget of $17 million, it would also be the most costly Warners movie ever.

---

* The happy seller of those screen rights was CBS, whose canny chairman William Paley had

My Fair Lady was the last great Broadway musical to receive lavish screen treatment. It was Jack Warner's extravagant swan song—his last production at Warner Brothers. Everything about it would be on a grand scale, starting with the casting. Warner wanted nothing but top-of-the-line stars in the leads, and he knew exactly which three he wanted most: Cary Grant as Higgins, James Cagney as Doolittle and Audrey Hepburn as Eliza.

Normally, if a great studio mogul set his sights on certain stars and the stars were available, that was it. No other input was needed. But neither Warner nor the industry reckoned on the unprecedented kibitzing of a group whose casting preferences were rarely heard or heeded: the public. Many of those thirty-two million owners of the original cast album were staunch fans of—and clamoring for—Julie Andrews. One of the staunchest was Alan Lerner who, after seeing her in *The Boy Friend*, had selected Andrews for the Broadway role and was now 100 percent behind casting her in the film. But Lerner had no contractual say in the matter.

Warner was criticized ever after for not giving Andrews the part, but he discussed it with her at least once by phone. "I'd love to do it," she reportedly told him. "When do we start?" Warner asked when she could come out for a screen test, to which Andrews replied, "Screen test? You've seen me do the part and you know I can do a good job." He said, "Miss Andrews, you're only known in London and New York. You've never made a movie and I'm investing a lot of money in this. I have to be sure you photograph and project well. Films are a different medium." But Andrews refused. Thenceforth, after Warner let it be known that he would hire a film actress, show-biz columnists around the country took up the standard, lamenting and lobbying for Julie.

No one was following the controversy more closely than Audrey. "I understood the dismay of people who had seen Julie on Broadway," she said later. "Julie made that role her own, and for that reason I didn't want to do the film when it was first offered. [But] I learned that if I turned it down, they would offer it to another movie actress [and] I thought I was entitled to do it as much as the third girl, so then I did accept."[5]

Audrey herself never revealed the name of that "third girl," of whom she was very fond: Elizabeth Taylor. ("Get me *My Fair Lady*," Taylor allegedly commanded Eddie Fisher and Kurt Frings—as if either of them could.) But as soon as Audrey entered the race, she won it. Never before had Jack Warner felt obliged to justify a casting decision, but such

originally invested a mere $400,000 in the stage production in exchange for exclusive rights to the cast album (which would sell 32 million copies). CBS subsequently became 100 percent owner of *My Fair Lady* by acquiring the interests of lyricist Lerner, composer Loewe and stage director Moss Hart.

was the outcry in this case that he publicly—and candidly—stated his explanation:

> With all her charm and ability, Julie Andrews was just a Broadway name, known primarily to those who saw the musical. But in thousands of cities and towns throughout the United States and abroad, you can say "Audrey Hepburn" and people instantly know you're talking about a beautiful and talented star. In my business, I have to know who brings people and their money to a theatre box-office. I knew Audrey Hepburn ... had given exhibitors a big money shot in the arm with *The Nun's Story*. For that picture, we gave her a guarantee of a quarter of a million dollars against ten per cent of the gross, and she came out with nearly one and a half million dollars—in other words, the film grossed $14 million, and that was remarkable.[6]

Audrey was Warner's idée fixe. Her name alone would ensure the film's success, he believed. The box-office difference between Andrews and Hepburn he calculated to be $5 million. A notoriously tightfisted man, he shocked Hollywood by agreeing to pay her $1 million for the role. Only three other stars belonged to the million-per-film club: Marlon Brando, Elizabeth Taylor and Sophia Loren. Frings arranged for seven annual installments of $142,957, to help Audrey with her taxes and to make the payout less draining on the studio's cash flow.

Warner faced rebellion on his choice of male lead, as well, but he at least kept that controversy from spilling over into the press. When director George Cukor approached Cary Grant about Higgins, Grant said, "There is only one man who should play this, and that's Rex. Any other actor would be a fool to try it.... Not only will I not play Higgins, if you don't put Rex Harrison in it, I won't go and see it."[7] Warner, amazingly, had also sounded out Rock Hudson on the role. At the opposite extreme, Cukor had spoken with Laurence Olivier and Peter O'Toole about it, but neither was available.

It was little known that Rex Harrison was actually the *fourth* choice for Higgins on stage (after Noel Coward, Michael Redgrave and George Sanders all turned it down). Nowadays, he was in England, in a comfortable position. He was not a man to get overly excited about behind-the-scenes casting maneuvers.

"I sat tight," Harrison recalled. "One evening George Cukor telephoned on a crackly line from California and asked me to make a photographic test for the part. I laughed. 'I'm not making any tests,' I told him. 'If you want me to play the part, then I'll come.' As a joke, I then sent him some Polaroid photos which had been taken while we'd been fooling about on my boat, in which I appeared stark naked, holding, in one picture, a Chianti bottle in front of me, and in another, a strategically placed copy of the *New Statesman.* 'You wanted a test,' I told him.... They saw that I was not as decrepit as they feared.''[8]

Harrison was in, and for more compelling criteria than his beefcake Polaroids. But Cagney was out. He took the opportunity to pay back Warner for past injustices and refused the role of Alfred Doolittle, which was then offered to Stanley Holloway, who accepted. So two of the three top stars would be the Broadway originators of the parts—their presence making Julie Andrews's absence even more noticeable.

Cukor had a nervous vibration. "The first time I talked to Audrey," he said, "she called me overseas from Switzerland and told me she was working on her cockney. She tried it out on the phone for me. 'Ao-ow-ow,' she said. I told her it sounded okay to me.... Actors always worry about the wrong thing."[9]

THE OVERALL TECHNICAL CHALLENGE OF *My Fair Lady* could be summed up by the word "look," and the specifics summed up by the word "Edwardian." Edward VII reigned just nine years, from 1901 to 1910. *Pygmalion* and now *My Fair Lady* were set in that dynamic era of Cubism, the Suffragettes, and the fall of Oscar Wilde. But it was the English king's personal style—everything from his eating habits to his effete Bohemianism—that defined the day, above all in fashion and manners.[10]

Flamboyant designer-photographer Cecil Beaton (1904–1980) had created the dazzling costumes for the show's New York and London stage productions and was engaged to reprise those designs for the film. This time, he would design the sets, too. Alan Lerner said of Beaton that, "When you looked at him, it was difficult to know whether he designed the Edwardian era or the Edwardian era designed him."[11]

Beaton and his ferocious ego were bursting with new energy. "It's a most exciting job, this," he said, "and one that I would very much have hated anyone else to have done!"[12] He was thrilled to be in charge of the whole of the visual production, and, in his compulsively kept diaries, left an almost minute-by-minute account of events, starting with the day in September 1962 when George Cukor tornadoed into his London house to research the period and to gloat that Audrey was "dying to do Eliza."[13]

Beaton flew to Hollywood and started work in February 1963, months before Hepburn and the rest of the cast arrived. He and Cukor were getting along swimmingly, exploring every aspect of the picture together. Most of all, they discussed the quality and quantity of costumes to be made—one thousand! Some four hundred of them, all black and white, were required for the Ascot Gavotte and ball sequences alone. Each one would be lovingly re-created from museum sources with the attention given to a principal's clothes.

Beaton took special care with the designs for Gladys Cooper as Higgins's mother. "We have decided not to make Mrs. Higgins into the conventional Marx Brothers dowager," he said, "but into an 'original,' a Fabian, an aesthetic intellectual." He wrote his friend Lady Diana Cooper, asking what her mother, the late great Duchess of Rutland, would have worn at Ascot. Lady Diana's reply was firm: "Certainly *cream*."[14]

On May 16, 1963, Audrey and her family flew to Los Angeles and set up housekeeping in a large rented villa in Bel-Air. Beaton, like everyone else, was excited and energized by the leading lady's arrival, as he recorded two days later:

"George, Alan and I went to pay a formal call on Audrey Hepburn Ferrer at tea time. Sean, her [three]-year-old son, was present, and it is obvious that this is the love affair of her life, and she of her son's." He could hardly wait 'til after tea to show her his designs:

She and Mel each sat with a book of sketches on their laps, and suddenly Mel held up a sketch of Eliza as the flower girl. "Look at that, Audrey! That's got it all. That's what it's all about." . . . Audrey closed her eyes and smiled. . . . "Oh, it's more than I thought it possibly could be. It's too much!" Such genuine enthusiasm thrilled me.

[Later] Audrey and Mel came with me to Wardrobe where they gasped at the first things they saw. . . . The combination of Audrey and these exaggerated clothes created comic magic. She wanted to pose for photographs in every one of them. "I don't want to play Eliza! She doesn't have enough pretty clothes. I want to parade in all these." And she did. . . . in a gay mood, making rubber faces, speaking in Eliza's cockney accent, joking with all the adoring helpers.[15]

A few days later at the studio, a lilting voice invited him to, "Come on in and see my secrets." It was Audrey in the Makeup Department. "Now, you see, I have no eyes!" she told Beaton. He didn't agree: "Without the usual mascara and shadow, Audrey's eyes are like those in Flemish painting and are even more appealing—young and sad. Yet it was extraordinary to see that it is simply by painting her eyes she has become a beauty in the modern sense. But having seen her without these aids, I will try to prevail upon her to do away with them in the earlier sequences for this will give an entirely new and authentic look—different from any we have seen before in her pictures. Her appearance without [eye makeup] will be a revolution and, let's hope, the end of all those black-eyed zombies of the fashion magazines."[16]

NIGHT AND DAY, ALL THAT mattered to Beaton was costumes and sets.

But the director and studio executives were far more worried about Audrey's songs and the recording process.

"When she began," said Cukor in a mid-production interview, "it was an agony for that girl to sing. But she is not afraid to make an ass of herself. She has the courage to do it, do it wretchedly at first, but do it."[17]

As a vote of confidence in Audrey's singing ability, that faint praise seemed a bit damning. But she was indeed working extraordinarily hard on every facet of her performance, often spending twelve hours a day in rehearsals. In addition to memorizing lines and sitting endlessly for costume fittings, she attended Hermes Pan's grueling dance rehearsals and took cockney lessons from UCLA phonetics professor Peter Ladefoged ("an American who probably knows London like I know Peking," she remarked).[18]

Most of all, she was working on her voice, determined as she was to perform and record all of her own songs. Singing coach Susan Seton was imported from New York and led her through vocal lessons for five weeks, sometimes five or six hours a day. But there were rumors that the studio was casting about for a dubber.

Audrey had been nervously aware of it—and in a kind of denial—from early on, as Beaton's diary entries of mid-May indicate: "After lunch, we accompanied [Lerner] to listen to a girl singing Eliza's songs, in case Audrey's voice proves to be too frail for one or two of the most operatic arias, and a few notes have to be dubbed."[19] Two days later, he wrote, "Suddenly Audrey asked, 'Are you going to use my voice for songs at all?'"

Beaton's analysis of the remark was upbeat to the point of delusional: "This was disarming and removed any awkwardness in approaching a difficult subject.... It was now easy to say that, quite probably, Audrey's voice will be used for many of the songs, but certain notes might be interpolated from another voice." Nevertheless, he was superstitious, and it "worried me when she said, 'This picture is one we must all remember. Wonderful talents, everyone right, everyone happy.'"[20]

Pre-recording now began, and on July 4 Audrey sang her first solo, shut up in a cubicle, while the orchestra played outside under André Previn. For Audrey, it was "an ordeal," said Beaton, "but if her voice is not up to standard she will be the first to admit it. Previn may appear as sleepy as a tapir, but coaxes the best from everyone with his intelligence and patience."[21]

Music director Previn was enthralled with Hepburn and did everything he could to help. He knew her musky mezzo voice was no finely trained instrument, but she had used it to good musical and emotional effect in *Funny Face*. The trouble now was that, since Rex Harrison was the master of parlando—a kind of half-spoken singing style—his Eliza had to trill like a bird.[22]

"Audrey's voice was perfectly adequate for a living room," Previn says. "If she got up around the piano with friends and sang, everybody would rightfully have said, 'How charming!' But this was the movie to end all movies, with six giant surround speakers. Even so, I was of the opinion that if you had bought Audrey Hepburn to play it, so she didn't sing so hot—it wasn't such a crime. But you can imagine how Lerner and Loewe felt—much more strongly than about *Paint Your Wagon* or *Brigadoon*. This was their statement for the ages."[23]

Hollywood dubbing was time-honored but erratic. In *Paint Your Wagon* (1967), for instance, Jean Seberg couldn't sing a note and *had* to have a substitute. It is claimed by some (and denied by others) that Lauren Bacall's voice double in *To Have and Have Not* was young Andy Williams.[24] Kitty Carlisle, a trained opera singer, had to sob loudly in Louis B. Mayer's office before MGM would let her sing her own songs in *Night at the Opera*. Juanita Hall, the original Bloody Mary in *South Pacific*, was dubbed in the film version for reasons not even director Joshua Logan understood. And Previn is still incensed that Ava Gardner was not allowed to sing in *Show Boat*. "When you heard her do 'Bill,' she broke your heart," he recalls. "But they couldn't see it."[25]

Previn thought the system was screwy, but he was stuck with it. So was Audrey, and so was one of the most "unsung" singers of the era, Marni Nixon—Dubber to the Stars. Nixon had sung for Deborah Kerr in *The King and I* (1956) and *An Affair To Remember* (1957), and for Natalie Wood in *West Side Story* (1961). She performed symphonic vocal repertoire as well, in concerts with André Previn and Leonard Bernstein.

"I did a lot of different people's voices in those days," Nixon recalls. "It was something one did to subsidize one's 'real' career. Audrey had been signed and everybody was upset Julie didn't get it. People kept calling me and saying, 'You'd be perfect—tell your agent to get you in!' But those things don't come from agents. They come from the music director."[26]

Previn knew Nixon was "a much more serious singer than people realized. I first heard her do an evening of Ives songs that was absolutely remarkable. She also had this peculiar, chameleonlike quality: She could 'do' everybody. You could hand her a piece of music and say, the first four bars are cockney, then it gets French—it made no difference, she could do it."[27]

Previn arranged for Marni to audition in Hollywood, telling her, "You'll have a number, and they're not to see you. We don't want any other information except the voice." She came, she sang and she got the job. What she did not get was a clear notion of whether she'd be singing all or only part of the songs. "I think Audrey knew 'I Could Have Danced All

Night' would probably be all me," says Nixon, "but if anything else was
decided, we didn't know about it." Exactly when Audrey learned of Nixon's
hiring is unclear, but it was a big blow to her self-confidence when she
found out. So was the process itself, which Nixon describes:

> Sometimes I would rehearse with her directly and hear what she was trying
> to do with the songs. Eventually, we both went into the recording studio
> and recorded what we had planned to do. We knew in some numbers, she
> was going to start, and I was going to carry on.... I would record and then
> she would record her portion of those songs. She kept going back to re-
> record certain parts and would say, "I can do these measures better now.
> Put my voice in."

It was painful, almost pathetic. Audrey's stepson Chris Ferrer remembered Audrey "coming home each day totally exhausted and discouraged
because she was trying so hard to do it right, but she could tell that it
was really not quite good enough."[28]

Did Hepburn ever turn to Nixon for vocal advice? Would she ever say,
"How should I sing this?" Or, "Am I forcing?"

"There was some of that," says Nixon. "They wanted me to help her
as much as possible. [But] I wasn't sure that what I would have told her
was any better than what Sue was telling her. It was a matter of me
singing it with her accent, and then her imitating me. I was imitating her
personality and trying to sing it as I thought she would have, then she
would correct my pronunciation. It was really a technical thing. She had
to have a lot of trust in me. The thrill I have is that I was able to pick up
on her. I really felt fused with her."

But Audrey was the victim of a lot of false hope along the way. "They
were all happy enough with 'Wouldn't It Be Lovely?' so that she actually
filmed that whole song to her track," Nixon recalls. "But I was always
doing the high notes for her, even in that. Later they decided it just
wouldn't match up. You couldn't have one voice for one song and one voice
for another. So they threw out her track, which was very discouraging to
her. In 'The Rain in Spain,' it wasn't clear how much would be me and
how much would be her [until] the last minute. Lerner was there. It was
his choice, not mine."[29]

Lerner was there, indeed—with some dubious brainstorms. He now
summoned his music director with what he thought was a surefire solution
to the Audrey vocal dilemma, as Previn recalls:

"Lerner said, 'She is extremely intelligent about herself. So I want you
to record her with the full orchestra, make her a beautiful arrangement.
And when she hears it back on those six surround speakers, she'll say,
Holy Jesus, and she won't do it.' I said, 'Alan—' He said, 'Trust me, I

know actresses.' I said, 'No, you marry actresses, but you don't know them.'

"Anyway, we did it and we played it back and it was not good and she said, 'I love it.' We were cooked. It didn't sound bad, but you wanted it to sound good. It was the musical film of the decade—the last great operetta—you wanted it to be perfect."[30] Beaton recorded an uncomfortable moment in June when Audrey sang part of the score to the assembled company—"a mistake," he said. "Audrey, seeing the brave smiles on everyone's face, had the feeling she was drowning."[31]

Harper McKay, Previn's assistant musical director, said one of his tasks was to help Audrey improve "despite the fact that the decision had already been made to have Marni dub her voice. Audrey dutifully worked on her vocalises for a half hour or so every morning, and the weeks went by.... Lerner, Previn or Cukor would drop by occasionally, listen to Audrey's singing and compliment her extravagantly on how well she was sounding. Audrey, unfortunately, began to believe them."

During the last day of rehearsal on the Covent Garden set, Audrey sang "Wouldn't It Be Lovely?" herself, and the extras and crew broke into loud applause. Afterward, during a meeting to discuss the next day's work, Audrey came in flushed with emotion. "Did you hear it?" she asked Cukor. "They actually applauded!"

"Audrey," Cukor said, "they thought it was you."

"George," she said, "It *was* me," and tears came to her eyes. The playback operator had mistakenly used her track instead of Marni Nixon's. Cukor, Lerner and Previn hadn't noticed.[32]

From that point on, says Previn, "it became a passing-the-buck thing. Warner wouldn't tell her. Lerner wouldn't tell her. Loewe was never around at all. They came to me and I said, 'Listen, fellas, I'm not the one to tell her.' So finally Cukor had to go. She was very hurt because she felt that if she had taken Julie Andrews's place and then couldn't sing, it would reflect very badly on her. But she never said a word. I'm sure she had tears about it, but not so you'd know."[33]

Her good friend Doris Brynner, wife of Yul, dissents. One of very few visitors allowed on the set, she denies Audrey was upset. "She *had* to be dubbed," says Brynner. "All that high soprano singing—how could she have done it? She never had any intention of singing."[34] But nobody else remembers it that way.

On hearing the bad news from Cukor, she said, "Oh!", and walked off the set. All the weeks of coaching, practicing and matching were down the drain: Virtually all her songs would be dubbed. The next day, she came back and apologized to everyone for her "wicked" behavior, saying she understood it had to be. "That was her idea of being very wicked," says Marni Nixon.[35]

"I'D DONE THE SHOW FOR so long in the theatre with Julie that *any* new leading lady was going to be a problem," said Rex Harrison. "Audrey also had to weather a great deal of adverse press publicity about how much she was being paid, for most of the press had sided with Julie, and had wanted Julie to get the part. Audrey is a very sensitive person, and could not fail to feel all this. It quickly leaked to the press that she was being dubbed [and] wasn't 'really' singing the part she'd wrested from Julie and for which she was being so highly paid."[36]

The sympathetic tone contained a certain amount of crocodile tears. Harrison, in fact, was in no mood to accommodate his "new" Eliza after discovering that, at $250,000, his salary was only a quarter of hers. In his opinion, it was *he* who had been responsible for the stage (and potential film) success of *My Fair Lady*, and he was incensed by the inequity. Even Cukor was getting more than himself ($300,000).Though he was hostile to Audrey at first, their relationship gradually warmed as he realized that her difficulties would enable him to dominate the film.[37]

Harrison's "outward self-assurance was only a cover-up for an even greater self-assurance underneath," said Previn. "There seemed to be only two ways to approach any problem: his way and the wrong way.... When Rex heard I had been engaged by Warners to serve as musical director, he flew into a rage. 'I won't have it, I don't want him,' he hissed at Alan Lerner. 'For the entire run of the play, both on Broadway and in London, we had Franz Allers conducting the orchestra. Franz knows exactly how I sing and how I speak, my cadences and my rhythms. There's no one like Franz, that's who I want, that's who we must get.'...

"Alan persuaded Rex to try—'just try'—recording a number with me. [If] it didn't work out, Rex could go to Jack Warner and have me replaced with Franz. [So] we scheduled the recording of 'Let a Woman in Your Life.' It went perfectly.... Rex had no problems, the orchestra and I had no problems, and the song was finished ahead of schedule. That night, Alan called Rex from New York: 'How did it go? Did you get any of it finished?' Rex interrupted him, 'Yes, yes, dear boy, it was terrific. I get along fine with André, and he followed my singing without the slightest trouble. In fact, he was certainly better than that Germanic son of a bitch we used to have in the pit!' "[38]

Previn today smiles at the recollection before delivering his final verdict: "Rex Harrison, who gave one of the most transcendental performances ever, was—and I don't say this lightly—the most appalling human being I ever worked with. He was charming and funny and a great raconteur but, Jesus Christ, what he did to people. Rex didn't like Audrey very much. He was mean *about* her, not *to* her. That was very much more his style."

He wanted Julie Andrews?

"No, he didn't want *anybody*. He felt whatever fuss was made about

Audrey or Julie was pointless, because nobody was interested in the girl. They were only interested in *him*."[39]

Others with firsthand experience confirm that appraisal. "I'd known Rex since I was twelve," says Roddy McDowall, who costarred with him on the New York stage and in two films, *Midnight Lace* (1960) and the calamitous *Cleopatra* (1963). "He was emotionally unstable, like a wanton child. You always had to approach him with a firehose. He was an exquisitely impeccable actor but a basic hysteric—and unconscionable to his fellow actors."

Evidence of that was provided by their joint appearance in Jean Anouilh's *The Fighting Cock* on Broadway. "Rex was all wrong for the general because he just viscerally could not be a victim," McDowall recalls. "Everything in him revolted against it. We had a great scene in which my character made a total ass of his character. It was imperative that he be humiliated in the second act so that he could be triumphant in the third. But he couldn't and wouldn't play it correctly. He was never where he was supposed to be, and I never knew what he would do next. He'd go downstage and mug and try to distract me—primitive tactics. It was his first Broadway appearance after *My Fair Lady*, and it ran for a month because of the advance sales. But it was agony."[40]

The *My Fair Lady* film script closely resembled the one he performed exactly 2,717 times on stage. But he insisted that all his musical numbers be performed and shot live—an unheard-of practice in Hollywood—and, as usual, he got his way. Harrison claimed he never sang a number the same way twice; he scorned the lip-synch technique. Thus a microphone was set in his tie and a transmitter strapped to his leg, so that his singing could be recorded over and mixed with the pre-recorded music—a technical problem of such magnitude that two unions demanded extra pay for it.[41]

"It made it much easier for him," says André Previn. "A lot of people said, 'That son of a bitch!' But he had a point. I was in his corner. What it left me with was that insane delivery of his without any accompaniment except the piano, which was fed into his ear. So I had this madman with the up-and-down voice and I had to put on earphones and chase him with the orchestra. That was hard work. Which he never acknowledged."[42]

PRINCIPAL PHOTOGRAPHY ON *MY FAIR LADY* began August 13, 1963, and continued for four and a half months on the majority of Warners' twenty-six soundstages. Only Mel, Doris Brynner, and Hubert de Givenchy were allowed onto the closed set. In Garboesque fashion, Audrey could not tolerate anyone in "eyeline" range while she was in Eliza mode. "Seeing a strange face looming beyond the cameras dispels the mood I'm trying to set," she said. "It throws me off balance."[43]

Obligingly, Cukor set up a series of black baffles with peepholes, screening off the action from all but the minimum necessary technicians. "Cukor always closed his sets off for those big lady stars," says Previn. "I don't think it was a device just for Audrey. He did it for Joan Crawford, Norma Shearer and Garbo before."[44]

Her husband complained that "she wouldn't even let *me* visit her on the set while she was in that bedraggled flower-girl characterization. But even at her dirtiest, she sprayed herself with a $100-an-ounce perfume, *Joy*. 'I may look dirty,' she'd say, 'but I aim to smell pretty.' "[45] Mel thought that was charming, but some thought it an indication of her subliminal unsuitability for the role.

Theodore Bikel, the film's sole surviving supporting star, thought Hepburn not just suitable but "the most enchanting figure that ever graced the screen." As diplomat Zoltan Karpathy, Bikel's one big moment was the ball scene in which he dances with Eliza. But the real-life Bikel was none too light on his feet.

"I was terrified," he recalls. "I said to George Cukor, 'I want dancing lessons. There can't be the slightest danger that I step on this gorgeous creature's toes.' But she was easy as pie —gracious and collegial and lovely. A true aristocrat."

Bikel's outstanding memory of the filming?

"Cukor asked me before we shot my first entrance, 'How would Karpathy greet Professor Higgins?' I said, 'Karpathy is a Hungarian, Mr. Cukor, and between the two of us, you're the Hungarian.' He said, 'Yes, but you're the actor.' So I said, 'All right, if you ask me, I would come in and kiss him on both cheeks.' And that's how it came about that I was the only male actor ever to make an entrance kissing Rex Harrison."[46]

The grimmest moment of the ballroom shooting occurred when veteran character actor Henry Daniell, a close friend of Cukor's and brilliant featured player in *Camille*, among other Cukor films, suddenly keeled over dead on the set.

My Fair Lady contained 165 scenes and seventeen musical numbers, each seeming to pose more difficulty than the one before. In a short early scene with just two lines of dialogue, for example, Higgins says to Pickering, "Shall we ask this baggage to sit down, or shall we throw her out the window?" Eliza yowls, "I won't be called a baggage when I've offered to pay like any lydee." It took twelve takes before Cukor was satisfied. Tempers were growing short all around, Previn recalls:

"Marni, after many days of recording . . . , became rather difficult and resistant to Alan Jay Lerner's instructions. To be fair, he gave six directions per syllable, so her reticence was not entirely unwarranted. But on this particular day, she took off the earphones, bridling, and snapped, 'Are you aware, Mr. Lerner, that I have dubbed the voice for Deborah Kerr and

Natalie Wood and dozens of others?' Alan's reply was prompt... 'And are you aware, dear, that all those ladies dubbed your face?' "[47]

Audrey herself had outbursts of temperament unprecedented in her career. During one August rehearsal of "Loverly," while dancing on the non-skid rubber cabbage leaves and mouthing the words to the song, she did the unthinkable: She stopped the scene twice herself, instead of letting director Cukor do so, stamping her feet in frustration and bursting into tears.[48]

On July 19, Beaton recorded:

> This past week has been a swine.... Audrey, George and I watched the latest tests. Deeply depressing.... Eliza's Ascot dress gave me a nasty jolt; the poppies on her hat became orange. But who would have guessed that in the long shots the black-and-white striped lacings and bows would appear green and yellow? As for today's attempt at glamour, Audrey's elaborate cloak is not suitable, as I had expected: on the screen it looks as if it were made of a tarpaulin. Her Ball hairdress looks like a bird's nest, while her makeup assumes the color of canned salmon.

It did not cheer him up to learn that the bill for the costumes he had made so far was $500,000.[49] "Everyone's nerves are explosive," said Audrey. "Everyone's on edge."[50]

Even so, Beaton grew more and more impressed with her characterization. On August 21, he observed that the flower girl was no longer just "sweet little Audrey Hepburn, dressed as a cute cockney with a dab of dirt becomingly placed on her nose: this was a wraughty guttersnipe, full of fight and determination, a real 'rotten cabbage leaf.'...

"Every dawn Audrey has to have her hair covered with grease, then with a lot of brown Fuller's Earth. The effect is really dirty, and psychologically must be very depressing. Tiring, too: it takes another hour to wash out the dirt before going home. Audrey said she was beginning to warm up in her part, but was sad that on the first day's shooting she didn't get into the right groove; had been too strident, her eyes bugged.... 'I see what it should be now that it's too late,' she laughed, wistfully."[51]

GEORGE CUKOR, MEANWHILE, WAS HAVING serious difficulties with Cecil Beaton. Through their mutual friend Greta Garbo, they had known each other for years but deeply mistrusted one another. After their initial "honeymoon" on the project, both of them came to regard Audrey as their personal property and began feuding over her. They were of clashing gay types—Cukor the closeted perfectionist, Beaton the extroverted egomaniac—and their struggle for control of Audrey and her affections escalated.

"George had a bungalow on the set," recalls André Previn, "and almost every day, one or the other would go slamming out of the screen door saying something that ended in 'cunt.'"[52]

The catalyst of the blowup was Cukor's order, in mid-production, restricting Beaton's access to photograph Audrey on the set. Beaton fumed; his monumental vanity was easily wounded. He had a keen sense of Hepburn's importance as a fashion icon of the mid-century, and of his own importance in packaging and marketing her. By this time, he had taken more than a thousand pictures of her in *My Fair Lady* costumes for lavish photo spreads that he sold to virtually all the major American and British magazines. Those pieces had generated tremendous advance publicity for the film and tremendous fees for himself. But he had a voracious appetite for more.*

"The reason George got so angry at him is because Cecil stored every person and experience in his life to exploit then or later," says Roddy McDowall, who knew both men well and observed them with a sharp eye. "He used people, and he was profligate." Greed headed the list of Beaton's character defects and offended Cukor's private and professional scruples. Two thousand photos to date? Enough was enough! Publishing intimate details of his sexual encounters with Greta Garbo? Unconscionable! Yet Cecil could boast of such affronts. After hearing him do so once during the 1959 New York run of *Look After Lulu* (designed by Beaton, costarring McDowall), Roddy asked, " 'Cecil, you'd sell your grandmother's fingernails, wouldn't you?' His reply was, 'Of course I would, dear.' He didn't see it as betrayal."

But Cukor did. He felt that Beaton had become a kind of monster, shamelessly abusing his well-paid position to make lucrative side deals; and that his intrusive presence on the set was distracting Audrey. "Cecil was Talleyrand, full of art and craft," says McDowall, "whereas George was a very just man—but if you did him dirt, he was unforgiving."[53]

Once Cukor came to believe that Beaton was taking advantage of him, the tension between them increased and so did the director's restrictions. During a set break in October, Beaton asked Audrey to pose and she agreed. But as soon as they began, assistant director Buck Hall informed Cecil, "Mr. Cukor doesn't want you to take pictures of Audrey while they are fixing the lights." Then when? he asked. "Mr. Cukor does not want you to photograph her on the set during any of her working days," said

---

* Though Beaton took full credit for sets, costumes, hairstyles, and virtually all other visual aspects of *My Fair Lady*, a great deal of work was done by art director Gene Allen, who went largely unnoticed as the film's co-production designer.

Hall. "*All* her days are working days," Beaton snapped. Looking very pained, Audrey said, "I can't be in the middle of this."[54]

By November, Beaton was having as much trouble capturing her with his palette as with his camera, and she was having troubles, too: "Audrey has no spare time to pose for a painting, so I suggested that [she] sit during her lunch interval. A great effort to slash paint on canvas while she ate her salad and talked of the sad things that happened to her over the weekend. Her son had been ill with a temperature of 103 degrees, the canary had flown away, and somebody had stolen from her mobile dressing-room a bag with her diamond wedding ring in it.... My painting just passable under the circumstances."[55]

On November 18, Mel called Beaton to say that "Audrey was completely depleted and was taking three days off to sleep and rest, and be treated by a doctor."[56] She returned to work on the blackest day in twentieth-century American history.

"We were filming the part where Eliza returns to Covent Garden with Freddy," recalled Jeremy Brett, when someone rushed up to their carriage with word that President John F. Kennedy had been murdered. "We sat in the carriage with the blinds down, holding each other and crying on stage seven at Warner Brothers."[57] George Cukor was too distraught to make the announcement. When no one else would do it, Audrey stoically volunteered.

For millions, America's innocence and idealism died with Kennedy on November 22, 1963. For Hepburn and her colleagues, it was the day the joy went out of *My Fair Lady* once and for all.

Shooting finished a few days before Christmas. Beaton bid a fond farewell to Audrey a week earlier: "They were shooting the scene where Eliza returns to Covent Garden Market after the row with Higgins... the sort of scene Audrey can do to perfection. She is at her best when portraying sweet sympathy and compassion.... I crossed the cobblestones towards Audrey. She had put a Shetland shawl around her shoulders, and looked forlorn."[58]

MARNI NIXON REMEMBERS WATCHING HEPBURN the actress at work, "listening and carefully taking all their directions and then, after they were through, doing it exactly the way she wanted. Everybody around the room said, 'Oh, isn't she wonderful, she took what I said to heart.' But to me, all she did was thread it through herself. She was just placating everybody."[59]

A legendary characterization of Hepburn is attributed to Dory Previn: "Audrey has a whim of iron." Hollywood folklore is a marvelous but often erroneous thing.

"The 'whim of iron' statement is wonderful," says Dory's ex-husband André, "but it was said by director Robert Mulligan—and not about Audrey but about Natalie Wood. Of course, it's true that what Audrey wanted, she got. The fact that she beguiled you into giving it to her, as opposed to bullying you like Joan Crawford, doesn't make much difference.

"One time on the set she went to Cukor and said, 'George, darling, could I possibly leave a little early after lunch?' She came up with some extraordinary reason and asked so circuitously. George said, 'Listen, honey, you're a big star. You want to fucking get out of here? Just say so.' She thought it was terribly funny. She always got what she wanted."[60]

Except—on My Fair Lady—what she wanted most. Before, during and after, she was never convinced that, except for a few high notes, she could not have sung the whole score.[61]

"There's a lot of her in 'Just You Wait, 'Enry 'Iggins,'" says Previn. "Every time it was humanly feasible, I would cut her in to the finished track. In 'Loverly,' there were a couple of things, and off and on in 'Show Me.' We used as much of her as we could. I used more than they were aware of at the time. But I couldn't get away with too much."[62]

In the final product, perhaps 10 percent of Eliza's singing, at most, was Hepburn's. When some publications claimed Audrey had sung "almost half" of the role, Nixon's husband issued an indignant denial, at which point Cukor lost patience and replied, "The whole thing is a great bore to me. It is mischievous and unattractive to make a Federal case out of it."[63]

Thirty years later, the evidence suggests that at the top level there was never any question about dubbing Hepburn's voice and that it was duplicity all along to let her think she would sing it herself. Testimony to that effect comes from Rudy Fehr, the executive in charge of post-production music and sound editing at Warner Brothers. Hepburn was allowed to make "a couple of tracks for her own satisfaction," says Fehr—essentially just to humor her—but as for any serious intention to use her voice, "Never. Nobody ever said anything about that, and I was with Jack Warner all the time."[64]

Asked if in fact they were just leading her on, Previn replies, "Very likely. But 'they' did not include anybody on such a low level as me. 'They' was probably Jack Warner and Rudy and some other executives, maybe George. We went through the same charade with Leslie Caron on Gigi. She was absolutely sure she was going to do it, and they knew bloody well she couldn't. Since she and I were close friends, they gave me the unenviable duty of saying, 'Leslie, you're not going to do it.'"[65]

"That was a disappointment," Caron reflects. "I tried to do a recording, but my voice was not trained and the studio unfortunately didn't take care of training me."[66]*

---

* "It's funny," Marni Nixon told interviewer John Barba. "Alan Jay Lerner said in his biography that I dubbed Gigi, which I didn't. It was Betty Wand."

Lost in the *My Fair Lady* dubbing shuffle was Jeremy Brett. "I know exactly how Audrey felt because the same thing happened to me," he said. "When I arrived on the set, I found to my horror that someone else [Bill Shirley] had sung my song ['On the Street Where You Live'].[67] What Audrey really had to contend with was the ghost of Julie Andrews."[68]

She was still contending with that ghost as late as 1991 on *Larry King Live:* "I did think the part of Eliza was right for me," she said, "but it was Julie Andrews's, so I had sort of an aching heart about that." When King asked her who did the singing, she replied—disingenuously or not—"I've forgotten her name, a lovely girl," and then added with a touch of real or mock irritation, "I sang a *bit* of it. Larry!"[69]

THE LONG-AWAITED, $17-MILLION *My Fair Lady*—nearly three hours in length—was released with great fanfare in October 1964. Audrey agreed to a heavy round of promotional appearances, attending premieres in ten cities on four separate trips to America.

The dubbing controversy would not go away. At the New York opening, she looked constrained but put the best face on it for the press: "I took singing lessons from a New York vocal coach and pre-recorded all of Eliza's songs," she said, "but the final result is a blend.[70] I must say, I take my hat off to the marvelous people in Hollywood who twiddle all the knobs and who can make one voice out of two."[71]

The critics did not let up. "Although miming to a canned voice has long been a tradition of film musicals, I still find the sight of a beautiful dummy singing someone else's head off rather less than enthralling," wrote Philip Oakes in the *London Sunday Telegraph.*

"With Marni Nixon doing the singing," wrote Hedda Hopper, "Audrey Hepburn gives only half a performance." Others criticized not so much the dubbing itself as the fact that Nixon received no screen credit for it and the implication that Warner Brothers was trying to hide the truth.* "I don't know what all the fuss is about," Jack Warner replied. "We've been doing it for years. We even dubbed Rin-Tin Tin."‡

Even so, Hepburn received praise from many quarters. But when the thirty-seventh annual Oscar nominees were announced in February 1965, *My Fair Lady*'s twelve nominations did not include one for Best Actress, and the news was treated as a scandal. "JULIE ANDREWS CHOSEN, AUDREY HEPBURN OMITTED," said the page one *Los Angeles Times* headline. *Variety* was blunt about the reason why: "Hepburn did the acting, but Marni Nixon

---

* Though she got no screen acknowledgement, Nixon did and does continue to get royalties from the sound track album.

‡ "Jack Warner had wit like shrapnel," notes Roddy McDowall.

subbed for her in the singing department and that's what undoubtedly led to her erasure."

Warner called it "outrageous" and took it as a personal affront. In typically quirky fashion, he thought it was due to the quality of Nixon's singing and released a statement saying, "The next time we have some star-dubbing to do, we'll hire Maria Callas." Julie Andrews, when tracked down by the press, said, "I think Audrey should have been nominated. I'm very sorry she wasn't." Rex Harrison said the same. Katharine Hepburn sent her a telegram saying, "Don't worry about not being nominated. Some day you'll get another one for a part that doesn't rate."[72]

Audrey was in Spain when word of the Oscar snub reached her, and immediately attributed it to the dubbing.

"The trouble was, Marni blabbed all over town that she was going to more or less 'save' the movie," says André Previn. "George Cukor, who along with all of us worshipped Audrey, got very angry. He said, 'Listen, you're getting a lot of money for this and you're going to get a lot of money from the recording. Why don't you shut up about it?' Marni got a little too much mileage out of the publicity. Audrey is the only one who never said anything negative about her. That was beneath Audrey."[73]

Nixon denies and bristles at the "blabbing" charge, as well as the subsequent reports that she was "blacklisted" for revealing her dubbing of Hepburn in *My Fair Lady*:

"I was upset that people thought Audrey didn't get nominated because I did the dubbing and [that] I was purposefully trying to push that knowledge out.... I did say that during the filming of *The King and I*, the PR department threatened that I would 'never work in this town again' if I let anyone know. But that was *King and I*. *My Fair Lady* was the last film dubbing job I did, but not because I was 'prevented'—only because that era was over and pictures like that weren't being made anymore."[74]

In fact, the main source of information about the dubbing of Hepburn was not Nixon but, rather, the aggrieved friends of Julie Andrews. No one particularly cared when Nixon dubbed Deborah Kerr or Natalie Wood; but they cared when she dubbed Hepburn, considering it insult to the injury of depriving Andrews of her rightful role. In any case, the beneficiary of the dubbing fracas was Julie Andrews, now the highly favored Oscar nominee for her performance in the saccharine *Mary Poppins*.

The ordeal, for Audrey, wasn't over. She was now faced with the Awards night itself—to go or not? If she didn't, Warner and Cukor would be upset and everyone would accuse her of bad sportsmanship. The decision was soon made for her: By tradition, Patricia Neal, the previous year's Best Actress winner for *Hud*, should hand out the current year's Best Actor award. But Neal was still recovering from a devastating stroke, and Hepburn was asked by the Academy to stand in for her. Under those circumstances, there was no way she could decline.

Cukor, the front-runner for Best Director, was her escort on the night of April 5 in the Santa Monica Civic Auditorium, and he won as expected—his first Oscar victory in five nominations over the decades. In his acceptance speech, he thanked "Miss Audrey Hepburn, whose magic makes it so easy for us to win these awards." Most of the other *My Fair Lady* winners did the same in the course of the evening.

All night long, the TV cameras took every opportunity to scrutinize and juxtapose the faces of Hepburn and Andrews, building up the "tension" over Best Actress. It was won by Andrews, who thereby achieved the instant (and lasting) film success that Warner believed she could never attain. After accepting the statuette from Sidney Poitier, Andrews delivered the most acerbic remark of the night: "My thanks to Mr. Jack L. Warner, who made all this possible."[75]

Her mellower assessment came later. "I'll never know to this day whether it was sentiment that won it for me or whether the performance in *Poppins* really did," she said in 1993, adding with a smile, "I think it was the sentiment, myself."[76]

Andrews's triumph and Hepburn's humiliation were now complete, it seemed. For Audrey, at least the worst was over. Next up was the Best Actor award, and she got a warm "consolation" reception when she stepped out radiantly—in gorgeous Givenchy gown—to present it. The name in the envelope was Rex Harrison's, and she read it out beaming with real joy, kissing him repeatedly when he reached the stage to take Oscar from her hands. Harrison seemed as pleased by Hepburn's pleasure as by the award itself. In his thank-you, he said, "I should actually divide the statue in half" to share it with her, ending diplomatically with, "I admire both my fair ladies."

Harrison later called the ceremony "very embarrassing." Warners' publicity department "spent a lot of time and effort trying to keep Julie and myself apart—at least in front of the photographers," he said. "It was awful—a make-believe scandal created entirely by the press and the PR."[77]

Harrison had won over stiff competition—Peter O'Toole and Richard Burton for *Becket*, Anthony Quinn for *Zorba the Greek*, and Peter Sellers for *Dr. Strangelove*—all of whom perhaps deserved it more. *My Fair Lady* swept a total of eight awards. Most important was Best Picture, Warners' first since *Casablanca*, and Jack Warner's first as a producer.* The picture's

---

* The other *My Fair Lady* Oscar winners were Harry Stradling for Best Color Cinematography; Gene Allen, Cecil Beaton and George James for Best Color Art Direction and Set Decoration; George R. Groves for Sound; André Previn for Best Music Adaptation; and Cecil Beaton (alone) for Best Color Costume Design. Supporting actor and actress nominees Stanley Holloway and Gladys Cooper lost out to Peter Ustinov (*Topkapi*) and Lila Kedrova (*Zorba the Greek*).

overall success was enough to let Audrey say, if not too convincingly, "This evening made up for everything."[78]

She'd done well to keep a stiff upper lip and survive the night with aplomb. But unwittingly, she capped it off with the worst faux pas of her public life—a lapse of protocol for which she herself was less to blame than the Oscar show's writers.

"I had been told that Audrey Hepburn would bestow the honor in my place and I couldn't wait to hear all the nice things she said about me," recalled Patricia Neal. "... But suddenly she was handing Rex Harrison his award, and she hadn't said a thing about me. It had to be a mistake. I pounded on the table with my good hand. 'God! God! Me! Not me!' "[79]

Neal and Hepburn had gotten along well on *Breakfast at Tiffany's*. "She was a fantastic woman, really," says Neal today. "But I was so angry that she didn't say, 'I'm here in her place.' I couldn't say the words. I could only stick out my tongue."[80]

Hepburn's failure to mention Neal caused yet another mini-scandal. "Audrey snubs ailing star," said the headlines. Neal's author husband Roald Dahl was thoroughly outraged on his wife's behalf. When reporters confronted Audrey at Kennedy airport on her way back to Paris, she was mortified by her oversight and ran immediately to phone Neal and apologize. Dahl answered and responded harshly: "I told her to bugger off," he said.[81]

Neal, as time went by, was more magnanimous. "The incident at the Academy Awards occurred under enormous pressure and has long since been forgotten," she would later say. "Audrey sent me a fabulous porcelain rose, which was very good of her. I guess it just didn't occur to her that night. I suppose she was distracted. One never knows how these things happen."[82]

She had felt a powerful need to prove Warners right in giving her the role, and, despite all the handicaps, many thought she succeeded. Bosley Crowther in *The New York Times*, for one, said she was "dazzlingly beautiful and comic." But the kudos were outnumbered by brickbats. Audrey's Eliza—dream role of the decade—was doomed by the much-publicized grievances of Julie Andrews, Marni Nixon and Patricia Neal. Hepburn had always been treated gently and respectfully by the press before. Now, the combined negative fallout from *My Fair Lady* left her stunned.

"The circus aspect of the profession demands that things be made into an 'occasion,' " says Roddy McDowall. "*My Fair Lady* was like *Catch-22* and *Waterworld*—a victim of enormous, injudicious advance hype. It had been 'the time' to do in Mike Nichols and Kevin Costner then, and *My Fair Lady*, by virtue of the peculiar circumstances, was Audrey's 'time.' "

Had Julie Andrews been unavailable or indisposed, Hepburn's casting as Eliza would not have raised a stir. But Andrews was alive and well and beatified by public sympathy after Warner took "her" role away. Audrey was punished first for not being Julie and later, ironically, for the very reason Rex Harrison was much praised: the inability to sing!

"Because she was so famous, so well-behaved and such an icon," says McDowall, "she was ripe for the fall."[83]

Eliza was an extremely difficult role because of the Big Transition midway: Most actresses pulled off either the guttersnipe or the transformed goddess, rarely both. Audrey was not terribly convincing—even to herself—as the flower girl. She had been cast primarily for the transformation, and she executed it deftly. "From 'I Could Have Danced All Night,' she takes off," said Jeremy Brett. "No one can touch her from there on."

In retrospect, music director Previn thinks *My Fair Lady* is not so much a movie as a stage show preserved in amber:

"I personally don't think it's very wonderful. I think it's endless. It has very little impetus. It doesn't get going often enough. By the time Lerner and Loewe got through telling us how to approach it, it had more traditions than *The Ring* at Bayreuth. 'Is it okay if we play this eighth note shorter?' Jesus, it's a *musical*. Everybody treated it like it was the Key to the Absolute. It was overreverential, and I think it shows."[84]

Even so, it was one of the ten all-time biggest moneymakers in film history, grossing more than $33 million.

"This picture is one we must all remember," Hepburn had said to Beaton, and it was—if for the wrong reasons. For Audrey personally, it was in many ways the zenith and, simultaneously, the nadir of her career.

DURING *MY FAIR LADY* PRODUCTION, all had not been well between the Ferrers, and crew members had reported hearing the sound of quarrels emanating from Audrey's dressing room.[85] "Her relationship with Mel is not all that easy, but she loves him," wrote Cecil Beaton in his journal at the time. "Her success is astonishing, and [yet] it comes second always to her private life, and the infinite trouble and finesse she manages in that strike me as being extraordinary."

Ferrer had not endeared himself to Audrey's *My Fair Lady* colleagues in general. "I didn't like Mel very much on those few occasions when he visited the studio," said Mona Washbourne, who played Higgins's housekeeper. "He was always rather condescending and patronizing towards me, probably because I played a small part and he thought that was a bit *infra dig*. I think he was wildly jealous of Audrey."[86]

To pacify Mel and enable him to be near Audrey during *My Fair Lady*, Warners paid him twice his usual fee to play a small role in *Sex and the Single Girl*, which was filming concurrently just a soundstage away from his wife, under that old rogue Richard (*Paris When It Sizzles*) Quine. No lesser light than Joseph (*Catch-22*) Heller had cowritten the script—based unrecognizably on Helen Gurley Brown's hit book —about an ace reporter (Tony Curtis) who sets out to expose a famous sex researcher (Natalie Wood). Henry Fonda and Lauren Bacall were the unlikely comic support. Wood is supposed to join Mel Ferrer for more research, but in the end she declares, "I don't want to be a single girl!" and happily abandons her career to marry Curtis. Mel was actually quite good, but the film wasn't, and few of the reviews even bothered to mention him.

Both Ferrers were more than ready to leave Hollywood. The professional and physical strains of the previous six months had been enormous, with reverberations that carried over into their private lives and seriously disrupted their relationship. "*My Fair Lady* was an ordeal," Audrey would say, "and when it was over, I nearly broke down from the exhaustion."[87]

She longed to rest; but she longed, even more, to preserve her marriage and now, shortly after returning to Switzerland, she undertook a monumental effort to that end: In the next eight months, instead of taking it easy at home, she made sixteen trips throughout Europe with Mel on his film shoots, rarely letting him out of her sight—in the hope of curtailing his interest, or at least the persistent rumors of his interest, in other women.

Ferrer's most important film project at that time was *El Greco*, shooting in Toledo, Madrid and Rome for 20th Century-Fox. He played the title role, and she spoke of it with glowing—if premature—optimism:

"It's a wonderful vehicle, and I am praying it turns out the way Mel hopes it to be. Apart from being the man I love, Mel is also one of the most talented actors in the world and I am immensely proud of him.... I thought if I went along, I could somehow help. I could try to make the beds comfortable, to disinfect the bath, and to make them cook something palatable.... I'm sure that any wife would have done the same."[88]

El Greco, a respectable but largely ignored movie, was never released in the United States. But Mrs. Ferrer's devotion to Mr. Ferrer's comfort and career was as ceaseless in Europe as in Hollywood. There, according to André Previn:

"When you'd go over to her house, she would end up running one of Mel's movies. It was kind of sad. She had small parties, always exquisitely done, amazing cooking from the Italian ingredients she brought over with her. It was the only time I had a truly amazing pizza—thin as a Kleenex!

"She would sometimes play the piano at the house, nothing formal, but she liked good music and had a reasonable record collection. That extraordinary mystique of hers made you think she lived on rose petals and listened to nothing but Mozart, but it wasn't true. She was quite funny and ribald. She could tell a dirty joke. She played charades with a great sense of fun and vulgarity, and she could be quite bitchy.

"Alan Lerner was married to a French girl at the time—I don't know which number, maybe number seven—a very hard piece of work. She came on the set one day when I was talking to Audrey and flounced over, dressed in the most peculiar clothes. Everything matched. She went on and on and then said, 'Oh, I must fly and meet Alan for lunch!' and walked away. Audrey looked after her, turned to me and said, 'I'll bet you didn't know that even Dior makes dogs.' I thought, wow! So she was not beyond that."[89]

Audrey's own image and sense of fashion were rather subtler, to say the least, and much more powerful for being so. In the sixties as in the fifties—and again without her quite realizing it—she virtually *defined* the feminine vogues of the decade, at least thus far. Her film and fashion image, as before, still derived largely from that "ideal" figure, which continued to be admired by millions, even if it wasn't to everyone's taste and even if some people joked about it.

"If I wanted to look at bones, I could always have my foot X-rayed," said one producer—evidently one of the few who wasn't enthralled with her.[90] "Standing next to Audrey Hepburn makes you hope against hurricanes," said *McCall's* reporter Art Seidenbaum, who watched her on the set of *My Fair Lady*. "She is that thin.... Structurally, she has all the curves of a piece of melba toast—viewed from the side."[91] But even Seidenbaum immediately went on to acknowledge that Hepburn was to *haute couture* "what Bardot is to bath towels."

Audrey's legendary slender build was integral to her physical image and fashion impact—the sine qua non, perhaps—but, alone, would never have brought her such massive celebrity: It was her personality that touched and intrigued people, and not just her vulnerable sweetness. Reticence and discretion were the other key ingredients of the Audrey Formula, more than ever after the stings of *My Fair Lady*.

"I have a great sense of privacy," she said. "Writers have to have an angle. If you say less than what you might tell your husband or your doctor, then you're 'mysterious.'... Basically, I don't enjoy the one-sided talk about myself. I don't enjoy the process of cross-examination; I find it absolutely sapping. [I've] been made mistrustful by being burned."

A cynic on the *My Fair Lady* set had joked, "Somewhere beneath that even-tempered exterior is an unadulterated ax murderess. It's a wonderful mask. You could be around her six months and still not know her." It was a European mask. "I've never lived in America, always in Europe," she said in 1964. "I'm still a British subject." Her favorite recent film was the emotional *Sundays and Cybele*, in keeping with her past favorites, *Waterloo Bridge* and *Camille*, all of which made her cry. And what of her current popularity? The thirty-five-year-old Hepburn laughed and said, "I'm amazed it's lasted as long as it has."[92]

Throughout the sixties, Hepburn was second only to Jacqueline Kennedy in the degree of flattery-by-imitation she inspired. "Watch this suit—the squareness, the uncompromising flatness on the body," said a typical *Vogue* caption beneath a Hepburn photo spread in November 1964. "It's the most important piece of Givenchy tailoring this season."[93] Women followed her every sartorial move, while men reacted to her much like André Previn:

"Whether Audrey was in jeans and a bandanna or all dolled up for the Oscars—she was so beautiful that you couldn't bear it. Audrey coming up and saying hello wilted strong men. Along with everybody, I would just drown in those eyes. I discussed this I suppose in a locker-room fashion with a few of my contemporaries, but there was almost never anything carnal in it. You wouldn't look at her and say, 'Boy, would I like to—' She didn't provoke that. My wife once said to me, 'How close were you to Audrey?' I said, 'I was hopelessly in love with her.' She said, 'Good,' because she knew it would never come to anything. . . .

"Audrey knew how to handle flattery when it was not connected with a come-on. Once we were talking, and I kept looking at her until she said, 'What's the matter, what are you looking at?' I said, 'Audrey, you're just so beautiful, I can't stand it.' She giggled and took my hand and said, 'Come to dinner.' I said, 'Okay.' It was wonderfully done."[94]

Her vulnerability was no longer childlike—but still very much a part of her. During one *My Fair Lady* recording session, Previn recalls going up to her and saying, "Audrey, when I turn to cue you in, you look like you've been caught in a deer snare. Could you keep the terror out of your eyes? You look like a fawn that's about to get shot." At the end of filming, she presented him with a heavy, silver ceremonial baton from Mendelssohn's day inscribed, *To André, Love from a Fawn.*

Hepburn's friend John McCallum, the Australian actor, opined that "Sex starts in the eyes. A film close-up of an attractive woman's face is far sexier than a close-up of naked breasts. There is an expression to the effect that men make love to women's faces, and I think there is a good deal of truth in it."

Audrey agreed, and once expressed her own opinion on the subject with a surprising *lack* of self-effacement: "Sex appeal is something that you feel deep down inside. It's suggested rather than shown. . . . I'm not as well-stacked as Sophia Loren or Gina Lollobrigida, but there is more to sex appeal than just measurements. I don't need a bedroom to prove my womanliness. I can convey just as much appeal fully clothed, picking apples off a tree or standing in the rain."[95]

Loren and Lollobrigida were hardly comparable to Hepburn. Leslie

Caron was. Their gamine personas were similar, despite which, says Caron, no rivalry existed between them:

"I'm not somebody who's jealous. I truly thought Audrey was magnificent, and I thought she had many qualities I lacked, and perhaps I had one or two she didn't have. I thought she was so gorgeous, so elegant, so refined, and so adorable. But I thought perhaps I had more sense of drama than she had."

In their twenties, Hepburn and Caron played many of the same parts, from Gigi to Ondine, but at this point, as actresses, they and their roles had totally diverged: Caron seemed to change. Hepburn seemed not to.

"It was partly a financial thing," says Caron. "She wasn't under contract. She was free. She earned a great deal more money than I and didn't need to adapt so much to circumstances, whereas I really did have to go on working out of necessity—and I'm glad of it. I developed a sort of second career as a sometimes outrageous, frivolous, middle-aged woman, and sometimes the opposite type of modest, subservient woman, as when I played the wife of Lenin. I was forced to become more versatile."[96]

There were reports that Hepburn had wanted the part of the pregnant French girl, superbly played by Caron in *The L-Shaped Room* (1963), but Caron says, "No, I don't think that's true."

Audrey and her image didn't need it.

THE ISSUES OF HEPBURN'S IMAGE and publicity were now causing problems with Mel and with her friend Henry Rogers. One of Hollywood's top publicists, Rogers had met her during *War and Peace* and, in the years since, had guided and protected her and played a large role in molding the public view of her. Rogers, in his memoirs, recorded intimate impressions of both Ferrers:

> She never had the burning desire to... remain a movie star, as do most actresses, but instead cared only for personal happiness, peace, love, her children, a husband whom she loved and who loved her. Rarely did I ever see her happy. It was no secret that her marriage with Mel was not a happy one. It seemed to me that she loved him more than he loved her, and it was frustrating for her not to have her love returned in kind. She had confided these feelings to me.... I always saw the sadness in her eyes....
>
> She wanted to work less and spend more time [with Mel and Sean]. She was filled with love. Mel was filled with ambition, for his wife and for himself. [He] had pushed her into the relationship... with me, and although we became close friends, she always bridled when I mentioned the need for an interview or a photo session.... I performed a constant balancing act between Mel's insatiable desire for Audrey's new publicity and her reluctance.[97]

The beginning of the end of the Hepburn-Rogers professional relationship came on a Sunday at the Ferrers' home in Switzerland where Audrey, Mel and Henry engaged in a heated discussion of her career. At issue was the new Givenchy perfume, L'Interdit.

"Mel," said Rogers, "resented the fact that she had given Givenchy her name and likeness to launch his first venture into the fragrance business. *Vogue, Harper's Bazaar, Town and Country* and other mags all over the world were carrying a magnificent portrait of Audrey, indicating that the fragrance had been created exclusively for her. Givenchy had built a multimillion-dollar business using Audrey—without compensating her."

At Mel's request, Rogers had stopped in Paris to meet with Givenchy's brother Claude and discuss compensation for the use of Audrey's likeness. Mel had said, "For Christ's sake, Henry, she doesn't even get a discount on the clothes he designs for her. As for the perfume, wouldn't you think he would send her gallons of it as a gift? She buys it herself—retail!"

Rogers now told the Ferrers about his meeting in Paris and said the Givenchys were agreeable to some payment. But Audrey said, "Neither of you seems to understand. I don't want anything from Hubert. I don't need his money. He is my friend. If I have helped him build his perfume business, then that's exactly what one friend should do for another.... Yes, I even want to walk into a drugstore and buy the perfume at the retail price."

At that tense moment, according to Rogers, the doorbell rang and yet another crisis presented itself in the form of Favre Le Bret, director of the Cannes Film Festival, with whom Audrey, Mel and Rogers had been friendly for years. He had come to ask Audrey to attend the opening night of that year's festival.

"Mel had asked me what I thought about it," said Rogers. "I told him I was opposed, that there was no reason for Audrey to attend the opening ceremonies. She didn't have a film that was being screened. She did not need or care about the publicity she would get out of it. [But] Mel kept insisting I talk to him."

Audrey left the room. "I'm going upstairs to see Sean," she said. "You fellows decide what to do." Rogers told Le Bret there had to be a reason for Hepburn to attend—and soon came up with one himself. The festival, he proposed, should create a new annual award—"a special tribute to one person, an actor, an actress, a producer, or a director who has made an outstanding contribution to [film]. This year it could be Audrey." Le Bret said he'd think about it. The next morning, Rogers's hotel phone rang and the sobbing voice at the other end was Audrey's.

"What's wrong?" he asked. "Is something wrong with Sean?"

"No, Henry, it's you. You know how much I care about you—how much I value your friendship. I'm crying because I have decided that I don't want you to represent me anymore.... I just can't stand any more of this. I just don't like what is happening to me, and my life and my friends.... First you embarrassed me with Hubert, [and last night] Favre Le Bret told me you had tried to blackmail him, that you told him the only way I would go to the Cannes Film Festival would be if he gave me some kind of phony, trumped-up award. Henry, I don't want you to work for me anymore. Will you still be my friend?"

Rogers was stunned. "Here was a lively, sensitive person, genuinely sobbing her heart out," he said. "She really did not want to be involved in the complex world which is part and parcel of the motion picture industry—the intrigue, the deals, the negotiations that go on behind the scenes." Of course they would remain friends, he told her, but "you must understand one thing. You have known me for many years. You know how I work. You know very well that I never tried to blackmail Le Bret. If he is stupid enough to interpret my proposal [that way], I never want anything to do with him again—and you shouldn't either."[98]

Hepburn and Rogers did remain friends. But the man who really instigated Rogers's dealings with Le Bret and Givenchy was Mel Ferrer—and he took her dismissal of Rogers hard.

CHAPTER 7

Nights Off for Givenchy
(1965–1967)

"I'm the only person alive who has attacked Audrey Hepburn, and in public.
I've tried to make up for it with a series of
heartwarming performances on public
television."

ALAN ARKIN

DIRE PREDICTIONS OF THE FERRERS' imminent marital collapse had been rife—and wrong—for a decade. The Givenchy and Le Bret flaps produced additional stress but did not prevent their agreement, with Sean's future in mind, on the major decision to leave Bürgenstock.

Sean would recall her saying that not least of the reasons why his mother chose to live in Switzerland was because "it was a place where there would never be a war." As a boy then (and long after), his term of endearment for her was *Mutti*, a German diminutive of mother.[1] Audrey loved the pet name but not much else about that language and what it represented for her: Bürgenstock was in the heart of the German part of Switzerland, and the idea of her son attending a German school was repellent.

The picturesque place to which the Ferrers relocated would remain Audrey's home for life: the village of Tolochenaz-sur-Morges, above Lake Geneva, fifteen miles from Lausanne and thirty from Geneva. There in the French-speaking canton of Vaud, Audrey—not Mel—purchased a fine old eighteenth-century farmhouse. It was an eight-bedroom villa built of the local peach-colored stone, surrounded by a white picket fence and situated on Tolochenaz's one and only street, Route de Bière, with beautiful Alpine vistas. It was called "La Paisible" (The Peaceful Place) and, for Audrey, would always live up to its name.

Tolochenaz dated back to an early Celtic settlement of lake dwellers, who built their homes on stilts.[2] Its current inhabitants—barely five hundred of them—were mostly farmers with fruit orchards and vineyards and a few cattle. It was quite near the Geneva-Lausanne highway but set back far enough to retain its quiet, isolated charm. A hardware shop and a grocery were pretty much the sole businesses on the sole street.

"Come with me, I want to show you the exact angle the moment I first saw the house!" Audrey told Anna Cataldi, a good friend of later years, on Anna's initial visit. Audrey led her into the garden and enthused, "I was here when I had the first glance of the house and it was spring and fruit trees were in blossom, and my heart stopped beating. I said, 'This is my place!'"[3]

It was a place where her domestic instincts and love of family life led her to an old-fashioned testimonial: "I have never gotten over the wonder of being married," she said. "Like many teenagers, I thought I was such an ugly thing that no one would ever want me for a wife.... Which is why I always say to Mel, 'Thanks to you I'm off the shelf!'"[4]

Within a year, she would get over the wonder and the home front would not be so blissful. But for now, in mid-1965, they were happy with their post-*My Fair Lady* rapprochement, which was based on her becoming a full-time wife and mother. She put her career on hold in order to "be there" every day when Sean came home from the two-room schoolhouse where he was fast adding French to the four other languages he knew (Italian, Spanish, English and German). Staying home was no sacrifice when the alternative was being miserable on a movie set. From now on, Tolochenaz was her "harbor," she said, "the absolute opposite of the life I led working. I was to a great extent left in peace. The Swiss press doesn't care what you do. If I had lived in London or New York or Hollywood, it would have been outlandish. I never liked the city. I always wanted the countryside."[5]

Life in Tolochenaz was made more *paisible* and pleasant by the presence of an artiste named Florida Broadway. "I once asked if that was her real name," says Leonard Gershe, "and she said, 'Would anybody make up a name like that?'"[6]

Florida was the African-American chef *par excellence*, hired by the Ferrers in California during *My Fair Lady* on Gershe's recommendation. "Audrey was so crazy about her, she took her to Switzerland," he recalls. Florida had previously worked for the likes of Joan Fontaine and Diahann Carroll, "but no one as nice as Miss Hepburn," she says. For two years, she created gourmet and everyday meals for the Ferrers and was a member of the family, as she recalls today in her soft-spoken, regal way:

I didn't like Mr. Ferrer at first—he was so stiff, where she was so warm and had a marvelous sense of humor. But I grew fond of them both. I was terribly lonely there at first. She'd invite me to go on walks, and I was allowed to make calls at least twice a week to my family in the U.S. They did other nice things—they let me use the chauffeur on my day off, and I'd go into the city and get lost.

Mr. Ferrer was a little fussy about food, but she ate everything and always wanted to experiment. If I was fixing something special for myself—something ethnic—she'd want to come back and have some of it. Like greens—collards. I'll never forget what we went through in Rome, trying to find this kind of smoked pork that I liked. Every time they went into the city, they'd come back with the wrong thing. It was never what I wanted. She kept trying and trying and finally found it—oh, I was ecstatic! I said, "I'm going back to my roots." She said, "After all this trouble, I've got to have some of this!" So she came back into the kitchen and sat down and enjoyed it the same as I did.[7]

A frequent visitor in those days was Audrey's mother, who "got a big bang out of her title," Florida thought. "The Baroness really liked goulash. Mrs. Ferrer, on the other hand, liked a good hearty soup and I made great soup." Sean she describes as "a very privileged little boy, and why not? His food was all prepared fresh. He turned out to be a chunky fellow—he liked a lot of bread and cake."

Mel was allergic to garlic. "Oddly enough, so was Ella," says Gershe. "They were also allergic to each other. Anyway, Florida had to find some other way to spice up the pasta."

It was her greatest culinary challenge.

"My God, how can you cook without garlic?" she says. "So I invented a spaghetti sauce using green olives instead of garlic. The olives, and the slow process of cooking it forever, did the trick. They really liked it. She used to say she had spaghetti all over the world but never quite as good as mine."

In the dessert department, Florida's dilemma was that "one of them liked chocolate cake and the other liked white, so I made an 'integrated cake' for them—half chocolate and half white. Mr. Ferrer got a big bang out of me calling it that. Some people treat their help as just hired hands, but they weren't like that. I only had one experience with her that I was upset about...."

Florida, out of loyalty and discretion, hesitates to tell the story but finally decides to do so:

The household was fully staffed. I was the chef. One day, on the maid's day off, Mrs. Ferrer came in and noticed a dirty spot in the kitchen. She asked if I would clean it up. Well, there wasn't a mop—and anyway, that wasn't my job. So I said that the girl would be back the next day to do it. She said, "Well, you could just get down on your hands and knees and do it yourself." I was horrified. I said, "You know something, Mrs. Ferrer, I only get on my

knees to pray." And she said, *"Well, pray the while!"* I was offended. It
sounded medieval, like a Shakespearean play. I thought, "What does she
mean?" Then it occurred to me she was saying, "Pray the while you're
down there!" So I said to her, "I would rather not." It was the only time I
got really angry with her. To me, that was like insulting my religious beliefs,
and I let her know it.[8]

This, by all accounts, was Audrey Hepburn at her most "vicious"—
and predictably, she felt guilty about it.

"I never did clean the spot up," says Florida. "She must have regretted
it because she did all sorts of little things for me that afternoon to kind of
make up for it."[9]

WHEN ASKED IF SHE EVER noticed any eating disorder on Audrey's part,
Florida Broadway responds with a categorical no:

"For a tiny woman, she had an enormous appetite. I really doubt those
bulimia or anorexia stories. She loved to eat, and they had all kinds of
things with butter and cream. They liked chocolate souffle, roast duck,
rich things. Once when Yul Brynner came to dinner, I made this roast
duck and, oh, you never heard such carrying on over a duck in all your
life."[10]

Brynner was married to Audrey's beloved Doris Kleiner, one of the
prominent, jet-setting Beautiful People of the day. Born in Yugoslavia, she
grew up in Santiago, Chile, came to Paris in the 1950s, and was working
there at Pierre Cardin's when she met Audrey. The Brynners married in
1960, during the making of *The Magnificent Seven*, and took up residence
in a beautiful lakeside property near Lausanne, just ten minutes from
Tolochenaz.

"We became close friends right away," says Doris. "Nothing happened
in my life without her knowing about it or in her life without my knowing
about it. Soul mates. It only happens once in a lifetime. Audrey really
cared and really listened. Most people don't. If you really listen, it's because
you really care. I don't listen to half of what I hear—but Audrey did."

She listened especially to Doris's daughter Victoria—her godchild.
Audrey was no figurehead godmother, but an actively functioning one
who "always gave incredibly sound advice whenever I had problems with
my parents or boyfriends or if I was scared about something," says
Victoria. "It was heaven, having this generous, adorable, loving person
who was never critical."

At one point Victoria considered becoming an actress and took Method-
acting classes in Paris. "I came back distraught and flabbergasted by the
system," she says. "They told me to imagine I was holding a cup of coffee

and how I would drink it, with my eyes closed sitting on a chair. When I related this to Audrey, she said, 'That seems funny—either you drink a cup of coffee in a natural way or you don't.' She was graced with such a natural talent herself, it made no sense whatsoever to her."[11]*

She always had time for Victoria who—like her mother—became an integral part of Audrey's family. As always, nothing was more important than family, Doris Brynner reconfirms:

"She wasn't a social person. Her biggest joy was being at home with her children or in the garden. That was where she wanted to be most. She was a great cook and loved her food. Yul didn't like pasta, so whenever he went on trips, Audrey would come to my house and we'd have pasta and vanilla ice cream and fudge sauce. That was our great treat. We lived more than twenty years within sight distance, just above her. She'd come up or I'd go down for walks with the dogs. . . . The prime time was to have a plate of spaghetti and chat, just the two of us."

Their lives were centered around their children and their homes, in the beautiful vineyard country near Lausanne, where the grapes ripen from the reflection of the sun off the lake. They left the area only rarely. "We weren't shoppers," says Doris. "Maybe twenty years ago, life was different, we would go to a party in Portugal or take off to get away for a bit. But that was long ago. Anybody who just gets on a plane to go shopping in Paris is a fool. Your priorities change over the years, thank God."[12]

BUT AUDREY, WE KNOW, ALWAYS had a weakness for Paris. She now flew there, in July 1965, not for a shopping spree but to make *How to Steal a Million* for director William Wyler—their third together—at the Boulogne Studios. The screenplay by Harry Kurnitz, from a story by George Bradshaw, was a light confection in the *Pink Panther* vein: Hepburn plays the daughter of art forger Hugh Griffith, whose flawless fake of a Cellini statue of Venus is about to be exhibited as the real thing. Ethical Audrey is so upset about it, and worried for her father's impending arrest, that she joins forces with burglar Peter O'Toole to steal it from the museum.

Wyler and 20th Century-Fox pulled out all the artistic stops: Master designer Alexandre Trauner of Hungary was hired to create the beautiful sets. He, in turn, hired expert copyists for the gigantic labor of creating all the phony Renoirs, van Goghs and Picassos needed for the film.[13]‡ Mel

---

* Victoria Brynner decided she wasn't cut out for acting—at least not *Method* acting. She would become a skilled photographer, instead (see photo 51).

‡ Fox would promote *How to Steal a Million* with a special Parke-Bernet exhibition in New York of forty brilliant forgeries that had been created for the movie.

had agreed to stay in Tolochenaz with Sean while Audrey worked in Paris and flew home on the weekends. Terribly fearful of kidnappers, she had bought a German shepherd (and later an Australian sheepdog) to guard their home and refused to let Sean be photographed by anyone. Her fears were increased in Paris when, one morning, a group of men in masks tied up the studio concierge and made off with the production's payroll.

But her consolation was Peter O'Toole—and the fun they had during the eleven days it took to shoot the sequence in which they are locked up together inside a cramped museum closet, awaiting the precisely timed moment to execute their heist.

"If you're not in a place like that with somebody you like, it can be very boring," she said. Years later, the very mention of O'Toole's name would make her burst into laughter. "My friend! He was very dear and very funny. I don't know why, but he used to call me the Duke of Buckingham...."[14]

O'Toole knew why. As he later explained to writer Ian Woodward, the reference was to the great nineteenth-century actor Edmund Kean and a colleague—both heavy drinkers—who were playing Richard III and the Duke of Buckingham in *Richard III*. Kean as the King tottered onto the stage, "thoroughly polluted with liquid light, started his soliloquy and the audience began to call and bawl 'You're drunk!' 'He's drunk!'... Kean glared at them and said, 'If you think I am drunk, wait till you see the Duke of Buckingham,' and, waiting at the side of the stage, was indeed the Duke of Buckingham on his hands and knees."

But what did that have to do with Audrey?

"We were filming an exterior in Paris and the weather turned round and became very, very cold indeed," O'Toole related. "Audrey had to walk across the street, get into a waiting car and drive off, but the poor child had turned bright blue with cold. The light was going and the shot was needed. I pulled Audrey into the caravan and gave her a shot of brandy. She went all roses and cream, bounced out of the caravan, radiated towards the motor car, hopped into it and drove off, taking with her five great big lamps [being used to light the scene], the trimmers of which had flung themselves on the cobbles out of the way. From then on she was my Duke of Buckingham."[15]

Director Wyler complained—but not too bitterly: "They react on each other like laughing gas, and the trouble is they're in almost every scene together."

Freewheeling O'Toole, an erstwhile drummer and banjo-player, was as fond of jazz and he was of drink, and obtained both in quantity at a Parisian bistro called Le Living-Room. More than once he helped shut the place down at its closing time (six a.m.). He attributed his nocturnal habits to childhood days of tagging along with his bookmaker father and falling asleep under the tables at which good Irish whiskey was consumed—and good horse-racing tips exchanged—into the wee hours.

Says a female cast member who wishes to remain anonymous:

"The three men who started out on that film—Hugh Griffith, Peter O'Toole and George C. Scott—were wonderful actors but often incoherent by eleven a.m. Scott said he was ill. They sent a doctor, but George threw him out bodily. So they fired George."

Scott was to play a crass American tycoon who has a fixation on the Cellini statue and is desperate to buy it—and Audrey. His role now went to Eli Wallach, imported on a kind of emergency leave of absence from the Broadway production of *Luv*.

"There was one scene in the movie where I had to kiss her," says Wallach, "and Audrey was quite tall. "She looked at me and smiled and said, 'I'll take my shoes off.' I said, 'I love you, I love you.' She took her shoes off and played the scene."[16]

The unlikely duo of Wallach and O'Toole were good friends on and off the set. "Peter was in his prime," says Wallach, "—a bright man who liked to tease. He had his evil spirits. The alcohol sent the editor of his brain home. But he had great respect for Audrey, which came across on the screen. And when he was finally told he had to stop drinking—he did. For good."

O'Toole was a cutup but also a good observer. He found Audrey to have a fine sense of fun but also "a modesty and a sadness" about her. And he was fascinated by Charles Boyer, who played the part of a gallery owner in the film.

"Charles had just lost his son," O'Toole recalled. "We had to shoot a gay scene. I wondered, at such a moment, if his memory would hold out. It did; Boyer thought of nothing but playing the scene well, but we all had tears in our eyes.... Bloody total perfection."[17*]

Of equal perfection in *How to Steal a Million* is the first memorable glimpse of Audrey Hepburn in her white suit, white gloves, white "bobby" hat, white stockings, white shoes and white sunglasses. Everything is white—except her flaming red sports car, for outrageous contrast. Soon after, she is lying sexily in bed (reading an Alfred Hitchcock mystery magazine) when she hears a burglar break into her father's art gallery below.

It's O'Toole, of course, and it's one of the film's funniest scenes: She catches and holds him at gunpoint. The gun goes off accidentally, and they both faint as a result of *his* flesh wound. "I'm a society burglar," he complains when revived. "I don't expect people to rush about shooting

* Michael Boyer committed suicide in 1965. Charles Boyer did the same in 1978, two days after the death of his wife.

me." He talks her out of calling the police and into driving him back to his hotel. She puts her go-go boots over her negligee and gripes, "This is crazy—you should be in jail, and I should be in bed." But she is smitten, inevitably, after his first bold kiss.

Hepburn is stunningly dressed by Givenchy in every scene, most notably in a black voile dinner dress and lace "mask" midway. Wyler's pace is leisurely—the film is two hours and seven minutes long. He gives the audience its money's worth of Audrey. She and O'Toole are as good as the script, which is not as Hitchcockian as it wants to be. In *Charade*, Hepburn was really a foil to Grant; in *Million*, O'Toole is the foil to Hepburn.

"Take off your clothes," he orders after they're locked inside the closet, handing her a scrubwoman's outfit.

"Are we planning the same sort of crime?" she enquires.

The closet scene was photographed with masterful irony by Charles Lang—just a narrow strip of lighted space in the middle of the huge, wide and otherwise pitch black Panavision frame. Such was their proximity and for so long, said O'Toole, that he had a hard time restraining himself. Romantic as well as funny, that sequence fueled press rumors of an affair, encouraged as usual by the film's publicists and, as usual, false.

Wyler had been pleased to make a comedy in the wake of his depressing previous picture, *The Collector*. But when it was released in July 1966, the critics were less pleased. "They have her repeat her characterization of the *jeune fille* undergoing romantic awakening, a role in which she is now expert to the point of ennui—a kind of upper-class Debbie Reynolds," wrote Richard Schickel in *Life*. Crowther in the *New York Times* called both the movie and the Givenchy wardrobe "preposterous." To look at it, one would never suspect that the glossy, lumbering *How to Steal a Million* was made in the raging middle of the Vietnam war. Wyler made only two more films before retiring in 1970.

Hepburn and O'Toole did not work together again, and in later years Audrey often expressed regret about it. Eli Wallach thinks the film never got proper credit for the fact that she was finally paired with a handsome lover her own age, instead of the older men with whom she was usually saddled.

The problem with *How to Steal a Million* was McLuhanesque: Its message was its medium, and its medium was entirely Audrey. There is a point in any star's career, says Caroline Latham, at which the real-life personality begins to dwarf or dominate the characters he or she plays. One solution is to mock the legend, playing on audience memories of the star's previous roles. In this case, Wyler played on her persona as a fashion statement—"High Audrey" all the way. "The absorption with Hepburn's looks and mannerisms," says Latham, "teeters on the edge of parody."[18]

When O'Toole surveys her in the shabby cleaning woman's disguise, he says, "That does it!"

"Does what?" she asks.

"Well, for one thing," he replies, "it gives Givenchy a night off."

BULLETIN, WIDELY PUBLISHED: "AUDREY HEPBURN and Richard Burton will star in the MGM musical remake of *Goodbye, Mr. Chips*, each to receive a salary of $1 million against 10 percent of the gross."

False bulletin. Her pal Peter O'Toole and singer Petula Clark would eventually take the roles, instead.

The role Audrey much preferred at the moment was that of gardener in Tolochenaz—and expectant mother. She was ecstatic about both, but in January 1966, her joy ended in a Lausanne clinic with another miscarriage. Once again, she was overcome by sorrow. The mediocre reception of *How to Steal a Million* did nothing to pull her out of it, but Mel was determined not to let her wallow in depression. His antidote, as always, was the therapeutic activity of a new project. For psychological and professional reasons alike, he thought she should update her film image to suit the times—which were a-changin'.

Of dozens of proposed scripts, the winning candidate was *Two for the Road*, to be directed by Stanley Donen. If she was going to do a real "makeover," it would be under the guidance of an old and trusted friend. The offbeat story concept, on the other hand, was quite new and untested. Writer Frederic Raphael and his wife, from the time they were childhood sweethearts, always went on holiday to the south of France. Going to the same places over and over, he sometimes had the sensation of passing a former version of himself along the same road. He asked Donen if a movie about the relationship of a man and woman—told in five different time bands as they traveled their holiday road—sounded interesting. Donen said it sounded wonderful.[19]

Two for the Road chronicled a faltering twelve-year marriage, not unlike the length and condition of Hepburn's own. It would be her daring departure, once and for all, from the fifties to the swinging sixties (now that they were half over).[20] Paul Newman was the director's first choice for her leading man. When he turned down the role, Donen offered it to Albert Finney.

The Angriest Young Man of the British new wave and one of its hottest properties was Finney, who had given brilliant performances in *Saturday Night and Sunday Morning* (1960) and *Tom Jones* (1963). Hepburn heard much about him from Peter O'Toole, his fellow student at London's Royal Academy of Dramatic Art. O'Toole had taken the lead in *Lawrence of Arabia* when Finney rejected it in favor of stage work in *Billy Liar* and *Luther*. At thirty, Finney was seven years younger than Hepburn, and she was the first real film superstar with whom he'd been teamed.

"Audrey Hepburn Swings? You're Kidding," said the incredulous *Ladies' Home Journal* headline, while shocking talk of miniskirts and nude scenes peppered the text beneath it. Audrey didn't need "a look," said the magazine. "She already *is* one." She would alter her style about as readily as Charles de Gaulle. "Why change?" she once said. "Everyone has his own style. When you have found it, you should stick to it." But that was then. Now, of her metamorphosis in *Two for the Road*, she was saying, "All convention is rigidifying. I think we should try to avoid being rigid—that does age one."[21]

Her revisionist declaration was a little stiff, but she was trying hard. Indeed, she would have to: Raphael's script called for adultery, a bathing-suit appearance, and a steamy bedroom scene in which she wore nothing at all. "It is inconceivable that it could have been submitted to me ten years ago," she said, "or even five," and her qualms were many. But when Mel read it, his advice was, "Take it right away."[22]

When we first meet the Hepburn and Finney characters, Joanna and Mark, their relationship is set: They're rampantly unfaithful to each another, but no time is wasted on background explanation. The issue is marital game-playing, and this marriage seems doomed at the outset—or maybe not, depending on the time frame.

Two for the Road's structure was revolutionary: The couple's shifting attachments unfold in episodic, non-sequential fashion. Donen cuts back and forth over a twelve-year period, with only the cars, clothes and hairdos to help us figure out the chronology.

Beyond that are the metaphysical implications—"the past's intrusion upon the present," says Donen biographer Joseph Casper, who calls the film "a pas de deux on wheels." Mark and Joanna sometimes even pass themselves surrealistically on the road. It was a "deconstructivist" narrative that helped introduce New Wave techniques to Hollywood, but the shooting was mostly in France. Audrey was introduced to Finney there in the summer of 1966 and was instantly struck by his muscular good looks and his sharp, unpredictable mind. Her impact on him was potent, too:

Audrey and I met in a seductive ambience [in] a *very* sensual time in the Mediterranean. We got on immediately. After the first day's rehearsals, I could tell that the relationship would work out wonderfully. Either the chemistry is there, or it isn't.... That happened with Audrey. During a scene with her, my mind knew I was acting but my heart didn't, and my body certainly didn't! Performing with Audrey was quite disturbing, actually.... With a woman as sexy as Audrey, you sometimes get to the edge where make-believe and reality are blurred. All that staring into each other's eyes.... People are always asking me when I'm going to marry her.... I won't discuss it more because of the degree of intimacy involved. The time spent with Audrey is one of the closest I've ever had.[23]

The usual reports of a romance between costars were quick in coming, with one significant difference: This time, it was true. When production moved to the French Riviera, Hepburn cut loose even more, frugging away with Finney in the local discotheques and otherwise cavorting with him in their off-hours.

The greater test of Audrey Hepburn's new "liberation" lay in those much-ballyhooed scenes in which she had to unveil most of her self-consciously thin body. The beach scene with Finney had her in a stew. She told Donen she didn't think she could do it. It was one thing for the younger, athletic Finney to run around in his swimming trunks; it was another for Audrey, at thirty-seven, to expose herself to the world. But Donen cajoled and talked her out of a body double, and she came through admirably.[24]

That left the final challenge of the "nude" bedroom scene, filmed at the Hotel du Golf in Beauvallon near St. Tropez: After all the publicity, it turned out to be much ado about very little, the total nudity consisting of her upper back. The rest of her was demurely covered by a sheet. Finney, for his part, was even more demurely covered—clad in a T-shirt throughout their postcoital pillow talk in the scene.

Audrey's biggest problem in *Two for the Road* was the reverse of what she originally feared: not what she had to take off but what she had to put on. With Mel's approval, Donen decided to dump Givenchy in favor of Audrey's new, "mod" look—not too far removed from the one Raphael conceived the previous year for Julie Christie in *Darling.* "The beautiful simplification of her life was gone when Givenchy wasn't to dress her," said one of Audrey's friends. "Mel was trying to tear away some of the cocoon which had been wrapped around her for too long."[25]

Most of her *Two for the Road* wardrobe would be purchased "off the rack" *pret-à-porter* at Parisian boutiques. Ken Scott was brought in as fashion coordinator, and she took a liking to his Ban-Lon prints. But Scott found her "extremely rigid," even about informal clothes. Red and most other primary colors were taboo. "I want to stay in fashion," she told an interviewer at the time, "but being young in spirit counts more toward looking young than dressing in a hippie style."[26] There was always a certain defensiveness in her comments on the subject.

Worn-out by arguing over every detail, Scott departed and was replaced by Lady Claire Rendlesham, who got along better with Audrey and worked hard to modify (and pad out) the selections, from miniskirts to swimsuits, according to her demands. Most of the clothes came from London's Mary Quant, supplemented by Paco Rabanne and other top "mod" designers of the day.

In the end, Audrey's new duds enhanced her performance and, in the opinion of costar William Daniels, helped liberate her not only from her inhibitions and from Givenchy, but also from Mel. She seemed relieved to be out from under his supervision and to become a kid again—or at least her own woman—after years of conforming to his wishes. Daniels recalled her as "constantly laughing, relaxed and joyous," often taking off with Finney to drink and dance at the bistros.[27] Novelist Irwin Shaw, an old friend, described his visit with her on the set:

"She and Albie had this wonderful thing together, like a pair of kids with a perfect understanding and a shorthand of jokes and references that closed out everybody else. It was like a brother-sister in their teens. When Mel was there... , Audrey and Albie got rather formal and a little awkward, as if now they had to behave like grown-ups."[28]

Stanley Donen said "the Audrey I saw during the making of this film I didn't even know. She overwhelmed me. She was so free, so happy. I never saw her like that. So young!... I guess it was Albie." Finney was youthful, frisky, impulsive and exciting—everything Mel was not.[29]

She could not go too far, of course. The attachment with Finney was strong but temporary. It could not be allowed to compromise or endanger her custody of Sean. Though separated, she and Mel were on civilized terms and had decided to give the relationship another try. During one of many phone calls, Mel told her he was taking Sean to a matinee of *My Fair Lady*. The next day, she phoned to ask if he'd had a nice afternoon.

"Yes," said Sean.

"Did you do anything special?"

"Yes, we had ice cream."

"Did you see a movie?" she prompted.

"Yes.... Mommy, why did you hate to take a bath?"[30]

It was time to go home, hold him in her arms, and explain things like Eliza's bathtub scene in person.

DONEN CALLS *TWO FOR THE ROAD* the first Audrey Hepburn movie to deal with the *aftermath* rather than the initial euphoria of falling in love. Essential to its success was her comic timing which, in the director's opinion, measured up nicely to Raphael's sharp dialogue (and helped earn him an Oscar nomination for it).

"When we married you were a disorganized, egotistical failure," Joanna tells Mark. "Now you are a disorganized, egotistical success."

Two for the Road ended with a shocking, two-word exchange between the two stars—shocking, at least, for an Audrey Hepburn film, and the closest thing to profanity in any of her films:

"Bitch!" says he.

"Bastard!" she replies.

As the insecure, egotistical architect, Finney had more difficulty than Hepburn, and his one-dimensional performance was somewhat grating. "Albie really can't bear playing a man with pleasant charm," said Donen. "He wants to play something more startling. He doesn't like to come in and win you with his pleasant ways."[31] Eleanor Bron, William Daniels and Gabrielle Middleton (the horrid daughter) nearly stole the film in their several hilarious episodes as the travel-companions-from-hell.

Many felt it was Audrey's best performance in years, and some even said it was the best in her entire career. One of the film's biggest fans is Audrey Wilder:

"I was crazy about *Two for the Road* and thought she really let her defenses down in it. That was a real person. She let herself be seen in not the best light—the bathing suit and all. Actresses all try to protect themselves usually. That's the nature of the beast. But she's really real in that."[32]

Films and Filming hailed it as "a combination of American expertise and European cool," adding that it would not have been nearly so convincing if Hepburn's role had been played by the more overtly sexual Julie Christie or Jeanne Moreau.

Two for the Road did moderately well at the box office—better in Europe than in America, where it was handled as a kind of "art film," just beyond mainstream appeal. But it was influential in changing the way Hollywood would treat the subject of marriage, and certain film historians still consider it "a veritable textbook on editing."

Donen's next film, the brilliant Faust-parody *Bedazzled* (1967), would employ a much sharper satirical touch. His personal judgment of *Two for the Road* is that it was "a good movie, but I don't think it should have been as sweet as it was."

"AUDREY CARED FOR FINNEY A great deal," says Robert Wolders today. "He represented a whole new freedom and closeness for her. It was the beginning of a new period of her life."

But given that the Ferrers were still trying to work out their marriage, the reports of her activities with Finney caused Mel concern. Audrey, for her part, was concerned about Mel and a fifteen-year-old Spanish dancer named Marisol.

Marisol had captivated both Ferrers a year or so earlier at a party given by the Duchess of Alba in Madrid. With fiery eyes and voluptuous breasts, Marisol thrilled that gathering with her remarkable singing and dancing. Soon after, Mel and Audrey began to plan a movie around her, *Cabriola*. Mel's story and screenplay were accepted by Columbia as a vehicle for Marisol and Spain's great bullfighter, Angel Peralta. The picture would be made primarily for the Spanish and South American markets.

Mel would direct.

Audrey took it upon herself to take Marisol to Alexandre of Paris, who restyled the girl's hair under Hepburn's supervision. During and after *Cabriola*, rumors of Ferrer's "affair" with Marisol abounded. With much weariness, Ferrer today denies it: "There was no romantic involvement; it was common knowledge that Marisol was involved with the Spanish producer of the film. Audrey and our son Sean were with me as we went from location to location in Madrid and Andalucia."[33]

Marital difficulties notwithstanding, he and Audrey decided to build a villa on the Spanish Riviera near Marbella. The Peter Viertels lived there, too, and often visited, Deborah Kerr recalls:

"It was a charming house, very simple, and of course everything was white. Wherever they went, everything was white. I always thought that was—not strange, but so indicative of her: Everything had to be white. The car was white. Even the baby was dressed in white."[34]

At the end of *Cabriola* filming, "We decided to stay on at the Marbella Club and have a little holiday with Sean," Mel recalls. "Audrey had brought a stack of unread scripts with her, and while she and Sean went for a stroll on the beach I tried to unwind by going through them." One of them came from Kay Brown, a friend of Mel's who had found Margaret Mitchell's *Gone With the Wind* in galley form and persuaded David O. Selznick to read it.

"The play Kay submitted was Frederick Knott's *Wait Until Dark*," says Ferrer. "When Audrey returned from her walk, I took Sean back to the beach and she read the play. We called Kurt Frings in California and set a deal that afternoon."[35]

KNOTT WAS THE AUTHOR OF *Dial M for Murder*, and—thanks to Kay Brown—Mel read his *Wait Until Dark* even before it opened on Broadway. He immediately pegged it as a tour de force for his wife—by far the most vulnerable of all the vulnerable roles she had played to date, or ever would: a blind girl terrorized in her Greenwich Village apartment by three vicious criminals.*

"*Wait Until Dark* was a pivotal moment in Audrey's career," Ferrer

---

* When Knott's thriller did open on Broadway, at the Ethel Barrymore Theater on February 2, 1966, it earned a Tony nomination for Lee Remick and enjoyed a 373-performance run.

contends. "She went from an ingenue to a leading woman in it, and it was one of the best films she ever made." Warners paid $1 million for the screen rights and provided Audrey with an exceptional supporting cast: Alan Arkin, Richard Crenna, Jack Weston, Efrem Zimbalist, Jr. and child-prodigy Julie Herrod. Mel was the producer and quickly signed up Britain's Terence Young for his Hollywood debut as director.

Young's very first film, it may be recalled, was the powerful war documentary *Men of Arnhem* (1944), which Audrey revered. More recent and spectacular were his three wildly popular James Bond pictures, *Dr. No, From Russia with Love* and *Thunderball.* Young was the man who had rejected Audrey for a part when she was a total unknown but predicted she would "make it" and asked her to let him direct a future film of hers one day. She now did so. Warners was nervous about his reputation for heavy gambling and habitually going overbudget. But he was the firm choice of both Ferrers, and they would have their way.

Young had wanted either George C. Scott or Rod Steiger to play the main villain who tries to kill Audrey, but both of them declined to take such an unsympathetic part and the role went to Alan Arkin—recently Oscar-nominated for his own debut in *The Russians Are Coming! The Russians Are Coming!* (1966). "Arkin may not have had the brutal, cold menace that Scott could have delivered," said Young, "but he gave it all sorts of new dimensions—the total lack of feeling and that memorable quality of evil."[36]

Audrey, meanwhile, did her homework. She studied first with a doctor in Lausanne whose specialty was teaching the blind and then in New York, where Mel had secured the cooperation of the Lighthouse Institute for the Blind to prepare her further for the role. She observed the behavior and movements of the sightless there and learned how to read Braille.

"Audrey and I both had lessons as blind people," recalled Young just before his death in 1995, "but Audrey was miles faster than I. She was quickly able to find her way, blindfolded, around the Lighthouse rooms and corridors. She mastered the routine of filling a kettle, lighting the gas, boiling the water, putting tea in the teapot and pouring it without spilling a drop. When it was my turn, every natural disaster took place."[37]

She learned to differentiate textures with her fingertips, to judge people's distance by a sound, to tell by the tapping of her cane whether she was walking on tile, wood or stone, and to put on makeup without a mirror. It was a profound experience, and one of the people who led her through it was college student Karen Goldstein, blind from the age of six.

"Karen came to the Warner Studios and was to run through the movements of the scenes so that Audrey could then copy her," said Young. "She picked up a lot from Karen—dialing a phone, judging the height and eyes of someone with whom she was speaking so that conversation was natural—all from the sound and direction of the voice. After a few days, she decided to work on her own. But being Audrey, she went to Jack Warner and persuaded him to pay Karen her full salary for the rest of the twelve-week schedule."[38]

Filming of *Wait Until Dark* began in New York City in early 1967. Mayor John Lindsay helpfully agreed to block off traffic in the Village for the ten-day shoot, as thousands of gawkers crowded the barricades for a glimpse of Audrey. Interiors were shot at Warners' Burbank studio, where technicians who had worked with Audrey on *My Fair Lady* thought she now looked tired and gaunt. For the second time in a row, her friend Hubert was passed over. "She went somewhere like Saks and bought her meager two costumes off the peg," Young remembered. "We settled on the most ordinary ones—she was blind and the colors weren't important. Givenchy was obviously not for this particular epic."[39]

When production chief Walter MacEwen saw the rushes, he thought Audrey's expressive eyes belied blindness. Contact lenses irritated her, but she agreed to them in certain close-ups when she could not avoid reacting with her eyes. "I ran picture after picture to see previous attempts of other actors playing blind and I never saw anybody nearly as good," said Young. "She was able to focus in the far distance, and to keep the focus so that even if she was talking to someone very near, her eyes would not refocus on that person."[40]

Young debunked the reports that MacEwen and Jack Warner were furious about Mel and Audrey's expenses: "Mel was an exceptionally efficient producer. Kurt Frings would have certainly got all of that worked out in her contract. He told me, with awe, that after [*The Nun's Story*] she returned several thousand dollars to the studio because she hadn't needed so much for her expenses. That had to be a unique occasion in the history of the cinema."[41]

Unique, too, was the formal English tea break taken daily at the stroke of four on the *Wait Until Dark* set. The ceremony was very elaborate. Audrey adhered rigidly to the rule of one spoonful of tea for each guest and one for the pot, with a steeping period of precisely ten minutes. Terence Young related how it came about:

Originally I had arranged for tea to be brought on the set for myself. Audrey said she would like tea as well, because the coffeemaker on the set got a little tired by the end of the day. The next stage was that Audrey bought a couple of mugs and hand-painted on them THE TOFF, which is what she had nicknamed me, and AUD for herself. Charles Lang, the cameraman, told us he much preferred tea, so a day later he joined the gang with his own mug. Richard Crenna and Jack Weston asked why they were being treated as second-class citizens and said they, too, wanted tea, which I'm sure they hated, but it was all part of the fooling around that went on off the set, which I strongly encouraged.

The weekend intervened, and I went to a tea party given by the actress Edana Romney, whom I had directed in my first film, *Corridor of Mirrors*. She was comfortably installed in Beverly Hills having brought her maid and in particular, her butler, Freddy, who was a terrific character. I invited Edana to tea at the studio and [asked her to] bring Freddy plus the solid silver tea service.... I had the Props Department lay out a square of fake grass with pedestals and huge vases at the four corners, filled with ghastly plastic flowers.

The white table had an umbrella, and Props unearthed some very delicate China to replace our mugs. The cast sat down and had tea as if they did this every day; the butler served them, everybody spoke with English accents, and then it was back to work. The Tea Garden was left intact on the stage, and all the cast brought something different—cakes, biscuits, you name it. The end of the week, at four o'clock, there were sounds of music from the direction of the garden. They had arranged a string trio, three elderly ladies, while Jack and Richard fox-trotted to the music of "Tea for Two." Thereafter, I gave up.[42]

"Thanks to Audrey, we shot on European hours," said Richard Crenna. "We came into the studio at eleven a.m. for makeup, never took lunch, and went home at seven. [At the four p.m. break] all the actors tried to outdo each other and put on a bigger and better tea. It got to a point where you just walked past the table and you gained ten pounds—except Audrey."[43]

In fact, she lost fifteen pounds during *Wait Until Dark*. The gossip columnists blamed it on her marital problems, but Young thought otherwise: "It was one of the most rigorous roles Audrey ever played. She worked herself so hard that you could see the pounds rolling off her each day."[44]

The final result was worth it: *Wait Until Dark* is a virtually perfect thriller—from the first to the last time Hepburn leaves her door unlocked. Charles Lang's moody lighting heightens the suspense at every turn. Audrey's frantic lightbulb-breaking scene became a classic, but no more than her deadly struggle with the psychopathic Arkin and his final, terrifying leap at her in the eerie light of the refrigerator.* By today's standards, the film was just mildly violent (brass knuckles, verbal abuse and a knife or two are the only weapons) but extraordinarily sadistic since the tormented victim was sightless. To test public reaction, worried

---

* Most, but not all, loved Arkin. Andrew Sarris complained about his mugging and noted the logical absurdity of his dressing up in wigs and disguises in order to fool a blind woman.

studio executives held a sneak preview—at which the audience shrieked repeatedly in that uniquely cinematic, disturbingly neurotic, commercially fantastic combination of horror and delight.

Warners left Young's picture exactly the way he made it.

Wait Until Dark opened in November 1967 to record-breaking grosses at Radio City—the ninth of Audrey's sixteen starring films to premiere there. It earned a hefty $11 million for the happy studio and a fifth Oscar nomination for the less happy but much acclaimed Hepburn. "That performance is so extraordinarily authentic," says costar Efrem Zimbalist, Jr. (the blind girl's kind but useless husband). "Working with her was heaven, even though she was going through hell with Mel."[45] Audrey withheld her true feeling until long afterward: "I was nominated for *Wait Until Dark* when I liked myself better in *Two for the Road* that year."[46] But playing the besieged, hysterical blind girl had been a vital catharsis, says Ian Woodward, "an emotional release far more purgative than any psychological 'remedy' dispensed by the average Hollywood headshrink."[47]

Maybe a little too purgative. It would be nearly a decade before Hepburn made another film.

"I HAD BEEN COMPLETELY MISERABLE while making *Wait Until Dark* because I had been separated from my son, Sean, for the first time," she would say.[48]

The Ferrers's working relationship was brilliantly successful during that production but, by its end, the only thing more painful to Audrey than Sean's absence was Mel's presence. MacEwen claimed one reason for the rift was Ferrer's "auditions" of way too many pretty models for the five-second bit-part of a girl found hanged behind a door. But Richard Crenna says, "It was only later we heard that Audrey was having a very difficult time in her marriage." Terence Young knew more about it because "both Audrey and Mel had confided [some] things to me. But they were a class act in every sense, and very little showed."[49]

One insight, à la *Upstairs, Downstairs*, comes from some unpleasant words overheard by chef Florida Broadway: "One time Mr. Ferrer wanted Mrs. Ferrer to work more than she wanted to. She felt she worked too much, and he was pushing and driving her more than she was willing. Something she said about being tired started it. They had their little tiffs and arguments."[50]

In addition to the stresses and strains of thirteen years of marriage, her miscarriages upset and occupied her obsessively. In January 1967 she sent a heartfelt condolence letter to Sophia Loren, strongly identifying with Loren's miscarriage that month.[51] Five months later, Hepburn herself was pregnant again, at thirty-eight, but soon miscarried once more. Losing those babies, she said, was her greatest trauma, "as painful as my parents' divorce."[52]

A few weeks later, she and Ferrer separated for good. Years earlier, Audrey had decided that 110 pounds was the ideal weight for her height. But she had now dropped down to ninety-five and, by one brutal assessment, resembled "an emaciated grasshopper."[53]

Mel was always accused of being a Svengali who called the shots and dictated her decisions. But in the end, it was Audrey who seemed to be in the driver's seat and to have been so, in many ways, from the beginning. "It's a problem when the wife outshines the husband as Audrey does me," Ferrer said, with painful candor, back in 1960. "I'm pretty sensitive when producers call and say they want to discuss a film with me, when in reality they're angling for Audrey and using me as bait."

The estimations of their friends differ widely.

"Mel was—probably still is—a hypersensitive person," says Leslie Caron, "and I think he gets hurt easily. I think that happened in his relationship with Audrey, although I cannot say too much about it because I wasn't 'holding the candle,' as we say—an expression in French. It means I could not see inside their private chamber."[54]

Yul Brynner, on the other hand, wondered how Audrey put up with Mel for so long: "I suppose she was so desperate to make it work [and] so sweet, loyal and human.... Mel was jealous of her success and could not reconcile himself to the [fact that] she was much better than he in every way, so he took it out on her. Finally, she couldn't take it any longer. God knows, she did everything a woman could do to save her marriage."[55]

Designer Ken Scott couldn't understand how Mel and Audrey ever got together in the first place. "She is so lively, charming and youthful," said Scott, "and he was a stick-in-the-mud, old beyond his years."[56]

Actor Robert Wagner's analysis is gentler:

"I met her when she first came to Hollywood with Mel. They used to come to our house when Natalie [Wood] and I lived on Beverly Drive. I think they loved each other very much, but two [high-profile careers] make a relationship more intense, and that intensity can work both ways. Mel was with her when she was very young, and it all changes as your life progresses."[57]

"Mel was the *sabio*—the guy that knew everything," says Peter Viertel. "Once he called me and said, 'You should forget this woman Gardner—she'll destroy you.' He loved to give advice. Audrey listened and was impressed by his knowledge of the movie business. She was a good wife and *believed* in being a good wife. That's what he wanted, and I suppose she lured him into thinking she could provide it. I think they just outgrew each other."

Mel Ferrer, now seventy-nine, says, "I don't think anybody could compete with Audrey [and there was no] sense in trying to. I had a great deal to do with her career, and I'm delighted I was able to contribute. But I didn't benefit from it."[58]

Documentarist Gene Feldman insists, "Mel was no ogre. He genuinely loved her. Obviously, he's a man of enormous ego and drive. Suddenly he became 'the husband,' which in our society is very difficult. Audrey understood that, and I think diminished herself incredibly so that she wouldn't threaten him. That's like walking stooped all the time. It's hard."[59]

For a long while they worked together well, says Rob Wolders. "Audrey had her most productive period then, in large part because Mel was looking after her. People conveniently forget that they made a lot of good choices together."

On September 1, 1967, their lawyers' jointly announced that Hepburn, thirty-eight, and Ferrer, fifty, would divorce. Mel was in Paris. Audrey was home in Switzerland with Sean. Much later she would say, "I hung on to my marriage because of Sean." She now sat him down for the much-dreaded talk. "We're not happy together," she said. "It's not going to affect you right now, but we've chosen not to live together anymore."

Sean developed a good understanding of it, says Rob Wolders: "It was extremely important to Audrey that the relationship between Sean and Mel should not suffer. Although she may have had certain negative feelings about Mel, she would never show them to Sean—or to anyone else. She never bad-mouthed Mel."

Like most things in her life, the divorce was conducted with what Sheridan Morley called "an avalanche of good manners."[60] Neither of them ever went public with their feelings. "Audrey never spoke about private, personal things and neither did I," says Mel. "It was kind of an agreement that we had."[61] In later years, Audrey would express a curious kind of guilt that the marriage had failed to work. Never having recovered from her parents' divorce, she would never quite recover from this one either.

Eva Gabor felt Mel indeed *tried* to dominate Audrey, "but I don't know that he got away with it, because Audrey was a very strong woman. She wasn't a weakling by any means. When you're in love, men get away with things. But only for a while. That's why I think they got a divorce."[62]

Audrey went into self-imposed exile with Sean at La Paisible and told Frings to stop sending scripts. She was depressed and indifferent about whether she ever worked again. "I thought a marriage between two good, loving people had to last until one of them died," she said. "I can't tell you how disillusioned I was. I'd tried and tried. I knew how difficult it [was to be] second-billed on the screen and in real life. How Mel suffered!

But believe me, I put my career second. [Even] when it was clear the marriage was ending, I still couldn't let go."[63]

In Audrey's mind, it was *her* personal failure and defeat.

CHAPTER 8

Roman Holiday II
(1968–1979)

"Please don't say I'm self-effacing. You
have to face something to be self-
effacing."

AUDREY HEPBURN[1]

A T THIRTY-NINE, HAVING MADE ALL (but one) of her great films, Hepburn retreated into motherhood. Her friend Doris Brynner threw various soirees to cheer her up. But soon enough, after Sean went off to school, the loneliness of Tolochenaz got to her.

She was, after all, single and "available" again—on the strength of which, she now felt free to make a delicate entry into the European jet set. In December 1967, for example, she met Prince Alfonso de Bourbon-Dampierre, a pretender to the Spanish throne, and enjoyed New Year's Eve with him in Madrid.

But most often, she flew to Rome, the site of her first great film triumph, *Roman Holiday*. There, she had a guaranteed welcome among friends established over the years—aristocrats who, like her, had time and money on their hands, such as Count Dino and Countess Camilla Pecci-Blunt, who often hosted Audrey in Tuscany in the summers. One of her most loyal Roman friends was Arabella Ungaro, a member of the "impoverished nobility" who these days worked for the *Corriere della Sera* and later sold a small house on her property to Audrey. Another close friend was Laura Alberti, whom Audrey called "my Roman Connie [Wald]."

They tended to be somewhat older, maternal women, and one of the most important of them to her at the time was Countess Lorean Franchetti Gaetani-Lovatelli, wife of Count Lofreddo ("Lollo") Gaetani-Lovatelli. She and Audrey met through Lorean's sister Afdera Franchetti, who was married to Henry Fonda at the time Hepburn and Fonda were filming *War and Peace* in Rome.

"I usually find cinema people boring," she says today. "But with Audrey, something clicked, and we became fast friends." A pillar of the Roman aristocracy, Lorean made her magnificent home available to

Audrey regularly from then on—and now more than ever. Melancholy celebrity exiles were her specialty, as the irrepressible Countess Lovatelli recalls:

> When her marriage finished, she called me and said, "May I come and stay with you?" I said, "Of course." She was very unhappy. She believed in marriage. When her marriage didn't work, she came here to hide. She needed a friend and she needed to be cheered up. She lived for eight months in my house during the divorce. I would give little dinner parties for her and there was always an extra man, but I won't tell you any names....
>
> She met all Rome through me. Everybody was enchanted by her. While she was staying with me waiting for the divorce, there was the revolution in Greece [December 13, 1967], and King Constantine and his wife had to leave in a hurry. They came to Rome with the mother, Queen Frederika, ran away during the night. They went to stay with Prince Henry of Hesse, their cousin, who has a beautiful villa in Rome. They were very depressed. It was rather gloomy, being kicked out of one's own country, leaving everything behind.
>
> Prince Henry is a great friend of mine—the nephew of King Umberto. He called me and said, "I have to do something to keep up their morale." So I gave a little dinner for them to meet Audrey. They were so enchanted with her that they kept coming back! She had just done *Wait Until Dark*, and Constantino hadn't seen it, so we screened it privately for them. They loved it. After the film, we went into the kitchen and had scrambled eggs with the king and queen.[2]

Audrey's arrival had thrown the Lovatellis' household staff into some confusion, as the Countess told interviewer John Barba:

"It was the time of the first Mary Quant very, very short skirts and frocks, which Audrey was one of the first to wear here. When she arrived, my maid took her to the guest room and then opened her valises to hang out her clothes. We were in the drawing room chatting, and my maid came and said, 'Signora, she must have forgotten some valise.' I said, 'Why?' The maid said, 'Because she only has blouses. I hung up twenty blouses.' I said, 'Those are frocks!' So short. We weren't used to them yet."[3]

The lady beneath the mod exterior was not a very happy one. The Countess has an astrological interpretation of her: "She was a real Taurus—a rather stuffy sign. I'm a Gemini—very flighty. That's why we went together so well. She was a very loyal, honest, serious person. If she hadn't been a film star, she would have been a stuffy matron, very normal and ladylike."

Hepburn was extremely fond of Count Lollo, who was "very Italian," his widow recalls. "He used to scold her because he wanted her to eat spaghetti and put on weight, she was so thin." During the first months, she begged not to go out in the evening but gradually acquiesced. "My husband would protect her, and she would hide under his wing when we went out."

What she much preferred was daytime walking. Lorean calls her "a maniac for fresh air," always in the company of her little dog. The Countess, presumably, strolled with her?

"As little as possible," she replies. "I hated walking. I used to follow her with the car. When she came to our house on the Isola del Giglio, every afternoon she would walk to the top of the mountain with my husband and children because I refused. I sat and watched."

Pundits in New York used to call Greta Garbo "a hermit about town." Something similar might have described Audrey Hepburn in Rome. But her semi-reclusion there was interrupted in April 1968 by the obligation to appear in Hollywood for the Academy Awards ceremony, at which she was both a nominee and a presenter.

The United States to which she returned was in chaos. Demonstrations against the Vietnam war were becoming more and more violent and, just four days before the Oscars, the murder of Martin Luther King, Jr., turned many American cities into riot zones. The awards were postponed for two days, and on April 10, under somber conditions, Audrey handed out the Best Actor award to Rod Steiger for his performance in the racially charged *In the Heat of the Night*. Audrey, as noted, lost to Katharine Hepburn amid deep sentiment over the death of Spencer Tracy. For the younger Hepburn, it was more of a chore than a triumphant night.

So, too, really, was the evening of the Tony Awards a week later in New York, where she was one of a half dozen recipients of a special lifetime-achievement Tony.* No one was quite sure why Audrey had been included. "Anyway you look at it," wrote Rex Reed, "a Tony Award to Audrey Hepburn for deserting the theatre for more money in Hollywood is preposterous."[4]

She couldn't wait to return to the warm embrace of the Lovatellis in Rome, where a fateful encounter awaited her.

AMONG THE GUESTS AT ONE of Lorean's soirees that May was Princess Olimpia Torlonia and her industrialist husband Paul-Louis Weiller, heir to a French oil fortune. The Weillers fell in love with Audrey on the spot and, before the night was over, invited her to cruise the Greek islands

---

* The other, more veteran honorees were Pearl Bailey, Carol Channing, David Merrick, Marlene Dietrich and Maurice Chevalier.

with them the following month. Their yacht and their money offered a service much like that provided by Aristotle Onassis to Jacqueline Kennedy at the same time—and with nothing better to do, Audrey accepted.

Also aboard that yacht in June 1968 was a handsome young psychiatrist named Andrea Dotti, an assistant professor at the University of Rome and director of his own clinic specializing in women's problems with depression. Dotti was an authority on psychopharmacology—drugs used to treat mental illnesses. Like the fictional Dr. Kildare, he was charismatic, gentle and a good listener. He was nine years younger than Audrey, despite—or because of—which, they took to each other immediately. They would soon be seeing a lot more of each other at the Lovatellis' Isola del Giglio estate, off the coast of Tuscany, where the Countess was none too pleased about the developing romance:

"She met Andrea, unfortunately, on the cruise, when she ought to have been in my house on the island. She said, 'I have eight days on Olimpia's yacht and then I will come.' So she met Andrea and then came to my house for the rest of the summer, and I had to invite Andrea too. I was very cross. I knew Andrea very well, and I knew he wasn't the man for her."[5]

Born in Naples on March 18, 1938, to Count and Countess Domenico Dotti, Andrea was a playboy as well as a psychiatrist. He claimed to have first met Audrey at age fourteen, during the filming of *Roman Holiday*, when he ran up to shake her twenty-three-year-old hand and then rushed home to tell his mother he was going to marry her. Allegedly, she was a recurring figure in his pubescent dreams after that. Nowadays, he was the attractive bachelor whom smart hostesses placed next to the likes of Christina Ford at Roman dinner parties. He said he and Audrey fell in love "somewhere between Ephesus and Athens. It was not [that she] came to cry on my shoulder about the breakup of her marriage or that I gave her comfort as a psychiatrist. We were playmates on a cruise ship with other friends, and slowly, day by day, our relationship grew into what it is."[6]

If Mel Ferrer was a proud, severe Spanish type of Latin, Dotti was the sensual, laid-back Italian variety.[7] "I will continue my career, and after a while all this interest in us will die down," he said, by way of wishful thinking. "I'm not a public figure and won't become one. I never think of Audrey as an actress but as a human being. Once anyone meets her, they forget she's a star."

His parents' marriage had ended in a civil annulment some twenty-five years before, leaving Andrea and his three brothers (a banker, an electrical engineer and a sociologist) to a largely fatherless childhood with which Audrey could identify. These days, Andrea's mother was Signora Paula Roberti, remarried to Vero Roberti, the London correspondent of the *Corriere della Sera*, and had a few words of her own on the subject of her son's wedding plans:

"For years and years, he talked of getting married and having lots and lots of children, but he continued to study and think about a career. But when he came back from the cruise, you could see he was in love. He made a film of the voyage and included everybody but Audrey. Love made him too shy even to photograph her. . . .

"Andrea has two distinct personalities. . . . He would shut himself off for hours to study; then, when his work was done, he would be very witty and social and dying to get out. I always encouraged my boys to have a good time when young."[8]

Young and old, Andrea Dotti would take his mother's advice to heart. He had the dignity of a professional but also an underlying sense of humor, which was highly appealing to Audrey in her unhappy state of mind at the time. "He made her laugh, he made her feel good about herself," says Robert Wolders.

Wolders believes Audrey was attracted to Dotti "because he was a cerebral man who at the same time did not take life that seriously—not because he was a psychiatrist and could 'assist' her. Audrey didn't have much difficulty understanding herself. She never voiced the feeling that there was any psychological manipulation on his part." More relevant was Dotti's large, colorful family—mother, brothers, in-laws—"people Audrey became very close to. This was true, too, with the Ferrers. Her sister-in-law Mary Ferrer stayed one of her closest friends for life. To become part of a family was extremely important to her. Her own family had lacked that kind of closeness."

THE WORST THING FOR AUDREY, as for most others dissolving a marriage, was the mind-numbing legal haggle over distribution of assets. When the Ferrers' divorce decree was finally issued, on December 5, 1968, all settlement details were kept under wraps except for the two things that mattered most to her: She got custody of Sean and the house in Tolochenaz (which, in fact, had been purchased by her). Mel would have unlimited visitation rights but could only take Sean out of Switzerland with her permission, and for no more than four weeks a year.

Years later, Ferrer would say, "I still don't know what the difficulties were. Audrey's the one who asked for the divorce and started the affair with Andrea Dotti."[9] At the time, however, he was involved with twenty-nine-year-old heiress Tessa Kennedy. In 1971, he would enter his lasting marriage with fourth wife Elisabeth ("Lisa") Soukhotine, thirty-four, a children's book editor. They remain together today in Carpinteria, California.

Ferrer never uttered a negative word about Hepburn in public, and Audrey was too thrilled with her new freedom and new romance to harbor any grudge toward Mel.

"Do you know what it's like when a brick falls on your head?" she said later. "That's how my feelings for Andrea first hit me. It just happened out of the blue. He was such an enthusiastic, cheerful person [and] as I got to know him, I found he was also a thinking, very deep-feeling person." The only potential problem was the one all the newspapers and magazines were harping on—age—which she addressed directly:

"I had lived longer than Andrea, but it did not mean I was more mature. Intellectually, he was older than I. His work had matured him beyond his years. Also, we were very close emotionally. So we met somewhere between [his] thirty-one and [my] forty![10] I was afraid of that age difference, that it might be a big handicap to a new relationship, let alone to a marriage."[11]

But it was easier to believe that love would conquer all. They conducted themselves and their relationship with discretion, Audrey sometimes flying to Rome and Andrea sometimes flying to Switzerland for their weekend rendezvous. On Christmas, Andrea presented her with a ruby engagement ring and surprised her soon after with a large solitaire diamond ring from Bulgari's. In the first week of January, their marriage banns were officially posted outside the little village post office in Tolochenaz.

Lorean Lovatelli tried to talk Audrey out of it, "but I didn't manage it," she says. "She wanted me to go to Switzerland to be her witness. I accepted. She gave me a beautiful necklace she had made for her witnesses, enamel with a little medal written 'Andrea and Audrey.' But at the last moment I called and said, 'I can't come. I don't want to be a witness. Forgive me.' Andrea was a friend of mine for years before, a very amusing fellow, but she was a sort of fairy princess and needed somebody who understood her. I don't know the other Dottis. I found Andrea quite enough."[12]

Audrey, on the other hand, knew and liked the other Dotti brothers, and they were likewise fond of her. Shortly before the wedding, one of them bluntly advised her: "Don't marry him. Just live with him." But it was a very Catholic country, and their plans—plus family pressure—called for children.

On January 18, 1969, six weeks after her divorce from Mel, Audrey Hepburn and Dr. Andrea Dotti were married in a private ceremony in the town hall of Morges, presided over by the town's clerk of records, Denise Rattaz. Nine-year-old Sean watched his mother and new stepfather exchange vows. Audrey looked perfect, as ever, in a pink jersey ensemble designed by Givenchy, with a matching scarf to protect her from the drizzle outside.

Instead of Countess Lovatelli, Audrey's maid of honor was Doris Brynner, who knew Dotti and approved of the marriage. The bride's other witness was Germaine Lefebvre, better known as actress Capucine from the popular *Pink Panther* series. The groom's men included the distinguished Italian painter Renato Guttoso—Andrea's uncle—and loveboat captain Paul Weiller.

At the reception, Paola Dotti Roberti was expansive: "Audrey will be an ideal daughter-in-law. She is such a delicious person, a dream. The age difference doesn't matter. She has become so much the perfect woman for Andrea that, for us, she doesn't have any age."[13] Audrey was bubbly, as well. After the ceremony, she phoned Givenchy in Paris to say, "I'm in love and happy again! I never believed it would happen to me. I had almost given up."[14]

There would be no formal honeymoon, just a quiet week at Tolochenaz before settling down in Rome. La Paisible would be kept as a weekend retreat and summer home, its staff to be supervised by Baroness van Heemstra, who now lived there year-round. Sean would attend the French Lycée Chateaubriand in Rome.

They were now looking for the perfect Roman home for three, and soon found it: a beautiful penthouse apartment by the Ponte Vittorio, overlooking the Tiber and Castel Sant'Angelo. It was said to have been the home of the mistress of a famous cardinal four centuries earlier, which increased its serendipitous cachet in the Dottis' minds. There, Audrey settled in to something like domestic bliss—while it lasted. Her greatest joy throughout the marriage was that Sean did not resent or reject Andrea. On the contrary, "the boys" liked each other a lot, thanks to Dotti's sensitivity and his wise decision to become the child's friend more than stepfather. "Sean's already got a father, and a very good father, whom he loves very much," Dotti would say.

Audrey grew gayer and more extroverted. "Now Mia Farrow will get my parts," she said cheerfully, "and she's very welcome to most of them.... After all, I worked nonstop from when I was twelve until I was thirty-eight. I feel a need to relax, sleep in the morning. Why should I resume work and the life I rejected, when I married a man I love, whose life I want to live?"[15]

She had no interest in being called "Countess," to which she was rightfully entitled. She was Signora Dotti, plain and simple, and their number was listed in the Rome directory. "I don't have a secretary, I don't have attack dogs, I don't go to parties or official functions, and I answer my own phone," she said.[16] She also did her own shopping and now discovered an up-and-coming young hairdresser who would become a good friend.

Sergio Russo, for a decade, had worked in the famous Parisian hair salon of Alexandre, where Audrey had been a client in her "high" film days. In 1969, Alexandre recommended his former assistant to her, now in Rome, as Sergio recalls:

> We had a little corner where we put up a dressing screen, behind which she would be seated for privacy. It was a little difficult because the shop was quite small. I was just beginning. After a few months she said, "Sergio, I am so ugly? You put me behind the thing. Why don't you take me with other people?" . . .
>
> She came to me not as a film star but as an Italian woman. We spoke in Italian and joked a lot together. She had a nice word for everybody. I worked with her all the years she lived here. She still had her *Sabrina* kind of short hair in 1969–70, and then she let it grow a bit and be kind of curly. Her hair never required a lot of daily care. Then she did the chignon, very simple. She used to say, "When I do the chignon myself, I use three hairpins. When you do it, Sergio, you use thirty or forty. Why?"[17]

She and Sergio chatted of everyday things—"the remodeling of the house, a lot about the garden, because we both loved gardens, and we both had a love for birds—she used to have a canary wherever she lived. She was not chatty about her personal feelings. She was British in that way—friendly, kind, but with that reserve of 'Don't get too close to me.' I cannot say what her relations were with her husband. I had too much respect for her. You could see she had a problem, but it wasn't discussed. I'm not that kind of hairdresser who trades confidences."[18]

Their conversation was never intimate until the day when Audrey gently confronted him about the fact that he seemed depressed. "She said, 'Sergio, I think you need my husband,' and she made an appointment for me with him. She arranged it. He took care of me."[19]

The "problem" between Audrey and Andrea, which Sergio was too discreet to probe, was a three-pronged one concerning sex. In the first place, her private eroticism consisted more of restrained tenderness than of the passionate abandon preferred by an Italian husband. Secondly, though she was nearing the end of her child-bearing years and had always had gynecological difficulties even when much younger, she was now—in May 1969, just four months after her wedding—pregnant again. Finally, on the heels of that exciting news and tending to spoil it, was the persistent rumor that Andrea was seeing other women.

"Rumor" was a euphemism. There was plenty of photographic evidence, thanks to the paparazzi, widely published for all who wished to see. Audrey was not among those who wished to see, but she could hardly avoid all the newspaper and magazine pictures of her husband in the company of some of the most striking and, in some cases, infamous Roman beauties.

Take the jet-set model Daniela Ripetti, for example, a favorite of photographers all over Europe for her guaranteed scandalous behavior on all occasions. She once interrupted a Beatles press conference in Milan to insist that the Fab Four listen to her sing and take her in as their Fab Fifth. Later, she became engaged to Brian Jones of the Rolling Stones, who died soon after of a drug overdose. She herself had spent nine months in prison on drug charges—and now, she was cavorting with Andrea in the hot nightspots of Rome.[20]

Dr. Dotti was snapped with many other female companions at the clubs. It was all the more galling to Audrey because she was in Switzerland expecting a baby at the time—a fact loudly trumpeted by the press. In the early months of her term, Audrey happily relaxed at the fashionable Gambrino Beach Club in Rome. But in the last six months, her confinement became exactly that, and on doctors' orders she stayed in bed or on a couch at La Paisible. It was during that period, predictably enough, that Andrea's nightlife skyrocketed.

Dotti's friends offered the creative excuse that what looked like fun and games were really part of his "research" for a book he was writing in his area of expertise—the use of psychotropic drugs for depression in women. "Major tranquilizers, but not LSD," he clarified. "We dispensed with [LSD] years ago. My approach to psychotherapy is closer to Freud's than to that of Jung, more physical and emotional than religious."[21]

Freudian or Jungian, it was the physical approach that had Audrey worried.

LUCA DOTTI WAS BORN ON February 8, 1970, by caesarean section at the Cantonal Hospital in Lausanne and named for his father's youngest brother. If Audrey and Dotti's family had been annoyed with Andrea for his indiscretions, things were now smoothed over, temporarily, by the joy of Luca's arrival. Once again, her most precious gift came from Sean: He not only failed to show any sibling rivalry toward the new baby but was actively fond of him and, from the start, developed a strong, avuncular relationship with his little brother that would last a lifetime.

The proud parents soon returned to Rome, where they showed off Luca to the adoring Dotti family and friends, and where Audrey now immersed herself fully in the dual role of mother and doctor's wife. There was no trace of the star in the woman who pushed the pram in the park, tossed her own special herbal pasta salads, and blended in comfortably with the Dotti family.

Author Dominick Dunne vividly remembers seeing her at "a large and boisterous spaghetti dinner" in Andrea's mother's home. "I watched her sit in dutiful daughter-in-law docility, drawing no attention to herself," Dunne recalled, "while her husband's mother reigned as the undisputed star of the evening."[22]

Journalist Anna Cataldi, who knew all three Dotti brothers and met Audrey through them, felt Audrey was deeply generous when faced with Andrea's reluctance to give up his practice in Rome and move to Switzerland, where she felt more secure:

"She adored her house in Switzerland, but to a big extent she gave it up for the life she was building for herself and Andrea in Rome. She took the role of the doctor's wife very seriously. She would help him when the lithium arrived and they had to measure out the doses. One time when Andrea was very sick after an operation—he developed an infection—the person who saved his life was Audrey. She was impeccable with him.

"It was a very strong, complicated relationship. When Audrey started to find out about his infidelity, she said, 'I'm going away.' He said, 'I promise it won't happen again,' and she believed him. She later found out he couldn't be believed, but I think he was genuine when he promised. I never met Mel Ferrer, but I think Andrea was more human. Certainly, he never wanted to promote himself through her."

Audrey increased her own efforts to make things work. She met him for institutional dinners at the hospital when he had to work late and otherwise accommodated him in every way. She let him and everyone else know she was fascinated by his work:

"It is most interesting being married to a psychiatrist," she said, and she wanted to hear all about his patients' case histories—anonymously, of course. Her own two-penny psychiatric theory was that most people's anguish stemmed from either the reality or the fear of loneliness.

Housewifery, to hear Audrey speak of it, was downright idyllic: "It's sad if people think that's a dull existence, [but] you can't just buy an apartment and furnish it and walk away. It's the flowers you choose, the music you play, the smile you have waiting. I want it to be gay and cheerful, a haven in this troubled world. I don't want my husband and children to come home and find a rattled woman. Our era is already rattled enough, isn't it?"[23]

Part of the motivation was guilt. It had struck her during *Wait Until Dark* that she could no longer "take the stress of being away from Sean."[24] From his birth in 1960 to 1967, she regretted missing much of his childhood and, in her highly self-critical way, felt she had shunted him aside to make movies. When Luca was born, she resolved to stay home and dote on him—with the full support of Andrea, in contrast to Mel's constant pressure to keep working. She would not repeat the "mistake" she felt she made with Sean, who was now almost out of her nest.*

Though Rome was home, a powerful kind of homesickness still lingered for La Paisible, and so she took Sean and baby Luca to Switzerland for the summer of 1970. Andrea visited on weekends and spent the whole month of August there, during which he and Audrey rebonded and rebounded from their rifts.

"If I could have had more than my two sons, if I could have had daughters as well—and dozens of them—then I certainly would," she said.[25] Andrea wanted a larger family, too, but Audrey's doctor advised against it, telling her, "You shouldn't tempt the devil."[26]

That advice matched Audrey's own instinct: She always felt profoundly grateful for what she had—but profoundly fearful of losing it. She expressed that in a *Vogue* interview, romantically titled, "The Loving World of Audrey Hepburn Dotti and Her Family in their Swiss Farmhouse," reflecting on her wartime experiences and the things for which she was now most thankful:

> That my child can eat three meals a day and be free and with no danger of somebody banging on the door. That I'm not afraid of somebody taking Andrea away or that he's going to be picked up in the street. Or if he's an hour late, maybe the Germans got him.... These things reassure me that I'm not going to be taken away, or my family taken away, as were millions of others who once lived around us....
>
> Love does not terrify me. But the going away of it does. I have been made terribly aware of how everything can be wrenched away from you and your life torn apart. That's why I guard against it so much. If I had known very secure nights all my life, if I had never seen or felt the fear of being tortured or deported or blown up into a million pieces, then I would not fear it....
>
> Today there are so many [things], and the more there is, the less I want. The more man flies to the moon, the more I want to sit and look at a tree. The more I live in a city, the more I search for a blade of grass.[27]

HER LIFE WAS NOT ENTIRELY a Roman holiday, of course. The paparazzi dogged her and her toddler's every move. "I could take him nowhere," she complained, "not to a park, not down the street, not put him on a terrace without paparazzi. [It] really drove me mad... to have pho-

---

* Sean's excursions outside that nest always worried her to death. While he was visiting his father in mid-1972, Audrey got a chilling call from Mel, informing her that Sean had been injured on an outing to the Los Angeles Wild Animal Park. A lion had reached out of its cage and slashed him on the back of his head—superficially, it turned out.

tographers jump out from behind trees and he would be howling because he was so startled."[28] Luca echoed that later. "I would get very angry," he said. "I wanted to walk around like other people."

To escape that nuisance, she and the children spent more and more time at her more isolated La Paisible. Which meant that Andrea, back in Rome, spent more and more time in the clubs and discos—photographic evidence usually appearing in the next morning's papers. But for that matter, even when Audrey was in Rome, Dotti was often out and about late at night without her. Hepburn, says Rob Wolders, "was humiliated."[29]

But she did her best not to show it, stuck doggedly to her home front, and continued to turn down one movie script after another—some of them plums. Offered the tsarina in *Nicholas and Alexandra*, she left it to Janet Suzman. William Wyler wanted her to play the divorcée in *Forty Carats*, but the studio would not agree to her request to film it in Rome. (Liv Ullmann finally took the role and Milton Katselas, not Wyler, directed.) It was reported in April 1971 that she would star in a film based on Anne Edwards's novel, *The Survivors*, to be directed by Terence Young. But it didn't happen. Neither did a Ross Hunter film planned for her, *The Marble Arch*, nor the movie version of Garson Kanin's novel, *A Thousand Summers*. Jeanne Moreau wrote and directed a screenplay called *Lumière*, hand-tailoring a role for Audrey. But Hepburn declined and Moreau did the part herself.

When confronted, through the media, with the disappointment of her fans, she protested, "I've never believed in this 'God-given talent.' I adored my work and I did my best. But I don't think I'm robbing anybody of anything."[30]

Over and over, to the same question, she replied with variations on the theme: "Some people think that giving up my career was a great sacrifice made for my family, but it wasn't that at all. It was what I most wanted to do." Sometimes the replies got a bit testy—or even sarcastic: "Let me put it simply. I have absolutely no desire to work. And it's not worth going to a psychotherapist to find out why."[31]

One defense was to cut down even further on the press's access to her. "I'm an introvert," she told Rex Reed. "You'd think after all these years I'd be accustomed to all the fuss, but it never gets any easier."[32] From now on, she would insist on limiting interviews to a thirty-minute maximum. "After that," she said, "the questions become personal." She once even canceled a scheduled interview on the *Today* show because, after so many years in Rome, she didn't know Barbara Walters and wouldn't discuss her personal life with a "stranger."[33]*

Audrey now occupied a curious existential and cinematic position, as Warren Harris points out: At forty-two, she and her primary peers— Elizabeth Taylor (thirty-eight), Leslie Caron (thirty-nine), Jean Simmons (forty-one)—were past the ingenue age. The women stars of the moment were Jane Fonda (thirty-three), Vanessa Redgrave (thirty-three), Faye Dunaway (thirty), Julie Christie (twenty-nine), Barbra Streisand (twenty-eight), Catherine Deneuve (twenty-seven) and Mia Farrow (twenty-five). One couldn't quite see Hepburn in any of the Oscar-nominated roles of 1970: Jane Alexander (thirty-one) for *The Great White Hope;* Glenda Jackson (thirty-four) for *Women in Love,* Ali MacGraw (thirty-two) for *Love Story,* Sarah Miles (twenty-nine) for *Ryan's Daughter* or Carrie Snodgress (twenty-four) for *Diary of a Mad Housewife.*[34]

It was both her glory and her problem that "she remained a young girl, even in her forties," said Leslie Caron, who around this time encountered Audrey and sons in Sardinia while Leslie was vacationing there with her own two children. But there was no movie talk. "We [just] compared and admired our respective offspring with motherly pride."[35]

Motherhood was indeed her occupation these days, but in 1971 she made a delicate "return," of sorts, to pictures in the TV documentary special, *A World of Love,* produced by UNICEF and hosted by Bill Cosby and Shirley MacLaine for broadcast at Christmas. The guest stars represented their state or country to illustrate UNICEF's work there: Audrey spoke for her adopted Italy; Richard Burton and Julie Andrews for Britain; Barbra Streisand for California; and Harry Belafonte for Florida. It was, in effect, Hepburn's first volunteer work for UNICEF.

Three months later, she agreed to one other professional appearance for exactly the opposite reason: lucre, not charity. She made four one-minute TV commercials in Rome for the Tokyo wig manufacturer "Varie" and received the amazing sum of $100,000 for two days work, which she reportedly invested in annuities for Sean and Luca. Written into the contract was a stipulation that the commercials would never be shown outside Japan where—ever since *Roman Holiday*—she had been a national idol.

She had been absent from the big screen for four years. But she could never be absent from the world of fashion. Her physical image, even in semi-retirement and divorced from movies, retained enormous power and influence, even though the object of all the attention viewed it in a strictly personal way.

"I depend on Givenchy," she said, "in the same way that American

---

* She changed her mind years later and did an in-depth interview with Walters in March of 1989 (see Chapter 10, p. 303).

women depend on their psychiatrists."[36] That statement was made on the record, and she meant it. But privately to Lorean Lovatelli, she confided, "Givenchy is so terribly expensive—can't you tell me of a good dressmaker in Rome?"

"Doesn't Givenchy give you things?" replied the Countess in surprise.

"No," said Audrey, "I insist on paying for everything. He pays when he goes to my movies, doesn't he?"

Lorean recommended a young dressmaker who had made a name for himself in Italy—Valentino [Garavani]. "I took Audrey to him," she says, "and she loved his designs. Now Valentino is so famous he doesn't do beautiful things anymore. Now he designs only for rich old women and Japanese."[37]

Audrey's friend New York designer Jeffrey Banks assesses that development in more professional terms:

"When she was married to Dotti, she wore some Valentino. She wore a Valentino costume to the Rothschilds' famous 'Remembrance of Things Past' masked ball, where everybody dressed as their favorite Proust character. I think she felt that since she lived in Rome, it was the right thing to do, and I don't think Givenchy felt abandoned....

"Givenchy told me that he had not altered the mannequin he made for her in 1954 in four decades. She had the same figure close to forty years later—an amazing thing. It was not a question of conflict or rivalry. It was a question of practicality, especially later when she wasn't making any money for the UNICEF work she was doing. Givenchy was more for special occasions, the tributes and salutes. Ralph Lauren's clothes [which she also wore later] were far less expensive and more practical in terms of the things she had to do.* I think she enjoyed wearing all three men's clothes."[38]

There were a few strands of grey in her hair now—she would never color it. But during the seventies, no less than in the two previous decades, what she wore and how she looked continued to fascinate millions of women, who clamored for her beauty secrets —which were few and not very secret: She washed her own hair every five days with a special shampoo from London trichologist Philip Kingsley. She used the skin-protective makeup products of Dr. Ernest Laszlo. That was about it. No magic formula.

"It's all in their minds," she said. "I use [the Laszlo] creams because I have dry skin, and I'm a nut on sleep. If I go without sleep, I feel like I have the flu.... In Italy, I get up early to get Andrea off to the clinic by seven-thirty, and he doesn't come home until after nine p.m. So we don't eat until ten and midnight is an early night, but it ain't early for me. I

---

* For Hepburn's meeting and relationship with Lauren, see Chapter 10, pp. 325–26.

have to make up for it by taking afternoon naps. I take care of my health, and this world takes care of my thoughts."[39]

"ROME IS A CESSPOOL NOW!" declares the ever-outspoken Countess Gaetani-Lovatelli today. "I'm sorry to sound snobbish, but it's true.   It used to be enchanting, when Audrey was married to Andrea and lived here. Everybody adored her. She was very, very popular."[40]

Not everyone agrees. Anna Cataldi says many people in the Dottis' Roman circle were not only "not nice to her, a lot of them were awful." It was sad, Anna thought, because "Andrea's friends fascinated her. Andrea's group was very different from the movie people. It was European society people like Paul Weiller, who was really a very boring man. She desperately needed to have friends and warmth, but she was the famous actress—'too much' for most of them. She didn't get much friendship. She was so nervous, she made *them* nervous."[41]

Cataldi remembers the summer of 1972, for example—still fairly early in Audrey's new life—as a time when "everybody in Rome was having a lot of fun doing *Andy Warhol's Frankenstein*," directed by Paul Morrissey. Warhol, Morrissey and everyone else, it seemed, rented villas in town, Carlo Ponti, Franco Zefferelli and Roman Polanski among them. "It was *la dolce vita* at the time," says Cataldi, "and sometimes Audrey was there, too, with Andrea, because he was very social." But Morrissey was quick to notice she was different from the rest. "She never integrated because she was not a gossip," he said. In those decadent circles, Audrey was the "straight" one—always up eighty-thirty a.m., perfectly dressed when the shops were barely open, shopping or sending her son off to school while the other Beautiful People in Rome's exclusive Parioli section were still sound asleep.

In today's parlance, she was "out of the loop." Years earlier, she had met Marcello Mastroianni and they had talked most of a night. "I was thrilled," said Audrey then, "because I'd been dying to meet him for years."[42] But much later, when asked why—despite all her years in Rome—she never worked with the great Italian actors, she replied, "I don't know people like Mastroianni or Vittorio Gassman very well," adding that even during *War and Peace* she and Gassman had virtually no contact.

Cataldi recalls shopping one day with Hepburn in Milan at La Rinascente, a Bloomingdale-type department store, "when a woman approached me and said, 'Is that Audrey Hepburn?' I was about to say yes, but Audrey became pale. 'Don't tell,' she said. 'Otherwise, people will gather around.'"

But chef extraordinaire Florida Broadway detected something more akin to approach-avoidance. In her opinion, "Miss Hepburn liked the limelight. She would have the dark glasses on, but she would enjoy it when we'd be out someplace and somebody recognized her. Sometimes I think she made sure that they did, although she was subtle about it."[43]

That seemed true, in a way, of Dr. Dotti as well. Unlike Countess Lovatelli and many of Audrey's other friends, Cataldi was fond of Andrea and much amused by him. In particular, she felt, Andrea was redeemed by his "enormous love for Luca," who was the idol of both his parents' eyes: "When we were in Tuscany, Luca broke his arm. It was in plaster, and he was so courageous. Another time in Gstaad in the winter, Luca was about four. All the paparazzi were around him, saying, 'Ah, you are the son of Audrey Hepburn?' And little Luca very proudly looked up at them from the snow and said, 'No, I am the son of Signora Dotti!' "[44]

In the long run, Signora Dotti's decision to give up all for Luca may or may not have been best for him or for the mother-son relationship. In later years, she would often call Sean "my best friend." She had dragged him back and forth across the ocean, on and off her movie sets, and yet those experiences seemed to make him a more urbane, secure adult. Luca would have more difficulty finding himself, perhaps somewhat suffocated by her doting, compared to the upbringing of her "buddy" Sean.

In November 1973, Hepburn and Dotti made a rare trip together to New York, where Audrey saw actress Marian Seldes for the first time since they had performed together in Ondine. "What did we talk about? Our careers? No, our children," said Seldes, who was thrilled when Audrey came to see her in Equus that week.[45] Speculation ran high that Hepburn's return to the States signaled a new movie, but she insisted she was really only accompanying Dr. Dotti to a medical conference in Washington— which was true.

Around the same time, on a shorter trip, she had a pleasant encounter with another face from her past. "The last time I saw her," says Lord James Hanson, "was with my wife at the opening of the Aga Khan's Costa Smeralda Hotel in Sardinia. We didn't know she and Dr. Dotti would be there. I'd been knighted by that time, and she'd heard of it. She just walked into the room and gave me a little smile and said, 'Haven't we done well!' That's how she was, always gracious and fun."[46]

But she was always anxious to get back home.

"I'm a Roman housewife, just what I want to be," she said. "Despite what you sometimes read, my marriage is working out beautifully, and watching my sons grow is a marvel. I'm also fully Italian now.... I never was part of Hollywood or anywhere else, and I've finally found a place that I can call home."[47]

Among many who were curious about the *inside* of that home was director Billy Wilder. During a visit to Rome, his wife Audrey paid a call on his other Audrey, and when she returned, Billy asked her what the place was like.

"I don't care who you were—compared to Audrey Hepburn, everybody felt too fat," says Audrey Wilder. "Most apartments in Rome are so heavy, with those heavy drapes and heavy, ornate paintings and gold. But Audrey's was totally different—bright and airy, lovely yellow and white. Her draperies were the kind of material that would lie on the floor. They actually *draped*. All those other apartments looked like lasagna by comparison."

She gave Billy a detailed report—the colors, the big windows, and so forth—and then finally came up with the precise one-word description she was looking for:

"It's 'non-fattening,' I said—just like Audrey."[48]

BY JUNE 1975, SEAN WAS a six-foot-three fifteen-year-old and Luca, at five, no longer a toddler. "The happiest I've ever been has been in the seventies," Hepburn said then. "I'm much less restless now, and no longer searching for the wrong values.... I've had so much more than I ever dreamed possible out of life—[no] great disappointments or hopes that didn't work out: I didn't expect anything much and because of that I'm the least bitter woman I know.... I've accomplished far more than I ever hoped to, and most of the time it happened without my seeking it.... I'm glad to have missed what's been happening in the movies these last eight years. It's all been sex and violence, and I'm far too scrawny to strip and I hate guns, so I'm better off out of it."[49]

She had stayed out of it since 1967—but was about to make her first commercial film in eight years. The screenplay that lured her back was written by James Goldman, who had won an Oscar in 1968 for *The Lion in Winter*. This one, *Robin and Marian*, gave similarly ironic but lyrical treatment to the final adventure of a once-swashbuckling couple who could still summon enough energy, and command enough allegiance, for one last stand.

Goldman's interest in Robin Hood actually predated *The Lion in Winter*, when he was researching twelfth-century ballads. Audrey had been his first choice for Marian, but it took four years to put the deal together and half a dozen tentative directors, including Arthur Penn and John Frankenheimer. The ultimate choice was Richard Lester, director of *A Hard Day's Night, Help!, The Knack... and How to Get It, The Three Musketeers* and other brilliantly offbeat films that did not particularly appeal to Audrey Hepburn. Film historian Kevin Brownlow sums him up best: "Lester can make a Beatles film, he can make an intimate film like *Petulia*, and he can do swashbuckling epics. He's an extraordinary filmmaker, whom one day people will recognize, but too late, of course."

This project would require less swash and more buckle. Lester recalls its genesis:

> [Columbia production chief] Peter Guber came to my office, sat down with a series of three-by-five cards, and said, "Columbia wants to make a picture with you," which doesn't happen very often. He started reading off scripts that were in turnaround and other ideas, one of which was "Robin Hood as an old man meets Maid Marian." I said, "I'll do it." He said, "Don't you want to see a script?" I said, "No, I think I know how to do that." I instantly thought it was the kind of thing I would like to do and would know how to do.[50]

Considering that the first film version of the Robin Hood legend was in 1909, it was high time the Merry Men came to grips with middle age.* How did they finish off their days? Did Marian remain a Maid? *Robin and Marian* was designed, wryly and perversely, to bring the tale to an end once and for all.

But as Audrey had not worked for years, "It was important that I fit what she had to do into a period that was convenient for her and her children's school," says Lester, "and that wouldn't interfere with their lives." That was Mission Nearly Impossible—but Lester accomplished it.

"Such a poetic idea, to find out what happened to Robin and Marian," Audrey enthused. "Everything I had been offered before then was too kinky, too violent or too young." She liked the idea of playing a woman her own age. Most of all, she liked the reaction she got from Sean and Luca: "They begged me to do the film. They were so thrilled at the idea of meeting James Bond."

Lester's initial casting idea was Sean Connery for Little John and Albert Finney for Robin Hood, but the latter was not available. The former, in the end, would be the ideal masculine rogue to complement Hepburn's ideal femininity.[51]

Both Robin and Marian were equally pleased with their costars, and Audrey packed her bags for Spain.

---

* Robin Hood has inspired a score of movies. Silent versions were produced in England (1909, 1912, 1913) and in the U.S. (1912, 1913). The first great large-scale rendering was Douglas Fairbanks's *Robin Hood* (1922). The best sound version was *The Adventures of Robin Hood* (1938) with Errol Flynn as Robin and Olivia de Havilland as Marian. Cornel Wilde played Robin's son (Robert Hood!) in *The Bandits of Sherwood Forest* (1946). Jon Hall was Robin in *Prince of Thieves* (1948). John Derek starred in *The Rogues of Sherwood Forest* (1950). Walt Disney's *The Story of Robin Hood and his Merrie Men* (1952) starred Richard Todd. Richard Greene was Robin in 165 half-hour episodes of the popular fifties television series.

"I took Luca with me," she said, "and he saw the Spanish countryside, played with horses and had a grand time."[52] She arranged for him to take archery and riding lessons from experts on the set and, all in all, pronounced it "a grand experience for a little boy.... He kept saying, 'Why isn't Daddy playing Robin Hood?' I told him that was impossible, and he said, 'I know why—because Daddy doesn't have the right suit.'"

Audrey, however, had her problems, starting with the fact that the script handed to her in Spain was very different from the one that had originally sold her on the project. She was especially annoyed by the way she was first informed of it: Upon arrival at the Madrid airport, she caught sight of producer Ray Stark going up an escalator as she was going down. "Hi, Audrey!" he yelled. "Wait 'til you see the new script!"[53]

She was also annoyed by the way Richard Lester first greeted her— offhandedly, through the fence of a tennis court, without interrupting his game. "Audrey could get along with Hitler," said a Columbia executive, "but Lester is not in her scrapbook of unforgettable characters."[54] Due to Lester's frenetic pace, she could not be accorded her customary star-status arrangements. He shot the picture in a lightning-like thirty-six shooting days.

"I'm prone to be impatient," he says. "*Hard Day's Night* was just under seven weeks. *Juggernaut* was six. *Musketeers* was seventeen weeks for the two parts, about eight and a half apiece. On *Robin*, I set out to shoot eight or nine pages a day. There were about fifty pages under a bloody tree, so why not?

"We had a location which suited the temperaments of the cast and, more important, their tax arrangements. There were five members of this distinguished English cast who couldn't set foot in England for tax reasons. In Nottinghamshire, where Sherwood Forest really is, there are very few trees left that aren't held up by hope and heavy bits of steel. So we shot in Spain."

Pamplona, some two hundred miles north of Madrid, "looks like everyone's idea of what England looked like in the twelfth and thirteenth centuries," says Lester. It had castles and forts much like those of Robin's time, plus "wonderful old oak trees, rocks, moss, waterfalls, wildlife and wildflowers."[55]

Liz Smith, who came on the set to interview Audrey, wasn't so impressed with the place:

"Pamplona is a man's town with macho in the air and leftover bull dung in the streets. It is sadly worn-out.... Nowhere evident is the enchantment that Ernest Hemingway wrote about in *The Sun Also Rises*. This is the last place one expects to find romance—legendary or real."

The interview took place on a path beside a brook. There, wrote Smith, when Audrey looked about "for a rock most suitable to her bony bottom," a press agent offered her his Louis Vuitton briefcase as a cushion. She let out a squeal of delight at the appearance of that unlikely item—and talked bravely.

"*Robin and Marian* was really worth waiting for," she told Smith, later adding, "There's a great need in films today for mature women to be seen playing mature women." Things had changed a lot since she made her last movie, *Wait Until Dark*, she said. The technical advances were amazing, "and Dick Lester is so fast and unencumbered by ego or dramatics. He is a whiz-bang with his many cameras and single takes."[56]

But behind the scenes, she and Lester were said to be having script quarrels. *Time* reported that Lester kept cutting down on the love story between Robin and Marian, and that Hepburn was fighting to retain some of her best romantic lines. "With all those men," she was quoted, "I was the one who had to defend the romance in the picture. Somebody had to take care of Marian."[57]

Lester denies it: "There was very little dialogue cut. We never had arguments or disagreements about cuts. It's true that I'm not sentimental in any way, either in life or in my films, and I don't think Jim [Goldman] was either. The picture is unsentimental, but I think it remains romantic and poignant."[58]

What he does not deny is that Audrey was "unaccustomed to working at that speed, and with a multiple camera technique. She had to adapt to that, and we had to try to adapt to suit her." Her greatest anxiety lay in not knowing how she now looked on the screen after such a long absence, because Lester did not run the daily rushes. "I never look at rushes," he says. "I stopped in about 1965, and it was important to me that nobody else looked, either. But this was unusual for her. Normally, she did."[59]

Adding to her insecurity was the fact that she had not been consulted about the choice of cinematographer—Lester's friend David Watkin, who preferred unfiltered close-ups that she feared would be unflattering.

"The first thing she said was, 'When are you doing camera tests?'" Lester recalls, "and David said, 'You'll have to take your chances like everyone else, won't you, dear?' And she did. It was difficult for her, because she had come from a studio system and she'd been dressed by Givenchy and photographed by the old masters. Here, we had two cameras working so her close-ups were being done at the same time as the long shots, and the scenes were being played theatrically.

"But to her credit, once she knew that this was the way I worked, and that all the other actors were happy with it, she tried to adapt to it, and I think did very well. What we did in exchange was to shoot the angles favoring away from her first. The other actors, like Sean, who liked to work quickly, would go first, giving her a chance, with her back to the camera, to perfect what she wanted to do."[60]

Audrey's initial reaction to Lester's techniques was the equivalent of a primal scream. "I was literally petrified the first day on the set," she said. "Even after a few days, I was still shivering and shaking before each take. My hands were clammy. Making movies isn't like riding a bicycle. It doesn't all come back to you at once."[61] She would later reflect that "even in the best artistic surroundings, in the end you are still alone."[62] And she didn't consider these the best surroundings.

But she wasn't alone on screen. Lester had done her the service of assembling one of the most distinguished casts of British actors ever: In addition to Connery, Robert Shaw (straight from *Jaws*) was the Sheriff of Nottingham, Nicol Williamson was Little John, Denholm Elliott was Will Scarlett, Ian Holm was King John, and Richard Harris played Richard the Lionheart. She got along famously with them all—best of all Connery, with whom she remained friends for life. Her major offscreen outing, says Lester, was the Sunday that Sean Connery took her to the running of the bulls:

"Someone arranged for an apartment with a balcony overlooking the street, and Sean and Audrey went. I stayed at home curled up in the fetal position, worrying about what I was going to do the next week." One would think she would have hated anything to do with bullfighting. "But it was just the running. The bulls have a pretty good track record—they kill more than get killed. They charge down the street and people hop about like idiots, blind drunk. It turns out they're mostly New Zealanders and they get gored so they can go home with a story."

Pamplona was experiencing a terrible heat wave that summer, and Audrey was among many in the cast who suffered both from the heat and from diarrhea. At one point, she offered fellow-sufferer Denholm Elliott some pills, with the observation, "They may not be the real answer, but they're a damn good cork. I've been using them all week."[63] Lester says "Denholm wouldn't stay in the hotel with the rest of us and found a monastery that made a rather serviceable red wine. He got into a monk's cell and decided to stay there because the wine was cheap."

It was reported that Audrey's doctors had instructed her to drink beer to keep her weight up. If so, says Lester, "the doctors must have told that to the entire crew, as well." In general, he doesn't remember her being in fragile health. On the contrary, the director had evidence that she was quite robust:

"We had a sequence where the wagon turned over in the water, which wasn't planned. The carriage, as it went across the muddy river, slowly fell on its side. Instead of redoing it, I decided to keep it in and shoot around it. We had Sean fish her out and put her on the bank in the next scene. She was in the water quite a while and managed it very well."

That scene got a good, cheap laugh in the theaters thanks to the line devised for Robin as he surveys Marian's toppled wagon in the water: "She never could drive."

Audrey's recollection was much less sanguine than Lester's. "It was actually very frightening even though the water wasn't very deep," she said.[64] "We very nearly drowned. I was scared to death, stuck under the canvas with that big horse bucking his legs out in front of me, and those nun's habits got terribly waterlogged and heavy and dragged us down even more."[65]*

Accidents aside, her mood throughout the shooting was upbeat, says Lester, as was his own. But when production was over, he would have—and lose—a major battle with the studio over the picture's title and the publicity department's slogan, "Love is the greatest adventure of all."

"I felt it was wrong to advertise the film as Columbia did," Lester says. "People expected another *Three Musketeers*, and when it ends up with the leading characters dead on a bed, they were confused. I always felt the one thing you have to do is to advertise a film accurately, so the audience knows what it's going to see. When they don't, there is a built-in resentment. Jim's original title was *The Death of Robin*. Everybody said, 'You can't have a film with "Death" in the title—it's depressing.' But that's what people were going to see. 'Love is the greatest adventure of all' was not what it was about."[66]

In March 1976, Audrey came to the United States for a promotion blitz to kick off *Robin and Marian*'s premiere in New York. There, the press went crazy over her emergence from retirement, showering her with questions about her "comeback" until her annoyance and defensiveness finally broke through.

"I never 'retired,' " she said. "I'm not Garbo. I always hoped to make another film. The time was right for me and the part was right, too.... I'm not one of those people who retire and then come back year after year. I'm not making a 'comeback' because I never consciously went away. And now that I've come back in *Robin and Marian*, I may not stay back."[67]

But, in fact, she *had* gone away "consciously"—for the very reason she went on to explain to that same reporter: Acting was simply "not that important to me," she declared, "not all that real. The home is the last stand—the last thing we've got."[68] At that New York press breakfast, "her hands shook noticeably and she smoked without letup," Jim Watters reported.[69] But Audrey endured, and pitched the picture in yeoman fashion.

"People associate me with a time when women wore pretty dresses in films and you heard beautiful music," she said. "Now people are frightened

---

* Hepburn's sackcloth habits were created by British designer Yvonne Blake, based on medieval originals.

by the movies. *Robin and Marian* is really about how much two people
love each other. It's an intimate story, and that's why I wanted to do it."

Despite her cooperation, Columbia had a serious problem. A private
survey had revealed, to the producers' dismay, that young people—who
comprised most of the potential audience—weren't quite certain who
Audrey was. Most of them were in the cradle at the time she made *Roman
Holiday* and *Funny Face*. But *everybody* knew James Bond—and thus Sean
Connery, of the two costars, was the more important draw. His role *in
Robin and Marian* was a major departure from Bond; among other things,
he revealed his baldness for the first time. He was now pressed into service
for the promotion and came through eloquently.

"I like films that dispel time," Connery told Liz Smith, "and this
appealed to me because not only it's an interesting legend, but also an
examination of the legend. It's tremendously concerned with dying.[70]
[Robin] at this point in his life is in his twilight. A ripe old age in his day
was anything over forty, and in our film he's something like fifty. But he's
an exceptional man. Remember, Joe Louis only came back for a couple of
rounds, but for those two rounds he was as good as ever!"[71]

A Columbia official put it even more—well, baldly:

"Let's face it, this is primarily a woman's film, and women are the
ones in our society who usually decide what movies the family sees, right?
On *Robin and Marian* we're leaning heavy on the romance angle, placing
a lot of thirty-second ad spots using the kissing scenes on daytime TV. All
the women watching soap operas are going to see themselves in Sean
Connery's arms."[72]

The night before the premiere, Columbia threw a lavish, medieval
supper-dance at which Audrey nibbled caviar until midnight. The next
day, *Robin and Marian* headlined the big Easter show at Radio City Music
Hall, where the Rockettes in white bunny suits frolicked to the tune of
"Cocktails for Two" with a dancing chorus of Day-Glo Easter eggs. Audrey
drew a standing ovation from the full house of 6,200, and long, rowdy
shouts of, "We love you!" From the stage, she told the crowd, "I keep
hearing that I am making a comeback. I don't think of it as that. It is a
homecoming."

Never having seen any rushes, it was literally her first glimpse of the
film and her performance as Marian. Asked later what she thought of
herself, she replied carefully, "I shall have to see it again before I decide."[73]

Nearly everyone else decided that Hepburn and Connery were well
matched—"silk and chain mail," said one critic—and superb together.

At the film's outset, a disillusioned Robin returns from the Crusades,
scarred and exhausted, to find things in very bad shape: Good King Richard
Lionheart is off his rocker, and the Sheriff of Nottingham is more entrenched
than ever. Marian, the love of his life, has gotten herself to the Kirkely

31. A definitive Cecil Beaton portrait of Audrey Hepburn as Eliza in his stunning costume design for her trial run in society—the famous Ascot scene of *My Fair Lady*. (ARCHIVE PHOTOS, COURTESY OF ERIC RACHLIS AND JANET SOMMER)

Act II

32. Fussy, dynamic Cecil Beaton is captured as he captures Hepburn in *My Fair Lady* costume for the April 1964 *Harper's Bazaar*. (PHOTO BY BOB WILLOUGHBY)

33. By the flickering light of the projector, conductor André Previn engages in a fine excruciating art: synchronizing the music of a thirty-piece orchestra with the corresponding images on film. (PHOTO BY BOB WILLOUGHBY)

34. Moody atmosphere fits moody Hepburn as she listens to a playback of her rendition of "Wouldn't It Be Lovely?" at one of many frustrating *My Fair Lady* recording sessions. (PHOTO BY BOB WILLOUGHBY)

35. Master photographer Bob Willoughby catches director George Cukor in the act of wagging his finger at a disgusted Cecil Beaton—a perfect tableau of their relationship. (PHOTO BY BOB WILLOUGHBY)

36. Something's missing: George Cukor, Rex Harrison, Audrey Hepburn and Jack Warner sport four smiles but only three Oscars in the *My Fair Lady* group-victory portrait after the Academy Awards. (PHOTOFEST)

37. The unforgettable profiles of the unforgettable *Charade* (1962): Hepburn and Cary Grant; below, the heroine is trapped and menaced inside a phone booth by James Coburn's matches in the film that defined a chic new mystery-comedy genre. (ARCHIVE PHOTOS)

38. In the heterosexual closet: Audrey and Peter O'Toole hide out among the art museum's janitorial supplies prior to their daring art-heist in *How to Steal a Million* (1966). (*VOGUE*/CONDE NAST, COURTESY OF CYNTHIA CATHCART & BRIAN BALTIN)

39. On the Riviera set of *Two for the Road* (1966): The normally restrained actress yucks it up in a big way with the normally somber actor Albert Finney —not such an Angry Young Man these days. (PHOTOFEST)

40. Detachment—actual and symbolic—in the body language: Hepburn is escorted by her psychiatrist-husband Andrea Dotti to the 1976 Oscars in Los Angeles. Swifty Lazar said she'd win Best Actress for *Robin and Marian*, but she wasn't even nominated. (ARCHIVE PHOTOS)

1. Middle-aging Sean
Connery and Audrey
Hepburn in the title roles
of *Robin and Marian*
(1975): Rekindling and
concluding the bittersweet
romance once and for all.
(PHOTOFEST)

2. *Robin and Marian*'s
rapid-fire director Richard
Lester: If the Beatles could
shoot a movie in seven
weeks, so could the
legendary Miss Hepburn.
(ARCHIVE PHOTOS)

43. An unlikely film just before an unlikely marriage: Sixty-two-year-old Merle Oberon and thirty-seven-year-old Rob Wolders in a steamy scene from *Interval* (1973). (BARRY PARIS COLLECTION)

44. Dashing Dutch discovery Robert Wolders got his first big film break in Universal's 1966 remake of *Beau Geste*. (BARRY PARIS COLLECTION)

45. Audrey sandwich: Rob Wolders between Mrs. Wilder and Miss Hepburn at Connie Wald's home, the evening he met Hepburn. "He was getting over the death of Merle," Hepburn said, "and it was the worst period of my life. We both cried into our beers." (COURTESY OF ROBERT WOLDERS)

46. Stark, classic simplicity: A late 1970s Hepburn portrait by Richard Avedon.
(COURTESY OF ROBERT WOLDERS)

47. Hepburn's sons—"my two greatest creations"—in 1979: Half-brothers Sean Ferrer, nineteen, and Luca Dotti, nine. (COURTESY OF THE AUDREY HEPBURN ESTATE)

48. "La Paisible," Hepburn's beautiful estate in Tolochenaz, Switzerland: Behind the rambling 1730-vintage farmhouse were expansive gardens where the mistress could be found blissfully digging away. (COURTESY OF THE AUDREY HEPBURN ESTATE)

49. At the home of her Swiss neighbor and intimate friend Doris Brynner: More amazing than Hepburn's love of animals was their reciprocal affection and comfort with her. (COURTESY OF DORIS BRYNNER)

50. Hepburn with Givenchy and Leendert de Jong, programming director of the Hague Film Foundation, at the opening of the "Film and Fashion" series on November 19, 1988—about to be nailed by a photographer lying in wait around the corner. (PHOTO BY PETER VAN MULKEN, COURTESY OF LEENDERT DE JONG)

51. Audrey's most upbeat UNICEF journey was her February 1989 trip to Central America, where she pleaded the case for children with the chief executives of Honduras, Guatemala and—most touchingly—the dying Salvadorean President, Napoleon Duarte. She and that mission were chronicled along the way by her photographer-godchild Victoria Brynner, Doris's daughter.

52. Role-reversal: Audrey with *Gardens of the World* series co-producer Julie
Leifermann during shooting of the segment at Tintinhull, England in 1990. "She
ended up becoming *my* caretaker," says Leifermann, Hepburn's personal assistant.
"In the backseat of a car with Audrey, I'd fall asleep. I'd wake up with my head on
her shoulder, and everyone would tease me about how I drooled on her."
(PHOTO BY BRUCE FRANCHINI)

53. The UNICEF Special Ambassador with her cherished friend and photographer John Isaac, Bangladesh, October 1989. In his view, "Audrey had no color, no race." (COURTESY OF JOHN ISAAC)

54. Ethiopia, 1988: There was a tender kind of magic between John Isaac and Audrey Hepburn in real life, and in the sensitivity–never sentimentality–of his photographs of her for UNICEF. (COURTESY OF JOHN ISAAC)

Holding a starving child at the refugee camp in Baidoa: This time, Hepburn cannot manage a smile, y an angry, sorrowful frown. (PHOTO BY BETTY PRESS, COURTESY OF UNICEF)

Audrey brightens up a boy at the feeding center and displaced persons camp in Baidoa, Somalia, tember 1992. (PHOTO BY BETTY PRESS, COURTESY OF UNICEF)

57. Audrey and Rob, just back from the rigorous UNICEF mission to Bangladesh in October 1989, at home in Tolochenaz with their adored Jack Russell terriers, Missy and Tuppy. (PHOTO BY JOHN ISAAC)

Abbey nunnery for the last eighteen years, and is now its abbess.

Lester and Goldman tantalize us—delaying her entrance for nearly thirty minutes. When it finally comes, Audrey as Marian looks haunting and perfect, and so is Goldman's dialogue. In her first encounter with Robin, she tells him her confessions were "the envy of the convent." He says, "I never meant to hurt you, and yet that's all I ever do." A pause. "You never wrote," she complains sadly. "I don't know how," he replies.

Their later love scenes are as fascinating as the sometimes bizarre lines. "Hurt me, make me cry!" says Marian before one big clinch. "I'd be twenty for you if I could.... I'd do everything for you but mourn."

One of the film's most beautiful scenes belonged to Hepburn and Nicol Williamson:

"You've never liked me, have you?" Marian asks Little John.

"You're Rob's lady," he answers with sullen fidelity, and then a quiet afterthought, "If you'd been mine, I would never have left you."

That scene with Williamson was "one of my favorites," says Lester. "When we shot it, we had a problem with the film stock, and in theory we should have gone back and shot it again. But I liked the original so much, I just said, 'I don't care what it looks like.' It played right the first time, and often, when you do it again, it doesn't come up to that original *frisson*. So I said, 'To hell with it, we'll just have it as it is.'"

Marian, as ever, is a pawn in the men's political games. More than once, Robin goes to her rescue, albeit more creakily than in the olde days. He is the world's first guerilla warrior, and the peasants still rally to his call. The final duel between him and the Sheriff is the last, sad, slow-motion battle of two aging titans. After a shocking murder-suicide denouement, the film ends on a grimly perfect shot of rotting apples.

Audrey later complained to Rex Reed about that final image, offended by the suspicion that it was designed to symbolize herself and Sean Connery. But there was no denying its impact, or the impact of the film overall.

"*Robin and Marian* is really a story about loss," wrote Caroline Latham, in which "Hepburn at last plays the part of a fully mature woman responsible for her own destiny."

"Am I old and ugly?" Marian asks Robin poignantly at one point. The answer is of course no, but that's not enough. In the end, rather than see him die in battle or crippled in bed, she commits the ultimate crime. Pauline Kael, for one, was appalled: "When Robin—who has survived body-smashing combat with the Sheriff—is poisoned by Marian, who has also poisoned herself, I was disgusted and angry."

Frank Thompson, in *American Film*, was less judgmental on the moral issue: "*Robin and Marian* is a sad and satisfying hymn to heroism, myth and lost youth.... Hepburn's Marian is the heart of the film; for once, neither fragile nor innocent. Her performance has steel in it, and a touch of madness."[74]

Audrey's portrayal was the triumph of her late career. Something about Marian inspired her—some identification with a woman who "gives it all up" for the cloisters but, finally, can't bear the isolation and must return to the world. Marian was spiritually close to Sister Luke in *The Nun's Story*.

Richard Lester's bottom-line characterization of Hepburn was as "a very hard, methodical, almost mechanical performer who worked at it very much the way dancers would, in that everything was blocked. Audrey was not the kind of person to whom, in the middle of a scene, you would suddenly throw a prop from off-camera and expect her to catch it with her left hand, carry on, and do a number with it."[75]

Robin and Marian was a jaundiced view of the heroism business among the formula-ridden action genres of the seventies. "It turned out to be much more of a success than we all realized at the time," said Audrey. "It had marvelous notices, but it was never 'commercial.'"[76] Yet it holds up remarkably to the test of time now—and of *Time* then:

"Audrey Hepburn has not made a movie in seven years. The moment she appears on screen is startling, not for her thorough, gentle command, not even for her beauty, which seems heightened, renewed. It is rather that we are reminded of how long it has been since an actress has so beguiled us and captured our imagination. Hepburn is unique and now, almost alone."[77]

After the New York premiere of *Robin and Marian*, Audrey flew to Hollywood for the Academy Awards ceremony, at which she was to present the Best Picture Oscar. Again as so often "out of the loop," she had to ask a reporter which movies had been nominated and, when informed, said, "Oh, yes—I have seen *Nashville* and *Jaws*."[78] (The other nominees were *Barry Lyndon*, *Dog Day Afternoon* and *One Flew Over the Cuckoo's Nest*.)

Her appearance March 29, 1976, at the Dorothy Chandler Pavilion in Los Angeles, in a dazzling pink Givenchy gown, drew a standing ovation. She was genuinely excited to announce *Cuckoo's Nest* as the winner, having known Michael Douglas, its producer, from his boyhood. Douglas later said that getting the award from Audrey was more important than the award itself. Jack Nicholson—named Best Actor for the same film—felt similarly. He considered Hepburn one of the few "un-phony" actresses of the times.

She was escorted that night by Dr. Dotti. Later, after the ceremony, they decided to skip the Governor's Ball in favor of Swifty Lazar's legendary Oscar bash in Beverly Hills. Swifty told her he'd seen *Robin and Marian* and that she would be the guaranteed winner of next year's Oscar race.

But when the time rolled around, she never even got a nomination.

AS ALWAYS, SHE WAS GLAD to get back home—for all its drawbacks. "It's difficult to live in Rome nowadays," she said, "but my roots are here now."[79]

She had agreed to be interviewed again by Jim Watters for *People* in the living room of her friend Arabella Ungaro's Monti Parioli home. Suddenly, the hostess rushed off to get them a glass of mineral water, apologizing that "there's not one drop of tap water in my house today." It was a typical aggravation of life in even the best parts of Rome. "From June to November I had no hot water," Audrey chimed in. "I had to bathe at my husband's office. You might say I went to Spain last summer to make *Robin and Marian* just so I could take a bath!"[80]

A much worse vexation was in vogue: kidnapping for ransom, to which the rich and famous in Rome were prey. Most notorious was the abduction—and grisly ear-slicing—of J. Paul Getty III. The danger was constantly, almost obsessively on her mind.

"It's a very anguishing period in Rome," she told Rex Reed. "They're even kidnapping tourists for $50 apiece, ransacking apartments and breaking into cars.... Some do it for political reasons, some for money, and [some just] for kicks. Two years ago, the joy of Rome was to walk around in the streets at night.... Not anymore. The whole world has changed."[81]

She was alarmed by a warning, evidently from the police, that Sean and Luca were being followed in the streets of Rome. Next came a serious of intimidating phone calls—for Audrey, the last straw. At dawn one morning, a car drew up at their home and took her and the boys at high speed to Leonardo da Vinci Airport. Two hours later, Sean and Luca were safely ensconced at La Paisible, where Audrey decided they should stay indefinitely, enrolling them in an exclusive academy at Le Rosey.[82]

She now had the stress of commuting even more frequently between her boys in Switzerland and her husband in Rome, since Andrea reiterated his refusal to give up his clinic and teaching in Rome. Audrey's fears for him increased—for good reason.

In broad daylight, as Dotti was leaving his clinic on the Via Ettore Ximenes, four men in ski masks jumped from a Mercedes and tried to drag him into the car. He struggled and got clobbered on the head with a gun butt but made enough noise to draw the attention of two guards outside the nearby Egyptian Embassy. The assailants fled. Dotti was taken to a hospital for seven stitches in his head.

Audrey was in Switzerland when it happened, and Dotti's close call confirmed and fueled her worst fears about Rome. From then on, she lived in a state of increased terror for him, for herself, and for the boys. Her insecurity—and a certain tension—came to the surface in a bantering but revealing way during the only joint interview she and Andrea ever did, in 1976, for *McCall's*. Asked if he thought Audrey's childhood under Nazi terror in Holland accounted for her fear of loss, psychiatrist Dotti replied with his belief that the search for security and the search for love go hand in hand.

"It's difficult to have both," said Andrea, "especially for women, since security is based on a fixed social and economic situation, a status quo with prearranged agreements or contracts, while love is wild, unfixed, unpredictable.... No doubt Audrey's childhood experiences intensified these drives.

"She's a perfectionist, with a strong need for security. She must have matters under control and she's afraid of surprises. For example, if she has to go to Geneva next month, she buys the ticket now. I do it the day before, and maybe then I'll change my mind and go to Sardinia."

Audrey interrupted him: "No, love, you wouldn't fly off *any*where, because for Sardinia there's *always* a waiting list."

Dotti responded brightly: "She's right—absolutely! So you see, we're good for each other. We compensate. I'm a curious Pisces and she's Taurus with both feet on the ground. That's very good for a marriage." He paused, with a twinkle in his eyes. "But for a love affair, Cancer is best."

Audrey: (coolly) "How exciting. Do tell us more."

Andrea: "She's composed of categories, like boxes. It's either good or bad. It can be done or it can't. In between, we don't discuss. That's good, too, since it makes for great mental economy."[83]

During the six weeks of *Robin and Marian* shooting, she had returned as often as possible to Rome on the weekends to be with Andrea. That still left him many free weeknight evenings to kill in the nightclubs, but she was tolerant to a fault:

"He's done it all his life. It's not as if all of a sudden he's breaking out at the age of thirty-seven to go to nightclubs. It's his way of relaxing, and I think it's important for him to feel free. I don't expect him to sit in front of TV when I'm not there. It's much more dangerous for a man to be bored."[84]

But the photographic reports of his infidelities hurt almost as much as the final miscarriage she now suffered, at age forty-five.

By way of consolation, her sons were making excellent progress at school. For distraction, she had only to go to her mailbox and ponder the endless stream of scripts submitted to her. Now and then one would cause her to linger wistfully. One such was the offer of female "lead" in Richard Attenborough's all-male war epic, *A Bridge Too Far* (1977), with Dirk Bogarde, Michael Caine, James Caan, Robert Redford, Sean Connery, Ryan

O'Neal and a battalion of others. Attenborough wanted her to play Kate ter Horst, a Dutch national heroine and mother of five who turned her home outside Arnhem into a secret hospital for the Allies. But Audrey could not bear the thought of re-creating the horror and violence of her girlhood.*

Most of the time Audrey could look back at the final result of such rejected projects as *A Bridge Too Far* and feel she had been correct to decline. But "the one that got away" was Herbert Ross's *The Turning Point* (1977). She was deeply intrigued by the part of the aging ballerina star and ideally suited to it because of her dance background. She would have been teamed with Shirley MacLaine, Mikhail Baryshnikov and Leslie Browne. But Anne Bancroft had evidently been cast in the part by the time Audrey learned of it. By another account, Hepburn was offered her choice of roles in the film but refused. In any event, she didn't appear in the picture—and always regretted it.

Also lamented was a project dear to the heart of her friend Anna Cataldi, who had spent a great deal of time in Africa, fallen in love with the continent, and wanted to do a movie about Karen Blixen ("Isak Dinesen"), the author of *Out of Africa.*

"The first person I contacted was Audrey," Cataldi recalls. "I went to Switzerland in 1977 and spent a few days with her, and she told me she wanted to do it. She knew everything about Isak Dinesen. But there were several different proposals for this movie. She said, 'If you want to do it, the person I would like you to see is Fred Zinnemann,' who had done *Nun's Story* with her and knew Africa. I went to London and had several meetings with him and discussed *Out of Africa.* Then Audrey said, 'Now go to Los Angeles and meet Kurt Frings.' And that was awful. He said, 'You want to put my client in a stupid adventure movie? Forget it. Audrey will never do another movie.' "[85]

DIRECTOR TERENCE YOUNG DESCRIBED THE elaborate *danse macabre* of approaching Audrey Hepburn with a movie project, in general, and with his current project, in particular:

"First of all you spend a year or so convincing her to accept even the principle that she might make another movie in her life. Then you have to persuade her to read a script. Then you have to make her understand

---

* The role went to Liv Ullmann, who seemed destined for Audrey's hand-me-downs: Ullmann also took the role Hepburn declined in *Richard's Things* (1980), written by Frederic (*Two for the Road*) Raphael. As for *A Bridge Too Far*, its lumbering, three-hour screenplay was filmed with scrupulous fidelity to Cornelius Ryan's book about the 1944 Allied airdrop in Arnhem. It had fine battle scenes but was relentlessly downbeat and did not do well at the box office.

that it is a good script. Then you have to persuade her that she will not
be totally destroying her son's life by spending six or eight weeks on a
film set. After that, if you are really lucky, she might start talking about
the costumes. More probably she'll just say she has to get back to her
family and cooking the pasta for dinner, but thank you for thinking of
her."[86]

Anna Cataldi was just as persistent as Young, if ultimately not as
persuasive. Refusing to give up on Audrey's participation in *Out of Africa*,
she shook off Kurt Frings's first rebuff and, the next day, made a second
stab and called Frings again.

"I'm rushing to Paris," he told her. "Audrey is doing a fantastic
movie!"

Cataldi was aghast. "Yesterday you said she would never work again,"
she protested.

"But this is an extraordinary movie," Frings replied, "with a fantastic
cast. Givenchy is doing the clothes!"[87]

When *Out of Africa* was eventually made in 1985 by director Sidney
Pollack, Cataldi got credit as an associate producer and the film won many
Oscars, including Best Picture. But it would be Meryl Streep and not
Audrey Hepburn in the lead role.

The picture she made instead, and the one Frings was so enthused
about, was *Sidney Sheldon's Bloodline* (1979). The self-promotional title of
that trashy bestseller pretty much told the whole story: She had chosen a
blatantly commercial mish-mash over a host of worthier offers under the
pressure of Terence Young and the enticement of a cool $1 million (plus
percentage) for just six or seven weeks' work. *Bloodline* was a multinational
coproduction designed, in large part, to provide its American and European
investors with a tax shelter. Much of its $12-million-dollar budget would
end up in the pockets of agents and travel bureaus. But that wasn't
Audrey's concern.

At the time, it seemed like a great deal. In retrospect, it wasn't nearly
enough. A certain cynicism about the whole project prevailed, as Nicholas
Freeling detected when he interviewed her at that time in Rome, in a
story called "Audrey Hepburn at 50":

The professionals of the movie industry do not want acting from Audrey
Hepburn. Leave that to Liv, dear. We have $4 million here [on *Bloodline*] in
pre-production costs and not a camera has yet turned.

Halfway through the interview comes a knock at the door. An Italian
photographer with a bunch of stills. "These pictures have to go off today. . . .
Come and look at them with me." [She] switches on a strong light above
her head and examines them through a glass with a lamp built in. She is in
profile to me. . . . On the curves of her jaw and cheekbones is a fine down.

Her throat muscles are strongly corded and the whole of the celebrated neck has the intensely plastic, exaggeratedly anatomical modelling, full of movement of a Michelangelo drawing....

It is obvious that the illusion of youth, around the eyes, demands a skilled make-up artist.

[But] why on earth did she take this film?[88]

The answer was complex: First of all, money. Andrea's earnings were respectable but insufficient to support the family in the style to which they were accustomed. Second, her longtime friendship and confidence in director Terence Young, who felt he had a certain "right" to her in view of the huge success of their *Wait Until Dark*. When he gave her Sheldon's book, she failed to read it; she only knew that her role was fairly small and that she would not have to "carry" the film herself. Third, the shooting locations would be close to home—mostly at Rome's Cinecittà, with runouts to Munich, Copenhagen and Sardinia.

The final factor was perhaps the most significant: a last-ditch effort to make Andrea mend his ways. It was the worst period of her marriage to Dotti, and her friends were unanimously encouraging her to get out of the house. In the past, she had threatened to go back to work if he did not stop seeing other women, but Andrea did not believe her.

This time, however, the press was rough on her. *The London Sunday Times*, for example, filed an acerbic report from Munich where, in November 1978, she flew for four weeks of shooting:

For the last three years Audrey Hepburn has done nothing more strenuous than strain spaghetti for her family: "I lead such a full life at home. I'm just like most women, caught up in household duties that keep me very busy...."

When she needs a match for a cigarette, the look on her face is like a deer on a rifle range. Clearly, if Hepburn hadn't brought along a friend from Rome [Arabella Ungaro], she'd feel completely lost on this set.... In conversation I had no trouble believing her claims to ordinariness.... For her, an interview seems as much of an ordeal as trying to convince a camera that she's 35.[89]

"I never gave a thought to the question of my age when I was asked to do this film," she maintained—but the producers did. Her role had been rejected by Jacqueline Bisset, Candice Bergen and Diane Keaton, among others, but Young "flattered her into believing she could pass for fifteen years younger" and assured her that the script "only needs ten pages changing" to conform to her age.[90] Such was the novel's depth! Sheldon dutifully rewrote it to make her thirty-five instead of the original twenty-three.

Bloodline was Sheldon's second novel to be filmed. Producers David Picker and Sidney Beckerman bought the screen rights for $1.5 million and hired Laird Koenig (author of the fine Jodie Foster film, *The Little Girl Who Lives Down the Lane*) to write the potboiler screenplay about industrial intrigue and murder. It had an international all-star cast to ensure a profit on the Continent. The one superstar was Audrey. There was James Mason for the British. Gert Frobe and Romy Schneider would make the Germans happy. Omar Sharif was an ersatz Italian. Irene Papas would please the Greeks. Ben Gazzara, Beatrice Straight and Michelle Phillips might draw in the Americans.

Heroine of the turgid tale was Audrey, a paleontologist who is first seen in *Bloodline* in the act of cleaning a dinosaur—symbolic of her task in the film. She is the object of a grand conspiracy, but her romantic involvement with Gazzara and most other elements of the plot end up submerged in random violence and a series of pornographic "snuff-film" murders.

When Hepburn finally realized, in mid-production, just how sleazy the film was really going to be, she complained—too late—to Frings, who told her sex and violence were necessary these days for a hit film and she should adjust to the times.

Audrey's periodic brushes with death are heralded by Ennio Morricone's corny "suspense" music, while an even cornier soprano chorus accompanies her romantic moments with Gazzara. Audiences didn't know which to dread more, the brushes with death or the bad dialogue of the love scenes: "Isn't it instantly plain to the naked eye I'm in love with you?" she tells Ben.

The ending is a combined rip-off of *Wait Until Dark* and *Charade*—cut phone lines, flames engulfing her house, Audrey forced to decide whether the real culprit is Mason or Gazzara.

The final credits clear up the most compelling question:

"Miss Hepburn's jewels by Bulgari."

DURING *BLOODLINE* SHOOTING, AUDREY TOLD a British journalist that Ingmar Bergman's *Autumn Sonata*, with Ingrid Bergman and Liv Ullmann, had moved her to tears. She identified powerfully with the introspective Ullmann character, "inwardly turned and tortured, psychologically crippled." Audrey knelt on the sofa, arms outstretched, miming the girl's anguish, then added a soft non sequitur: "I am a very interior person." There was an unspoken sense that her own career had run into a dead end.[91]

On *Bloodline* location in Sicily, Audrey had several bodyguards, said a cast member, "until she realized that even kidnap by the Mafia would be preferable to having to finish this script."[92] The critics were correspondingly merciless.

Variety: "It's a shock to see Hepburn playing a role that even Raquel Welch would have the good sense to turn down."[93]

New York Daily News: "*Bloodline* offers the chance to see Hepburn on the screen again but under what rotten circumstances. As a team, she and Ben Gazzara evoke no spark, no charisma."[94]

Denver Post: "Hepburn is showing the passage of time."[95]

Devastated by the reviews, Audrey wondered if she'd lost her touch for picking winners. What remained of her confidence was deeply shaken. It occurred to her that Mel's input, overbearing as it often was, was something she rather missed.*

The only thing more disastrous than *Bloodline* was her marriage, whose instability hadn't been helped by reports during filming that she and Gazzara were becoming involved. Ben (né "Biago") Gazzara was a year younger than Audrey, a product of Lee Strasberg's Actors Studio and, for a while, thought to be a potential new Brando. He'd starred on Broadway in *Cat on a Hot Tin Roof* and *A Hatful of Rain* and had a hit TV show, *Run for Your Life* (1965–68). He was separated from Janice Rule at the time he and Audrey met, and their relationship became the object of great press speculation during *Bloodline*.

But an "affair"? Her friends, and possibly Audrey herself, relished the rumor for giving Andrea a taste of his own medicine. But if her brief infatuation with Gazzara was anything serious or profound, Hepburn never mentioned it—then or later—to her confidantes Connie Wald or Doris Brynner or anyone else.

Andrea was, in fact, disturbed by the Hepburn-Gazzara gossip, but not enough to renounce his ways. His extracurricular socializing continued unabated, and so did the Roman public's fascination with him. His favorite haunts were Bella Blue, Rome's most chic private nightclub, and Jackie O, just 150 meters away. The man who knew and followed his movements most closely—and whom Dr. Dotti loathed above all others—was a genial working stiff named Tony Menicucci.

---

* Mel Ferrer's career is unrelated to Audrey's at this point, but perhaps the reader will indulge our footnote efforts to keep up with its highlights: Adnan Kashoggi, the Saudi Arabian financier and later go-between for U.S.-Iran arms deals, had asked Mel to head up the Entertainment Division of his Triad company and, later, to undertake the Arab-financed film epic, *Mohammed: Messenger of God* (1977). Ferrer counter-proposed a better project newly under option: *Little House on the Prairie*, starring Michael Landon, with NBC as partner. But Triad opted for the $10 million *Mohammed*, starring Anthony Quinn and Irene Papas. In mid-production, King Hassan gave the company twenty-four hours to get out of Morocco—he had royal objections to the script's religious content. The film was completed elsewhere but lost its whole investment. *Little House on the Prairie*, on the other hand, is still in reruns.

"I am not a paparazzi!" Menicucci declares in Rome. "I am a *photojournalist*. Paparazzi shoot people when they are shopping or with friends—unimportant times." Menicucci shoots them when they're somewhere, or with someone, important. That is his legal right, he declares, going on to defend it at length. It's a sensitive issue—and his occupational hazard. But as one of Europe's greatest celebrity catchers, he is proud of his work, in general, and of his extensive knowledge of Dr. Dotti's nocturnal habits, in particular. Typically, he says:

> Dr. Dotti went to the movies at eight p.m., then to eat about ten-thirty, then the nightclub. He very much liked the nightlife—to stay up after work, go to the clubs and meet a girl. At one-thiry or two, he'd leave. I took my pictures a lot at two to three a.m., when people were coming out of the clubs. He went mostly with other women, not with Audrey. I remember only one time Audrey went to "Jackie O" with him. She didn't like to go out. With Audrey, he went only to restaurants, where they stayed two-three hours, to eat slowly. To the clubs, he went with married and single women both.[96]

What was it about Dr. Dotti that so many women loved?

"I don't know," the photographer replies. But it seems to have been his mind more than his body, and Dotti, in turn, seems to have been more interested in their company than in sex. Says Menicucci, with the investigative certainty of a Woodward-Bernstein: "I know he didn't take them to his house."

Even if Audrey knew that, it was small consolation to her in view of the immense publicity, for even a partial list of Dotti's outings and the women who appeared on his arm in those days is staggering. On an elegant Roman coffee table, Menicucci lays out an immense stack of photographs of Dr. Dotti taken during his marriage to Hepburn: Some are with Luca and Sean and Audrey. A few are with such celebrities as Ringo Starr and Olivia de Havilland. But most are with the beautiful young women "who were important in his life then," Menicucci says, of whom the following are but a Whitman's Sampler:

Actress Daniela Trebbi (1979, et al.); Lupua Yerni and actress Karin Shubert (1979); Countess Coppotelli Latini at Bella Blue (1979); actress Christiana Borghi, one of Dotti's favorites, in Bologna and Rome (1980, et al.); Beatrice Corri of Italian TV and French actress Carol André (1975); Manuela Croce (1976); actresses Dalila Di Lazzaro and Marinella Giordana (1978); Countess Iliana Coritelli Lovatelli (Lorean's daughter) at Bella Blue (1980); actress Marilù Tolo (1982).

The pictures go on and on.... They appeared in *Novella*, *Ava Express*, *Stop*, *Oggi*, *Gente*, *Gioia*, *Annabella* and *Paris-Match*, to mention only a few.

Menicucci's most dramatic encounter with Dotti produced "a sentiment that was not friendly," says the photographer, with a classic Italian shrug. "Son of a bitch!" Dotti yelled at him. "Don't you ever go to sleep? I don't want pictures!" With actress Dalila Di Lazzaro, especially, he became as "wild as a hyena" and would run to his car in an effort to hide her.[97]

Anna Cataldi felt it was "as if Andrea somehow wanted to provoke Audrey. It was a neurotic relationship. Audrey was a strong person. She set limits and was rather inflexible, and Andrea suffered for that. But Andrea had a rather schizophrenic personality. One side was looking for glamour. The other was a serious person who was a good doctor, a good father, a brilliant man. I think his relationship with Audrey had the same schizophrenia. One part of him was very impressed with the 'Audrey Hepburn' glamour but also battling against it. The other part had a real relationship with a real human being.

"Andrea had enormous respect for her. 'Audrey is a very straight person, very honest,' he would say. But Andrea destroyed Audrey's dream to have a little family and house when Luca was born. He disappointed her enormously and had some kind of rebellion against her."[98]

Some of the Dottis' mutual friends were struck by Andrea's attentiveness to Audrey in many ways. Others, such as actor David Niven, were struck by the opposite:

"When Audrey married Dotti and was swept off to Rome, she was, I think, determined to be a very good wife to this very socially minded Roman, [but] the longer it went on, many people felt she was much too good for him and that he took incredible advantage of her and that she gamely played the wife of the social Roman and really let her career just stand still, on purpose, to help him."[99]

Billy and Audrey Wilder's opinions are always of interest.

"He didn't make any impression on me," says Mr. Wilder.

"They didn't go together," says Mrs. Wilder. "You look at two people and you say, yes or no, and this was no."[100]

Hepburn's friend Camilla Pecci-Blunt thought the same, even though, like Anna Cataldi, she knew and liked Andrea very much. "It seemed to me they didn't belong together at all," says the Countess. "They just led very different lives. He was a very good father, and he has grown up a great deal since then. But he was rather childlike in those times."[101]

Eli Wallach has the last word: "She seemed to have a tendency to get involved with men who didn't take good care of her. I don't know exactly what happened, but when she married that Italian psychiatrist, she went dotty."[102]

CHAPTER 9

Dutch Treat
(1980–1989)

> "A wife entirely preoccupied with her af-
> fection for her husband, a mother entirely
> preoccupied with her affection for her
> children, may be all very well in a book
> (for people who like that kind of book)
> but in actual life she is a nuisance."
>   GEORGE BERNARD SHAW

AUDREY HEPBURN WAS HAUNTED BY the trauma of her first marital breakup and almost fanatically determined to avoid another one. In sadder but wiser hindsight, she assessed the situation as follows:

"I decided that if and when there was a second marriage, I would not let my fame or anything at all get in the way of personal happiness—for myself, for him, for my son and for the second child I hoped for. [Andrea] and I had what you could call an open arrangement. It's inevitable, when the man is younger. I wanted the relationship—the marriage—to last. Not just for our own sake, but for that of the son we had together.... I still believe the child has to come first.[1]

"[Divorce is] one of the worst experiences a human being can go through. I tried *desperately* to avoid it.... I hung on in both marriages very hard, as long as I could, for the children's sake, and out of respect for marriage. You always hope that if you love somebody enough, everything will be all right—but it isn't always true."[2]

It was time to act on a statement of principles she had made four years earlier to journalist Curtis Bill Pepper:

"Marriage should be only one thing: Two people decide they love each other so much that they want to stay together.... So, if in some way I don't fulfill what he needs in a woman—emotionally, physically, sexually, or whatever it is—and if he needs somebody else, then I could not stick around. I'm not the kind to stay and make scenes."[3]

Audrey, says Anna Cataldi, "behaved fantastically. She even stayed in

Rome after they separated because she wanted Luca not to be split between his father and mother."[4]

Dr. Dotti would later tell a *People* magazine reporter, "I was no angel—Italian husbands have never been famous for being faithful. But she was jealous of other women even from the beginning."[5] Hepburn would later come to a less Italian conclusion. "Those open marriages don't work," she said. "If there's love, unfaithfulness is impossible."[6]

"THE DIFFICULTY WITH STARS," SAYS Billy Wilder, "is, what do they do at fifty or fifty-five?"[7]

It struck Audrey—as it had stricken the critics and millions of her fans—that *Bloodline* was no proper way to end such a grand film career. Her next picture, if she ever made one, might well be her last and had better be good. Among those clamoring for her film presence was director Peter Bogdanovich, who flew her to Los Angeles in January 1980 and instantly charmed her with his personality and with a script idea.

The title *They All Laughed* was borrowed from a Gershwin song composed for Fred Astaire and Ginger Rogers in *Shall We Dance* (1937). The story was a quirky romance-suspense caper concerning four private detectives in New York whose love lives get mixed up with their sleuthing.

Barbra Streisand, after working with Bogdanovich in the hilarious *What's Up, Doc?*, called him "a horny bastard but brilliant." He had been in a slump since the poorly received *Daisy Miller* (1974) and *At Long Last Love* (1975)—starring his paramour, Cybill Shepherd. He spent the next three years breaking up with her, and then made *Saint Jack* (1979), Paul Theroux's novel of a Singapore pimp, starring Ben Gazzara.

"Benny couldn't get a job in a feature to save his life then," Bogdanovich recalls. "None of the majors wanted him. I said, 'Fuck it,' I was fed up with the whole system, so I went to Roger Corman and we made *Saint Jack* for under $2 million. When I screened it for Barry Diller and Michael Eisner in my projection room in Bel Air, they both flipped over Ben, and the next day—literally—they cast him in *Bloodline*."

Thenceforth, Gazzara was an unsolicited hotline of information. During *Bloodline*, Bogdanovich recalls, "he was constantly calling me about Audrey.... 'Is she wonderful? Oh, Jesus, an angel come down from heaven!' They fell in love, he said. But Benny was going through a very bad time. His divorce was about to start. He would tell me these things candidly.

"So I wrote *They All Laughed* for Audrey, knowing what I knew because Ben had told me. I wrote those things into the script, and she knew it when she read it. It was what she was going through, an unhappy marriage, ten-year-old kid—all written for her based on what was happening in her life.

"The original idea of the detectives getting involved with their own clients was much like movie people who get involved romantically during their movies. It's an occupational hazard. So it was really a thinly veiled picture of our own lives."[8]

Cinema à clef. David Susskind bought the first draft of the script, but by the time it got to production, "it was totally different—almost unrecognizable except for the title," says the director, "and Susskind was going crazy." The project was sold to Time-Life Films, a new arm of the media conglomerate, which was looking for its first big hit and felt Audrey was the star to launch it. If *They All Laughed* even approached the success of *Paper Moon* or *What's Up, Doc?*, everyone would be in clover.

The first version of the script was melancholy. In it, the detective played by John Ritter was still getting over a girl based on Shepherd. "It was going to be just Cybill's photograph," says Bogdanovich. "That was the joke. She and I had just broken up. But in November [1979], I met Dorothy, and she and I fell madly in love. Her original part was just one scene. But I decided to stretch her story out into a happy ending, and I rewrote the whole thing from the middle on."[9]

Gorgeous Dorothy Stratten, a twenty-year-old Canadian model, was *Playboy's* 1980 Playmate of the Year. When Bogdanovich met her at a Hugh Hefner party, all thoughts of Cybill Shepherd vanished from his mind. Stratten's previous film work consisted of one unreleased film and one that should have remained unreleased—*Galaxina* (1980), a kind of *Star Wars* spoof in which she played a robot. But Bogdanovich was smitten and determined to make her a star. He also wanted to marry her, but she was already married to (though separated from) a small-time Los Angeles hustler named Paul Snider. While Stratten was shooting in New York, Snider was enraged by press stories of her affair with the director. He bought a shotgun and told friends, "I'm going to kill Bogdanovich," but nobody paid attention to his threats.

Another marriage was breaking up, as well. The Dottis had begun divorce proceedings by the time Hepburn arrived in New York City in mid-1980 to begin filming *They All Laughed.* She was depressed about that, and her life in general. Gazzara's casting had been reason for her acceptance of the film: She was happy to be reunited with him, though she was distressed by the new round of tabloid stories blaming her for Gazzara's divorce from Janice Rule. That subject was avoided in a *New York Times* interview with Michiko Kakutani on June 4, 1980, at the Cafe Pierre, where she sounded her "family values" theme once again but otherwise limited the discussion to her role.

She would be playing a Euro-millionaire's wife in search of a Manhattan escapade—"witty and fragile and strong," said Bogdanovich. "What I think is interesting is bringing an actor and character together so you don't know where one leaves off and the other begins." Audrey went along with it. "You have to refer to your own experience," she told Kakutani. "What else have you got?" That—and her directors, whom she credited, as always, for her film success:

"I'm not trying to be coy. I really am a product of those men. I'm no Laurence Olivier, no virtuoso talent. I'm basically rather inhibited and I find it difficult to do things in front of people. What my directors have had in common is that they've made me feel secure, made me feel *loved*. I depend terribly on them. I was a dancer and they managed to do something with me as an actress that was pleasing to the public."[10]

She still tried to control her wardrobe, at least. But in the case at hand, Bogdanovich recalls, "I came up to her room one day at the Pierre, laid out all her clothes, and said, 'I like this shirt, these pants, this scarf.' She said, 'Fine.' No Givenchy. Blue jeans, a pea coat, a silk shirt. Everything she wore in the movie was what she walked around in normally."

Several scenes in the film were shot on Fifth Avenue in the middle of the day, and the actors had to mill around in the stores during the setups. There were no luxury trailers for the stars, but "Audrey complied without a sigh," says Bogdanovich, and "never threw her weight around. Everyone knew her, of course, so after ten minutes, she would come out of a shop beaming: 'Just look at what they gave me, Pete-ah. Look at this lovely umbrella! This wonderful handkerchief!' I told her, 'You can work the other side of the street tomorrow.'"

As she never asked for special treatment, she also never asked for any of her lines to be changed. Instead, says the director, if she didn't like her dialogue, "What she'd do in her own sweet way [was] simply change the line. She'd say, 'Oh! Terribly sorry, Pete-ah. I thought that *was* the line.'[11] . . .

"I caught onto it after a while. I'd say, 'That's not the line.' She'd say, 'Oh, isn't it? I'm so sorry. I'll say the line—what was it?' I'd say, 'No, yours was better.' She'd say, 'Oh, no, no. Are you sure?' I'd say, 'Yes, darling . . .'"[12]

Bogdanovich did her other favors during production, not least of which concerned her son Sean. The previous year, at nineteen, he had decided that one semester at the University of Geneva was enough and that he'd rather go to work—in films. With his mother's intercession, he was hired as an assistant director on the Terence Young film *Inchon*, a Korean war epic produced by the Reverend Sung Myung Moon's Unification Church, starring a deeply uncomfortable Laurence Olivier as General Douglas MacArthur (and, coincidentally, Ben Gazzara in a supporting role). On one of Sean's first days on the Korean set, an extra was killed in a crowd scene, and it fell to young Ferrer to collect the body.

"Audrey worried so much and wanted Sean to banish it from his mind," recalls Rob Wolders. "But it was the school of hard knocks. He really wanted to make his own way."

Before production of *They All Laughed* began, Audrey invited Bogdanovich to an intimate family dinner. It was clear that he was not just to have supper but also to see if a place for Sean might be found on the picture:

"It was love at first sight. I sat next to him and you looked into his eyes and you wanted to hug him. He was the most adorable kid you've ever seen. I thought, 'I'd like to look at him every day,' so I asked if he wanted to be my assistant. He said yes, and that was it. He carried my script, my cigars, woke me up at six o'clock, made omelets for me on a hot plate—he's a brilliant cook—drove me, whatever I had to do. He was my guy.

"And then I wrote him into the picture. There was a Latin guy named José, and I said, 'Why don't we have Sean play it? He'd be great.' Sean said, 'I don't think I can act.' But he became that part, got so many laughs based on his attitude—totally Sean. At one point, he's walking with Colleen Camp and she says, 'You're very rich,' and he says, 'Rich? Oh, a little...' A nothing line. I don't think it was even in the script. But the way he delivered it was fabulous."[13]*

The four private eyes in the film are played by Gazzara, Ritter, Blaine Novak and George Morfogen, who all work for the Odyssey Detective Agency and fall in love with the women they're trying to follow. The audience, for its part, must try to follow a plot with more twists and turns than the Pacific Coast Highway.

Ritter was then regarded as a hot property from his *Three's Company* TV series, but his physical-shtick comedy in *They All Laughed* is unfunny and progressively more annoying, providing an example of Bogdanovich's weakness for choosing actors on the basis of looks. But on the other hand, his casting of the unknown Blaine Novak (as dope-smoking Arthur) and George Morfogen (as the boss detective, Mr. Leondopoulos) was inspired. Morfogen and Novak were coproducers as well as costars of the film, as Bogdanovich recalls:

"George Morfogen was an old friend of mine. In *What's Up, Doc?*, he had a small part but got big laughs as the wine steward in the banquet scene.... I'm for having the actors get involved. George was particularly good with scripts, and we were rewriting as we were shooting. We would

---

* Bogdanovich also provided small parts in the film for his own daughters, Antonia and Alexandra, as Gazzara's daughters.

all sit around—George, Benny, me—and then we added Blaine, who had worked for [John] Cassavetes on the distribution of *Woman Under the Influence*.

"Blaine was a long-haired, weird kind of hippie-radical kid, and so was his character in the film. In real life, he had six or seven girlfriends all the time—in this macho, fucking-around scene that I'd never been a part of. It was new to me, but I was getting into it. The film reflected that scene."[14]

During *They All Laughed* shooting, Novak and Sean Ferrer became close friends. As Sean always called his mother "Mutti," Novak started to call Audrey "Mutti," too. "She didn't mind at all," says Bogdanovich. "She thought Blaine was funny."[15]*

Blaine *was* funny—in life and in *They All Laughed*—but the film, overall, was not. Its few good flashes of comedy called for Madeline Kahn and Ryan O'Neal, rather than Colleen Camp and John Ritter, while the Gazzara-Hepburn romance element of the story was Grade B *Two for the Road*, at best.

Years later, the question still remains: What was the sex appeal of Ben Gazzara? On-and offscreen, why were beautiful women so eager to jump into bed with him? He seems so devoid of charm, so wooden, so unjustifiably smug.

"You see more of his charisma in *Saint Jack* than in *They All Laughed* because of his sad character," says Bogdanovich, "but Audrey helped supply what he was missing. She knew how to pick up on the weak point of another actor and compensate for it without destroying her own performance."[16]

But there was too much art imitating too much life. To an intimate new friend, she confided that Gazzara was just "walking through" his part, giving her nothing to work with. In the end, even Bogdanovich knew that Gazzara and Hepburn didn't click. "Ben was going through his divorce," he says, "and had started an affair with another woman he ended up marrying later.‡ I think when Audrey realized all that, she was very disappointed."

Gazzara felt Hepburn was pursuing him, and was alarmed. She was "the marryin' kind," and marriage was the last thing he wanted at that point. "I'd work with her anytime, anywhere, anyhow," he said. "She's a beautiful, sexy, talented woman."[17] But there would be no new romance between them, if indeed there had ever been one in the past.

Hepburn's "rejection" by Gazzara, however, was a blessing in disguise.

---

* Novak and Sean Ferrer later convinced several actors to work for deferred payment in their jointly produced film, *Strangers Kiss* (1984), a remake of Stanley Kubrick's *Killer's Kiss* (1955), which was a critical but not a commercial success.

‡ Thirty-three-year-old German photographer Elke Krivat.

While *They All Laughed* was still shooting in New York, another man
would not only console her but would eventually provide her with the
happiest and most stable relationship of her life. Everyone assumed his
name was Bogdanovich.

"The newspapers hinted there was something going on between Audrey
and me," says the director today with a chuckle. "Audrey and I kidded
about it because something was going on with her, and Audrey knew
that something *was* going on with Dorothy and me. So when it appeared
that we were having an affair, we kind of encouraged it with some
intimate photos taken when we were shooting on Second Avenue—me
sitting in my chair, her sitting in my lap—that made it into the papers.
We were very huggy and kissy. I absolutely adored her. Our relationship
was very close, but of course it never got near an affair."[18] Bogdanovich
was in love with her, all right—professionally:

> I've never seen anybody change so much in front of a camera as Audrey.
> In life, you'd think, 'How is she going to get through the day or even the
> hour?' Her hands are shaking, she's smoking too much, she's worried, she's
> being kind of desperately nice to everybody, she's so fragile—how the fuck
> can she survive? But between the time she stepped in front of the camera
> and you said 'Action!,' something happened. She pulled it together. A kind
> of strength through vulnerability—strength like an iron butterfly. You
> couldn't possibly get her to be any righter. You could only say, 'a little faster,
> a little slower.' The performance was true, never weak, always strong and
> clear. It was an amazing thing to watch, this professional completely in
> charge of her instrument without even thinking about it. I think it was all
> second nature.[19]

Bogdanovich's personal, as opposed to professional, love was reserved
for Dorothy Stratten, whom he encouraged to watch and learn from
Audrey Hepburn on the set. Stratten did so and was fascinated by Audrey's
discipline. There were reports that the two women became very close.

"Not at all true, unfortunately," says Bogdanovich. "I don't think
Dorothy and Audrey ever spoke. Dorothy was extraordinarily shy and
awed by Audrey. They passed in one scene on Fifth Avenue—the only
time you see them together. Dorothy looked like she wanted to talk to
her, but it didn't happen."

Back in California in August 1980, a few weeks after shooting on *They
All Laughed* was completed, Stratten was staying with Bogdanovich in Bel
Air when she decided to pay a visit to her estranged husband for the
purpose of expediting their divorce. Bogdanovich was later criticized for
letting her go alone, but that was with the advantage of hindsight:
Deranged and wildly jealous, Paul Snider terrorized her at gunpoint before

blasting her in the face and then killing himself as well.

Actor Tony Curtis, who knew Stratten from Hefner's Playboy Mansion in Los Angeles, remembers her as "very naive about the profession she was getting into and easily manipulated by any guy who made an overture—and in those days everybody made overtures to everybody. She's the perfect example of a tragedy that didn't need to happen."[20]

Hepburn was extremely supportive after the murder and described her as a very sweet kind of angel, says Bogdanovich, who quoted Audrey in his book about Stratten, *The Killing of the Unicorn:* "It's as though she just came down long enough to make this picture, and then she was gone."[21]

"It broke my heart," he says.

The murdered Stratten thus became the tragic star of *They All Laughed,* and the film itself an object of morbid curiosity instead of a pleasant romp. "When Dorothy was killed, the picture was killed," Bogdanovich says. "The melancholy story of Audrey was supposed to be juxtaposed with the happy story of Dorothy, but now there was no way to look at it without it being almost unbearable."*

Even morbid curiosity failed to generate much attendance, and neither did the reviews. "It's aggressive in its ineptitude," wrote Vincent Canby. "It grates on the nerves like a 78 rpm record played at 33 rpm." *Newsweek* called it "an aimless bust, unencumbered by a visual or structural scheme. It wanders through a series of *boîtes*, boutiques and hotel lobbies in the vagrant hope of witnessing a privileged moment.... At 52, the eternal gamine has become a figure of icy chic."

"They all laughed, but you won't," said the *Providence Journal,* griping that Hepburn "can't have had more than 10 pages of dialogue" in the film.[22]

Bogdanovich pleads nolo contendere:

"If I had not been struck by a terrible calamity, I think I would have edited it better. The director's cut is clearer.... I lost $5 million of my own money on that picture, which was why I went bankrupt in 1985. We never could get it booked. You can't fight the majors. I was so shellshocked—I went into therapy after that and found I was trying to destroy myself."[23]

Bogdanovich is hard on himself and the film, but in fact it was acclaimed in such prestigious quarters as the Venice Film Festival and in *Variety,* which called it "probably Bogdanovich's best film to date." One of the most appreciative critics was Bill Cosford in *The Miami Herald:*

"Imagine Woody Allen's *Manhattan* without the *angst.* [*They All*

---

* Stratten's life and death inspired two lurid films: *Death of a Centerfold: The Dorothy Stratten Story* (1981), hastily produced for TV, starred Jamie Lee Curtis and Bruce Weitz. *Star 80* (1983), with Mariel Hemingway as Stratten, was much better directed by Bob Fosse (his last movie) and highlighted by Eric Roberts's brilliant, chilling performance as the psycopathic Snider.

Laughed] recalls Manhattan just a little because it is a romantic comedy not just about people but about the city of New York, which always makes a good costar when properly handled.... This one should have been a hit.... For a flop, this is one interesting film."[24]

The Atlanta Journal reviewer called it "oddly disjointed" but concluded, "I can probably forgive a movie almost anything if it allows me even a glimpse of Audrey Hepburn."[25]

The next-to-the-last glimpse on film, as it turned out. Bogdanovich sums up the *They All Laughed* experience—and Audrey —with brutal candor:

> If it hadn't had been for Audrey, we couldn't have done it. And she didn't want to do it that badly. Finally when I said, "Audrey, I wrote the whole picture for you!", she said, "Oh, all right." Even when I decided to use Sean, it wasn't definite that she was going to do it....
>
> She understood how to marshal everything she had. It was an extraordinary mechanism. Maybe she got tired of moving that mountain. She was very insecure. She was also so hurt. I noticed that she was somebody who had been wounded many times, and when you're wounded in the same area, you grow scar tissue. She was a survivor, but it was painful. There was a sense of lost gaiety around Audrey that she could never quite recapture. I felt it was from all the guys that had treated her badly....
>
> I sensed this would be her last film, which is why I did the ending as a montage of all those shots of her. I felt it was a farewell to that Audrey Hepburn. As the helicopter took her away, I thought, 'The world is taking her away.' I had a strong sense that she didn't really enjoy making pictures anymore. The fun had gone out of it for her. She didn't think it was important anymore.[26]

Hepburn and Bogdanovich "almost" made another picture together. In 1991, "I tempted her with *Noises Off*," says the director. "She thought about it for a while, but then she said no." The part went to Carol Burnett.

AUDREY WAS DECIDEDLY "DOWN" DURING much of *They All Laughed* shooting, Peter Bogdanovich recalls, but "it became a happy thing. It started to happen for her, toward the end of shooting, when she met Robbie."[27]

Robert Wolders, seven years younger than Hepburn, had been a costar of the popular television western series *Laredo*, and the fourth husband of the recently deceased Merle Oberon.

"I happened to be in New York when Audrey was doing the Bogdanovich movie," says Anna Cataldi, "and she was very mysterious about this new man. When I went back to Italy, Andrea told me, 'Audrey has found somebody!' He was terrible about it. Everybody assumed it was either Bogdanovich or Ben Gazzara."[28]

The fateful meeting of Hepburn and Wolders came about through Connie Wald, widow of the celebrated producer-writer Jerry Wald. She was Audrey's closest friend and regular hostess in Los Angeles. Hepburn loved her beautiful but unpretentious stone house in Beverly Hills, with its wood-paneled library and state-of-the-art screening room full of Jerry's film memorabilia, including his 1948 Irving Thalberg Award.

Connie had also been a good friend of Merle Oberon, and of Rob Wolders, for more than a decade. She was struck then, and still is, by his "intense caring and devotion to Merle," especially after Oberon had open-heart surgery.

"Merle and I used to go to Connie's often," Wolders recalls. "Merle had died about two months earlier, and Connie felt I should be with friends because I had been keeping to myself. She said, 'Come to the house for dinner. It's just family.'"

Wolders arrived to find that the "family" included Billy and Audrey Wilder, William Wyler—and Audrey Hepburn, Connie's current houseguest. ("We always had Billy and Willie together when Audrey came," she says. "It was a love fest."[29]) Also present were Kurt Frings, Lenny Gershe and Sean Ferrer.

Some claim that Connie was actively matchmaking. "Heavens no," she says today. "That never works." In any case, Wolders recalls, "Audrey was extraordinarily sweet with me that night. We spoke Dutch and talked about Merle a great deal. Sean was wonderful with me, too. Later he said he remembered that I seemed to be hiding behind a certain chair. Connie took a picture of the two Audreys on either side of me [see photo 45]. That evening helped me considerably."

Audrey later told interviewer Glenn Plaskin, "I was charmed with him that night, but he didn't register that much. He was getting over the death of Merle, [and] it was the worst period of my life, one of the low ebbs. We both cried into our beers."[30]

Four months later, Wolders had to go to New York and Connie said, "Audrey's doing a picture there—you should call her."

He did so.

"She seemed pleased to hear from me but when I asked her to dinner, she said they were doing night shooting and it would be impossible," he says. "I thought it was a gentle, subtle way of rebuffing me. But I was in New York two more weeks and, on my last night there, I was dressing to go to a small party with some friends when the phone rang. It was Audrey, saying she wasn't shooting that night and would I like to have dinner? I said I had another commitment and asked if she'd like to join us. She said, 'No, thank you, but would you like to come by for a drink?' I said, 'Great.' I wanted to see her again.

"So I met her at the Cafe Pierre, we sat down for a drink, and before I knew it, an hour had passed. Audrey said, 'Do you mind if I have some pasta?' I said no, of course. So she had a huge plate of pasta. An hour and three quarters passed, and I realized I was quite late. I joined my friends and had to leave early the next morning for Los Angeles. But after that, we spoke almost every day and got to know each other on the telephone."

Those conversations in the beginning, he says, "were not romantic tête-à-têtes. She was counseling and advising me and then gradually, she started to talk about her own life and began to seek *my* counsel. I was the one calling her, but then one day, she called me, which gave me an entirely different feeling about her. It meant that she cared enough to speak to me, whereas, up to then, I thought perhaps she was just 'accommodating' me. That's when I went back to New York and we began a kind of clandestine relationship, which she went into very reluctantly."

Her main concern was for Luca, not Andrea. When she returned to Rome, Dotti said, rather flippantly, "You look very beautiful—you must be in love." She replied, rather daringly, "I am!" Their marriage was by then irreparable, but it wasn't entirely Andrea's fault. To Rob, she confided an example of the problems caused by her own emotionalism a few years earlier:

"She was extraordinarily close to her makeup man, Alberto de Rossi, and to his wife, Grazia. When he died, Audrey was destroyed—not only for Grazia. Her own pain was so intense that Andrea thought it excessive. He could not comprehend the depth of her sorrow, and that contributed to their rift; Audrey's melancholia was so intense that it became difficult for Andrea to deal with, and he criticized her, she told me. Without making herself the victim and him the villain, she was investigating where she might have failed. I think she was also keen to find out what had made Merle's and my marriage so successful."

ROBERT WOLDERS WAS BORN ON September 28, 1936, in Rotterdam, the son of a KLM airline executive. He was four years old during the Nazi destruction of Rotterdam, after which a farmer friend of his mother's said, "You can bring your children here." Dutch people in those days used to take their china and silver into the countryside to trade with the farmers for food. Rob and his sister spent the terrible *Hongerwinter* of 1944 with that farm family in a tiny village near Zwolle, just ten miles from Arnhem.

"There is a great irony in the fact that Audrey and I were so close to each other then," he says. Later, in discussing the impact of the war on their childhood, they found that they both shared the odd feeling that "this was the way things had to be. An occupation wasn't anything unusual. I thought everybody lived like that. We thought America was someplace up in heaven—it didn't really exist. Audrey frequently pointed out, and I experienced it, too, how close families grew to each other and the humor we found in everything—her mother's extraordinary dedication to her and her grandfather and her aunts. She said those were, in a sense, among the best years of her life."[31]

After the war, several members of his family emigrated to Rochester, New York. Rob joined them in 1959, with a goal of becoming an actor. He enrolled at the University of Rochester, where he founded an avant-garde theatrical group called "Experiment '60." He was much praised for his production of Samuel Beckett's *Endgame* and for his bold direction of Ghelderode's *Escuriel*—a "triumph that should elevate him to professional echelons," wrote one Rochester critic. On the strength of three successful seasons as the leading figure and guiding spirit of that group, Wolders was accepted by the American Academy of Dramatic Arts in New York, where he studied for two years. He was then engaged, in July 1963, as a novice at the Spoleto Festival, where he directed (and played "Greeneyes" in) a much-admired production of Jean Genet's *Deathwatch*, supervised by Jerome Robbins.

By 1966, Wolders was costarring with Neville Brand and Philip Carey in the NBC-TV series *Laredo*, where his appearance in some fifty episodes drew raves. *Variety* hailed him as "a very suave addition to the Texas Rangers." *The Hollywood Reporter* said he set a record "for authoritative audacity" on the show.[32]

Soon enough, he got a movie contract. "Handsome Dutch Import Groomed as Star," read one headline. Said Monique James, a talent scout for Universal: "We have started a momentum for him by introducing him importantly in *Beau Geste* and following it up with a good role in the forthcoming *Tobruk*. I have no doubt that his face will register immediately with the movie public, but we want him to be an experienced, knowing actor."[33]

Sadly for Wolders, neither film lived up to expectations. *Beau Geste* (1966), costarring Rob with Telly Savalas, Guy Stockwell, Doug McClure and Leslie Nielsen, was the least successful version of that French Foreign Legion adventure. *Tobruk* (1967), directed by Arthur Hiller, costarred Wolders with Rock Hudson and George Peppard in a World War II action tale of the destruction of Rommel's fuel supply in the Sahara. It was better than *Beau Geste* but sabotaged by its slow pace.

In 1970, at thirty-four, Wolders met and became involved with the veteran star Merle Oberon, then fifty-nine. Soon after, she emerged from retirement to produce and costar with him in her final film—a steamy "vanity picture" called *Interval* (1973).

Shot in and around the Mayan ruins of Chichen-Itza, Mexico, *Interval* was the tale of a globetrotting older woman, on the run from her past, who finds true love with a much younger man—Rob Wolders. Their common bond is purely existential: both are caught in the "interval between being born and dying." Oberon looks nowhere near her sixty-two years, and hunky Wolders makes a noble effort to be fascinated by her; their modestly undraped love scenes are tasteful enough (see photo 43). Oberon and screenwriter Gavin Lambert deserved credit for at least *trying* to address the age issue.

"You've been very kind to me these last few days," she says to Rob at one point, "but surely you want to be with young people."

"Are you afraid of the past?" he asks.

"Not at all," she replies. "I'm faced with it. Most of it's not worth remembering."

As tearjerkers go, *Interval* was no *Intermezzo* or even *Interlude*, and the critics were brutal. But the film's failure did not diminish the offscreen ardor of its costars. Oberon and Wolders were married two years later, in 1975, and took their places in the international jet set, where Rob thenceforth tended to her and her career instead of his own.

One of Oberon's closest friends was Mignon Winans, who often stayed with her in Acapulco during those years and watched the progress of her relationship with Wolders:

"He's such a kind, serious person, and Merle thought he was just wonderful. He understood women—the tender side of women. Some do and some don't. They were certainly a happy couple. More than any of her marriages, this was the one that made her the happiest. His refinement is what she was very much attracted to. There aren't too many men who have that quality, that aura. He gave her a lot."[34]

Rob was ever gentle, says Eleanor Lambert, who was also a friend of Oberon's. "In a way, when he was with Merle, he was her slave. Not a slave of passion, but her adorer. If she had something within reach, she'd ask him to cross the room and hand it to her. That's how courtly he always was."[35]

Now and then, the words "gold digger" came up; some assumed Wolders married Oberon for her money. The truth was otherwise. "Because Merle was married to a wealthy industrialist, the presumption was that she was very wealthy, which was not the case," says Wolders. "When she left Bruno Pagliai, a man she loved a great deal, she did not ask for a major settlement."*

---

* Merle Oberon inspired many colorful myths. It was said she came from the slums of Calcutta but

Merle Oberon died on Thanksgiving Day 1979. Five months later, her legendary jewel collection netted $2,446,000 at a Christie's auction. Some $1.4 million of that was divided into equal trust funds for her adopted daughter and son, Francesca and Bruno Pagliai, Jr. The remaining $1 million was bequeathed to the Motion Picture Country Home and Hospital. Wolders got not a penny of it—by his own request, five years earlier, at the time Oberon made out her will. He was left only with the Malibu beach house which they had purchased jointly. It was reported that, shortly before her death, Merle had instructed him to find and marry someone else and not spend the rest of his life alone.

"This thing about 'instructions'... ," says Wolders, shaking his head. "I had told close friends that when I said to Merle she couldn't leave me because my life would be ruined, she became perturbed with me. She expected me to have more courage. She said, 'You owe it to me to be happy, to restart your life.' But instructions to find another woman to marry? No."

But it was true, he says, that Merle and Audrey had known and much liked one another:

"Audrey talked to me a great deal about Merle. Once while Audrey was married to Mel and not having a very positive attitude, she saw Merle at Doris Brynner's house. Audrey said she spent most of that day with Merle and it turned her around. One of the reasons why she extended herself to me so much at our first meeting was because of her admiration for Merle."

It was a curious coincidence that both women had played the same role in *The Children's Hour* for William Wyler, but Wolders says they never commented on each other's performances: "Neither Merle nor Audrey talked very much about their film work, but what struck me was the openness and vulnerability in both of their faces in that part. They both had a similar type of naturalness and innocence." To some extent, they even looked alike, with their high cheekbones and exotic, slightly slanted eyes.

The early stage of the Wolders-Hepburn match was complicated by the Hepburn-Gazzara gossip. "Her family was together at Christmas when

pretended to be an aristocrat and hired her own mother as a maid (keeping her identity a secret). The facts: She was born Estelle Merle O'Brien Thompson in Bombay in 1911, to a Ceylonese mother and a British father. She grew up in India and went to school in Katmandu before the family moved to Tasmania. The maid story derives from Michael Korda's book (later film), *Queenie*, a fictional version of Oberon's life. Korda's uncle, director Alexander Korda, saw her in London when she was a teenager working under the name "Queenie O'Brien," and married her in 1939. It was Korda who wanted to suppress her ethnic background because he feared it would harm her career. They divorced in 1945, after which she married cinematographer Lucien Ballard. Bruno Pagliai was her third husband and Rob Wolders her fourth.

those stories surfaced," says Wolders, and despite the fact that the divorce was well along, "Andrea was consumed by jealousy. She resented that very much at the time. But we could laugh afterwards over her supposedly having an affair with Gazzara, when she and I were well into our relationship by then."

A few months later, he began to visit her in Rome, where he rented an apartment because "Audrey and I, for Luca's sake, didn't consider it quite right to live openly together." Audrey's fondest wish was that Luca and Rob would like each other, which was inevitably the case. Except for Mel Ferrer and Andrea Dotti, no one in or out of Hepburn's family ever disliked Rob.

"Robert made Audrey so happy," said their friend, the late Eva Gabor. "She and I both chose very badly as far as men are concerned, as most actors do, because one doesn't have time to give it a chance. But Robert was wonderful, very European and genteel—a true gentleman in every way."[36]

Wolders' integrity and devotion were a revelation to Hepburn: Here, after so many years, was a gentle spirit who had no interest in dominating her, only in taking care of her and accepting her wishes. She had, says Wolders, "almost a child's need or capacity to trust and to entrust herself to someone. Once she trusted someone, she would give them her life."[37]

Audrey felt like a new woman with new enthusiasm. There were things to do and places to go with a wholly sympathetic companion who would help her come to terms with the loose ends of her life, while retaining his own life and independence. They decided from the start to avoid the legal entanglements of marriage and to keep their finances completely separate. After years of Andrea's tricks, she now had a Dutch treat.

CHIEF AMONG AUDREY'S "LOOSE ENDS" was her kinfolk. During her ten years of marriage to Dotti, she had been preoccupied with him and Luca to the extent of neglecting her own relatives in favor of his. Now, with Rob's stolid Dutch support, she once again turned her attention to them. Wolders has described Audrey's mother as "a superior woman" but "biased and intolerant and critical of most everyone, including Audrey. She did, fortunately, have extremely demonstrative aunts."[38]

Her favorite was Miesje, widow of Otto, who was shot during the war. Miesje never hesitated to embrace and give her physical affection, says Wolders, and "Audrey regarded her almost as more her mother than Ella." When Miesje moved to Switzerland in her seventies, Audrey and Rob visited her often and, when she became ill, went to see her daily.

They got her into a special nursing home in Morges, where she died—in Audrey's arms—in 1986.

She was equally attentive to her youngest aunt, Jacqueline, the former lady-in-waiting to Princess Juliana. "It's amazing what Audrey did for her aunts," says her cousin, Hako Sixma van Heemstra, in the Netherlands. Audrey looked after Jacqueline until her death in 1990 and made her last years livable.

Infinitely more complex, however, was Audrey's relationship with Joseph Hepburn-Ruston—her father. Rob Wolders has a strong opinion on the subject:

> It's not true Audrey was trying to hide the truth about him over the years, or that she thought of him as a skeleton in the closet. If it was important at all to her career, it was from about 1948 to 1952. After *Roman Holiday*, you could have had it on the front page and it would not have hurt her. With me, she seemed eager to talk about it and get my feelings, perhaps in part to explain why she couldn not love her parents as unconditionally as I or others loved theirs. But it didn't wreck her life; it made her more just and fair. Audrey fought the tendencies to reject her parents. She was extremely good to both of them.[39]

The melodramatic story that she never saw her father after he abandoned her in the 1930s has been shown to be untrue. It is known that, after the war, Audrey learned through the Red Cross that he was alive and eventually mustered the courage to see him in Dublin in 1959. *Unknown* is the fact that he came to visit her in Switzerland in the late sixties and that, ever after, she kept a photo of him and herself from that visit in her dressing room.

In October 1980, when Hepburn received word that her father was gravely ill, she desperately wanted to see him again but was full of trepidation. She asked Rob to come with her.

"We flew to Dublin, and it was an amazing experience," Wolders recalls. "He reached out to me with the knowledge—I'm convinced—that what he conveyed to me, I would convey to Audrey. He said extraordinary things about her and about his regrets for not having given her more in her childhood, for not showing his love for her."

Joseph Hepburn-Ruston died the next day, October 16, 1980, at the age of ninety. The funeral was private, and there were no obituaries. His fascist past would be buried with him.

"What's important," says Wolders, "is that she had no bitterness toward him. She felt a certain pity for his having been simplistic enough to believe in fascism, but her anger was directed toward the movement, not him.... I regret that Audrey chose not to do an autobiography. I wish the public would have known her feelings about her father. She didn't hate him for his fascism, but she became what she was in reaction to it."

During an interview ten years later, Phil Donahue observed that at least her father "died knowing you loved him."

"Yes," she replied, "and I knew that he loved me. It's always better late than never."[40]

THE PROBLEM WITH HER MOTHER was entirely different.

"She taught me to stand straight, sit erect, use discipline with wine and sweets, and to smoke only six cigarettes a day," was Audrey's wry summary. "She opposed both my marriages, maybe knowing neither man was going to be totally good to me. But I must say, she adored Robbie."[41]

Ella was bedridden during most of the time Wolders knew her, but they spoke a lot of Dutch together, he recalls, and as with Audrey's father, "I had the satisfaction of knowing that I was a sort of conduit between her and [Audrey]. Her mother, I think, suffered a great deal because she was unable to show her sentimentality. But Audrey's father's second wife, after his death, forwarded to us a series of letters her mother had written to him, talking of her extreme pride in Audrey. They were able to express it to one another, but not to Audrey."

The greatest insight into Ella van Heemstra comes from an unlikely source—*Funny Face* author Leonard Gershe:

"I met her when we were shooting the musical numbers in Paris. The two most unnecessary things on a set are the star's mother and the writer, not in that order, so the two of us would go off and have a Dubonnet in a café. That's how our friendship began, and it flowered from there.

"She stayed with me in Los Angeles when she was trying to decide where to settle out here in the early sixties. I didn't know the Greg Pecks then—they're good friends of mine now, but this was a long time ago—and one day, Ella got a call from Véronique Peck. 'She wants to take me to lunch tomorrow,' Ella said. 'Will you tell her how to get here?' I got on and gave her directions —second right, then the first left, etc. . . ."

The next afternoon, when Gershe asked Ella how her luncheon had gone, she said Véronique had been almost an hour late to pick her up, and then supplied the details:

Véronique made a wrong turn and went to the wrong house. A housewife in her apron answered, and Véronique said, "Hello, I'm Mrs. Gregory Peck," and the woman invited her in. She sat down. The woman said, "Would you like something?" Véronique said, "Are you going to have something? All right." The woman told her how much she liked Gregory Peck, and they chatted about his pictures. Finally, the woman said, "Mrs. Peck, are you here about some charity?" "No," she said, "I'm waiting for Baroness van Heemstra." The woman said, "Oh, is she coming, too?"[42]

Ella found it hilarious. "She had great humor and so did Audrey," says Gershe, "but unfortunately they didn't have it together—they didn't share laughs. I adored her mother, but Audrey did not like her very much. She told me Ella had been a fascist, had gone along with her husband, and when she got rid of him, she got rid of that, too, and was ashamed of him. I was always perplexed about that. If Audrey said it, it was true. Audrey did not lie. But the Ella I knew was nothing like that."

Ella eventually picked San Francisco over Los Angeles as her residence through the early seventies. There, she did volunteer work and "came to all of us, including Audrey and me," says Gershe, "to raise money for the boys coming back from Vietnam, who weren't getting proper benefits because it was an undeclared war. The Ella I knew was working her ass off in a VA hospital."

Once or twice a year, she came back to Los Angeles to visit her friend Mildred Knopf, wife of producer Edwin, and to be entertained by George Cukor, among others. "Ella was a very dignified and commanding presence," recalls Connie Wald, "quite majestic."[43] Gershe was struck by the fact that both the mother and the daughter stuck rigorously to their roles:

Ella played the role of stern mother. She was a different person when she talked about Audrey—judgmental—and she took her role of Baroness quite seriously. She was proud, in the pejorative sense. You could tell by the way she walked into a room that she felt slightly superior to everyone else. It was not one of her endearing qualities, but there it was. It embarrassed Audrey, who was exactly the opposite, and that was another one of the walls between them.

On the other hand, Ella could be very silly when she wanted to be, and so could Audrey. But Audrey never knew that woman. They didn't know they were really very alike. There was always that hand held up—"Don't come any closer!" ... Ella thought Audrey was a wonderful actress, but she couldn't tell her that. She was very proud of being the mother of Audrey Hepburn. That was even better than being a baroness. Ella once said to me, "When I was young, the three things I wanted most to be was thin, beautiful and an actress. Isn't it ironic that I should have a daughter who's all three?"

Audrey once told me she never felt loved by her mother, but Ella did love her, believe me. Often, people can't tell the object of their love they love them; they'll tell other people, instead. I probably would have hated Ella as a mother, but I loved her as a friend.

In the last letter she wrote to Gershe, from Tolochanaz in 1982, Ella enclosed a picture of herself and said, "We hope to see you over here after the snow leaves us. We shall have the garden in bloom and plenty of butterflies, and they should be free."* The letter ends with, "I love you, Lenny!"

"She never wrote that before," says Gershe, "and I never heard from her again."

Baroness Ella lived with her daughter at La Paisible in Tolochenaz for the last ten years of her life. She died there, on August 26, 1984.

YEARS LATER HEPBURN WAS ASKED, "Since your marriage to Mel Ferrer in 1954, you've always lived with a man. What have you learned about them?"

"Nothing," she replied. "What can one learn about them? They're human beings, with all the frailties that women have. I think they're more vulnerable than women. I really do. You can hurt a man so easily....

"I love Robbie very, very much. It's not *Romeo and Juliet*; we've had our tiffs, but very few. It's a wonderful friendship; we *like* each other.... He is solid in every way. I can trust him. I trust his love; I never fear I'm losing it. He reassures me. We like the same life, being in the country, the dogs, making trips together.... He's absolutely there for me."[44]

Said Wolders at the time: "It's important that I convince Audrey that love is still possible, because I think she must have begun to feel that it's not in the cards for her anymore."

Rob had moved in with her at Tolochenaz much earlier, even though her divorce was not finalized at the time. Andrea had been dragging his feet, insisting that Luca remain in his custody in Rome while he continued to attend school there.

"I witnessed her pain during the process of the divorce, and it was heartwrenching," says Wolders. Such was her hypersensitivity that she identified with Dotti's pain as well.

"Audrey told me, 'I suffered so much for Andrea,'" says Anna Cataldi. "She used that exact phrase. For her, Andrea was so important. She said, 'If Andrea would ask for my skin, I would give it to him.' I never, never heard her say anything negative about him. I think she knew it was quite negative for Andrea's career to be with such a famous woman. He was a doctor, not a real-estate agent, after all. The publicity, he was looking for in the beginning, but he got more than he bargained for."[45]

---

* In addition to his successful screenplays, Leonard Gershe wrote the Tony Award-winning play *Butterflies Are Free* (1969).

The divorce finally came through in 1982.* For all the depth of her relationship with Wolders, she was in no mood for another wedding. Journalists kept asking when she and Rob were going to get married, and if not, why?

"We're happy as we are," she said.

Wolders's elaboration was wise: "Everyone knows how unhappy her marriage to Mel was, and the second, to Andrea, was even worse. It would be like asking someone who has just got out of an electric chair to sit back on it again."[46]

THOUGH AUDREY WAS ESSENTIALLY RETIRED these days, Eleanor Lambert thought she had a tempting little non-film offer that might appeal to her. Lambert was a prominent publicist, writer and consultant whom Hepburn credited with helping shape and promote her image in the very beginning.

"I'd known Audrey for a long time," says Lambert, "and she was still a sort of symbol of Tiffany's because of the film." Lambert handled Tiffany's publicity, and when the store expanded in 1981, she suggested Audrey as the perfect spokesperson and guest of honor at the opening of Tiffany's new branches. "They thought it was a lovely idea," says Lambert, and so did Audrey. Lambert sent her a detailed itinerary—press conferences, photo shoots, ribbon-cutting appearances—and Hepburn agreed.

"But suddenly, she changed her mind," says Lambert. "She was traumatized about being photographed candidly. She would [only] pose for photographs. She was too timid to appear in a casual way—which she later did extensively [for UNICEF]. But that relaxed way of seeing herself must have come through years of thinking it over."[47]

The bridge between her movie career and her next vocation would not be a commercial gig for Tiffany's, although it did involve public appearances: a series of retrospectives for some dear friends in the film and fashion worlds. However nervous such affairs made her—and they did—it was time to pay back old favors in that most valuable currency, her presence.

First of the lot was the American Film Institute's 1981 tribute to Cary Grant in Washington, for which she wrote and delivered a lyrical poem on friendship, dedicated to Grant, "a very special player who's also been my friend." Thrilled and moved by her appearance, Grant wept at the end

---

* Andrea Dotti never remarried, but in the months following their divorce, his celebrity dating picked up steam. The ever-vigilant Tony Menicucci dogged his footsteps and, in 1983 alone, photographed him with Daniela Trebbi, Marilu Tolo, Denise Pardo, Roberta Balsano, Lynn Wyeth, Donatella Zegna, and Italian TV personality Elizabeth Vigili, among many others.

of it, even as he traded hugs with Ron and Nancy Reagan.

Over the next five years, Audrey materialized at four separate testimonials for her favorite—Hubert—in New York, Tokyo, Los Angeles and San Francisco. She was honorary chairperson of the affair in Los Angeles, where Givenchy received the first California Lifetime Achievement in the Arts Award at an event that raised a half million dollars for the Los Angeles County High School for the Arts.

In May 1983, she cochaired a Givenchy retrospective at the Fashion Institute of Technology in New York, where designer Jeffrey Banks, who had fallen in love with her at age eleven when he saw *Funny Face*, couldn't wait to meet her. They were introduced by his friend John Rizzuto, President of Givenchy America, but the longed-for meeting fell short of Banks's expectations:

> I was a little disappointed. She was perfectly cordial but she seemed distant. It wasn't the magical moment I had created in my head. John called me the next morning and explained that Audrey's mother had fallen and hurt herself just before Audrey left Switzerland, and she really didn't want to leave. She got up several times during the evening and called her. Every other time I saw her, she made you feel like you were the only person on earth. She was just totally preoccupied with her mother that night.[48]

The decline and death of her mother had been preceded by the 1979 death of her brother Alexander, at fifty-eight, in a freak domestic electrical accident in Spain.[49] It was a time of milestones: She was distraught about David Niven, her old British pal and neighbor of the last twenty-five years. In happier days, they used to visit Noel Coward together in Paris. Now, she and Rob were making sickbed calls as he suffered through the final stages of Lou Gehrig's disease. Niven died at seventy-four in the village of Chateau d'Oex, near Gstaad, in August 1983.

William Wyler had passed away two summers before. In 1985, at the request of his daughter Cathy, Hepburn went to New York to participate in a PBS documentary tribute to Wyler. There, she was interviewed by *New York Post* reporter Stephanie Mansfield at the Algonquin, on the condition she not be asked personal questions. But there was nothing to prevent Mansfield from reporting a Kodak moment she witnessed at the end of their chat:

"She leaves the suite, slings her purse over one bony shoulder, and meets Sean, a tall, handsome twenty-four. Standing in the elevator, she gazes at him with obvious pride. In the lobby, she links her arm through his and dons an enormous pair of Holly Golightly–style black sunglasses."[50]

"Best friends" Audrey and Sean had always been close but now seemed to draw even closer. Sean's career in film production was advancing. Later that year, he married Italian designer Marina Spadafora, daughter of the scion of a leading continental fashion company. The two twenty-five-year-olds were wed at St. Peter's Church in Los Angeles, and both of the groom's parents were present—the first time they'd been seen together since their divorce.* Audrey's wedding gift to the newlyweds was a $375,000 house in the Hollywood Hills, which they would not occupy together for very long.[51] Sean and Marina were divorced in 1989.

The year 1986, for Audrey, held a new spate of high-profile galas, starting with her first appearance at the Academy Awards in some years. There to hand out the award for best costume design (to Emi Wada for Kurosawa's *Ran*), she got a standing ovation and stole the show in her stunning, pink, sari-type Givenchy gown, edged in sparkling gold, offset by an audacious set of triple-tiered earrings.

A few weeks later, she hailed a beloved mentor at the American Film Institute's "Salute to Billy Wilder." She also appeared, in these years, at no fewer than four separate tributes to Gregory Peck.

"We wanted to interview her for a biography of Gregory Peck," says documentary filmmaker Gene Feldman, "so I called her agent, Kurt Frings. A woman answered and said, 'One moment, please.' Well, it was fourteen or fifteen minutes that I waited. Finally, a voice came on and I could hardly distinguish it. Mr. Frings had had a stroke and could barely speak. But he was still her agent. In this cutthroat, miserable business, that was an insight into the unique kind of woman she was. People were telling her, 'You must get a new agent.' But she refused."‡

For that shoot at the Pierre Hotel in New York, Audrey showed up at the appointed hour of ten a.m. but said, "Oh, Gene, I have a problem. I forgot earrings. One minute, I'll be right back." She returned a few minutes later, Feldman recalls, "and with her was a very burly man who I thought was some friend she had met on the elevator. He came in and stood there eyeballing her the whole time. She had gone down to Bulgari's in the lobby and borrowed clip-ons worth $45,000, and they had sent up this man to guard her while she did the interview."[52]

George Eastman House in Rochester held a tribute to Gregory Peck during a week in 1987 when Rob and Audrey were visiting Rob's mother there. As a surprise, "we sneaked Audrey in through the back door," says Wolders. The honoree beamed as she recalled the thrill of being "cast opposite Gregory Peck—the beautiful, quiet, gentle hero of countless

---

* Continuing our footnote bulletins on Mel Ferrer: His "date" at his son's wedding, properly enough, was Lisa, his wife of fourteen years. Everyone was charmed by Lisa. Ferrer's career was on the upswing, thanks to his role as the smooth-talking lawyer friend (and eventual husband) of matriarch Jane Wyman in the popular television series *Falcon Crest*.

‡ Hepburn remained loyal to Frings until his death in 1990.

marvelous movies. In my innocence I thought he'd be just like that in real life. He was."

She was the honoree herself that October, in New York, at the annual benefit tribute of the Museum of Modern Art to raise money for its Film Preservation Fund. She had lost none of her drawing power: At $1,000 a ticket, a sellout crowd showed up for screenings of *Roman Holiday*, *Sabrina*, *Funny Face*, *Breakfast at Tiffany's*, *My Fair Lady* and *Robin and Marian*.

The following April, 1988, she was back for the sixtieth annual Academy Awards to present the Oscars for Best Original Screenplay and Screenplay Adaptation (John Patrick Shanley for *Moonstruck* and Mark Peploe and Bernardo Bertolucci for *The Last Emperor*) in the company of Greg Peck.

"I hated going out to those black-tie things," says Rob, "and so did Audrey, but they were obligations. We would steel ourselves to get through it and, when it was over, rush home and tear off the formal clothes. You'd be on your best behavior and then get the hell out of there. But Audrey knew it was usually her last opportunity to pay tribute to the colleagues she loved, people like Fred Astaire and Cary Grant. In a sense, it was fun and one looked forward to it—until you had to go."

Much more fun than usual for both of them was a major festival in Holland, "Film and Fashion," arranged by Leendert de Jong of The Hague's Filmhouse, to honor film costume designers such as Yves St. Laurent, Edith Head and of course Givenchy.

"I wrote to her," says de Jong, "and a week later, I got a call from a man who spoke Dutch and said, 'We would like to know more.' I thought he was her agent or something and forgot to ask his name. The next time he called, I said, 'I'm sorry, but who the hell are you?' He laughed and said, 'Audrey and I have lived together for years.' I blushed to the phone. After that, he was amazing. He organized everything with so much calm and humor."[53]

Audrey opened the festival on November 18, 1988 and spent four days in The Hague with Rob. De Jong decided to kick off the series with *Funny Face* because "it is of course the best fashion film. Beforehand she said, 'I hope you find a good print and that the colors are still bright.' I said, 'When was the last time you saw it?' She said, 'At the premiere.' She hadn't seen it since then, and Robert had *never* seen it! I was amazed."

After *Funny Face*, the Filmhouse held an auction of couture dresses and a big bottle of Givenchy's perfume, the money from which was given to UNICEF. A wide variety of Dutch film and political celebrities was present, and there was a tense moment when a woman showed up for the auction in the exact same Givenchy dress that Audrey was wearing. "Everyone said, 'Oh my God, she's got on the same dress!' But Audrey just laughed and said, 'Let's take a picture.' She told the other lady, 'It suits you well.' "

The next day, she opened an exhibition titled *Givenchy, Worn by Audrey Hepburn* at the Municipal Museum of The Hague, to which she had contributed four suitcases of her own clothes.

When it was time to leave, de Jong drove Hepburn and Wolders to Schiphol International Airport and, on the way, got an unexpected insight into—of all things—Audrey's late mother:

"As we neared Amsterdam, we saw a windmill, and it reminded Audrey about visiting Holland with her mother in the early '60s. Her mother had pointed and said, 'Audrey, that is the last windmill in Holland.' Audrey said, 'No mother, there are a lot of windmills.' She said, 'No, you're wrong. This is the very last one.' She thought all the rest were destroyed."[54]

There are, of course, hundreds of beautiful windmills remaining in Holland. But Ella van Heemstra believed otherwise, and no one could dissuade her from that conviction.

DOMINICK DUNNE IN *VANITY FAIR* told a fine anecdote from around this time: At one of Swifty and Mary Lazar's famous Academy Award parties, Dunne watched Hepburn and Elizabeth Taylor give each other a warm embrace, after which Audrey pointed to one of Elizabeth's enormous jewels and asked, "Kenny Lane?"

"No, Richard Burton," replied Taylor, and both stars screamed with laughter.[55]

Their friendship was nurtured by Doris Brynner, a good friend of Taylor's. "We did a fund-raiser for AIDS in Basel," says Brynner. "Elizabeth was cochairing it, and Audrey came because I asked her to, if I may take credit. Audrey and Elizabeth had tremendous respect and admiration for each other."[56] The following year, at an event honoring Taylor for her AIDS work, Audrey delivered a moving tribute:

"Never have I been more heartbroken than by [seeing] babies with AIDS. I will be haunted by the unspeakable suffering in the eyes of their mothers." If and when a vaccine is found, it would be thanks to tireless researchers but "above all, to the determination and love of one woman, Elizabeth Taylor, who at a time when AIDS was spoken of only in whispers, had the courage to speak out with such force that we were obliged to listen."[57]

When in Hollywood, says Doris Brynner, "Audrey might see Elizabeth or Billy and Audrey Wilder or the Jimmy Stewarts, whom she was very fond of, and have dinner with them. But she really wasn't the Hollywood type. She worked there—rented a house, did the job—and then came back to Switzerland."[58]

These days, Audrey had no pressing financial need to work. Nevertheless, in February 1987 she agreed to make her first film in seven years and first TV film in thirty years—*Love Among Thieves*, directed by Roger Young. Some said she was motivated by the desire to let her aging, ailing agent Frings collect his commission on her $750,000 fee. But her costar Robert Wagner debunks the idea that she did it as an act of charity: "Kurt was pretty well financially set. Audrey was always in demand and would always have given the fee to Kurt, no matter what."

Together with Jeffrey Hunter, Robert ("R.J.") Wagner shared the "Prince of 20th Century-Fox" crown in the 1950s, playing a variety of juvenile roles. In the end, however, he was not well served by his studio, which seemed determined to keep him from developing into a full-fledged leading man. "I was left there," he once said, "with a tennis racket in one hand and a beach ball in the other."[59] But he eventually found great success in several television series, *It Takes a Thief* (1968–70), *Switch* (1975–78) and—most of all—*Hart to Hart* (1979–84).

The last of those happened to be one of Audrey's great favorites. "I love *Hart to Hart*," she told a reporter, "and I've seen every episode on TV in Switzerland." But why would she choose an ABC-TV film above all other proposals? It was because of executive producer Karen Mack, she said: "I wasn't really all that keen to work. I've become very lazy. But I was tempted and said I would like to do something if it was going to be fun, something cheerful. Karen came up with [*Love Among Thieves*], and when she threw in R. J. Wagner, that did it."[60]

They had long known each other, both in Hollywood and in Gstaad, where Wagner had a chalet and saw her on and off. But they had never worked together. Now, when he heard she wanted to appear with him, "I was very flattered. I read the script and said, 'Show me where to go for makeup and let's get started.' Working with Audrey was one of the highlights of my career."[61]

It was a mystery-heist story with elements of *Charade* and *How to Steal a Million*: Audrey, a baroness and concert pianist, is now also a thief—forced to steal some priceless Fabergé eggs and deliver them to ransom her kidnapped fiancé in Latin America. Wagner, her seatmate-from-hell on the airplane, is relentless with the wisecracks and the running gag of annoying Hepburn with his cigar. Their adventures take place in the fictional country of "Yaruba"; the actual location was a kingdom called Tucson.

"I'm not very elegant," said Audrey of herself in the role. "I only have one dress, and it was filmed in Tucson, where it was 102 degrees."[62] Wagner, who had a home there, recalls "a lot of running around in cars in the heat. Audrey arrived every morning looking absolutely terrific, with her dogs."[63] But on film, she didn't look quite so terrific in either of her two Givenchy creations—the black and white gown at the beginning (concert pianists do not wear hats!) or an unflattering red one at the end. She looked all fifty-eight of her years, in fact—but was none the less effective for that. Wagner most remembers the shooting of the finale in a government building in San Francisco:

"They brought in one hundred dress extras and at one a.m., when she came out to do her concert-pianist thing, they all stood and applauded her for three minutes. At that hour! She treated everybody so beautifully and created such a positive atmosphere around her. What you saw is what she was, in everything—my God, even her garden looked like her! I raise horses, and when she left to go back to Europe she gave me a wonderful painting of a horse, which I cherish and have hanging in my bedroom. She's probably the most wonderful woman I ever met."[64]

Contemporary critics were likewise enthralled with Hepburn but not with *Thieves Like Us*—a prototypical "TV-movie" shot mainly with commercial breaks in mind. By appearing in it, she was "stooping way down to conquer," said *Variety*.[65]

"Audrey Hepburn can do no wrong," wrote John Leonard in *New York* magazine. "She can, however, be done wrong [as in] *War and Peace*, which was Tolstoy for morons. In the thirty years since her last appearance in an original television production [*Mayerling*], nobody at Lorimar seems to have learned anything.... *Love Among Thieves* wants to be witty and just sits there with a drool."[66]

R. J. Wagner sighs and says, "I thought the critics were rather harsh with the picture. They were going for the ratings on TV and put it up against some pretty heavy stuff. Maybe they expected too much from it."[67]

"IF A WOMAN OF FIFTY is very thin, she can pass for years younger," said Audrey Hepburn around 1979.

But what about a woman of sixty?

"Audrey was so beautiful, of course," says Audrey Wilder. "But when you get older and you're that thin, it doesn't usually become you."[68]

"She was too, too skinny when I saw her at parties," insists Zsa Zsa Gabor.[69] She had always been thin, but some thought she was now looking almost emaciated. In any case, it wasn't her look but her health that mattered. The "A"-word was bandied about privately—anorexia—and a more aggressive series of interviewers got close to saying it when they questioned her.

"Why are you so thin?" asked Barbara Walters in March 1989.

"I was born thin," Audrey replied. "My grandmother on my father's side—we have exactly the same figure. I eat very well and I eat everything I want...."

"And nothing puts the weight on?"

"No."

"May I ask what you weigh?"

"Fifty kilos. A hundred and ten pounds."[70]

By current medical standards, a healthy woman of Audrey's height (five-foot-seven) should weigh 127 pounds. She was thus only about 14 percent below "normal," not enough to be clinically defined as anoretic.

"I don't put on weight—it's not part of my metabolism," she told an Australian TV reporter in 1988.[71] "I was just *born* this way," she protested to another interviewer.[72] Phil Donahue drew her feistiest responses to such personal probing in 1990:

DONAHUE:	You never became an egomaniac?
HEPBURN:	How do you know?...
DONAHUE	You are sixty.
HEPBURN	Sixty, yes—not sixteen, no.
DONAHUE	And you've had no cosmetic surgery?
HEPBURN	Naturally—not. [Applause; she turns to address the audience.] They said he was so great and so friendly. He's asked me about my age and cosmetic surgery, and we haven't done two minutes yet!
DONAHUE	And you've never had a weight problem?
HEPBURN:	No.... If I get nervous, I don't eat. I like to eat. But I need not to be nervous to eat. I'm very nervous, you see. I'm nervous now.[73]

Leslie Caron thought she had, if not anorexia, at least some kind of eating disorder. "Shirley MacLaine told me that [during *The Children's Hour*], all she had for lunch was a hard-boiled egg. I would think that at times, when she was very nervous, she was almost anorexic. I've had that throughout my life. In times of stress, I can become anorexic if I don't counterattack."[74]

Laurie Stone in the *Village Voice* had a feminist take. In the fifties and sixties, wrote Stone, "No one talked publicly about anorexia; no one, in describing Hepburn, discussed the impulse to escape [gender stereotypes] expressed in radical dieting.... Her image was fabricated to suppress evidence of struggle."[75]

But Givenchy and virtually all her other friends maintain that Hepburn *never* adhered to any tyrannical diet. "Hubert told me she would make huge plates of spaghetti and eat it quite enthusiastically," says Leslie Caron.[76]

"I know some people that eat nothing but salad and vinegar," says Audrey Wilder. "But not her. She was always eating spaghetti or a version of it." Billy nods in agreement, adding, "She was so thin because she was a dancer."[77]

Some claimed that her problem was bulimia, evidenced by the frequent hoarseness of her voice. Others say no—she was merely a smoker, easily tired by interviews. "I never saw her jump up and run to the bathroom at dinner affairs," says Jeffrey Banks. "She was just one of these people who was blessed with being basically thin, and a lot of people were jealous of that."[78]

Doris Brynner gets irate on the subject:

"How dare they say she was anorexic? She loved her food and her spaghetti and her ice cream. She was just lucky that she didn't put on weight; we all do after a certain age, but she never did. She adored her food."[79]

Eating disorders range widely, of course, and "anorexic" is a loaded cultural term when used loosely as an adjective. Its informal adjectival meaning is lack of appetite; almost everyone is "anorexic" when sick, for instance. Anorexia nervosa, on the other hand, is a serious psychological or personality disorder—an aversion to food and obsession with weight loss or body image, for reasons of vanity or self-denial. "There's a fine line between 'fashionably thin' and neurotic," says diet authority Marilynn Gump. "Audrey obviously *chose* to be thin, but that's no evidence that she had any clinical inability to nurture herself or repulsion to food."[80]

Later Hepburn chroniclers would make strong assertions of anorexia.[81] But the fact was, Audrey's eating pattern never really varied over the years, and neither did her weight.

"THE CITIES ARE NOT A place for you if you are famous," she said. "With the paparazzi in Rome, there is no privacy.... It is because I live in the country in Switzerland that I can lead a totally unself-conscious life and be totally myself.[82] ... I have a delightful rose garden and I have an orchard and jams and jellies to preserve. Sean is grown and married now, but he's still very much a part of my life. Luca attends boarding school in Switzerland but is home every weekend."

She was very much "a citizen of the world," says Doris Brynner, "but Switzerland was home, and for such a long time. She adored her house."*

Tolochenaz is just forty minutes from Geneva by train—a little local

* Audrey's actual citizenship was British, as it had always been. She also had a United Nations *laissez-passer* that enabled her to travel virtually everywhere without visas and a Swiss permit allowing her to live (but not work) in Switzerland.

that changes at Nyon. As it treks northward, a wide expanse of land unfolds before the sparkling lake; beyond that are the Swiss Alps with their snow-covered caps. Clusters of new apartments are interspersed with great stretches of carefully maintained grapevines and row upon row of meticulously espaliered fruit trees. It is agriculture *très fin*, indeed.

There is no "station" at Tolochenaz, just a small sign, a walkway up to the road, and no indication whether the town is off to the left or to the right. It's to the left—a fifteen-minute walk—and on a typical Sunday, there's not an open shop or a soul to be seen. Empty, quiet, shuttered. One passes straight through in a minute or two.

Off the main drag to the west, up a rigorous climb, is the first of several entrances to a stunning estate: On a stone herald, in a script muted by centuries of rain, are inscribed the words *La Paisible*. The house at first doesn't seem charming, imposing or even *caractéristique*. It looks ordinary. Why would Audrey Hepburn choose a home so close to the road—perhaps fifty feet away—and such a busy road at that?[83]

The answer lay within and behind the rambling, 1730 vintage farmhouse, especially in its expansive orchard and gardens where the mistress of the manor could usually be found digging. "Wonderful therapy being down in the dirt," she said. "I couldn't *bear* to live a social life.[84]

"I can take long walks, as I understand Greta Garbo does, and no one interferes with my thoughts and tranquility. Come to think of it, the other day I was on Fifth Avenue [in New York] and I saw a woman who could very well have been Garbo; I was a bit tempted to go up to her, but then I thought, 'My God, practice what you preach! If it is her, you'll be intruding—just the thing you don't like yourself.' "[85]

In her orchard, she declared proudly, "every fruit you can imagine grows. First it's the cherries, then come the plums, the greengages, apples, pears and quinces. And the berries, too, the raspberries. It takes a lot of care."[86]

Her gardener, Giovanni Orunesu, was a former shepherd and the brother of her housekeeper Giovanna, who served her through the years with Ferrer, Dotti and Wolders over two decades. "Audrey took him and his wife in after a terrible drought in the seventies when his whole herd died and he had no place to go and a child on the way," says Wolders. "Audrey and Giovanni worked closely together on the garden ever after."

Inside, the house was comfortable, balanced and pleasing. "It was beautiful and spectacular, but it wasn't for show," says garden enthusiast (and PBS producer) Janis Blackschleger, who visited her in September 1989. "It was for use."[87]

On the solid white walls in the main hall was a huge painting of her grandfather and his brother with their dogs. On a nearby bureau sat photos of Audrey hugging Sean, her father on horseback, her brothers as children, Colette, Connie Wald, and—the only solo portrait of herself—a signed Cecil Beaton shot. On the ground floor was a room containing nothing but baskets, where she arranged her flowers. Overall, the furnishings were sparse, but "she loved every piece of furniture there," says Anna Cataldi. "She would say, 'I bought this dining table when I got married,' and then tell you about it. Everything was white and beautiful in that house....

"My daughter Giaccaranda was in a Swiss boarding school then and sometimes spent the weekend at Audrey's. My other daughter was a manic depressive [in a clinic at] Lausanne. They asked, 'In case of emergency, who is the person to contact first?' The name was always Audrey. We all asked too much of her."[88]

By then, Audrey had lived in Switzerland for more than a quarter of a century.

"I love it," she told Dominick Dunne. "I love the country. I love our little town and going to the open market twice a week. And Robbie and I are potty about our dogs.... They are totally dependent on you, and therefore completely vulnerable. And this complete vulnerability is what enables you to open up your heart totally, which you rarely do to a human being. Except, perhaps, children. Who thinks you're as fantastic as your dog?"[89]

She was also very fond of ducks, and had a great number of duck decoys scattered about the house, though she hated the idea of hunting. For that matter, she had no real interest in any sports, including—to the amazement of the Swiss—skiing. She and Rob shared not only interests but disinterests. "We talked about the fact that in our Dutch childhood, skiing was for the elite," says Wolders, "and you had to have money—which we didn't—to go to Austria or Switzerland to do it."

She was much more interested in the quietude of her home and the people she cared about, one of whom was Leendert de Jong. When he took her and Rob to the airport at the end of the 1988 "Film and Fashion" festival in Holland, she had kissed him and said, "Leendert, you must visit us in Tolochenaz." He thought she was just being polite but found out otherwise in 1989:

I called and said, "Audrey, my friend and I are going to the Venice film festival. Can we drop by?" She said, "You're very welcome." So we drove to Tolochenaz and stayed for four days. We just shared their daily routine— the market, shopping, meals together in the evening. We spoke about her mother and children ... personal things ...

She liked to get up very early. She said, "I have some sins," and one them was smoking. She was smoking cigarettes and answering letters in her white dressing gown with her hair loose, no makeup. She said, "I'm sorry,

I don't wear makeup at home." I said. "Of course not." She would take us to the kitchen and make breakfast.... One night at dinner when I asked her something about "stardom," she said, "Oh, come on, I'm not a movie star. Liz Taylor is a movie star." I think she really meant it. She said, "You chose to be in films as a programmer of an art house. I happened to be an actress. It was not my first choice, but I did my best to do it as well as I could. I became this, you became that, another person becomes a carpenter...." As a movie buff, I wanted to hear some stories, but she didn't like to speak about that so much. My friend was a big Montgomery Clift fan and he said, "Did you ever meet Monty?" She said, "Oh, yes, a darling man." And then she walked into the kitchen, and that was the end of the discussion....

On Sunday when we were leaving for Venice, she said, "I'll make lunch so you can eat it on your way." We said no, don't bother. "No, no—what do you like on your bread?" I said cheese and butter, and my friend said, no butter. She gave us two Chanel bags and we thanked her, kissed goodbye. Halfway to Venice we stopped and opened the bags. There were real glasses inside and two pieces of paper, one with my name and one with my friend's—with and without butter. She was always taking care of people.[90]

Swiss society and geography lent itself to a kind of selective intimacy. "Everybody respected everybody else's privacy," says Rob Wolders. "Even with someone like Hubert, a great friend of forty years, months went by when we wouldn't see him. But then he and Audrey would pick up right where they left off. She had very strong friendships like that. The strongest was with Doris Brynner, though Doris used to be annoyed with us because she thought we were antisocial sticks-in-the-mud. But from the time Audrey and I met, we basically made time only for each other and didn't go out much. We loved films and I got tapes of everything of any consequence, which we watched."

Watching movies on TV was her favorite pastime, she told *Wichita Eagle* film writer Bob Curtwright at the time.[91] She loved Gerard Depardieu's *Cyrano* "because they kept it intimate," and Spielberg's *ET*, and "anything with Michelle Pfeiffer in it. I like to watch them in my *bed*—that's the best place! I just saw Robert De Niro and Jeremy Irons in *The Mission* and thought that was a lovely film. And I very much liked *Prizzi's Honor*."

When asked to name her favorite contemporary actresses, she cited Pfeiffer, Meryl Streep, Julia Roberts and Cher (see Cher's letter to Hepburn, Chapter 10, pp. 328–29.) "Cher has an enormous scale of emotions and total lack of inhibition, which I haven't," she said. "Meryl Streep is a phenomenon. She can make herself look any way she wants and become so many different people. She can do anything she wants. I can't."[92]

Wolders was fascinated by the way Audrey influenced people like Julia Roberts and Liza Minnelli. "Like so many of the younger actresses I saw

with Audrey, she and Liza had this wonderful hugging thing—this trust."
Nastassia Kinski encountered Audrey for the first time in Paris, at the
French Oscars. "I felt a tap on my shoulder," says Rob, "and this demure
little girl whispered, 'Can I meet her?' Audrey turned around at that
moment and they recognized each other. Kinski took Audrey's hands and,
not quite knowing what to do, just held her hands to her face and kissed
them like a child."

On the few occasions when she went into Geneva, Rob or Doris would
drive her. Doris had a boutique there. But something about Geneva did
not appeal to her—perhaps its obsession with money. *"C'est juste"* is one
of the most common expressions there, meaning "That's right," as when
correct change is given. Like most things in Geneva, it implies an economic
transaction. The better shop doors, with their POIGNÉE AUTOMATIQUE signs,
open by themselves at your approach to make it easier to buy. In that
haven of commercialism, it seems that few ideas and even fewer feelings
are exchanged. Thousands of elderly women ("Greta Garbos," some call
them) walk around in fur coats, often talking to themselves. The great
Swiss banking culture has created not only a *prix fixe* for everything but
great social distance.[93]

In subtle ways, it reinforced Hepburn's reluctance to go there more
than necessary. Doris Brynner was better equipped and more adept at
dealing with it, but even she understood the social and professional
implications for her friend: "We were always pushing Audrey to make
another movie," Doris says, "but the only thing she really looked forward
to was staying home."

ROB WOLDERS LOOKED FORWARD TO the same thing, bewitched by
Audrey and everything about her—not least, conversing with her in their
native tongue. "She was the only person I ever knew who made Dutch
sound beautiful," he says. They spoke it frequently "because there are
Dutch expressions that just don't exist in English. Audrey was able to do
various Dutch accents very well, especially the more vulgar dialects, which
amused her very much. She would break me up. Sometimes we used
Dutch to say things we didn't want anyone else to understand. Her Dutch
was heavenly. the most palatable I ever heard—the kind spoken prior to
the war, learned from her mother and grandfather." Says Rob's brother-
in-law, Dr. Ronald Glegg: "When she went into Dutch, her sense of humor
came through more. Her tone of voice changed, and she became more
childlike and endearing." But linguistics were only the most obvious of
their many cultural and emotional ties.

"Robbie is totally Dutch," she told Alan Riding of *The New York Times*
Paris bureau. "The two of us discovered how much pride we had in our

roots and the respect we have for the Dutch.... They've always had an immensely practical and courageous way of dealing with things. They're not fussers, they're solid and very liberal.... Rob has a lovely Dutch family—umpteen sisters and a wonderful mother. As you get older, it's nice to feel you belong somewhere—having lived a rather circus life."[94]

Audrey instantly connected with the Wolders clan, most of all with Rob's mother, Cemelia, whom she would soon call "Mama." They developed a strong, surrogate mother-daughter relationship, says Dr. Glegg, husband of Rob's sister Grada: "The Wolders family is very tightly knit. Audrey recognized that and fit in closely on many warm occasions in Rochester around the dinner table with a dozen relatives." Otherwise, her favorite place there was most unlikely: the huge, suburban Irondequoit Mall.

"It's the most beautiful one I've ever seen!" she'd exclaim. "Can we go?" Glegg recalls her "teenager's pleasure there—and she looked like a teenager, too, in her jeans and sweater." He savors, even more, her visits with him and Grada at their home on Longboat Key in Florida: "She loved the pristine beauty, the birds, the barefoot walks in the sand. She tended to take charge of our kitchen, and that lady in the kitchen with no makeup and curlers in her hair didn't mind being seen that way."[95]

All of her life she had been searching for a man capable of returning her love unequivocally. In Rob, she had finally met "her spiritual twin, the man she wanted to grow old with.[96] It took me a long time to find [him, but] it is better late than never. If I'd met him when I was eighteen, I wouldn't have appreciated him. I would have thought, 'That's the way everyone is.'

"I still feel I could lose everything at any moment. But the greatest victory has been to be able to live with myself, to accept my short-comings.... I'm a long way from the human being I'd like to be. But I've decided I'm not so bad after all."[97]

Her need for the quiet life was fully in sync with his own, says Wolders: "Sometimes, Audrey would become exasperated because Doris or somebody would say, 'What do you *do* all day?' We found that the day would fly by because the things we were involved with took a lot of time—the market, and so forth. You cook a meal carefully, hours go into that. For our own sake, but mostly for the dogs, we'd go to the lake and take our walks there. On a Sunday afternoon, if the weather allowed, we would have a swim, take some sun—invariably, at some point, Audrey would disappear and come back with a basket of fruit or vegetables."

Wolders recalls the summer of 1990 when the huge, seventy-year-old willow tree outside their home keeled over and crashed to the ground— "this thing that we both loved. It was so big that even lying on its side, the branches were still higher than the house. Then Tuppy, our Jack

Russell terrier, died." Those events might strike others as trivial, "but they were tragedies for us. It's amazing how such things become so important when you lead that kind of life. Luca once laughed his head off because adjacent to the house was the little village church, and its bell would sound on the hour and half hour. It was a major part of our lives, but they were doing some renovation and we missed those wonderful sounds. One day, the bells started to peal at noon and we both yelled. We were so delighted. Luca thought we were nuts. But it was a part of our lives that had been restored."

Life in Tolochenaz, after all, was simple.

"We would go to town to shop," Rob recalls, "which meant going to the dry-goods store, the stand where we bought our mushrooms, etc. Audrey loved shopping—and she was a maniac in a supermarket. She said it harked back to the starvation days when you needed a coupon to get an ounce of butter in Holland. The supermarket in Tolochenaz didn't exist until about five years ago, but she loved it. She was like a child, and we would end up with a lot of stuff we didn't need. In the smaller shops, she'd settle into a discussion with the owners, and I preferred those places because she wouldn't go bananas."

When asked what, for her, would constitute the perfect day, Audrey once replied, "It's going to sound like a thumping bore, but my idea of heaven is [having] Robert and my two sons at home—I hate separations—and the dogs, a good movie, a wonderful meal and great television all coming together. I'm really blissful when that happens. [My goal] was not to have huge luxuries. As a child, I wanted a house with a garden, which I have today. This is what I dreamed of. I'd never worry about age if I knew I could go on being loved and having the possibility to love. If I'm old and my husband doesn't want me, or my children think me ugly and do not want me—that would be a tragedy. So it isn't age or even death that one fears, as much as loneliness and the lack of affection."[98]

There was no danger of her children rejecting her, and no lack of affection from Rob. Paradoxically, for *not* being her husband, she found she could count on him even more.

CHAPTER 10

Apotheosis
(1988–1993)

> "Somebody said to me, 'You know, it's re-
> ally senseless what you're doing. There's
> always been suffering, there will always
> be, and you're just prolonging the suffer-
> ing of these children [by rescuing them].'
> My answer is, 'Okay, then, let's start with
> your grandchild. Don't buy antibiotics if
> it gets pneumonia. Don't take it to the hos-
> pital if it has an accident.'"
>
> AUDREY HEPBURN

I AM SORT OF MARRIED TO Robert," she told his hometown newspaper, the Rochester *Democrat & Chronicle*, in 1989. "We're always together and we have been for almost ten years now."[1]

She turned sixty that May, and it was assumed that her film career was finished. But she now surprised everyone by agreeing to a cameo role in a new Steven Spielberg movie.

"She was as uncertain and nervous and undecided about her last film as she had been with *Roman Holiday*, her first," says Wolders.[2] Hepburn and Spielberg had never met. But she finally accepted the job because she admired his films and because he promised her it could be done in just a few days that summer.

"We left everything behind and got on a plane [for] Montana," she said.[3] By the time she arrived, costar Richard Dreyfuss had finished most of his own shooting and now turned over the house he was renting—a wonderful log cabin in the Montana woods—to Audrey and Rob.

Always (1989) starred Holly Hunter, John Goodman and Brad Johnson, as well as Hepburn and Dreyfuss. It was pure, nostalgic Spielberg—a remake of Victor Fleming's World War II "morale booster," *A Guy Named Joe* (1943), in which flier Spencer Tracy, killed in action, returns as a friendly ghost to watch over his girl, Irene Dunne, and her new romance with Van Johnson. Spielberg transposed his version to the present-day

American west; the soldiers in battle became firefighters in a national forest.

The original had been written by Dalton Trumbo, who also wrote *Roman Holiday*, thus providing an alpha-omega bracket to her American career. But Audrey's tiny role in this one was hard to describe. "Nobody knows what I am," she said, "even Steven Spielberg! I would say I'm a spirit.... but not an extraterrestrial. It's just plain old me with a sweater on."[4]

Wolders recalls it as "a fantastic experience for Audrey. She worked a great deal over the phone with the writers, who wanted to tailor it to Audrey and get her input. Then Spielberg and Dreyfuss came to this lovely house in the woods, and they sat around and talked about what was she going to wear. I even went into the little town, Libby, to see what was in the shops there. All they had were hardware stores that also sold clothes. They finally decided on a simple turtleneck instead of wings."

The typical Spielbergian opening is full of suspense: Dreyfuss's plane is out of fuel but he manages to land. The gripping forest-fire scenes employ spectacular footage taken during the 1988 fires at Yellowstone National Park. But soon enough, after Dreyfuss executes a brilliant midair rescue of Goodman, his own plane catches fire and explodes.

Enter Audrey as "Hap"—a New Age angel in slacks, sent down to assist the freshly deceased Dreyfuss. Quietly, she explains that he must return to earth to inspire others and that true love means letting go. Only Hepburn's sincerity redeems her platitudinous dialogue: "The love we hold back is the only thing that follows us here." The "here" is evidently heaven—a meadow. "Time's funny stuff," she tells him.

Down below, dispatcher Holly Hunter grieves for Dreyfuss as she listens to their painfully ironic theme song—"Smoke Gets in Your Eyes." Hunter is the best thing in the film, exuding erotic presence and an exquisite sense of longing. In the movie's most haunting moment, she dances in a seductive white dress with Dreyfuss' ghost, without ever touching.

Hunter and Hepburn had no scenes together but enjoyed each other off the set. Wolders has fond memories of the time it was arranged for the whole cast and crew to go on a special outing to Coeur d'Alene Lake, just across the Idaho border from Spokane:

"They hired two huge busses to accommodate one hundred people, and it tells you something about Audrey and Holly that—as good professionals—they were the first ones on the bus. But only about six other people showed up, probably because they didn't think Audrey or Holly or anybody else 'important' would go. While we were sitting there waiting, the radar thing in the bus kept beeping, and finally Holly yelled, 'Shut that fucking thing up!' Audrey found that extremely funny, and we spent a lovely evening on the boat with Holly that night."

With its overbearing John Williams musical score, *Always* is sweetly sappy, imbued with Spielberg's penchant for the supernatural and his simpleminded conviction that death, evil and everything else can be overcome through wishful thinking.

Variety opined that Audrey was "alluring as always, but corny as a live-action fairy godmother."[5] Leonard Maltin said *Always* suffered "from a serious case of The Cutes." Pauline Kael in the *New Yorker* was most severe:

> Was there no one among Steven Spielberg's associates with the intellectual stature to convince him that his having cried at *A Guy Named Joe* when he was 12 was not a good enough reason for him to remake it? [He] has caught the surface mechanics of '40s movies [but has] no grasp of the simplicity that made them affecting. He overcooks everything, in a fast, stressful style.
>
> Audrey Hepburn... delivers transcendental inanities in the cadences that have stoned audiences at the Academy Awards and other film-industry shebangs; people see her, rise to their feet, and applaud. She's become a ceremonial icon, ravishing and hollow. Where has the actress gone—the one who gave a magnificent performance in *The Nun's Story*? There's no hint of her in this self-parody....
>
> In 1943, it was the finality of death that was being repressed. What the New Age hell is being repressed now?[6]

But Audrey was thrilled by her ten-day close encounter with Spielberg: "I loved it, and I wouldn't mind if he asked me again, like next summer. I'd be right back. I had really one of the best times of my life."[7] The admiration was mutual. Spielberg said one of the greatest thrills of his life was to have worked with Audrey. Universal lobbied to get her a Supporting Actress Oscar nomination, but *Always*—and the last performance of Audrey Hepburn—were overlooked.

The final tally was twenty-nine motion pictures, counting her two TV films—a modest total for such a stellar career.

In the second of her two scenes in the Spielberg film, Hepburn gently lectures Dreyfuss: "What we gave you is a chance to say, 'I'm glad I lived, I'm glad I was alive'... and a chance to say goodbye."

AUDREY'S DEEP INVOLVEMENT WITH UNICEF actually began a year before she made *Always* (and will be chronicled in detail below). But though all her UNICEF work was dramatic, no *formal* dramatic performance had been asked of her until an unusual benefit with the CBC Vancouver Orchestra in December 1988.

"This evening brings together all the things I love—children, music and UNICEF," she began, in English and French. Then, with conductor Bruce Pullan and the Bach Children's Chorus, she took part in a superb new *Winnie the Pooh* oratorio by David Niel for orchestra and children's chorus. Between musical sections, she read selected *Winnie* tales, as kids clustered around her onstage, mesmerized by a voice perfectly suited to A. A. Milne. "Pooh was doing his stoutness exercises before the glass... ," she began, and smiles instantly appeared on every young face. Words and music alike were magical.

Live concert-stage performances made her just as nervous as any other kind of public speaking. But that one set an important precedent for a more potent musical collaboration to come. "It came about because of Audrey's desire for it," says conductor-composer Michael Tilson Thomas. Hepburn would read selections from *The Diary of Anne Frank*, integrated into an original orchestral work by Thomas, using themes from the kaddish, the Jewish mourner's prayer. A series of benefit concerts for UNICEF would take place in March 1990 with Thomas's Miami-based New World Symphony Orchestra in five American cities, plus a performance with the London Symphony Orchestra in 1991.

"Anne's story is my own," she often said. "I knew so many girls like Anne. This child who was locked up in four walls had written a full report of everything I'd experienced and felt."

She had resisted all previous invitations to portray Anne Frank. But at this point in her life, with Thomas's encouragement, she changed her mind. In a quavering voice, she tried to explain why to Larry King:

"When the liberation finally came, too late for Anne Frank, I took up my ballet lessons and went to live in Amsterdam with my mother in a house we shared with a lady writer, who one day handed me a book in galley form and said, 'I think you'd like to read this.' It was in Dutch, 1947: *The Diary of Anne Frank*. I was quite destroyed by it. [Later, when] I was asked to do the picture and the play, I was never able to.[8] There were floods of tears. I became hysterical. I just couldn't deal with it.[9]

"But now, I think it is a wonderful occasion to pay tribute to this child, and I think Anne Frank would be very happy that today her words will be used to bring solace to so many children in conflict, and in aid of UNICEF."[10]

Her emotional resistance had been overcome by the format and by the nature of her psychological approach. "The difference now is I'm not 'playing' Anne Frank," she said. "I'm just relaying her thoughts. I'm reading. I still wouldn't play her. It would have been like putting me back into the horrors of that war."[11] Even just reading the excerpts was painful, but she would do it. Composer Michael Tilson Thomas illuminates the process:

We both read the diary and made notations of the passages we liked most. We discovered there were a number of passages we both agreed on, and I asked Audrey to make me a tape of her reading those sections. I listened to that and started to think about how the music would work—to put order into it, how it would flow. But so much of the music, I realize now, was influenced by hearing the way she read, her voice, her personality. The piece is as much about Audrey as about Anne Frank.[12]

Thomas's result, *From the Diary of Anne Frank*, was a set of symphonic variations created "in a kind of stream of consciousness way," he says. He had precious little time to put it together—two months to write nearly thirty minutes of music. Holed up with a coffeepot in Miami, he called Audrey now and then for moral support and completed the piano score. They then met in Zurich, where Thomas was conducting with the London Symphony. He played it through for her, for the first time.

"She was blown away," says Thomas, with no hint or need of modesty. "She had no idea what it was going to be like. I think she was terrified that it would be some giant, bizarre, dissonant, horrible thing."

What she heard, instead, was one of the century's most moving, melodic and muscular requiems, its tragic angularity both subtle and soaring. "She was relieved," says the composer. "But it was still a major stretch for her to relate to this very intricate music. She didn't read music; she didn't have a musical education. She heard it in a very different way. It was an arduous process. She was nervous to do something like this live. It was a huge act of daring and devotion on her part.[13]

Frank's diary, Thomas's music and Hepburn's speech merged in a richly creative way. It was her first true stage appearance in thirty-five years—in many ways more powerful than any film role she ever played. She read with astonishing simplicity and understatement, the melody of her voice an unpredictable delight. Her intensity brought audiences to tears. She had said she wasn't going to "play" Anne—but that, in the end, was precisely what she did.

"It was an amazing kind of inward acting," says Thomas, as if she was "imagining the cadences of the thought that the words represented, rather than 'playing' it to the audience." Rob Wolders was with her at every rehearsal and performance and says, "In my mind, she became Anne Frank almost against her wishes, in the expression of emotion, her whole comportment, not just the voice. It's a pity there is no videotape."*

---

* There is a "bootlegged" audiotape which at least preserved the sound. Thomas wanted to make a proper recording, "but I was still playing with it, and Audrey wasn't certain. We should have gone for it. We just thought, 'This is a work in progress. We'll do it later.' " Thomas later worked with Leslie Caron on a similar project, *The Martyrdom of Saint Sebastian*, with D'Annunzio's text and Debussy's music. He and the London Symphony Orchestra made a beautiful Sony recording of it.

Thomas's favorite moment was just before the premiere, when she was debating what to wear: "She said, 'I can't decide if I should wear the pantsuit or the dress. Let me model them for you.' She went into the next room and came back wearing this very elegant pantsuit and struck some tomboyish poses. Then she got very serious and said, 'Now, I'll show you the dress.' She disappeared and came back wearing this stunningly understated Givenchy creation which hugged her gorgeous frame. I was absolutely dumbstruck. I just stood there with my mouth open, speechless. After a moment, she looked at me very kindly and said, 'I guess you prefer the dress.' "[14]

From the Diary of Anne Frank premiered in Philadelphia on March 19, 1990. There, and throughout the tour, she was touched by the groups of schoolchildren who greeted her and gave her flowers and scrolls with messages to deliver—somehow—to children in the Third World. The production moved on to Miami, Chicago and then Houston.

"We were 'down' after some mediocre reviews and had to travel to Houston the next day, changing planes, everybody exhausted," says Rob. "The moment we got there, they had an interview set up for Audrey, who was terribly tired. But it was one of the best she ever gave." Indeed, the delicate questions of KTRK-TV producer Shara Fryer on March 22 drew her out to an unusual degree. She sat unabashed in her wrinkled shirt and slacks and sneakers from the plane and, among other things, made an extraordinary statement on the subject of emotional pain.

"Do you carry the memory of hardship with you?" Fryer asked.

"There's a curious thing about pain or hardship," she replied softly. "In the beginning, it's an enemy, it's something that you don't want to face or think about or deal with. Yet with time it becomes almost a friend. If you've lost someone you love very much, in the beginning you can't bear it, but as the years goes by, the pain of losing them is what reminds you so vividly of them—that they were alive. My experiences and the people I lost in the war remain so vivid for me because of the pain. Being without food, fearful for one's life, the bombings —all made me so appreciative of safety, of liberty. In that sense, the bad experiences have become positive in my life."[15]

The last concert destination in the United States was New York City, where *Anne Frank* was performed for the United Nations General Assembly on March 25, 1990, and where her thoughtfulness and sense of fun lifted everyone's spirits.

"It was exciting," maestro Thomas remembers, "because Audrey had become so friendly and involved and generous with all these young musicians by then. The last night in New York after the concert, I said, 'There's an orchestra party. Would you like to go over?' She said, 'Of course!' By the time she arrived at the hotel, this big disco party was going strong, everybody acting like twenty-three-year-olds. When they saw Audrey, there was a groundswell—everybody wanted to dance with her. She got right out on that dance floor with the double bass player, the cellist.... She did the requisite rock 'n' roll and rhythm 'n' blues numbers, too. I couldn't believe she did that for us all."

Only Thomas and Wolders knew how much every performance took out of her. "Narrating *Diary of Anne Frank*," she said, was "terrifying. To get up in front of a big concert hall with ninety professional musicians behind you and narrate for half an hour.... I've suffered from stage-fright all my life in the worst way. It affects my stomach, I get headaches. It's awful. But when I'm shivering backstage and Michael is conducting the overture or first piece he's doing, already I feel better.... I stand there absolutely petrified. And then the first strains of music make you forget yourself."[16]

During the engagement in London, she revealed a trade secret about how she managed it: "I act the same way now as I did forty years ago... with feeling instead of technique. All my life I've been in situations where I've had no technique, but if you *feel* enough you can get away with murder."[17]

The critics called her May 1991 *Anne Frank* with the London Symphony Orchestra "heartbreaking." On the recommendation of Leonard Bernstein, Thomas had reworked and improved the finale. That Barbican concert hall performance constituted Audrey's first London stage appearance in forty years, and her last. She had received a letter from Eva Schloss, Anne Frank's half-sister in England, asking her to become a patron of the new Anne Frank Educational Trust, to which she agreed. Schloss—an Auschwitz survivor—came backstage after the Barbican concert, deeply moved. "She and Audrey had a very emotional encounter," says Rob. Audrey, through the Trust, issued an emotional statement:

"The memory of Anne Frank is with us today as it will be forever, not because she died but because she lived—just long enough to leave us her undying message of hope, of love, and above all forgiveness."[18]

That London experience featured a joyous reunion. While studying dance with Rambert in the late forties, Audrey had lived briefly in a rooming house across the hall from London Symphony violinist Patrick Vermonth, who took care of her when she was sick. At the first "Anne Frank" rehearsal, she spotted him. "My God, Patrick!" They had a grand embrace. She cherished him most in relation to England's chronic postwar shortages. "Patrick had an airline-steward friend," says Thomas. "He flew to the Bahamas a lot in those days—and always brought back nylons for Audrey."

Michael Tilson Thomas pauses long, when asked for a final summation, before formulating it:

"She was the dearest soul I ever met or worked with. She had that quality of 'recognizing' you even when meeting you for the first time. She looked at you in those first seconds with a delicious surprise—as if, 'My dearest friend, you've suddenly appeared, how wonderful to see you again!' She made you feel there was some special secret you shared with her, some beautiful melody playing that perhaps just the two of you could hear."

Thomas wanted to do more performances with her, "but when I'd ask, 'What are you doing on February 25, 1997?' she'd just laugh. She couldn't believe how far in advance the music world worked." The last time he saw her was a year later in Gstaad, when she made him a pasta dinner. "We were eating," he recalls, "and I said, 'Listen, how about it? We'll do the concert again and record it then.' She said, 'Well, the old girl's not getting any younger. I don't know if I should still be going on stage.' I said, 'Oh, please—of course you're going to do it.'"

The "futuristic" dates Thomas had in mind were April and May of 1995, for New York and Rotterdam. She was particularly intrigued by the latter venue, for obvious reasons. But it would be Debra Winger and Dutch actress Pauline van Rhenen, not Audrey Hepburn, who would do those performances.

DURING THE MIAMI PORTION OF her *Anne Frank* tour came shocking news from Europe about someone close to Audrey—a mysterious beauty with no surname.

Capucine, the striking French actress-model with the Nefertiti-like features, was born Germaine Lefebvre, in 1933, into a middle-class family in Toulon. She earned a degree in foreign languages and modeled for such haute couture houses as Dior and Givenchy. Her first meeting with Hepburn in Paris at Givenchy's was the start of an intimate forty-year friendship.

In the late fifties, Capucine left France for Hollywood, under contract to producer Charles K. Feldman, and settled on her odd solo pseudonym: Capucine ("kap-u-SEEN") was the French word for nasturtium. Her sultry beauty and deep voice led some to hail her as a possible new Garbo. The picture that really launched her was Edward Dmytryk's deliciously lurid *Walk on the Wild Side* (1962), in which she turned in a memorable performance as the oppressed call girl in lesbian Barbara Stanwyck's bordello. She then moved successfully upward in such stylish international hit comedies as *The Pink Panther* (1964) and *What's New, Pussycat?* (1965). She was also in demand for a host of European features, including *Fellini Satyricon* in 1970.

Privately, she lived in Lausanne, not far from Audrey, in a small and troubled world. Audrey's friend Anna Cataldi recalls living in Capucine's apartment building as a student—the same building whose penthouse was occupied by Yul and Doris Brynner. More than once, Cataldi bumped into actor William Holden in the elevator, on his way up to tryst with Capucine. Their stormy affair had begun years earlier, during the making of two adventure films together, *The Lion* and *The Seventh Dawn*.

In the late seventies and eighties, when her film heyday was over, Capucine came to visit Audrey and Rob in Tolochenaz at least twice a week. On her good days, she and Audrey did all sorts of things together. But there were many bad days, related to her declining career, compounded by depressing memories of Holden.

For all his romancing of Audrey, Capucine and a dozen other women, Holden had remained married to Brenda Marshall for thirty tempestuous, unfaithful years—often separated but just as often reunited. Capucine had helped—or tried to help—him through many of his alcoholic binges. Blake Edwards recalls seeing Holden and Capucine at a screening of *Days of Wine and Roses*, after which Holden turned to Capucine and said, "Was I that bad?"

"Worse," she said.

"Did I put you through that?" he asked.

"More," she replied.

Holden's sexual fidelity to her was zero but his financial help was substantial after the flop of her later European films. The persistent, bizarre reports that Capucine was a transsexual seem to have been debunked by Holden, whose amorous preferences were decidedly and conventionally macho.

In November 1981, William Holden fell and hit his head, in a drunken stupor, and bled to death in his Santa Monica apartment. Both Holden and producer Feldman—and possibly Darryl Zanuck and Peter Sellers, as well—"generously remembered" Capucine in their wills. Holden, in fact, remembered her to the tune of $50,000, enabling her to continue living fairly well in Lausanne.

But these days she was lonely and unhappy and worried about sliding into old age, without a mate or a source of income. She seemed to live in the past, often threatening suicide. "Cappy was a great friend of mine as well," says R. J. Wagner. "She did some *Hart to Hart* episodes with me, and I loved her very much. But she was a very disturbed person."

Rob Wolders often drove her to her clinic. "She was a manic-depressive," he says. "Audrey had many trying times with her. They were very close, but it was the kind of friendship that rested largely on Audrey's compassion." Wagner says Audrey and Rob once saved Capucine's life from an overdose of pills, but "when she came to, she was disappointed."[19] Rob, too, felt she resented them for helping thwart the attempt. "I'm weary," she said. "I'd like to work, but the enthusiasm is gone. But then, so are the opportunities."[20]

The grim call came on March 19 to Audrey's hotel room in Miami, where *Anne Frank* was being performed that night. "Audrey answered the phone and turned ashen," says Wolders. "She managed to get out the word—'Capucine.'" At fifty-seven, she had finally succeeded in killing herself that afternoon, leaping from a window of her eighth-floor apartment in Lausanne.

Some weeks later, after they returned home to Switzerland, Audrey and Rob were visited by Capucine's psychiatrist, a kind man they knew through many "Cap crises." He told Audrey something that shocked her: "The pain Capucine was suffering was so immense, this was really the best solution." Only then, says Rob, did Audrey make her peace with it.

In death, Capucine made an extraordinary gesture to Audrey. She was largely broke, her money from Holden long gone. Her sole asset was a modest equity in her apartment. She stipulated in her will that, when it was sold, half of the money was to be given to the Red Cross and the other half to UNICEF, both gifts in honor of Audrey's work. It was about $100,000 apiece, and Audrey was asked to designate the projects to which it should go.

Capucine's obituary in *The New York Times* concluded with, "Her only known survivors were her three cats."

PERHAPS WITH CAP ON HER mind, she said, "All I really want now is not to be lonely, and to have my garden."[21]

She often said she wasn't much of a gardener and that her only real skill was "pulling weeds." But that was, of course, more self-effacement. Her beautiful grounds at Tolochenaz contained a fruit-producing orchard and extensive vegetable and flower tracts. She was far more serious about gardening than the world knew. But it was about to find out.

"What fascinated me from the very beginning was, when you would just say, '*Gardens of the World* with Audrey Hepburn,' people's faces would light up," says Janis Blackschleger. "It was such a pleasing combination and such a natural one."

Blackschleger, a Peabody Award-winning documentary maker, was executive producer of that stunning six-part series, first proposed in January 1989. British garden authority Penelope Hobhouse and American garden writer Elvin McDonald were hired as consultants, and so was the perfect host. "I think [coordinating producer] Julie Leifermann was the first to utter Audrey's name," says Blackschleger. "She loved the idea. I think the appeal for her was to be out in and around beauty, and to bring that to people. With Audrey involved, you set a certain expectation, and our job was simply to fulfill that expectation."

Who better to stroll down a garden path with than Audrey? The ambitious *Gardens of the World* series would take viewers on an around-the-world expedition exploring the greatest gardens on the globe—from Europe to North and South America and the Far East. Hepburn was filmed among the luxuriant cypresses of Tuscany, the bare rocks of Saiho-ji in Kyoto, and the perfect geometrical lines of the Jardins de Luxembourg in Paris, examining their philosophies and styles as she went. Each half-hour episode focused on a botanical genre: "Roses and Rose Gardens," "Tulips and Spring Bulbs," "Formal Gardens," "Flowers and Flower Gardens," "Country Gardens" and "Public Gardens."

Her narration, elegantly written by Glenn Berenbeim, contained a lot of Hepburn's input. It was not to be a garden history, producer Stuart Crowner made clear. It was about *being there*, responding to the gardens and figuring out how and why they were created. But at the outset, there was a bit of concern when Audrey said she thought the series should be "poetic."

"We didn't quite know what she meant," Blackschleger recalls. "We were a little afraid of it at first. We thought it might mean 'sentimental.' But we came to understand that her definition of poetic was the fusion of image, idea, music, art. She meant poetic in the fullest sense of lyrical.

"From when we first met with her, it was clear that Audrey favored a more natural style of garden. She wasn't so enthralled with formal gardens and the notion of perfection. Our job was to reconcile Penelope's discriminating requirements with Audrey's more folksy, less rigorous ideas."[22]

The professional and the amateur ended up a fine team. When work on the series began, Hepburn was sixty and Hobhouse was fifty-nine. "Penelope adored Audrey and thought, 'I'm going to learn how to be sixty from Audrey,'" Blackschleger recalls. "Together, they were as conscientious as two sixth-grade schoolgirls. If you've never been one yourself, you might not know just how conscientious that is." Hobhouse supplied the expert's grand pronouncements, Hepburn the layperson's warm enthusiasm.

Their itinerary was jammed tight, and gardens have no respect for production scheduling. They barely made it from Italy to England, for instance, in time for the once-a-year blooming of the old roses in the walled garden at Mottisfont Abbey. Then it was on, quickly, halfway across the planet to the Dominican Republic, where Gustavo Tavares led her among the six-foot vanda orchids of Villa Pancha, the exquisite "jungle" his family had been cultivating there for sixty years.

"That was the one venue that lacked a good hotel," says Julie

Leifermann, "and the first time Audrey stayed with a garden owner. She had a lovely time. Every evening when the sun would start to set, Gustavo made rum old-fashioneds and we all sat on his wonderful veranda and talked about the day."*

Leifermann had many duties on the production, but her primary job was to keep Audrey happy and functional. Audrey did not have or want an entourage—no hairdresser, no makeup or wardrobe person, no personal maid. "I'm a big girl," she said. "I don't need all those people fussing over me." As her liaison to the production, Julie tried to help her with such things and to watch over her in general. But soon enough, the tables started to turn, Leifermann recalls:

> She ended up becoming *my* caretaker. When she got comfortable with you and cared about you, she had this need to fuss over you, do things for you.... It became a running gag. I was always dashing back and forth from Europe to L.A. during the production and having perpetual jet lag. Invariably, sitting in the backseat of a car with Audrey, I'd fall asleep. I'd wake up with my head on her shoulder, and everyone would tease me about how I drooled on her. But she would say, 'Come on, just put your head down on my lap,' and cover me with her blue cape and I would sleep on her with her arms around me. She knew a little snooze would keep me going. So I slept on Audrey Hepburn through many weeks of travels around the world.[23]

The first location shoot on "Gardens of the World," in April 1990, was in Holland for the tulip episode. It was a homecoming, of course, and Netherlanders took advantage of the opportunity to honor her with the official christening of "the Audrey Hepburn tulip"—a luminous white one—in a ceremony at her family's ancestral home in Doorn, now a museum. There, she saw Baroness Jacqueline van Heemstra, her eighty-seven-year-old maiden aunt and last of her mother's siblings, for the final time. "It was a very emotional moment," Leifermann says. "Her aunt was in a wheelchair and they hugged and kissed and spoke in Dutch." Hollanders take their tulips seriously. Doorn was full of spectators and news media, Julie recalls, and the ceremony full of protocol:

> There was a big pedestal with the tulip in a beautiful glass vase on a pillow. But the moment the ceremony began, a huge black cloud rolled in out of nowhere and the wind knocked the vase off just as the tulip was to be handed to her and named in her honor. It started to downpour, and everyone said, 'Oh, my God, what do we do?' But Audrey just laughed and ran around

---

* The Dominican Republic segment was not among the original six episodes aired. The final two parts, "Tropical Gardens" and "Japanese Gardens," were released in the spring of 1996.

the podium after the tulip, grabbed it, stuck it back in the vase, and put it all back. Then the cloud moved off, the sun came out, and everything was fine. She had taken charge and righted it all.[24]*

In their three months together on the road, Audrey's ministrations to Julie continued to the end:

When I got sick in Italy, she was constantly checking to see if I had a temperature, sticking a cough drop in my mouth—the mother hen fussing over her chick. In England, on our last location, I ran out of clothes. We had a half day off and Audrey wanted me to go shopping with her in a little village called Broadway—spend the afternoon together and do girl stuff. I said, "I have to get my clothes cleaned and ironed for tomorrow." She said, "Bring them with you. We'll figure it out." So I did. My hotel washed them, but they wouldn't iron them.

So we went and did our shopping, and then we went back to her room, and she said, "Give me your pants and your shirt, I'm going to iron them."

I said, "You can't iron my clothes."

She said, "Do you know how to iron?"

I said, "Not very well, but I'm going to try."

She said, "Give me those."

I said, "No, if anyone finds out you ironed my clothes, I'm in trouble." We were fighting over my pants.

"Give me them."

"No."

"Now, stop it, and let me have them."

So I gave in and she stood there happily ironing my pants and shirt, folded them beautifully.

"There you go," she said. "Now we don't have to look at you in wrinkled clothes tomorrow."

And that was that.[25]

Leifermann found the sophisticated star easily delighted by a bug or a bird. "It wasn't a put-on. She genuinely loved the beauty of small things. She was connected to the simplicity of how life could work and tried not

---

* An official "Audrey Hepburn rose" was also developed during *Gardens of the World* production. "Audrey liked the whites and pinks," says Janis Blackschleger, "so we asked Clare Martin to find one that was pastel. He found a beautiful rose in America, done by Gerry Toomey at Springhill nursery, with a perfect icing-on-a-cake shaped bud, but when it opens, it gets blowzy and informal, with a red heart. It goes from formal elegance to a more casual apple-blossom pink—perfect for Audrey." When Dr. Ron Glegg asked her how she felt about the naming of a new rose in her honor, "Her eyes lit up as in a scene from *Breakfast at Tiffany's*, and she said, 'It is the most romantic thing that could ever happen to you.'"

complicate it." Her love of problem-solving reached a comic peak in Paris at the Jardins de Luxembourg, where Audrey had a big trailer in which to change clothes and relax when she wished. Midway in shooting, Julie had to go to the bathroom, and Audrey said she'd go along. They walked through the park to the motor home but, once there, couldn't find the driver, who had the key:

I said, "I really have to go." Audrey said, "I do, too—come here!" She takes me around to the back end of the trailer and says, "I'm going to boost you up. Go through the window and unlock the door." So there's Audrey down low, hoisting and pushing—trying to get me up high enough to grab onto something. "You'd better hurry," she says. "We've got a crowd around us." I pull open the window, get halfway through, legs flailing, half of me is in, half out. She's pushing me and I don't know what I'm falling into. Finally she shoves me through—and the crowd starts to applaud! I ran around, opened the door and she scooted in. It was, "Image be damned! I have to go to the bathroom!"[26]

Audrey wanted to be sure the series made a statement about the environment—"something people hadn't heard before," says Blackschleger. "So we had her write up what she wanted to say, and we decided to open and close the series on that statement."

It declared that, "Gardens remind us of the beauty we are in danger of losing. The arts of the garden nurture and comfort the human spirit, [offering] man a chance to regulate at least one aspect of his life... and show himself as he wishes to be."

Hepburn's favorite site in Japan was Kyoto's Saiho-ji, the contemplative monastery garden, created in 1339 by a Zen Buddhist priest, with hundreds of different mosses and sculpted evergreens in bamboo-enclosed seclusion. Its "grammar of formality," she said, beautifully demonstrated that each garden, like each country, had a unique language. So did Hepburn herself, says Blackschleger—a language of distinct gender:

One of the things Audrey brought to the world was a feminine point of view. If we had a language that ended in o's and a's, if we understood masculine and feminine in those fundamental terms—but we don't. How few words we have that end in "a." How few feminine visions. Tropical gardens, for instance, do not have a linear history the way most European gardens do. We wanted to tell the tropical story as one of beauty and fragility, not conquest. That is essentially a more feminine idea. We don't have that clear masculine-feminine distinction in our cultural view of the world, which is really more pleasing to both. We go to the extreme of feminist, which is something different.[27]

"WHEN YOU WERE WITH AUDREY you felt prettier, better about yourself and your own possibilities," Blackschleger says.[28] Millions felt the same—especially seeing her in *Gardens of the World*, dressed in the stylishly casual designs of Ralph Lauren.

Like Givenchy, Lauren had both a personal and professional relationship with her, though of much more recent vintage. They had met three years earlier in his New York flagship store at Seventy-second Street and Madison Avenue.

"She came in with Rob," the designer recalls, "and my wife Ricky said, 'Ralph, you'll never believe it. Audrey Hepburn's in the store. Do you want to meet her?' I said, 'I'd love to, but let her go through the store.' Later, she came up to see me. I said how much of a fan I was, and she said, 'Well, I'm a fan of yours,' and asked for my autograph. I wanted *her* autograph!"

On a subsequent visit to his store, she told Lauren the clothes she wore as a girl were "simple, European classic"—the exact quality she liked in his designs. "She knew my clothes before I knew her," he says. "She knew exactly what she wanted. Nobody could tell her what to wear."

He found that out firsthand. One day in the store when he approached her with a suggestion, she cut him off with, "All right, Ralph, you can go now." Lauren was offended: "I thought, so this is what Audrey's really like—bossy. It was the manner I didn't like. I walked out very angry at her."

Earlier, Audrey and Rob had accepted Lauren's invitation to spend a three-day weekend at his house in Jamaica, and Ralph didn't see her again until their departure for Kingston.

"On the plane, she was very effervescent," he recalls. "I said, 'Audrey, I want you to know I'm angry at you,' and I told her why. She said, 'Ralph, I really felt I was holding you up—it must have come out the wrong way. I'm very sorry.' I was always very direct with her. I think she valued that in people."

Lauren says many of his conversations with Audrey were left unfinished or interrupted by other people. That didn't bother her but it did him, and one day he gave her his theory: "I said, 'Audrey, you don't really want to listen. You're too tight.' She said, 'What do you mean?' I said I felt she wasn't receptive to hearing certain things. She said, 'That's insecurity, Ralph.... All my life, I was too tall, long neck.... I never thought I was pretty.' I said, 'How could you think that?' But she did. She was a very protected person. She was assured about who she was but, at the same time, insecure in so many ways."[29]

When *Gardens of the World* came up, it was Lauren she called upon for her wardrobe. "I love Givenchy for night," she told him, "but I love your sport clothes for daytime." Today, when asked to elaborate on the differences between his and Givenchy's fashion, Lauren chooses his words carefully:

"Givenchy is a charming, elegant man, and they had a fine connection. But I must say, you could take Audrey into Sears Roebuck or Givenchy or Ralph Lauren or an army-surplus store—it didn't matter, she'd put something on and you'd say, 'It's her!' Very few people can do that. Clothes look great or not so great, depending on who's wearing them. I truly feel Audrey gave *Givenchy* a look. As time went on, they collaborated, but I think she picked what was Audrey out of Givenchy. The same for my clothes. She just picked from them what was right for her."[30]

One delightful result, in the *Gardens of the World* series, was her outfit—with its feminine hint of a military collar—worn during the tour of George Washington's gardens at Mt. Vernon. Surely, it was an original designed for that occasion?

"No," Lauren replies. "We just went through the store and she picked it out. They were all existing designs."

A partial preview of the *Gardens* series and high tea in Audrey's honor were held at Cartier's New York headquarters in March of 1991. "They wanted to be able to say, 'She has breakfast at Tiffany's, but she has high tea at Cartier's,'" Blackschleger recalls. "Audrey said, 'I've had breakfast at Tiffany's and high tea at Cartier's—I guess this means I have to have dinner at Bulgari's.' She knew how to weave all those commercial interests together and make everybody happy.

"Audrey and Robbie paid attention to all the details. They were amazing together. It was incredible to see two human beings be so elegant and responsible but also kind and caring."

Julie Leifermann recalls asking Audrey, "'How do you and Rob do it? How do you spend all this time together, travel together, live together, without killing each other?' She said, 'We just enjoy going through the world together.' It was the sweetest thing to see their little jokes—that playful, mischievous side of her. She was so smart, so well-read, spoke gazillions of languages. No wonder Robbie never got bored with her."[31]

SHE WOULD MAKE NO NEW movies, but neither would she forsake the past. It was a time to look back and pay tribute: Between 1989 and 1992, Audrey was an honored guest, or guest of honor, at no fewer than sixteen film galas. The full list would be taxing, but the highlights provide insight into the depth of her friendships.

She once said that the first thing she saw when she arrived in America was the Statue of Liberty—and the second was Richard Avedon. On January 14, 1989, at the Council of Fashion Designers salute to Avedon in New York, she appeared in a red strapless gown, her neck and shoulders drawn but proud, and lionized him:

"For Richard, I've happily swung through swings, stood in clouds of steam, been drenched with rain, and descended endless flights of stairs without looking and without breaking my neck.... Only with Richard have I been able to shed my innate self-consciousness in front of the camera. Is it his sweetness? Is it his sense of fun? The assurance that you know you're going to end up looking the way you wished you looked?... How many unknowns like myself were put on the map by Richard Avedon?"[32]

The next year she was thrilled, in view of her advocacy for children, to stand on a Broadway stage for the first time in forty years and hand out a 1991 Tony award to little Daisy Egan for *The Secret Garden*.

But most affecting personally was the Film Society of Lincoln Center's "Gala Tribute to Audrey Hepburn" of April 22, 1991, at Avery Fisher Hall in New York, with tributes delivered by Billy Wilder, Stanley Donen, Gregory Peck, Alan Arkin, Tony Perkins, Harry Belafonte and many others.

What did the Lincoln Center tribute mean to her?

"I don't know what it means," she replied. "It's a huge honor."

What had her career meant?

She struggled for an answer before concluding that the key thing was the "experiences with other performers who somehow make you open up to them. For me, it always has to do with some kind of affection, love, warmth. I was born with an enormous need for affection and a terrible need to give it. That's what I'd like to think maybe has been the appeal. People have recognized something in me they have themselves—the need to receive affection and the need to give it. Does that sound soppy?"[33]

That fund-raising event was the most successful since the first Lincoln Center Film Society tribute, in 1972, to Charles Chaplin. Tickets were sold out months in advance, and hundreds of checks had to be returned to disappointed Hepburn fans. Avery Fisher Hall seated 2,700 but, "We could have done this in Shea Stadium," said one Lincoln Center publicist. Gala chairman Ralph Lauren set the evening's tone by, professing a lifelong adoration of Hepburn. Stanley Donen topped him by noting, "My passion for her has lasted through four marriages—two of hers and two of mine." He was topped in turn by Billy Wilder, who said he fell in love with her within five seconds of meeting her on the set of *Sabrina*, and then reprised one of his best lines: "I talk in my sleep, but fortunately, my wife's name is Audrey." Alan Arkin got an even bigger laugh—the biggest of the night—following a film clip from *Wait Until Dark* (see opening passsage of Chapter 7, p. 222). Wendy Keys, who programmed and directed the

Lincoln Center tribute to Hepburn, recalls certain delicate, behind-the-scenes moments—with Anthony Perkins, for instance:

"I was nervous because I didn't have or want any clips from *Green Mansions*. I said, 'I hope you don't mind, but I don't have an excerpt from the film.' He said, 'I'm thrilled.' "[34] Yet when he spoke that night, Perkins told the audience he had given up an offer to costar in Billy Wilder's *Some Like It Hot* for the chance to meet and work with Audrey in *Green Mansions*.[35]*

One of very few invitees who failed to attend was Sean Connery, then shooting a film in Mexico. Another was a person only Rob Wolders expected to show up: "Cher was a great personal favorite of Audrey's. When Wendy pointed out we had all men and no women, I suggested her as a surprise for Audrey, who adored her in *Moonstruck*." But forty-eight hours before the event, Cher got sick and, on April 20, 1991, had to send Audrey her regrets:

> This is a very hard letter for me to write because what I had dreamt of doing all my life was to be able to tell you in person.... the profound effect you have had on my life.
>
> On the night I won the Oscar, you touched my hand and said you were glad I'd won.... You can never imagine what that meant to me. Since I was a little girl you have been my idea of a "star" and it was partly because of you that I became an actress.
>
> You were a brilliant light for me in a sometimes dark childhood. I so wanted to be like you in "Breakfast at Tiffany's" that I put my hair in 2 ponytails, bought huge sunglasses, and wore the closest thing to "you" I could put together. I got suspended from school for the sunglasses....
>
> Someone once said to me that I was like a "3rd World Audrey Hepburn"— I'm not sure how they meant it, but it's one of my favorite comments. [Your work] has inspired me again and again. I love you [and] you will never know how sad I am to miss this opportunity to say it in person.

Audrey's own little speech that night was, of course, the climactic last act on the bill. Ralph Lauren saw her backstage just before she went on and was amazed that "she was so nervous... pacing back and forth, smoking, her hands ice cold."[36]

Wendy Keys has a similar recollection:

---

* The idea of Anthony Perkins in the Tony Curtis role of *Some Like It Hot* is bizarre—and "not true," said Wilder in Beverly Hills recently. "I wouldn't have wanted a man who had that affair with his dead mother in *Psycho!* It would have cast a shadow over *Some Like It Hot*." Never mind that *Psycho* (1960) was made after both *Green Mansions* and *Some Like It Hot*. Wilder's remark is cosmically if not literally true.

"If there's a frozen moment, just one image I keep in my mind, it's the view of her leaving from backstage to go out to the center of the Avery Fisher stage at the end of her tribute: She threw her shoulders back, and this beautiful white chiffon skirt swirled around her legs as she walked out to greet these people who were so thrilled to see her. It was heightened by the fact that she was so nervous. The sight of her back, with that beautiful French twist and those shoulder blades like nobody else's—it was a moment I'll never get over."[37]

Once on stage, her words were no less gracious and rather more humorous than usual. She thanked all the directors, costars and technicians who made a "marketable commodity out of a skinny broad."

The post-tribute dinner at Tavern on the Green in Central Park presented a dilemma. The restaurant's tables held a maximum of ten, but many times that number had come to pay tribute to her and she was worried that there wouldn't be enough room for them all at her table. "If there was a chance of their feeling slighted, Audrey would not allow it," says Professor Richard Brown, one of her favorite interviewers, who was a guest and witness.[38]

On this night above all others, says Keys, "She had to make sure that everyone who had come long distances sat close to her, but she couldn't bear to decide who should or shouldn't. So she had us make one tremendous table by pushing ten together into a giant oval that went on for miles. It was perfect. Nobody's feelings were hurt. It never happened before or since at one of those events, because most people don't care. But Audrey did."[39]

Keys felt that quality carried over onto the screen:

"One thing she portrays on film so sharply is hurt feelings. You're so overcome by her beauty you don't really acknowledge the acting that goes on behind it. In *My Fair Lady*, when Higgins abuses her, you can see her hurt feelings and how honest they are. It was something close to her surface, that vulnerability I saw Rob react to in private. He would be so devastated when he saw that wounded expression—that look in her eye when she was struck down by something."[40]

RALPH LAUREN'S BLUNT, SOMETIMES CONFRONTATIONAL way of dealing with Audrey not only didn't alienate her but seemed to draw them closer. His enormous affection for her was known by all, and Hepburn was the obvious choice to present him with the Council of Fashion Designers' Lifetime Achievement award on February 3, 1992 in New York. Audrey's was the most emotional of many emotional tributes to Ralph Lauren that night:

"You've not only created a total concept of fashion and style, but by your consistency and integrity, protected it, always reminding us of the best things in life. As a designer, you conjure up all things I most care about—the country, misty mornings, summer afternoons, great open spaces, horses, cornfields, vegetable gardens, fireplaces and Jack Russell terriers.

"As a man, I respect you for your total lack of pretension, for your gentleness, kindness, sincerity, simplicity. And as my friend, I love you."[41]

When Lauren's turn came at the end, he said, "You want to know the lifetime achievement?" Then, addressing his best pal from boyhood, "Steve, remember we went to the movies in the Bronx thirty years ago? Remember the princess? I got her!"

As noted, Hepburn graced no fewer than four tributes to Gregory Peck.* "How much could they say about each other?" asks Rob Wolders rhetorically. But Audrey always found something more, notably at the Kennedy Center in December 1991:

> Gregory Peck is the most authentic actor of our time.... Because he was willing to fight the studio executives when they didn't want to take the risk, we have *Gentlemen's Agreement* and its landmark exposure to anti-Semitism. Only because he wanted to play the part did they make *To Kill A Mockingbird*. Dearest Greg, to your generosity, I owe my career. For your courage and integrity, you have my deepest respect. For your friendship, your goodness, and your humor, you have all my love.

Six months later, she was honorary chairperson of the American Cinematheque's tribute to Sean Connery. Their mutual friend Terence Young, who directed Connery's great James Bond hits, sent regrets by telegram: "There are only two great stars in my recollection who've not been changed by great, massive success: Sean Connery and Lassie."[42] Said Audrey:

"Like every actress in the world, for years it was my dream to work with Sean Connery—marvelous-looking, superb acting, warm, versatile and wildly sexy. I got my wish. But I was cast as a nun. Nevertheless, once Robin was back from the crusades in all his splendor, the nun's veil just seemed to melt away."

At the Academy Awards that year—1992—Hepburn substituted for Mother Teresa in presenting an honorary Oscar to the ailing Indian director Satyajit Ray. Audrey got a standing ovation when she appeared in her Indian-style, off-the-shoulder Givenchy dress to introduce Ray's pre-

---

* At Eastman House in Rochester in 1987; at the American Film Institute on March 15, 1989; at the Kennedy Center in Washington on December 26, 1991; and at Lincoln Center in April 1992.

recorded acceptance speech from his hospital bed in Calcutta.*

A few months earlier, when honored in Dallas by the U.S.A. Film Festival for her own contribution to motion pictures, she was asked how she felt about all the lavish praise.

"It's wonderful," she replied, "but at the same time... you just die in a way. I mean, all those compliments. You wish you could spread it over the year. It's like eating too much chocolate cake all at once. You sort of don't believe any of it, and yet you're terribly grateful."[43] She was deeply immersed in her "second career" with UNICEF by then, and—she told Dominick Dunne in *Vanity Fair*—she felt the same about the praise she was receiving for her UNICEF work:

"It makes me self-conscious. It's because I'm known, in the limelight, that I'm getting all the gravy, but if you knew, if you saw some of the people who make it possible for UNICEF to help these children survive. These are the people who do the jobs—the unknowns, whose names you will never know.... I at least get a dollar a year, but they don't."[44]

On the other hand, she said, "I'm glad I've got a name because I'm using it for what it's worth."[45]

"HER CAREER CAN BE SPLIT into two chapters," says her friend Leslie Caron. "In the first part she received all the glory she could hope for, and in the second part she gave back, in spades, what she had received."[46]

On the heels of the Allies' liberation of Arnhem in 1945 came UNRRA, the United Nations Relief and Rehabilitation Administration, forerunner of UNICEF, bringing desperately needed food, medicine and clothing. Audrey, we know, was one of the first beneficiaries, and her emotional commitment to that agency began then and there. "There is a moral obligation," she would say, "that those who have should give to those who don't."[47]

The death of actor Danny Kaye in March 1987 left a void at UNICEF. For the previous twenty years, he had roamed the world as its most popular Goodwill Ambassador. Only someone extraordinary could replace him or, at least, take over part of his work.

Now that her sons were grown, in 1988, instead of retiring in comfort to the jet set, Hepburn began the job that would occupy the last five years of her life: Special Ambassador for the United Nations Children's Fund. "I auditioned for this job for forty-five years," she would say, "and I finally

---

* Academy president Jack Valenti introduced Audrey that night. He attempted to apply President Kennedy's remark about Jefferson to Audrey—one person doing the work of twelve— but garbled it and said the reverse. Afterward, blissfully unaware of his gaffe, he told Hepburn and Woders they should "go on the road" with their act. "I couldn't say, 'Not if you mess up your lines,'" says Rob.

got it.[48] I always felt very powerless when I would see the terrible pictures on TV. But I was offered a wonderful opportunity to do something [and it is] is a marvelous therapy to the anguish I feel."[49]

How long did it take her to accept the position?

"About two minutes," she said. "I've always had an enormous love of children. When I was little, I used to embarrass my mother by trying to pick babies out of prams at the market. The one thing I dreamed of in my life was to have children of my own. It always boils down to the same thing—of not only receiving love but wanting desperately to give it."[50]

There was an even simpler way to put it: "It's something I'd do for my child, so why not for others?"

The waters she first tested were in Macao, where UNICEF Portugal asked her to be guest of honor at a benefit concert in October 1987. In the beautiful Church of St. Lorenzo there, she delivered brief remarks—exactly two minutes—gently reminding her audience that 40,000 children die every day from preventable causes. She sat down briskly at the end, turned to Rob and asked, "Did I do all right?" It was her first real appearance for UNICEF, Wolders recalls: "She knew little about what was expected of her and was pacing outside in her evening dress beforehand because it meant the world to her."

She had done all right, indeed.

Back at Macao's Mandarin Oriental Hotel, Audrey shed her evening gown in favor of jeans for a late-night meeting with Jack Glattbach, UNICEF's Regional Information Officer. ("Why did I think she looked better in T-shirt and jeans?" he wondered to himself.) She told him she was content in Switzerland and didn't really want to travel much but would be glad to help UNICEF again—"if they ask me." He made sure that she *was* asked, and over the next five years she often said, "It's all Jack's fault for getting me into this!" That, says Glattbach, "is the best thing I've been blamed for in all my years at UNICEF."[51] Indeed, he helped launch her on the course that would redefine her life.

Two months later in Tokyo, she was the "warmup act" for UNICEF director James P. Grant at a benefit concert by the World Philharmonic Orchestra—musicians from fifty-eight countries, under the baton of Giuseppe Sinopoli. It was there that she met Christa Roth, chief of UNICEF's Geneva office, who soon became one of her closest friends and helpmates.

"She had a tremendous following in Japan," Roth recalls. "It was mind-boggling. In Tokyo we organized a press conference in a normal hotel room. We thought maybe a few journalists would come, but there were tenfold—we had to change rooms to accommodate them all."[52]

For Roth, as for so many, Hepburn had been a role model. "I'm fifty-four," she says, "so when I was a teenager, it was the time of Brigitte Bardot—and I was as skinny as Audrey. I thought, if it's not wrong for her, why should I feel bad about looking like that?" From now on, back in Switzerland, it was Christa who assisted her in a hundred ways, taking care of logistical details and helping her fight for the things she wanted.

After her successes in Macao and Japan, requests began pouring in from the UNICEF committees of Turkey, Finland, Holland, Australia—"and in our enthusiasm, we accepted all of them," says Wolders, including one from Ireland. Dublin was a melancholy place, and after accepting the invitation, they had misgivings based on the memory of the previous sad visit with her father. But it turned out to be a cherished experience.

When they arrived there on September 30, 1988, the Irish committee chairwoman told her, "There's a lady who says she knows you from your childhood. We didn't want to tell her to go away." It turned out to be the elderly Greta Hanley, Audrey's nanny in Brussels half a century before—a woman she adored. Their emotional reunion was the first of many, through UNICEF, that brought her closer to her "extended family" all over the world.

Hepburn's commitment to UNICEF grew stronger, and quickly. "It's hard to be too late, to see a child that already has polio." she said. "It shouldn't happen anymore, [nor should] a child be a victim of war. That's why we have to get on with it. It is a question of time for so many children. They don't have time to wait." She often quoted Charles Dickens: "In the little world in which children have their existence, nothing is so finely perceived and so finely felt as injustice."[53]

In later years, the powerful images of Audrey Hepburn in the Third World would leave the rest of the world with the impression that she made dozens of UNICEF pilgrimages. In fact, over four years, there were just eight missions—but of increasingly profound impact.

THE FIRST JOURNEY: ETHIOPIA—MARCH 1988

Audrey's first field-trip assignment for UNICEF was designed "to attract attention, before it was too late" to the poorest country in the world. Ethiopia was in dire distress. Millions were starving from famine, drought and civil war. One in four Ethiopian children was dead by age five. Those who survived were grossly malnourished, many of them blind from vitamin A deficiency. The refugee centers, filled to overflowing, were potential death camps due to epidemics.

The logistics were complicated by many stops and unreliable transportation. "We flew across the country in comfortless, clattering transport aircraft," said UNICEF board member John Williams, who went along. Audrey would sit next to the pilot, gazing down at the dry riverbeds, naked mountains and occasional patches of green, teeming with people. "She was awed. By the second day she knew the name and background of each of the twenty people accompanying her—European pilots, Ethiopian minders, American journalists and UNICEF officials."[54]

One of those people was UN photographer John Isaac, a soft-spoken veteran of many such hardship missions, with whom she and Rob formed a deep bond. This was Isaac's fifth trip to Ethiopia in four years, and during their week together in Eritrea and Tigré—the areas hardest hit by drought and civil war—she soaked up every tidbit of information he gave her, educating herself on the technical problems of food transport and water.

Isaac explained to her that the drought was due to the lack of dams to hold rainwater, and that a new one was being constructed. Audrey wanted to see it.

"Ethiopians are very proud," says Isaac. "They don't want handouts. This was a very good program where they would do a day's work for a certain amount of grain. We watched thousands of people carrying water and rocks on their backs, mixing the mud and building this huge dam with their own hands. The pictures from there are very biblical."

Isaac had traveled with Harry Belafonte and Liv Ullmann and other fine UNICEF ambassadors, but Audrey and her sense of humor were different, he says: "I told her, 'When the plane lands, I want to get out first to get a shot of you.' I was nervous— it was my first big 'event' with her—and as I was getting out, my camera fell with the battery pack and wires and everything connected to me. Audrey was behind me and said, 'John, you dropped your—equipment. Well, thank God it's still attached. Can I get it up for you?' Everybody cracked up."[55]

The fact that Hepburn met John Isaac early on "is what colored much of Audrey's feelings towards UNICEF," says Rob Wolders. "He really inspired her. He spoiled us. We were looking for more people like that, and they don't exist."

Isaac, a native of India, had been one of the UN's most brilliant photographers for twenty years. His first assignment was the war in Lebanon; his second, the Vietnamese boat people, followed by ten years of work in Iran, Iraq, Kuwait and Ethiopia. His personality and philosophy had a profound impact on Audrey:

"For me, human dignity is more important than getting that 'great' picture," he says. "I try not to take anybody's dignity away. One of the boat people in Thailand was a little girl who was raped by twenty pirates, her father was shot, her mother committed suicide. I saw her washed up on the shore. A nurse said, 'She hasn't spoken a word. She just stares at me.'

"I didn't want to photograph her. I went back to the hotel, bought some chocolates. I had some Vietnamese music and brought back my tape recorder, sat next to her, and played the music for her. After about ten minutes, she put out her hand and I gave her some chocolates. To me, that was worth ten thousand pictures. I told some nuns, 'You have to rescue this girl,' and they took her to California. A lot of people said, 'That's not your job.' Well, I'm a human being first. I don't care about the Pulitzer prize."

Audrey, too, had to adjust to the emotional as well as physical stress, and to the political constraints of the job.

"Working with the UN is sometimes very frustrating," says Isaac, "because you're in the middle. You can't support this or that side. Initially, she was flustered by that. You want to sympathize. But she took a stand on a lot of things. She was so worried about her first UNICEF press conference."[56]

In preparation for that, back in Addis Ababa, "she was determined to master every nuance of the labyrinthine politics of war and drought," says John Williams, who spent hours drilling questions and answers with her."[57] Videotapes of the press conference show she was not only nervous but on the verge of tears—hands shaking visibly when she sipped a glass of water—as she tried to explain to the media what she had seen. In the end, she was powerfully articulate and moving.

The only one who thought she could have done better was Audrey herself. Everyone else sat up and took notice, including the Marxist government of Ethiopia, which found reason to criticize her, thus provoking a second round of international publicity during which she declared, "A child is a child is a child, whether his parents are Marxists or Nazis."

The challenge was just beginning. Preparing to leave her Addis Ababa hotel, she suddenly realized she had sent down the bags containing all of her clothes. She was in her underwear, recalls Rob, who obligingly gave her his raincoat, which hung down to her ankles. She wore it on the plane home and during her press conference at the Rome airport. Italy was the first stop of an exhausting postmortem press tour of America, Switzerland, Finland and Germany, talking about Ethiopia in as many as fifteen interviews a day. "I think," she said, with typical modesty, "it made people aware that there were needs."[58]

WHETHER IT WAS A TWO-MINUTE speech at the Oscars or a two-hour one for UNICEF, "it scares the wits out of me," she said.[59] "My stomach goes to pieces and my head starts to ache." She had such stage fright, says her daughter-in-law Leila, "that you could literally see her knees knocking behind the podium."[60] While accepting her Golden Globe award in 1990, "I was terribly concerned that the mike would pick up the thumping of my heart while I was speaking," she said. "My epithet will be, 'It's nerves what done her in,' as Eliza Doolittle would say."[61]

Even so, she was getting better at it fast, and at thinking on her feet. In her first BBC interview, asked for proof that UNICEF's food distribution efforts ever succeeded, she thought a moment and replied sweetly, "If a famine is *averted*, you don't hear about it, do you?"[62]

Cannily, she and Christa Roth began to refine her dealings with the press. "Many times," says Roth, "people would ask for an interview about UNICEF when they really just wanted to talk about movies. She would talk an hour about, say, Ethiopia and five minutes about films, but the story would be 10 percent UNICEF and 90 percent movies. It bothered her a lot. So we started to restrict the interviews to publications that gave her solid footage. It worked out quite well. She got a lot of a coverage."[63]

More coverage than any other UNICEF ambassador before or since. That convinced her to be even better prepared and to write all her own speeches. As her conscientiousness increased, so did her impact. She told a Congressional subcommittee:

"In Ethiopia, I went to the orphanage in Mecalee... five hundred children, whose parents died in the drought of 1985... which is run by Father Chasade of the Catholic Church. It was he who in desperation said, 'If you can't send me food for my children, then send me the spades to dig their graves.'"[64]

UNICEF, she said dramatically, chose to send the food.

"There is a science of war, but how strange that there isn't a science of peace," she declared, paraphrasing Maria Montessori. "There are colleges of war; why can't we study peace?"[65] She articulated that more passionately in replying to a question about how Ethiopia had affected her personally:

I have a broken heart. I feel desperate. I can't *stand* the idea that two million people are in imminent danger of starving to death, many of them children, [and] not because there isn't tons of food sitting in the northern port of Shoa. It can't be distributed. Last spring, Red Cross and UNICEF workers were ordered out of the northern provinces because of two simultaneous civil wars....

I went into rebel country and saw mothers and their children who had walked for ten days, even three weeks, looking for food, settling onto the desert floor into makeshift camps where they may die. Horrible. That image is too much for me. The "Third World" is a term I don't like very much, because we're all one world. I want people to know that the largest part of humanity is suffering, that starvation exists even in a wealthy country like America— which is scandalous, a true disgrace.... [66]

I think that, today, never has there been more suffering in more places all at once. At the same time, never has there been so much hope. We've had the greatest gift mankind could possibly give to children, which is "The Convention on the Rights of the Child." Two hundred and fifty thousand children die every week—last week, next week—and nobody really talks about it. It's the greatest shame and tragedy of our times. And it must stop.[67]

The Convention on the Rights of the Child was based on the "Declaration on the Rights of the Child," proclaimed by the UN in 1959, calling on all nations to guarantee children's rights to health, education and protection in time of war. It was to be adopted into national legislation everywhere. She talked it up wherever she went and confronted the cynicism head on. In New Zealand, for instance, a patronizing interviewer praised its idealism but doubted that politicians could ever be convinced to care and do something about it.

"If you and I are convinced, they're going to be convinced too," she shot back. "Somebody said to me the other day, 'You know, it's really senseless, what you're doing. There's always been suffering, there will always be suffering, and you're just prolonging the suffering of these children [by rescuing them].' My answer is, 'Okay, then, let's start with your grandchild. Don't buy antibiotics if it gets pneumonia. Don't take it to the hospital if it has an accident.' It's against life—against humanity—to think that way."[68]

THE SECOND JOURNEY: TURKEY—AUGUST 1988

Hepburn's next trip, to Turkey, coincided with an international children's festival there and a shift in UNICEF's agenda from food to health. The priority in Turkey was immunization against the six main child-killing diseases: measles, tuberculosis, tetanus, whooping cough, diphtheria and polio. UNICEF and the World Health Organization had set a joint goal of universal child immunization by 1990, and their high-gear efforts were now saving three million young lives each year.

Audrey called Turkey "the most lovely example" of UNICEF's ability to provide brilliant organizational skills in partnership with cooperative nations:

"We notified the government that their infant mortality was very high. The Turkish government sent a group to New York to study the program we had completed in Colombia. The group went back, and a total immunization program was planned in four months. The Turkish president and prime minister went on TV, the school teachers spoke from their desks, and the imams from their pulpits. The army gave us their trucks, the fishmongers gave their wagons for the vaccines, and once the date was set, it took ten days to vaccinate the whole country. Not bad."[69]

Not bad at all. Good consolation for the local TV programming in Ankara. "Because it was a state visit, they had an Audrey Hepburn festival," Rob Wolders recalls. "One night we turned on the television, and there was *My Fair Lady*. I had never seen it and was looking forward to it. But it was in Turkish. The combination of Audrey speaking in Turkish and Marni Nixon singing was too much. I had to turn it off."

THE THIRD JOURNEY: SOUTH AMERICA—OCTOBER 1988

Street children and education were the focus of her South American tour a few months later. In Venezuela and Ecuador, she later told Congress, "I saw tiny mountain communities, slums, and shantytowns receive water systems for the first time by some miracle—and the miracle is UNICEF. "I watched boys build their own schoolhouse with bricks and cement provided by UNICEF."[70]

Most intently, she studied projects designed to aid children living on the street. That situation appalled her as much as it did Roger Moore, her friend and fellow UNICEF colleague (she had helped to recruit him), who was now viewing the far worse "violence of neglect" in Brazil. "First they ignored the street kids," said Moore, "and now they've started killing them."

He had met thirteen-year-old prostitutes, living in the streets, who used the money they earned to buy toys. So relentlessly grim was his report that he felt obliged not to end it on a totally depressing note: "I get one dollar a year for this—a whole dollar—but I have to wait a year to get it. UNICEF is receiving that interest on that dollar, you realize."[71]

Audrey found it harder to leaven her remarks with humor. Her ferocity could be frightening. When she learned something shocking, she demanded that the world learn it, too. "Do you know how many street children there are in South America?" she would later ask in New York. "All over the world?... But especially in South America and India? It's something like a hundred million who live and die in the streets."[72]

THE FOURTH JOURNEY: CENTRAL AMERICA—FEBRUARY 1989

She had met many dignitaries on her previous trips but had not been drafted for "summit meetings" until now, on the most upbeat UNICEF journey she ever made, in Guatemala, Honduras and El Salvador. In Central America—while Colonel Oliver North covertly stoked Nicaragua's Contra war with arms from Iran—Audrey pleaded the case for children in many forums, but most remarkably in a series of meetings with the chief executives of Honduras, El Salvador and Guatemala.

"Bienvenida Audrey Hepburn," read hand-lettered signs all along the way, *"los niños te saludan!"* (Welcome—the children salute you!) She was everywhere at once, it seemed, weighing babies at a new maternal-care clinic, turning on the spigot for the first time at a mountain village's water project, handing out press awards for excellence in covering children's issues in Tegucigalpa. No frown troubles her features in the documentary footage—just joyous scenes of gorgeous, fairly healthy and happy children, whom she snatches up for hugs.

In flawless Spanish, she delivered a lovely message on breast-feeding to the television cameras: *"Soy Audrey Hepburn. Soy madre. La leche materna es el mejor regalo que una madre puede dar a su hijo. Es para toda la vida."**

The "summits" went flawlessly, as well. She charmed the presidential pants off Honduras's Jose Azcona Hoya and Guatemala's Roberto Carpio. Most touching was her meeting with Salvador's ailing President Napoleon Duarte, who died shortly afterward.

Having accomplished all that, she got the kind of reward she liked best: a private evening with Rob, her UNICEF companion Teresa Albanez, and her photographer-godchild, Victoria Brynner, Doris' daughter. Together they all attended a gathering in San Salvador, where Audrey sang and played the guitar with a group of local musicians. When the party was over, the adoring minstrels followed her outside and kept on singing. "They were still serenading her as we were driving off," says Wolders. "So much love for Audrey there."

Victoria Brynner grew up with Audrey and often photographed her, but never "officially." This was "a great opportunity for me to be with her in the context of her work," says Brynner, "and to watch her deal not only with the suffering people in the field but with all the UNICEF officials, the governments, the media, constantly bouncing from one to the other. It was so impressive to see how giving and patient she always was."

After one wrenching inspection of Quito's most poverty-stricken areas, the two women stopped into the magnicifent La Compañía church. "We stood there next to each other and held hands and each said our own little prayer," Victoria recalls. "After what we'd just seen, it was very moving. A few months later, on my birthday, she came to our house with

---

* "I'm Audrey Hepburn. I'm a mother. Mother's milk is the best gift that any mother can give to her child. It's for his whole life."

a little basket, and in the basket was a bird's nest she had found in her garden, and in the bird's nest was a little hand-painted paper bird, and under the bird was an unbelievable cross set with diamonds and rubies. The card said it was for that moment we spent in the church in Quito. I have worn it every single day."[73]

AS AN INSPECTOR IN THE field, the lady of fashion dressed down and traveled light: Two suitcases and a carry-on held all the jeans, sneakers, sweatshirts and Lacoste pullovers she required. For UNICEF, as for *Gardens of the World*, she pressed her own clothes in the hotels, did her own hair and makeup, and never made a late entrance. On the road, she needed no one to hold her hand, literally or figuratively, except Rob.

As a lobbyist in Washington, D.C., however, she reverted to type—and to nerves. On April 6, 1989, smartly attired in a sleeveless black Karl Lagerfeld dress, she was jittery, clinging to the arm of U.S. UNICEF Committee President Lawrence Bruce as she entered a Capitol conference room to testify before the House Select Subcommittee on Hunger.

As John Isaac had told her early on, UNICEF spokesmen were in a tricky position because they could not take political stands. But in the bellicose Reagan-Bush eighties, politics and economics were at the heart of most human disasters worldwide and could hardly be ignored. Walking that tightrope, the UN staff had devised the idea of a "1 percent for Development Fund" and was now trying to sell it to the world community. Audrey was one of its first and greatest saleswomen:

"Less than one-half of one percent of today's world economy would be the total required to alleviate the worst aspects of poverty and would meet basic human needs over the next ten years," she told the congressmen. "We cannot ignore the economic issues that have made the 1980s into a decade of despair....

"The heaviest burden of a decade of frenzied borrowing is falling not on the military nor on those foreign bank accounts nor on those who conceived the years of waste, but on the poor who are having to do without the bare necessities.... When the impact becomes visible in the rising death rates among children, then what has happened is simply an outrage against a large section of humanity. Nothing can justify it.... The burden of debt must be lifted to a degree where the developing countries can cope with debt repayment."[74]

It costs $5 to vaccinate a child for life, six cents to prevent death from dehydration, and eighty-four cents a year to stop a child from going blind. "How is it that governments spend so much on warfare and bypass the needs of their children, their greatest capital, their only hope for peace?"[75]

It was a strong political stand, carefully worded. UNICEF, she went on, was the one international organization with the infrastructure and diplomatic leverage to channel aid directly to children and not through governments.

When she finished, UNICEF executive director Jim Grant spoke bluntly to the committee of Audrey's import to the cause:

"At the heart of whether we succeed is public opinion.... It isn't the question of funding anymore. In the Sudan, it's public opinion that is going to keep the pressure on the two sides to allow the supplies to move.... Ms. Hepburn will be going to Sudan next week to keep world public attention on it. [With her,] we have a new capacity to talk to people. Television picks up a picture in the Sudan and says, 'Ms. Hepburn is there ... children are dying but there is still time to do something about it.' Last fall, the media weren't able to get in there. Then, you saw only the bodies of the dead four months later."[76]

It's just a six-minute drive from the Capitol to the White House, but a much greater distance psychologically. After her congressional appearance, Audrey and Rob were invited to a state dinner there for Israeli Prime Minister Shamir. "Bush was very considerate," Rob recalls. "He put Audrey on his left."

He was doing himself a favor, of course. But it gave Audrey a perfect chance to speak with him about what mattered to her. When she mentioned her forthcoming "emergency" trip to Sudan, he introduced her to Cable News Network's Bernard Shaw and suggested that his network ought to cover it. (Bush was an avid CNN fan.) Before leaving, Audrey arranged to come back for a private chat with the woman of the house, as Barbara Bush remembers:

Audrey came to call on me the next day to talk about her work with UNICEF. I had met her once before in Rome at a luncheon when George was vice president. Audrey felt passionately about two things, both of which mattered to me also: She loved children and became an advocate for young people in distress around the world; and she adored dogs.... She played with Millie's puppies, and I was slightly surprised that Millie let her pick them up without even a small protest.... How the world admired that lovely creature![77]

THE FIFTH JOURNEY: SUDAN—APRIL 1988

Just days after that White House visit, Hepburn and Wolders found themselves in Sudan to witness the start of a miraculous UNICEF-sponsored relief effort called "Operation Lifeline."

"Sudan is an outpost of despair, but it has astounding beauty," Rob recalls. "I remember Audrey looking down from the plane at where the Blue Nile and the White Nile branch out and saying she had this great feeling of gladness. It's wrong to think we'd go to a place like that and immediately be immersed in misery. There was a period of assimilation."

UNICEF's Jim Grant had been appointed special envoy to the Sudan and was largely responsible for the negotiations that led to Operation Lifeline. Its goal was to ferry food to southern Sudan, which was cut off from all aid because of the civil war. Audrey and Rob watched the first ship with food and medical supplies leave Khartoum for Kosti on the Nile.

The next day, while visiting a remote Sudanese refugee camp, Audrey noticed a fourteen-year-old boy lying on a dirt floor and asked what was wrong with him. The answer was terribly familiar: acute anemia, respiratory problems and edema, due to malnutrition. "That was exactly the same way I finished the war—that age, with those three things," she said, noting that even when fed, starving children often never recover from the neurological damage. "I thought, how strange to hear those same three things. But it was also a moment of glory for me, because just then a big UNICEF truck came by full of food and medicine."[78]

Be it famine in Ethiopia, civil war in El Salvador, or ethnic massacre in the Sudan, "I saw but one glaring truth: These are not natural disasters but manmade tragedies for which there is only one manmade solution—peace." Just in the past month of this most brutal civil war, "20,000 starving orphan boys have fled from the Sudan into Ethiopia," she said. "Many of them never make it. They either die of hunger on the way [or] drown in the river which divides the Sudan from Ethiopia."[79]

In the Sudan, with Rob's help, she would again employ her "summit" skills, as Wolders relates:

"There was a meeting arranged for Audrey, me and Sadique, the man in power, who didn't usually deal with UN people. But he wanted to see Audrey, and he was gracious to her. It was our intention to go to the refugee camp in El Mereim, where 16,000 people had died. Sadique sent his minister of health along with us, and we got to an area just on the border with the Christian south. From there we were supposed to go with the Moslem minister of health into rebel country, the city of Juba, which was totally surrounded by government troops. But they said they couldn't guarantee safety and they made us go back to Khartoum.

"It was very frustrating. We said we were willing to take a chance, but the UN officials overruled us. So rather than go home with our tail between our legs, we got a Red Cross plane to fly us from Khartoum to Nairobi—a night flight over Uganda—and then they sent one of rebel leaders to Kenya to fly us back into Sudan. It illustrated Audrey's determination. Without that corps of journalists along, we could speak our minds more bluntly to the leaders there, and we did. It produced some results.

"Some places we went to over the years were run-of-mill, but this was one of the truly exotic places we'd heard about as children—Khartoum. We smuggled in a bottle of scotch, by the way, since it was a Moslem country."

SOMETIMES IT GOT TO HER. "If everybody just decided to *do* something about it, we wouldn't be here *talking* about it," she said in frustration. She had to reinvent the wheel constantly—as at the Canberra Press Club, where the question was, "What do you *really* do for UNICEF?"

"My task is to inform, to create awareness of the needs of children," she replied politely, as if for the first time. "It would be nice to be an expert on education, economics, politics, religions, traditions and cultures. I'm none of those. But I am a mother and will travel."[80] UNICEF had only 2,000 paid employees, she said. It consisted mostly of volunteers, such as herself. "I fly around the world on tickets donated by airlines, stay in hotels free of charge—in great luxury, I might add."

It was a rueful inside joke at UNICEF that people so often congratulated her for her work with *UNESCO*. Over and over, she explained the difference between the two organizations, chiefly that "UNICEF has no permanent allocation. We get no funds from the UN. By definition, we are a *fund*, not an agency."[81]

Hepburn provided a phenomenal boost to the fund-raising campaigns of the national UNICEF committees everywhere. Also, every year between 1988 and 1992, she hosted with Roger Moore the *Danny Kaye International Children's Special* in Holland, which was broadcast worldwide and drew enormous donations.

"Jim Grant told me they got $1 million in contributions every time she made an appeal on Barbara Walters or wherever," says John Isaac. "She made such a huge impression."

Isaac and Hepburn had become important figures in each other's lives by then. After their Ethiopia trip, she had written to say how much she enjoyed traveling with him and the photos he had taken. She now told him Bangladesh was her next choice for a UNICEF visit, and she wanted him to come with her.

THE SIXTH JOURNEY: BANGLADESH—OCTOBER 1989

"Everybody was calling Bangladesh 'a basket case,'" Isaac says, "because of the constant mishaps they had with floods, famine—you name it. But when everybody else was throwing up their hands, Audrey said, 'I want to go there and be with them and promote their cause.' I thought that was amazing."

Together, he and Audrey and Rob first visited projects for poor children in Bangkok, then quickly moved on to Bangladesh.

"She traveled to every little corner," Isaac recalls. "In one town, she leaned over to me and said, 'John, do these people know or care who I am?' I said, 'You'd be surprised.' As we were talking, I heard this one man say to another, 'I think that is Miss Hepburn.' When I told her that, she turned around and asked, 'Do you know me?' The guy said, 'I have seen *Roman Holiday* ten times!' In the middle of Bangladesh!

"Often the kids would have flies all over them, but she would just go hug them. I had never seen that. Other people had a certain amount of hesitation, but she would just grab them. Children would just come up to hold her hand, touch her—she was like the Pied Piper."

Cole Dodge was the UNICEF representative in Bangladesh, and it was his job to show Audrey and Rob the health-related projects connected to UNICEF. At one stop, he recalls, a crowd surrounded Audrey—as always—when she stepped from her car:

"She smiled at the children, and some of them came forward to stroke her arm and hold her hands as we walked through the village. To the side of the path, just ahead, a small girl sat by herself under the shade of a coconut tree. The little one caught Audrey's attention, and she asked, 'Why doesn't she join the others?' Walking over, Audrey knelt down and spoke with her. Then, picking her up, she hugged her close. The child's legs, crippled by polio, dangled uselessly. Carrying the little one, Audrey walked towards us, her eyes filled with tears. None of the rest of us had taken notice of that child."[82]

A few weeks later, back in the United States on *Larry King Live*, a caller asked, "How do we know when we send money that it actually gets there?"

"I know it gets there because I've seen the results," she said. "UNICEF money goes straight to projects and never to governments.[83] I just came back from Bangladesh [where] contaminated water is the biggest killer of children. In the last eight years, we have sunk 250,000 tube wells there.... It's not enough to know there's been a flood in Bangladesh and 7,000 people lost their lives. *Why* the flood? What is their history? How are they going to survive?"[84]

Isaac was most struck by the fact that, at any given moment, "she dealt only with what she was doing. Audrey had no color, no race. She went to Bangladesh at a time when the main crisis was over, but it was still an ongoing thing. 'I want people to be reminded,' she said. Today, we forget what happened yesterday with all the satellite technology. Today you are here, tomorrow there, the next day, somewhere else. How soon people forget the previous tragedy. But she never did."

RISKS HAD TO BE WEIGHED before every trip—even to the United States. After the Pan-American disaster over Lockerbie, European fears of airline terrorism reached panic levels. But Audrey had agreed to a six-city American fund-raising tour for UNICEF, including Atlanta, where former president Jimmy Carter was to give her an award. She and Rob flew first to Los Angeles to see Connie Wald and there, at dinner one night, they met former ambassador Anne Cox Chambers and her good friend William Banks. Chambers, the publishing heiress and daughter of 1920 Democratic presidential nominee James M. Cox, turned out to be chairperson of the Atlanta UNICEF event—a pleasant coincidence with a pleasant outcome: She offered Hepburn and Wolders a "lift" in her private plane, to spare them another commercial flight.

"Audrey asked what time," recalls Chambers, "I said, 'Oh, around noon, but there's no hurry. Just come when it suits you.' When we arrived at noon, she was already there—this radiant creature standing at the top of the steps in the doorway with that lovely smile, saying, 'Welcome aboard your own airplane!' " As the plane was revving up, William Banks said half-facetiously, "I always say a prayer at takeoff," and Audrey replied, "Oh, I just hold Robbie's hand." The Hepburn-Wolders friendship with Chambers and Banks was instant: All four of them had not only UNICEF in common, but also gardens—and dogs.[85*]

At the Atlanta ceremony, Jimmy Carter presented her with her award and said, "When I was young, guess who I wanted to be? You may think Thomas Jefferson or Andrew Jackson—not at all. I wanted to be Humphrey Bogart or Fred Astaire or Cary Grant, I was so filled with envy of them being kissed by Audrey Hepburn." Audrey replied, "I'll fix that," and gave him a big kiss. They would often work together later on UNICEF causes.

William Banks was as impressed with Rob as with Audrey and, even more, with their relationship. "It was obvious that he adored her and she adored him," says Banks, a courtly southern gentleman. "I've never seen

---

* The following year, Anne chambers and Audrey were both honorees at the annual ASPCA gala in New York. "I was delighted to accept," Hepburn began her speech, "because, after all, I had dogs long before I had babies." She said she and Rob slept with their two Jack Russell terriers. Why? "Because we couldn't find a basket big enough for the four of us," she explained.

a better marriage, even though they were not married. When the cameras converged on Audrey, Rob always stepped out of range in the most graceful way. He basked in the admiration people felt for her. He was self-effacing but not self-abnegating, and she looked up to him so."[86]

Rob was always there, says John Isaac, in every way:

"She would see him running around and say, 'Isn't he wonderful? I don't know what I'd do without my Robbie.' Always 'my Robbie.' Day in and out, he made sure everything was right." Audrey often declared, "I could never have done all this work with UNICEF without Robbie.... He does a million things."[87]

Jeffrey Banks summed it up: "The overwhelming thing about Audrey was that men wanted to protect and shield her from all the bad in the world. That was my instinct at age eleven, for instance. But Rob's the one who truly *did* it."[88]

Wendy Keys enjoyed watching their "sense of playfulness" together: "At the Peninsula Hotel after they'd just flown in, Rob and I were talking across a coffee table. She was busy unpacking, but he said, 'Audrey, could we move these flowers? I can't see Wendy.' She swept them away and then plunked down a teeny little flowerpot instead and said, 'Now can you see Wendy?' She took advantage of the moment and the prop. It was delicious.

"Another time, she and I were gossiping with our legs swung over our respective sofas, yakking away. Rob came out of the shower in a terry-cloth robe and sat down to reveal a beautiful leg. She winked at me, and the two of us started to giggle. One of those moments—that constant twinkle in her eye.

"They shared a lot of things—their commitment to other people and to UNICEF. Rob's own enormous UNICEF commitment was rarely acknowledged, and he didn't want it to be. But he was certainly the best man in her life. The others were appalling, or normal, depending on your point of view. What a wonderful thing that she and Rob found each other."

The press, meanwhile, kept asking the same old question: Were they going to get married?

"Why bother?" she replied to one reporter. "It's lovely this way... more romantic. It means we're together because we want to be, not because we have to be. It's a slight difference, but maybe it's a very good one."[89]

THE SEVENTH JOURNEY: VIETNAM—OCTOBER 1990

Of all Audrey Hepburn's remarkable UNICEF journeys, the least remembered is her visit to Vietnam. Unlike the others, it received little coverage except in France, whose ties to Vietnam were historic. For America and the American media, more recent wounds were still unhealed. Audrey was too apolitical to get the virulent criticism dealt to Jane Fonda for going to Vietnam during the war itself. Instead, she got the silent treatment.

The Vietnam trip had been suggested in 1987 by UNICEF's Jack Glattbach, who now accompanied her on what turned out to be a highly useful mission. As in Bangladesh, the main purpose was to get the government behind the UNICEF-supported immunization and water programs. And as in Bangladesh, Audrey went everywhere.

At Mo Vang Commune in Hoang Lien Son Province, the children handed her flowers and performed a martial-arts demonstration in her honor. "How do you say thank-you in Vietnamese?" we hear her ask in the video documentary footage. "Ka-mun," she is told—and thereafter uses it freely. A child hands her a rose, whose stem pricks Audrey's finger. "All roses have thorns," she smiles. Priming a new pump, she splashes water on her face and proudly proclaims that UNICEF supplied the materials but that the wells "have all been made by the Vietnamese themselves."

The tour was going so well that, midway, Glattbach briefed her on Vietnam's unique "structural adjustment" policies and asked if she would emphasize that in the documentary they were shooting. "Oh, that's too complicated for me," she replied. "Really, if I don't understand it, I can't speak it." Glattbach said fine, never mind. But soon after, he recalls, "watched by a few hundred Vietnamese villagers and with absolutely no 'fluffs,' she spoke four minutes to camera and covered every point from the discussion she 'didn't understand.' It was one of the best summaries I ever heard. It got seven minutes on ABC prime-time news and incredible TV pickup around the world."[90]

The video footage shows it clearly: Everywhere she goes in Vietnam, Hepburn is greeted lovingly and the mood is upbeat, with no recriminations about the war. She meets the heads of several unions, all of them women. But her most important meeting is the last—a "summit" indeed, with General Vo Nguyen Giap, Vietnam's deputy prime minister and great war hero, the field commander most responsible for defeating the mighty United States.

"This general and UNICEF—we have a lot in common," she said formally, in his presence. "We have both fought many battles for children. I just hope we will be as triumphant as you have been, and conquer all the children's diseases."

Giap said UNICEF's help was crucial to a country that had suffered so many years of war. In response, she said, "I find your country miraculous, and I think UNICEF has never had a more ideal situation to take care of children because you always have given children the priority in spite of war.... Your education and literacy are very high, and immunization almost completed."

Clearly charmed, General Giap smiled and said, "You have so many praises! But we feel we have so much more work to do."

AUDREY'S OWN WORK TOOK MANY forms, including the artistic. A UNICEF Christmas card these days was adorned with her sketch of an Ethiopian mother carrying a baby, simply but beautifully done. The original was donated to the Finnish UNICEF committee and sold at auction in Helsinki for $16,500.

"It was a fund-raiser for camels," says Rob Wolders. "For the vaccination campaign in Chad, they used camels with solar-energy panels in order to keep the vaccine refrigerated. They could buy a lot of camels with that $16,500."

The following year, she launched the UN's "Rights of the Child" postage-stamp series in Geneva with a first-day philatelic envelope of her own design.

In August 1990, she went to Oslo, Norway, to cohost the "Concert for Peace," sponsored by the Elie Wiesel Foundation, with Jimmy Carter, François Mitterrand and Nelson Mandela among the participants. Audrey introduced Václav Havel and James Galway, and conductor Lukas Foss led the Oslo Philharmonic. Havel made a great impact on her and, soon after, she deftly worked his significance into her remarks at UNICEF's Universal Child Immunization kickoff ceremony in Rome:

"I didn't think I'd live to see the end of [the Cold War]. I had grown up with it and it was part of all our lives. Then the world changed dramatically. Like the Berlin Wall and the Soviet empire, the old order has come tumbling down. We now have something that is so rare in the course of civilization: a second chance....

"UNICEF and the World Health Organization [have] achieved their goal of universal child immunization by 1990. This is the miracle of this decade. It does not mean we have immunized every child. It does mean that 80 percent of the world's one-year-olds have been immunized against the six major child-killing diseases—four out of five children on the whole planet!... In 1974, only 5 percent of the developing world's children were vaccinated.

"The day people can count on having two children survive, they will have two instead of having nine in hopes that two will live.... China,

Indonesia, Thailand and Mexico have proven that population can be slowed [through] education and family planning. Letting children die is not the remedy to overpopulation."[91]

The immunization campaign had been the most monumental global mobilization in the history of UNICEF—if not the history of the world. But ironically, she told Harry Smith on *CBS This Morning*, the immunization rate in America was *decreasing*. In North Africa, 79 percent of all children were now vaccinated against measles; the figure was 58 percent in Houston and 52 percent in Miami! When her time was up, she would not let Smith cut her off. "May I tell you one more thing?" she pressed. "Rotary International has raised three-quarters of a billion dollars for immunization over ten years—an extraordinary example of what people can do."

A sweet smile of triumph crossed her face: She had managed to slip in one last plug.[92]

In view of those measles statistics and the fact that one in five American children lives in poverty, Smith asked if we should be more concerned with our own kids, rather than the world's. "I think we can do both," she replied. "Sure, we take care of our own children first. Charity begins at home. But there's no reason why we can't have love or time or money or food for children in Africa.[93] It's the endless wars that have destroyed what we've tried to do [there]. Adults fight and children die. Peace is what I'm pleading for, because until there's peace we won't be able to construct."[94]

That was the message she took to Washington once again in June 1991 for her second congressional appearance, at the invitation of senators Philip Leahy of Vermont and Nancy Kassebaum of Kansas, to urge a boost in aid for Africa.

"We tried to plan a time when she and I could both be in Africa together," recalls Senator Kassebaum, "but we never could get it worked out. She was very shy, and she looked very frail. She did such a tremendous job of calling attention to the plight of children in ways that nobody else could."[95]

THE LAST JOURNEY: SOMALIA—SEPTEMBER 1992

Somalia, torn to shreds by war and famine, was hell on earth —eight million people in a land the size of Texas, most of them starving to death. Hepburn had wanted to go there a year earlier but the New York office thought other assignments more urgent and Somalia too unsafe. Now, as she and Rob left Switzerland, Somalia was still on the back pages of the papers. But Audrey Hepburn's last mission was about to rivet the world.

"Apocalyptic," she called it. "I walked into a nightmare.... I have seen famine in Ethiopia and Bangladesh, but I have seen nothing like this—so much worse than I could possibly have imagined. I wasn't prepared for this. It's so hard to talk about because it's unspeakable."[96]

Among many images that haunted her was the first, from the air, as they flew into Kismayu from Nairobi over the desert:

"The earth is red—an extraordinary sight—that deep terra-cotta red. And you see the villages, displacement camps and compounds, and the earth is all rippled around them like an ocean bed. And those were the graves. There are graves everywhere. Along the road, around the paths that you take, along the riverbeds, near every camp—there are graves everywhere."[97]

Kismayu's huge displaced-persons camp held 20,000 people, but it took a while for it to dawn on Audrey that there was something missing. "There were no babies and practically no infants, because they are the most fragile," she said.[98] "They were just all snuffed out like candles."[99] At the feeding center in Baidoa, "One of the first sights I saw was that they were loading the bodies of that night onto a truck, and most of them were very small. Just one night's dead. Around a hundred. Children were sitting around waiting to be fed, but they were beyond wanting food. Some of them had to be more or less force-fed with little tiny spoonfuls. They are just totally spent."[100]

Many of the children and adults were maimed. Those who could still walk looked like ghosts, caught between the worst drought in history and a horrifying civil war that had destroyed whole families, whole villages— the whole country. There were no highways, no phones, no sanitation. You didn't need a visa to get in because there was no government to care. "There's nothing left," Hepburn said. "The cattle are dead, the crops are gone, whatever there was has been looted. Anarchy. It's a country without a government—a mayhem of marauding bandits who are likely to hold up a convoy or loot a storehouse.[101]

"This is the first in history that a country has been totally held together by individuals, by relief workers, these incredible, heroic people [from] Save the Children, Care, Oxfam, Médecins Sans Frontières. But there are very few of them."

Hepburn's presence in Somalia coincided with that of her journalist friend Anna Cataldi, who confirmed Audrey's assessment in the story she sent back to Milan:

"The volunteer workers with Médecins Sans Frontières [Doctors Without Borders] look at us with dazed expressions. Clearly, they are in a bad way. Malaria, amoebas, and now that they've had so much contact with blood, they are testing them for AIDS as well. These brave people stayed in Somalia even during the bombardments, when everyone else had left."[102]

The brighter side was that food was now arriving under the protection of UN peacekeepers and the U.S. Navy. Audrey was profoundly moved during a visit to the USS *Tarawa* aircraft carrier and its 2,400 sailors and Marines. "We were there for less than an hour and at the end were handed a check for $4,000, which the boys had collected," she said, weeping at the recollection. "You see, there I go again. But I don't want people to feel helpless. Everything is needed—blankets, clothes. The rains are coming now. Rain brings more death. In one camp where one night the death toll was sixty, it rose to over one hundred the next night because of the rain, because they're so fragile, and the chill—it's just too much for them."[103]

Bryant Gumbel on the *Today* show later asked if, in view of the anarchy, any amount of assistance was more than just a Band-Aid?

"Survival means much, much more than a Band-Aid," she said. "I wouldn't call a good doctor that saves your child from dying a Band-Aid. You may say that only tiny numbers of people can be helped. But the numbers are getting bigger. I go through my soul-searching. What can I do? What am I going to go and do there? But for all of us there's something we can do. It's true you can't take care of 1,000. But finally, if you can save one, I'd be glad to do that."

Among her challenges was to try to explain a complex colonial history—the difference between Somalia and Somaliland, for example, so named by the territory's Italian and British conquerors, respectively. "Are we not reaping the mess we made so many years ago when we enriched ourselves?" she said. "We didn't do a hell of a lot for those people, did we? That's why it's right that we do now."[104]

Audrey was asked not to dwell on that with the press, as UNICEF was now getting money from both the Italian and British governments. But Cataldi was able to be more fierce about the politics of it: "We Italians are responsible for Somalia," she wrote, as a result of which, hundreds of thousands of people were now dying "without even knowing *why* they are dying. They can't comprehend the ocean of rhetoric surrounding them, because this people of poets doesn't know how to read. Illiteracy in Somalia is the highest in the world: 95 percent."[105]

Why had the world been so slow to react? Audrey made a telling comparison. "People in Florida complained bitterly when aid took five days to get to the area hit by the hurricane," she said. "We've always been too late. In Ethiopia—a million people were dead before the BBC ever showed those pictures. In the Sudan, a quarter of a million died. Perhaps we're too late in Yugoslavia.... You could not get into Somalia to know really what was going on—to get inland and see the extent of the devastation.... You can't show pictures or write stories until you can go there and tell the world about it.[106] I came to Somalia because there cannot be enough witnesses."

Before leaving Africa, she held a press conference in Nairobi on September 22 and then granted a private interview to Nairobi TV reporter Katherine Openda—perhaps the most poignant she ever gave. "Somalia is one of the worst tragedies ever," she said. "It has gone over the edge. I want to be very careful how I say this. I don't want to sound overly dramatic. But you really wonder whether God hasn't forgotten Somalia."

Openda asked how she personally coped with it, and she replied, "Perhaps I don't. I give in sometimes. It is heartbreaking.... You never walk away from it, ever again. It's an image you carry with you for the rest of your life."

Hepburn's Somalia mission was followed by press conferences in London, Geneva and Paris and a host of television appearances in the United States. Not least of her skills was that she could speak with reporters in a variety of languages. More than any other, this round of interviews generated an unprecedented amount of international coverage and captivated the world. In all of them, she looks a bit tired but otherwise healthy, betraying no hint of the fact that she had just fifteen weeks to live.

Some of the news media, flippantly but fondly, called her "Mother Teresa in designer jeans." Columnist Liz Smith was one of the first to refer to her as "Saint Audrey." Sally Jessy Raphael recalled the day she appeared on Raphael's program to talk about Somalia: "The people who work with me are pretty tough cookies. But during the interview with Audrey, [everyone] showed such love and such respect. The crew lined up afterward and she went down the line shaking hands. I've never seen anything like it. Those hardened men and women almost wept. It was as if they knew they would never see her again."[107]

Shortly afterward, the United States military went into Somalia in full force. "She was very glad when they did," says Christa Roth. "I think that was something she prompted."

NEVER BEFORE IN FILM HISTORY had so great a star lent herself so vigorously to such an urgent crusade. But the toll was enormous. "She suffered terribly inside," said Elizabeth Taylor. When she saw the things she did in Somalia, "she didn't reflect that to the children," says Roger Moore. "She hid from them what was going on inside her. It doesn't do to show a person who is suffering that you're terribly upset by it."[108]

She spoke of that agonizing problem herself:

"There's this curious—embarrassment or timidity that comes over one when you walk into a feeding center like that. I feel I shouldn't be there. I think I should leave them alone. It's like walking into somebody's room who is dying, and only the family should be there. [You long] to pick up one of those children and give it some kind of warmth.... They're so frail that I worry I am going to break their little body and—and it's unbearable. It just is so totally unacceptable to see small children die in front of your eyes."

Somalia was the worst. "She came back and said, 'I've been to hell,'" says her son Sean, "and every time she spoke about it, she had to relive it. Nothing ever prepared her for going to a camp and meeting a little kid and coming back the next day and he wasn't there anymore. You're supposed to go back to your hotel room and drink bottled water? Get on a plane and go back to your regular life? It throws your whole world out of balance."

In the end, says Anna Cataldi, "she had this rage. The more she saw, the more rage she had. In Somalia, she was really furious with what she constantly was seeing."[109]

Audrey used the same word: "I'm filled with a rage at ourselves. I don't believe in collective guilt, but I do believe in collective responsibility."[110] Buckminster Fuller, the great philosopher-inventor, once said, "Politics is simply a function of the inequitable distribution of food and other basic life necessities." It was Hepburn's principle as well.

"Taking care of children has nothing to do with politics," she would say. "Politics has nothing to do with one's helping a dying child. Survival, that's what it's about.[111] ... I think perhaps with time, instead of there being a politicization of humanitarian aid, there will be a humanization of politics."

She and Rob were "closet politicians" in many ways. During the Gulf War, while most Americans were tying yellow ribbons on their mailboxes and celebrating the fact that only seventy-five Americans died, Hepburn and Wolders were concerned about the enormous brutality and the real statistics—concealed by both Saddam Hussein and George Bush—that 150,000 Iraqis, mostly civilians and many of them children, were killed in the American bombings.

A week after that conflict began, Audrey and Rob attended a meeting of the UNICEF national committees in Geneva, where Jim Grant spoke optimistically about what could be done for Iraqi children once the war was over.

"He didn't talk about the horror of the war or what the overall results might be from a historical perspective," Wolders recalls. "We were aghast. It was as if he were talking about Grenada. Audrey was as close to depression as I'd seen her over the whole situation, and when it came her turn to speak, she said it was UNICEF's duty to speak out against the injustices that *caused* such misery, and not simply to help out after the damage was done. There wasn't a single person who didn't come up to thank her. They thought there was something wrong with Jim for making no mention of the significance of the war, which we felt was going to interfere immensely with UNICEF's work."

In 1992, when asked to identify UNICEF's single greatest problem, Hepburn's one-word answer was, "War." Currently, she said, "the developing countries spend about $150 billion on arms each year. Meanwhile, the five permanent members of the UN Security Council sell 90 percent of the world's arms."[112]

She was no figurehead ambassador. "The work Audrey does for UNICEF is imperative for us," said Lawrence E. Bruce, Jr., the president of the United States Committee for UNICEF. Under Bruce's leadership, the U.S. Committee had more than doubled its fund-raising revenue, from $18 million in 1985 to $46 million in 1992. Audrey was extremely fond of him.[113]

"He was very warm and generous," says Jill Rembar, who worked for him for four years. "He had much to do at UNICEF, but Audrey always came first with him because she was so important to fund-raising, and because, personally, he just adored her."

Bruce died at forty-seven, on Christmas Eve 1992, of AIDS.

Rembar remembers the video footage of Audrey's first UNICEF trip with Bruce, to Ethiopia: "Audrey was walking around the refugee camps, reaching out to people. Emaciated babies, flies on their eyes. She's picking them up, kissing them, without knowing what diseases they might have. I said to Rob, 'It looks like Audrey didn't care what was the matter with them. She had no thought for herself.' Rob said, 'Well, you'd be the same.' A chill went through me. I thought, 'I don't think so.' But that's how he was—and that's how she was, too."[114]

THE HORROR OF SOMALIA WAS indelible. But, even so, it would be wrong to think that Audrey Hepburn saw only misery in her last years. "It wasn't all heartache," says Rob. "We weren't endlessly traveling for UNICEF. We'd always come back to the haven at home. UNICEF took over a certain part of our lives, but that didn't mean there wasn't time for the other things we enjoyed. In the last year, we spent a great deal of time in Gstaad in the mountains, where Audrey had a small condominium-chalet. We had missed going there for a few years, but during that summer, Audrey was bursting with energy and we took walks that we had planned to take for years."

Michael Tilson Thomas remembers one such occasion, just three weeks before she left for Somalia, when he visited Audrey in between performances with the London Symphony Orchestra on its tour of Switzerland:

> She took an immense delight in having a quiet dinner with friends and saying, 'Oh, it's still light, let's go for a walk'—a walk which was off the roads, down the cow tracks, up and down, over and across everything, very swift. Not exactly a leisurely stroll. She liked to *move*, very much appreciating each environment she came to—the smell of the flowers, the wonderful disorder of a harvested field —and she got you to appreciate it as well.
>
> Those walks were wonderful. She talked about her friends and her concern for them, for me—was I working too hard? She was aware of the enormous pressure that people in 'the business' are under. She felt that even people who seemed to be perfectly fine were in danger psychologically. She was always looking at everyone and thinking, "Are you okay? Is there any way I can help?"[115]

Perhaps due to Thomas's influence, she had undertaken a recording project of Saint-Saëns's *Carnival of the Animals* and Ravel's *Mother Goose Suite* for Dove Audio Tapes in May 1992—her last professional endeavor. The result was *Audrey Hepburn's Enchanted Tales*, conducted by Lalo Schifrin and hailed by *Publishers Weekly* as "a perfect introduction to classical music."[116] Its proceeds went to the ASPCA.

"Audrey was a great cutup—very impish and playful," says Wolders. "It's a quality you find in children and in puppies, which might explain why she was so drawn to animals—and perhaps had more trust in animals than in human beings. Sometimes when she would show a great deal of love for someone on whom I felt it was wasted, I'd say, 'Don't you expect something in return?' She would say, 'No. My love for them doesn't mean I expect anything back. It's like with an animal.'"[117]

John Isaac recalled that, "no matter where we went, even in Bangladesh, she would say, 'Oh, look at those pooches!' She'd be reminded of her puppies at home. She loved animals, people, trees—she basically just loved *life*."

The catalyst for her involvement with *Carnival of the Animals* was Roger Caras, president of the American Society for the Prevention of Cruelty to Animals. He had met her in 1991 when she flew in to New York to attend an ASPCA fund-raiser. Later, pianist Mona Golabek asked if he would put her in touch with Audrey for the *Carnival* recording, and he did. It would win a Grammy award. Caras's fondness for her is boundless:

> Her desire for privacy was very real. She didn't want to live like Madonna. Once I walked down a hallway at the St. Regis Hotel with her, and in all

my years working with the press, I'd never been so blinded. I'd never seen photographers jump on someone as when Audrey Hepburn walked in that room in New York City. She was on my arm and I had to steady her. About five hundred flash bulbs went off in our faces. They went crazy. I never saw that kind of adulation.

She had a quality I found in Eleanor Roosevelt. When Audrey said to you, 'How are you, dear?' she looked in your eyes and wanted an answer. It was not a form of salutation. It was a question from someone who cared. It was that one-on-one quality that electrified everyone. When Audrey was talking or listening to you, you possessed her totally and she possessed you. There were differences between her and Eleanor, but they both built instant bridges to anyone they were with. What they wanted was your *soul*.[118]

BY SOME ACCOUNTS, AUDREY FIRST started to suffer from abdominal pain and colitis in the summer of 1992—before leaving for Somalia—but refused to heed her Swiss doctors' advice to go in for tests and, once in Somalia, "kept clutching her stomach and wincing in pain."[119] Rob Wolders denies it: "We had no idea Audrey was sick when we went to Somalia. There were no warning signs of illness until we'd been back several weeks."

It is true that, in some of the photographs, Audrey looks almost as thin as the starving children she is holding. But in her subsequent European and American press conferences, she appeared to be fine and there seemed no cause for alarm.

With Somalia behind, she had returned to Switzerland with Rob for a few weeks before setting off again for the United States in October to honor two long-standing engagements, one at the George Eastman House in Rochester and the other in New York two days later. Following that, they planned to spend ten days in the Caribbean on a much-needed holiday.

As she wanted to see Sean, they flew first to California for a short stay with Connie Wald. "The pain became intense in Los Angeles," Rob recalls. "We rushed her to the doctor and she underwent every conceivable test. But they couldn't find anything and they said it would be all right to travel. They knew it was important to us. Perhaps it shouldn't have been that important."

The events in Rochester, October 24 and 25, 1992, were rather more grueling than either she or Rob had expected. On the first evening, she met with the press at six o'clock—looking pained during the photo session—and attended a long dinner and social afterward, which began at eight and was still going on when she and Rob left much later in the evening.

She rallied the next night for the presentation of the Eastman Award, following a screening of *Breakfast at Tiffany's*. Aware that she was in some pain, Eastman director James Enyeart had proposed limiting the postfilm question-and-answer session to half an hour. It was agreed that Rob would give Audrey a sign when the half hour was up. She looked frail in her somber black satin Givenchy gown. But she got caught up in the spirit of the event, buoyed by a pleasant surprise midway and then by a series of intelligent questions on Somalia. When Rob signaled her that the half hour was up, she didn't want to stop and kept going.

The surprise took the form of an old pal. A woman in the audience stood up and asked if Audrey remembered the gentleman sitting next to her. Audrey stared in amazement: "Yes, absolutely! Of course I remember you! My God, you haven't changed a bit! Nick Dana, ladies and gentlemen, a fabulous dancer! We danced together in *High Button Shoes* in 1948!... You were awfully good, flipping across that stage at the Hippodrome!"

Dana recalls that "Rob was crouched down the whole time on the side of the organ, checking on her, waiting to see if she got too weak." But her adrenaline was flowing, and she was determined to make everyone happy and answer all the questions she could—including a nasty one from a man demanding to know why she had left the previous night's event so quickly.

"Forgive me for leaving early last night," she said, "but I'm still very jet-lagged."

That was partly true. "She didn't want to say, 'I'm also in great pain,'" says Rob. "Nobody knew how ill she was—how could they? I didn't, either. It was quite heroic what she did that night. They never had such a turnout and couldn't accommodate everyone in the [Dryden] Theater. They had to use the ballroom, with a closed-circuit TV, and Audrey made it a point at the end to go to the other hall and greet the people there as well."

The next day, a call came from the doctors in Los Angeles saying that the test results indicated Audrey had an amoeba. She was given a prescription—essentially, a massive purge—which made her feel so terrible that she stopped taking it after the first few pills. They went on to New York City, where she did several more interviews and accepted a Maria Casita Award from Ralph Lauren at the Plaza Hotel. In just twenty-four hours, they were to leave for Antigua. But her pain became so intense during dinner that they canceled the holiday and decided to fly back to Los Angeles for urgent medical attention.

The following morning on their way to the airport, despite her pain, Audrey insisted on stopping first at Larry Bruce's apartment for a brief visit. He was dying, and she knew it.

GUILT AND HINDSIGHT GO HAND in hand.

"People said Audrey knew she was ill, but I absolutely know she didn't," says Anna Cataldi. "She had a routine checkup in August in Geneva, including a colonoscopy, *before the trip to Somalia*, and they said she was okay."

Cataldi had her own Somalia assignment for *Epoca* magazine in Milan, and for the rest of August, she and Audrey spoke frequently on the phone about what they had to do to prepare:

"Audrey did all the vaccinations—even meningitis. I did only yellow fever and tetanus, but she did everything. If a person knows she's sick, she would not go through all those vaccinations. Audrey led a healthy life, lived in the country, went to bed early. She was very careful. We were not protective enough towards her because she was always so healthy. People didn't think there was any reason to worry about her."[120]

At the beginning of October, Cataldi stopped by Audrey's room in Nairobi's Intercontinental Hotel to say farewell before she left Africa for her press obligations in Europe. "When I hugged her," Anna recalls, "I was scared. I had a shiver. She said, 'War didn't kill me, and this won't either.' But I had the feeling that sooner or later, war kills you. She was so skinny. I felt something was really wrong."

In their last conversation there, Cataldi recalls, "She told me what shocked her more than anything was Kismayu, because every child was dead. She said, 'I have nightmares. I cannot sleep. I'm crying all the time.' She had seen a lot of terrible things with UNICEF, but she broke in Somalia. I went back in a state of shock myself."[121] John Isaac, too, felt "it took a heavy toll on somebody as sensitive as Audrey," adding that "I'm still recovering from Rwanda. I had to go for therapy. I couldn't function. I was totally stunned."

Cataldi claims Audrey's beloved maid Giovanna "hated UNICEF" for its harmful impact on Audrey's health. "Andrea Dotti also felt it was UNICEF's fault in a way," Cataldi says, "because when Audrey started to look bad, everybody just said, 'Oh, she looks terrible because she is emotionally stressed.' Robert once asked me, 'Do you think I made a mistake in letting her go?' I told him, 'You didn't make her go. She had a need to go. She would have gone even if she had known that she had only a year to go.' She told me, 'I have this obsession because of the children.'"

In a dark corner of the New York restaurant where she is recounting those last days, Anna Cataldi kneads her handkerchief and takes a minute to compose herself before concluding:

"I witnessed a human being—the famous Audrey Hepburn—at the moment she had everything she wanted. She finally had the right man. She had a beautiful home. She said, 'I would like to take a year and enjoy

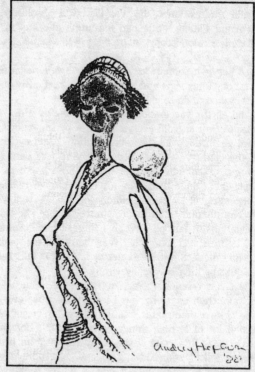

Audrey Hepburn's drawing of an Ethiopian mother and
child, 1990 UNICEF card.

my garden, my house, Robbie, my children.... I worked since I was twelve
years old. Now it's time to rest.' "

Doris Brynner expresses a similar view:

"She certainly did her job. She did get everything a human being could
do for UNICEF. It was even more physically exhausting than making
movies and much more emotionally involved. Whenever she came back
here to Switzerland, all she wanted was to stay at home. She was going
to give up the United Nations. She was tired—emotionally and physically
drained."[122]

To Alan Riding of *The New York Times* Paris bureau, Audrey said, "I
decided to do as much as possible in the time that I'm still up to it. Because
I'm running out of gas.... I've done it on a constant basis because I know
I cannot keep it up for long."[123]

CHAPTER 11

Farewell

"Audrey [had] grace and manners—things
you cannot take a course in. She could say
something risqué, but the way she did it
had an elegance that you could not, under
any circumstances, mistake for Madonna
reading the line. What is needed to really
become a star is an extra element that God
gives or doesn't give you. You cannot
learn it. She just was blessed. God kissed
her on her cheek, and there she was."

BILLY WILDER

UDREY HEPBURN, AT SIXTY-THREE, was running out of gas.
In Los Angeles, Sean and Rob immediately checked her into
Cedars-Sinai Medical Center, where three days later, on November
2, 1992, she underwent surgery. A malignant tumor required the partial
removal of her colon and a hysterectomy. The cancer had begun in her
appendix—extremely unusual—and then formed a vise around the colon.
The situation was quite serious, but her physicians were initially optimistic.
"There is a strong feeling," said a hospital spokesman, "that surgeons
removed all of the malignancy and that none of her organs were com-
promised."

The tabloids sensationally claimed otherwise. *The National Enquirer* said
her cancer could not be treated and that she only had three months to
live.

"I spoke with her after the operation," said Hubert de Givenchy. "She
was dumbfounded that she had cancer. She had been convinced that she
had contracted a virulent amoebic infection during her work in [Somalia].
She was so totally loved that I never stopped hearing from friends—and
strangers—who knew of such and such a doctor who could save her. 'Go
see him,' they would say. 'We're all going to fight this together.'"

Luca flew from Rome to Los Angeles. He and Sean and Rob felt the same, to the point of denial: They would all somehow find a way to lick it.

Audrey's own reaction was colorful and controversial, under the circumstances. According to a family member, when told she had cancer, she just said stoically, "Oh, shit." Mel Ferrer denies that and says Sean does too. Wolders says, "I remember more than anything, not what she said, but her trying to make it easier for us by trying to make light of it."[1] Later, she once broke down and asked Sean, "Where am I going to get the courage?"[2] But most of the time she was tremendously brave.

Among those rallying to her cause was Leonard Gershe, who thought humor might be the best medicine:

"When she was in the hospital, I spoke to Rob and he said, 'If they'd only stop sending flowers, each one vying with the next for the bigger arrangement. There's no room. She barely knows who sent what.' I wanted, if I could, to make her laugh, so I sent her Madonna's *Sex* book with a card saying, 'Flowers fade away, but great works of art live forever.' Later, she called me: 'Lenny, you made me the most popular patient in the hospital. Doctors I never heard of were stopping in. Luca will not get off my bed.' Sending it to Lana Turner wouldn't have been funny. But for Audrey, it was funny—like sending it to Queen Elizabeth."[3]

But her condition deteriorated with shocking speed. Just a day or so after the initial surgery, it was learned that the cancer had spread to her stomach. A medical team at that point implanted a Hickman catheter in her chest to administer chemotherapy and painkillers. She had a strong desire to leave the hospital and try to recuperate at Connie Wald's, which, toward the end of November, she was allowed to do.

"I couldn't believe she was so ill," says R. J. Wagner, who initialized their conversations in more ways than one. "To the very last, I'd call her up and say, 'A?' She'd say, 'R? Are you okay?' I'd say, 'Fine. I love you so much.' She'd say, 'I love you too. Goodbye, R.' I'd say, 'Goodbye, A.'"[4]

Rob and Sean asked the doctors not to tell Audrey the extent of the disease—certainly not that it was terminal. In fact, they themselves were not aware of the full truth. "*The National Enquirer* bribed someone in the operating room," says Rob, "and they had a more detailed report in that damned magazine than we were given! Sean, Luca and I made a statement saying Audrey was going to be all right, and the public tended to believe us rather than the *Enquirer*. But it was one occasion where they were speaking the truth and we were telling the lie. We made up the lie to give ourselves strength."

UNICEF, for its part, was in full denial and refused to acknowledge she was gravely ill until the last possible moment.

In early December 1992, as if she hadn't enough to worry about, it was time for the Presidential Medal of Freedom. Audrey had been selected for the honor much earlier, but the White House was only now getting around to the arrangements. Just a few days after Audrey's release from the hospital, Rob got a call at Connie's house from Laurie Firestone, George Bush's personal secretary, asking if Audrey could speak to the President.

"I said, 'It's difficult,'" Wolders relates. "'In her room, there is no phone.'" Bush then asked to speak with Wolders, who explained and asked if he could hold on. "'By all means, take all the time you need,' he said. I went to Audrey's room and she did come and take the call. But it didn't sink in with Bush just how ill she was. His last words to her were, 'I'll be seeing you in two weeks then.' And she said, 'I'll be there if I can.'"

When they were in Bangladesh together, recalls John Isaac, "Audrey asked me my beliefs [about death] and I said, 'I think I have the right to decide about my own life.' She said, 'For me, the same. I wouldn't want to be dragged on.' When she decided not to go through chemotherapy, I told Rob and Sean about this discussion. They believed she should go through with it—maybe there was a chance. But she didn't want that."[5]

On December 9, Audrey went back into the hospital for new exploratory surgery that revealed nothing more could be done. Christmas was not far off. She wanted to see Switzerland and La Paisible for the holidays, and Rob and Sean decided to take her home. On the night they left, December 20, they asked a few of her closest friends to come by Connie Wald's to say goodbye. Billy Wilder describes the scene:

> She, Rob, the nurse and the dogs were all staying at Connie's. She wanted to say goodbye to me and Aud, and also to Gregory Peck and Véronique. She was in a white blouse, I remember, and was smiling all the time. But once in a while, she pushed her elbow into something under the blouse which injected the morphine, because she did not want us to see her suffering. She pushed it to release the drip.
>
> Meanwhile, Rob was organizing the big limousine to get the dogs and the nurse and the luggage in. We said goodbye and went outside, and there behind Connie's big palm trees on Beverly Drive was a cameraman. Peck got very angry and said, 'You leave now or I'll call the police,' and the guy disappeared. It was very emotional. The end was never mentioned, but we all knew it was hopeless.[6]

Much to Rob's relief, Givenchy had arranged to lease a private Gulf-stream jet for the trip to Switzerland, thus sparing Audrey the hassle and publicity of a commercial airliner. It left Los Angeles carrying a woman who now weighed less than ninety pounds and relied on intravenous morphine to relieve her pain.

Faithful Christa Roth went to see her the day after she returned to Tolochenaz, and found her in pretty good spirits. "I'm so glad I'm home," she told her. "I can see my trees again." It was a cold but beautiful Swiss December, and Roth came regularly to chat and bundle her up and take her for walks in the garden. "She would still go into the garden every day, even when she was very ill," says Doris Brynner. "That was her biggest pleasure until those shit photographers took that away from her."[7] The paparazzi lay in wait behind the fence and took grim photos.

"I came to love Doris a great deal more in those last few months," says Rob. "She was extraordinary with Audrey and helped her tremendously. Doris came through for her."

On Christmas Eve, at Rob's request, Audrey did a little reading for Sean and Luca of *Time-Tested Beauty Tips*, author Sam Levenson's wise letter-poem to his grandchild:

For attractive lips, speak words of kindness.
For lovely eyes, seek out the good in people.
For a slim figure, share your food with the hungry.
For beautiful hair, let a child run his fingers through it once a day.
For poise, walk with the knowledge you'll never walk alone....
People, even more than things, have to be restored, renewed, revived, reclaimed and redeemed and redeemed....
Never throw out anybody.
Remember, if you ever need a helping hand, you'll find one at the end of your arm.
As you grow older, you will discover that you have two hands. One for helping yourself, the other for helping others.

She told her sons, "You are the two best creations I ever made."[8] Wolders felt she summoned superhuman courage to help him and the boys deal with losing her: "She didn't leave until she knew we were in full accord about everything. She died, not leaving anything unsolved. She became almost stronger than the disease.... It never altered her character. There was no bitterness, not for a moment."

Sean Ferrer agrees. "She left everything in perfect order," he says, "as if she knew she wasn't going to be around long."

The prospect of death did not frighten her?

"No," Sean replies. "We were much more angry about it than she was, about the fact that it was so unjust. She said, 'It's not injustice, it's the way nature is. It has nothing to do with me or with injustice. It's the process.'"[9]

They all agreed to celebrate Christmas, as usual, and Rob had gone to the village to get some gifts. "The feeling of desolation," he says, "—to be there by myself just before Christmas. The merchants kept asking, 'How is madame?' Those were the saddest hours, the Christmas shopping. I came back extremely down and Audrey said, 'What's the matter?' I said, 'It was horrible to be in town without you.' She was quietly angry with me because it meant I was losing courage—that if she left me, she would be responsible for my unhappiness. There was a parallel in her attitude and in Merle's."

On Christmas Day, Audrey came downstairs, with difficulty, and presented everyone with a little gift. "She gave me a beautiful Givenchy scarf," says Christa Roth. The day went well and, at the end of it, Rob took her back upstairs.

"That last Christmas is one of the most wonderful recollections for me," he says. "It was so important to her to have the boys and me together. We were able to sleep in the same bed until the day she died, and once we shut out the lights, we were in our own world and felt very peaceful. It was just us. I remember that voice in the dark saying, 'This is the happiest Christmas I've ever had.' "

ONLY A WEEK OR SO before her death, she called Michael Tilson Thomas, whose parents had recently died within a few weeks of each another. "You're so lucky," Audrey told him. "If only I could have loved my parents as freely as you did yours." He tried to express his concern for her, but she wouldn't talk about herself: "It was, 'Are you all right, Michael? I'm sorry I haven't contacted you sooner. You must take strength in your music.' So typical of her gentility and enormous care."[10]

Hubert de Givenchy arrived from Paris. "They were so, so close," says Leslie Caron. "There was a deep symbiosis between them." On their last stroll together in her garden, she had to rest every ten steps. There, Givenchy recalled, "I noticed the fragrance of apples. I had to know where it came from, so I asked a servant. A part of the cellar was filled by the harvest of the previous autumn, which they were preparing to send, at Audrey's wish, as in previous years, to the Salvation Army. She thought constantly of others."[11]

As a last gift, she had bought three quilted coats, one for Sean, one for Rob and a navy-blue one for Hubert. As Givenchy was leaving, she asked for the coat to be brought to her and presented it to him, touching her lips to it with a little kiss and murmuring, "Think of me when you wear it."[12]

Around New Year's of 1993, the Academy of Motion Picture Arts and Sciences announced that Audrey (and Elizabeth Taylor) would be the recipient of the Jean Hersholt Humanitarian Award at the next Oscar ceremony in April. But that was eons away in time and space. More immediate was the Screen Actors Guild Achievement Award, which she was to receive in Hollywood on January 10. She had sent an acceptance letter to be read by Julia Roberts, whose character in *Pretty Woman* at one point drifts off to sleep in a hotel room while watching *Charade*. "One would *never* fall asleep watching Audrey Hepburn," Roberts apologized, and then read Hepburn's last public statement:

> As a child I was taught that it was bad manners to draw attention to yourself and make a spectacle of yourself. I then went on to make a rather nice living doing just that—with a little help from the greatest directors, the best writers, the most fabulous stars, glorious photography, terrific scores, super clothes, and the best crews in the industry. My job was to be on time and know my lines. [Others] helped and honed, triggered and taught, pushed and pulled, . . . guided and nurtured a totally unknown, insecure, inexperienced, skinny broad into a marketable commodity. I am proud to have been in a business that gives pleasure, creates beauty and awakens our conscience, arouses compassion and perhaps most importantly, gives millions a respite from our so violent world.

In Switzerland that same day, January 10, Audrey took her last walk around the gardens at La Paisible, supported by Rob and Doris, stopping at each plot to remind them what was planted there and what kind of attention it would require come spring.

"Those last weeks would have been sheer hell if it hadn't been for Audrey's attitude," says Rob. "Even a few days before her death she was trying to make me laugh and said, 'Smile for me, Robbie.' I tried, for her sake."

Of the pain, she would say, "It's not that bad," but even with medication, it was terrible. At last, when she was slipping in and out of consciousness, Sean remembered, "She kept saying people were expecting her—angels or Amish people working in the fields were waiting for her."[13] Rob clarifies:

> They turned up the morphine, and the progress of the disease was resulting in hallucinations—but almost always peaceful ones. At one point, Audrey and I were together and she was looking intently at my side of the bed. I said, "What do you see?" She said, "It's very beautiful. . . . like something from that Peter Weir movie." I said, "*Witness?*" She adored that film and talked about it a lot. "Yes," she said, "they're all simple, spiritual-looking people."

She was very calm. "I'm sorry, but I'm ready to go," she told Luca.[14] In the end, she survived the first operation by just seventy-nine days—

even less than the three months her doctors had predicted. Audrey Hepburn died at home at seven p.m. on Wednesday, January 20, 1993.

INEVITABLY, THERE WAS MORE GUILT and more hindsight.

"Would it have been better for Audrey to have been at home all the time, instead of having to deal with an American hospital and the *National Enquirer*?" Rob wonders. "I keep going around in circles. I had so many misgivings. About three weeks before her death, I asked Audrey, 'Would it have been better, instead of working for UNICEF, if we would just have been together here with the dogs?' She said, 'Think of all we would have missed. Think of what we did together!' But I had to ask myself, if she hadn't done it, would that have been better for her?"

There is no answer, of course. It is equally possible that Hepburn's UNICEF work prolonged, rather than shortened, her life.

Wolders speaks of a certain existential angst she had—not about death but about life, and "living it correctly." Her ASPCA friend Roger Caras observes, "You can come out of her kind of background one of two ways, hard or soft. She came out soft. She wasn't hardened by her difficult experiences in life."[15]

Sean recalls that, "My mother used to say, 'Let us say that we are sitting in our house and we hear the terrible sound of screeching tires... and we run outside and find that a child has been hit by a car.... You pick him up and you run all the way to the hospital. You don't stop and wonder who ran the red light or who should have looked both ways before crossing.'"[16]

Audrey cited the same parable to reporter Alan Riding when he asked her if she was "a person of faith."

"Enormous faith," she replied, "but it's not attached to any one particular religion.... My mother was one thing, my father was another, in Holland they were all Calvinists. That has no importance at all to me.... The minute something happens to a child, you pick it up and take it to a hospital. You don't think about religion or politics."[17]

Her mother's Christian Scientism was not a huge influence on her, "but something about it might have remained with her," says Rob, "perhaps involving an acceptance of fate. She never talked about religion. Not long before her death I brought it up, and she said, 'My only religion is a belief in nature.'"

She said many things in her last weeks, says Sean, but one stands out most memorably: "The last time we all walked in the garden, Giovanni, her gardener, came up and said, 'Signora, when you get better, you'll come and help me to trim and to plant again.' She smiled and said, 'Don't worry, Giovanni, I will help you—but not like before.'"[18]

AUDREY HEPBURN'S DEATH OCCURRED ON the day of President Bill Clinton's inauguration and interrupted all the news broadcasts of those proceedings. It was also, oddly enough, the day on which rock 'n' roll was declared the official music of the White House. There was no connection—except that four United States presidents sent letters of condolence to Rob Wolders.

The day she died, Tiffany's stores around the world put her photograph in their windows and placed memorial advertisements saying only: AUDREY HEPBURN—OUR HUCKLEBERRY FRIEND—1929–1993.

By coincidence on the following day, January 21, Audrey was seen by millions in the first of PBS-TV's six-part *Gardens of the World* series. Many papers carried the *Garden* reviews and Audrey's obituary in the same issue. The show was "off the charts," producer Janis Blackschleger recalls: "We were in complete denial. We were insisting on this life-affirming statement she made in *Gardens*, and we had a lot of ads we were planning to do for the series. But still, to this day, it just doesn't feel right to say 'the late' Audrey Hepburn."

For Anna Cataldi, the news and the denial were even more intense. After parting with Audrey in Somalia, she had gone on immediately to Bosnia to observe the UNICEF-proposed ceasefire for which Audrey had made a video appeal, with Serbo-Croatian subtitles, that was broadcast twelve times a day in Yugoslavia.

"I went to Bosnia because of Audrey," says Cataldi. "She did an appeal for the 'Week of Tranquility' at the end of October, to help the children in Sarajevo before winter arrived. There she was on TV—when we had electricity—such a vision. I think if Audrey had been well, she would have gone to Sarajevo herself."

Cataldi stayed there a month before escaping by car with two other journalists and a ten-month-old baby with an amputated leg. "They shot at us," she says, "but we drove through the mountains and finally we arrived in Croatia, where there was peace. I saw a little restaurant. I'd been cut off from the world.... My first call was to my family. The second was to Audrey. I was going to tell her that I saved a baby, which I knew would make her happy. I said, 'Giovanna, give me la Signora.'"

But la Signora could not come to the phone, and Anna would not see her again.

Cataldi arrived in Tolochenaz the night before the funeral. "The house was full of people—Givenchy, all the Ferrers, the Dotti clan, everybody," she recalls. "At one point, Giovanna said, 'La Signora... she is in the living room.' I opened the door, nobody there. In the middle of the room was Audrey's coffin, closed. That beautiful white living room—white floor and couches, impeccable, everything exactly the way Audrey kept it. Just one little vase with one rose."[19]

In Tolochenaz, funerals were not allowed on Sunday, but the rules had been changed. A huge number of people lined the way from the house to the church, and from there to the cemetery. Audrey's simple pine coffin was carried from La Paisible to the church by Sean, Luca, Givenchy, Rob, Audrey's brother Ian, and her longtime friend and lawyer Georges Müller. Mel Ferrer, seventy-five, walked behind them. Sean saw him waiting in line. "Come, Papa," he said, hugging his father as they entered the stone church.[20] Some six hundred villagers listened outside via loudspeaker to the service presided over by eighty-three-year-old pastor Maurice Eindiguer, who had married Audrey and Mel in 1954, baptized Sean in 1960, and given Audrey the last rites just two hours before her death.

Rob had asked UNICEF's Prince Sadruddin Aga Khan to deliver a eulogy, and he did so with extemporaneous eloquence. "She was an extraordinary star in every sense of the word," said the Prince, who had known and loved her from their first meeting after a performance of *Ondine* forty years before. He spoke of what she symbolized to the world—of her ability to touch everyone who came in contact with her and of her insistence that the welfare of the children was the adult world's most solemn responsibility.

"To know the affluence of places like California and then suddenly to be placed in the Sudan was a tremendous shock," he said. "When she came back from one of those trips, you could see it had taken a lot out of her, physically and morally. But at the same time, she felt we could somehow turn things around. She kept going. Always, there was her underlying optimism."[21]

Sean then read the Sam Levenson poem she liked so much and added, "Mummy believed in one thing above all: She believed in love. She believed love could heal, fix, mend, and make everything fine and good in the end."

At the end of the thirty-minute ceremony, hymns were sung by a children's choir from St. Georges International School in Montreux. At the village cemetery, she was laid to rest atop a small hill overlooking Lake Geneva. Her grave would be marked by a plain pinewood cross.

"SHE LEFT THE BIGGEST VACUUM anybody could leave," says Doris Brynner. "A great big black empty hole."[22] But it was Audrey's "three men" that Anna Cataldi worried about most. She speaks of them with maternal bluntness:

"One hour after the funeral, Sean was putting on the California New Age act, talking so esoterically. And poor Luca, just out of art school.... When my book, *Letters from Sarajevo*, came out in Italy, he did the cover design. He's very good. When Luca was with Andrea, he was shy. But when he was with Audrey, he behaved like a Hell's Angel, speaking Italian with an accent of Roman suburbs, in front of his mother!... But can you imagine, to lose a mother like Audrey?"[23]

John Isaac says "Robert was completely devastated. He was pretty strong until the last moment when they lowered the coffin. That's the first time I saw him just break down."

All those men without Audrey—Rob, Sean, Andrea, Luca. "Audrey was the focus," says Anna. "She was surrounded by men."

Audrey had called Sean "my best friend"—mature even as a child. "He's been a rock in my life, enormous support," she said. "He was born with a marvelous nature. He's one of the nicest human beings I've ever met.... I'm totally crazy about my sons." The feeling was mutual. "I still carry her every day in my heart," he says, "so she is still my best friend, too."[24] A year after her death, in Tolochenaz, Sean Ferrer assesses his mother in remarkably candid terms:

She always followed the program and her life was very continuous. She tried to get up and eat and take her walks and go to sleep at the same hour. She saved up strength like you would save up a handful of water for your last drink. Instead of using it to do commercials or whatever, she used it for the kids, because that's what mattered to her.

I think that connects back to her childhood—to the loss of her father and the fears that never left her. First it was fear of a tough mother, fear of being alone and being abandoned by the father, fear of the war. And then she was damned scared all her life through her career. She was scared to death, man. She was scared to death.[25]

Was it a fear of potential loss?

No, of being up there, of having to perform—afraid she wasn't good enough, wasn't as beautiful as all the other women and had to work harder and know her lines better than anyone, get up earlier and have the best makeup person and the best costume man and the most beautiful clothes. They were almost like an armor in which she was protected....

In her case, the motivation was fear, and love for her family. From her youth, she never saw herself as we did. She thought it was a gift that could go away any day. Most artists believe that somehow they're going to be "found out"—models most of all. They're all glitz on the outside but on the inside they're [trying] to keep up this exterior cupola that may crash if you remove the center stone....

That's why people love her on the screen, because when she cries, she really is feeling it, really living through it. She is believing, reliving—she's actually there. And you want to take her in your arms and hug her.[26]

Sean attended the March 1993 Oscar ceremonies to accept Audrey's Jean Hersholt Award. "On her behalf," he said, "I dedicate this to the children of the world"—his own, included. Soon after Audrey's death, Sean and Leila learned they were about to become parents. "My God, how Audrey would have loved that!" Doris Brynner exclaimed. Emma Audrey Ferrer, born in Tolochenaz, inherited a closet of hand-embroidered baby clothes worn by her father and a nursery that was her grandmother's dressing room.

"She missed seeing her first grandchild," says Sean. "But there's a little bit of her in that baby."[27]

Sean Ferrer continues in the film-production business, commuting from Switzerland to Los Angeles and New York. Luca the graphic artist works with computers, shares his mother's desire for privacy, and lives quietly with his boarding-school sweetheart, Astrid, in Paris.

Robert Wolders lives in the Rochester, New York, suburb of Irondequoit, near his mother and sister Claudia who, like his older sisters Margaret and Grada, were very close to Audrey. He travels a great deal, tending to commercial and UNICEF interests —and to the memory of Audrey Hepburn.

The Wolders home is an elegant "Dutch" environment in white. It is no maudlin shrine but contains enough images of Audrey to ensure that her presence is strongly felt. Something else ensures that in a lively way— tiny little "Missy," the Jack Russell terrier who cuddles into the sleeves of Rob's sweater and never leaves him as he sits and talks. Audrey gave him the dog five years ago, and Missy is a precious living link to her now.

Shortly after her death, Wolders was asked by UNICEF to put together a film from video footage he had taken in the field. The resulting documentary, *Audrey Hepburn in Her Own Words*, was modest in length (twenty-three minutes) but soaring in content—the most moving film record of her last years' work. Soon after that, he immersed himself in the preparation of a marathon, three-hour "Audrey Hepburn Memorial Tribute" benefit concert at the United Nations General Assembly in New York—the most star-studded performing-arts event in UN history.* "They all came in without even a rehearsal," Rob recalls. "Henry Mancini didn't

* A partial list of those performers on April 30, 1993: Roger Moore (remarks), Yo Yo Ma (Bach cello solo), American Boychoir with Atlanta Brass Ensemble (Dufay's "Gloria"), Frederica Von Stade (Mozart selections), Harry Belafonte (remarks), Pinchas Zuckerman and John Browning (Brahms sonata), Barbara Walters (remarks), Henry Mancini ("Moon River"), Tokyo String Quartet (Schubert scherzo), Michael Tilson Thomas (Ravel's "Pavane for a Departed Princess"), Gregory Peck (film tribute), Carol Vaness (Puccini aria), Tatiana Troyanos (DeFalla and Brahms songs), Hugh Downs (remarks), Terry Cook ("Deep River" spiritual), Elizabeth Taylor (film remarks), Cicely Tyson (reading), and Dave Brubeck & Ensemble (his 1954 tune "Audrey," written—he said—with the image of Hepburn in her garden in his mind).

quite know what he was going to play. I kept begging him to do 'Moon River.' He heard Frederica von Stade was going to sing it and didn't want to do it twice—but then he did it anyhow, with a 'special stamp' on it for Sean and Luca and me."

Wolders' business interests include a longtime association with Public Storage Partners, a conglomerate with its own management company, and he continues to give as much time as he can to UNICEF. But his friends worry about him.

"Every time we speak on the phone, he always comes back to, 'Should I have done this or that?'" says John Isaac. "I say, you can't blame yourself. You were helping her. That's what she wanted. She did what she wanted."

Wolders muses constantly on that, and on Audrey.

"They say the pain lessens with time," he says. "But it's not true."

HEPBURN AND WOLDERS NEVER MARRIED and kept their finances scrupulously separate. He had suffered after the death of Merle Oberon from false reports characterizing him as a gold digger, and he was determined not to let it happen again.

"People assume Audrey was wealthy, but they forget that she hadn't worked for years and that she educated and supported her two children largely by herself," Wolders says. "Long before her death, I insisted that I *not* be part of her estate."

That decision startled Hepburn's sons. But Wolders did agree to serve on the board of directors of a new foundation created by Sean and Luca to carry on their mother's work.

The Audrey Hepburn Hollywood for Children Fund is located at 4 East 12th Street in New York's Greenwich Village. "We originally thought we could become a subcommittee of UNICEF," executive director Rose Ganguzza told film writer Maria Ciaccia. "But the bureaucracy was mindboggling. We wanted to be able to work on things more efficiently, to be a storefront operation— to have a lasting effect, something ongoing and grass roots."[28] The Fund's member-advisors include Martin Short, Whoopi Goldberg and Jim Carrey, plus many others who have never before loaned their names to such a cause.*

---

* Among them: Dan Ackroyd, Richard Avedon, David Bowie, Matthew Broderick, Leslie Caron, Harrison Ford, Hubert de Givenchy, Marvin Hamlisch, Gregory Peck, Nancy Reagan, Julia Roberts, Winona Ryder, and Donald Trump. Hollywood for Children also has a "Kids Board," with such child-celebrity members as Raven Symone from *Hangin' with Mr. Cooper*, Shawn Toovey of *Dr. Quinn, Medicine Woman*, Emily Hart from *Tommy*, Zachary Ty Bryan from *Home Improvement*, and Laura Bertram and Lani Billard of *Ready or Not*.

UNICEF's institutional nose is a little out of joint. "Our understanding at first was that we would be one of the beneficiaries," says a UNICEF official, "but Sean has not yet made a clear decision where funding will be going. He wants to create a foundation to benefit various organizations, including places where UNICEF is not operating, like the United States and England. He wants it to be independent."

Many, including the chief director's father, think it should be relocated to the West Coast. "I've been giving Sean a lot of free advice," says Mel Ferrer. "There's no point calling it 'Hollywood for Children' and having it based in New York."[29]

One of its goals is to be a conduit to other charities. The organization is still embryonic, but Hepburn's sons are "caring individuals," says Ganguzza, "and they'll find the way. She left them her loving legacy. It's a lot to live up to."[30]

The sons are constantly asked to testify to that legacy, beyond just UNICEF. The little matter of her film career was at the forefront in 1994, with the $600,000 restoration of *My Fair Lady*. Over thirty years, the film had deteriorated to the point that it was in danger of total ruin. Its glorious color had faded and spotting of the negative was serious. Typical of the cinematic dermatology was a three-second spot on Audrey's face, which cost $10,000 to fix. Film restoration experts Robert A. Harris and James C. Katz had done handsome reconstructions of *Lawrence of Arabia* and *Spartacus*, but *My Fair Lady* was an even bigger job—literally—the first rescue of a Super Panavision 70 film.

"I am so very moved," Sean told the jammed audience at the *My Fair Lady* gala "re-premiere" in New York, September 19, 1994. "One day our little Emma will be able to look up and see her grandmother... see her, feel her, and love her."

Jeremy Brett, better known by then as PBS's Sherlock Holmes, was one of the very few surviving costars in attendance. ("I got better notices for Freddy this time around than I did before," he said.[31]) The refurbished print was gorgeous, but most in the audience felt the highlight of the night came during the final credits: As a fine postscript, the restorers added the soundtrack of Audrey's own rendition of "Wouldn't It Be Loverly?"

Silenced for thirty years in the vaults, she finally got to sing it herself.

MY FAIR LADY'S RESTORATION WAS just the beginning. In the two years since, the postmortem fascination with Audrey Hepburn has burgeoned into a major cultural and commercial phenomenon. Countless Hepburn film retrospectives, on network and cable television and in theatrical screenings across the country, have recaptivated millions of old fans and created generations of new ones. What accounts for such renewed and renewable popularity? One simple answer comes from Patricia Davis, a program-scheduling executive at American Movie Classics: "You always felt good after you saw Audrey Hepburn."[32]

Contemporary Hollywood, meanwhile, having fashioned a new *Sabrina* in 1995, is also planning a remake of *Two for the Road*, to star Meg Ryan and to be written by Carrie Fisher. A 1991 Asian-American film production by Sharon Jue was called *My Mother Thought She Was Audrey Hepburn*. The most worshipful new project, similarly titled, is *Why Can't I Be Audrey Hepburn?*, a comedy tentatively set for production by Steven Spielberg's new "Dreamworks SKG" company, with Téa Leoni starring as a woman obsessed by Hepburn. Producer Robert Evans has something similar in development called *Golightly*, whose heroine is fixated on Holly in *Breakfast at Tiffany's*.

Audrey-obsessed films and books seem to constitute a whole new genre. The most serious entry is Alan Brown's novel, *Audrey Hepburn's Neck* (Pocket Books, 1996), film rights to which have been bought by director Wayne (*Smoke*) Wang. In this tale, it's not a woman but a young man who is mesmerized by Audrey. The setting is a semi-surreal Japan, where the rural womenfolk eat grilled eel while watching their beloved Hepburn movies.

Audrey isn't the first film icon to be embraced by whole societies and woven into their artistic and psychological fabric. The Swedish sphinx preceded her and inspired such "personal" works of art as the fine Anne Bancroft film *Garbo Talks* and an intriguing novel *The Girl Who Loved Garbo* by Rachel Gallagher. But otherwise, the only comparable icons are Valentino, Harlow, Dean and Monroe, whose cults have one great morbid prerequisite in common: an early, tragic, preferably violent death.

There was no such imperative in the case of Audrey Hepburn, whose sphere of influence went far beyond film. An au courant example is the list of "Most Fascinating Women of Our Time" in the July 1996 issue of Britain's influential *Harpers & Queen*: The surprise is not Hepburn's inclusion but her ranking—number one. That corresponds to her powerful, ongoing force in fashion and advertising. More à la mode now than ever, her look and her look-alikes again dominate the runways of Prada, Calvin Klein and, of course, Givenchy and Lauren, and adorn the toniest European and Madison Avenue advertisements from L'Interdit fragrance to Nicole Miller scarves. There's no end to the phenomenon, but there's a final item of note for the pop-music scene:

The thirty-five-year-old movie containing Audrey's only smash musical success, "Moon River," provided both the title and the whimsy for a major hit tune of 1996—the offbeat love song "Breakfast at Tiffany's," by Texas band Deep Blue Something. Songwriter Todd Pipes, who was born well after the movie was made, estimates that he has seen it more than fifty times.

AUDREY WOULD NOT WRITE HER autobiography. Over and over she was asked, and over and over she said no. "In the last year," she told Ed Klein, "I've had seven requests from publishers for the Audrey Hepburn story— you know, the definitive book. It's an idea [I hate:] How boring to have to sit there and write your whole life.... The other thing that makes me hold back is that you cannot write your life as if you'd live in a [vacuum]. You've lived with lots of other people. So perforce you have to talk about others. I have no right to do that nor would I."

And to other interviewers: "Memoirs? I don't want to relive it, nor do I need the psychotherapy—get on with it!"[33]

Sean had encouraged her to write a book, "if for no one else, then for Luca and myself," and because it might have guaranteed her financial security for the rest of her life. "But you and Luca already know everything," she replied.

Her "three men" respected that decision. But after her death, a spate of Hepburn books appeared, one of which outraged and mobilized them into legal action: Diana Maychick's *Audrey Hepburn: An Intimate Portrait* (Birch Lane Press, 1993), made much of Hepburn's alleged anorexia, but its greater offense, in the family's view, was Maychick's claim that Audrey had actively cooperated with her in a series of phone interviews.

"Never, ever did Audrey speak with her," Wolders insists. "I keep very careful records, and I even got hotel phone records where we stayed. Maychick claims to have had interviews when, in fact, Audrey was dying." The suspect book was optioned for a possible TV miniseries, now stalled pending resolution of the Estate's litigation against Maychick and her publisher.

Rob Wolders strokes little Missy on his lap and looks out his living-room window in Rochester at the ever-present snow, still on the ground in April. He has just read two other film-star biographies and is troubled by the problematic contrast he sees in trying to capture Hepburn's life on the page.

"Audrey was in a sense an open book," he says finally. "She was not enigmatic like Louise Brooks or Greta Garbo. There was a wonderful darkness in their personalities—a 'mystery' to be uncovered. There's nothing like that with Audrey."

Back in 1954, British critic Clayton Cole had called her not just a "weird hybrid with butchered hair" but also "insincere" as an actress.[34] As the years went by, however, most people felt sincerity was her biggest asset. "Hepburn was first of all a human being," says Eleanor Lambert.[35]

It was her personality more than her acting that made her a star.

Her early films were fairy tales, of course. "One would like to see her play stronger parts which would broaden her," said a fan magazine in the early fifties. "Could she play the daughter in *The Glass Menagerie* or Sally in *I Am a Camera*? Only her future acting will answer that."

The answer seems to have been no.

"I've never been driven," she said, except "by the need to provide for my mother and myself."[36] Even that drive soon disappeared "because I had the luxury of not needing it. After *Roman Holiday*, the offers came in. It was not in my nature to be terribly ambitious or driven because I didn't have the confidence.... My confidence came and went with each movie."

A psychiatrist who "shrank" her for *Good Housekeeping* in 1959 asserted that her early life contained a dozen things that might have driven a less controlled person to an analyst.[37] "She shared her joys with friends, but kept her unhappy moments to herself," said Hubert de Givenchy.[38] And at least she knew the source of her problems.

"People all have fears," she said, "but mostly they are distant and unknown to them. They are afraid of death, which they haven't gone through; they are afraid of getting cancer, which they don't have; they are afraid of getting run over, which hasn't happened. But I've known the cold clutch of human terror. I've seen it, I've felt it, I've heard it."[39]

Phil Donahue jumped to the conclusion that "living under the Nazis left you very insecure?"

"That is not what left me insecure," she answered. "My father leaving us is what left me insecure.[40] [It] has stayed with me through my own relationships. When I fell in love and married, I lived in constant fear of being left.... Whatever you love most, you fear you might lose."[41]

Yes, yes—she had always wanted the security of love and children more than her career. So much so, that she could never quite face or self-efface her enduring screen presence:

"Many years ago, my mother said to me, 'Considering that you have no talent, it's really extraordinary where you've got.'[42] She said it in the middle of all the successes I was having. She wasn't putting me down. She was saying how fortunate I was. She was right. I don't have this huge talent. I'm not a Laurence Olivier or a Meryl Streep.... I landed in this business because I had to earn a living.[43]

"The acting was a surprise to me. It still is. I wanted to be a ballerina, that's all.... It's easier to be a shy ballerina than a shy actress. You don't have to talk. You can hide yourself in your music and just forget about yourself. That I became an actress is something of an accident."

Michael Tilson Thomas marvels at how realistic she was about her good fortune: "She said, 'I didn't really have to do much. I just had to be myself and it worked.' She had the best head on her shoulders. She could easily have bought into Hollywood and everything that it represented. Instead, she emerged as what she was: Her integrity and personal qualities were more powerful than all the films and good works."[44]

Hepburn's total output (just twenty starring films in forty years) was as modest as Garbo's (twenty-six), and of comparable impact. Also comparable were their continental ways, which seemed to evade a nationality, and their mesmerizing "low" voices: Garbo's was nearly a baritone; Hepburn's, a velvety contralto of "purred elegance," said Peter Bogdanovich—a voice "that barely made the acquaintance of consonants," as distinctive in accent as in the idiosyncratic way she used it.

"Audrey had a little speech pattern all her own," says costar Eli Wallach. "Nobody else could do it." Its tone had an unusual, emphatic kind of upward swing when she finished a sentence. Cecil Beaton called it "a singsong cadence that develops into a flat drawl, ending in a childlike query."[45]

Unfortunately, that voice lost most of its meaning to millions in the non-English-speaking world, with or without dubbing. But Audrey had something that rose above the Tower of Babel and crossed all international barriers of language: her eyes. "From *Sabrina* on, she was like no other actress," Theodore Bikel told John Barba. "Innocence and mischievousness, wrapped into one—an extraordinary mixture, acted with her eyes."[46]

There was a recurring holy trinity of words in the litany of her screen appeal. Bikel intoned the first—"innocence"—and is bolstered by Bogdanovich: "Audrey Hepburn became the last true innocent of the American screen." The second is "gamine"—the boyish but sexy waif with impish European style. The third word, "vulnerable," is the quality most often attributed to both her real and screen character. One critic referred to it as her "indestructible frailness." Director Fred Zinnemann considered it very real: "In her private life, she was emotionally vulnerable to [everyone, but especially] her mother, her brothers, and Mel."

Rosalie Crutchley was dubious: "Audrey, vulnerable? Yes, maybe.... The one thing that is rather unpleasant about acting is that you have to reveal certain things about yourself through a character, and I don't think Audrey liked doing that."[47]

That contributed both to her ambivalence about making movies, and to the limitation of her roles. Richard Lester, after *Robin and Marian*, had described her as "a very methodical, almost mechanical performer. I would not say she was a varied actress. She was a star. She was always more or less Audrey in the way that John Wayne was always John Wayne. The qualities she had in person were the qualities she had on the screen."[48]

They were the qualities that Gregory Peck exalted: "Audrey is a magical combination of high chic and high spirits."[49] And they were the qualities, coupled with her later UNICEF work, that made her one of the most beloved actresses of her time.

"When Nick Dunne was doing his piece on Audrey for *Vanity Fair*," William Banks recalls, "I said to Rob, 'Aren't you a little nervous, because he can be so bitchy?' Rob said, 'Nobody can be bitchy about Audrey.' And of course, Dunne wasn't."[50]

But then, in the bottom of the ninth, up steps Nora Sayre to spoil the no-hitter—in *Running Time: Films of the Cold War:*

"Many adolescent girls of the fifties were almost tyrannized by the image of Audrey Hepburn: Hers was the manner by which ours was measured, and we were expected to identify with her, or to use her as a model. . . . Flirtatious yet almost sexless, Hepburn appealed because she was utterly unmenacing to men. [The adulation of her] seemed to tell us that young women ought to be well-heeled, submissive and sexually spotless—sophisticated at parties, perhaps, but free of genital vibrations. . . . Why did we rush pell-mell to choose a haughty pre-anorexic upon which to pattern ourselves, so slavishly and for so long?"[51]

IS IT POSSIBLE TO SEPARATE the actress from the flesh-and-blood woman? Nora Sayre didn't like *either* of them: Demure morality and the tyranny of the skinny waist were not to everyone's taste. There was a lot going on in the fifties and sixties that Audrey Hepburn represented, and a lot that she did not. Her type—especially her sexual type—was not the unanimous preference of all or even most men. Nobody put Marilyn Monroe out of business but herself.

But in the end, unlike most of her peers, the *personal* Audrey was even stronger than the screen Audrey. Even her "worst" traits were spoken of fondly. UNICEF's Horst Cerny, for instance, sheepishly cites "two things kind of contrary to her image: She smoked, which—for a non-smoker and for UNICEF—surprised me. The other thing was her enjoyment of whiskey."

Billy Wilder calls her "that unique lady! She's what the Latin calls *sui generis*—the original, no more examples, and never will be." Dominick Dunne asked her if she was surprised by the excitement she always caused wherever she went. "Totally," she replied. "Everything surprises me. I'm surprised that people recognize me on the street. I say to myself, 'Well, I must still look like myself.' . . . I don't understand it. At the same time, I'm terribly touched by it."[52] It was all the more surprising since she had deliberately distanced herself. Many considered her a snob because she held so aloof from the public and the media—and most of all, from Hollywood.

"I certainly did not intend to be untouchable," she replied to that charge. "I came to work every day ... terribly nervous ... terribly insecure, was I going to get the words right, was I going to do it properly? And ah, the relief when they said, 'Print,' and Willie [Wyler] or Stanley [Donen] was happy. And then I went home at night and had my bath and my supper and learned my lines and got up again at four a.m."

Ironically, Donen—whom she was so eager to please—confirms her untouchability. "I longed to get closer," he said, "to get behind whatever was the invisible but decidedly present barrier between her and the rest of us, but I never got to the deepest part of Audrey. ... She always kept a little of herself in reserve, which was hers alone, and I couldn't ever find out what it was, let alone share it with her."[53]

Dr. Ron Glegg, Rob Wolders's brother-in-law, perceived much the same thing: "I sensed a sort of reserve, a hesitancy in her relationship with people. She was always prepared to withdraw from any event or discussion—she could quickly, almost abruptly, bring it to an end. I'd give her an 'A' in closure! It made her not less but more interesting."[54]

Audrey acknowledged that quality in herself but felt that, at least in her film work, it wore off as soon as "I discovered the [other] actors were just as insecure as I was, however famous and however long they had been at it. Gary Cooper used to get clammy hands like I did. Cary Grant and Rex Harrison worried like mad ... because people were expecting a lot of them, which they weren't of me, though I was expecting a lot of myself."

She had had no huge disappointments or unfulfilled hopes. "I am the most un-bitter person in the world," she told Rex Reed. "I was asked to act when I couldn't act, to sing in *Funny Face* when I couldn't sing, to dance with Fred Astaire when I couldn't dance, and do all kinds of things I was not expecting and was not prepared for. Then I tried like mad to cope with it."[55]

But there was one thing that she sought and never quite achieved—serenity: "I don't think it exists. [You] can be perfectly serene, then you spend two minutes thinking about the Kurds and want to shoot yourself. I mistakenly thought that with age comes serenity, when your job is done, maybe you have earned enough money so you can be secure and the children are okay. ... Perhaps the only time you can be serene is when you are very small, when you don't know all these things."[56]

But if serenity was elusive, love was not—and that was Audrey Hepburn's open secret:

"Actors, directors, technicians ... there's something in some of them that makes you open up to them. With me, it always has to do with some kind of affection they convey—a message of affection, love, warmth. I was born with an enormous need for affection. I have always been terribly aware of it, even when I was small. And a terrible need to give it, like every child—they all want a dog, they want a cat, they all want a horse, they all want to cuddle a baby. That has been very strong with me.... Much more important than receiving affection is giving it."[57]

"THERE'S NEVER BEEN A HELLUVA lot to say about me," Audrey once declared, but the world begged to differ.[58]

A great deal was said about her in Arnhem on April 23, 1994, at the dedication of a bust by Dutch sculptor Kees Verkade in Burgemeesters Plaza, near "Human Inference Street"—a midtown neighborhood of neat red brick houses characteristic of prewar Arnhem. Hundreds came to see the unveiling that sunny afternoon, as a dozen blue and white UNICEF flags snapped in the wind.

It was very much a family affair. Rob, Sean, Luca, Hubert de Givenchy and Audrey's brother Ian sat together in the front row listening to the speeches, all in Dutch. Popular performer Paul van Vliet, who had been inspired by Audrey to become UNICEF's goodwill ambassador in Holland, read an original poem:

I drink to the people who never play safe, who begin things without knowing how they will end.
I drink to the people whose joy is erased and who don't give a damn what's around the next bend...

The bust itself is—well, a bust in all ways. "It's not Audrey," says Van Vliet. "It has no warmth in the eyes and mouth." Indeed, with its distended neck and hollow eyes, it looks more like the blind girl Suzy in *Wait Until Dark* than the real Audrey Hepburn. The crowd's subdued reaction registers its disappointment. But the release of a dozen white doves, soaring gracefully up and away, provides a touching end to the ceremony.

Fame, Audrey said, "creates a certain curiosity. People want to see you. I'm using that curiosity for the children."[59] In her lifetime, millions of curious people stared at Hepburn differently from the way they stared at other movie stars.

When someone said Hollywood wasn't very romantic any more, she replied, "Well, I am.... I could never be cynical. I wouldn't dare. I'd roll over and *die* before that."[60] She was a romantic, all right, but at the same time, says Gene Feldman, her film documentarist:

She was a woman of enormous substance. She always described herself as not knowing, not being sure. But when she made a decision, it was totally fixed. When I saw her talking on Somalia, that was *ferocity*. That was a Golda Meir. Her performance as a human being was even greater than her performance as an actress. She activated something in us all. She was not some 'vulnerable' or pathetic figure. There may have been moments in her life when she was battered or drawn to the wrong people. But she had the courage to pick herself up and go on to maintain her work, her kids, the man she loved, Rob, her basic notion of who she was: an independent woman. It wasn't God-given. She did it herself, and with a nobility of spirit.[61]

Some movie stars have an impact greater than the medium can explain, and Hepburn was one of them. She was part of our shared cultural experience—a huge influence on the way women looked and played the feminine role.[62] Our image of her really stems less from her films than from the fashion magazines. In any case, glamour queens, like good strippers, must keep something hidden to retain the audience's attention. If all is revealed, the show is over.[63] Hepburn, for that reason and others, chose to keep her personal life as private as possible.

"We think we know all about Elizabeth Taylor's weaknesses [for] men and food," says Caroline Latham, "or Doris Day's love of home, children and dogs; or Marilyn Monroe's troubled search for love. But few of us attach any such intimate characteristics to... Audrey Hepburn. If the result is somewhat two-dimensional in personal terms, it is all the more powerful as an icon."

Her friend Leslie Caron says Audrey "conducted her life as discreetly as the way she dressed." The irony is that Hepburn's fabulous "look" was essentially just something that evolved over time to camouflage what she considered her faults. But still today, decades after her peak, if a designer exclaims, "It's so 'Audrey'!", everyone knows exactly what he means.[64]

"Through the years," says designer Michael Kors, "Audrey Hepburn has projected an image of style and not of fashion." Though she was not an American, Hepburn's style reflected the great American designs: "She became the symbol for what we all talk about today in fashion—a woman who has independence, confidence to do what she wants when she gets dressed," offers Rebecca Moses. "She was the beginning of minimalism," maintains Isaac Mizrahi. According to Christian Lacroix in Paris, "Audrey Hepburn didn't simply epitomize the style of Hubert de Givenchy. She symbolized a generation."[65]

Dwight MacDonald's verdict back in 1960 was that "she is not an actress, she is a model, with her stiff meager body and her blank face full of good bone structure. She has the model's narcissism, not the actress' introversion." Others, too, call her more a figure of fashion than of film. But her defenders—such as the late Eva Gabor—vehemently reject that view:

"That annoys me, because she was a wonderful actress. The blind girl in *Wait Until Dark*? That was not a fashion model. *War and Peace*—the scene where her brother gets killed? That was acting, not fashion."

But she was *also* a fashion legend, of course:

"She always underdressed instead of overdressed," says Eva. "Nobody in the world looked better in plain white pants and a white blouse. Whatever she put on became perfectly elegant. Without a stick of jewelry, she looked like a queen. The queen should look so good. I mean, the perfume this woman used—everything about her was perfect. Those wonderful eyes, the sweetness, the genteel soul. I can't imagine Audrey with a bad thought. Maybe she was too good to be here. Maybe the Lord decided he wanted her up there."[66]

Divine references abound when people talk about her. "She was taken too young—a gift from God," says R. J. Wagner.[67] "Hepburn as actress and woman seemed a gentle emissary from a better world than ours," wrote Richard Corliss. "She taught, by example, what a lady was: a vessel of grace and gravity, ready wit, eldritch charm; a woman whose greatest discretion was to hide her awareness of her splendor."[68]

After she won her Academy Award for *Roman Holiday*, "she was not highfalutin," says Billy Wilder. "She did not play 'The Oscar Winner.' She was humble. She listened intelligently. She made what she said and felt so true that her partner—whether it was Holden or Bogart or Cooper—had to react the proper way. She drew them in. She could say something risqué, but the way she did it had a kind of elegance that you could not, under any circumstance, mistake for Madonna reading the line.

"Audrey was known for something which has disappeared, and that is elegance, grace and manners—things you cannot take a course in. You're born with it or not. What is needed to really become a star is an extra element that God gives or doesn't give you. You cannot learn it. She just was blessed. God kissed her on her cheek, and there she was."[69]

In the characters she played on film, most of Hepburn's leading men didn't realize her allure until the end, says Wendy Keys—"but *we* knew all along."[70] No actress ever pleaded more earnestly with her screen suitors not to admire her, or to so little effect.[71] "Everything about her," wrote Marjorie Rosen in *Popcorn Venus*, "worked toward a female dignity."

But oddly enough, there were few other females in her films. "She always had fathers or uncles—no mothers, children or girlfriends," says Keys. "Audrey was always bouncing off a variety of men."[72] Accepting her 1990 Golden Globe Award, she said there were always "too many names in thank-you speeches, so I'll only mention a few." As a joke she then reeled off, fast as she could, the names of thirty-four people crucial to her film career—of whom Shirley MacLaine and Lillian Gish were the only women.

In her "other" career with UNICEF, however, it was women with whom Audrey identified most profoundly. While men fought and children starved, women grieved and did all the work. In Somalia, she said, "women are respected—it's a matriarchy. I spoke to a wonderful Somalian woman lawyer who said, 'Women can bring peace to this country because we're strong.' Their status is unusual for a Muslim country. They have the vote and the 'say' at home. They can stop their husbands and children from carrying guns and shooting each other."[73]

Only a woman and a mother could have felt Somalia so viscerally—and communicated it so directly to the world.

WILLIAM HOLDEN—IN ONE OF his rare, non-self-referential remarks—came up with an insight into Audrey: "I think people love her off the screen for the same reason they love her performances—a kind of orderliness and formality."[74]

It is the film star's grim duty to age in front of the public. Hepburn did so with characteristic dignity and order, without resorting to the usual extremes—over-the-hill "guest" shots and commercials, or pathological withdrawal.

"I never expected to be a star, never counted on it, *never even wanted it*," she once said. "Not that I didn't enjoy it all when it happened. [But] it's not as if I were a great actress. I'm not [Ingrid] Bergman. I don't regret for a minute making the decision to quit movies for my children."[75]

But millions of others regretted it. "I think she retired much too early," says Leslie Caron. "It's a pity she didn't move on to more mature parts. She would have given something so heavenly. There's grace and beauty to be shared at every age, and she had that above everyone else. It's a loss."[76]

Audrey herself had twinges. "I'd have loved to have done a movie with Jimmy Stewart because we've known each other for so many years [and] I've always had an enormous rapport with him," she said in 1991. "I'd have loved to have made a picture with Philippe Noiret [and] I'd have liked to have done a picture with de Sica.... He wanted to do *Camille*, but I didn't want to do it because I didn't dare follow Garbo's footsteps."[77]

Kurt Frings had wanted to reteam her and Gregory Peck for a *Roman Holiday* sequel in which the princess (now a queen) and the reporter (now a successful novelist) have a daughter and son who fall in love. Just fifteen months before her death, she wanted to do a picture with Peck "the way we are now," she said.[78] "And I'd love to do a picture with Michael Caine or Michael Douglas—actors who have style but aren't pompous about it." As late as December 1992, unaware of how ill Audrey was, Julia Roberts was still looking for a project she and Hepburn could do together.

"There's a luxury in being able to retire before it's time to retire," said

Audrey, while admitting in the next breath: "It would be fun to do another part before I roll over."[79]

She held out. In the end, she played her greatest part not on a movie set but on the vast and more dramatic stage of Africa.

"AUDREY AND CARY GRANT ARE the only people I ever knew who had no age," says Ralph Lauren.[80] Nothing is more quickly dated than high fashion, yet for all her importance in that realm over the decades, Hepburn seemed to have no time. At the last of her life, instead of trying to simulate youth, she was unashamed to look like the sixty-three-year-old woman she was, "which is to say, better than any sixty-three-year-old woman who's pretending that she isn't," said The New York Times. "Would that she were going to be around longer, to teach us all how to grow old."[81]

One of those celebrated Two Women is among many in Italy with deep emotional attachments to her. "Audrey was meek, gentle and ethereal," says Sophia Loren, "understated both in her life and in her work. She walked among us with a light pace, as if she didn't want to be noticed. [I regret losing her] as a friend, as a role model and as a companion of my youthful dreams."[82]

From Rome, Valentina Cortesa, the star of Hepburn's first important film, Secret People, laments, "I miss her. Well, we all miss her. . . . Carina, carina, deliziosa. La piccola cerbiatta."[83] Audrey meant so many different things to so many different people. "We shared our lives for 15 years," says Rob Wolders, "but I'm only now becoming fully aware of how important a figure she was in her generation and for future generations."

Her reality was shaped by the horrors of World War II, when people needed and tried to help one another. But once it was over, she said, "they were just the same—gossipy and mean."[84] If that was the rule, she wanted to be the exception. She had learned something and didn't want to be the same. Her sorrows were the desertion of her father and an inability to please her mother. After the war, the roles were switched: Audrey would became the "nurturer"—for her parents, then for her own children and, finally, for the children of the whole world.

She wanted only to be a dancer. By the standards of the day, she couldn't manage it—but her dancer's discipline turned her into a superb technician for life. Later as a film star, some inner voice told her she was unworthy of such great acclaim. She could never quite reconcile the public adulation with her private self-image or her mother's impossibly high standards.

The case history was not unusual, but the way she resolved it was: No Garboesque reclusion for Hepburn. No booze or pills. She had a secure place, early on, as a major cultural icon in film and fashion. She could have comfortably remained there with no additional effort. But in her centeredness, she figured out that the one thing she could do and should do was give back.

She lived her last thirty years in an age when cynicism largely displaced idealism. "She was too good for Hollywood," says her gentle friend Efrem Zimbalist, Jr., "but somehow she graced it, her life shone on it, and it became a different place while she was around."[85] People called her "Saint Audrey"—fondly, sarcastically or both. She told Rob Wolders she did not want to be remembered that way. She was no saint—just a human being with the heart and the will to rise above her frailties.

Once when she was asked to pick a single word to describe herself, Audrey Hepburn smiled and replied, "Lucky."[86] So, too, was the world.

AUDREY HEPBURN
1929–1993

Our huckleberry friend

TIFFANY & CO.

EPILOGUE

AUDREY HEPBURN'S EPILOGUE IS CONTAINED in the continuation of her work on behalf of the world's children. To obtain more information or make contributions, please contact the Audrey Hepburn Hollywood for Children Fund, 4 East 12th Street, New York, N.Y., 10003 (212–243–5264) or the Audrey Hepburn Memorial Fund for UNICEF, 3 UNICEF United Nations Plaza (#H6F), New York, N.Y., 10017.

FILMOGRAPHY

1. *Nederlands in Zeven Lessen [Dutch in Seven Lessons, or Dutch at the Double]* (1948). Netherlands, G-B Instructional Production. Produced by H. M. Josephson. Directed by Charles Huguenot Van der Linden. With Koes Koen [Wam Heskes] (George), A. Viruly (KLM pilot), AUDREY HEPBURN (KLM stewardess).

A girl-crazy English cameraman has just one week in which to film a rather dull travelogue of Holland. Running time: 79 min.

2. *One Wild Oat* (1951). Great Britain, Eros-Coronet. Produced by John Croydon. Directed by Charles Saunders. Written by Vernon Sylvaine and Lawrence Huntington from the play by Sylvaine. With Robertson Hare (Humphrey Proudfoot), Stanley Holloway (Alfred Gilbey), Constance Lorne (Mrs. Proudfoot), Vera Pearce (Mrs. Gilbey), June Sylvaine (Cherrie Proudfoot), Andrew Crawford (Fred Gilbey), Irene Handl (Audrey Cuttle), Sam Costa (Mr. Pepys), Robert Moreton (Throstle), Charles Grove (Charles), Joan Rice (Annie), AUDREY HEPBURN (unbilled extra).

A barrister tries to discourage his daughter's love for a scoundrel but is blackmailed instead. Running time: 78 min.

3. *Young Wives' Tale* (1951). Great Britain. Associated British Pictures. Produced by Victor Skutetzky. Directed by Henry Cass. Written by Ann Burnaby, from the play by Ronald Jeans. Photographed by Erwin Hillier. Music by Philip Green. Edited by E. Jarvis. Music Direction by Louis Levy. Art Direction by Terence Verity. With Joan Greenwood (Sabina Pennant), Nigel Patrick (Rodney Pennant), Derek Farr (Bruce Banning), Guy Middleton (Victor Manifold), Athene Seyler (Nanny Gallop), Helen Cherry (Mary Banning), AUDREY HEPBURN (Eve Lester), Fabia Drake (Nurse Blott), Irene Handl and Joan Sanderson (Nurses), Jack McNaughton (Taxi Driver), Brian Oulton (Man in Pub), Carol James (Elizabeth).

A timid boarder becomes infatuated with one of the married men living in the same house. Running time: 79 min.

4. *Laughter in Paradise* (1951). Great Britain. Associated British Pictures. Produced and directed by Mario Zampi. Written by Michael Pertwee and Jack Davies. Photographed by William McLeod. Music by Stanley Black. Edited by Giulio Zampi. Art Direction by Ivan King. With Alastair Sim (Deniston Russell), Fay Compton (Agnes Russell), Beatrice Campbell (Lucille Grayson), Veronica Hurst (Joan Webb), Guy Middleton (Simon Russell), A. E. Matthews (Sir Charles Robson), Joyce Grenfell (Elizabeth Robson), Hugh Griffith (Henry Russell), Anthony Steel (Roger Godfrey), John Laurie (Gordon Webb), Eleanor Summerfield (Sheila Wilcott), Ronald Adam (Mr. Wagstaffe), AUDREY HEPBURN (Cigarette Girl).

An eccentric millionaire bequeaths his money to four selfish relatives, on the condition that they first carry out his humiliating requests. Running time: 93 min.

5. *The Lavender Hill Mob* (1951). Great Britain. Ealing Studios. Produced by Michael Balcon. Directed by Charles Crichton. Written by T. E. B. Clarke. Photographed by Douglas Slocombe. Music by Georges Auric. Edited by Seth Holt. Musical Direction by Ernest Irving. Art Direction by William Kellner. With Alec Guinness (Holland), Stanley Holloway (Pendlebury), Sidney James (Lackery), Alfie Bass (Shorty), Marjorie Fielding (Mrs. Chalk), John Gregson (Farrow), Edie Martin (Miss Evesham), Clive Morton (Sergeant), Ronald Adam (Turner), Sydney Tafler (Clayton), AUDREY HEPBURN (Chiquita), Robert Shaw (in his bit-part screen debut).

A mousy shipping clerk, aided by his boarding-house crony, concocts and executes a brilliant scheme to steal a fortune in gold from his employers. Running time: 82 min.

6. *Secret People* (1952). Great Britain. Ealing Studios. Produced by Sidney Cole. Directed by Thorold Dickinson. Written by Dickinson, Wolfgang Wilhelm and Christianna Brand, from a story by Dickinson and Joyce Carey. Photographed by Gordon Dines. Music by Roberto Gerhard. Edited by Peter Tanner. Art Direction by William Kellner. Costumes by Anthony Mendleson. Choreography by Andrée Howard. With Valentina Cortesa (Maria), Serge Reggiani (Louis), Charles Goldner (Anselmo), AUDREY HEPBURN (Nora), Meg Jenkins (Penny), Irene Worth (Miss Jackson), Reginald Tate (Inspector Eliot), Norman Williams (Sergeant Newcome), Michael Shepley (Manager), Athene Seyler (Mrs. Kellick), Sydney Tafler (Syd Burnett), Geoffrey Hibbert (Steenie), John Ruddock (Daly), Michael Allan (Rodd), John Field (Fedor Luki), Bob Monkhouse (Barber).

After the assassination of their father, a Central European refugee and her innocent ballet-dancer sister in London are caught up in a violent political conspiracy. Running time: 96 min.

7. *Monte Carlo Baby* [*Nous Irons à Monte Carlo*] (1952). France. GFD/Favorite Pictures. Produced by Ray Ventura. Directed by Jean Boyer and Lester Fuller. Written by Boyer, Fuller, and Alex Joffe. Dialogue by Serge Veber. Photographed by Charles Suin. Music by Paul Misraki. Edited by Franchette Mazin. Art Direction by Robert Giordani. Music and lyrics by Misraki and Geoffrey Parsons. Sound by A. Archimbault. With AUDREY HEPBURN (Linda Farrell; Melissa Walter in French version), Jules Munshin (Antoine), Michele Farmer (Jacqueline), Cara Williams (Marinette), Philippe Lemaire (Philippe), Russell Collins (Max), John Van Dreelan (Pianist), Ray Ventura and his orchestra.

A touring musician is mistakenly given custody of a movie star's child. Running time: 89 min.

8. *Roman Holiday* (1953). Paramount. Produced and directed by William Wyler. Written by Ian McLellan Hunter and John Dighton, from a story by Hunter. Photographed by Frank F. Planer and Henri Alekan. Music by Georges Auric. Edited by Robert Swink. Art Direction by Hal Pereira and Walter Tyler. Costumes by Edith Head. With Gregory Peck (Joe Bradley), AUDREY HEPBURN (Princess Anne), Eddie Albert (Irving Radovich), Hartley Power (Mr. Hennessy), Laura Solari (Hennessey's Secretary), Harcourt Williams (Ambassador), Margaret Rawlings (Countess Vereberg), Tullio Carminati (General Provno), Paolo Carlini (Mario Delani), Claudio Ermelli (Giovanni), Paolo Borboni (Charwoman), Heinz Hindrich (Dr. Bonachoven), Gorella Gori (Shoe Seller), Alfredo Rizzo (Taxi Driver), John Horne (Master of Ceremonies), Giacomo Penza (Papal Nuncio), Eric Oulton (Sir Hugo Macy de Farmington).

A bored and sheltered princess escapes her guardians and falls in love with an American newsman in Rome. Running time: 119 min.

9. *Sabrina* (1954). Paramount. Produced and directed by Billy Wilder. Written by Wilder, Samuel Taylor, and Ernest Lehman, from the play *Sabrina Fair* by Taylor. Photographed by Charles Lang, Jr. Music by Frederick Hollander. Edited by Arthur Schmidt. Art Direction by Hal Pereira and Walter Tyler. Costumes by Edith Head. Music and lyrics by Wilson Stone, Richard Rodgers, Lorenz Hart, Harold Lewis, Louiguy, Edith Piaf, Frank Silver, Irving Cohen and John Cope. With Humphrey Bogart (Linus Larrabee), AUDREY HEPBURN (Sabrina Fairchild), William Holden (David Larrabee), Walter Hampden (Oliver Larrabee), John Williams (Thomas Fairchild), Martha Hyer (Elizabeth Tyson), Joan Vohs (Gretchen Van Horn), Marcel Dalio (Baron), Marcel Hillaire (The Professor), Nella Walker (Maude Larrabee), Francis X. Bushman (Mr. Tyson), Ellen Corby (Miss McCardle), Marjorie Bennett (Margaret, the Cook), Emory Parnell (Charles, the Butler), Kay Riehl (Mrs. Tyson), Nancy Kulp (Jenny, the Maid), Emmett Vogan, Colin Campbell (Board Members).

A chauffeur's daughter falls in love with one of two rich brothers, is packed off to cooking school in Paris, returns a sophisticate, and becomes the object of both brothers' affections. Running time: 114 min.

10. *War and Peace* (1956). Italy/U.S.A. Ponti-De Laurentiis Productions/Paramount. Produced by Dino De Laurentiis. Directed by King Vidor. Written by Bridget Boland, Robert Westerby, Vidor, Mario Camerini, Ennio de Concini, Ivo Perilli and Irwin Shaw, from the novel by Leo Tolstoy. Photographed by Jack Cardiff and Aldo Tonti. Music by Nino Rota. Edited by Stuart Gilmore and Leo Cattozzo. Music Direction by Franco Ferrara. Art Direction by Mario Chiari, Franz Bachelin and Giani Polidori. Costumes by Maria de Matteis. With AUDREY HEPBURN (Natasha Rostov), Henry Fonda (Pierre), Mel Ferrer (Andrei), Vittorio Gassman (Anatole), John Mills (Platon), Herbert Lom (Napoleon), Oscar Homolka (General Kutuzov), Anita Ekberg (Helene), Helmut Dantine (Dolokhov), Barry Jones (Count Rostov), Anna Maria Ferrero (Mary Bolkonsky), Milly Vitale (Lise),

Jeremy Brett (Nicholas Rostov), Lea Seidl (Countess Rostov), Wilfrid Lawson (Prince Bolkonsky), Sean Barrett (Petya Rostov), Tullio Carminati (Kuragin), May Britt (Sonya), Patrick Crean (Denisov), Gertrude Flynn (Peronskaya), Gualtièro Tumiati (Pierre's Father), Mauro Lanciani (Young Prince Nikolai Bolkonsky).

The great love story of young Natasha for Prince Andrei—and the unrequited love of bastard Pierre for Natasha—set in the panorama of Napoleon's invasion of Russia. Running time: 208 min.

11. *Funny Face* (1957). Paramount. Produced by Roger Edens. Directed by Stanley Donen. Written by Leonard Gershe, from his musical libretto, *Wedding Day*. Photographed by Ray June. Music by George Gershwin, Ira Gershwin, Edens and Gershe. Edited by Frank Bracht. Musical Direction by Adolph Deutsch. Art Direction by George W. Davis and Hal Pereira. Costumes by Edith Head and Hubert de Givenchy. Choreography by Fred Astaire and Eugene Loring. With AUDREY HEPBURN (Jo Stockton), Fred Astaire (Dick Avery), Kay Thompson (Maggie Prescott), Michel Auclair (Professor Emile Flostre), Robert Fleming (Paul Duval), Dovima (Marion), Virginia Gibson (Babs), Suzy Parker, Sunny Harnett (Specialty Dancers in "Think Pink"), Don Powell, Carole Eastman (Specialty Dancers), Sue England (Laura), Ruta Lee (Lettie), Iphigenie Castiglioni (Armande), Elizabeth Slifer (Madame La Farge), Nesdon Booth (Southern Man), Jerry Chiat (Man on Head).

A Greenwich Village bookworm is turned into the fashion sensation of the decade by the editor and star photographer of a glitzy, *Vogue*-like magazine. Running time: 103 min.

12. *Love in the Afternoon* (1957). Allied Artists. Produced and directed by Billy Wilder. Written by Wilder and I. A. L. Diamond, from the novel *Ariane* by Claude Anet. Photographed by William Mellor. Music by Franz Waxman. Edited by Leonid Azar. Art Direction by Alexander Trauner. Costumes by Hubert de Givenchy. With Gary Cooper (Frank Flannagan), AUDREY HEPBURN (Ariane Chavasse), Maurice Chevalier (Claude Chevasse), Van Doude (Michel), John McGiver (Monsieur X), Lise Bourdin (Madame X), Bonifas (Commissioner of Police), Audrey Wilder (Brunette), Gyula Kokas, Michel Kokas, George Cocos, Victor Gazzoli (Gypsies), Olga Valery (Lady with Dog), Leila Croft and Valerie Croft (Swedish Twins), Charles Bouillard (Valet at the Ritz), Minerva Pious (Maid at the Ritz), Gregory Gromoff (Ritz Doorman), Janine Dard, Claude Ariel (Existentialists), Guy Delorme (Gigolo).

The cellist-daughter of a detective falls for the playboy-lothario whom her father is investigating. Running time: 125 min.

13. *The Nun's Story* (1959). Warner Brothers. Produced by Henry Blanke. Directed by Fred Zinnemann. Written by Robert Anderson, from the book by Kathryn C. Hulme. Photographed by Franz F. Planer. Music by Franz Waxman. Edited by Walter Thompson. Art Direction by Alexander Trauner. Costumes by Marjorie Best. With AUDREY HEPBURN (Sister Luke, Gabrielle Van Der Mal), Peter Finch

(Dr. Fortunati), Dame Edith Evans (Mother Emmanuel), Dame Peggy Ashcroft (Mother Mathilde), Dean Jagger (Dr. Van Der Mal), Mildred Dunnock (Sister Margharita), Beatrice Straight (Mother Christophe), Patricia Collinge (Sister William), Eva Kotthaus (Sister Marie), Ruth White (Mother Marcella), Niall McGinnis (Father Vermeuhlen), Patricia Bosworth (Simone), Barbara O'Neil (Mother Katherine), Lionel Jeffries (Dr. Goovaerts), Margaret Phillips (Sister Pauline), Rosalie Crutchley (Sister Eleanor), Colleen Dewhurst (Archangel), Stephen Murray (Chaplain), Orlando Martins (Kalulu), Errol John (Illunga), Jeannette Sterke (Louise Van Der Mal), Richard O'Sullivan (Pierre Van Der Mal), Diana Lambert (Lisa), Marina Wolkonsky (Marie Van Der Mal).

A nursing nun in the Belgian Congo struggles with her own worthiness and—after the death of her father—whether she should give up the sisterhood to fight the Nazis. Running time: 149 min.

14. *Green Mansions* (1959). Metro-Goldwyn-Mayer. Produced by Edmund Grainger. Directed by Mel Ferrer. Written by Dorothy Kingsley, from the novel by William Henry Hudson. Photographed by Joseph Ruttenberg. Music by Hector Villa-Lobos and Bronislau Kaper. Edited by Ferris Webster. Art Direction by William A. Horning and Preston Ames. Costumes by Dorothy Jeakins. Choreography by Katharine Dunham. With AUDREY HEPBURN (Rima), Anthony Perkins (Abel), Lee J. Cobb (Nuflo), Sessue Hayakawa (Runi), Henry Silva (Kua-Ko), Nehemiah Persoff (Don Panta), Michael Pate (Priest), Estelle Hemsley (Cla-Cla).

A political fugitive in Venezuela meets Rima the Bird Girl, mysterious beauty of the jungle, whom he views as the ideal of innocence but whom the superstitious natives believe to be evil and set out to kill. Running time: 104 min.

15. *The Unforgiven* (1960). Hecht-Hill-Lancaster Productions, United Artists. Produced by James Hill. Directed by John Huston. Written by Ben Maddow, from the novel by Alan LeMay. Photographed by Franz F. Planer. Music Direction by Dimitri Tiomkin. Edited by Russell Lloyd. Art Direction by Stephen Grimes. With Burt Lancaster (Ben Zachary), AUDREY HEPBURN (Rachel Zachary), Audie Murphy (Cash Zachary), John Saxon (Johnny Portugal), Charles Bickford (Zeb Rollins), Lillian Gish (Mattilda Zachary), Albert Salmi (Charlie Rawlins), Joseph Wiseman (Abe Kelsey), June Walker (Hagar Rawlins), Kipp Hamilton (Georgia Rawlins), Doug McClure (Andy Zachary).

An orphan is caught between the prejudices of the white family that adopted her and a bloody Kiowa uprising. Running time: 120 min.

16. *Breakfast at Tiffany's* (1961). Paramount. Produced by Martin Jurow and Richard Shepherd. Directed by Blake Edwards. Written by George Axelrod, from the novel by Truman Capote. Photographed by Franz F. Planer. Music by Henry Mancini. Edited by Howard Smith. Costumes by Edith Head. Music and lyrics of "Moon River" by Mancini and Johnny Mercer. With AUDREY HEPBURN (Holly

Golightly), George Peppard (Paul Varjak), Patricia Neal ("2E"), Buddy Ebsen (Doc Golightly), Martin Balsam (O. J. Berman), Mickey Rooney (Mr. Yunioshi), José-Luis De Villallonga (José), John McGiver (Tiffany Salesman), Dorothy Whitney (Mag Wildwood), Stanley Adams (Rusty Trawler), Elvia Allman (Librarian), Alan Reed Sr. (Sally Tomato), Claude Stroud (Sid Arbuck).

Holly Golightly, a New York Bohemian girl for hire, falls in love with a budding novelist. Running time: 114 min.

17. *The Children's Hour* (1961). United Artists. Produced and directed by William Wyler. Written by John Michael Hayes, from the play by Lillian Hellman. Photographed by Franz Planer. Music by Alex North. Edited by Robert Swink. Art Direction by Fernando Carrere. Costumes by Dorothy Jeakins. With AUDREY HEPBURN (Karen Wright), Shirley MacLaine (Martha Dobie), James Garner (Dr. Joe Cardin), Miriam Hopkins (Mrs. Lily Mortar), Fay Bainter (Mrs. Amelia Tilford), Karen Balkin (Mary Tilford), Veronica Cartwright (Rosalie).

A vicious student accuses the two owners of her girls' school of lesbianism, with tragic results. Running time: 107 min.

18. *Charade* (1963). Universal. Produced and directed by Stanley Donen. Written by Peter Stone, from the story *The Unsuspecting Wife* by Stone and Marc Behm. Photographed by Charles Lang Jr. Music by Henry Mancini. Edited by James Clark. Art Direction by Jean d'Eaubonne. Costumes by Hubert de Givenchy. Music and lyrics by Mancini and Johnny Mercer. With Cary Grant (Peter Joshua), AUDREY HEPBURN (Regina Lambert), Walter Matthau (Hamilton Bartholomew), James Coburn (Tex), George Kennedy (Scobie), Ned Glass (Gideon), Jacques Marin (Grandpierre), Paul Bonifas (Felix), Dominique Minot (Sylvie).

A stylish widow is hounded by a quartet of unsavory characters—plus savory Cary Grant—all of them in pursuit of her late husband's hidden fortune. Running time: 113 min.

19. *Paris When it Sizzles* (1964). Paramount. Produced by Richard Quine and George Axelrod. Directed by Quine. Written by Axelrod, from the story by Julien Duvivier and Henri Jeanson. Photographed by Charles Lang, Jr. Music by Nelson Riddle. Edited by Archie Marshek. Art Direction by Jean d'Eaubonne. Costumes by Hubert de Givenchy and Christian Dior. With William Holden (Richard Benson), AUDREY HEPBURN (Gabrielle Simpson), Gregoire Asin (Police Inspector), Raymond Bussieres (Gangster), Noel Coward, Tony Curtis, Marlene Dietrich, Mel Ferrer (Themselves!).

Long-in-the-tooth American in Paris bounces bad literary fantasies off primarily prim, periodically provocative typist in wild, wacky effort to produce wild, wacky screenplay within forty-eight hours. Running time: 110 min.

20. *My Fair Lady* (1964). Warner Brothers. Produced by Jack L. Warner. Directed

by George Cukor. Written by Alan Jay Lerner, from the musical play by Lerner and Frederick Loewe, and the play *Pygmalion* by George Bernard Shaw. Photographed by Harry Stradling. Music by Loewe. Edited by William Ziegler. Production Design by Cecil Beaton. Musical Direction by André Previn. Art Direction by Gene Allen. Costumes by Beaton. Choreography by Hermes Pan. With AUDREY HEPBURN (Eliza Doolittle), Rex Harrison (Henry Higgins), Stanley Holloway (Alfred P. Doolittle), Wilfrid Hyde-White (Colonel Hugh Pickering), Gladys Cooper (Mrs. Higgins), Jeremy Brett (Freddy Eynsford-Hill), Theodore Bikel (Zoltan Karpathy), Henry Daniell (Prince Gregor of Transylvania), Isobel Elsom (Mrs. Eynsford-Hill), Mona Washbourne (Mrs. Pearce), John Alderson (Jamie), John McLiam (Harry), Marni Nixon (singing voice of Audrey Hepburn), Bill Shirley (singing voice of Jeremy Brett), Grady Sutton, Allison Daniell, Betty Blythe (Ascot/Ball Guests).

Eliza Doolittle, that lovable Cockney guttersnipe, is transformed into a lady by phonetics professor Henry Higgins, that lovable mysogynist. Running time: 170 min.

21. *How to Steal a Million* (1966). 20th Century-Fox. Produced by Fred Kohlmar. Directed by William Wyler. Written by Harry Kurnitz, from the story *Venus Rising* by George Bradshaw. Photography by Charles Lang. Music by Johnny Williams. Edited by Robert Swink. Production Design by Alexander Trauner. Costumes by Hubert de Givenchy. Makeup by Alberto de Rossi. With AUDREY HEPBURN (Nicole Bonnet), Peter O'Toole (Simon Dermott), Eli Wallach (David Leland), Hugh Griffith (Charles Bonnet), Charles Boyer (De Solnay), Fernand Gravey (Grammont), Marcel Dalio (Señor Paravideo), Jacques Marin (Chief Guard), Francois Moustache (Guard), Bert Bertram (Marcel).

An art forger's daughter and a private eye set out to steal her father's fake Cellini sculpture before it is discovered by insurance appraisers. Running time: 127 min.

22. *Two for the Road* (1967). 20th Century-Fox. Produced and directed by Stanley Donen. Written by Frederic Raphael. Photographed by Christopher Challis. Music by Henry Mancini. Edited by Richard Marden and Madeleine Gug. Art Direction by Willy Holt and Marc Frederic. Set decoration by Roger Volper. Costumes by Hardy Amies, Ken Scott, Michele Posier, Paco Rabanne, Mary Quant, Foale and Tuffin. Makeup by Alberto de Rossi. With AUDREY HEPBURN (Joanna Wallace), Albert Finney (Mark Wallace), Eleanor Bron (Cathy Manchester), William Daniels (Howard Manchester), Gabrielle Middelton (Ruth Manchester), Claude Dauphin (Maurice Dalbret), Nadia Gray (Francoise Dalbret), Georges Descrieres (David), Jacqueline Bisset (bit), Irene Hilda (Yvonne de Florac), Kathy Chelimsky (Caroline).

A couple in the south of France spin down the highways of infidelity in their troubled twelve-year marriage—doing so in non-sequential segments. Running time: 112 min.

23. *Wait Until Dark* (1967). Warner Brothers. Produced by Mel Ferrer. Executive Producer, Walter MacEwen. Directed by Terence Young. Written by Robert Carrington and Jane Howard-Carrington, based on the play by Frederick Knott. Photographed by Charles Lang. Music by Henry Mancini. Edited by Gene Milford. Art Direction by George Jenkins. Set decoration by George James Hopkins. Music and lyrics by Mancini, Jay Livingston and Ray Evans, sung by Bobby Darin. Makeup by Gordon Bau. With AUDREY HEPBURN (Susy Hendrix), Alan Arkin (Roat), Efrem Zimbalist Jr. (Sam Hendrix), Richard Crenna (Mike Talman), Jack Weston (Carlino), Samantha Jones (Lisa), Julie Herrod (Gloria), Frank O'Brien (Shatner), Gary Morgan (The Boy).

A blind woman is terrorized by criminals seeking a heroin-filled doll that was given to her husband. Running time: 107 min.

24. *Robin and Marian* (1976). Great Britain. Columbia. Produced by Denis O'Dell. Directed by Richard Lester. Written by James Goldman. Photographed by David Watkin. Music by John Barry. Edited by John Victor Smith. Production Design by Michael Stringer. Art Direction by Gil Parrando. Costumes by Yvonne Blake. With Sean Connery (Robin Hood), AUDREY HEPBURN (Maid Marian), Robert Shaw (Sheriff of Nottingham), Richard Harris (King Richard), Nicol Williamson (Little John), Denholm Elliott (Will Scarlett), Kenneth Haigh (Sir Ranulf), Ronnie Barker (Friar Tuck), Ian Holm (King John), Bill Maynard (Mercadier), Veronica Quilligan (Sister Mary), Victoria Merida Roja (Queen Isabella).

Robin Hood, aging none too gracefully, returns exhausted from the Crusades to woo and win Maid Marian one last time. Running time: 112 min.

25. *Bloodline* (1979). Paramount. Produced by David V. Picker and Sidney Beckerman. Directed by Terence Young. Written by Laird Koenig, from the novel by Sidney Sheldon. Photographed by Freddie Young. Music by Ennio Morricone. Edited by Bud Molin. Production Design by Ted Haworth. Costumes by Enrico Sabbatini. With AUDREY HEPBURN (Elizabeth Roffe), Ben Gazzara (Rhys Williams), James Mason (Sir Alec Nichols), Claudia Mori (Donatella), Irene Papas (Simonetta Palazzi), Michelle Phillips (Vivian Nichols), Maurice Ronet (Maurice), Romy Schneider (Helene Martin), Omar Sharif (Ivo Palazzi), Gert Frobe (Inspector Max Hornung), Beatrice Straight (Kate Ehrling).

Snuff films and skullduggery in the pharmaceutical industry—a rare and insane combination—ensnare a fragile paleontologist in Givenchy designs. Running time: 116 min.

26. *They All Laughed* (1981). Time-Life Films/20th Century-Fox. Produced by George Morfogen and Blaine Novak. Directed and written by Peter Bogdanovich. Photographed by Robby Muller. Music by Douglas Dilge. Edited by Scott Vickrey. Art Direction by Kert Lundell. With AUDREY HEPBURN (Angela Niotes), Ben Gazzara (John Russo), John Ritter (Charles Rutledge), Colleen Camp (Christy

Miller), Patti Hansen (Sam the Taxi Driver), Dorothy Stratten (Dolores Martin), George Morfogen (Mr. Leondopoulos), Blaine Novak (Arthur Brodsky), Sean Ferrer (José), Linda MacEwen (Amy Lester), Glenn Scarpelli (Michael Niotes), Vassily Lambrinos (Stavros Niotes), Antonia Bogdanovich (Stefania Russo), Alexandra Bogdanovich (Georgina Russo), Sheila Stodden (Barbara Jo), Lisa Dunsheath (Tulips), Joyce Hyser (Sylvia).

Four New York private detectives—each quirkier and hornier than the other—fall in love with the women they're assigned to follow. Running time: 115 min.

27. *Always* (1990). Universal-United Artists. Produced by Steven Spielberg, Frank Marshall and Kathleen Kennedy. Directed by Spielberg. Written by Jerry Belson, from the screenplay *A Guy Named Joe* by Dalton Trumbo; story by Frederick Hazlitt Brennan, Chandler Sprague and David Boehm. Photographed by Mikael Salomon. Edited by Michael Kahn. Music by John Williams. Production Design by James Bissell. Art Direction by Chris Burian-Mohr. Costumes by Ellen Mirojnick. Choreography by Bob Banas. With Richard Dreyfuss (Peter Sandich), Holly Hunter (Dorinda Durston), Brad Johnson (Ted Baker), John Goodman (Al Yackey), AUDREY HEPBURN (Hap), Roberts Blossom (Dave), Keith David (Powerhouse), Ed Van Nuys (Nails), Marg Helgenberger (Rachel), Dale Dye (Fire Boss), Brian Haley (Alex), James Lashly (Charlie), Michael Steve Jones (Grey).

A fire-fighting pilot saves his best friend's life but loses his own, subsequently watching over the woman he loves from beyond. Running time: 121 min.

TELEVISION

1. "Rainy Day in Paradise Junction," an episode of the *TV Workshop* series. (CBS, April 13, 1952)

2. "Mayerling," *Producers' Showcase* special. Produced by Fred Coe. Directed by Anatole Litvak. With AUDREY HEPBURN (Maria Vetsera), Mel Ferrer (Prince Rudolph), Raymond Massey (Emperor), Diana Wynyard (Empress). The heir to the Hapsburg empire enters into a suicide pact with his mistress. (NBC, February 4, 1957)

3. *A World of Love*, UNICEF documentary special. Produced by Alexander Cohen. Cohosted by Bill Cosby, Shirley MacLaine, AUDREY HEPBURN, Richard Burton, Julie Andrews, Barbra Streisand and Harry Belafonte. (Christmas 1971)

4. "Love Among Thieves," ABC-TV movie. Produced by Robert A. Pazazian. Directed by Roger Young. Written by Stephen Black, Harry Stern and Sally Robinson. With AUDREY HEPBURN (Caroline DuLac), Robert Wagner (Mike Chambers), Jerry Orbach (Interpol Agent), Samantha Eggar (Solange), Ismael Carlo (Mazo).
   An elegant baroness, who also happens to be a concert pianist, steals a priceless Fabergé egg to ransom her abducted fiancé and ends up in the wilds of South America with a wisecracking Yankee adventurer. (February 23, 1987)

5. *Gardens of the World*, Parts I–VI, PBS. Perennial Productions, Inc. Produced by Janis Blackschleger. Directed by Bruce Fanchini. Written by Glenn Berenbeim. Photographed by Jeri Sopanen. Hosted by AUDREY HEPBURN. Narrated by Michael York. (January 1993)

5a. *Gardens of the World*, Parts VII–VIII, PBS. Tropical and Japanese gardens. (June 1996)

STAGE

1. *High Button Shoes*. The Hippodrome, London. Opened December 22, 1948, for a 291-performance run. Produced by Archie Thomson. Directed by Jack Hylton. Music by Jule Styne. Choreography by Jerome Robbins. With Lou Parker, Alma Cogan, Kay Kendall, Nickolas Dana, AUDREY HEPBURN.

2. *Sauce Tartare*. Cambridge Theatre, London. Opened May 18, 1949. Produced and directed by Cecil Landeau. With Renee Houston, Jack Melford, Alma Cogan, Joan Heal, AUDREY HEPBURN.

3. *Sauce Piquante*. Cambridge Theatre, London. Opened April 27, 1950. Produced and directed by Cecil Landeau. With Norman Wisdom, Muriel Smith, Douglas Byng, Moira Lister, Bob Monkhouse, David Hurst, Joan Heal, Marcel le Bon, AUDREY HEPBURN, Aud Johanssen.

4. *Gigi*. Fulton Theatre, New York. Opened November 24, 1951. Produced by Gilbert Miller. Directed by Raymond Rouleau. Written by Anita Loos, adapted from Colette's novel. Settings by Raymond Sovey. With AUDREY HEPBURN (Gigi), Josephine Brown (Mme. Alvarez), Cathleen Nesbitt (Alicia de St. Ephlam), Doris Patston (Mother), Michael Evans (Gaston), Francis Compton (Victor), Bertha Belmore (Sidonie). Closed May 31, 1952. Hepburn also did the road-show tour, which began October 13, 1952, in Pittsburgh and continued through Boston, Cleveland, Chicago, Detroit, Washington and Los Angeles, closing May 16, 1953, in San Francisco.

5. *Ondine*. 46th Street Theatre, New York. Opened February 18, 1954. Produced by The Playwrights Company. Directed by Alfred Lunt. Written by Jean Giraudoux, adapted by Maurice Valency. Settings by Peter Larkin. Costumes by Richard Whorf. Lighting by Jean Rosenthal. Music by Virgil Thompson. With AUDREY HEPBURN (Ondine), Mel Ferrer (Ritter Hans), John Alexander (Auguste), Edith King (Eugenie), Alan Hewitt (Lord Chamberlain), Marian Seldes (Bertha), Robert Middleton (The Old One). Closed June 26, 1954.

SOURCE NOTES

CHAPTER 1

1. John Maynard, "Audrey's Harvest of the Heart," *Photoplay*, September 1956, p. 115.
2. Cecil Beaton, "Audrey Hepburn," *Vogue*, November 1, 1954.
3. Caroline Latham, *Audrey Hepburn* (London and New York: Proteus Publishing, 1984), pp. 6–8.
4. James Robert Parish and Don E. Stanke, *The Glamour Girls* (New Rochelle: Arlington House Press, 1975), p. 319, and introduction by Rene Jordan, pp. 16–17.
5. Frank Thompson, *American Film*, May 1990, p. 55.
6. Joseph J. O'Donohue IV letter to BP, February 26, 1996.
7. Quoted in "Audrey Hepburn— Angel of Love," undated Dutch article, translated by Sandra Homner.
8. Alan Riding, *New York Times* Paris bureau, interview with AH, April 12, 1991.
9. Quoted in *Audrey Hepburn Remembered*, video documentary, Wombat Productions (1993), Gene Feldman producer.
10. Quoted in Ian Woodward, *Audrey Hepburn* (New York: St. Martin's Press, 1984), pp. 9 and 19.
11. Robert Wolders, in outtakes of *Audrey Hepburn Remembered*, video documentary, Wombat Productions, 1993, Gene Feldman producer.
12. Quoted in Warren Harris, *Audrey Hepburn* (New York: Simon & Schuster, 1994), p. 16.
13. Wolders, *op. cit.*
14. Martin Abramson, "Audrey Hepburn," *Cosmopolitan*, October 1955, p. 30.
15. Riding, *op. cit.*
16. *De Gelderlander* article, December 24, 1993.
17. Harris, *op. cit.*, p. 20.
18. Glenn Plaskin, "Audrey Hepburn," *US* Magazine, October 17, 1988, p. 44.
19. Edward Klein, "One Woman's Search for Love: A Profile of Audrey Hepburn," *Parade*, March 5, 1989, p. 5.
20. Plaskin, *op. cit.*
21. Sidney Fields, "Success Is Not Security," *McCall's*, July 1954, p. 62.
22. Riding, *op. cit.*
23. *Ibid.*
24. Alfred Heineken III to BP and John Barba, Amsterdam, December 1993.
25. Dominick Dunne, "Hepburn Heart," *Vanity Fair*, May 1991, p. 197.
26. Klein, *op. cit.*
27. *Somalia: The Silent Children*, October 1992, by AH, Christopher Dickey transcript for *International Newsweek*.
28. AH on *Donahue*, January 31, 1990.
29. Quoted in Harris, *op. cit.*, p. 25.
30. Riding, *op. cit.*

31. David A. Heringa letter to BP, March 27, 1994, from Edmonton, Alberta, Canada.

32. "Audrey Hepburn—Angel of Love," *op. cit.*

33. Quoted in Harris, *op. cit.*, p. 32.

34. "Audrey Hepburn: Angel of Love," translated by Sandra Homner.

35. Annabel Farjeon, "The Dutch Journal: The Sadler's Wells Ballet in Holland, May 1940" (Part One), *Dance Chronicle: Studies in Dance and the Related Arts*, Volume 10, No. 3, 1987.

36. *Ibid.*

37. Dunne, *op. cit.*

38. Jane Edgeworth to John Barba, March 4, 1994.

39. Elizabeth Kennedy to John Barba, January 22, 1994.

40. Quoted in Woodward, *op. cit.*, p. 24.

41. *The Lion Rampant: The Story of Holland's Resistance to the Nazis*, by L. de Jong and Joseph W. F. Stoppelman, (New York: Querido, 1943).

42. Harris, *op. cit.*, p. 36.

43. AH on *Donahue*, January 31, 1990.

44. de Jong and Stoppelman, op. cit.

45. Quoted in *De Gelderlander*, December 24, 1993.

46. Quoted in *The Philadelphia Inquirer*, May 13, 1990.

47. Paul Vroemen to BP, December 9, 1993.

48. *De Gelderlander*, *op. cit.*, et al.

49. AH on *Donahue*, January 31, 1990; and Curtis Bill Pepper, "The Loving World of Audrey Hepburn Dotti," *Vogue*, April 1, 1971, p. 94.

50. Paul Vroemen to BP, *op. cit.*

51. Hako Sixma van Heemstra to BP, January 3, 1995.

52. Scott Harris, "Audrey Hepburn, Actress and Humanitarian, Dies," *Los Angeles Times*, January 21, 1993.

53. AH on *Donahue*, January 31, 1990.

54. *Ibid.*

55. Quoted in *De Gelderlander*, December 24, 1993, by Helene van Beck.

56. David Heringa to John Barba, February 20, 1995.

57. Quoted in Parish, *op. cit.*, p. 321.

58. Paul Vroemen to BP, April 28, 1994, Kamerik, Holland.

59. Quoted in J. D. Podolsky, "Life with Audrey," *People*, October 31, 1994, p. 104.

60. Jerry Tallmer, "Audrey's N.Y. holiday," *New York Post*, April 22, 1991.

61. "Audrey Hepburn—Angel of Love," *op. cit.*

62. AH to Henry Gris, quoted in Higham, p. 18.

63. "Audrey Hepburn—Breakfast at UNICEF," *Philadelphia Inquirer*, May 13, 1990.

64. "Audrey Hepburn," *Coronet*, January, 1954.

65. "Before This, She Starved," *This Week* magazine, *New York Herald Tribune*, August 30, 1953, p. 20.

66. Quoted in Harris, *op. cit.*, p. 39.

67. AH on *Larry King Live*, January 25, 1990.

68. Houston interviews, 1990.

69. William Hawkins, interview with

AH, *Dance Magazine*, October 1956, p. 19.

70. *Magriet* translation by Sandra Homner, plus Willems with John Barba, April 1994.

71. Willem van Hall to Paul Vroemen.

72. Quoted in Woodward, *op. cit.*, p. 30.

73. AH to Henry Gris, quoted in Woodward, p. 31.

74. Quoted in Latham, *op. cit.*, p. 11.

75. "Princess Apparent," *Time*, September 7, 1953.

76. Michael Quarles to John Barba, February 26, 1994.

77. Anita Loos, "Everything Happens to Audrey Hepburn," *The American Weekly*, September 5, 1954; and *The American Weekly* (1958).

78. Hawkins, *op. cit.*, p. 17

79. Anthony Deane-Drummond, *Return Ticket.* (London: Collins, 1967).

80. Quoted in Harris, *op. cit.*, p. 42.

81. Hawkins, *op. cit.*

82. Terence Young to BP, April 24, 1994.

83. Hawkins, *op. cit.*

84. Sidney Fields, "Only Human," *Daily Mirror*, November 27, 1951.

85. Plaskin, *op. cit.*; also Plaskin, *Richmond News Leader*, May 24, 1991.

86. "UNICEF AMBASSADRICE VOELDE ZICH VAAK MACHTELOOS IN DE RAMPGEBIEDEN" [undated Dutch news article, c. January 1993.]

87. Klein, *op. cit.*

88. Quoted in Latham, p. 11.

89. AH on *Larry King: TNT Extra*, October 18, 1991.

90. AH to Tex McCurdy, "Cover Story" radio interview, January 10, 1954.

91. AH to Terry Wogan, BBC, 1988.

92. *Somalia: The Silent Children*, October 1992, by AH, Christopher Dickey transcript for *International Newsweek*.

93. *Philadelphia Inquirer*, May 13, 1990.

94. Hawkins, *op. cit.*

95. Riding, *op. cit.*

96. Pauline Swanson, "Knee-Deep in Stardust," *Photoplay*, April, 1954.

97. Quoted in Parish, *op. cit.*, p. 322.

98. AH on *Donahue*, January 31, 1990.

99. Terence Young to BP, April 24, 1994.

100. David A. Heringa letter to BP, March 27, 1994, from Edmonton, Alberta, Canada.

101. Quoted in Harris, *op. cit.*, p. 50.

102. "Audrey Hepburn—Angel of Love," *op. cit.*

103. Anneke van Wijk Koppen to John Barba, April 17, 1994.

104. Alfred Heineken III to BP and John Barba, December 8, 1993.

105. *Magriet* article, translation by Sandra Homner.

106. *Ibid.*

107. Ida de Jong to John Barba, March 4, 1994.

108. *Ibid.*

CHAPTER 2

1. Alan Riding, *New York Times* Paris bureau, interview with AH, April 12, 1991.

2. AH to Terry Wogan, BBC, 1988; and Glenn Plaskin, "Audrey Hepburn," *US* magazine, October 17, 1988, p. 44.

3. Quoted in Ian Woodward, *Audrey Hepburn* (New York: St. Martin's Press, 1984), p. 41.

4. Quoted in Henk van Gelder, "Hepburns Nederlandse filmdebuut" ("Hepburn's Dutch Film Debut"), *NRC Handelsblad*, January 22, 1993 [translated by Paul Vroemen].

5. Leendert de Jong to BP, January 8, 1994.

6. Warren Harris, *Audrey Hepburn* (New York: Simon & Schuster, 1994), p. 57.

7. Quoted in *The New Yorker*, December 8, 1951, p. 32.

8. Ella to Cecil Beaton, in *Cecil Beaton's 'Fair Lady'*, p. 57.

9. AH on *Donahue*, January 31, 1990.

10. Riding, *op. cit.*

11. Angela Dukes Ellis to John Barba, January 24, 1995.

12. Quoted in William Hawkins, interview with AH *Dance Magazine*, October 1956, p. 19.

13. Plaskin, *op. cit.*

14. Quoted in Plaskin, *ibid.*

15. Quoted in Caroline Latham, *Audrey Hepburn* (London and New York: Proteus Publishing, 1984), p. 12.

16. Ida de Jong to John Barba, March 4, 1994.

17. Ronald Hynde to John Barba, May 1, 1995.

18. Quoted by Dennis Washburn, *Birmingham News*, February 22, 1987, and by Mal Vincent, *Norfolk Virginian-Pilot*, February 22, 1987.

19. Quoted in Joyce Waldman, "Audrey's Fantastic Figure," *Cosmopolitan*, June 1959, p. 61.

20. Quoted in UNICEF video of the Universal Childhood Immunization Achievement Celebration, October 8, 1991.

21. Quoted in Hawkins, *op. cit.*

22. AH to Tex McCurdy, "Cover Story" radio interview, January 10, 1954.

23. Nickolas Dana to BP, October 28, 1994.

24. Quoted in Woodward, *op. cit.*, p. 55.

25. *Ibid.*, p. 56.

26. *Ibid.*, p. 60.

27. AH to David Lewin, quoted in Woodward, *op. cit.*, p. 54.

28. Quoted in Woodward, *op. cit.*, pp. 58–59.

29. Dominick Dunne, "Hepburn Heart," *Vanity Fair*, May 1991, p. 198.

30. AH remarks, Eastman House, Rochester, N.Y., October 25, 1992.

31. Quoted in Sheridan Morley, *Audrey Hepburn: A Celebration* (London: Pavilion Books Limited, 1993), p. 38.

32. Gene Finggold, "AH Added Post-Hitler Realism to the Movies' Image of the Child-

Woman," *Films in Review*, December 1971, p. 587.

33. Outtakes from "Audrey Hepburn in Her Own Words," Robert Wolders video documentary, 1994.

34. Holloway autobiography, quoted in Woodward, p. 62.

35. Quoted in Morley, *op. cit.*, p. 38.

36. Kevin Brownlow to BP and John Barba, London, December 3, 1993.

37. Cited in Morley, *op. cit.*, p. 38.

38. Charles Saunders to John Barba, April 17, 1994.

39. Harry Haun, "That's Our Fair Audrey," *New York Daily News*, April 21, 1991.

40. AH to Bill Collins, Australia, 1989.

41. *New York Times*, November 12, 1951, p. 21.

42. Quoted in Harris, *op. cit.*, p. 68.

43. Lord James Hanson to BP, London, December 3, 1993.

44. Zsa Zsa Gabor to Maria Ciaccia, November 12, 1994.

45. Lord James Hanson to BP, London, December 3, 1993.

46. Valentina Cortesa to John Barba, February 15, 1995.

47. *Ibid.*

48. Quoted in Robert Parish and Don E. Stanke, *The Glamour Girls* (New Rochelle: Arlington House, 1975), p. 325.

49. Latham, *op. cit.*, p. 17.

50. Cited in Woodward, *op. cit.*, pp. 94–95.

51. Terence Young to BP, April 24, 1994.

52. Quoted in Woodward, *op. cit.*, p. 77.

53. Valentina Cortesa to John Barba, *op. cit.*

54. Nickolas Dana to BP, October 28, 1994.

55. Ringgold, *op. cit.*

56. *New York Times*, May 19, 1954.

57. Anita Loos, *A Cast of Thousands* (New York: Grosset & Dunlap, 1977), pp. 157–164.

58. Harris, *op. cit.*, p. 75.

59. Anita Loos, *op. cit.*

60. Gilbert Miller, "The Search for Gigi," *Theatre Arts*, July 1952, p. 50.

61. Quoted in Latham, *op. cit.*, p. 20.

62. Valentina Cortesa to John Barba, *op. cit.*

63. Quoted in Harris, *op. cit.*, p. 77.

64. Axel Madsen, *William Wyler* (New York: Thomas Y. Crowell Co., 1973), p. 309.

65. AH to Bill Collins, Australia, 1989.

66. Quoted in Harris, *op. cit.*, p. 77.

67. Parish quoting from Madsen, *op. cit.*

68. "Princess Apparent," *Time Magazine*, September 7, 1953.

69. *Ibid.*

70. Quoted in Woodward, *op. cit.*, p. 87.

71. Cited in Morley, *op. cit.*, p. 46.

CHAPTER 3

1. Martin Abramson, "Audrey Hepburn," *Cosmopolitan*, October 1955, p. 26.
2. *Ibid.*
3. AH at "Council of Fashion Designers '88" salute to Richard Avedon, January 14, 1989.
4. Charles Higham, *Audrey: The Life of Audrey Hepburn* (New York: Macmillan, 1984), p. 45.
5. Anita Loos, *A Cast of Thousands* (New York, Grosset & Dunlap, 1977), pp. 157–164.
6. Quoted in Ian Woodward, *Audrey Hepburn* (New York: St. Martin's Press, 1984), p. 89.
7. Joseph Wood Krutch, *The Nation*, December 15, 1951, p. 530.
8. *Gigi* text published in *Theatre Arts*, July, 1952. pp. 43–44, 52.
9. Quoted in "Princess Apparent," *Time*, September 7, 1953, p. 62.
10. Quoted in Warren Harris, *Audrey Hepburn* (New York: Simon & Schuster, 1994), p. 84.
11. Quoted in Higham, *op. cit.*, p. 48.
12. Quoted in "Princess Apparent," *Time*, September 7, 1953, p. 62.
13. Quoted in Norton Mockridge, "Explosive European Beauty," *New York World Telegram and Sun*, October 27, 1951, p. 3.
14. Sheridan Morley, *Audrey Hepburn: A Celebration* (London: Pavilion Books Limited, 1993), p. 48.
15. Quoted in Woodward, *op. cit.*, p. 90.
16. Sidney Fields, "Success Is Not Security," *McCall's*, July 1954, p. 61.
17. Quoted in Woodward, p. 91.
18. Quoted in Caroline Latham, *Audrey Hepburn* (London and New York: Proteus Publishing, 1984), p. 24.
19. Walter Kerr, *Commonweal*, December 14, 1951, p. 254.
20. Wolcott Gibbs, "One Birth, Two Obituaries," *The New Yorker*, December 1, 1951, p. 87.
21. *Newsweek*, December 3, 1951, p. 60.
22. *Gigi, Theatre Arts*, February 1952, p. 71.
23. Graham Payn and Sheridan Morley, eds. *Noel Coward Diaries*, April 26, 1952 entry, (Boston: Little Brown and Co., 1982), p. 192.
24. Quoted in "Everybody's Etiquette: You Look Lovely," *New York Herald Tribune*, 1952 (undated clipping, Billy Rose Collection).
25. "Audrey Is a Hit," *Life*, December 10, 1951, p. 104.
26. "Stars Who Danced," *The Saturday Review*, November 15, 1952, p. 29.
27. Louis Sheaffer, "Audrey Hepburn, Who Has to Live Her Part as 'Gigi'," *Brooklyn Eagle*, January 22, 1952, p. 6.

28. Quoted in "Princess Apparent," *Time*, September 7, 1953, p. 62.

29. Courtesy of Jane Sherman and Ned Lehac.

30. Quoted in "Stars Who Danced," *The Saturday Review*, November 15, 1952, p. 29.

31. Fields, *op. cit.*, p. 62.

32. Jack Gaver, "Sparks Cinderella Tradition," publication unknown, c. December 1951.

33. Lord James Hanson to BP, London, December 3, 1993.

34. *Ibid.*

35. Quoted in Radie Harris, "Audrey Hepburn: The girl, the gamin and the star," *Photoplay*, March, 1955, p. 99.

36. Quoted in Woodward, *op. cit.*, p. 93.

37. "Princess Apparent," *Time*, September 7, 1953, p. 62.

38. Nicholas Drake, ed., *The Fifties in VOGUE* (New York: Henry Holt & Co., 1987). Foreword by Audrey Hepburn.

39. Drake, *ibid.*

40. Quoted in Eleanor Ringel, "Appreciation—Audrey Hepburn," *Atlanta Journal*, January 21, 1993.

41. Molly Haskell, "Our Fair Lady: Audrey Hepburn," *Film Comment*, March–April 1991, p. 10.

42. Quoted in Woodward, *op. cit.*, p. 95.

43. Latham, *op. cit.*, p. 32.

44. Quoted in Morley, *op. cit.*, p. 49.

45. Quoted in *Audrey Hepburn Remembered*, Wombat Productions, 1993.

46. AH to Professor Richard Brown, 1990.

47. Quoted in Woodward, *op. cit.*, p. 103.

48. *Directed by William Wyler*, video documentary, May 1986.

49. *Directed by William Wyler*, video documentary, May 1986; and AH to Professor Richard Brown, 1990.

50. Gregory Peck at SAG Achievement Award, quoted in *Screen Actor*, Fall 1993.

51. Lawrence Cohn, "Turnaway Crowd Honors Audrey Hepburn," *Film*, April 19, 1991, p. 12.

52. Quoted in Morley, *op. cit.*, p. 51.

53. *Directed by William Wyler*, video documentary, May 1986.

54. Quoted in Higham, *op. cit.*, p. 59.

55. Quoted in *Audrey Hepburn Remembered*, Wombat Productions, 1993.

56. Lord James Hanson to BP, London, December 3, 1993.

57. Quoted in Anita Loos, "Everything Happens to Audrey Hepburn," *The American Weekly*, September 12, 1954, pp. 11–12.

58. Quoted in James Parish, *The Glamour Girls* (New Rochelle: Arlington House, 1975), p. 327.

59. Quoted in Woodward, *op. cit.*, p. 115.

60. Zsa Zsa Gabor to Maria Ciaccia, November 12, 1994.

61. Lord James Hanson to BP, *op. cit.*

62. *Ibid.*

63. Quoted in Dorothy Kilgallen, "H.R.H. Audrey Hepburn," *The American Weekly*, September 27, 1953, p. 7.

64. Molly Haskell, "Our Fair Lady Audrey Hepburn," *Film Comment*, March–April 1991, p. 17.

65. Frank Quinn and Fred Zepp, "Rise of Audrey Hepburn, Up from Anti-Nazi Underground," *Mirror*, March 26, 1954.

66. Quoted in Mike Connolly, "Who Needs Beauty!", *Photoplay*, January, 1954.

67. Gregory Peck at SAG Achievement Award, *Screen Actor*, Fall 1993.

68. Lord James Hanson to BP, *op. cit.*

69. Richard Buckle, ed., *Self-Portrait with Friends: The Selected Diaries of Cecil Beaton, 1926–1974*, July 23, 1953, entry (New York: Times Books, 1979), p. 262.

70. Mel Ferrer to BP, February 24, 1995.

71. *Ibid.*

72. James Coburn to BP, Los Angeles, February 1, 1995.

73. Joseph J. O'Donohue IV letter to BP, February 26, 1996.

74. *Ibid.*

75. Mel Ferrer to BP, February 24, 1995.

76. Joseph J. O'Donohue IV to BP, *op. cit.*

77. Mel Ferrer to BP, February 24, 1995.

78. *Ibid.*

79. Mel Ferrer, "The La Jolla Players," *Theatre Arts*, August 1951, p. 4.

80. Mel Ferrer to BP, February 24, 1995.

81. Mel Ferrer to BP, February 1, 1995.

82. Mel Ferrer to BP, February 24, 1995.

83. Mel Ferrer to BP, February 1, 1995.

84. Mel Ferrer to BP, February 24, 1995.

85. *Ibid.*

86. *Newsweek*, April 3, 1951, p. 54.

87. Leslie Caron to BP, December 8, 1993.

88. AH press release, The Playwrights Company, c. Fall 1953: William Fields, Press Representative, New York.

89. "Audrey Hepburn Exclusive," press release, c. Fall 1953.

90. AH press release, The Playwrights Company, December 29, 1953: William Fields, Press Representative, New York.

91. Parish, *op. cit.* p. 330.

92. Quoted in Joe Hyams, *Bogie* (New York: The New American Library, 1966), p. 167.

93. Quoted in Maurice Zolotow, *Wilder in Hollywood* (New York: G. P. Putnam's Sons, 1977), p. 254.

94. Higham, *op. cit.* p. 66.

95. Fields, *op. cit.*, p. 62.

96. Quoted in Higham, *op. cit.* p. 68.

97. Audrey Wilder to BP, Beverly Hills, January 30, 1995.

98. Donald Zec, *Sophia: An Intimate*

Biography (London: W. H. Allen, 1975), p. 130.

99. Quoted in Harris, *op. cit.*, p. 118, and Woodward, *op. cit.*, p. 120.

100. Higham, *op. cit.* p. 66.

101. Quoted by Glenn Plaskin, "Audrey Hepburn," *US* magazine, October 17, 1988, p. 43.

102. Quoted in *People*, "Our Fair Lady," February 1, 1993.

103. Billy Wilder to BP, Beverly Hills, January 30, 1995.

104. Audrey Wilder to BP, Beverly Hills, *op. cit.*

105. Billy Wilder to BP, Beverly Hills, *op. cit.*

106. "Princess Apparent," *Time*, September 7, 1953, p. 60.

107. "Audrey Hepburn, Many-sided Charmer," *Life*, December 7, 1953, p. 131.

108. Quoted in Fields, *op. cit.*

109. Otis L. Guernsey, Jr., "A New Star Comes to Town," *New York Herald*, c. October 1953.

110. Higham, p. 61.

111. Quoted in *My Fair Lady* restoration program, 1994; and Hubert de Givenchy to BP, May 15, 1995.

112. Quoted in Harris, p. 104.

113. Audrey Wilder to BP, Beverly Hills, January 30, 1995.

114. Quoted in Parish, *op. cit.*, p. 331.

115. *Ibid.*

116. Radie Harris, *op. cit.*

117. Quoted at New York Film Critics Award, New York, host Ben Grauer, November 19, 1957.

118. Pauline Swanson, "Knee-Deep in Stardust," *Photoplay*, April, 1954, p. 103.

119. Harris, *op. cit.*, p. 108.

120. Radie Harris, *op. cit.*

121. Marian Seldes, *The Bright Lights* (Boston: Houghton-Mifflin, 1979).

122. Marian Seldes to BP, January 19, 1995.

123. Quoted in Jared Brown, *The Fabulous Lunts: A Biography of Alfred Lunt and Lynn Fontanne* (New York: Atheneum, 1986), p. 385.

124. *Ibid.*

125. Eric Bentley, "Giraudoux & Others," *New Republic*, March 8, 1954, p. 21.

126. "First Nights," *Newsweek*, March 1, 1954, p. 71.

127. Radie Harris, *op. cit.*

128. Quoted in Brown, *op. cit.*, p. 385.

129. Eva Gabor to BP, Los Angeles, December 12, 1994.

130. Gibbs, *op. cit.*, pp. 74–75.

131. Quoted in Brown, *op. cit.*, p. 385.

132. Richard Hayes, *The Commonweal*, April 2, 1954, p. 650.

133. Henry Hewes, "Nymph Mania," *Saturday Review*, March 13, 1954, pp. 26–27.

134. Harold Clurman, *The Nation*, March 6, 1954, p. 206.

135. Celeste Holm to John Barba, February 1, 1995.

136. Quoted in Fields, *op. cit.*

137. Abramson, *op. cit.*

138. Harris, *op. cit.*, p. 114.

139. Unidentified newspaper clipping, April 3, 1954, New York (Billy Rose Collection).

140. Frank Quinn and Fred Zepp, *op. cit.*

141. Philip Wuntch, "Audrey Hepburn Reminisces," *Dallas Morning News*, March 2, 1991.

142. Quoted in Woodward, *op. cit.*, p. 5.

143. Unidentified newspaper clipping, April 3, 1954 (Billy Rose Collection).

144. Quoted in Mary Worthington Jones, "My Husband Doesn't Run Me," *Photoplay*, April, 1956, p. 105.

145. Carl Clement, "Look Where You're Going, Audrey," *Photoplay*, June 1957, p. 84.

146. Abramson, *op. cit.*

CHAPTER 4

1. Radie Harris, "Audrey Hepburn—The girl, the gamin and the star," *Photoplay*, March 1955, p. 100.

2. Quoted by Billy Wilder to BP, January 30, 1995.

3. "Audrey Hepburn," *Movie & T.V. Album*, July 1957, p. 31.

4. Eleanor Harris, "Audrey Hepburn," *Good Housekeeping*, August 1959, p. 117.

5. Caroline Latham, *Audrey Hepburn* (London and New York: Proteus Publishing, 1984), p. 114.

6. AH press release, The Playwrights Company, December 29, 1953: William Fields, Press Representative, New York.

7. Quoted in Eleanor Harris, *op. cit.*

8. "Audrey Hepburn," *Movie & T.V. Album, op. cit.*

9. Earl Wilson, "Is Hollywood shifting its accent on sex?", *Silver Screen*, July 1954, p. 40.

10. Cynthia Lowry, "Audrey Hepburn Seems to Be Sensation of Decade," *Louisville Courier Journal*, March 21, 1954.

11. Nicholas Drake, ed., *The Fifties in VOGUE* (New York: Henry Holt & Co., 1987).

12. Pauline Swanson, "Knee-Deep in Stardust," *Photoplay*, April 1954, p. 103.

13. Mel Ferrer to BP, February 24, 1995.

14. Quoted in Ian Woodward, *Audrey Hepburn* (New York: St. Martin's Press, 1984), p. 131.

15. Quoted in Bert McCord, "AH Is Sought by Helen Hayes for 'Mary'," *New York Herald Tribune*, August 17, 1954, p. 31.

16. AH to Tex McCurdy, "Cover Story" radio interview, January 10, 1954.

17. Mel Ferrer to BP, *op. cit.*

18. Billy Wilder to BP, *op. cit.*

19. Bosley Crowther, *New York Times*, September 23, 1954, p. 43.

20. Frank Thompson, *American Film*, May 1990, p. 55.

21. Quoted in Latham, *op. cit.*, p. 37.

22. Clayton Cole, *Films & Filming*, October 1954, p. 20.

23. Mel Ferrer to BP, *op. cit.*
24. *Ibid.*
25. *Ibid.*
26. *Ibid.*
27. *Newsweek*, July 30, 1956, pp. 53–56.
28. Quoted in Warren Harris, *Audrey Hepburn* (New York: Simon & Schuster, 1994), p. 129.
29. *Newsweek, op. cit.*
30. *Newsweek, ibid.*; and Parish, *op. cit.*, p. 333.
31. Quoted in Latham, p. 43.
32. Fred Zinnemann, *Fred Zinnemann: An Autobiography* (New York: Charles Scribner's Sons, 1992), p. 154.
33. Quoted in *Newsweek, op. cit.*
34. Jeremy Brett to Maria Ciaccia, December 20, 1994.
35. Quoted in Woodward, *op. cit.*, p. 142.
36. AH video interview with Bill Collins, Australia, 1989.
37. Quoted in Harris, *op. cit.*, p. 132.
38. Quoted in Mary Worthington Jones, "My Husband Doesn't Run Me," *Photoplay*, April 1956, p. 105.
39. Nicholas Drake, ed., *The Fifties in VOGUE* (New York: Henry Holt & Co., 1987), p. 97.
40. Mel Ferrer to BP, *op. cit.*
41. Quoted in Jones, *op. cit.*
42. Carl Clement, "Look Where You're Going, Audrey," *Photoplay*, June 1957, p. 84.
43. Quoted in Jones, *op. cit.*
44. *Ibid.*
45. Tony Curtis to BP, March 15, 1996.
46. Quoted in Woodward, *op. cit.*, p. 141.
47. Theodore Bikel to John Barba, December 14, 1994.
48. Quoted in Higham, *op. cit.*, pp. 98–99.
49. Unidentified clipping (Billy Rose Collection), April 1956.
50. Quoted in *Photoplay* (1957).
51. Leonard Gershe to BP, December 12, 1994.
52. Quoted in Woodward, *op. cit.*, p. 146.
53. Quoted in Leonard Gershe's *Funny Face* liner notes, July 1956.
54. AH in *Voice of America* interview, c. mid-1956.
55. Harris, *Good Housekeeping, op. cit.*
56. Mel Ferrer to BP, *op. cit.*
57. Quoted by William Hawkins, *Dance Magazine*, October 1956, p. 19.
58. Quoted in Mark Nichols, "Audrey Hepburn Goes Back to the Bar [sic]," *Coronet*, November 1956.
59. *Ibid.*
60. Leonard Gershe to BP, *op. cit.*
61. AH introduction to Stephen Silverman's biography of Stanley Donen, *Dancing on the Ceiling* (New York: Alfred A. Knopf, 1995), p. xiv.
62. AH to Williams Banks, quoted to BP November 3, 1994.
63. AH to Sarah Giles, quoted in Morley, *op. cit.*, p. 81.
64. Quoted in Latham, *op. cit.*, p. 47.
65. Quoted in Higham, *op. cit.*, p. 106, and Harris, *op. cit.*, p. 141.

66. Leslie Caron to BP, December 8, 1993.

67. Sheridan Morley, *Audrey Hepburn* (London: Pavilion Books, 1993), p. 79.

68. Latham, *op. cit.*, p. 48.

69. Quoted in Harris, *op. cit.*, p. 139.

70. "Moanin' for Donen," *Film*, January/February 1961.

71. Joseph Andrew Casper, *Stanley Donen*, Filmmakers, No. 5. (Metuchen N.J. and London: Scarecrow Press, 1983), p. 96.

72. Arthur Knight, "Choreography for Camera," *Dance*, May 1957, pp. 14–21.

73. *Audrey Hepburn Remembered*, Wombat Productions, 1993.

74. Janet Maslin, "Audrey Hepburn's Party," *The New York Times*, April 21, 1991.

75. André Previn to BP, Pittsburgh, January 12, 1995.

76. "Audrey Hepburn," by Frank Thompson, *American Film*, May 1990, p. 55.

77. Quoted in *Audrey Hepburn Remembered*, Wombat Productions, 1993.

78. Givenchy in *My Fair Lady* restoration program.

79. Hubert de Givenchy in *Audrey Hepburn Remembered*, Wombat Productions, 1993.

80. Ralph Lauren to BP, April 26, 1995.

81. Leslie Caron, "Audrey, Darling," *Vogue (UK)*, April 1993, p. 183.

82. "That Girl with the Eyes," *Inteview* magazine, August 1990, p. 99.

83. Elizabeth Wilson, *Sight and Sound*, March 1993.

84. Leonard Gershe to BP, December 12, 1994.

85. Quoted in Woodward, *op. cit.*, p. 149.

86. Quoted in Woodward, *op. cit.*, p. 150.

87. Quoted in Carl Clement, *op. cit.*

88. Sophia Loren letter to John Barba, March 28, 1995.

89. Sidney Skolsky, "Hollywood Is My Beat," *New York Post*, August 26, 1956, p. M3. "Audrey's Advice: Have Fun, Let Hubby Wear the Pants," *New York Journal-American*, August 19, 1957, p. 6.

90. Quoted in Martin Abramson, *Cosmopolitan*, October 1955, p. 30.

91. Quoted in John Maynard, "Audrey's Harvest of the Heart," *Photoplay*, September 1956, p. 113.

92. Glenn Plaskin, "Audrey Hepburn," *US* Magazine, October 17, 1988, p. 44.

93. Abramson, *op. cit.*

94. Rowland Barber, "The Delightful Riddle of Audrey Hepburn," *Good Housekeeping*, August 1962, p. 61.

95. Quoted in Maynard, *op. cit.*, p. 114.

96. *Ibid.*

97. Quoted in Carl Clement, *op. cit.*.

98. Audrey Wilder to BP, January 30, 1995.

99. James Parish, *The Glamour Girls* (New Rochelle: Arlington House, 1975), p. 348.

100. Quoted in Higham, p. 111.

101. Charles Higham, *Audrey* (New York: Macmillan, 1984), p. 109.
102. "Why Not Be in Paris?," *Newsweek*, November 26, 1956.
103. Frank Thompson, *American Film*, May 1990, p. 54.
104. Parish, *op. cit.*, p. 347.
105. Quoted in William Pepper, "Audrey Keeps Park in a Stir," *World Telegram*, August 16, 1957.
106. Liza Wilson, "Audrey: the girl with the hop-skip-and-jump marriage," *The American Weekly*, September 29, 1957, p. 12.
107. Quoted by Jane Wooldridge, *Miami Herald*, December 3, 1989.
108. Alan Riding, *New York Times* Paris bureau, April 12, 1991.
109. Doris Brynner to John Barba, Geneva, December 13, 1993.
110. *Larry King: TNT Extra*, October 18, 1991.
111. "Scandal in Rehearsal," *Life*, February 4, 1957, p. 56.
112. Quoted in Harris, *op. cit.*, p. 147.
113. Quoted in Parish, *op. cit.*, p. 347.
114. Quoted in Latham, *op. cit.*, p. 52.
115. Morley, *op. cit.*, p. 89.
116. Peter Viertel to BP, April 17, 1996.
117. Quoted in William Pepper, *op. cit.*
118. Richard Corliss, "Serene Majesty," *Film Comment*, Vol. 29, No. 2, 1993, p. 4.

CHAPTER 5

1. James Robert Parish and Don E. Stanke, *The Glamour Girls* (New Rochelle: Arlington House, 1975), p. 349.
2. Fred Zinnemann, *Fred Zinnemann: An Autobiography* (New York: Charles Scribner's Sons, 1992), p. 155.
3. Mel Ferrer to BP, February 24, 1995.
4. Quoted in Caroline Latham, *Audrey Hepburn* (London and New York: Proteus Publishing, 1984), p. 55.
5. Zinnemann, *op. cit.*, p. 157.
6. Warren Harris, *Audrey Hepburn* (New York: Simon & Schuster, 1994), p. 153.
7. Patricia Bosworth to BP, March 17, 1996.
8. Quoted in Ian Woodward, *Audrey Hepburn* (New York: St. Martin's Press, 1984), pp. 164–165.
9. Zinnemann, *op. cit.*, p. 166.
10. *Ibid.*, p. 163.
11. "Audrey Lives a Nun's Life," *This Week* magazine, April 6, 1958, pp. 36–37.
12. Zinnemann, *op. cit.*, pp. 166–167.
13. Eleanor Harris, "Audrey Hepburn," *Good Housekeeping*, August 1959, p. 119.

14. Zinnemann, *op. cit.*, p. 166.
15. Quoted in Bob Thomas, "Hollywood: Jungle Girl... Audrey Hepburn Goes from One Safari to Another," *Newark News*, August 4, 1958.
16. Zinnemann, *op. cit.*, p. 167.
17. Zinnemann, *ibid.*, pp. 168–169.
18. Zinnemann, *ibid.*, p. 167.
19. *Ibid.*
20. Quoted in Woodward, *op. cit.*, p. 165.
21. Elaine Dundy, *Finch, Bloody Finch* (New York: Holt Rinehart Winston, 1980), p. 231.
22. Dorothy Alison, quoted in Trader Faulkner's *Peter Finch: A Biography* (London: Angus & Robertson Publishers, 1979), p. 205.
23. Quoted in Eleanor Harris, *Good Housekeeping, op. cit.*
24. Quoted in Bob Thomas, "Hollywood: Jungle Girl, *op. cit.*
25. Eleanor Harris, *Good Housekeeping, op. cit.*
26. Zinnemann, *op. cit.*, p. 166.
27. *Ibid.*, p. 169.
28. Rudy Fehr to John Barba, September 27, 1994.
29. Quoted in Eleanor Harris, *Good Housekeeping, op. cit.*
30. *Ibid.*
31. Quoted in David Zeitlin, "A Lovely Audrey in Religious Role," *Life*, June 8, 1959, pp. 141–144.
32. Frank Thompson, *American Film*, May 1990, p. 56.
33. Simon Brett, *Films & Filming*, March 1964, pp. 9–12.
34. Stephen Whitty, *San Jose Mercury News*, March 12, 1993.
35. Quoted in *Audrey Hepburn Remembered*, Wombat Productions, 1993.
36. Zinnemann, *op. cit.*, p. 162.
37. *Ibid.*, p. 171.
38. Gene Ringgold, "Audrey Hepburn," *Films in Review*, December 1971, p. 597.
39. Quoted in "Audrey Hepburn Denies Planning to Become Catholic," *New York Post*, October 13, 1959 (Reuters wire-service report).
40. Quoted in Woodward, *op. cit.*, p. 166.
41. Fred Zinnemann FAX to BP, May 4, 1995.
42. Joe Hyams, "The Fawn That Loves Audrey," *This Week* magazine, November 2, 1958, pp. 8–9.
43. Quoted by Eleanor Harris, *Good Housekeeping, op. cit.*
44. Quoted in Woodward, *op. cit.*, p. 175.
45. Quoted in Joyce Waldman, "Audrey's Fantastic Figure," *Cosmopolitan*, June 1959, pp. 60–64.
46. Quoted in Eleanor Harris, *Good Housekeeping, op. cit.*, p. 121.
47. Bob Willoughby to BP, May 5, 1995.
48. Quoted by Eleanor Harris, *Good Housekeeping, op. cit.*
49. Katharine Dunham to BP, February 16, 1994.
50. Quoted by Gene Ringgold in *Films in Review*, December 1971, p. 598.

51. Quoted in Woodward, *op. cit.*, pp. 172–173.

52. Quoted in Latham, *op. cit.*, p. 61.

53. Brett, *op. cit.*

54. Wendy Keys to BP, New York, October 11, 1994.

55. Mel Ferrer to BP, February 24, 1995.

56. *Ibid.*

57. Eleanor Harris, *Good Housekeeping, op. cit.*, p. 121.

58. Radie Harris, "Audrey Hepburn—the girl, the gamin and the star," *Photoplay*, March 1955, p. 100.

59. Pauline Swanson, *Photoplay*, April 1954, p. 102.

60. John Huston, *An Open Book* (New York: Alfred A. Knopf, 1980), p. 283.

61. Cy Egan, Jr., "Ferrer Tells How Audrey Broke Her Back," *New York Journal American*, January 31, 1959.

62. Quoted in Warren Harris, *op. cit.*, p. 168.

63. Quoted in *Photoplay*, May 1959, p. 100.

64. Quoted in Eleanor Harris, *Good Housekeeping, op. cit.*

65. *Ibid.*

66. Quoted in Earl Wilson, *New York Post*, March 24, 1959.

67. Doug McClure to John Barba, October 26, 1994.

68. Huston, *op. cit.*, p. 284.

69. Quoted by Robert Wolders, October 21, 1994.

70. Molly Haskell, "Our Fair Lady Audrey Hepburn," *Film Comment*, March/April 1991, p. 14.

71. Quoted in Dominick Dunne, "Hepburn Heart," *Vanity Fair*, May 1991.

72. Quoted in Edward Klein, "One Woman's Search for Love: A Profile of Audrey Hepburn," *Parade*, March 5, 1989, pp. 5–6.

73. *Ibid.*, p. 6.

74. Quoted in Woodward, *op. cit.*, p. 183.

75. *Parool*, October 2, 1959 (translated by Sandra Homner).

76. Quoted in Morley, *Audrey Hepburn: A Celebration* (London: Pavilion Books Ltd., 1993), p. 103.

77. Quoted in Woodward, *op. cit.*, p. 183.

78. Charles Higham, *Audrey* (New York: Macmillan, 1984), p. 144.

79. AH on *Larry King Live*, January 25, 1990.

80. Quoted in *Look*, November 8, 1960.

81. Quoted in Higham, *op. cit.* p. 147.

82. Quoted in Joseph Barry, "Audrey Hepburn at 40," *McCall's*, July 1969, p. 57.

83. AH at George Eastman House, Rochester, N.Y., October 25, 1992.

84. Quoted in Richard Zoerink, "Truman Capote Talks About his Crowd," *Playgirl*, September 1975, pp. 50–51, 54, 80–81, 128.

85. Quoted in Morley, *op. cit.*, p. 106.

86. *Patricia Neal, As I Am* (New

York: Simon & Schuster, 1988), p. 213; and Patricia Neal to BP, March 20, 1995.

87. Henry Mancini in "Audrey Hepburn Remembered," Wombat Productions, 1993.

88. Ginny Mancini to BP, Los Angeles, December 12, 1994.

89. Quoted in Warren Harris, *op. cit.*, p. 185.

90. Frank Thompson, *American Film*, May 1990, p. 56.

91. Herbert Feinstein, "My Gorgeous Darling Sweetheart Angels: Brigitte Bardot and Audrey Hepburn," *Film Reviews*, Spring 1962, p. 68.

92. Quoted in Rowland Barber, "The Delightful Riddle of Audrey Hepburn," *Good Housekeeping*, August 1962, p. 112.

93. *Ibid.*

94. M. Thomas Inge, ed., *Truman Capote: Conversations*, University Press of Mississippi, Jackson and London, 1987; *Playboy* interview, Eric Norden, March 15, 1968, 51–53, 58–62, 160–170.

95. Michael Sragow, *San Francisco Examiner*, December 7, 1990.

96. Deborah Kerr to BP, April 17, 1996.

97. Vito Russo, *The Celluloid Closet: Homosexuality in the Movies* (New York: Harper & Row, 1981), p. 139.

98. Quoted in Latham, *op. cit.*, p. 84.

99. Quoted in Russo, *op. cit.*, p. 140.

100. *Ibid.*, pp. 140–141.

101. Barber, *op. cit.*, p. 61; and "The

Two Audrey Hepburns," by Eliot George, *Silver Screen*, August 1964, p. 51.

102. Billy and Audrey Wilder to BP, Beverly Hills, January 30, 1995.

103. George Axelrod to BP, March 25, 1996.

104. Quoted in Higham, *op. cit.*, p. 155.

105. Quoted in Woodward, *op. cit.*, p. 199.

106. Quoted in Higham, *op. cit.*, pp. 155–156.

107. Quoted in Morley, *op. cit.*, p. 117.

108. Tony Curtis and Barry Paris, *Tony Curtis: The Autobiography* (New York: William Morrow & Co., 1993), p. 214.

109. Quoted in Higham, *op. cit.*, p. 158.

110. Graham Payn and Sheridan Morley, eds., *The Noel Coward Diaries* September 25, 1962 entry, (Boston: Little Brown and Co., 1982).

111. Michael Quarles van Ufford to John Barba, February 26, 1994.

112. George, *op. cit.*

113. Billy and Audrey Wilder to BP, *op. cit.*

114. Quoted in Joseph Andrew Casper, *Stanley Donen*, Filmmakers, No. 5. (Metuchen N.J. and London: Scarecrow Press, 1983), p. 166.

115. James Coburn to BP, Los Angeles, February 2, 1995.

116. Quoted in Casper, *op. cit.*, p. 167.

117. *Cary Grant, The Lonely Heart,*

Charles Higham and Roy Moseley (New York: Harcourt Brace Jovanovich, 1989), p. 274 and pp. 270–271.

118. AH quoted in Stephen Silverman, *Dancing on the Ceiling*, pp. xiv–xv, and in Warren Harris, p. 193.

119. James Coburn to BP, *op. cit.*

120. *Ibid.*

121. Quoted in Warren Harris, *op. cit.*, p. 195.

122. James Coburn to BP, *op. cit.*

123. Quoted in Charles Higham and Roy Moseley, *op. cit.*, p. 272.

124. Quoted in Look, December 17, 1963, p. 90.

125. AH video interview with Bill Collins, Australia, 1989.

126. Quoted in Warren Harris, *op. cit.*, p. 194.

127. James Coburn to BP, *op. cit.*

128. *Ibid.*

129. Casper, *op. cit.*, p. 177.

130. Quoted in Parish, *op. cit.*, p. 356.

CHAPTER 6

1. Ian Woodward, *Audrey Hepburn* (New York: St. Martin's Press, 1984), p. 205; and Charles Higham, *Audrey* (New York: Macmillan, 1984), p. 161.

2. AH to Henry Gris, *Modern Screen*, January 1965, pp. 24–27.

3. Higham, *op. cit.*, p. 163.

4. Rex Harrison, *A Darned Serious Business: My Life in Comedy* (New York: Bantam Books, 1991), p. 121.

5. Quoted in Philip Wuntch, *Dallas Morning News*, March 2, 1991; and AH to Barbara Walters, March 29, 1989.

6. Quoted in Woodward, *op. cit.*, p. 208.

7. Quoted in Harrison, *op. cit.*, p. 156.

8. *Ibid.*, p. 156.

9. Quoted in Cleveland Amory, "The Phenomenon of '*My Fair Lady*,'" *Vogue*, November 11,

1964, pp. 153–155.

10. Cyril Connolly, "The Happy Times When Edward Was King," *Ladies' Home Journal*, January/February 1964, p. 78.

11. Quoted in Rex Harrison, *op. cit.*, p. 122.

12. *More Loverly Than Ever*, video documentary, "Designs for a Lady" featurette to promote MFL.

13. "The Filming of MFL," by Cecil Beaton, Oct. 18, 1964.

14. Cecil Beaton, "My Fair Lady," *Ladies' Home Journal*, January-February 1964.

15. Cecil Beaton, *Cecil Beaton's 'Fair Lady'* (New York: Henry Holt & Co., 1964), pp. 50–52 (diary entry of May 18, 1963).

16. *Ibid.*, p. 62 (diary entry of July 3, 1963).

17. Quoted in Art Seidenbaum, "Audrey Hepburn," *McCall's*, October 1964, p. 182.

18. Art Seidenbaum, "Audrey Hepburn," *McCall's*, October 1964, p. 182.
19. Beaton, *op. cit.*, p. 47 (diary entry of May 16, 1963).
20. *Ibid.*, p. 50 (May 18, 1963).
21. *Ibid.*, p. 65 (July 3, 1963).
22. André Previn, *No Minor Chords: My Days in Hollywood* (New York: Doubleday, 1991), p. 115.
23. André Previn to BP, Pittsburgh, January 12, 1995.
24. Previn, p. 129.
25. Maria Ciaccia to BP and André Previn to BP, Pittsburgh, January 12, 1995.
26. Marni Nixon to John Barba, New York, September 20, 1994.
27. André Previn to BP, *op. cit.*
28. Chris Ferrer to Marni Nixon at *My Fair Lady* restoration premiere, New York, September 19, 1994.
29. Marni Nixon to John Barba, *op. cit.*
30. André Previn to BP, *op. cit.*
31. Beaton, *op. cit.*, p. 53 (diary entry of June 4, 1963).
32. Harper McKay, "Wouldn't It Have Been Loverly?" *Opera News*, October 1994, p. 18.
33. André Previn to BP, *op. cit.*
34. Doris Brynner to John Barba, December 13, 1993.
35. *More Loverly Than Ever*, video documentary.
36. Harrison, *op. cit.*, p. 158.
37. Alexander Walker, *Fatal Charm: The Life of Rex Harrison* (London: Weidenfeld & Nicholson, 1992), p. 267.
38. Previn, *op. cit.*, pp. 116–117.
39. André Previn to BP, *op. cit.*
40. Roddy McDowall to BP, Philadelphia, February 23, 1996.
41. Joe Hyams, "Hollywood: 'Good... Now Do Another,'" *New York Herald Tribune*, September 29, 1963, pp. 35, 37.
42. André Previn to BP, *op. cit.*
43. Quoted in *Silver Screen*, August 1964.
44. André Previn to BP, *op. cit.*
45. Eliot George, "The Two Audrey Hepburns," *Silver Screen*, August 1964, pp. 22–25, 50–51.
46. Theodore Bikel to John Barba, December 14, 1994.
47. Previn, *op. cit.*, p. 115.
48. Seidenbaum, *op. cit.*
49. Cecil Beaton, "My Fair Lady," *Ladies' Home Journal*, January-February 1964.
50. Beaton, *op. cit.*, p. 69 (diary entry of August 6, 1963).
51. Beaton, *ibid.*, p. 73 (August 22, 1963).
52. André Previn to BP, *op. cit.*
53. Roddy McDowall to BP, *op. cit.*
54. Beaton, *op. cit.*, p. 106 (October 11, 1963).
55. *Ibid.*, p. 119 (November 11, 1963).
56. *Ibid.* (November 18, 1963).
57. Jeremy Brett to Maria Ciaccia, December 20, 1994.
58. Beaton, *op. cit.*, pp. 125–126.
59. Marni Nixon to John Barba, *op. cit.*
60. André Previn to BP, *op. cit.*
61. McKay, *op. cit.*
62. André Previn to BP, *op. cit.*
63. Quoted in Woodward, *op. cit.*, p. 209.
64. Rudy Fehr to John Barba, September 27, 1994.

65. André Previn to BP, *op. cit.*

66. Leslie Caron to BP, December 8, 1993.

67. *More Loverly Than Ever*, video documentary, *op. cit.*

68. Jeremy Brett to Maria Ciaccia, *op. cit.*

69. AH on *Larry King Live*, June 5, 1991.

70. Quoted in *Look*, February 25, 1964, p. 60.

71. *More Loverly Than Ever*, video documentary, *op. cit.*

72. N. C. Chambers, *Films in Review*, May 1965.

73. André Previn to BP, *op. cit.*

74. Marni Nixon to Maria Ciaccia, New York, March 2, 1995.

75. Quoted in Parish, p. 359.

76. *More Loverly Than Ever*, video documentary, *op. cit.*

77. Rex Harrison, *op. cit.*, p. 159.

78. "De Twee Fair Ladies," *De Telegraaf*, April 8, 1965.

79. Patricia Neal, *As I Am* (New York: Simon & Schuster, 1988), p. 213.

80. Patricia Neal to BP, March 20, 1995.

81. Woodward, *op. cit.*, pp. 216–217.

82. Patricia Neal to BP, *op. cit.*

83. Roddy McDowall to BP, *op. cit.*

84. André Previn to BP, *op. cit.*

85. Herb Sterne, quoted by Charles Higham, *Good Housekeeping*, October 1984, p. 307.

86. Quoted in Woodward, *op. cit.*, p. 213.

87. M. George Haddad, "My Fair Lady," *Hollywood Studio Magazine*, September 1979.

88. AH to Henry Gris, "A Man to Hold—A Child to Love," *Modern Screen*, January 1965, p. 24–27.

89. André Previn to BP, *op. cit.*

90. Quoted in Woodward, *op. cit.*, p. 173.

91. Seidenbaum, *op. cit.*, pp. 183–184.

92. *Ibid.*

93. "Givenchy: Audrey Hepburn's choices from his new collection," *Vogue*, November 1, 1964, p. 142.

94. André Previn to BP, *op. cit.*

95. Quoted in Woodward, *op. cit.*, p. 173.

96. Leslie Caron to BP, *op. cit.*

97. Henry C. Rogers, *Walking the Tightrope* (New York: William Morrow and Co., 1980), pp. 216–217.

98. *Ibid.*, pp. 219–220.

CHAPTER 7

1. J. D. Podolsky, "Life with Audrey," *People*, October 31, 1994, p. 104.

2. Warren Harris, *Audrey Hepburn* (New York: Simon & Schuster, 1994), p. 216.

3. Anna Cataldi to BP, New York, October 4, 1994.

4. AH to Henry Gris, *Modern Screen*, January 1965, p. 24–27.

5. Alan Riding, *New York Times*

Paris bureau, interview with AH, April 12, 1991.

6. Leonard Gershe to BP, December 12, 1994, and January 14, 1995.

7. Florida Broadway to BP, January 11, 1995.

8. *Ibid.*

9. *Ibid.*

10. *Ibid.*

11. Victoria Brynner to BP, March 26, 1996.

12. Doris Brynner to John Barba, December 13, 1993.

13. Violette Leduc, "Hepburn and O'Toole," *Vogue*, April 1966, p. 172.

14. AH on *Today*, March 23, 1988.

15. Quoted in Ian Woodward, *Audrey Hepburn* (New York: St. Martin's Press, 1984), pp. 221–222.

16. Eli Wallach to BP, April 28, 1995.

17. Violette Leduc, *op. cit.*, p. 207.

18. Caroline Latham, *Audrey Hepburn* (London and New York: Proteus Publishing, 1984), p. 96.

19. Joseph Andrew Casper, *Stanley Donen*, Filmmakers, No. 5., (Metuchen N.J. and London: Scarecrow Press, 1983), p. 180.

20. Sheridan Morley, *Audrey Hepburn* (London: Pavilion Books Ltd., 1993), p. 138.

21. "Audrey Hepburn Swings? You're Kidding," *Ladies' Home Journal*, January 1967, p. 60.

22. Quoted in Robert Parish, *The Glamour Girls* (New Rochelle: Arlington House, 1975), p. 361.

23. Quoted in Charles Higham, *Audrey* (New York: Macmillan, 1984), pp. 180–81.

24. *Ibid.*, p. 182.

25. Quoted in Woodward, *op. cit.*, p. 226.

26. Quoted in *Ladies' Home Journal*, *op. cit.*

27. Quoted in Higham, *op. cit.*, pp. 180–181.

28. Quoted in Woodward, *op. cit.*, p. 227.

29. *Ibid.* pp. 227–228.

30. Quoted in Leonhard Dowty, "Audrey Hepburn Makes the Scene," *Good Housekeeping*, August 1967, pp. 85–86.

31. Quoted in Casper, *op. cit.*, p. 183.

32. Audrey Wilder to BP, Beverly Hills, January 30, 1995.

33. Mel Ferrer to BP, February 24, 1995.

34. Deborah Kerr to BP, April 17, 1996.

35. Mel Ferrer to BP, *op. cit.*

36. Terence Young to BP, April 24, 1994.

37. *Ibid.*

38. *Ibid.*

39. *Ibid.*

40. *Ibid.*

41. *Ibid.*

42. *Ibid.*

43. Richard Crenna at Golden Globe Awards, January 1990.

44. Quoted in Woodward, *op. cit.*, p. 233.

45. Efrem Zimbalist, Jr., to BP, March 25, 1996.

46. Quoted in Philip Wuntch, "Life imitates film art as Audrey meets press," *Dallas Morning News*, March 20, 1976.

47. Woodward, *op. cit.*, p.233.
48. Quoted in Philip Wuntch, *op. cit.*
49. Terence Young to BP, *op. cit.*
50. Florida Broadway to BP, *op. cit.*
51. Donald Zec, *Sophia: An Intimate Biography* (London: W. H. Allen, 1975), p.196.
52. Quoted in Glenn Plaskin, "Audrey Hepburn," *US* magazine, October 17, 1988, p.43.
53. Quoted in Woodward, *op. cit.*, p.235.
54. Leslie Caron to BP, December 8, 1993.
55. Quoted in Harris, *op. cit.*, p.231.
56. Quoted in Joseph Barry, "Audrey Hepburn at 40," *McCall's*, July 1969, p.57.
57. Robert Wagner to BP, March 1, 1995.
58. Quoted in Podolsky, *op. cit.*, p.105.
59. Gene Feldman to BP, New York, October 5, 1994.
60. Quoted in Morley, *op. cit.*, p.145.
61. Mel Ferrer to BP, February 1, 1995.
62. Eva Gabor to BP, December 12, 1994.
63. AH to Henry Gris, quoted in Higham, *op. cit.*, p.190.

CHAPTER 8

1. Quoted in Jim Watters, "The Voice, the Neck, The Charm: They Just Don't Make Movie Stars Like Audrey Hepburn Anymore," *People*, April 12, 1976.
2. Lorean Lovatelli to John Barba, December 7, 1994.
3. *Ibid.*
4. Quoted in James Parish, *The Glamour Girls* (New Rochelle: Arlington House, 1975), p.363.
5. Lorean Lovatelli to John Barba, *op. cit.*
6. Joseph Barry, "Audrey Hepburn at 40," *McCall's*, July 1969, p.57.
7. Charles Higham, *Audrey* (New York: Macmillan, 1984), pp.191–192.
8. Quoted in Barry, *op. cit.*
9. Quoted in J. D. Podolsky, "Life with Audrey,"*People*, October 31, 1994, p.105.
10. Quoted in Curtis Bill Pepper, "The Return of Audrey Hepburn," *McCall's*, January 1976, pp.94 and 126.
11. George Haddad-Garcia, "Hepburn's Back!", *Sacramento Bee*, January 10, 1982, p.D10.
12. Lorean Lovatelli to John Barba, *op. cit.*
13. Quoted in Warren Harris, *Audrey Hepburn* (New York: Simon & Schuster, 1994), p.238.
14. Quoted in Barry, *op. cit.*
15. AH to Henry Gris, quoted in Higham, *op. cit.*, p.197.
16. Quoted in Rex Reed, "Our Fair Lady Is Back, and It's Spring," *New York Sunday News*, March 21, 1976.

17. Sergio Russo to BP, Rome, December 16, 1993.

18. *Ibid.*

19. *Ibid.*

20. Parish, *op. cit.*, pp. 364–365; and Higham, *op. cit.*, p. 199.

21. Quoted in Barry, *op. cit.*

22. Dominick Dunne, "Hepburn Heart," *Vanity Fair*, May 1991, p. 136.

23. Quoted in Harris, *op. cit.*, p. 244.

24. AH to Barbara Walters, March 29, 1989.

25. Quoted in Sheridan Morley, *Audrey Hepburn* (London: Pavilion Books Ltd., 1993), p. 103.

26. Quoted in Podolsky, *op. cit.*

27. Quoted in Curtis Bill Pepper, "The Loving World of Audrey Hepburn Dotti," *Vogue*, April 1971.

28. AH to Professor Richard Brown, American Movie Classic inter-view.

29. Quoted in Podolsky, *op. cit.*

30. AH to Henry Gris, quoted in Higham, *op. cit.*, p. 200.

31. Quoted in Ian Woodward, *Audrey Hepburn* (New York: St. Martin's Press, 1984), p. 241.

32. Quoted in Rex Reed, *op. cit.*

33. Jim Watters, *op. cit.*

34. Cited in Harris, *op. cit.*, p. 243.

35. Leslie Caron, "Audrey, Darling," *Vogue (UK)*, April 1993, p. 183.

36. Quoted in Barry, *op. cit.*

37. Lorean Lovatelli to John Barba, *op. cit.*

38. Jeffrey Banks to BP, November 15, 1994.

39. Quoted in Rex Reed, *op. cit.*

40. Lorean Lovatelli to John Barba, *op. cit.*

41. Anna Cataldi to BP, New York, October 4, 1994.

42. Quoted in Woodward, *op. cit.*, p. 249.

43. Florida Broadway to BP, January 11, 1995.

44. Anna Cataldi to BP, New York, October 6, 1994.

45. Marian Seldes, *The Bright Lights* (Boston: Houghton-Mifflin, 1979).

46. Lord James Hanson to BP, London, December 3, 1993.

47. Quoted in M. George Haddad, "My Fair Lady," *Hollywood Studio Magazine*, September 1979.

48. Audrey Wilder to BP, Beverly Hills, January 23, 1995.

49. Quoted in Rex Reed, *op. cit.*

50. Richard Lester to BP, London, December 4, 1993.

51. Richard Corliss, "Serene Majesty," *Film Comment*, Vol. 29, No. 2, 1993, pp. 3–4.

52. George Haddad-Garcia, *op. cit.*

53. Quoted by Robert Wolders to BP, Rochester, October 19, 1994.

54. Quoted in "Champions," *Time*, March 22, 1976, p. 78.

55. Richard Lester to BP, *op. cit.*

56. Quoted in Liz Smith, "Audrey Hepburn on Location," *Rocky Mountain News*, September 7, 1975.

57. Quoted in *Time*, March 22, 1976, p. 78.

58. Richard Lester to BP, London, December 4, 1993.

59. *Ibid.*

60. *Ibid.*
61. Quoted in Philip Wuntch, "Hepburn is back!", *Houston Post*, March 21, 1976, and in *Dallas Morning News*, March 20, 1976.
62. Quoted in Morley, *op. cit.*, p. 154.
63. Quoted in Harris, *op. cit.*, p. 252.
64. Quoted in Wuntch, *op. cit.*
65. Quoted in Donia Mills, "They Came to Hail Hepburn and Her Yorkshire Trifle," *Washington Star*, March 21, 1976, p. B6.
66. Richard Lester to BP, *op. cit.*
67. Quoted in Bill Diehl, "Here Comes Robin Hood," *St. Paul Pioneer Press*, February 1, 1976; and in "No Comeback, Insists Audrey," *Salt Lake Tribune*, March 9, 1976.
68. Quoted in *Salt Lake Tribune*, *op. cit.*
69. Watters, *op. cit.*
70. Quoted in Smith, *op. cit.*
71. Quoted in Diehl, *op. cit.*
72. Quoted in Mills, *op. cit.*
73. Quoted in *Time*, March 22, 1976, p. 78.
74. Frank Thompson, *American Film*, May 1990.
75. Richard Lester to BP, *op. cit.*
76. Quoted in Alan Riding, *New York Times* Paris bureau, April 12, 1991.
77. *Time*, March 22, 1976, p. 78.
78. Quoted in Mills, *op. cit.*
79. Quoted in "Audrey Hepburn in Middle Age," *London Sunday Times*, November 12, 1978.
80. Quoted in Watters, *op. cit.*
81. Quoted in Rex Reed, *op. cit.*
82. Woodward, *op. cit.*, p. 259.
83. Quoted in Pepper, *op. cit.*
84. *Ibid.*
85. Anna Cataldi to BP, New York, October 4, 1994.
86. Quoted in Morley, *op. cit.*, p. 157.
87. Anna Cataldi to BP, *op. cit.*
88. Nicholas Freeling, "Audrey Hepburn at 50," *Telegraph Sunday Magazine*, No. 139, May 20, 1979.
89. *London Sunday Times*, November 12, 1978.
90. *Ibid.*
91. Freeling, *op. cit.*
92. Quoted in Morley, *op. cit.*, p. 161.
93. *Daily Variety*, quoted in Harris, *op. cit.*, p. 264.
94. Ernest Leogrande, "*Bloodline* a pallid and vacant tale," *New York Daily News*, June 29, 1979.
95. Rena Andrews, "*Bloodline* Grand-Scale Jumpy Soap of Pop-Novel Kind," *Denver Post*, July 3, 1979.
96. Tony Menicucci to BP and John Barba, Rome, December 16, 1993.
97. Quoted in Woodward, *op. cit.*, p. 263.
98. Anna Cataldi to BP, *op. cit.*
99. Quoted in Woodward, *op. cit.*, p. 251.
100. Audrey Wilder to BP, January 23, 1995.
101. Camilla Pecchi-Blunt McGrath to BP, January 11, 1996.
102. Eli Wallach to BP, April 28, 1995.

CHAPTER 9

1. Quoted in George Haddad-Garcia, "Hepburn's Back!" *Sacramento Bee*, January 10, 1982, p. D10.
2. Quoted in Glenn Plaskin, "Audrey Hepburn," *US* magazine, October 17, 1988, p. 47.
3. Quoted in Curtis Bill Pepper, "The Return of Audrey Hepburn," *McCall's*, January 1976, p. 126.
4. Anna Cataldi to BP, New York, October 4, 1994.
5. Quoted in J. D. Podolsky, *People*, October 31, 1994.
6. Quoted in Plaskin, *op. cit.*
7. Billy Wilder to Gene Feldman, in video documentary "Audrey Hepburn Remembered."
8. Peter Bogdanovich to BP, August 25, 1995.
9. *Ibid.*
10. Quoted in Michiko Kakutani, "Why Has She Done So Few Films in Recent Years?" *The New York Times*, June 4, 1980.
11. Quoted in Natalie Gittelson, "Audrey Hepburn," *McCall's*, August 1989.
12. Peter Bogdanovich to BP, *op. cit.*
13. *Ibid.*
14. *Ibid.*
15. *Ibid.*
16. *Ibid.*
17. Quoted in Ian Woodward, *Audrey Hepburn* (New York: St. Martin's Press, 1984), p. 271.
18. Peter Bogdanovich to BP, *op. cit.*
19. *Ibid.*
20. Tony Curtis to BP, March 15, 1996.
21. Quoted in Peter Bogdanovich, *The Killing of the Unicorn* (New York: William Morrow & Co., 1984), p. 162.
22. *Providence Journal*, August 22, 1981.
23. Peter Bogdanovich to BP, *op. cit.*
24. Bill Cosford, "They All Laughed deserves a better reputation," *Miami Herald*, December 24, 1982.
25. Eleanor Ringel, *Atlanta Journal*, January 7, 1983.
26. Peter Bogdanovich to BP, *op. cit.*
27. *Ibid.*
28. Anna Cataldi to BP, New York, October 4, 1994.
29. Connie Wald to BP, Beverly Hills, January 31, 1995.
30. Plaskin, *op. cit.*, p. 43.
31. Rob Wolders to BP, Rochester, October 19, 1994.
32. *Hollywood Reporter*, October 10, 1966.
33. Richard Whorf, "Handsome Dutch Import, *Tobruk* Actor, Groomed as Star" (unidentified, undated clipping).
34. Mignon Winans to BP, January 11, 1996.
35. Eleanor Lambert to BP, October 11, 1994.
36. Eva Gabor to BP, Los Angeles, December 12, 1994.
37. Robert Wolders, in outtakes of *Audrey Hepburn Remembered*, Wombat Productions, 1993.
38. *Ibid.*
39. Robert Wolders to BP, Rochester, October 19, 1994.

40. AH on *Donahue*, January 31, 1990.
41. Plaskin, *op. cit.*
42. Leonard Gershe to BP, December 12, 1994 and January 14, 1995.
43. Connie Wald to BP, *op. cit.*
44. Quoted in Plaskin, *op. cit.*
45. Anna Cataldi to BP, *op. cit.*
46. Quoted in Sheridan Morley, *Audrey Hepburn* (London: Pavilion Books Ltd., 1993), p. 166.
47. Eleanor Lambert to BP, October 1994.
48. Jeffrey Banks to BP, November 15, 1994.
49. Michael Quarles van Ufford to John Barba, February 26, 1994.
50. Stephanie Mansfield, "Audrey Hepburn, Eternal Waif," *New York Post*, August 31, 1985.
51. Warren Harris, *Audrey Hepburn* (New York: Simon & Schuster, 1994), p. 275.
52. Gene Feldman to BP, New York, October 5, 1994.
53. Leendert de Jong to BP, January 8, 1994.
54. *Ibid.*
55. Dominick Dunne, "Hepburn Heart," *Vanity Fair*, May 1991, p. 136.
56. Doris Brynner to John Barba, December 13, 1993.
57. AH at Elizabeth Taylor AIDS Award, 1991.
58. Doris Brynner to John Barba, *op. cit.*
59. Maria Ciaccia, *Dreamboats: Hollywood Hunks of the '50s* (New York: Excalibur Publishing, 1992), p. 141.

60. Quoted in Dennis Washburn, "AH is very busy, even while not making movies," *Birmingham News*, February 22, 1987.
61. Quoted in Yardena Arar, "Wagner, Hepburn team in TV romance," *Los Angeles Daily News*, February 23, 1987.
62. Quoted in Mal Vincent, "To moviegoers, AH will always be 'My Fair Lady,'" *Norfolk Virginian-Pilot*, February 22, 1987.
63. Robert Wagner to BP, March 1, 1995.
64. *Ibid.*
65. *Variety*, March 11, 1987.
66. John Leonard, "Thin As Thieves," *New York* magazine, February 23, 1987, p. 121.
67. Robert Wagner to BP, *op. cit.*
68. Audrey Wilder to BP, Beverly Hills, January 30, 1995.
69. Zsa Zsa Gabor to Maria Ciaccia, New York, November 12, 1994.
70. AH to Barbara Walters, March 29, 1989.
71. AH to Terry Wogan, BBC, 1988.
72. Jim Watters, *People*, April 12, 1976.
73. AH on *Donahue*, January 31, 1990.
74. Leslie Caron to BP, December 8, 1993.
75. Laurie Stone, "In Thin Air," *Village Voice*, April 23, 1991.
76. Leslie Caron to BP, *op. cit.*
77. Audrey and Billy Wilder to BP, Beverly Hills, January 30, 1995.
78. Jeffrey Banks to BP, *op. cit.*
79. Doris Brynner to John Barba, *op. cit.*

80. Marilynn Gump to BP, Wichita, Kansas, October 8, 1995.

81. Diana Maychick, *Audrey Hepburn: An Intimate Portrait* (New York: Birch Lane Press, 1993), p. 118.

82. Quoted in Vincent, *op. cit.*

83. John Barba, "C'est Juste: The Geneva Story," May 9, 1995 [published privately].

84. Plaskin, *op. cit.*

85. Quoted in Woodward, *op. cit.*, p. 268.

86. Quoted in Jane Wooldridge, *Miami Herald*, December 3, 1989.

87. Janis Blackschleger to BP, November 22, 1994.

88. Anna Cataldi to BP, *op. cit.*

89. Dunne, *op. cit.*, p. 199.

90. Leendert de Jong to BP, *op. cit.*

91. Bob Curtwright, *Wichita Eagle-Beacon*, January 15, 1987.

92. AH on *Larry King: TNT Extra*, October 18, 1991.

93. John Barba, "C'est Juste," *op. cit.*

94. Alan Riding, *New York Times* Paris bureau, interview with AH, April 12, 1991.

95. Dr. Ronald E. Glegg to BP, November 18, 1995.

96. Quoted in Podolsky, *op. cit.*

97. Quoted in Edward Klein, "One Woman's Search for Love: A Profile of Audrey Hepburn," *Parade*, March 5, 1989, p. 6.

98. Quoted in Plaskin, *op. cit.*; Riding, *op. cit.*; and Pepper, *op. cit.*

CHAPTER 10

1. Quoted in Angela Fox Dunn, "Audrey Hepburn Is a Class Act," *Rochester Democrat & Chronicle*, December 21, 1989.

2. Rob Wolders, in outtakes of *Audrey Hepburn Remembered*, Wombat Productions, 1993.

3. Alan Riding, *New York Times* Paris bureau, interview with AH, April 12, 1991.

4. Quoted in Dunn, *op. cit.*

5. *Variety*, December 20, 1989.

6. Pauline Kael, *The New Yorker*, January 8, 1990, p. 92.

7. AH on *Larry King Live*, January 25, 1990.

8. *Ibid.*

9. Quoted in Jane Wooldridge,

Miami Herald, December 3, 1989.

10. AH to Larry King, *op. cit.*

11. Quoted in Wooldridge, *op. cit.*

12. Michael Tilson Thomas to BP, November 3, 1994.

13. *Ibid.*

14. Michael Tilson Thomas at "A Tribute to Audrey Hepburn" concert, April 1993.

15. AH to Shara Fryer, KTRK-TV, Houston, March 22–23, 1990.

16. Riding, *op. cit.*

17. AH to Lesley Garner, *Sunday Telegraph*, quoted in Morley, p. 172.

18. Quoted in February 1, 1993, letter to Robert Wolders from Gillian Walnes, executive direc-

tor, Anne Frank Educational Trust, Hertfordshire, England.

19. Robert Wagner to BP, March 1, 1995.

20. Quoted in *The Hollywood Death Book*, p. 215.

21. AH to Rex Reed, quoted in Morley, p. 158.

22. Janis Blackschleger to BP, November 22, 1994.

23. Julie Leifermann to BP, December 8, 1994.

24. *Ibid.*

25. *Ibid.*

26. *Ibid.*

27. Janis Blackschleger to BP, *op. cit.*

28. Quoted in Warren Harris, *Audrey Hepburn* (New York: Simon & Schuster, 1994), p. 283.

29. Ralph Lauren to BP, April 26, 1995.

30. *Ibid.*

31. Julie Leifermann to BP, *op. cit.*

32. AH at "Council of Fashion Designers '88" event honoring Richard Avedon, New York, January 14, 1989.

33. Riding, *op. cit.*

34. Wendy Keys to BP, October 11, 1994.

35. Quoted in Lawrence Cohn, "Turnaway Crowd Honors Audrey Hepburn," *Film*, April 19, 1991, p. 12.

36. Ralph Lauren to BP, *op. cit.*

37. Wendy Keys to BP, *op. cit.*

38. Professor Richard Brown, "Audrey," in *My Fair Lady* restoration program.

39. Wendy Keys to BP, *op. cit.*

40. *Ibid.*

41. AH to "Council of Fashion Designers Award '91," February 3, 1992.

42. American Cinemathèque tribute to Sean Connery, July 1992.

43. Quoted in Philip Wuntch, *Dallas Morning News*, March 2, 1991.

44. Quoted in Dominick Dunne, "Hepburn Heart," *Vanity Fair,* May 1991, p. 136.

45. AH to Peter Jennings, ABC "Person of the Week," April 1991.

46. Leslie Caron, "Audrey, Darling," *Vogue (UK)*, April 1993, p. 183.

47. Quoted in Natalie Gittelson, *McCall's*, August 1989, p. 36.

48. Quoted in Dominick Dunne, *op. cit.*, p. 198.

49. Quoted in Glenn Plaskin, *US* magazine, October 17, 1988.

50. *Audrey Hepburn in Her Own Words*, Robert Wolders's video documentary, 1994.

51. Jack Glattbach to BP, November 28, 1995.

52. Christa Roth to BP, January 1, 1995.

53. Audrey Hepburn, "Children First: Building a Global Agenda," *The Commonwealth*, February 17, 1992.

54. John Williams, "Elegance with an Elf Inside," *International Herald Tribune*, January 26, 1993.

55. John Isaac to BP, New York, October 6, 1994.

56. *Ibid.*

57. John Williams, *op. cit.*

58. Alan Riding, *New York Times* Paris bureau, interview with AH, April 12, 1991.

59. Dunne, *op. cit.*

60. Quoted in J. D. Podolsky, *People*, October 31, 1994.

61. AH on *Donahue*, January 31, 1990.

62. AH to Terry Wogan, BBC, 1988.

63. Christa Roth to BP, *op. cit.*

64. AH at hearing of the Select Committee on Hunger, House of Representatives, Washington, D.C., April 6, 1989.

65. *Audrey Hepburn in Her Own Words, op. cit.*

66. Quoted in Plaskin, *op. cit.*

67. *Audrey Hepburn in Her Own Words, op. cit.*

68. AH to New Zealand interviewer Ian Fraser, 1988.

69. Audrey Hepburn, *The Commonwealth, op. cit.*

70. AH at hearing of the Select Committee on Hunger, House of Representatives, Washington, D.C., April 6, 1989.

71. Quoted in UNICEF video, "Universal Childhood Immunization Achievement Celebration," October 8, 1991.

72. Quoted in Warren Harris, *Audrey Hepburn* (New York: Simon & Schuster, 1994), p. 281.

73. Victoria Brynner to BP, March 25, 1996.

74. AH at hearing of the Select Committee on Hunger, House of Representatives, Washington, April 6, 1989.

75. AH statement to the UN staff at "The 1% for Development Fund" meeting, Geneva, June 13, 1989.

76. Hearing of the International Task Force, Select Committee on Hunger, House of Representatives, Washington, April 6, 1989.

77. Barbara Bush, *Barbara Bush: A Memoir* (New York: Charles Scribner's Sons, 1994), p. 285.

78. Quoted by Scott Harris, *Los Angeles Times*, January 21, 1993.

79. AH at hearing of the Select Committee on Hunger, House of Representatives, Washington, April 6, 1989.

80. Bill Collins, Australia, 1989, Canberra Press Club speech.

81. Riding, *op. cit.*

82. Cole Dodge to BP, January 3, 1996.

83. AH on *Larry King Live*, January 25, 1990.

84. Quoted in Harris, *op. cit.*, pp. 279–280.

85. Anne Cox Chambers to BP, New York, November 8, 1994.

86. William Banks to BP, New York, November 8, 1994.

87. Dunne, *op. cit.*

88. Jeffrey Banks to BP, November 15, 1994.

89. Jane Wooldridge, *Miami Herald*, December 3, 1989.

90. Jack Glattbach to BP, November 28, 1995.

91. AH statement to the UN staff at "The 1% for Development Fund" meeting, Geneva, June 13, 1989.

92. Video coverage of the Universal

Childhood Immunization Achievement Celebration, October 8, 1991.

93. AH to Harry Smith, CBS *This Morning*, June 3, 1991.

94. AH on *Larry King Live*, June 5, 1991.

95. Senator Nancy Kassebaum to John Barba, Washington, D.C., March 31, 1995.

96. AH to Bryant Gumbel, *Today*, September 29, 1992.

97. *Somalia: The Silent Children*, October 1992, by AH, Christopher Dickey transcript of one half hour discussion for *International Newsweek*.

98. AH to Katherine Openda, TV interview, Nairobi, September 22, 1992.

99. AH to Christopher Dickey, *op. cit.*

100. AH on *Good Morning America*, September 27, 1992.

101. AH to Bryant Gumbel, *op. cit.*

102. Anna Cataldi, "Somalia 1992," *Epoca*, Milan, October 1992.

103. AH to Katherine Openda, *op. cit.*

104. AH to Christopher Dickey, *op. cit.*

105. Anna Cataldi in *Epoca*, *op. cit.*

106. AH to Katherine Openda, *op. cit.*

107. Quoted in Harris, *op. cit.*, p. 286.

108. RM to Gene Feldman in "Audrey Hepburn Remem-

bered" video documentary, Wombat Productions, 1993.

109. Anna Cataldi to BP, New York, October 6, 1994.

110. AH at George Eastman House, Rochester, October 25, 1992.

111. Quoted in "Audrey Hepburn: Breakfast at UNICEF," *Philadelphia Inquirer*, May 13, 1990.

112. Audrey Hepburn, *The Commonwealth*, *op. cit.*

113. "Losing a Leader: Lawrence E. Bruce, Jr., 1945–1992," *Thursday's Child*, publication of the United States Committee for UNICEF, Spring/Summer 1993.

114. Jill Rembar to BP, October 12, 1994.

115. Michael Tilson Thomas to BP, November 3, 1994.

116. *Publishers Weekly*, November 16, 1992, p. 25.

117. Rob Wolders, in outtakes of *Audrey Hepburn Remembered*, Wombat Productions, 1993.

118. Roger Caras to Maria Ciaccia, New York, August 31, 1994.

119. Ian Woodward, "Audrey Hepburn: The Star of Pure Class Dies at Age 63," (unidentified publication), January 1993.

120. Anna Cataldi to BP, *op. cit.*

121. *Ibid.*

122. Doris Brynner to John Barba, December 13, 1993.

123. Riding, *op. cit.*

CHAPTER 11

1. Rob Wolders to BP, December 13, 1994.

2. Quoted in J. D. Podolsky, *People*, October 31, 1994.

3. Leonard Gershe to BP, December 12, 1994.

4. Robert Wagner to BP, March 1, 1995.

5. John Isaac to BP, New York, October 6, 1994.

6. Billy Wilder to BP, Beverly Hills, January 30, 1995.

7. Doris Brynner to John Barba, December 13, 1993.

8. Eva Gabor to BP, Los Angeles, December 12, 1994.

9. Sean Ferrer to Ivo Niehe, Dutch TV interview, Hilversum, January 20, 1994.

10. Michael Tilson Thomas at "A Tribute to Audrey Hepburn" concert, United Nations, April 30, 1993.

11. HdG to Gene Feldman in "Audrey Hepburn Remembered" video documentary, Wombat Productions, 1993.

12. Quoted in Leslie Caron, *Vogue (UK)*, April 1993.

13. Quoted in Podolsky, *op. cit.*

14. *Ibid.*

15. Roger Caras to Maria Ciaccia, New York, August 31, 1994.

16. Sean Ferrer in *My Fair Lady* restoration program.

17. Alan Riding, *New York Times* Paris bureau, interview with AH, April 12, 1991.

18. Sean Ferrer in *My Fair Lady* restoration program.

19. Anna Cataldi to BP, New York, October 6, 1994.

20. Quoted in J. D. Podolsky (et al.), "Adieu to the Lady Next Door," *People*, February 8, 1993, p. 54.

21. Prince Sadruddin Aga Khan to John Barba, December 13, 1993.

22. Doris Brynner to John Barba, *op. cit.*

23. Anna Cataldi to BP, *op. cit.*

24. AH and Sean Ferrer both quoted in Dutch TV interview with Ivo Niehe, Hilversum, January 20, 1994.

25. Sean Ferrer to BP, October 27, 1994.

26. *Ibid.*

27. Sean Ferrer to Ivo Niehe, Dutch TV interview, *op. cit.*

28. Rose Ganguzza to Maria Ciaccia, New York, November 12, 1994.

29. Mel Ferrer to BP, October 31, 1994.

30. Rose Ganguzza to Maria Ciaccia, *op. cit.*

31. Jeremy Brett to Maria Ciaccia, December 20, 1994.

32. Anna Holmes, "Hollywood Golightly," *Entertainment Weekly*, Vol. 321, April 5, 1996, p. 24.

33. AH to Shara Fryer, KTRK-TV in Houston, March 23, 1990.

34. Clayton Cole, *Films and Filming*, Vol. 1–2:7, November 1954.

35. Eleanor Lambert to BP, October 11, 1994.

36. Riding, *op. cit.*

37. Quoted in Eleanor Harris, "Audrey Hepburn," *Good Housekeeping*, August 1959, p. 118.

38. Quoted in Leslie Caron, "Audrey, Darling," *Vogue (UK)*, April 1993, p. 183.

39. Quoted in Curtis Bill Pepper, *Vogue*, April 1, 1971, p. 94.

40. AH on *Donahue*, January 31, 1990.

41. Quoted in Edward Klein, "One Woman's Search for Love: A Profile of Audrey Hepburn," *Parade*, March 5, 1989, pp. 4–6.

42. *Ibid.*

43. Quoted in Angela Fox Dunn, *Rochester Democrat & Chronicle*, December 21, 1989.

44. Michael Tilson Thomas to BP, November 3, 1994.

45. Quoted in Warren Harris, *Audrey Hepburn* (New York: Simon & Schuster, 1994), p. 11.

46. Theodore Bikel to John Barba, December 14, 1994.

47. Quoted in Ian Woodward, *Audrey Hepburn* (New York: St. Martin's Press, 1984), p. 168.

48. Richard Lester to BP, London, December 4, 1993.

49. GP to Gene Feldman in "Audrey Hepburn Remembered," video documentary, Wombat Productions, 1993.

50. William Banks to BP, New York, November 8, 1994.

51. Nora Sayre, *Running Time: Films of the Cold War* (New York: Dial Press, 1982.)

52. Quoted in Dominick Dunne, "Hepburn Heart," *Vanity Fair*, May 1991, p. 136.

53. Quoted in Stephen M. Silverman, *Dancing on the Ceiling: Stanley Donen and His Movies* (New York: Alfred A. Knopf, 1986), pp. 296–297.

54. Dr. Ronald E. Glegg to BP, November 18, 1995.

55. Quoted in Rex Reed, "Our Fair Lady Is Back, and It's Spring," *New York Sunday News*, March 21, 1976.

56. Riding, *op. cit.*

57. Quoted in Dunn, *op. cit.*

58. Quoted in Woodward, *op. cit.*, p. vi.

59. Quoted in Eleanor Ringel, *Atlanta Journal*, January 21, 1993.

60. Michiko Kakutani, *The New York Times*, Wednesday, June 4, 1980.

61. Gene Feldman to BP, New York, October 5, 1994.

62. Caroline Latham, *Audrey Hepburn* (London and New York: Proteus Publishing, 1984), p. 113.

63. Rene Jordan, introduction to *The Glamour Girls*, by James Robert Parish and Don E. Stanke (New Rochelle: Arlington House Press, 1975), p. 22.

64. Stephen Schaefer, *Boston Herald*, January 21, 1993.

65. Kors, Moses, Mizrahi and Lacroix quoted in "That Girl with the Eyes," *Interview* magazine, August 1990.

66. Eva Gabor to BP, *op. cit.*

67. Robert Wagner to BP, *op. cit.*

68. Richard Corliss, "Serene Majesty," *Film Comment*, April 1993.

69. Billy Wilder in *Audrey Hepburn*

Remembered, video documentary, Wombat Productions, 1993.

70. Wendy Keys to BP, October 11, 1994.

71. Janet Maslin, "Audrey Hepburn's Party," *The New York Times*, April 21, 1991.

72. Wendy Keys to BP, November 10, 1994.

73. AH to Katherine Openda, TV interview, Nairobi, September 22, 1992.

74. Quoted in "Audrey Hepburn, Many-sided Charmer," *Life*, December 7, 1953, p. 131.

75. AH to Barbara Walters, March 29, 1989.

76. Leslie Caron to BP, December 8, 1993.

77. Riding, *op. cit.*

78. AH on *Larry King: TNT Extra*, October 18, 1991.

79. Quoted in Edward Klein, *op. cit.*

80. Ralph Lauren to BP, April 26, 1995.

81. *New York Times*, January 23, 1993, p. 20.

82. Sophia Loren letter to John Barba, March 28, 1995.

83. Valentina Cortesa to John Barba, February 15, 1995.

84. Quoted in Robert Parish and Don E. Stanke, *The Glamour Girls* (New Rochelle: Arlington House Press, 1975), p. 322.

85. Efrem Zimbalist, Jr., to BP, March 25, 1996.

86. AH to Shara Fryer, KTRK-TV, Houston, March 23, 1990.

BIBLIOGRAPHY

ANDERSON, LINDSAY. *Making a Film: The Story of "Secret People."* London: Allen & Unwin, 1952.

Arce, Hector. *Gary Cooper: An Intimate Biography.* New York: William Morrow and Co., 1979.

BEATON, CECIL. *Cecil Beaton's Fair Lady.* New York: Henry Holt and Co., 1964.

BOGDANOVICH, PETER. *The Killing of the Unicorn.* New York: William Morrow & Co., 1984.

BROWN, JARED. *The Fabulous Lunts: A Biography of Alfred Lunt and Lynn Fontanne.* New York: Atheneum, 1986.

BUCKLE, RICHARD, ED. *Self-Portrait with Friends: The Selected Diaries of Cecil Beaton, 1926–1974.* New York: Times Books, 1979.

BUSH, BARBARA. *Barbara Bush: A Memoir.* New York: Charles Scribner's Sons, 1994.

BRYNNER, ROCK. *Yul: The Man Who Would Be King.* London: William Collins Sons & Co., 1989.

CASPER, JOSEPH ANDREW. *Stanley Donen.* Metuchen, N.J., and London: Scarecrow Press, 1983.

CHEVALIER, MAURICE. *Bravo Maurice!* (translated by Mary Fitton). London: George Allen & Unwin Ltd., 1973.

Ciaccia, Maria. *Dreamboats, Hollywood Hunks of the '50s.* New York: Excalibur Publishing, 1992.

CURTIS, TONY, AND BARRY PARIS. *Tony Curtis: The Autobiography.* New York: William Morrow and Co., 1993.

DEANE-DRUMMOND, ANTHONY. *Return Ticket.* London: Collins, 1967.

DE JONG, L., AND JOSEPH W. F. STOPPELMAN. *Lion Rampant: Holland's Resistance to the Nazis.* New York: Querido, 1943.

DOMINIC, ZOE, AND JOHN SELWYN GILBERT. *Frederick Ashton: A Choreographer and His Ballets.* Chicago: Henry Regnery Co., 1973; London: George G. Harrap & Co. Ltd., 1971.

DRAKE, NICHOLAS. *The Fifties in Vogue.* Foreword by Audrey Hepburn. New York: Henry Holt & Co., 1987.

DUNDY, ELAINE. *Finch, Bloody Finch.* New York: Holt Rinehart Winston, 1980.

FAULKNER, TRADER. *Peter Finch: A Biography.* London: Angus & Robertson Publishers, 1979.

FRANK, ANNE. *The Diary of a Young Girl* (translated by B. M. Mooyaart).

New York: Bantam Books, 1993. First published as *Het Achterhuis* [The Secret Annex], Amsterdam, 1947.

HARRIS, WARREN H. *Audrey Hepburn: A Biography*. New York: Simon & Schuster, 1994.

———. *Cary Grant: A Touch of Elegance*. New York: Doubleday, 1987.

HARRISON, REX. *A Darned Serious Business: My Life in Comedy*. New York: Bantam Books, 1991.

HIGHAM, CHARLES. *Audrey: The Life of Audrey Hepburn*. New York: Macmillan, 1984.

———, AND ROY MOSELEY. *Cary Grant: The Lonely Heart*. New York: Harcourt, Brace, Jovanovich, 1989.

HIRSCHFELD, GERHARD. *Nazi Rule and Dutch Collaboration: The Netherlands Under German Occupation, 1940–1945* (translated by Louise Wilmot). Oxford: Berg Publishers Ltd., 1988.

HUSTON, JOHN. *An Open Book*. New York: Alfred A. Knopf, 1980.

INGE, M. THOMAS, ed. *Truman Capote: Conversations*. University Press of Mississippi, Jackson and London, 1987.

KARNEY, ROBIN. *Audrey Hepburn: A Star Danced*. London: Bloomsbury, 1993; and New York: Arcade Publishing, 1995.

LATHAM, CAROLINE. *Audrey Hepburn*. London and New York: Proteus Publishing, 1984.

LLOYD, NORMAN. *Stages: Of Life in Theatre, Film and Television*. New York: Limelight Editions, 1993.

LOOS, ANITA. *A Cast of Thousands*. New York: Grosset & Dunlap, 1977.

Madsen, Axel. *William Wyler*. New York: Thomas Y. Crowell Co., 1973.

MAYCHICK, DIANA. *Audrey Hepburn: An Intimate Portrait*. New York: Birch Lane Press, 1993.

McDOWALL, RODDY. *Double Exposure: Take Four*, New York: William Morrow and Co., 1993.

MORLEY, SHERIDAN. *Audrey Hepburn: A Celebration*. London: Pavilion Books Ltd., 1993.

NEAL, PATRICIA. *Patricia Neal: As I Am, An Autobiography*. New York: Simon & Schuster, 1988.

PARISH, JAMES ROBERT, AND DON E. STANKE. *The Glamour Girls*. (Introduction by René Jordan). New Rochelle: Arlington House, 1975.

PAYN, GRAHAM, AND SHERIDAN MORLEY, EDS. *The Noel Coward Diaries*. Boston: Little Brown and Co., 1982.

PREVIN, ANDRÉ. *No Minor Chords: My Days in Hollywood*. New York: Doubleday, 1991.

PRYCE-JONES, DAVID. *Unity Mitford: A Quest*. London: Weidenfeld and Nicholson, 1976.

ROGERS, HENRY C. *Walking the Tightrope: The Private Confessions of a Public Relations Man*. New York: William Morrow and Co., 1980.

RUSSO, VITO. *The Celluloid Closet: Homosexuality in the Movies*. New York: Harper & Row, 1981.

RYAN, CORNELIUS. *A Bridge Too Far*. New York: Simon & Schuster, 1974.

SAYRE, NORA. *Running Time: Films of the Cold War*. New York: Dial Press, 1982.

SELDES, MARIAN. *The Bright Lights*. Boston: Houghton-Mifflin, 1979.

SILVERMAN, STEPHEN M. *Dancing on the Ceiling: Stanley Donen and His Movies* (introduction by Audrey Hepburn). New York: Alfred A. Knopf, 1986.

SWINDELL, LARRY. *The Last Hero: A Biography of Gary Cooper*. Garden City, N.J.: Doubleday & Co., 1980.

VAN KLEFFENS, E. N. *The Rape of the Netherlands*. London: Hodder and Stoughton Ltd., 1941.

VROEMEN, PAUL, AND HEN BOLLEN. *Het Ende* [*The End of Five Years of Terror in Holland*]. Holland: Europese Bibliotheek, 1990.

WALKER, ALEXANDER. *Audrey: Her Real Story*. London: Weidenfeld and Nicolson, 1994.

———. *Fatal Charm: The Life of Rex Harrison*. London: Weidenfeld and Nicolson, 1992.

Woodward, Ian. *Audrey Hepburn*. New York: St. Martin's Press, 1984.

YULE, ANDREW. *The Man Who "Framed" the Beatles: A Biography of Richard Lester*. New York: Donald I. Fine, Inc., 1994.

ZEC, DONALD. *Sophia: An Intimate Biography*. London: W. H. Allen, 1975.

ZINNEMANN, FRED. *Fred Zinnemann: An Autobiography*. New York: Charles Scribner's Sons, 1992.

ARTICLES

ABRAMSON, MARTIN. "Audrey Hepburn." *Cosmopolitan*, October 1955, pp. 26–32.

AMORY, CLEVELAND. "The Phenomenon of MY FAIR LADY." *Vogue*, November 11, 1964, pp. 153–155.

BARBER, ROWLAND. "The Delightful Riddle of Audrey Hepburn." *Good Housekeeping*, August 1962, p. 61.

BARRY, JOSEPH. "Audrey Hepburn at 40." *McCall's*, July 1969, p. 57.

BEATON, CECIL. "My Fair Lady," and Cyril Connolly, "The Happy Times When Edward Was King." *Ladies' Home Journal,* January/February 1964, pp. 78–128.

BROWN, PROF. RICHARD. "Audrey." *My Fair Lady* restoration program.

CARON, LESLIE. "Audrey, Darling." *Vogue (UK),* April 1993, p. 183.

CLEMENT, CARL. "Look Where You're Going, Audrey." *Photoplay,* June 1957, pp. 46–47, 82–84.

CORLISS, RICHARD. "Serene Majesty." *Film Comment,* Vol. 29, No. 2, 1993, p. 3–4.

DICKEY, CHRISTOPHER. "Somalia: The Silent Children," interview transcript for *International Newsweek.*

DUNN, ANGELA FOX. "AH is a class act." *Rochester Democrat & Chronicle,* December 21, 1989.

DUNNE, DOMINICK. "Hepburn Heart." *Vanity Fair,* May 1991.

FARJEON, ANNABEL. "The Dutch Journal: The Sadler's Wells Ballet in Holland, May 1940" (Part One). *Dance Chronicle: Studies in Dance and the Related Arts,* Volume 10, No. 3, 1987.

FERRER, MEL. "The La Jolla Players." *Theatre Arts,* August 1951, p. 4.

FIELDS, SIDNEY. "Success Is Not security." *McCall's,* July 1954.

FREELING, NICHOLAS. "Audrey Hepburn at 50." *Telegraph Sunday Magazine,* No. 139, May 20, 1979.

GEORGE, ELIOT. "The Two Audrey Hepburns." *Silver Screen,* August 1964, pp. 22–25, 50–51.

GITTELSON, NATALIE. "Audrey Hepburn." *McCall's,* August 1989.

Gris, Henry. "A Man to Hold—A Child to Love—I Won't Let Them be Taken Away." ["by Audrey Hepburn as told to Henry Gris"]. *Modern Screen,* January 1965, p. 24–27.

HADDAD, M. GEORGE. "My Fair Lady." *Hollywood Studio Magazine,* September 1979.

HARRIS, ELEANOR. "Audrey Hepburn." *Good Housekeeping,* August 1959, pp. 61, 117–121.

HARRIS, RADIE. "Audrey Hepburn—the girl, the gamin and the star." *Photoplay,* March 1955.

HARRIS, SCOTT. "Audrey Hepburn, Actress and Humanitarian, Dies." *Los Angeles Times,* January 21, 1993.

HASKELL, MOLLY. "Our Fair Lady Audrey Hepburn." *Film Comment,* March/April 1991, p. 9.

HAWKINS, WILLIAM. Interview with Audrey Hepburn. *Dance Magazine,* October 1956, pp. 17–19, 64.

HEPBURN, AUDREY. "Children First: Building a Global Agenda." *The Commonwealth*, Feb. 17, 1992.

HYAMS, JOE. "The Fawn That Loves Audrey." *This Week* Magazine, *New York Herald Tribune*, November 2, 1958, pp. 8–9.

JONES, MARY W. "My Husband Doesn't Run Me." *Photoplay*, April, 1956, pp. 53, 104–106.

———. "The Small, Private World of Audrey Hepburn." *Photoplay*, February 1957, pp. 66–67, 94–97.

KLEIN, EDWARD. "One Woman's Search for Love—A Profile of Audrey Hepburn." *Parade*, March 5, 1989, pp. 4–6.

KNIGHT, ARTHUR. "Choreography for Camera." *Dance*, May 1957, pp. 14–20.

LEDUC, VIOLETTE. "Hepburn & O'Toole." *Vogue*, April 1966, p. 172.

LOOS, ANITA. "Everything Happens to Audrey Hepburn." *The American Weekly*, September 5, 1954.

MAYNARD, JOHN. "Audrey's Harvest of the Heart." *Photoplay*, September 1956, pp. 42–43, 113–115.

McKAY, HARPER. "Wouldn't It Have Been Loverly?" *Opera News*, October 1994.

McVAY, DOUGLAS, AND TOM VALLANCE. "Gotta Sing! Gotta Dance!" *Film*, Summer 1964, p. 9.

MILLER, GILBERT. "The Search for Gigi." *Theatre Arts*, July 1952.

PEPPER, CURTIS BILL. "The Loving World of Audrey Hepburn Dotti and Her Family." *Vogue*, April 1, 1971, p. 94.

Plaskin, Glenn. "Audrey Hepburn." *US* magazine, October 17, 1988, pp. 43–47.

PODOLSKY, J. D. [et al.] "Adieu to the Lady Next Door." *People*, February 8, 1993, pp. 53–54.

PODOLSKY, J. D. "LIFE WITH AUDREY." *People*, October 31, 1994, pp. 100–109.

REED, REX. "Our Fair Lady Is Back, and It's Spring." *New York Sunday News*, March 21, 1976.

RIDING, ALAN. *New York Times* Paris bureau, interview with Audrey Hepburn, April 12, 1991.

RINGGOLD, GENE. "AH Added Post-Hitler Realism to the Movies' Image of the Child-Woman." *Films in Review*, December 1971.

SEIDENBAUM, ART. "Audrey Hepburn." *McCall's*, October 1964, pp. 96–98, 182–85.

SWANSON, PAULINE. "Knee-Deep in Stardust." *Photoplay*, April 1954.

TALLMER, JERRY. "Audrey's N.Y. holiday." *New York Post*, April 22, 1991.

THOMPSON, FRANK. "Audrey Hepburn." *American Film*, May 1990, pp. 54–56.

WALDMAN, JOYCE. "Audrey's Fantastic Figure." *Cosmopolitan*, June 1959, pp. 60–64.

WATTERS, JIM. "The Voice, the Neck, The Charm: They Just Don't Make Movie Stars Like Audrey Hepburn Anymore." *People*, April 12, 1976.

WHITESIDE, KATHERINE. "The Grand Garden Tour." *House & Garden*, January 1991, pp. 41–44, 123.

WILLIAMS, JOHN. "Elegance with an Elf Inside." *International Herald Tribune*, January 26, 1993.

WILSON, ELIZABETH. *Sight and Sound*, March 1993.

WOOLDRIDGE, JANE. "At this stage of her life, Hepburn's still a fair lady." *Miami Herald*, December 3, 1989.

VIDEO

Audrey Hepburn in Her Own Words, Robert Wolders, 1993.

Audrey Hepburn Remembered, Wombat Productions, Gene Feldman producer, 1993.

LIFE Remembers, December 1993.

More Loverly Than Ever: The Making of "My Fair Lady," Galler West Productions, 1994.

ACKNOWLEDGMENTS

I have always depended on the kindness of strange friends and archivists—and on the facts and favors they provide me over the years of researching and writing a biography such as this. There is no nice way to "group" people; doing so by location is perhaps least offensive. So those mentioned in the Foreword now join all the others for a full geo-alphabetical listing below.

Biography is a mosaic, and a mosaic is an arty jigsaw puzzle: Random pieces arrive in no sensible order. Some pieces never arrive at all; many turn out to belong to somebody *else's* puzzle and thus a colossal waste of one's time. Gradually, some shape or outline is discernible, and then patches of the whole that may or may not connect. Not even the biographer himself knows what the picture will look like until it's done—unless his picture is preconceived, in which case he's not to be trusted.

Each of the people and institutions below supplied pieces of the Audrey Hepburn mosaic or helped me figure out where they belonged. With every project, I am always amazed anew by the generosity of the folks I ask for help. I am fondly grateful to everyone listed below, and I think George Coleman would approve of sharing this book's dedication with all of them.

NEW YORK

Teresa Albanez, Jeffrey Banks, Dolores Barrett, Michael Barson (Putnam), Theodore Bikel, Patricia Bosworth, Professor Richard Brown, Charles Busch, Roger Caras, Cynthia Cathcart (Conde Nast), Horst Cerny, Maria Ciaccia, Jocelyn Clapp (Bettmann), Howard Cutler, Nickolas Dana (Rochester), Jody Donahue, Dominick Dunne, Gene Feldman, Mary (Mrs. José) Ferrer, Rose Ganguzza, Robert Gottlieb, Jane Halsman (Philippe Halsman Estate), Rose Hayden, Robert Heide, Mary Hernandez (Unilever), Celeste Holm, John Isaac, Roger Jones, Martha Kaplan, Wendy Keys, Ed Klein, Eleanor Lambert, Owen Laster (William Morris Agency), Ralph Lauren, Wayne Lawson (*Vanity Fair*), Lorraine Martindale (Putnam), Camilla Pecci-Blunt McGrath, Stafan de Mistura, Eric Myers, Patricia Neal, Marni Nixon, André Previn (Bedford Hills), Eric Rachlis (Archive Photos), Jill Rembar, Richard Schmidt, Marian Seldes, Deborah Solomon, Eli Wallach, Shelley Wanger, Victoria Wilson, Ron Wisniski and Robert Wolders (Rochester).

CALIFORNIA

George Axelrod, Janis Blackschleger, Peter Bogdanovich, Florida Broadway, James Coburn, Stuart Crowner, Tony Curtis, Rudy Fehr, Mel Ferrer, the late Eva Gabor, Zsa Zsa Gabor, Rick and Deborah Geary, Lenny Gershe, Kirk Hallem, Charles Higham, Judd Klinger, Della Koenig, Gavin Lambert, Richard Lamparski, Jack Larsen, Julie Leifermann, Leonard & Alice & Jessie Maltin, Ginny Mancini, the late Doug McClure, Roddy McDowall, Joseph J. O'Donohue IV, Wallace Potts, David Stenn, R. J. Wagner, Connie Wald, Billy & Audrey Wilder, Cara Williams, Mignon Winans, Efrem Zimbalist Jr., and the inspiration of Marcia Davenport.

PITTSBURGH

Dr. Tom Allen, Stephen Baum, Ken & Betty Behrend, Bill Bollendorf & Dr. Madalyn Simasek, Patti Burns, Judi Cannava, Jim Cunningham, Ron & Lynn Curry, Dan & Barbara Ernsberger, Janet Fanale, Lucy Fischer, Albert French, Doris and Josie Kalina, Tim Menees, Ruth Ann Molloy, James and Queen Christina O'Toole, Myrna Paris, Ben Paris, Merica Paris, Christopher Rawson, Sylvia Sachs, Shirley and Morris Shratter, John Ezra Schulman, Bob Simeone, Marilynn Uricchio, Laura Wallenchek and that wild, wacky Egyptologist Tim Ziaukas (in Bradford, Pennsylvania).

WASHINGTON

John & Margie Barba, Ken & Denise Cummins, Patricia Heberer (Holocaust Museum), Sandra Homner-van Damme, Senator Nancy Kassebaum, Madeline F. Matz (Motion Picture, Broadcasting and Recorded Sound Division, Library of Congress), Liz Mays, Jacqueline Pessaud, and James Lee Auchincloss.

ELSEWHERE IN THE U.S.

William Banks and Anne Cox Chambers (Atlanta); Steven Bach (Vermont); Bob Curtwright (*The Wichita Eagle*); William Donati (Memphis); Katharine Dunham (East St. Louis, Illinois); Grada [Wolders] and Dr. Ronald E. Glegg (Sarasota, Florida); Marilynn Gump (Wichita, Kansas); Cathy Henkel

(Seattle); H. R. Hutchins (Royal Dutch Shell, Houston); Ned Lehac and Jane Sherman (Englewood, New Jersey); Pamela, David, Todd, Heather and Paris Loyle (Wichita, Kansas); Nancy & Wyoming B. Paris, Jr. (Bel Air, Maryland); Wyoming B. Paris (Wichita); Trever Patton (Wichita); Yvonne Quarles van Ufford (Manchester, Massachusetts); Margaret Schouten (Sarasota, Florida); Teller (Las Vegas) and Michael Tilson Thomas (Miami).

THE NETHERLANDS

Charles H. André de la Porte; Martin Appelmann (Bosch & Kuening Uitgevers, Baarn); Mrs. G. A. Bechtold; Vim Borawitz (The Hague); Leendert de Jong (The Hague Film House); Alfred Heineken III (Amsterdam); Ida de Jong; Ph. Kamphuis (chief of Army Staff section, Military History Dept., The Hague); Jascht Kulom (Dutch Film Archives, Amsterdam); Michael Quarles van Ufford (Breda); B. Melis of Shell International (The Hague); Hako & Christine Sixma van Heemstra (Vetuphen); Cornelus Tieleman (The Hague); Hesje and Willem van Hall; Countess Klarien von Zuylen van Nyenveldt; Anneke van Wijk; Paul van Vliet; author-historian Paul Vroemen and Coos and Rocky (Et Kamerik); and Rose-Marie Willems.

ENGLAND

Mark Austen (Kompass Training Centre), Maria Avgoulis (William Morris Agency), the late Jeremy Brett, Kevin Brownlow, Sappho Clissit, Ninette de Valois, Jane Edgeworth, Angela Dukes Ellis, Annabel Farjeon, Maude Gosling, Peter and Catherine Green and families, Lord James Hanson, Penelope Hobhouse, Ronald Hynde, Elizabeth Kennedy, Richard Lester, Charles Saunders, Hugo Vickers, and Fred Zinnemann.

FRANCE

Michele Amon, Alain Barthot, Marie-Claude Benard, Leslie Caron, Hubert de Givenchy, Roland Petit, Gabrielle Hayat-Gelber, Bethany Haye, Veronique de Moussac, Marie-Christine Protoy, Alan Riding (International Herald Tribune), Ian and Yvonne Quarles van Ufford, Bob Willoughby, and the late Terence Young.

SWITZERLAND

Doris Brynner (Geneva), Sean Ferrer (Tolochenaz), Jack Glattbach (Geneva), Prince Sadruddin Aga Khan (Geneva), Christa Roth (Geneva); and my faithful friends Peter Viertel and Deborah Kerr (Klosters).

ITALY

Antonio, Bice & Giovanni Abbadessa, Enzo Amato, Anna Cataldi, Valentina Cortesa, Countess Lorean Gaetani-Lovatelli, Sophia Loren, Tony Menicucci, Grazia de Rossi, Sergio Russo, and Arabella Ungaro.

ELSEWHERE GLOBALLY

Cole and Marilyn Dodge (Nairobi, Kenya); David Heringa (Edmonton, Alberta, Canada); Ian MacLeod (Capetown, South Africa); Victor Soler-Sala (Madrid, Spain); Christine Sparagana (Santiago, Chile); and Gustavo Tavares (Dominican Republic).

INDEX